Annette Young was born in Sydney and grew up on Sydney's northern beaches and north shore. She studied music from an early age and it has remained a lifelong passion. Annette holds an honours degree in History from the University of Sydney and a Doctorate in English Literature from the University of New South Wales. She now lives in Maitland, New South Wales with her husband, Francis, and their 'quartet' of boys. *A Distant Prospect* is her first novel.

A
Distant
Prospect

Annette Young

ISBN 978-0-9874351-0-1

National Library of Australia Cataloguing-in-Publication entry:

Young, Annette
A distant prospect / by Annette Young
ISBN 9780987435101 (pbk.)
A823.4

Cover:

Grace Cossington Smith
Australia 1892–1984
The bridge in-curve 1930
tempera on cardboard
83.6 x 111.8 cm
National Gallery of Victoria, Melbourne
Presented by the National Gallery Society of Victoria, 1967
© Estate of Grace Cossington Smith. Used with permission.

Distant Prospect Publishing
8 Roy Street
Lorn NSW 2320
Australia

www.adistantprospect.com

Acknowledgements

A special thank you to Professor Christine Alexander, Ruth Hutchison, Dr Susan Moore and my aunt, Judith Bennett, whose constructive criticism during the various stages of writing proved invaluable.

To my husband, Francis, for his help with the cover design and publication. His ongoing love and support throughout has been nothing short of inspirational.

To Toni Stevens, whose careful reading and commentary of the final manuscript, assistance with the synopsis and encouragement during the latter stages of preparation is deeply appreciated.

And to Dorothee Uí Chleirigh, Cóilín McDonagh, Máire Uí Iarnáin and Paula Ní Ríogáin for their assistance with the Irish.

For my Mother,
Margaret Lyne Nelson née Cameron

And my Grandmother,
Yvonne Lyne Cameron née Murray
(1906–1994)

To each his sufferings: all are men,
Condemned alike to groan;
The tender for another's pain,
The unfeeling for his own.
Yet ah! why should they know their fate?
Since Sorrow never comes too late,
And happiness too swiftly flies.
Thought would destroy their paradise.
No more; where ignorance is bliss,
'Tis folly to be wise.

Thomas Gray
'Ode on a Distant Prospect of Eton College'

1

It was the third time that morning Daid had called. After breakfast he called to remind me not to dally getting ready. He called again when I started playing my 'cello, informing me of my train's departure. Now he called and knocked at my bedroom door and announced that as far as he was aware, the Good Lord would not be stopping the sun for my sake as He did for Joshua. I sighed, unscrewed my bow and reluctantly laid down my instrument. Bach would have to wait till later. I reached for the cover and fitted my 'cello inside before resting it carefully back on the floor. Then I swivelled around in the chair, leant across, and gripped the end of my bed. I pulled myself up hard to standing position. As I did, I made a tentative glance at my reflection in the cracked glass of my wardrobe mirror. Today I was dressed for school in a black box-pleated tunic, a not very white shirt and a black and white tie.

There had been precious little money to spare on that uniform for most of it had been taken up in the purchase of not one, but two pairs of boots. The boots, as usual, had been custom-made by the orthopaedic man and had cost a small fortune, whereas the uniform had been acquired second or third hand for a few pennies. So, unlike my brand new boots – solid, shiny and sensible, their laces not yet frayed – my tunic was still redolent with the smell of the vinegar that had been used in the attempt to remove ancient stains and three old hemlines. My shirt should have been white. Instead it was more parchment in colour, the fabric soft from years of scrubbing. Somehow the collar and cuffs had survived another starching, and the shirt, despite its aged condition, had been ironed to perfection.

'Luighseach!'

Daid knocked again. I opened my bedroom door and followed my father into the corridor.

He looked me over. There was a mixture of pride and concern on his face. Then he relaxed somewhat and ran his hand through his hair which typically was a tousled mass of charcoal locks, and a stark contrast to the pristine neatness of his trim-fitting waistcoat and pinstriped trousers, striped shirt and necktie, and round, silver rimmed glasses.

''Tis the first day of school, lassie,' he smiled. 'Will you not have your photograph taken?'

Daid should have known better. I shook my head.

'But 'tis a special day to be sure, Luighseach,' Daid continued in his gentle brogue.

Again I shook my head, looked down at my boots and sighed.

''Tis the camera's set up in the parlour there. Will you sit for a portrait, lass? Head and shoulders and nought more than that. You can take your glasses off if you want.'

Take my glasses off? What good would that do? It wouldn't change the rest of me.

'I'm thinking Sister Ignatius would like a photo of yourself in your uniform. And did you write to thank her for the help she gave you to win the scholarship?' I had not written and Daid knew it. 'What's more 'tis myself would like a new picture of my lass to put on my desk in the studio. 'Tis more than eight years old, you know, the one that sits there.'

But I liked that photograph, and if I had any say in it, it was not going to be replaced by what would undoubtedly be an inferior piece. I refused a fourth time.

Daid, in resignation, took my blazer from the hallstand and helped me put it on. He picked up my satchel and fitted it over my head, arranging my long black braids so that they fell down my front instead of being thrown back over my shoulders. My hat, too, he set carefully on my crown. I stretched my hands into a pair of black gloves. Together we walked to the front door. Daid took some holy water from the font near the doorpost and made the sign of the cross on my forehead. He stood at the top of our front steps and watched me leave.

'Will you not let me drive you, Luighseach?' he asked.

I carefully worked my way down one, two, three, four steps. On the fifth, however, I stumbled. Before I even realised I was falling my father was at my side. He steadied me and helped me down to the gate.

'Bíodh lá maith agat, a Luighseach,' he said quietly. 'You'll be all right, will you not?'

'Aye, I will, Daid,' I replied.

And so it was, one February morning in 1928, that I was on my own for the very first time since arriving in Sydney from Ireland a little over seven years ago. It was not yet eight o'clock and already the air was soaked with heat. Slowly I began my walk up Watkin Street, which was the street where we lived.

Had I been able, I would have run past Mrs Murphy's house which was next door to our own. But I could not and I prepared myself for the inevitable. Sure enough, I heard the front door open and my name called.

I stopped.

'Lucy!' Mrs Murphy waddled down the path. 'I was hoping I'd see you before you left. And don't you look smart in your uniform! Who would have thought you'd ever be off to school and on a scholarship too! Why, I remember when you first came home from the hospital. Nineteen twenty-two it was, two months after dear Mr Murphy, God rest his soul, passed away. The good Lord took him on St Joseph's day, you know, so he was well taken care of. He always had a strong devotion to good St Joseph, Mr Murphy did. My, what a frail, thin little lass you were with those braces on your legs. And now look at you, fifteen years old – I never thought you'd grow so tall. But child—' she paused. 'You're only wearing a brace on one leg.'

It was typical of Mrs Murphy to notice that. If Daid had noticed, he had wisely kept silent. But Mrs Murphy made it her business to talk about everything.

'I'm not needing the other calliper,' I replied, 'for I'm walking fine without it now.'

'And what does the doctor say about that, dear?'

The doctor did not know.

'Well, I hope you don't come to harm. It's a wonder your dear father's let you go out like that. Dear me,' she sighed, and pulled something from her apron pocket. 'Now Lucy, I've kept this for you. It's a devotion to St Jude. You pray to him for protection and strength.'

She pressed the holy picture into my hand.

'He's bound to help you,' Mrs Murphy continued. 'Why only the other day, I was talking to old Mrs Quinn down the lane and she said that since praying to St Jude her rheumatism's far better. Then there's Arthur Harrison who was gassed in the War. Well, St Jude's seen that he's finally on the mend. So you can be sure he'll listen to a crippled child like you, dear.'

This syllogism, such as it was, disclosed the pith of Mrs Murphy's argument and purpose.

'And what is *that* to do with it, I'm asking?'

'But Lucy, the sick and the needy are always in God's mind.'

'Are they now, Mrs Murphy? Well, if the Almighty's arranged things so, there bees no need for yourself, St Jude or anyone else who's walked the face of the earth to be troubling on it.'

And sending a glare in the woman's direction, I scrunched up the devotion and silently challenged her as to whether or not I would actually throw it away. I pulled my leg into line and resumed my hike up the hill towards King Street.

'Mother of God, that girl!' I heard Mrs Murphy mutter as she waddled back down the path. Only when I was satisfied I was out of her sight did I open my satchel and stuff the devotion inside.

The Rugby Hotel stood at the corner of Watkin and King Streets and, when I finally reached it, I leant against the wall to catch my breath. St Dominic's, the school I was to attend, was in Strathfield and to get there I had to take a train. Newtown station was still a long walk away. Down King Street I wandered amidst a hubbub of wheels and hoofs and trousers and skirts and shoes and bells and horns. At Daid's studio, I paused again to rest my legs and studied the photographs exhibited in the front window. Some were Daid's and others were the work of Mr Birstall, his associate. Thomas' book and music store was a few more doors along, and there I spent time peering through the glass, trying to make out the tune of a song displayed in the window. Then there was the butcher's which did not serve Catholics, and Bray's music where the 'cello lived. I ate an orange outside Bray's.

Finally I arrived at the top of the railway stairs in time to watch my train steam under the bridge and down the track. Another locomotive chugged by. I edged down endless steps and was saved from what might have been serious falls by a sudden show of hands and words of caution. Two fast trains sped past before, with unsolicited assistance, I boarded the slow train to Strathfield and took refuge in a corner of the carriage.

The train rounded the track past St Joseph's church. A little further along was the convent. I could not see it from my carriage seat, but it was where my education had been taken care of for the last few years. Sister Mary Ignatius, a Sister of Charity, was the nun who had been given the responsibility. With considerable vigour she bent my mind round the arts and sciences. That was, until she abruptly announced that she was soon to take care of a group of postulants.

'As for yourself,' she remarked in her forthright Cork accent the day she broke the news, 'You ought to sit for a scholarship. It would be good for you.'

So was castor oil. As far as I was concerned, I was required to do too many things that were 'good' for me.

'Well, and what will you be doing with the life God's given you?' she probed. 'Will you work in your father's shop when you've finished your studies?'

I had never given the matter any thought. According to Sister Ignatius, it was about time I did.

'If you received a scholarship, you could sit for matriculation,' she continued. 'If you matriculate well, you could win a scholarship to the varsity. If you go to the varsity, you'll be able to study the mathematics you want to study. You'll get ahead. You need to get ahead. It's important.'

However obstinate I may have appeared regarding her lofty ambitions, Sister Ignatius was assured of one thing: I could not resist aceing a test. So she prepared me for the scholarship. I sat the examination and was duly rewarded.

I should have been proud of my success. Everyone else was. But for me the achievement was tainted with the prospect that I was to join my peers in the pursuit of learning. That was quite another matter entirely. Aside from very brief exchanges after Sunday Mass, I had precious little to do with other girls. I pulled my tunic further over my knees and hugged my satchel. A lady sitting in the opposite seat smiled at me and I looked away. With each stop I grew more apprehensive. By the time the train pulled in at Strathfield, I was physically sick.

To my relief I found St Dominic's deserted. Had I arrived punctually, I knew the grounds would have been swarming with girls: staring, gossiping, giggling girls.

Now I was faced with the task of finding and entering my class.

A door to the right of the central archway directed me to an office. I entered and stood at the desk. An elderly nun came to my assistance.

'May I help you, child?'

'You may.'

'And you are?'

4

'My name is Luighseach Ní Sruitheáin.'

'You're the lame girl, aren't you?' She glanced over her pince-nez, across the desk and down to my boots. 'Tut, tut. Sister Bellarmine, the head mistress, has been waiting for you this past half hour. Why are you so late?'

'I missed my train.'

The nun shook her head. 'I'm afraid Sister Bellarmine has gone to teach now. What a pity! She wanted to introduce you personally.'

That may have been Sister Bellarmine's desire, but it was definitely not mine.

'I can find my class myself, you know.'

'Well, you're going to have to now. Let me see, you're in the fourth form. South wing, top of the stairs, turn right, first right.'

'The south wing was it you said?'

'Through the main archway,' she explained in a tone that suggested she had given those directions many a time. 'Across the quadrangle, up the stairs, turn right, first right.'

I waited awhile outside the classroom and took as long as I could to remove the gloves which were glued to my fingers with sweat.

I knocked.

'Enter.'

The voice had to repeat the command before I had courage enough to turn the handle. I opened the door and pushed my head inside. Facing me was a beach of desks strewn with seaweed clumps of girls in tunics.

'How may I help you, child?' A nun, rather like a great white walrus, occupied a desk on a platform.

'Don't be shy so,' she lilted with a gentle smile.

I swallowed.

'Gabh mo leithsceál. An bhfuil—'

'Why bless me! You speak the Irish!' exclaimed the nun, stopping short the chattering girls. 'Come inside, come inside! Welcome to this holy place.'

Now came the dreaded moment in which I had to stand before my class. Sickening, I removed my hat and sidled inside, and in doing so revealed everything I wished so desperately to hide. Twelve pairs of eyes stared at my shiny brown boots, noting how different they were to the shoes with straps fixed to the twelve pairs of legs which were crossed under the desks. They stared at my left boot with its built up heel. They stared at my legs, long and spindly, and at the calliper with its metal shafts and leather straps and buckles. They stared at the black, hand-knitted woollen stockings I wore to stop the straps rubbing against my skin, and they began to whisper.

'I'm afraid it's only Sister Comgall in the convent who speaks Irish here,' the nun explained. 'Now, I am Sister Mary Magdalene. Who might you be?'

'It's Luighseach I am. Luighseach Ní Sruitheáin,' I answered.

Sister Mary Magdalene perused her roll then eyed me quizzically.

'I'm afraid we don't have anyone by that name in this class, child,' she apologised.

'But 'twas in the office they told me the fourth form it was I had—'

Sister gently raised her hand to halt me.

'Be calm, dear child. We do, however, have a Lucy Straughan,' she said. 'Now would that be yourself?'

They had anglicised my name.

'Then welcome, Lucy,' Sister proceeded. 'You will find your desk in the centre there,' and she indicated the spot with her ruler.

'Can— can I not sit here?' I asked, indicating the desk pressed against the wall, closest to where I was standing.

'No, no, my child,' smiled the nun. 'That desk is being sent for repair. Your desk is the one I pointed out.'

It was always hard to begin walking without holding some form of support, and it was even harder when my legs were tired. I looked anxiously at the nun. She gave me an anxious smile in return while her eyes gently encouraged me to my seat. Slowly, I lifted my right leg high from the knee in order to clear my foot. Then I swung my shorter left leg, held rigid by the calliper, from the hip. Lift and swing, lift and swing, I limped towards my seat. The nun requested someone to help me. A small, slender girl volunteered. She stood and pulled out my chair for me.

'I can do it myself,' I muttered, and I took the seat without as much as a glance at her, fixed my braced leg into a bent position and stared at the pattern of woodgrain spirals on the desk.

There was an equation for spirals… Did any of the woodgrains make a golden spiral?

Sister Mary Magdalene resumed her lesson. It appeared to be a history lesson on the Counter-Reformation and the Jesuit saints had been selected for study. When at last I had the courage to look up from my spirals, I noted the various dates and names listed on the board: St Ignatius Loyola, St Francis Xavier, St Aloysius Gonzaga; the Spanish Inquisition: 1481.

I mulled over that number. 1481 was an interesting number. It was a prime number. Were there any other prime numbers on the board? I began to look over the dates and do calculations: if the sum of the digits was divisible by three a number would not be prime. Were any numbers divisible by seven? Eleven? Thirteen? What other numbers were there?

The lesson continued. 'Now who can tell me about St Peter Canisius?' Sister asked the class. 'Yes, Della, that is quite correct. He was only recently canonised and his canonisation is a reminder that God wants us all to live holy lives. Now, do you all remember the Lutherans?'

I continued with my calculations. That was, until Sister Mary Magdalene decided it was time I answered a few questions.

'Lucy?' she called.

I looked up. There were giggles. Clearly this was not the first time the nun had called my name. I blushed.

'1597,' prompted Sister. 'Could you tell me what happened?'

I gazed at the number that was now written on the board. The class silently waited for my reply. It seemed that everyone knew the answer I should give. But I did not know anything that happened in 1597. I only knew about the number one thousand, five hundred and ninety-seven.

''Tis a Fibonacci number,' I said.

The bell sounded. Sister concluded her class with a Hail Mary and left the room. I had not the chance to fully stand with rest of the class, and had barely taken my seat when I was encircled.

'A what number?' asked one girl who was very pretty and fair-haired.

'If ye're needing to know, Miss Frances Mahony,' a shrill Ulster-Scots voice sounded, and everyone turned in the direction of the diminutive nun who stood at the door. 'A Fibonacci number is a number which is the sum of two preceding numbers in a Fibonacci sequence, the pattern being 0,1,1,2,3,5,8 and so forth. Hail Mary full of grace the Lord is with thee. Blessed art thou among women and blessed is the Fruit of thy womb, Jesus.'

The class demurely prayed the response, although vague undertones of 'Fibonacci' and 'new girl' could be heard.

'Our Lady of the Rosary.'

'Pray for us.'

'St Dominic.'

'Pray for us.'

'Now, given that Miss Mahony would not be likely to have dabbled in pure mathematics over the course of the summer, I can only assume that such rare interest in the subject owes itself to another source. You there,' the nun adjusted a pair of round, black spectacles and eyed me carefully. 'Would ye be Miss Fibonacci perhaps?'

'Oh no, Sister Augustine,' piped up Frances Mahony. 'That's Lissie.'

'You don't say it like that, Fanny,' corrected a large, heavy-set girl. 'It's Lushie.'

'Lushie? That's not how *she* said it, Kathleen,' a third girl interposed.

They would have bickered over my name *ad infinitum* had not Sister quickly restored order with several raps of her ruler.

'To be sure Miss Fibonacci can speak for herself, Mary Byrne,' said Sister Augustine to the third girl. 'Well, is there a tongue in yer head?' she asked me. 'And will ye not stand when ye're spoken to?'

'She can't stand up, Sister Augustine,' Kathleen explained before I had chance either to stand or speak for myself. 'She's crippled.'

At this, I clenched my jaw and pushed my hands hard on my desk. It took me three attempts, but stand I did.

'Ah-ha, now ye must be Miss Lucy Straughan,' remarked the nun who pronounced my surname with a heavy guttural emphasis on the last syllable instead of softly blending the vowels. 'Pray and what will ye tell us about the Fibonacci sequence?'

Immediately I replied, my response revealing my own softer West Country accent. 'Mathematically, the Fibonacci sequence would be represented as $F_n = F_{n-1} + F_{n-2}$. 'Tis a numerical sequence whereby the ratio of two consecutive numbers converges on the golden ratio. You can see fibonacci patterns in nature, in the arrangement of petals in flowers or branches on trees. The sum of—'

'Very good indeed,' remarked Sister Augustine. 'Ye may sit now, Miss Straughan.'

I glanced sideways. Fat Kathleen looked at me with a very perplexed expression.

Now who was the cripple, I thought, as I sat.

Sister Augustine wrote the sequence on the board and explained how it occurred in the petal configuration I had mentioned.

'The sequence underlines,' said she, 'the order that exists in this world, which as ye all should know is one of St Thomas' five demonstrations of the existence of God. I beg yer pardon, Lucy Straughan?' the nun jutted her angular chin in my direction.

I had not expected Sister Augustine to hear what I had muttered. Again I was made to stand.

'Well?' inquired Sister Augustine.

'But what of the disorder?' I blurted.

'Disorder was it, ye said?' she echoed.

'Aye, I did. 'Tis all very well to talk of order showing God's existence. But what of the disorder? How does that show God exists now, can you tell me that?'

'Disorder?' queried Sister Augustine, shaking her head and suppressing the surrounding giggles. 'Our God is not a God of disorder. There's no such thing as disorder, Lucy Straughan. Only a more profound order.'

'But—'

No further discussion was permitted, for Sister immediately directed the lesson towards the quadratic formula.

The next bell apparently signalled morning tea. Curiously, the class left me alone and walked out in groups, making comments about 'spastic' and 'Sister Augustine' and 'maths' the while.

'Care to join us?' asked a girl whom I recognised as the one who earlier had offered to help me.

I shook my head.

'I suggest you go outside though. If a prefect sees you in here, you'll run the risk of a detention.'

I told her I cared not for going outside and that such things as prefects and detentions could go to the devil.

'Don't say I didn't warn you.'

She disappeared. I turned the page of my mathematics book and embarked on the homework that had been set, until an older, red-headed girl ousted me from the room.

The following lessons suffered such a prolonged discussion of my name and physical predicament that I regretted ever being born, let alone sit for a scholarship. Save for lunch, which I also spent inside until ejected, the day passed in a regular pattern. White-robed nuns pounded their lessons on an increasingly sleepy shore of students. Between each wave of instruction, however, the girls popped out of their seats like gangs of crabs and scuttled across the room in pursuit of pleasure. Otherwise, like pippies, they burrowed deep in gossip and stayed submerged until wrenched to the surface by the next instructress. I, meanwhile, remained stiff as a pole, fixed to my seat, firmly resisting and resenting even the tiniest semblance of attention.

The last bell sounded. The 'Sub Tuum Praesidium' was prayed and girls and mistress drifted away.

Finally, silence.

The sultriness with which the day began had not diminished, and by the time I alighted from the train the sky had become a threatening blue-grey. Dollops of summer rain flopped onto my boots as I trudged homeward. I opened the gate, and the rain wept down a thick, silver curtain.

Our house was dark and silent as always. I hung my blazer and hat on the hallstand, opened my bedroom door and dragged my chair to the foot of my bed. I picked up my 'cello from its place, removed the bow and cover, flung the cover on the bed, sat in the chair and slotted the spike into a groove in the floorboards. The bow I tightened with six deft twists and rubbed with rosin. Taking a deep breath, I removed my glasses, closed my eyes and sighed into the strings. One by one the fingers of my left hand planted themselves on the fingerboard and rocked into a vibrato. It was pouring now and I thudded my fingers in a series of chromatics, each sequence progressing higher and higher. My bow began to sweep across the strings and I felt my shoulders loosen. My 'cello and I were one great muscle of sound, and we mourned with all our might through Bach's D minor Prelude while outside the thunder rolled and heavy rain pounded the roof.

Daid returned. A brief question and the reply that all was fine sealed our conversation. Tea was had, Rosary prayed, homework done, legs massaged, and I was left atop my bed to prepare for the next day's encounter.

2

'Spastic.'

It was tittered on the station platform, giggled at the gate, whispered up and down lines of waiting girls and shouted from the verandahs. By the end of the second day of school, it had become a fully-fledged chant which dogged me wherever I went:

'Spastic! Spastic! Legs like matchsticks!'
'Spastic! Spastic! Legs like matchsticks!'

The only way I could escape the jeers and taunts was to arrive late and leave late, which I did the following day. That meant I risked a detention, but anything was to be preferred to the teasing, the comments, the giggles and stares.

The teasing continued in class. My classmates did not resort to the spastic jeer, although they employed the word quite frequently when talking about me. Instead, they seemed to relish anything that exposed my differences. If I needed to get to my desk, big Kathleen Doherty, whose seat was in my path, would sit back and stick out her legs as far as she could. I then either had to change direction – something I found difficult to do – and face the obstacle of Mary Byrne's legs, or else request Kathleen to please move her legs out of the way. Kathleen would then pretend not to hear, and I would be pressed to speak more forcibly which, of course, drew attention to my accent. Othertimes when I passed, Frances Mahony would cause a pencil or eraser to fall. Politely she would ask if I wouldn't mind picking it up, and she seemed strangely satisfied when, after several unsuccessful attempts, I had to confess that I could not. Particularly frustrating was that items seemed to disappear from my desk. Much to the annoyance of the mistress conducting the lesson, I would have to ask permission to retrieve my book, my ruler or my pen from my satchel, and face yet another course of obstacles in the fruitless trek there and back, only to find the objects in question already on my desk when I returned.

For some peculiar reason, the class found my involvement in mathematics highly amusing. In the third lesson, I again decided to challenge Sister Augustine who had written incorrectly a solution to one of the problems on the blackboard. Sister Augustine, who did not appear accustomed to such a level of interference, requested I come to the board and explain.

I refused.

'You refuse? In a subject devoted to truth, ye dare let error reign? Aye, ye're a traitor, Lucy Straughan.'

'I'm nothing of the sort for I said there was a mistake. On the third line it is.'

Giggles.

'Then ye're lazy and disobedient,' concluded Sister Augustine. 'I've asked ye to demonstrate on the board and I expect ye to come, gammy legs or no.'

I needed Sister's help to mount the platform. After that, there was no end to the giggles and whispers that accompanied our discussion of the mistake and my chalked up version of the quadratic equation in question. Tiny Sister Augustine made me explain her every step of the problem as I worked it through. By the time I finished, nearly every girl was doubled up in silent laughter. I looked over the blackboard. There was my answer, logically and legibly written on the upper half, and Sister Augustine's workings on the lower half of the board. It was only a quadratic equation. What was so funny?

But I had no chance of finding out, for the class rapidly dispersed into the grounds the moment it was dismissed. Since I could neither descend nor ascend the stairs as nimbly as my peers, I remained on my own during recess, ever on the lookout to avoid any girl who might pass me and tease. My sole objective very quickly became a desperate hunt for a refuge. At lunch, I found it: a disused cloakroom not far from the classroom. There, seated on an old trunk, with glasses laid aside and engrossed in my book, I could be secret, silent and secure.

Within minutes, however, someone discovered my hiding place.

'I say! What in heaven—!' came the crisp voice of the intruder.

I reached for my glasses. The voice belonged to the small, slender girl.

'Don't tell anyone!' she panted as she leant against the door. 'We're playing hide and seek. Mary's on the hunt. Pretend I'm not here!'

Down she ducked and covered her face with her hands.

The girl did not maintain her invisibility for long.

'I'm sorry I startled you,' she said.

'You didn't.'

'Yes I did. And your hand's been shaking ever since.'

To prove my hand was not shaking, I found my pencil, took off my glasses and began to scribble a few calculations.

A cough. She would not go away.

'I say, Luighseach,' her voice lilted my name, softening the 's' to 'sh' the way it should be softened. So far, no one had made any effort to say my Irish name. I looked over the top of *Amusements in Mathematics* and peered at the girl who was now at my feet.

'Have you heard the news?' she asked.

I confessed I had not heard 'the news', whatever it was.

'You know, about the *airman*,' she chirped with excited emphasis.

I shook my head and found my place. There was a quick tap on my leg. Apart from my father and members of the medical profession, nobody ever touched my legs.

'Look at this.' She raided her pocket. Numerous chocolate wrappers were piled onto the trunk before she produced a carefully folded piece of newspaper. 'Bert Hinkler's arrived in Rome. He left Croydon a couple of days ago. He's flying here, to Australia.'

She was English. Why was she telling me this?

'He's going to break the Smiths' record,' she continued as she unfolded the paper and sat down beside me. I put my glasses back on and studied her.

'The Smiths?' I asked.

'You know, Sir Ross and Sir Keith Smith. They're aviators—Well, they *were* aviators, or at least one of them was. The other one still is, I think. Wally knows all about it. Wally's my brother. Do you have brothers?'

I shook my head. What a chatterbox she was.

'Well, anyway, *I* think he's going to break the Smiths' record. I laid bets last night with Wally that he would. I'll get The Captain's medals if he does, and he's going to, *I'm* sure of it. Imagine flying all that way! We travelled to Australia from England by boat only a couple of years ago. It took six whole weeks! By 'plane it could take only three! It's exciting, isn't it?'

Then followed a thorough explanation regarding what she called Mr Hinkler's 'box of tricks' or devices that would assist him to fly the 'plane, and the route he had proposed. As she spoke, her tiny, delicate hands danced expressively, and to my surprise, occasionally touched my own.

She was fair and fine-featured. A halo of wavy, blonde hair, fashionably bobbed, framed a small, pert face. On her nose perched a pair of dainty glasses, ovular in shape, with an intricate pattern engraved on their gold frames. The glasses magnified gentle eyes of a pale blue-green. Although prim, her lips concealed a smile of such warmth it made her whole person glisten and glow.

The girl continued, candidly, to talk. She flitted from aeroplanes to what I was reading; from her family to the homework we had; from where she lived to where I lived, in such a way that I could not help but be entertained, even though I wished to return to my book.

'Shh! Voices,' she warned with a grab of my hand. 'I say! That's the bell. Game's over and they didn't find me! Ha, ha! Let's go.'

She watched me hoist myself up then slipped her hand in my arm. She barely reached my shoulder. Together we walked to the classroom. A quick 'Cheerio' ended the encounter and she hopped off to join the whirligig of social activity in the far corner.

Her name was Mary Arondelle Sotheby, called Della or Dell for short, and from that moment she seemed determined to take me under her wing regardless of whether I wanted her to or not. After Latin, she landed on my desk and pleaded for help on the accusative ablative. When class was dismissed, she followed her friends and gently banged me a good-bye as she passed.

The next day there was no escaping her attentions. She popped in and out of my world as cheerfully and sporadically as martins do when building their nests. First, it was a greeting; next, a query over homework. She cornered me at morning tea to pass on the latest snippet of aeronautical news. A note even made its way during History.

By lunch, I was permitted some peace in the cloakroom.

The afternoon bell sounded. I put my book down and reached for my glasses. They were nowhere to be found.

There was a giggle.

'Holy Mother! What did you do with them? Where are they? What did you do with my spéaclaí?'

'Stop groping, you funny thing! Here they are,' and I felt the familiar form of my thick, round, black-rimmed spectacles pressed into my hands. I put them on and peered into Arondelle Sotheby's pixie face.

'And how did you get in here?'

'Same as you, silly, only I got in first! I say, do you always read like that? You might as well be a mole made of marble.'

She imitated me reading, nose inches away from the page. Quickly she looked up and smiled, melting my icy glower until I could look no more.

3

Never did a weekend pass so slowly. In principle, it should have passed the same as any other weekend. On Saturday, as usual, I studied and practised in my room while Daid worked at the studio and photographed weddings. My father returned in the afternoon whereupon I was obliged to accompany him to Confession at St Joseph's. Daid confessed his sins and I passed the time doing crochet until Benediction. After that, there was tea, then Rosary, then bed. On Sunday we heard Mass, walked home, and spent the day quietly: Daid gardened and I practised. No one barged into my room with questions and chatter, no one stole my spectacles, no one giggled; no one paid me any attention at all. That weekend, my typically seamless progression of study, handwork and 'cello practice became, without Della Sotheby, a prolonged and painful regime of pointless activity.

So it was that by the time Monday came around, I found myself a little more inclined towards attending school than not. If there was the possibility of more of Della's company, I was prepared to weather the teasing, whatever it might be. As I dawdled down to the station, late as usual, I thought about what I could tell Della when I saw her, and stopped to buy a paper to see if it contained any news of her beloved aviator. Sure enough, there was a small article. I read it carefully, tore it out and read it again. Thus I arrived, equipped with the latest aviation facts, only to find Della Sotheby absent.

She was ill.

'Sick again,' groaned the class when the roll was called.

Apparently Della was often sick. The general consensus was that there had not been a single term in which she had not been sick. Della was sickly, always had been. Frances then reported that her aunt was sickly; Elizabeth Fitzgerald said her sister's constitution was poor; Kathleen informed that her grandmother had pneumonia. Then, there was Fanny's father's cousin's step-brother's son who had died of the Influenza after the War. Nearly everyone had a story about the Influenza and nearly everyone had a story about the War. But nobody knew what the matter was with Della.

Three more long, lonesome days dragged by and Della still had not returned. When she did not appear a fourth, I was convinced she had something serious.

I decided to pay her a visit.

Experience had furnished me with a good recipe for convalescence: puzzles and barley sugar. Puzzles were a sure means of alleviating the boredom of confinement, while barley sugar, despite having caused the demise of two of my teeth, was an effective palliative for castor oil. Convinced that puzzles and barley sugar were suitable comforts for anyone recovering from illness, I pulled my favourite book from my shelf, purchased tuppenceworth of my favourite sweet, and set off.

She had told me she lived opposite the park, two streets down from the station. That Friday afternoon I wandered along a wide, tree-lined avenue, graced on one side with stately homes. Della lived in one such abode. Which one, I did not know. I took a gamble on a large, gabled structure. The maid who answered directed me four doors further.

There I was faced with the most majestic of mansions. It stood in regal splendour amidst a court of roses, magnolias, azaleas and camellias carefully pruned. A plaque with 'Halcyon' engraved in gold letters proclaimed its name. I rang the bell and studied the kookaburras etched in the glass side-panels.

'May I help you, miss?' asked a maid smartly starched in a uniform of coffee brown with a cream cap and apron.

'Aye, you may. Would it be here that Miss Arondelle Sotheby lives?'

'Yes, she lives here. Is she expecting you?'

'She isn't. But I'd like to see her if you wouldn't mind.'

'I will tell her you are here. Who may I say has come?'

She departed, leaving me to peruse the vestibule at leisure. I was so absorbed with the patterns and colours of the majolica urn which stood on the hall table that I failed to notice the maid's return. Another voice – light, pretty and as polished as the chocolate and white tiles which paved the floor – brought me to attention.

'Who did you say it was, Nellie?'

'A Miss Leeshack Neeshroohoon, ma'am. Come to see Miss Della.'

A small, svelte woman entered. Her hair was neatly bobbed, like Della's, and fell with the same elegant wave. It was not blonde, however, but a rich Titian red. She looked up at me and smiled gracefully. She had large eyes, and they were a glorious teal blue. Her face should have been freckled, I thought, but I could not see any freckles for she wore face paint which had been meticulously applied. I removed my hat, pushed my glasses back up my nose and let my satchel fall in front of my legs. As I did, I noted her covered shoes, her embroidered costume of rose and lilac silk, her Chinese fan, her necklaces, pearls and rings.

'How do you do,' she held out a beautifully manicured hand. 'I am Della's mother, Mrs Sotheby.'

My 'how do you do' was a poor attempt at sounding English. As for the hand I held out, it was stained with ink.

'Nellie tells me you wish to see Della,' Mrs Sotheby inquired.

I nodded.

'But it's five o'clock! You do realise you have come a little late in the afternoon for visiting?'

I had not realised that at all.

'Do you have a letter of introduction?'

All I wanted was to see Della. It had never occurred to me that I required formal presentation. I shook my head and bit my lip.

'I—I heard that Della Sotheby was sick, ma'am,' I apologetically explained.

'She is quite well, thank you,' Mrs Sotheby surveyed my neat but shabby uniform with its yellowed shirt and worn pleats, and my boots now scuffed and dusty. '*We* receive visitors on Wednesday afternoons between two and four o'clock. Nellie, kindly show Miss Neesh— the door.'

Nellie obeyed with a glare at the mistress of the house. She opened the front door and was about to show me out when Della's voice was heard.

'Has someone come to see me?' she called. 'Luighseach! Well I never!' she exclaimed.

She neither looked nor sounded sick.

'I thought you were sick,' I remarked.

'I'm much better now, thank you. Not at all contagious,' she added with a smile. 'I say, how did you get here?'

'I walked.'

'Like that? In this heat? It must be a hundred degrees out there. Goodness gracious! You poor thing! You look worn out. Would you like a drink?'

'I'm not needing a thing,' I excused myself.

'Fiddlesticks,' she replied. 'Besides, *I* could do with some refreshment. Nellie, could you prepare us some lemonade? It's far too hot for tea.'

'With pleasure, Miss Della,' nodded Nellie, with a sideways smirk at Mrs Sotheby.

'Della dear,' Mrs Sotheby intervened, 'it is nearly time for dinner.'

'Why, dinner's not till seven, Mummy. There's plenty of time.'

'Very well,' sighed Mrs Sotheby who was clearly too hot to argue. 'Bring some lemonade, Nellie.'

'Very good, ma'am,' Nellie closed the front door and offered to take my things.

I pulled the book and barley sugar from my satchel before passing it to her.

'I brought you these,' I said, and handed my gifts to Della.

'Why thank you,' she was quite surprised. 'Ooh, yummy!' she exclaimed as she opened the bag. 'Care for one? Come, I'll show you to the verandah. And what's this? Dudeney, *The Canterbury Puzzles*. How very unusual.' She opened the book and saw my name on the fly leaf. 'It's yours. I'll take good care of it, I promise. Cross my heart. I say, it's not maths is it?'

'Aye.'

'You know we all call you Lucy Fibonacci, don't you?'

I shook my head. I had no idea at all.

'Is that why you laugh in the maths classes?' I asked.

'In part,' Della replied with a smile. 'I'll tell you more someday,' she added, dispelling some of my concern with a kindly look. Della, at least, meant no harm. 'Well, Lucy Fibonacci, I'm afraid I'm not very good at puzzles and that sort of thing, but I'll try. How very thoughtful you are! Do sit down,' she indicated a cane lounge framed by potted palms and littered with papers. 'Fancy thinking I was sick. Mind you, I did catch the Influenza when I was six. Apparently, I nearly died.

Have you ever been sick?'

I looked away at the canary trilling in an elaborate cage at the opposite end of the verandah.

'You've been very sick, haven't you?'

Eventually, I nodded, silently admitting to the fact.

'I say, did you have the Influenza too?'

I shook my head.

'Then what did you have?'

The canary hopped to a lower perch, pecked out some seed and began again to sing.

'Is it why your legs are a bit— well— a bit crippled?' crept the fourth question.

'If you really need to know,' I replied, "Twas Polio I had when I was two years older than yourself when you had the Influenza, and aye, it made my legs gammy.'

'I say, that is bad luck,' she remarked. Then, in an attempt to mix sympathy with optimism, she added brightly, 'Never mind.'

'Never mind?' I scoffed. 'Is that all you can say? Well, you weren't in hospital for more than a year, were you now? And you didn't spend the last—'

'Heavens! What a thundercloud you are!' Della gently cut me short. 'Still, I'm very glad to see you did get better – well enough in fact to pop in for lemonade on a summer afternoon. It's lovely having you here! Now take a look at my scrapbook. I've been getting it up to date.'

She pushed aside a paste pot and passed me her much-loved book.

I tried to push my cares aside by fishing out the newspaper article from my blazer pocket.

'Mr Hinkler, you know, reached Ramieh in his flying machine,' I began as I handed it to her.

'Why, thank you. Yes! And now he's headed for India! He'll be here soon. Seems as if I'll get my bet. Take a look! Here's a picture of the 'plane.'

She showed me the photo in question and we continued to leaf through the album, Della effusive with Hinkler talk. Nellie appeared with a silver platter bearing the requested lemonade and some unrequested, but very well received, slices of chocolate cake. I had not indulged in such luxuries in years and we ate and drank amidst happy conversation.

'Now you must meet Kismet,' she announced as she wiped her hands with her serviette, her mouth still full of cake. Della helped me up and brought me to the birdcage.

'Psst! Shoo, Ming!' she ordered a sleek Siamese cat which was watching the cage from behind a chair. The cat did not obey without first nonchalantly wrapping itself around Della's legs, then mine, leaping onto a table, then to the verandah rail and finally into the garden. With many chirrupy noises, Della coaxed the canary onto her finger and took it out.

'He's such a carefree little fellow. He makes me very, very happy. Sometimes too happy, I'm afraid,' she added after a pause. Then the chirrupy talk resumed.

'Come on now, who's a pretty boy? Who's a pretty boy? Hop to Luighseach. There's a darling.

'He's very tame,' she continued. 'But he gets very, very excited when the big birds come down for their feed. They'll be here later this afternoon. Then you should hear him sing! He always wants to go and join them, but he has to stay in his cage. He wouldn't survive if he was let out. It would be different if he'd been born in the wild, wouldn't you agree?' Della did not wait my answer. 'Back to mummy now, sweetie. There's a boy. Here we are! Now, let me show you round.'

We passed through a double door framed by gold-girdled curtains, and entered a spacious drawing room, the abode of a piano of the grandest proportions. The room was prettily papered in the palest shell-pink silk, which in turn was patterned with peacocks and cherry blossom and delicate pagodas. White chaise lounges and elegant armchairs were upholstered in pink and gold brocade. Against the far wall stood two lacquered cabinets, and upon these were posed a pair of vases enamelled with dragons. The back garden, brimful with roses, and the distant pavilion were reflected in an enormous gold-framed mirror which hung above the fireplace.

Della noticed me biting my lip. 'You must think we're frightfully rich. Dear, dear. But it's true, I'm afraid. The furniture's Louis Quinze style and the cabinets and vases are from China. Daddy's frightfully well-travelled, you see. He was brought up in India, but he's lived all over the world.'

'He's Indian, your father?' I could not imagine Della's father being dark-skinned.

'Oh no, he's as English as John Bull.'

'And what is it he does to earn his bread?'

'He's retired now, although he still imports antiques and has quite a lot to do with property and shares and all that sort of thing. And he sails and plays golf. But they're hobbies. In fact, I think everything Daddy does is a hobby. He once told me, though, that he was a self-made man, whatever that means, but I don't really know what you could say he actually does.'

She opened the folding doors and we entered a smaller room decorated with the same wallpaper and furniture. Fans patterned with oriental motifs had been mounted and framed and arranged in a pleasing array on the wall. An ornate carriage clock, its gold cogs busily marking time, stood in the centre of the mantlepiece.

Something familiar caught my attention.

''Twas my Daid painted that.' I indicated the large portrait of Mrs Sotheby which hung directly above the clock. ''Tis his signature upon it.'

Della looked at me, astonished and excited.

'Mummy's portrait? *Your* father? I say, is he an artist?'

'Aye. He's a photographer by trade. From time to time, though, he paints portraits, which is what he likes doing most.'

Well, well! What a small world! I say, does he really drive a motorcycle?'

'Aye,' I nodded.

'Wally was frightfully impressed with the motorcycle. He wanted to take it apart while your father was busy and I was at my wits' end persuading him not to. Anyway, we both spent hours trying to copy his accent. As for Mummy, she was thoroughly delighted with the picture. Look where it's hanging – pride of place in the drawing room. I love that painting. It's so very Mummy, right down to her boots.'

I gave the painting a second look. Somehow I could not imagine Mrs Sotheby wearing boots.

She gave my arm a tug. 'Come, I'll show you round some more.'

Della led me across the hall and into another room. Unlike the living room, which was such a delicate blend of France and the Far East, the dining room boldly evoked an exotic Araby. Again I could only admire the richly textured wallpaper, this time a magnificent turquoise, and the curtains patterned in orange, turquoise and ivory, with their sumptuous swags and heavy gold girdles. At the far end was a polished walnut sideboard replete with crystal decanters. Above the sideboard hung a painting, surprisingly modern in style, of a bare-breasted girl in exotic Turkish costume reclined like a Venus on tasselled cushions. Grapes and peaches and plums spilled from a silver bowl in the centre of the dining table, which also was polished walnut and was set with crockery and silver for the night's repast.

'Daddy bought the dining table during last year's trip,' explained my guide. 'Mummy was so delighted with it she had to redecorate the room and order a dinner service to match. As for the painting—it's a bit risqué don't you think? I say, would you like to stay to dinner?'

Immediately, Della went in search of her mother. We found her coming down the stairs, having changed into evening attire, fixing pearl bracelets around her wrists.

Della repeated her request:

'I say, Mummy, would it be all right if Luighseach stayed to dinner? Please? I'm certain Cook won't mind.'

'Cook?' echoed Mrs Sotheby. 'Darling, Cook has nothing to do with it. What will your parents say?' At that point she caught sight of the calliper. I edged behind Della. 'Surely you have a home to go to, dear?' Mrs Sotheby seemed to imply that I might be orphaned.

'I'll be needing to ask my Daid,' I answered. 'If it's not putting it out of you, 'twould be a grand treat to stay.' I did not fancy the trek back to the station and the long trip home, particularly if there was a good meal to be had. There might even be dessert: ice cream perhaps.

'Please, Mummy,' Della begged. 'Luighseach's been so kind as to visit. It's only right we should ask her to dinner.'

'But Della, it's not proper. What on earth will her parents think?'

'My Daid won't mind,' I added.

19

'Please, Mummy.'

Daid was telephoned. Much to Mrs Sotheby's surprise, he granted permission.

'Oh, I say! Topping!' Della exclaimed when she heard the verdict. 'Let's go out and feed the birds.'

She brought me out to the back garden where, at an old wooden table, Della ladled a mixture of bread and honey into some battered tin plates.

'This is for the big birds. Here.'

Within minutes, I was transformed into a tree for at least ten brash, brightly coloured creatures. Not having ever been subjected to conduct of this sort, I could not help hunching under the grip of claws and wincing at the noisy pushing and nibbling that accompanied their meal. Della, however, assured me that such behaviour was quite natural and joined her canary in song. I was only too glad when we were summoned for dinner.

I now had the opportunity to meet the rest of the Sotheby family. Mr Sotheby was an able-bodied, splendidly dressed, rather ruddy man whose most distinctive features were a dashing moustache with waxed ends, bushy sideburns, and a thick goatee in numerous shades of ochre, umber and oxide. He appeared to be in his late fifties, which made him substantially older than his pretty wife. Wally, Della's older brother, was in his final year at school. Tanned, blond and blue-eyed, with a reserved manner but athletic mien, he was at least a foot taller than his sister. Leila, who was about ten, possessed her mother's red hair, and with her bold look made it quite clear she was her own custodian. Eight-year-old Henry, also redheaded and freckled, gave the impression that he was hiding a good many things inside his cheeks and pockets.

Our introductions concluded we sat down at table. Instinctively I made the sign of the cross and said grace:

> Beannaigh sinn, a Dhia
> Beannaighe àr mbia is àr ndeoch
> Ós Tú a cheannaigh sinn go daor
> Go saora Tú sinn ó gach uile olc.

Only when I finished did I realise that my prayer had been a solo performance. The Sothebys looked on in silence.

'Are you a nun?'

That remark was made by Henry.

'I told you, Harry, Luighseach's a school friend,' Della explained, trying to be patient.

'Spotty dog, sitting on a log!' teased Henry in a sing-song chant.

'Anyway, whatever gave you that idea?' Della ignored the taunt.

'She did this,' and Henry made a poor imitation of my sign of the cross. 'That's what the nuns do.'

Leila, evidently, was of a similar mind. 'She must be a nun. She said grace in Latin. All the nuns say it in Latin.'

'That wasn't Latin, stupid,' interjected Wally.

'How would *you* know?' Leila retorted. 'You don't even *do* Latin.'

'Luighseach speaks Irish,' Della explained, proud that she could make the final, definitive remark and prove that she, for one, was not stupid. 'That was Irish, wasn't it?' she whispered to me.

'Aye,' I replied.

At that moment, I was presented with a platter of succulent fillet steak. I stared at it, stunned, for it was Friday and that meant a day of abstinence. I had never, ever eaten meat on a Friday.

'Are you not Catholic?' I whispered to Della.

'It's a little complicated,' she replied. 'I'll explain later.'

'Nuns are Irish,' Henry decided to link the latest snippet of information with his earlier observation.

'Of course they're Irish, silly,' Leila thought Henry deficient. 'They're Catholics.'

'No they're not,' corrected Della. 'Sister Scholastica isn't. I—I mean she's Catholic, of course. But she's not Irish.

'Must you always talk about nuns?' Mr Sotheby complained. 'Really, not a single meal passes without some mention of the creatures.'

'One shouldn't discuss religion at table, children,' Mrs Sotheby mildly remonstrated, supporting her husband. 'It's not proper.'

'We're not discussing religion at the table,' argued Wally.

'You were talking about the nuns again, dear,' replied Mrs Sotheby.

'That's not *discussing* religion,' insisted Wally. But Mrs Sotheby did not pay attention.

Mr Sotheby decided to redirect the course of conversation. He carefully patted his moustache with his serviette and slipped me a smile.

'Well, Luighseach,' he began. 'I must say you have quite a brogue. From which part of Ireland do you come? North or south?'

'Neither it is.'

'Luighseach's from Galway, Daddy,' Della spoke for me.

'Ah! So you're from the Gael— what do you call it?' asked Mr Sotheby.

'The Gaeltacht,' I answered. 'Aye, although 'twas in Belfast I was born.'

'I see,' Mr Sotheby rested his elbows on the arms of his chair and circled his forefinger over the enormous amber stone of a heavy gold dress ring. 'I visited Ireland many years ago. When was it now?' He fingered through his goatee for the necessary facts. 'Must have been back in the 'nineties. Let me see, was it 'ninety-four or 'ninety-five?' The goatee finally produced the answer. ''Ninety-five. I stayed mainly in the north. Visited Belfast,' he gave me a nod. 'Then travelled along the Donegal coast. I suppose it's rather changed since then.'

'I wouldn't know, sir, for I've not been around that long.'

Mr Sotheby confined his smile with a small sip of wine and proceeded with a flourish of his serviette. 'It was a pretty place in those days. Full of old-fashioned charm. And the sea views were spectacular if memory serves me well. On the whole, I found it all quite quaint.'

'You're thinking it's quaint, sir?'

'You don't think so?'

I felt my lips twitch as a hundred replies raced through my mind. But not one could find voice. I pushed some peas around my plate instead and stared suspiciously at my untouched portion of steak.

Mr Sotheby eyed me over his wineglass. 'I gather you were there during the uprisings?' he eventually asked.

'Aye.'

'Uprisings?' echoed Mrs Sotheby with some alarm.

'Were your family involved?' inquired Mr Sotheby.

'They may have been.'

'In a *revolution*?' added Mrs Sotheby. 'Bless me! I do hope you're not a radical.'

'Oh help! Now we're talking politics!' exclaimed Wally. 'All we have to do is talk about sex and we've covered the whole trinity of dinner table taboos.'

'Thank you, Wally,' interposed Mr Sotheby. 'I think that's sufficient impertinence for one evening.'

Wally curled his lip in a manner which suggested that given the opportunity there was plenty more impertinence to be had.

'Now Mummy,' Della made an effort to appease her mother. 'I'm sure Luighseach is not going to go round throwing bricks through anyone's window.'

'But, Della, she's a Bolshevik!' Mrs Sotheby's alarm had not subsided.

Mr Sotheby smiled at her reaction. 'Are you a Bolshevik?' he asked, still smiling, this time at me.

I looked back at him and, unable to resist his sport, smiled a little and shook my head.

'There, Letty dear, you don't need to worry. Our Irish dinner guest is not a Bolshevik.'

'Well, she really couldn't be could she, Desmond? After all, she is lame so she couldn't possibly throw bricks through our window,' Mrs Sotheby concluded. 'I couldn't help but notice your legs, dear,' she added.

At that moment, I wanted to throw twenty bricks through the Sotheby's window.

'Luighseach had polio when she was eight, Mummy,' Della was again the provider of vital information.

'Oh, what a shame,' lamented Mrs Sotheby. Conversation had now been successfully deflected from politics. 'But how on earth do you come to be at St Dom's?'

Why did people always assume that because there was something wrong with my legs, there must also be something wrong with my head?

'I'm on a scholarship, ma'am,' I explained.

22

'Really? You must be clever,' replied Mrs Sotheby. 'How very charitable of the sisters to provide such an opportunity. I suppose you'll go on to teach, although I don't know how you'll manage being crippled like that. Maybe you could learn to type? But the sisters don't teach typing at the convent, do they Della?'

'I beg your pardon, Mummy?' Della took leave of her whispered conversation with Wally who, at the mention of the nuns, had seized the opportunity to make an underhand comment about discussing religion at the table.

'Do the nuns teach typing?' inquired Mrs Sotheby.

'No, Mummy,' Della replied in a very matter-of-fact tone.

'Thank heavens,' responded a relieved Mrs Sotheby. 'Then perhaps you might be called to join the good sisters. They've always an eye out for recruits and they do favour the clever ones. After all, you'll probably never marry.'

'Mummy!' Della protested.

'What is it, dear?'

'Don't chatter so! Consider what Luighseach's feeling listening to you organise her life like this!'

'Della darling, why must you always think of everyone else? Have you even considered what *I* am feeling? It's been a frightfully hot day, and at the end of it all second hand Rose comes visiting out of the blue and you have the hide to invite her to dine. Then we find out she's political. How do you think *I* feel? I don't know *who* she is.'

'Well, if it's any consolation, Mummy, Luighseach's father painted *your* portrait.'

'Really? How nice! Did you hear that, Desmond?'

Mr Sotheby looked up from his meal.

'What was that, my dear?'

'My portrait! The one with the kimono you brought me from Japan for our anniversary. Such divine fabric! Julia Mahony thought it the most exquisite she has ever seen. Her garden party invitation arrived today. Now, I really do need an Easter bonnet for the occasion. I simply cannot wear last year's.'

'Why don't you wear the one you wore the year before?'

'Oh Desmond, do be serious.'

While Mrs Sotheby indulged her husband in descriptions of costumes, Leila and Henry became engaged in a game of marbles using the peas that remained on their plates. Della and Wally, on the other hand, saw a perfect opportunity to enjoy a conversation that seemed very much their own:

'It looks like Bert Hinkler is going to make it, Wally,' my companion whispered.

'He's not here yet, Dell, so I still keep my medals.' Wally emphasised his point with a thrust of his knife.

'*Your* medals? The Captain's you mean.' Della thrust her fork in reply.

'Major,' her brother corrected.

'Captain.'

'Major. He was promoted to Major after he won the Military Cross in 1915,' asserted Wally with considerable authority.

'Don't tell me you're talking about that wretched aviator again!' Mrs Sotheby angrily interrupted.

'Well, seeing it's nothing to do with religion, politics or sex, I reckon we can discuss "that wretched aviator" as much as we like,' Wally retorted, cuttingly. 'By the way, speaking of aviators, I'm off to the airfields tomorrow.'

'What about cricket?' Mr Sotheby laid down his knife and fork.

'I'm not playing.'

'You're *what*?' Mr Sotheby was far from pleased.

Wally repeated his declaration.

'Not playing cricket? *Not playing cricket*? How long's this been going on for?'

'I haven't played all season, or haven't you noticed?'

'The boy's gone mad!' Mr Sotheby exclaimed. 'First, he's kicked out of military school; now, he's opting out of cricket. You do realise you're not being educated to do as you please?'

'I couldn't agree more,' Wally replied as he rose from the table, tucked in his chair and walked to the door.

'And where do you think you're going?'

'Where do you think? I've finished dinner, I don't want dessert and I've an essay to knock off before I get to the airfields tomorrow. I'm going to my room. Any objections?'

Wally did not give his father time to raise any. The door was quickly shut and Mr Sotheby's attention was immediately taken by a pea which had misfired from Henry's plate and had hit him square on the shirt front.

Dessert was consumed in silence. Since we did not require coffee or port, Della and I were given permission to be excused.

We journeyed upstairs to her room.

Della's bedroom was a true bower, cluttered with knick-knacks and books. White satin swans on willow-lined ponds floated across a wallpaper of wedgwood blue. A breeze had scattered sheets of music all over the floor and a violin had been tossed amidst a pile of broderie cushions on a white four-poster bed. Also on the bed lay a violin case and a large paisley silk scarf. I picked up the instrument.

'Do you play?' Della inquired as she stationed herself next to a globe which she took no small delight in spinning as fast as she could.

'Aye.'

'Really? Violin?'

'Not any more,' I shook my head. ''Tis the 'cello I play.'

''Cello? With your legs like that? You're joking!' Della laughed in a surprised way and then quickly pursed her lips.

'Well, I suppose you really do have the physique for it, and you have to sit to play,' she considered as she spun the globe even harder. 'My violin teacher also plays the 'cello. She's tall with strong shoulders like you. You have to be to play the 'cello. I couldn't play it if I tried. Why, if it wasn't for getting sick, I imagine you'd be rather good at sport. Have you ever played?'

'I— I— '

Della cut my stutter short. 'I'm sorry. I didn't mean to make you feel bad. It's only that you look very capable, athletic even, despite that heavy brace and your legs being so thin.' She took my arm. 'Let me show you a few things.'

I opened the case and carefully placed the violin inside. As I did, I froze at the sight of a picture glued to the case's velvet lining.

Della was smiling fondly at it. It was a photograph of a man in military attire. 'That's The Captain,' she explained.

'Your uncle is it? Or a brother, perhaps?' I inquired after some hesitation. 'He looks like your brother.'

'Wally? Do you think so? Hmmm, I suppose you're right. Wally with a moustache,' she giggled. 'No, he's my father.'

That was impossible. The photo did not look at all like Mr Sotheby.

Della observed my disbelief.

'No,' she smiled, 'Daddy's my step-father. The Captain, my real father, was in the Royal Flying Corps. You see, I wasn't quite two when he went to the War and I saw him only a couple of times after that. It's all a bit of a blur, I'm afraid. He was shot down in France, I know that much. Anyway, Daddy's been as much of a father as any real father could have been, so we call him Daddy and we call my real father The Captain. Wally and me, that is. Leila and Harry are my half-sister and half-brother. Everyone called him The Captain. Captain Ralph William Ponsonby was his name. He was Irish, actually, like you.'

'Irish is it? Like myself?' Nothing could have been more absurd. ''Tis no Irish name that, for Irish names are O's and Macs. 'Tis an English name and Ascendancy to be sure.'

'Well, my father *was* an Irishman, I know that much. He was born there, although he was educated in England, Wally says. What on earth do you mean anyway?'

'Well, I'll put it like so, Della Sotheby. If we were both in Ireland now, it's yourself would be riding after foxes and myself would be tilling your fields.'

'Oh?' Della replied. 'Well, thank heavens we're not in Ireland. We can be friends,' she added cheerfully.

'Do you be Catholic?' I queried.

'Catholic? Of course I am. Why do you ask?'

'But 'twas steak your mother served on a Friday like the Protestants.'

'I know. But I did mention it was a little complicated. Mummy *is* a Catholic. Well, she's sort of a Catholic,' she added, noting my look of disbelief. 'I mean, she doesn't always go to Mass. In fact, she only goes when she's got a new hat. Daddy doesn't go at all.'

'Does he not buy hats?' I asked.

'No,' Della laughed. 'He only buys them for Mummy. Daddy isn't a Catholic. He's the one who insists on meat being part of every meal. Wally isn't either; nor is Harry. Daddy was adamant that the boys be brought up Church of England and attend grammar schools—well, they both attend grammar school now, but Wally went to the Royal Military School when we lived in England. Anyway, what I meant to say is that only the girls are Catholic – Leila and me, that is. But I'm the only one who goes to Church. I mean, I go to Church when I can. I try to go every week, but it's not easy when your parents don't bother. I do believe, though. After all, one has to believe in *Something*. Don't you agree?'

'Agree with what?'

'That one has to believe in Something.'

'Aye,' I replied. 'But it has to be the right something.'

'What do you mean by that?'

'Well, I been taught my catechism but that doesn't mean I believe it. Let's say that God's a bit more explaining to do before I'm doing any more believing.'

Leila barged in. 'Hey, Sister Spastica, you're father's here,' and she disappeared as quickly as she entered, slamming the door behind her.

'Leila!' Della shouted as she ran to the door. 'Of all the nasty things to say! Oh, I'm so very, very sorry. Oh, how awful!' She was blushing.

'I best be going now,' I replied.

'She didn't mean it, Luighseach. She's thoughtless.'

That was a lie. Leila Sotheby meant every word. I made for the door.

Della insisted upon seeing me downstairs.

Daid was waiting with cap in hand, his pinched, elfin features attending to yet another of Mrs Sotheby's glowing descriptions of the kimono she was wearing in the portrait. The moment he saw me, however, he politely excused himself, gave me his arm and helped me down the final step.

'Dia dhuit, a Luighseach,' he whispered as he signed the cross on my forehead and kissed my cheek. 'Did you have a grand time now?'

'Oh, we've had a lovely time,' gushed Mrs Sotheby, who quickly showed us the door. 'Why, she's such a clever girl. On scholarship, I hear. And so very kind to Della. It was so nice to have you, dear. Do come again.'

Della, on the other hand, saw my father and me to our motorcycle. She watched Daid help me into the sidecar and giggled a little at the sight of us both in goggles and gloves. We set off, and she stood alone in the driveway and waved us good-bye.

4

A small fish, a stray cow and a little kindness were three things that should always be returned, and Daid did not lose time in pointing this out when we returned from the Sotheby's. I gave the matter some consideration and arrived at St Dominic's on the following Monday in a quandry as to what to do.

Della Sotheby was quality. Any act of hospitality I could offer would be no match for her fine china and fillet steak. Besides, I had been the one to extend the kindness of visiting someone supposedly sick. So by rights reciprocation fell to Della, not to me.

Would Della respond? The probability that she would even remember, let alone return my favour became increasingly remote as the week progressed. Della was consumed with Hinkler-mania. The closer the airman flew to Australia, the more enthusiastic she became. She took particular delight in singing the 'Hinkle Hustle' at the top of her voice and choreographing appropriate actions. It was a little number she performed at every opportunity between lessons, and the class wasted no time in joining her. The moment a nun vacated the platform, Miss Sotheby and chorus would claim that spot as their stage, singing and dancing over and over until warning signals sent them scurrying back to their seats and the next sister entered the room.

I could not bring myself to break into that tight-knit troupe. The class had made it quite clear that it thought me odd and preferred to have as little to do with me as possible. All I could do was to draw Della a picture of her hero for her scrapbook, leave it in her desk with a short note of explanation, and watch and wait and hope.

I was rewarded with a cheeky, charming smile during History. It was later followed by a lunchtime visit to my cloakroom.

'I say, Luighseach,' she announced as she entered, picture in hand. 'Did *you* draw this?'

'Aye. And what is so remarkable about that?' I questioned.

'Simply, that it's awfully good! You've certainly got your father's talent. What a likeness!'

''Tis easy when it's from a photograph,' I shrugged. ''Twas a grid I ruled over the picture and copied each square across.'

'Well, it's very, very good however you did it. I say, can you draw from life? I mean, could you draw me if I sat for you?'

I shifted a little. 'I don't like drawing people from life.'

'Life gets in the way, I suppose,' Della gently observed. She could not have made a more apt comment.

I nodded and recommenced my reading.

'Luighseach,' she interrupted, 'I wanted to ask you something. Do you like the theatre?'

A very long time had passed since I had gone to the theatre.

'Well,' Della continued, '*Twelfth Night* is on at the Conservatorium and I have two tickets for the matinee this Saturday. Fanny, who was going to come, can't. I— I was wondering if you might like to join me.'

She paused.

I looked at her. She seemed very downcast.

'Fanny's organised a tennis party,' Della resumed. 'Everyone's going— everyone except me, that is,' she sighed as she flopped down on the trunk beside me. 'I wasn't invited. I know I'm hopeless at tennis, but I'm as much her friend as anyone. Anyway, she had promised to come to the theatre with me. Fanny said she didn't invite me because she knew I had another commitment, but I know it's because she's invited Wally. You remember Wally my brother, don't you? Well, Fanny's frightfully keen on Wally, you see, and she doesn't want me around at the same time. It's not very nice, is it?'

Della was fighting back tears.

'Well, if it's any consolation to you, Della Sotheby,' I replied, 'Frances Mahony didn't invite myself either.'

'What good would you be at a tennis party?' she laughed as she wiped a tear away.

'Not much good at all, I'm afraid,' I lamented.

'Well, that makes two of us,' Della replied, smiling again as she nudged me in the side. 'So then, what about the theatre? Care to come?'

'I don't know—I—'

But Daid, when he read Mrs Sotheby's letter of invitation, thought it would do me good. He was familiar with the venue and was convinced that it presented no obstacles as far as my legs were concerned. A lengthy telephone conversation followed whereby my father received the assurance from Della's mother that I would enjoy the performance from the comfort of a seat near the aisle, and that transport to and from the Conservatorium would be courtesy of the Sotheby car.

So at the appointed time, I was greeted at our front door by a quaint figure proudly sporting two military medals. They seemed a curious adornment for the white linen frock, silk stockings, pearls, gloves and rose trimmed hat which otherwise comprised her attire.

'Hinkle Hinkle little star, sixteen days and here you are! He made it! They're mine!' Della exclaimed as she accompanied me down the front steps. 'Wally didn't want to let them go, but he had to. Aren't they wonderful? That's the Distinguished Service Order and that's the Military Cross. And this is Hammond, although he calls himself 'Ammond,' Della indicated the middle-aged man smartly dressed in a brass-buttoned uniform, cap and gloves, who was waiting beside the Bentley. 'He's Mummy's chauffeur and gardener. He's married to Cook.'

Della especially enjoyed the performance, and by the time the play finished she was in very high spirits. Heedless of my objections, she insisted upon visiting my house. After all, I had visited hers and without invitation too.

'Hammond won't mind waiting and I don't have to be home till dinner,' she told me. 'Isn't that right, Hammond?'

'Your mother said 'ome by six, Miss Della,' answered the chauffeur.

'I say, do you like Shakespeare, Luighseach?' she continued while I was helped into the car. 'You didn't laugh very much.'

I was too busy with the calliper to reply in detail.

'I—I find it a little hard to follow,' I admitted.

'It is a little tricky,' agreed Della, 'but it does help to read the play before you see it. I've read *Twelfth Night* many times. Actually, Daddy bought me a miniature theatre so that I could act it out. It had cardboard cut outs of all the characters which you could move around the stage. I enjoyed doing that. Now, I wonder where that's got to? It must be still in a box somewhere. Have you read it?'

'Have I read what?'

'Have you read the play? *Twelfth Night?*'

I shook my head.

Sensing that I did not share quite the same literary interests, Della modified her conversation.

'I used to like reading Lambs' *Tales from Shakespeare*. Have you ever read Lambs' *Tales?*'

I did not reply immediately.

'Some—Somebody read them to me once.'

'I say, old thing,' Della took me by the elbow and again adjusted the course of conversation. 'Wasn't the drinking scene funny?' She began to imitate Sir Andrew. '"Begin, fool: it begins 'Hold thy peace.'"'

Della cut short her merry song. 'Mind you, you can't laugh too loud or too long, and anyone who does ends up making a fool of himself for lack of sensitivity.'

'And what are you meaning by that?'

'Well, take Malvolio for instance. I mean at the end of the play. They shouldn't have treated him like that, and anyone who laughs too much shows himself up.'

'Well, I'm thinking Malvolio got all he deserved,' I responded.

'Really?'

'And I wouldn't be saying otherwise that he was the greatest fool of them all, smiling and making himself superior so and donning them silly stockings. Yellow as your canary they were and with garters all criss-crossing. 'Tis no one in their right mind would be as foolish as that, and himself taking offence at the end of it all. A very fool for the reckoning he is.'

'Luighseach, you're too hard.'

'I amn't.'

She tightened her hold on my arm. 'I think you were embarrassed by him. You could hardly look at him when he came on stage cross-gartered.'

'That's not the truth.'

'Yes it is. Merely because there was something peculiar about his legs. Why, you've gone red as beetroot!'

I pulled away from her and looked out the window. Totally undaunted, Della persevered with her observations.

'But Luighseach, he couldn't help it. Personally, I think that if anyone should have been hard done by it should have been Sir Toby.'

'And why is it you think that now?'

'Because he was a very clever man but he used his cleverness to prey on others' weaknesses and make fools of them for his own sport. Anyone who does that is very, very cruel, and ultimately very foolish.'

'Nothing of foolish, Della Sotheby. Sharp he bees.'

'You're joking.'

'The devil I'm not. 'Tis Sir Toby Belch knows what he's about and he does fine for himself by the end. A wise man is Sir Toby Belch.'

'How can you say something like that?'

'I've a tongue in my head, have I not?'

'But you can't be serious,' she protested. 'You're playing devil's advocate, surely?'

'And what if I am? Who, then, would you consider to be a wise man, Della Sotheby?'

My question was silently mouthed.

'One who perceives the truth and orders his actions towards it,' crept from her lips.

''Tis Sir Toby does that.'

'He does not.'

'Aye he does. Sir Toby Belch knows them other characters inside out. He knows how to get what he wants from Sir Andrew and he knows his niece, and he admires Maria for he sees she knows how to make a fool of Malvolio. And because of that, Sir Toby does quite well for himself.'

'But he's so low!'

'But do you not agree he perceives the truth and orders his actions towards it as you said yourself?'

'Yes—'

'Then I'm saying Sir Toby's a wise man.'

'No he's not!'

'Prove it me, then!'

Della put a finger to her chin and deliberated over the matter. Then her eyes widened and she clapped her hands and pointed the finger in my face. 'Because his knowledge of the truth is limited! Sir Toby only sees weaknesses and faults.

That might be part of the truth but it's not all the truth. And all he's interested in is his own self and how he can use people for his pleasure. And all that is, is drinking and making a mockery of others. He never rises above his own baseness, nor does he allow others to do the same. And that, in the long run, I think is truly very foolish, for it does a lot of harm and very little good. Oh, Malvolio and the others were foolish too, but for one reason or another they couldn't help it. But Sir Toby, given to drink though he was, was still very much a master of his own actions and for that I think him a fool, moreso than Malvolio ever could have been.'

'Then,' I ventured a conclusion. 'Would you not agree that Sir Toby Belch is worldly wise?'

Della stopped to consider my pronouncement more carefully and closed her eyes. 'All right,' she sighed. 'I'll give you that one. Sir Toby Belch is *worldly wise*. Which is probably the most foolish thing of all!'

'Listen to you! You'd think you'd be counting yourself among the seers as live high upon mountains with nought but their souls for company and a little bread for to eat.'

'Nonsense! I'll join the heroes who fly to the heavens!' she laughed. 'I say, here we are already! Now are you going to invite me inside? Hammond can wait. Thank you, Hammond.'

'Arrah!' I muttered the moment I was helped to the pavement. 'Don't look!' I commanded Della, who was looking over the terrace houses which jostled onto the street, and was smiling and nodding at whatever neighbours chanced to be in their front gardens.

'What's up?' she asked.

I pulled her closer to me and whispered. 'Well, if you look over there you'll see Mrs Murphy sitting on her front porch.'

'Who's Mrs Murphy?' she asked.

'An old cow.'

'What rot,' Della replied, disbelievingly.

'And if you catch her eye,' I continued to caution, 'Mrs Murphy'll start to talk, for she's always looking about to see what I'm up to, and when she catches me up she starts talking. So let you look down so and walk on.'

'I wouldn't worry,' Della observed as we neared our front gate. 'She seems to be having a nap.'

'Whisht! Put your head down!' I commanded through my teeth.

The gate squeaked and scraped across the paving.

'Yoohoo! Lucy!' Mrs Murphy called from her chair.

'Oh my Jesus!' I groaned.

'Hello!' Della sent her a cheery wave.

'Lucy!' Mrs Murphy called again as she waddled down to the fence. I continued to mount the front steps. Della, meanwhile, decided to introduce herself.

'I was wondering if you needed some milk?' inquired Mrs Murphy.

"Tis milk we have aplenty, thank you, Mrs Murphy,' I curtly replied from the top step. 'We've no need of a cow,' I added as I watched Mrs Murphy take her leave and strike up a conversation with the Sotheby's chauffeur.

'Luighseach, you're rude!' scolded Della in an angry whisper.

'Rude is it you're saying? Well, I'll be telling you, Della Sotheby, that if you had your way you'd be standing there in the heat listening to the woman preach on about suffering and the Lord's mercy and the like of every devotion to every saint in Heaven.'

'Really?' Della replied. 'I thought she was very kindly offering some milk. I wish we had neighbours like that.'

'Offering milk!' I scoffed. 'She's always offering milk. And if it isn't milk, it's marmalade, and if it isn't marmalade, it's mending and if it isn't mending it's washing and if it isn't washing it's something else, you can be sure of that. And you can also be sure that if she's come with her milk and marmalade, she's come with preaching and prayers and stories of saints and sinners enough to last you this life and Purgatory put together.'

'I'm sure she means well,' remarked Della. 'She seems very nice.'

'Well, she can go and seem very "nice" at your house.'

'She seems to be very fond of you,' continued Della.

'She helped look after me when I came out of hospital,' I reluctantly admitted. 'And I'm not very fond of herself.'

I opened the door to our white gabled cottage. Della took time to admire our tiny flower garden before she entered.

'Why Luighseach, you have swallows!' she exclaimed.

'We do not.'

'Look, a nest!' she grabbed my elbow and pointed. 'Up there.'

Sure enough in the far corner, under the eaves, there was plastered a nest.

'Hadn't you noticed it before?'

'Not ever.'

'Why, they must have been there all summer. We have swallows too. Mr and Mrs Swallow make a nest at our place every year. Look! There's one now!'

A small bird playfully darted past.

The creak of our footsteps on the floorboards was the only welcome we received as we passed into the house.

'Where may I put my things?' she whispered.

'Over here,' I showed her the hallstand. 'Now why do you be whispering?'

Her eyes widened and she continued to whisper. 'I don't know. It's as if someone's sleeping and I don't want to disturb them.'

'Well you needn't whisper so 'cause 'tis no one here save ourselves. Would you care for a cup of tea now?'

Della gladly agreed and followed me down the corridor, through the dining room to the kitchen. I filled the kettle and placed it on the stove. I was about to strike the match when she interrupted.

'May I? I've never lit a stove before.'

I looked at her incredulously, handed her the matches and guided her through the motion.

'And is it something to eat you're after?' I asked.

'Yes thank you.'

'Then 'twill be bread and marmalade for you. We're not ones to keep cake.'

'Bread and marmalade would be lovely. Is it Mrs Murphy's marmalade?'

'It is.'

I took out the bread and the knife as Della studied my every move.

'Let me do that,' she urged.

I handed her the implement and left her energetically sawing the loaf while I did my utmost to combine unmatching cups, saucers and plates from the dresser.

Two thick, clumsy slices of bread were placed on the plates appointed for the purpose. I smeared them with soggy butter and lumped marmalade on top while Della's fingers dabbed up the crumbs that had escaped the vigorous assault of her knife. The kettle boiled. Throwing an old cloth over the handle, I sent the water splashing into the pot. Della pulled the milk from the cooler.

'Stop sin—!'

'Pardon?'

'Stop, I'm saying, for I'll be testing it before you pour.'

I took the jug from her, smelt it and dipped my finger in to taste. My wrinkled nose pronounced the verdict.

'Sour it is.'

'Oh dear. Would you like me to go to Mrs Murphy's house to get some?' Della suggested. 'I don't mind going.'

'And if you did, you'd never come back. Will you be taking it black now?'

'Oh, very well. I've never had black tea before.'

'And will there be sugar for you?'

'Four, thank you.'

These graceless introductory rites performed, we took our preparations into the dining room, sat down beneath a faded 'Last Supper' and continued the ritual.

'Where are your parents?' she asked at length.

'My Daid's at work. He does be at weddings on Saturdays, taking photographs.'

'And your mother?'

I looked down at the tablecloth. There was a stain on it that I had been unable to remove. Nearby was a hole that had not been patched. One of the plates was chipped. In a little while, I knew I would have to prepare the potatoes for tea.

'I haven't got—'

'Oh dear. Did— did she get sick like you?'

I shook my head. 'The polio happened after. She died before we left Ireland. Will there be more tea for you?'

'No thank you.'

I took her cup and saucer to the basin and left Della picking the crumbs off her plate. I had barely finished wiping my eyes on the tea towel when she appeared behind me.

'Where can I put the plates?'

'Over there,' I squinted at her and indicated the sink with my glasses.

In went the plates, soap was lathered, and all was washed and dried and returned to the dresser.

Despite my objections, Della dearly wanted to see my room.

She saw no swans on my walls. There was a crucifix instead. Della cautiously reached past the cane-crutches that leant against the wall near my bed and fondled the glass-beaded rosary that was slung round one of the bed knobs. She scanned my desk and saw nothing save the lamp and inkstand. She walked down to the wardrobe and glimpsed her face in the cracked mirror on its door. She lifted the seat of the chair on the opposite wall near the washstand and quickly closed it, embarrassed to find that it was a commode. Then she noticed my 'cello lying on its side on the rag rug. She wandered over to the music stand and pursued its contents.

'Dotzauer,' she observed. 'Looks dry as dust and difficult.'

'Aye.'

'And what's underneath? Beethoven 'cello sonatas? Good heavens! I'm learning the *Spring Sonata* at the moment. Which one are you playing?'

'The A major one it is.'

'How long have you been learning it?'

'Since last year,' I replied. ''Twas some practice I was doing this morning. I've a lesson on Monday and Mrs Epstein will rouse on me surely if I'm behind with it for 'tis too much Bach I been playing of late.'

'Did you say Mrs Epstein?'

'I did.'

'Does she live in Petersham?'

'Aye she does.'

'Is she tall and dark?'

'Aye.'

'With tortoiseshell glasses?' Della's questions became more excited.

'Aye.'

'And sort of bulgy, googly eyes?'

'Aye,' I couldn't help smiling at that description.

'I don't believe it!' Della exclaimed. 'Why! She's my teacher too! Well, I never! How long have you been learning from her?'

'Five and a half years it would be now.'

'Goodness gracious! To think we've only now begun to know each other. I've never seen you at a recital. I would have known you straight away if I had. Where *have* you been hiding? I say, would you play me some?'

I shook my head.

'Please,' she begged, 'I'd love to hear you. You don't often get to hear a 'cello, and it's such a beautiful instrument. Come on, sit down and show me. Can you play *The Swan*? I love *The Swan*!'

Della patted her hand on the seat of the chair and passed me my bow which she herself had tightened. I slid my thumb up and down the neck of my instrument then worked a phrase over the fingerboard. I lifted my bow. But it only took one glance at Della's eager face and my fingers disintegrated. Any tune I had intended to play completely vanished from my memory.

'I— I can't do it.'

'Nervous? Never mind, I know that feeling,' she smiled. 'That's a very pretty bedspread,' she remarked, stroking the colourful patchwork of lacy crochet that covered my bed. 'Who made it?'

'Myself,' I replied.

'Did you really? My, you're clever! I could never do anything like that! Much to Mummy's dismay, I'm all thumbs when it comes to needlework.'

'I made it when I was in hospital,' I explained. ''Twas the nuns taught me.'

'It's very big. Why, it reaches all the way to the floor! It must have taken you ages to make.'

'I was in hospital for ages.'

'Are these your books?' Della changed the subject.

I owned very few books for what little literature I read I acquired through exchange at the bookshop up the road. Aside from my *Canterbury Puzzles*, which was still in Della's possession, and *Amusements in Mathematics*, which lay on my bedside table, there was only one other volume remaining in my bookcase: a beautiful book of Botticelli prints which I had been unable to part with. Piles of 'cello music were stacked on the lowest shelf, along with numerous sketchbooks which documented my other artistic endeavours over the past years. These were filled with still lifes: detailed studies of teapots, cups, glasses, fruit and flowers, which my father had used to teach me how to draw and paint. Other pages were devoted to careful copies of works by great masters that Sister Ignatius had set me on a regular basis. On top of the bookcase was a metronome.

Della happily perused these belongings. Not being competent at drawing herself, she was fascinated by my sketches and had me explaining how Daid had shown me how to achieve such realistic effects by observing tonal variation and using different grades of lead. She pronounced my meagre library 'very, very strange'. *Amusements in Mathematics*, she declared, was an oxymoron.

'But don't you have *any* other books?' she asked, with a very worried expression. I shook my head.

'Don't you *like* reading?' she asked again, not believing that anyone could not enjoy one of her favourite pastimes.

''Tis not that I don't like reading,' I replied. 'I prefer puzzles and paintings and music is all.'

'I say, you're not scared of reading are you?' she probed.

Whatever gave her that idea? I silently resolved not to answer that question and my resolution was made the easier when I noticed my companion's wristwatch.

'Faith it's late! You'll do best to leave that and get along home now. Let them bits alone and I'll put them back myself. Your driver will be wondering what's become of you.'

'What's in here?' she asked as we passed down the hall.

'Ná hoscail an—! You cannot go in there!'

I had barely uttered the first word when she opened the parlour door and walked inside. She stood transfixed, staring at the statues of the Sacred and Immaculate Hearts that held vigil on either side of the fireplace. Each was honoured with flowers at their feet. Two pre-dieu were stationed nearby, a little further out from the two armchairs.

Like a pilgrim entering a shrine, Della walked to each, silently, wondrously. Devoutly she gazed at the images which adorned the surrounding wall and mantelpiece: a watercolour of myself and one of my mother on the opposite side, both painted by my father. There were photos of me dancing and on my pony; my first Holy Communion picture; my parents' wedding portrait; pictures of my uncles and aunts, and of my mother: sitting by the lake, writing at her desk and curled up in her favourite chair, book in hand, by the fire. Mam dressed up fine, Mam in apron and rolled up sleeves, Mam in the garden, Mam making lace. There were pictures of Galway and Belfast; watercolours and sketches of old buildings and towers, craggy outcrops and stone-hedged fields.

'I told you not to go in there!' I protested.

'Why not?' Della gently questioned. 'Why, it's a lovely room! There's such warmth and happiness here! Such peace!'

She turned to study the wedding portrait. 'Apple blossom!' she softly exclaimed. 'Is that apple blossom in your mother's hair? I haven't seen apple blossom since we left England. Mmmm! I can smell it now! Oh, how beautiful she is!' Della looked Mam up and down. 'Such sweet, simple beauty with her hair in that solitary braid. What colour was her hair, Luighseach? It's not dark like yours.'

''Twas gold,' I eventually whispered. ''Twas a sort of light, reddish-gold.'

'And your father's so handsome! He has a magical smile, doesn't he?' she marvelled at Daid, pictured there without his glasses. 'I say, he doesn't seem more than nineteen or twenty at the very most!'

Full of thought, Della wandered away from that watery, sketchy, sepia world and her eyes fell upon the statue of St Patrick in the corner. Then she noticed, in the opposite corner, the wheelchair and walking frame.

It was as if she had picked up a ring of keys. With a sad, puzzled look, she gazed at me in supplication, as if searching the lock to see if it would tell her which would fit.

'I— I think her soul is in Heaven, old thing.'

'Heaven you're saying? So 'tis prophet you turned now, is it? Will you not get out!'

'Oh don't be like that! Why, your mother seems such a tender person: so kind and good, and so much loved. Why should she not be there? And why should God deny her such a place when you have suffered so?'

'Because God doesn't care!'

'Well I care if that's any consolation.'

I turned away. Gently, she touched my hand.

'I suppose I ought to go home now.'

Not a word passed between us as I helped her with her things and walked her to the front door. I opened it for her. Della did not leave, however. She stood on the threshold and gazed at me, her large eyes moist.

'Goodbye, Luighseach,' she squeezed my hand. Her voice was barely audible. 'And— thank you. Thank you very much.'

She drifted down the steps, and, with a last look and fleeting wave, climbed into the car and was driven away.

5

The next day, Daid and I heard Mass at the Cathedral. When Mass finished, I waited while my father prayed a Rosary at the foot of the cross.

From the shadow of my pew, I looked up at the rose window on the other side of the church. It featured Christ in the centre surrounded by the twelve apostles. The window served as a great jewelled filter for the sun-sent sermon that splashed over parts of the transept and nave. In rainbows of colour, glittering with the morning light, it confidently proclaimed the unity and solidity of the church as a vessel of salvation. That massive wheel was complete in itself, without beginning or end, and radiant with the mighty message it contained. And in that message our hope was supposed to lie. Hope? It was all very well to hope, but to hope in what and for what? Hope that we would attain Heaven where we would be happy for eternity. At least that was what I had been taught. But as far as I was concerned, such hope was a mere palliative. It did nothing to ease the painful reality of the present. The light and glass could glisten and dance as much as it liked, but I still sat by myself on the hard bench, with a brace on my leg, boots on my feet and no mother to love.

A tap on the shoulder from Daid indicated that he had finished his prayers. We left the cathedral and drove out to South Head.

After a picnic of bread and cheese, my father removed jacket, collar and tie and took up his painting knapsack.

I watched his tall, thin form as he wandered away in search of subjects. From time to time he paused as if mesmerised. Then, once he found a place that appealed to him, he sat and set about organising his sketchbook and watercolours. He took out his flask, filled a small cup with water, and before long was absorbed in painting. His activity attracted the attention of a few boys. Soon, an inquisitive little bunch of children watched my father sweep the colour across the paper. A harbour scene emerged, much to the fascination of his audience.

I, too, rose from my spot, walked to the other side of the head and gazed out across the sea. Somewhere way over the waves was another world – a world I had known well but which had paled and powdered into the horizon. It was hard to conceive that the creature that now stumbled awkwardly over the uneven ground, half helped and half hindered by a brace and boots, and the sure-footed, lithe little character that had bounded barefoot across Galway's cliffs and crags, were one and the same. Between us lay a vast, billowy space, thinly bridged by makeshift memories that merged the two of us into the one person.

Galway had been a verdant, vibrant place – a place into which I had cosily fitted: A world of music and dance, fields and farms, of fireside tales and talk in pubs, of piping hot pies and fresh brown bread, of fishing boats and nets, of students and summer visitors, of lakeside rambles and strolls along the river. And all of a sudden, it had become unstitched and torn from me. One by one, folk had died at the hand of the Goddam Black and Tans. Villagers first, then Father Griffin was found in a bog with a bullet through his head. Uncail Breandán and Uncail Ruaidhrí were tortured and shot; Uncial Ciarán was killed by his own countrymen; and finally Mam, who died while trying to smile.

And then I was tossed into an angry sea and made sick.

Some seemed to think that, like the prophet Jonah, I had been spared by Providence. More likely, though, Providence had greater concern for the moon that regulated the tide than for me, who for seven long years lay submerged and forsaken, at the mercy of pounding waves and the pull of currents of daily life. A cold, wintry world it had been, one of white-washed walls and iron-headed beds, of splints and plasters, of callipers, crutches and chairs, a world of doctors and nursing sisters, of long, lonely hours and orderly routines.

In Galway, it used to happen that a body would wash its way onto the rocks. Usually the fisher folk who discovered it had no way of knowing who it was, so thoroughly had the sea wiped away its features. Sometimes the only way they could tell the village or the family it was from was by the pattern of the guernsey.

In a similar way had I been coughed ashore. I had drifted to a faraway place with the flotsam and jetsam of a few pages torn from time. Like those ancient people, no one here had any means of knowing who I was. An Irish brogue and a calliper told them something about what I was and where I was from, but they said nothing about me. I was little more than a corpse.

But now it seemed that winter, with her storms and whiplike waves, had slowed and softened into a gentle spring. The sea, dusted with diamonds from the sun and emblazoned with white crests, danced under a lucid azure heaven. And as in days gone by, the swallows had come. They had nested under the eaves of our house just as they used to do in the thatch of our Galway cottage. But not only was it in our house they had made their nest. One little swallow had daubed a nest in my heart. And her name was Arondelle Sotheby.

Perhaps there was some hope after all.

6

Had it not been for Della, my days at St Dominic's would have been a misery. Overall, I found the lessons easy for I had covered as much and more of most subjects through my private tuition at the convent. With Sister Ignatius, my schooling had moved at my own pace for four mornings a week, whereupon I could read, study, rest and practise as I pleased. Now, at St Dominic's, I was obliged to comply from dawn to dusk, day in and day out, with a curriculum that was not of my own devising.

What occurred during the lessons themselves was nothing less than torture, particularly in Maths. Every time I answered Sister Augustine's questions, the class would giggle, especially if it involved saying any number with 'three'. I decided to combat this simply by not answering any more questions. But the class counteracted with the same tactics, silently driving Sister Augustine to ask me and forcing out a reply.

My habitual lateness was also called into question. When I was late again on Monday morning, I was requested to report to Sister Bellarmine. Given my physical condition, she decided to be lenient and issue a caution, but if she heard of any further instance, my father would be notified. To my knowledge, Daid was unaware that I was taking my time over getting to school. Now I had to catch the train with other girls and put up with their looks and comments and callous attempts to mimic my limp. Worst of all, I had to walk past Frances Mahony and her friends as they flirted with Wally Sotheby and his mates on Strathfield station, and endure snide glances not only from girls, but also from boys.

Furthermore the long days, coupled with the long journeys, were taking their toll on me physically. At the end of a day of school, my legs and hips and back would ache so badly that Daid would often come home to find me already in bed, still dressed in my uniform. One night never seemed enough time to recover. But a day at home meant a day in Mrs Murphy's company and that was to be avoided at all costs.

The most punishing aspect of the school regime, however, was the Thursday afternoon sports lesson. I was required to attend despite being unable to play.

On the first lesson, Sister Catherine Bernard – young, confident and able – took one look at me and decided it was her duty to provide me with every opportunity for exercise. Since there was nothing wrong with my arms, she observed, I was quite capable of participating in a throwing game. So it happened that my usual claim to the right to be included in every possible normal activity, to my horror was used to demand that I take part in something I had no wish to take part in at all. I had to stand in a circle with the rest of the class. They then had to put up with me missing the ball. Every time I missed I had to chase after it, try and pick it up (if I had not already fallen in the process) and throw it back. The only person to whom I had any courage to throw the ball was Della, who was standing next to me.

At first the class giggled, then became exasperated by my ineptitude. Most girls avoided throwing the ball to me; but others, like Frances and Kathleen, made it a game within a game, threatening with a look to throw the ball my way before throwing it to someone else. Or else they made as if to throw it to another and instead tossed it at me. I became increasingly fearful and my fears only served as the bait they needed to continue the torture.

The second week's lesson was made worse by Della's absence. We had to take partners. Since no one in the class was prepared to be my partner, Sister Bernard assumed the role and took advantage of the position to 'teach' me how to throw the ball. The exercise was humiliating and tiresome. When it finally finished and I was permitted to sit, I decided never to attend physical education again. Fortunately, I did not have to the following Thursday, for it rained and supervised study was scheduled instead.

I missed my 'cello. For weeks now I had been unable to enjoy entire afternoons devoted to practice. Instead, there was homework to complete. On the odd occasion that I had little homework to do, I was too tired from walking home to attempt any serious 'cello work. Serious 'cello practice had been relegated to Saturdays.

So, when Thursday afternoon came round a fourth time, I decided to play truant. My plan was to leave school after lunch. Rather than go home, which risked detection by Daid since I had to walk past the studio, I intended to avoid the exhausting hike up King St by spending the afternoon at Bray's music.

What music I did not borrow from Mrs Epstein, I bought at Bray's. I enjoyed sitting in a corner of the store and browsing through a pile of tunes. Sometimes, I had the pleasure of listening to someone trying out pieces of music on the piano. Bray's music had the further attraction of a number of 'cellos for sale. They were kept in a workroom behind the shop and Miss Bray usually gave me permission to try them out.

Miss Bray did a slow trade with 'cellos. Instruments came and went at a very leisurely pace. There was one 'cello, though, which no one had wanted to buy for years. It was old and it looked as if had been literally hacked out of a cupboard. Its *f* holes were crudely carved, and the wood was dark and without the fancy varnishing that featured on most other instruments. But when I played it, it made a soulful, syrupy sound.

I loved that 'cello. During the train trip back to Newtown, I thought through the pieces I wanted to try out: the Beethoven sonata, some Saint-Saens and a few bits of Bach. They were melodies that had been spiralling inside my head for weeks; and aside from being drummed by my fingers to the rhythm of a steam engine, they had received little expression.

I pushed open the door to Bray's and was immediately gratified with some wonderful sounds. Someone was playing the piano. The music was glittering and rhapsodic and its performance had attracted an audience. That was good. It meant that I could creep in without anyone noticing. I managed to reach undetected the shelf with the 'cello music, and from a safe and shadowy distance I joined the gathering which had congregated around the instrument.

I could not believe what I saw.

I expected an adult – someone strong, authoritative and professional. Instead, the pianist was a child, a girl about the same age as myself. Equally intriguing was the fact that she was dressed in the same school uniform.

A scintillating ripple of notes ended the performance and the girl twirled round to receive the applause.

'What did you play, dear?' a lady inquired.

'*Waldesrauschen*,' the girl replied. 'It's one of Liszt's concert études.'

'Excuse me,' another lady politely interposed and handed the girl a sheet of music. 'I was wondering if you wouldn't mind playing this for me.'

The girl studied the music. '*Wedding Day at Troldhaugen*,' she read.

'Do you know it?'

'No. But I can play it,' she answered as she continued to study the music.

'Would you? I would be most obliged.'

The girl turned back to the piano, fixed the music stand, positioned the music and prepared herself.

It was hard to believe she was sight-reading. I gulped in astonishment. Sight-reading was my weakness. The music always seemed to play tricks with my eyes and invariably I became confused by the boggle of notes and fingerings. I found it easier to play by ear. Watching another sight-read with such facility brought me to the piano.

The girl was engrossed in the music. Her face was engaged in animated parley with the notes on the page and her hands flexed and leapt over the keys with astonishing agility.

But the magic disappeared when Miss Bray, who served as page-turner, turned a page too late. The girl made a mistake. For one brief moment, she looked away from the music and straight at me. She stopped playing. Her lips parted slightly and she stared at me. With her saucy dark curls, her light olive complexion and damask cheeks, she was very pretty indeed. I looked away.

'Why Lucy, how lovely to see you,' smiled Miss Bray. 'Have you met Phoebe Raye?'

All eyes were now directed my way. Before I could reply, Miss Bray, who fully knew the reason for my visit, took the initiative.

'The 'cello is still here, Lucy. I'll go and fetch it. Maybe Phoebe could play the piano for you. We've lots of music, of course.' She made her way to the back room where the 'cello lived. 'Cello and piano, such a divine combination!' she marvelled as she went, 'And how nice to have a soirée in the store!'

Miss Bray's enthusiasm was shared by the other ladies. They looked at me and at the girl at the piano and began to talk among themselves.

'What would you like to play, dear?' one lady asked me. From the piano, Phoebe Raye's pretty face silently seconded the question.

Play? In front of all these people? With a piano? It was bad enough playing each week in front of my teacher.

I backed away.

'I—I cannot play with a piano. I'm not knowing any pieces. I—I'm not good enough to play. I cannot do the like of that,' I muttered, holding on to the piano to disguise my limp.

I left the store and resigned myself to hiking homewards without even touching the 'cello.

I did not realise that I had been followed until I reached my front gate. A sneeze prompted me to look up. Peeping out from behind a lamp-post on the other side of the road were some dark ringlets and a portion of box-pleated tunic.

The next morning, Phoebe Raye and I coincided in a railway carriage. We had both caught a later train than we ought – me because I had fallen on the steps at Newtown station, she for her own private reasons. It was at Stanmore that she boarded and she sat on the bench opposite. I continued to study the mazes in Dudeney's *Amusements* and took advantage of a page turn to look her over, only to find that she was studying me. Her eyes, which were a deep mahogany, were fixed in my direction. The only way to avoid her gaze was to keep focussed on my book, and this became increasingly difficult with the knowledge that I was being scrutinised from head to toe.

I was not released from the examination until the train approached Strathfield. Phoebe Raye rose from her seat and sent her curls frolicking over her shoulders. She picked up a battered violin case and hugged it tightly while she waited for the train to halt. By the time I landed on the platform, having grappled with supports and steps, she had disappeared.

During the next few days, whenever I walked to or from the school, it seemed that Phoebe Raye was never far away. What was particularly strange about it was that she was never part of the tittering groups of girls who made the 'spastic' comments.

In fact, given the unique way she wore her uniform, Phoebe was as much an anomaly as I was. Whereas everyone else wore their tunics belted at the hip, Phoebe had cinched hers very neatly at the waist. Her hem did not fall on the knee as it should. It fell below her calf. On her feet was a pair of well-fitting button up boots with smart heels, not the typical flat, brown shoes with straps worn by every other girl save myself. Instead of a plainly tailored shirt, Phoebe preferred a blouse with full sleeves that were daintily gathered at the shoulder and cuff. She did not bother with a tie. As for her hair, that cascade of dark curls was loosely fastened with a large, scarlet, satin bow. It was never braided as required. How Phoebe had managed to escape correction from the like of such dragons as Sister Augustine had me baffled. Quaintly and rather mysteriously old-fashioned, she was always alone: a singular, solitary, silent figure that seemed to have a penchant for being my shadow.

'Really Luighseach, you're absolutely paranoid,' Della replied after I confided the matter in her.

'I'm nothing of that,' I retorted. ''Tis been going on for days, you know. Wherever I look, she's there, looking at myself. Sometimes she's hiding, othertimes she's right before me, standing and staring.'

'Luighseach, you would have me believe you're a mantis under a magnifying glass the way you carry on. How many girls are in this school? A hundred? And we cross each other's paths on a daily basis. How can you possibly say she's following you? Does she tease?'

I shook my head. Phoebe did not tease. But in many ways, what she was doing was equally as bad.

'Then stop worrying yourself silly,' Della concluded.

I shrugged my shoulders. There was no point confiding any further.

'I'll not be attending Physical Education again this afternoon,' I announced.

'Do you want me to cover for you?' asked Della by way of amendment.

I didn't want Della's help in anything.

'What are you going to do?'

''Twill be none of your business.'

Della sighed.

'Are you coming with me on Sunday?' she inquired.

'And what will you have me do on Sunday?'

'Have you forgotten already? Bert Hinkler's arriving in Sydney! You are coming to see him aren't you?'

'And you want me to come?'

'Why of course, old thing. Meet me on the eight o'clock train. We'll catch the tram from Railway Square.'

'The tram is it?'

'Yes. Tram: T-R-A-M. What on earth's the matter with the tram?'

'I cannot catch the tram.'

'Why—? Oh, nonsense, of course you can! I'll help you, silly. So promise me you'll come. Promise.'

'Aye.'

Thursday afternoon once again saw me at Bray's music. This time there was no one in the store.

'And how are you today, Lucy?' Miss Bray asked me.

I replied that I was fine.

'And how is your father?' she added with a smile. Miss Bray always asked after Daid and always smiled too much when she did.

'My Daid's fine too. The 'cello's here is it not?'

'In the workroom as always, Lucy. You may go in. Mr Hunt is not here today.'

Mr Hunt was an elderly gentleman who repaired instruments.

I opened the door to the workroom and saw the 'cello in its usual spot, alone in the corner.

'You're still here, you poor laddie,' I said to him as I pulled him out. 'And 'tis been no one to play you these past weeks. Well, I'm back again. Shall we not show them fancy fiddles on the shelf there what a 'cello sounds like?' And I looked disparagingly at the cabinet full of slender violins, all dolled up with smart coats of varnish.

I found the bow Miss Bray always kept for me and arranged my chair. I picked up the 'cello and fondly stroked his shoulder. Mr Hunt had been keeping him polished and he had developed a deep, warm glow, rather like the leather of a pair of much worn and loved work boots.

I would have played Bach first. Bach was usually first because Bach made the world right again. But I did not feel like playing Bach today, and I was too tired for Saint Saens or Beethoven. So I fiddled around with favourite phrases from many different pieces until I felt sufficiently warmed up to play the tune that had been wandering through my mind since Della had come to visit. It was a tune I never would have dared play at home. But Miss Bray's workroom was both secluded and anonymous, and therefore was the perfect place to indulge in very private matters. I took off my glasses, closed my eyes, tried to feel again the warmth of my mother's arms, and began.

At first I played 'Danny Boy' simply, the way Mam used to sing it when she sang me to sleep in the chair by the fire. I played it three more times and then I began to improvise. I liked improvising. I liked to manoeuvre my fingers over the strings and experiment with different tones and harmonies; and I liked to sweep my bow across double and triple stops and sculpt the sound. Variation after variation I tried, stopping and starting, repeating chords and progressions that appealed, until finally I arrived at a satisfying version. I played through 'Danny Boy' one last time.

'Can you play the Brahms *Double*?' asked a voice.

I quickly put my glasses on and saw Phoebe Raye, of all people, come out from behind a cupboard.

She must have been hiding there the entire time. Phoebe had heard everything. She'd heard me talking to the 'cello. She had heard me playing. She had heard

'Danny Boy'.

I threw down the bow.

'First, you follow me home! Then you follow me round school and now you spy on me in the music shop! Will you not leave me alone?'

'I— I wanted to see where you lived,' she began lamely and very taken aback. 'I didn't m—'

'Well, I'm telling you, I'm fed up with being followed and picked on and—'

'Oh, who'd want to play with you anyway?' she shouted, visibly upset. 'You clumsy, crippled, gauche—'

'Get out!'

'And that's the ugliest, most horrid, stupidest 'cello I've ever seen in my life!' she added petulantly and stormed out of the workroom.

That night, Daid sent silent prayers to Heaven while potato peels spiralled to the paper on the table. I pummelled the peas from their pods. No matter how hard I tried, I could not block out Phoebe Raye's hurt face: her full lips quivering and those mournful eyes that seemed to ask a thousand questions.

'Luighseach,' Daid began, ''twas Sister Bellarmine from school who telephoned today. A mitching you been these two weeks past is it?'

'Aye.'

'Well, they'll put a punishment on you tomorrow and rightly too. A day away from school, a day away from work and a Sunday— '

'Without the Holy Mass is three things will never return.' How many times had I heard that? Normally, however, I heard it on Sunday mornings, not Thursday evenings. 'Besides,' I shrugged. ''Twas but an afternoon that I mitched.'

There was silence.

I looked up and caught the full force of my father's glacier blue eyes. Light glinted from the fragile, silver rims of his glasses as he spoke.

'And were it but the smallest part of an hour, Luighseach, by God's good grace, ná déan é sin arís.'

'And I'll be damned if I know what learning I'm getting being pressed into playing sport!' I pulled each pea from the pod and, one by one, threw them into the pot.

'Sport is it?' was all Daid said in reply.

The following morning, Daid made a telephone call to Sister Bellarmine, and later that day I was summoned to her office. Sister Bellarmine chastised me for truancy and issued me with a detention. She then announced, to my relief, that I would no longer be required to attend sport on Thursday afternoons. Instead, I was to make myself useful to Sister Scholastica who taught the fourth class in the prep school. There, I was to help some of the slower students with their reading and spelling. For the second part of the afternoon, I was to go the school chapel to assist Sister Comgall with folding the altar linen and preparing the vestments and vessels for Mass.

'And I hope that with the grace of God you will perform these duties responsibly and well, Lucy Straughan,' she concluded, her wimpled face stern but strangely benign.

I declared that I would. But privately I included my own caveat: on the one condition that neither Sister Scholastica nor Sister Comgall would try to make me a nun.

7

Della could not contain herself. Bert Hinkler's arrival generated such a degree of nervous energy that she could think or talk of little else. She wriggled around in her seat, fidgeted more than usual and opened and closed her desk innumerable times to mark off the days, hours and minutes until the big event. No mistress saw the front of her head, for when it was not ducked under the desk-lid it was turned towards the window in eager anticipation of the aeroplane which was to fly in on Sunday. Moving her had no effect at all and any detention received was deemed a small sacrifice to pay. In response to such corrective measures, she lapsed into a cheery humming of 'Hustling Hinkler', cast her eyes to the ceiling, swung her feet, bobbed her head from side to side and tapped her pencil in time.

My brief journeys from classroom to cloakroom now involved increased risks. Invariably I was swooped upon when, with arms outstretched in imitation of Hinkler's 'Baby Avro', Della would race around me, grab me and try to spin me round. More than once her dive-bombing ended in disaster by catching me off-balance and sending me crashing to the ground; and in spite of my pleas not to do it, she still could not help herself.

On Friday, however, Della arrived late and spent the entire morning with her head on her desk. Not even Sister Augustine could induce her to move. She and I endured lunch inside fulfilling our respective detentions, and while penning pious observations on the evil of truancy, I glanced across and found her crying.

'What's ailing you?' I whispered.

'Lucy Straughan, silence!' barked Sister Catherine Bernard.

Della looked down and cried all the more.

Upon our release, the answer flooded out with much heaving of shoulders, stifled sobs and wringing of lace handkerchief.

'Mummy won't let me see Bert Hinkler!'

'And why would that be now?'

'Well, I asked Wally if he wouldn't mind taking us,' she began.

'You did what?'

'I asked Wally if we could go with him, but he said no. Anyway, Mummy overheard us talking about it and found out.'

'Did you not tell her what you were doing?'

'Oh, I've tried but she's never interested. She's too busy choosing fabric for her garden party costume. But this morning she found out and said I couldn't go because it wasn't proper, especially since I was planning to travel on public transport. I then asked if we could have Hammond. Mummy got furious about that and told me I was impertinent. Well, I'm afraid I told Mummy that the real reason she didn't want me to go was because it was to do with 'planes, which she hates, because they remind her of The Captain.'

It was then that I noticed she was wearing a different pair of glasses to the fine gold framed ones she normally wore.

'Did you break your glasses, Della?'

Della nodded.

'I'm afraid Mummy became so angry with me she threw a book at me. I—I didn't duck in time.'

With that, Della again burst into tears.

'She doesn't care!' she sobbed. 'She would prefer my father never existed. I can never talk to her about him! As far as Mummy's concerned, The Captain and the War never happened and I don't understand how she can turn her back on it all like that.'

Della could no longer stifle her tears. All I could do was put my arm around her and let her cry.

'I'll be all right, old thing,' she eventually composed herself. 'Really, Luighseach,' she reassured me, 'there's nothing to worry about, absolutely nothing. My glasses will be fixed today and Mummy will have quite forgotten about this morning. Thank you, old thing. Everything will be all right. You'll see.'

And, oddly enough, that seemed to be the case.

Our 'phone rang late on Saturday night. With spirits fully revived, Della warbled such a torrent of jubilation that it took some time to methodically piece the details together. In short, she was going to see Bert Hinkler after all. Her step-father was taking her, and if I still wished to come I would be collected next morning.

Della arrived to find Daid and me in the thick of an argument. I had awoken that Sunday to the sound of my father tending the fire in my room, and the smell of the woollen blanket he was warming to prepare my legs for the day's events. But neither blanket wraps nor massage provided any relief at all. My legs remained stiff and sore, totally worn out by yet another week of walking, of waiting in line, of stumbles and falls and climbing stairs. Much to my annoyance, Daid telephoned the Sotheby's upon our return from first Mass to inform them that I was not well enough to attend.

Fortunately he rang too late. Della and her step-father had already departed, so Daid had to wait to tell Della in person.

Daid answered Della's knock and repeated to her the contents of his earlier telephone call.

'I'm fine!' I protested as I walked down the corridor.

'Fine is it?' he queried. 'With a limp like that? You'll be needing your other calliper, Luighseach.'

'I'm not needing it!' But Daid had already gone to retrieve it from my room. I followed him.

An intense discussion in Irish ensued.

'Then for the love of God have the humility at least to take a walking stick,' Daid concluded as he left my room, calliper still in hand. The walking stick was pulled from the hallstand. I brushed it aside.

'Let you put it away. I'm a'going, Daid.'

'Aye, and you'll regret it. We're sorry to keep you waiting, lass,' Daid apologised to Della. 'Dia dhuit, a Luighseach,' he sighed and waved us off with the calliper.

'What on earth was all that about? Aren't you well?' Della asked as we walked to the car.

'I'm fine!' I replied.

'Hurry up, Della!' called Mr Sotheby. 'We've waited long enough.'

Della quickly escorted me to the back seat. Henry Sotheby, complacently munching an apple in the front, turned round.

'You remember Luighseach, don't you Harry?' said Della as she settled in.

Harry bit and sucked his apple in acknowledgment and faced the front again.

'Well, say hello,' his sister urged.

Something like 'Hello Lishack' emerged.

'Mummy discovered yesterday evening that Wally was going and there was another row,' Della rapidly explained. 'This time Harry found out what was going on. He threw a tantrum and demanded to be taken. So Daddy agreed. Luckily, we were permitted to come for the ride. I say, I didn't realise you had to wear a brace on your other leg.'

'I don't need it!' I replied.

Della sighed and looked out of the window. Something soon caught her attention and she clapped her hands in glee. 'I say, let's play "I spy". I spy with my little eye, something beginning with "C".'

'Cloud!' called an enthused Henry.

'No.'

'Cable,' said Mr Sotheby.

'No.'

The game occupied them all the way to the airfield and the espied objects became more cryptic and minute with every round. Finally we neared Mascot and formed part of a grand vehicular procession out to pay tribute to Mr Hinkler and his 'plane. Della quivered with excitement and hopped across the back seat, her whole body squirming north, south, east and west in search for a place to park. She burst out indications, suggestions and cautions with such rapidity and intensity that Mr Sotheby had to apply very firm words to calm her down.

Park we soon did, and pulling a rug, some cushions and a hamper from the boot, we trekked across the paddocks in the quest for a suitable picnic spot.

But the irregularity of the turf made walking even more difficult than usual; and matters were not helped by the cooler, damper weather and the effect it had on my already tired legs. My clumsy passage, with its frequent trips and stops, interspersed with 'Luighseach, are you quite sure you're all right?' or 'Luighseach, careful,' from Della, gave rise to particular interest on the part of Henry who could not help looking at my spindly lower limbs and peculiar gait.

'What's that meccano thing on your leg?' he asked loudly, pointing.

Tact, in any shape or form, was unknown to him. Another near fall. I felt myself colour and tightened my free fist inside my cardigan pocket.

'Well, what is it?' he insisted.

''Tis none of your business.'

'Is too. What is it?'

'A call-i-per it is,' I returned in a slower, more emphatic brogue.

'Calliper?' he repeated. 'What's it for?'

Della's look was almost tangible.

'It helps Luighseach to walk,' she explained.

'How?'

'I don't know exactly how but her poor leg is crippled.'

'How?'

Now Mr Sotheby contributed his tuppenceworth.

'Polio,' he said with certainty. 'It's a disease that paralyses you. It stops your limbs from moving properly.'

'How?'

'It appears to be due to a virus.'

'What's a virus?'

'It's a germ.'

'How does it get in? Do you eat it?'

'Not really. They don't know how it gets in. But when it does get in it attacks the brain.'

'Is something wrong with her brain too?'

Henry's incessant questions and Mr Sotheby's attempted explanations trailed into the distance.

'Don't worry, Luighseach,' said Della as we bumbled through an increasing amount of legs, holes, clods and stones. 'Henry simply has to know everything about everything. And he'll remember it all, too. So get ready. He'll be onto you about polio with the first opportunity.'

'Aye, with "How this" and "How that" about my legs and boots and callipers and limp and all. And what about "Why", Della Sotheby?'

'Why what?'

'Why the Polio? 'Tis easy to explain how. But why? Why? Why is it that *I* have Polio? Will you tell me that now?'

Della was taken aback. 'I— I really don't know, Luighseach. I don't think anyone really knows the answer to that. You might as well ask why the sky is blue.'

'That's not the point,' I replied.

'Well, why do you always feel so sorry for yourself?' Della retorted.

Neither of us said anything more until we found Mr Sotheby who by this time was comfortably seated in a folding chair and reading the *Herald*. Fortunately

51

Henry's interest had now been diverted to a group of rival boys and he had run off to sort them out. I refused Della's offer of a chair and sat on the rug. As for Della, she pressed her lips together and scowled at me, organised a chair for herself and began to read.

I gradually grew tired of studying the geometry of the rug's tartan checks and looked over at the cover of Della's book.

'Don Quicksote is it?' I asked at length.

Della smiled.

'Really, Luighseach, for all your cleverness you can be such a bumpkin. Everyone knows it's Don "Kee-*Ho*-tay", silly,' she replied, unable to resist laughing.

I blushed. 'Well, I proved you wrong,' I returned and pulled Dudeney from my satchel.

Mr Sotheby put down his paper. 'Are you reading *Don Quixote*, poppet?' he asked. 'Why, I read that when I was a boy. Very revealing of the Spanish character as I later found.'

'Did you go to Spain, Daddy?' said Della.

'Yes, many years ago,' he consulted his beard. 'In 'eighty eight to be precise.'

'I say! Daddy, have you been to Seville?' she asked.

'Most certainly. Why Seville?'

'Sister Magdalene was telling us about Seville only the other week. Apparently it has the most beautiful cathedral. It's full of gold, Daddy.'

'Plundered from Peru, I believe.'

'The conquistadors brought it back from the New World,' Della rephrased her step-father's remark to make it concord with what we had been taught in history. 'Didn't they, Luighseach?'

'Aye,' I replied as I leafed through my book. But I had not paid quite the same attention to that lesson as Della. Della sensed my indifference and decided to move the conversation along by herself.

'Did you see the procession when you were there, Daddy?'

'I beg your pardon?' replied Mr Sotheby.

'The procession in Passion Week when they take out the floats of Our Lord and Our Lady and parade them through the streets,' Della eagerly explained.

'Hmmm,' remarked Mr Sotheby.

'Sister Magdalene told us all about it. The floats are carried by men dressed in long black robes with hoods so that you can't see their faces. Sister Magdalene said it was a great privilege for a young man to carry the floats, but because of the heat and the weight of the floats, it was also a great penance. The townspeople play music while they march, and when the trumpets blow, the men carrying the Lady float make it sway from side to side to make the Virgin dance. They do that to console her for her sorrows at seeing Our Lord suffer. That's what Sister Magdalene said. Our Lady's dressed in lace like a bride and has tears in her eyes. Do you remember what they called her, Luighseach?'

I shook my head and gave my attention to a problem concerning bets on horses.

'Do you, Daddy?' Della queried.

Mr Sotheby replied in the negative and turned back to the *Herald*.

'What did you think of the procession, Daddy? Were you moved?'

'Frankly, Della,' remarked the *Herald*. 'I thought it a load of sentimental, heathenish barbarism. The things those nuns teach you in that school.'

That observation pierced Della like a sword. She cringed and coughed. But she was not to be undermined.

'Well, I was very moved,' she replied. 'Anyway, Luighseach, I don't know how you can possibly believe that God doesn't care about you or anything when you hear of Our Lord's Passion played out the way Sister Magdalene told us.'

I considered my calculations while mulling over the geometry of the picnic rug. 'Because, Della Sotheby, I don't understand how God can create an ordered world, as Sister Augustine says, and make such a mess of it.'

'Because the world isn't made merely of silly numbers, that's why!' came Della's frustrated outburst. 'Why do you always have to read that wretched book?'

'Because I like it, is why.'

Mr Sotheby laid his paper aside. 'What's that, Lucy?'

I held up *Amusements in Mathematics*.

'Ah, Mr Dudeney!' he rubbed his hands. 'I used to enjoy doing his puzzles in *The Strand*.'

'I don't know why you waste your time on such absurdities,' scolded Della. 'I mean, who cares how many cats rid Bury St Edmunds of umpteen million mice?'

'Come, Poppet,' coaxed Mr Sotheby. 'Puzzles are the very marrow of life. After all, what is life but a puzzle to solve?'

'Daddy, I have enough trouble solving life's puzzles without having Mr Dudeney add to them,' Della retorted. 'Cats and mice!' she huffed.

'Well, it's two hundred and thirty-nine,' I remarked.

'Two hundred and thirty-nine what?' echoed an exasperated Della.

'Cats it is,' I replied. 'It takes two hundred and thirty-nine cats to rid Bury St Edmunds of one million one hundred and eleven thousand one hundred and eleven mice if each cat caught the same number of mice and the number of cats was fewer than the number of mice caught by each.'

'Oh, Luighseach! Does it really matter?'

'Aye, it does to myself, and if it doesn't matter to you, may I have my *Canterbury Puzzles* book back?'

'No, you can't,' Della looked decidedly uncomfortable.

'And why not? 'Twas *my* book after all I lent you,' I demanded.

'Wally's reading it,' she replied.

'Your brother's reading my book?' I was incredulous.

'Listen,' she retaliated. 'I'm not an only child like you. I can't keep everything to myself. Wally wanted to read it so I lent it him. What does it matter to you? Ask Wally for it if you want it back that much.'

I folded my arms and stared at the squares.

'Luighseach, you're not scared of boys are you?' Della asked after a pause.

I continued to stare at the squares.

'Really!'

'What about some lunch?' suggested Mr Sotheby as he opened the hamper and glossed over its contents.

'Did cook make Scotch Eggs?' asked Henry who reappeared the moment the lid was raised.

A Scotch Egg was produced. Henry crammed his face with it and hurried off to join his newfound friends.

We had not quite taken our tea when an announcement came over the speakers. It could not be heard distinctly at first. Eventually the message repeated and its contents gave rise to a whoop of glee from Della.

'Joy rides! Oh Luighseach, can you imagine? What fun! Let's go and watch! Daddy, may we go?'

'Certainly.'

'May we borrow the binoculars?'

The binoculars were passed across with a strict instruction to be careful with them.

Della insisted I get up.

We picked our way through picnics and surreptitious games of two-up before reaching a thoroughfare filled with vendors and souvenir sellers. A jazz band had started and a few enthusiasts had taken the initiative to clear their own dance floor for foxtrots. Bert Hinkler and his 'plane was read in every eye, in every smile, in every lick of ice cream and sip of soda; was felt in the rhythm of every step and in the tap of every shoe. Mascot was charged with Hinkler fever.

On we pushed past shoes, skirts and trousers until we found ourselves before a barrier.

Della was not in the least deterred. She pulled herself up and sat, her legs swinging to and fro. With her father's binoculars pressed to her glasses, she surveyed the scene before her. I folded my arms, leant against the barricade and surveyed the grass below.

'It's wonderful up here, Luighseach! You really should see it! So many people and it looks as if some 'planes are getting ready. I say, what's the matter with you today? You're awfully moody.'

'I amn't.'

'Come on, pull yourself up here. You can do it.'

I sighed and shook my head.

Della shrugged her shoulders and returned to the binoculars. I returned to examining the appliqué of mud and grass stitched to my boots.

'I don't believe it!' she exclaimed.

'What is it now?' I wearily asked.

'Wally!'

'And you're seeing him through them glasses?'

'Yes. *And* he's smoking! Bad boy! Yes, and there's Archie.' The survey continued. 'Goodness gracious, Fanny's appeared! She's started to talk with Eric. Now they're both talking with Wally. And there's Beth. Heavens! And is that Kate with Archie? I think it's Kate. Yes, it's Kate's hat. And what's Mary doing there? Mary, of all people! I had no idea they were all going. Oh, thank goodness.'

'What happened?'

'Wally put out his cigarette. Now he's laughing.'

Then she gasped in horror and lowered the binoculars. 'Frances Mahony!'

'What is it?'

'How dare—!'

'What is it, Della Sotheby? What happened?'

'They kissed! Who do they think they are?'

She wriggled off the barrier in disgust and pulled me away.

'Joy rides, my foot! Honestly, I don't know what's gotten into my brother. Sacked from school! Stopped playing cricket! Sneaking off here and there, smoking on the sly, and now he's flirting! Luighseach, I tell you, the last few months he's been absolutely impossible!'

Weaving our way in and out of the crowd, we returned to our spot.

The *Herald* rustled an enquiry. 'You didn't see Harry at all?'

'No,' Della sighed. 'Don't worry, Daddy, he'll be nearby. Oh, I say, loop the loops! Take a look.'

The aeronautical stunts of two daredevil pilots were now the sole attraction.

'Did you see that?' Della gasped as a 'plane spun towards the earth and then swept up to the sky. 'How I would love to be up there! Wouldn't you?'

'I would not,' I returned to cross-hatching the mud on my boots with a stick. 'I think I'd be sick if I went up there.'

A small hand on my foot interrupted my labours and Della's face gazed into my own. She shook her head. 'Oh no you wouldn't, you'd love it. I don't mean doing side slips and all those tricks, but flying over land and sea. Think of the view you'd have! You'd see the world as it really is: how everything has a part to play in a divinely orchestrated masterpiece. You'd be able to tell the direction of rivers and mountain chains and see that they lead somewhere. So many questions would be answered if you viewed the world that way. Why, it would be wonderful! And to think The Captain saw all that!'

Delight touched her eyes with tears.

'And that's why you're flying mad is it?'

Della, enraptured with the whole idea, had gone back to the binoculars. Suddenly she gasped.

'Oh! He's coming! Luighseach, get up and take a look! Hold tight. Come on. Here.'

Small spots had indeed appeared on the skyline and were slowly gliding towards a now spellbound crowd. Larger and larger they grew until the faint forms of twelve 'planes were barely visible.

'And yet you have made him little less than a God!' she enthused.

'What was it you said?'

'Don't you think it magnificent?'

'I do, but I'm not going to go that far.'

'But to think he crossed the world in that tiny 'plane! It's marvellous!' And she stared at the spots in the heavens in wonder, one hand shading her eyes, the other trustingly slipped in my elbow.

I followed her gaze. Men, yes men, were up in the air. Yet upon beholding their 'planes: those flimsy, fragile things that grew and grew as they bobbed their way through a sea of sky; those men never seemed more mortal than now. I thought of Breughel's *Icarus*.

'And what if he failed, Della Sotheby? What if he'd fallen somewhere, never more to be seen, and the world didn't stop to care. Would you still be saying the same?'

'Luighseach, how can you say such a thing as that?' She then grew thoughtful and tightened her hold on my arm. 'But yes. Yes I would say the same. I would say he and anyone who did that was truly great and wondrous. Why certainly Hinkler's achieved something great and is having his greatness rewarded here and now. I suppose anyone with a bit of pluck, a good machine, and the luck of winds and weather could have done the same. And, I daresay, many will do far more than he and in time his greatness will be next to nothing. But that's not what is important. Why he's a man like the rest of us: a little man who's flawed and frail and at the mercy of all the elements. Yet in spite of everything, he reached for the stars. It is for that reaching I would count him great. It's not because he succeeded, it's because he strove. Luighseach, we're not meant to live with our eyes glued to the ground. We're meant to aspire to the highest heaven, to soar like eagles to the sun! And be it known that I, too, wish to fly sky high like Bert Hinkler.'

Nearer they came, fourteen in all, and we stood with our heads turned skywards and watched them circle. Then the Avro swooped low and smooth, whirred loud and swept its shadow wide upon us. A spray of hats leapt high and waves of white handkerchiefs welcomed the hero of the day. Horns stormed and a wild, windy cheer burst upon the air. Hinkler's 'plane rose again, spiralled slowly and glided to the ground. More cheers and horns sounded when a speck of a man climbed a ladder. He waved round and madly Della waved in reply.

Bert Hinkler disappeared again.

There was another cheer from the crowd.

'He must be on the platform!'

The screech of a microphone confirmed Della's suspicions and we turned towards the clubhouse. Nothing came forth.

'What's happening, Daddy?'

'I think the Premier's giving his address.'

We listened. More screeches than words issued from the speaker. There was a pause, another screech and then silence. Finally the Premier made mention of Hinkler's magnificent achievement and Australia's pride.

Della added her part to the wild applause and shouts of 'We want Bert' which met the Premier's welcome. A cheered crescendo set the scene for the airman's reply:

'My heart is too full for many words. From the bottom of my heart I must thank you. More I cannot say.'

Nothing more needed to be said. Hinkler could have said anything that day and it wouldn't have mattered. Again a chorus of cheers, horns and thunderous clapping rose high and gradually diminished when the hero left the microphone.

A few more speeches and that was it. No more Hinkler. No more 'planes. No more marvels. We were now faced with the task of heading back to the car.

There was no sign of Henry.

With crowds milling around us, we waited and waited to no avail. Della began to grow anxious and her father impatient.

A muffled message came from the speaker.

'That's him,' said Mr Sotheby.

Henry Sotheby, so it turned out, had managed to get in the front line, had seen the 'plane land and had seen Mr Hinkler up close. He reported that the airman wore a suit and tie, and had black hair and smiled. Aware that he had outdone his sister with his achievement, he repeated the facts over and over before insisting she give him something to eat. Della dug round the hamper, produced an apple and Henry, munching in triumph, held onto his father and was heard no more.

'Daddy, what's a woman aviator called?' Della asked as we reached the car.

'Oh, I don't know, an aviatress or an aviatrix, I suppose, if there is such a thing.'

She sighed wistfully, leant forward and rested her head and hands on the back of her father's seat. 'That's what I'm going to be: an aviatrix.' She lingered on that last word. 'I'm going to fly, fly up past the clouds, fly up to the sun and fly all round the world. And I'll fly to all the places you've been, Daddy, and more, and see all the wonderful things there are to see...'

Mr Sotheby gave a short laugh. 'And the next thing we know, you'll be fighting windmills on hilltops. Della, you're a dreamer. You have no hope of flying a 'plane!'

'I don't see why not.'

'Come now, Poppet,' he teased. 'You know there's more to flying than simply flapping your wings. There's quite a degree of skill involved, not to mention mathematics. You know everything about Bert Hinkler. You know he's an engineer. You need to be good at maths for that.'

'Mathematics! If I hear anything more about mathematics, I will scream!' Mr Sotheby may have intended a jest, but Della was in no mood for sporting with such a topic. She hung her head and sighed.

'I will never understand anything about mathematics!'

'That may be so, Della Sotheby,' I remarked. 'But 'tis myself understands a thing or two.'

'You and your silly numbers!' she blurted, visibly upset. 'You don't even care!'

But that was not so.

8

The duel was over. In a display of indifference I bounced my bow too hard against my boot and the force of the rebound caused me to lose my hold. The bow clattered to the floor. In the skirmish that followed, my 'cello teacher Mrs Epstein snatched it away.

Mrs Epstein had very weak, dark eyes. They were much magnified and distorted by the heavy tortoiseshell glasses she wore. Whenever she looked at anything, her eyes always appeared askew, and this strange, oblique gaze seemed to intensify if she had something important to say. It was such a look which now held me at dagger point, raised me upright and forced me back behind my 'cello. Thus pinned, I was at her mercy. She sat opposite, with one hand firmly positioned around the neck of her own instrument, her own bow well out of my reach, and mine pointed in my face. Still glaring, she sliced my soul with every thrust.

'This time Luighseach— and don't look away from me when I am speaking to you— you are going to play in a string quartet and I am not going to take "no" in any shape or form for an answer. I do not believe you when you say you do not want to play in a group. I know you like the music too much. I know you are not content merely to listen to gramophone recordings, and I do not believe you when you say you have enough to do because you always make time for the things you want. Now I can understand your being nervous about joining with others a year ago, but now you're at school, it shouldn't be so daunting. And most importantly, I cannot and will not accept that you are not even willing to try. Were you to give me any of those reasons after having a go, I might have accepted them. But to say "I will not" or "I am not" or "I shall not" from the outset like this is not going to hold. You will come on Thursday afternoon, you will meet the others, you will collect the music, you will learn your part and you will make an honest effort to try.'

She laid her 'cello aside, opened the drawer of her bureau, put my bow inside, locked it and placed the key in her pocket.

'You can have your bow back on Thursday.'

'Holy Immaculate Mother! You cannot do that, Mrs Epstein! 'Tis *my* bow you put in there! You're not being fair!'

'I'm not being fair? *I* am not being fair? You're the one who's not being fair, my girl. You're not being fair to me as your teacher, you're not being fair to the others who wish to form a group, and most important of all you're not being fair to yourself.'

'Let you ask someone else for I don't want to do it.'

'There *is* no one else, Luighseach. Listen, you have made more progress in five years than most good musicians would make in ten. You have nothing to worry about. Furthermore, it is an uncommon thing to find four musicians in the one school of a similar age, sound ability and the capacity to play well together. To throw something aside like this is to throw away a priceless jewel. You would be a fool to do that. All I am asking is that you try. Take one little step forward. Is it that difficult?'

'It is!' I declared.

This was not the first time Mrs Epstein had confiscated my bow. She had done so on many occasions to make me listen to what she had to say or demonstrate instead of playing or pretending not to pay attention. But the bow had only disappeared during the lesson. Now it was going to disappear for two whole days. It was not fair.

And Mrs Epstein was wrong. She did not know how difficult it was to put one little step forward like that. She did not know what it was like. Nobody knew. Nobody understood. Not even Della.

Della and I had had a fight. Sunday's aeronautic excursion and March's sudden burst of chill nights had made my legs worse, to the point that putting one foot in front of the other was nearly impossible. By the time I returned from the airfield I could no longer walk, so I spent the remainder of the afternoon and evening in bed. I would have stayed in bed on Monday, but that would have meant that Mrs Murphy would be in to keep an eye on me. Since this was to be avoided, I was determined to go to school regardless of effort, aches or time.

That Monday morning, Daid spent more than an hour working my legs. His efforts at first were futile and exhausting. I begged him continue. My legs began to revive a little, and as far as I was concerned that was sufficient for me to attend school. I made my preparations.

Daid, however, made other plans. When I emerged from my room, supported on crutches and dressed in my uniform, I came face to face not only with my father and the wheelchair, but with the old cow herself.

I insisted Daid drive me to school. Daid refused. He had an appointment on the other side of town and already he was running late. I was instructed to keep my tongue in my jaw and my toe in my pump and spend the day at home.

One would think that after years of looking after me, Mrs Murphy would be sufficiently skilled in the art of preparing my porridge the way I liked it: soft and creamy with mounds of brown sugar and butter. I ate but two spoonfuls. Mrs Murphy, sleeves rolled up ready to do some laundry, asked me if I wanted a cup of tea.

'Aye. And two pieces of toast,' I answered, pushing aside my bowl.

'You've not finished your porridge,' she observed.

'I'll no more of it, for there's no salt in it and 'tis lumpy besides,' I complained.

'You'll still be finishing it and offering it up for the Holy Souls,' Mrs Murphy advised as she examined Daid's Sunday shirt for stains.

'I already offered it up for the Holy Souls,' I replied.

Mrs Murphy stopped examining Daid's shirt and looked at me with a mixture of surprise and hope.

'They didn't want it,' I continued, looking at Mrs Murphy's flabby arms, 'for 'twas not enough salt in it.'

'It's a pity you don't remember the Great Hunger,' Mrs Murphy cautioned. 'The stories my mother told. 'Twas a feeling you never forgot,' she said. 'My mother would have been glad for that porridge when she was your age. And I'm sure there are thousands of children in Africa who would be the same.'

'And they're welcome to it,' I muttered as Mrs Murphy took my bowl.

'What was that?'

'I said I'll take black tea, and strong.'

Mrs Murphy set about making my tea and toast. As she did, she commenced her limited repertoire of hymns. 'Be Thou my vision' was first off the mark. My tea and toast were served and Mrs Murphy retired to our washtub.

There began the worst of the hymns. Mrs Murphy vigorously soaped and scrubbed while she sang 'Hail Queen of Heaven the ocean star' at the top of her voice. I put my hands over my ears, but that was poor protection for 'Pray for the wanderer, pray for me' which Mrs Murphy sang both shrill and flat. She began the second verse. Unable to bear more, I pocketed the toast, picked up my crutches and left for school.

The trip took me the entire morning. Since I was determined to enter the classroom unaided, I hid the crutches in the cloakroom. But my arrival in the middle of Maths did not pass unnoticed as I would have liked. Instead, it caused pandemonium. And Mary Arondelle Sotheby was among those who laughed loudest.

'Well, you're not too black and blue,' she said playfully after the lesson had finished. 'There's a little bit of ink on your sleeve, that's all.'

'Ink on my sleeve is it? And down my front besides.'

'On a black uniform? Who's going to see? Besides, you can get it clean again.'

'Aye, easy for yourself to say with your servants and your quality ways. Now let me be,' I returned to the Maths homework.

Della remained leaning over my desk.

'Luighseach, if only you could have seen yourself. Honestly, it was very, very funny. There we all were, immersed in awful algebra and Frances Mahony had that enormous bottle of ink. The door opened and you poked your head inside and looked around like a mole coming out of a hole. You didn't think anyone had noticed so you edged your way through a mere crack. And the care you took to shut the door and make sure it was shut was as if you were a master burglar in a rich man's house at midnight. Little did you know everyone was watching as you limped in, and your being tall and so very thin exaggerated everything. I suppose you were trying so hard with your walking that you didn't see Fanny.' Della began to giggle again. 'Crash!' she laughed. 'What a mess! Books here! Papers there and ink everywhere! Serves Fanny right for being lazy about filling the inkwells. Luighseach, you couldn't have picked a better target! Honestly, I thought I was going to die laughing! Oh dear, it was very, very funny!'

'It was not funny, Della Sotheby,' I interrupted Della's laughter.

'Luighseach, no one was laughing at you, it was the whole situation. In fact, we were laughing at Frances more than anything else. Did you see the blotch she had? All over her face and all through her hair! And she's so fair! She looked like a black and white minstrel! Or should I say a blue and white minstrel? Come on old thing, don't be such a stick in the mud.'

'Stick in the mud is it? And how would you like it if you were tripped? For 'twas Kathleen Doherty put her legs out as I passed.'

'Oh, don't be ridiculous!' Della replied, still laughing at the memory. 'How could anyone be so heartless as to do that?'

'Well that is what she did, Della Sotheby.'

'I don't believe it. You're having another bad day. Now come on, come outside and have some lunch.'

'I will not.'

'Luighseach, come on.'

She pulled my pencil and book from me and I pulled them back.

'I'll not come.'

She tried again.

'Let me be, I'm saying!'

'I won't let you be.'

'You will!' I shouted. 'You're mean! You're like the rest of them! You're mean! So get you away and leave me alone!'

'Very well!' she planted her hands on her hips. 'If that's how you want it, I will. Stay locked up in your own self-pity. And don't think you can tell me what I am or am not allowed to laugh about. I did not mean to be unkind. Nobody meant that.' And with a thump of her fist on my desk she walked out, slamming the door as she went.

The remainder of the day was utterly miserable. To make matters worse, by the time school finished, the spasms in my legs had intensified to such a degree that I could not move from my desk. Sister Magdalene noticed that I did not stand and leave with the rest of the class and arranged to get help. Daid was called, and I was faced with the humiliating task of explaining to him and to Sister where I hid my crutches. In turn I was scolded for failing to honour my father by leaving home without permission.

I vowed I would never go back to school again.

Normally my 'cello lesson was on Monday, after tea. My ailments, however, made attendance that evening impossible. Since Daid ruled that I was not to attend school on Tuesday, my 'cello lesson was rescheduled for midday that same day. It was to be my one respite from Mrs Murphy and her hymn singing. But instead of being an hour of pleasure, it became an hour of tortuous interrogation and argument, culminating in the confiscation of my bow.

I spent Wednesday at home with Mrs Murphy. To avoid any contact with the woman, I shut myself in my room after breakfast. Ordinarily I would have spent much of the day practising, which was my usual technique for avoiding Mrs Murphy, but without my bow practice was not possible, so I lay on my bed the entire day. By the end of the day I wanted my bow back more than ever.

Mrs Epstein telephoned that evening. Clearly, Daid found my teacher's arguments far more convincing than mine as to why I should come to her place on Thursday afternoon. Since I wanted my bow back, I was prepared to oblige. Daid had a free afternoon that Thursday, so he agreed to take me.

I arrived at Mrs Epstein's house with the sole intention of retrieving my bow.

'It's good to see you could come,' said Mrs Epstein as she opened the door.

'I'm only here 'cause I come for my bow.'

'Step inside, Luighseach,' Mrs Epstein sighed. 'Would you like a cup of cocoa?'

''Tis my bow I want.'

'Then wait in the music room.'

Della was there.

'Hello, old thing,' she said with a smile. 'How are you feeling?'

I did not reply.

'Della is going to be one of our violinists, Luighseach,' Mrs Epstein explained. 'Help yourself to something to eat.'

I sat in an armchair and hugged a tasselled cushion. Della continued to dismember the bun she was in the middle of when I entered. It was a very deliberate process. She held up the object, ascertained the section she wished to attack and picked off tiny bits of it, usually sultanas, which were popped into her mouth. From time to time, she licked her sticky fingers, gazed abstractedly at the elaborate nine branched candlestick on the sideboard and resumed her pecking.

I ran my fingers over the chair. It was covered in a rich tapestry of oak leaves and acorns in russets, ochres and umbers and edged with braid which was falling off in some places. An intertwining pattern, again of oak leaves, was carved on its arms. I fiddled with the tattered pieces of braid.

The doorbell rang and the voice of the visitor was heard as a heavy stride accompanied it up the hall.

'G'day Mrs Ep. Sorry I'm late. Had a tennis match.'

A hand gripped the doorknob, twisted it and threw the door open with such strength that it rebounded.

'Hey Della! Haven't seen you for a while.'

'Hello, Pim. How are you? Care for some bun?'

Della passed the plate of delicacies to the carroty-haired visitor who swiped an éclair for herself.

'So much for Lent,' she replied as she threw half the éclair into her mouth and herself into the chair.

Mrs Epstein reappeared with some cocoa for Della and the other girl.

'Good, Pim, I see you've made yourself at home. I would like you to meet our 'cellist, Luighseach Straughan. Luighseach, this is Pim Connolly. Pim plays the viola.'

It was now that the visitor noticed my presence. With her mouth full of éclair, half nodding in acknowledgment at Mrs Epstein and half at me, she grunted a greeting.

I did not reply.

Mrs Epstein made to leave.

'Luighseach, are you sure you won't have a cup of cocoa? There's some for you if you want.'

'I don't want any cocoa! I want my bow!'

'You may have it later,' Mrs Epstein brusquely replied as she closed the door.

I resumed my study of the armchair, conscious that the eating sounds made by the newcomer were directed at me.

'Seen you around school,' she began. 'You're new, aren't you? You settling in all right?'

I shrugged my shoulders and continued to fiddle with the tattered braid.

'Hope you don't mind me asking,' continued the confident, carroty-haired girl. 'But were you born crippled like that or did you have an accident?'

'I'm not crippled!'

'Ha! And my hair's blue,' she laughed.

'Luighseach had poliomyelitis when she was eight,' Della explained.

'Mother of God! Can you not mind your own business?'

'She was only asking—'

'And was I asking her if she was born with them pimples and freckles there or were they put on her face by accident? Was I asking that now, Della Sotheby?'

Della made a face, licked her fingers and wriggled further into her chair. Pim Connolly reddened and helped herself to another éclair.

'Well, if that isn't an Irish temper,' she muttered.

'She's in a filthy mood,' Della replied.

'Let you stop—'

'You know, Dell,' the other girl pushed some cream from the side of her lips. 'They thought I had polio once.'

'Did they Pim?' Della took a spritely interest.

'When I was six. My sister Gracie and I had a skipping contest to see who could jump rope the most times. Got up to over a thousand. Anyway, the next day we couldn't move so Dad took us to hospital. They kept us there for the weekend. Had a ball. Played games, got spoiled by the nurse, ate sweets. Then it was clear we weren't sick so we were sent home. When Dad found out what really happened he hit the roof. Nearly gave us the strap but he couldn't 'cause we were still sore.'

'You're joking.'

'Dead serious. Cross my heart. How's Wally?'

'Don't ask. He went to see Bert Hinkler last Sunday, though. Did you go?'

'Nah, too busy helping out at home. Saw the 'plane over the harbour but. Beaut, wasn't it? Say, I thought your brother was playing cricket this year.'

The conversation returned to Wally. From there, under the guidance of Miss Sotheby, it darted along a giddy course of parties, plays, and frocks. The very sound of her prim little English voice drove me mad. She was pretending. Every ounce of what she said was pretence.

The other girl consumed two more buns, slurped her cocoa and crashed the cup to the plate every time she put it down. Mrs Epstein came in with more cocoa and she drank a second cup. She had two stories for every one of Della's; laughed loudly and showed a huge array of horsy teeth when she did; stretched her legs a lot and folded her arms behind her head in hearty enjoyment of the conversation. Despite the cold, she was still in short sleeves; and in the light, her muscular arms and legs glowed with health. I looked at my long, thin, pale hands and my wasted legs in their stockings and sighed.

The doorbell rang again and Mrs Epstein's quick footstep was heard in the corridor. Again the drawing room door opened and in walked none other than Phoebe Raye.

More introductions were made. Della was friendly, the carroty-haired girl less so. Phoebe drew a little closer to Mrs Epstein and stared in reply. She glared at me.

Mrs Epstein took charge.

'I have taught you all for some time, and now that Luighseach and Phoebe have come to school I think you are all in a position to try some quartets. I will not say it will be an easy job. It will be a very challenging one and I am convinced you will find it extremely satisfying. But you must be prepared to work. If you do, you will find a rich reward lying in store for you. It is good to see you here and I believe that that is because you are willing to have a try.'

Mrs Epstein glanced in my direction and quickly continued.

'Now, it is going to take a little while for you to get used to one another and the way you each play. I thought we should begin with a fairly straightforward piece to help you to concentrate on listening and playing together. Playing in a group is very different from playing solo. Then, after you've mastered it, we'll look for something you might like to perform...'

Perform? Mrs Epstein wanted us to perform? Never had I played in public and I was never going to do so. Time and again, Mrs Epstein had tried to include me in her annual concerts and soirées and I had always refused. This was another of her plots to make me play in front of others. Mrs Epstein was using it to push me in front of people and I was not going to do it.

'I'll not do it!'

'I beg your pardon, Luighseach?'

'You cannot make me do it, Mrs Epstein! I'll not perform! You're wanting me in it for to make me perform!'

'Luighseach, for goodness' sake,' interrupted Della.

'I'm not doing it! Not ever! I don't want to do it at all at all. And I want my bow back!'

'Luighseach, calm down,' interrupted Mrs Epstein. 'Performance, *if* there will be any performance, is something way down the track. We will cross that bridge when we come to it. Listen. All I want you to do is to try.'

'But we will perform, won't we?' Phoebe questioned.

'We'll see in time,' replied Mrs Epstein.

'Oh but we must! To play without performing – why, it's too stupid for words!'

'Phoebe! That is enough! There will be time for everything, but first you must reach a standard that is suitable for performing and that is going to take work.'

'What do you mean standard? Don't you think I'm good enough?'

'You might be very capable, Phoebe, but there's more to this than mere virtuosity. You won't be playing solo.'

'Then I hope, Mrs Epstein, you've not asked me to play with anyone who hasn't got some degree of talent, because *I* won't do it.'

'You little snob!' exclaimed Pim.

Mrs Epstein quickly intervened. 'I assure you, Phoebe, that is not the case.'

'It better not be, Mrs Epstein, because *I* won't play with a spastic!' she hissed, her eyes smouldering in my direction.

That was it. I pushed myself out of the chair.

'The devil with string quartets, Mrs Epstein, and you can keep my bow in your drawer for all I care. I'll pluck my strings instead. I'll not change, I'll not perform, and I'll not ever play with the like of them that are here now. Not a one will I play with on any account!'

I left. A small stretch of carpet swallowed my slow clump and creak across the floorboards as I plodded down the corridor. Onto the street and up the hill I staggered, picking my way over the pavement, pausing at poles and posts, avoiding the polished shoes of passersby and the calls of boys with cricket bats. I heard my name and I tried to quicken my pace. But all was in vain. My right knee crumpled and I crashed to the ground.

'Luighseach!' the voice called, and Della, panting and coughing, came to my side. 'Luighseach, are you all right?'

I tried to pull myself up and winced with the pain. It had been a bad fall.

'I say, you're hurt. What happened?'

I could not answer and I bit my lip hard to keep the tears at bay.

'Is it sore?'

I nodded.

'I'll go back and get some help.'

'I don't need any help!'

'Nonsense! You can't get up and even if you could you can hardly walk. I saw you. You could barely lift your good leg. You couldn't even stand on it without steadying it with your hands. I know what! I'll go back and get Mr Epstein. He'll be able to carry you.'

"Tis nothing of the sort you'll do for 'tis here that I'll wait for my Daid.'

'You can't wait in the dust for your father. It's getting dark and cold. Come back and have something warm to drink. You're sick.'

I refused. 'I don't want to go back there! Do you hear? I'm not going back!' Della stamped her foot.

'Luighseach!' she began. 'I hate to say it, but you really are a spastic.'

'Don't say that!'

'Spastic!' she taunted. 'Legs like matchsticks! Yes you are – even more than you think. You're a spastic!'

'Stop it!' I implored, no longer able to hold back my tears.

'Very well, I'll stop it. But it doesn't change the fact that you're crippled – and I don't mean your legs. I mean your heart. Your heart's crippled. For someone who can be so kind, you can be so cruel to others when they try to be kind to you. In fact, you're cruel to yourself. How you can force yourself to walk in that painful way without a stick or a crutch to help you is nothing short of torture. Anyway, is it really that big a crime to show you some compassion? Is it a sin to try and help you?'

'I don't need any compassion! And I don't need any help!'

'Honestly, the way you carry on one would think that a mere glance at your legs merited eternal condemnation.'

'And how would you like it, Della Sotheby, to find people always staring and prying? Or calling you names, or laughing, or talking about you as if you couldn't hear, or making it hard for you to walk when it's hard enough already or copying the way—'

'I daresay I wouldn't,' retorted Della. 'Nor am I excusing anyone. Listen, I know people haven't been very nice. My own sister's one, and our class hasn't gone out of its way to make friends. Even today, Phoebe shouldn't have said what she said. It was very, very nasty. Mrs Epstein gave her such a talking to after you left. Vowed she would wash her mouth out next time she spoke like that and forbade her to go, and Pim was so angry with Phoebe it was all Mrs Epstein could do to keep them apart. And I know I laughed at you at school on Monday, but I said I didn't mean it. You weren't well and I didn't think. And I'm sorry for not believing you when you said you were tripped. I didn't think Kathleen could be so mean. Mary saw what happened, however, and you were right. Kathleen did trip you,' she sighed. 'But Pim on the other hand, Pim was only trying to be friendly when she spoke to you this afternoon and you were positively uncouth. She didn't mean any harm. All she did was break a big rule, a rule which governs your relationship with every living soul. Not only did she look. Even worse: she asked. She asked you about your legs.'

'And she has a right to know, does she?' I cried.

'Yes she does! Only you take offence where none is intended and you throw people's hearts back in their faces if they make a wrong move. Any comment or look you blow out of proportion. Look at you now! I've seen that scowl a hundred times: a tempest of anger and fear and hurt and defiance raging inside the moment your legs are mentioned, the moment anyone so much as blinks at you.'

'But why does everyone have to look and talk and tease?' I blurted. 'Why can't they leave me alone?'

'Because they don't understand, and in one way or another they want to. They simply don't know what to do. And you don't make it any easier. Anyway, you don't really want them to leave you alone. You want to be part of their world, don't you?'

I conceded with a sniff. 'But I don't need anyone's help for doing that.'

'No?' queried Della. 'Then get up and prove to me that's the case. Go on! Get up.'

But I could not get up, and I began to cry all the more. Della tried to put her arms around me and I pushed her away.

'Fair enough,' she remarked. 'And seeing that you don't want comforting and you're not going anywhere soon, you can listen to me instead. Crippled though you are, Luighseach Straughan, *I* don't care. I don't care about your skinny legs. I don't care about the calliper. I don't care that you limp. I don't care about any of that. *I* care about *you*. And you're much, much more than a pair of twiggy legs.'

'You're not being true, Della Sotheby.'

'I am, Luighseach. I am!

'But you laughed at me!'

'And I said I didn't mean to hurt you. Can't you forgive for Heaven's sake?'

There was a peal of thunder. We looked up at the sky. It had darkened considerably, and not only because it was late afternoon.

A few drops of rain began to fall.

'I'm sorry,' Della began in an attempt to resolve the predicament. 'Really, old thing, I'm very sorry. Call it pax?'

'Aye,' I nodded, although I was not quite so reconciled to the idea, 'Pax.'

'Shall we go back to Mrs Epstein's?'

'I'm not going back there.'

'Why not? It's starting to rain for Heaven's sake! Is it because someone has to carry you?'

'I don't want to be carried! And I don't want to play in the quartet. Mrs Epstein will make me play if I go back there, and I'm not going! Not ever!'

'Nonsense! If it's causing you this much upset, Mrs Epstein won't make you do anything. Besides, I don't think Pim or Phoebe would possibly toler—'

'I don't care what they think!'

'Don't you? And what about me? Do you care what I think?'

Seeing I did not respond, Della continued. 'Well, *I* think you should play. Why, I couldn't imagine a better opportunity. People will only think you're like them if you behave accordingly, and by playing in a quartet you have a perfect chance to give them cause to think precisely that. Otherwise, I know two people at least who will think of you as nothing more than a poor little cripple who was too timid even to try. And you don't want that. You might have trouble walking, but I bet you play well – I've seen some of the music you play, so you must play well – and that's going to stand in your favour. Besides, I would like very much to play in a quartet with you. I know Pim a little bit, but I don't know Phoebe at all, and frankly I'm a bit scared of playing with them myself. But you change everything. Why, you're—you're—'

Della's lips began to tremble.

'Luighseach, you're my *friend*.'

'Your friend?'

'Yes. You're my friend.'

I looked into her large, pale eyes. They were filling with tears.

'Do you really mean that, Delleen? Do you really mean it in your heart?'

'Of course I do!'

'And you're not saying it because I'm—'

'A moody, morose, math-minded Malvolio? No, I'm not. To be quite frank with you, I never would have picked you for a friend. You couldn't be more different from me if you tried. But I've grown to love you with all your melancholic ways and I cannot bear to see you suffering like this.'

Gently I stroked the tear that trickled down her cheek.

'Malvolio am I?' I queried, quite puzzled by her description. 'But Delleen, Malvolio's a Puritan is he not?'

'Yes,' she nodded and laughed through her tears, 'A poor puritan who has been most notoriously abused.'

Her tender, trusting smile edged across her face as again Della cast her eyes into mine and gulped.

'Shall I get some help now, old thing?'

Della presently returned with Mr Epstein and a couple of umbrellas. Back we trudged. Della pushed open the door to the music room. Everyone went quiet as Mr Epstein set me down in a chair and rested my injured leg on a footstool. Mrs Epstein gave me one of her looks. Pim's face rolled over the arm of her chair and her eyes showed their whites like a faithful dog. Phoebe sat pertly, arched her brows and took a sip of cocoa. Della stood next to me and placed her hand on my shoulder.

'So, we have a string quartet after all,' concluded my teacher. 'We'll meet here next Thursday *punctually* at half past four, with instruments. Della, could you please distribute the music? It's Haydn's *Fifths*. Concentrate on the Menuetto for now. Phoebe, I think you have something to say?'

Phoebe placed her cup and saucer on the table, then stood and glared at me.

'I apologise for calling you a spastic.' The way she pronounced that last word eliminated any contrition that may have accompanied the apology. Almost immediately she turned to Della. 'Where's my music?' she demanded as she snatched her part and waltzed away, before Della, stunned, could respond.

Pim mentioned something about tea and bade us good-bye.

'Listen,' she said as she passed me, 'I didn't mean to be a sticky beak. No ill feelings, I hope?'

I sighed and shook my head.

Mrs Epstein made me a hot cocoa and Della and I studied our music together until Daid arrived.

'I think you've forgotten something, Mrs Epstein,' I remarked as my teacher showed us to the door.

'Have I, Luighseach?'

'Aye. 'Tis my bow that's locked in your bureau, and if I'm going to practise quartets I need it back.'

It took some time to relocate the key. We were about to leave when Mrs Epstein reappeared, victoriously brandishing the bow.

Her black eyes deepened as she passed it to me. 'I trust it will be put to good use,' were her only words as we drove away.

9

I did not see Della again until the following Monday afternoon when she paid me a visit. We sat together in the parlour, sipping the tea Daid had served.

'I thought you'd be back at school today,' she remarked. 'You've been absent a week.'

''Tis Luighseach says she's not going back to school, lassie,' Daid explained.

'I beg your pardon?' Della stared incredulously at Daid, then at me.

'But—But you can't sit in that wheelchair all day,' she protested. 'You'll go out of your mind.'

''Tis a job I can get, you know,' I replied.

'Aye,' Daid interposed. 'And you'll still be using both your callipers and your crutches too. Doctor's orders they be and you're needing to accept that. You're not to overwork them legs. The trouble's not going to go away, Luighseach.'

'Ah!' Della responded with a very knowing expression. 'So Fanny Mahony was right.'

The very mention of Frances Mahony made me clench my fists and jaw. Della gleamed at my reaction.

'Fanny said you were absent from school because you were either too scared or too sick or both. Well, I guess she's right.'

'I'm neither of the sort!'

'So why aren't you coming?' asked Della. 'Everyone's been asking after you. You've no idea the effect the ink incident's had on our class. At first Fanny was the one to get all the attention as usual, and she was furious with you for falling on her and making her spill the ink. But then Mary, who saw what really happened, got mad at Kathleen for tripping you up. So, when Fanny heard that, she got mad at Kathleen for causing all the trouble and getting ink on her. Then everyone got mad at Kathleen and Fanny for being so cruel to you and thinking only of themselves. Now everyone wants you back so they can make up. Even some of the younger girls – the ones you help with reading down in the prep – came up especially to ask me where you were. As for Sister Augustine,' she continued, 'she's despairing over the lot of us. We're despairing over us! No one can explain maths like you do! Do please put us out of our misery and come back.'

I smiled at her gossipy argument.

'Anyway, if you really are scared, old thing, remember you're my friend and I'm going to stand by you. If it's teasing you're afraid of, well, I'm not going to let them. They'll have to get past me first. I say, what's so funny?'

'Delleen,' I replied, 'I'm nearly five feet ten. And yourself? Why you're no more than five feet to be sure. The very thought of having to get past you—'

'They're still going to have to try,' she replied, puffing out her small frame as best she could. 'I say, do you really have to wear a calliper on your good leg?'

Reluctantly, I nodded. 'My good leg's not too good at the moment, for I've been walking too much without the calliper. 'Twas the doctor said I'm to wear the other calliper all the time now. He was mad as a Kilkenny cat when he found out I'd been going to school without wearing it.'

'Silly girl. Why didn't you wear it in the first place?'

'Because I can walk fine without it!'

'Luighseach, you're delusional,' scolded Della.

'It makes my leg stiff! I hate my good leg being all stiff! 'Tis bad enough with a calliper on my gammy leg. And besides, everyone looks and talks and makes me different. What will they say now if I'm wearing two callipers? 'Twill only make me more different than ever and I want to be the same. Della, I'm the same!'

'I know, old thing. I think you're wonderful the way you get about. And as for everyone looking and talking— well, you're going to have to prove to them that you are the same, however many callipers you have to wear. Anyway, wouldn't it be that much easier if you wore both the callipers? You can't go around in pain the way you've been doing. That's not normal.'

'Easier?' I scoffed. 'You're talking through your hat, you are. And how am I going to climb all them stairs with crutches and callipers on both my legs? Will you tell me that?'

'You can manage the stairs, lass,' encouraged Daid. ''Twas months ago we made sure of that.'

'I'll help you,' Della confidently chimed.

'And at the station? What about the station steps? And the train?'

'You'll not be fretting about them station steps for now,' Daid reassured me. 'Let's work on getting you back on your feet again. I'll take you to school. Will you meet her at the gate and help her along, Della?'

'Of course I will,' Della replied. 'So I'll see you tomorrow?'

Della's jaw dropped in dismay when she saw me that Tuesday morning. Daid helped me out of the sidecar, making sure I was properly supported on my cane-crutches. Both my legs were now locked from feet to thighs in heavy metal braces. A slow, mechanical, straight-legged step replaced the irregular lift and swing gait she had grown accustomed to seeing.

'Oh Heaven!' she quietly exclaimed as I neared. 'Luighseach, I had no idea it was that bad.'

'I told you you were talking through your hat. So you're going to blame yourself for making me wear both my callipers so?'

Della overcame her initial shock and set about her mission as my protector. While we tramped down the drive, she was full of conversation over matters aeronautic and twirled and danced around me as she would a maypole. Occasionally she raced ahead and dashed back to entice me to a pleasure she had found: the honeysuckle vine near the front gate, a few golden leaves newly fallen, some birds sporting with the statue of St Dominic. When anyone passed us, she sang a friendly hello before they so much as noticed my legs and insisted I do the same. Hiding behind her and shrouding myself in silence, in her authoritative opinion, only served to draw attention to what I so dearly wished to conceal. There was no need to be afraid, she reasoned. If they saw I was not afraid of them, they would not be afraid of me, and if they found me friendly they would be friendly in return.

'I know they stare and talk and sometimes they say things that aren't very nice,' she observed, 'but it's only because they want to know and they don't know how to handle something unusual. It's only natural. Smile and say "hello". You'll be amazed at the effect it has. Do try, old thing.'

'Lucy!' called a small voice and my sleeve was grabbed. It was Sophie, one of the younger girls in the prep. She seemed quite undaunted by my crutches.

'Are you coming to help me read on Thursday afternoon?' she asked. 'You didn't come last week.'

I knew that Daid had made arrangements for me to have half days this week, so I would not be helping out. But one look at Sophie's eager face and bouncing curls compelled me to decide otherwise.

'Aye, I'll be there,' I answered. 'And you'll remember your book will you not?'

'Oh yes, of course.' And off she ran.

'She's coming! She's coming!' little Sophie yelled to her friends, two of whom I also helped.

'She's such a spastic,' sneered another girl in the group as she watched me struggle along the path.

'Stop it, Ruby,' I heard Sophie retort. 'She might walk funny, but she's nice. So don't say mean things about her.'

'See?' said Della.

My classmates were too stunned to comment much. Besides, Della did not give them a chance. The moment we entered the classroom, she maintained a steady stream of conversation while she helped me to my desk, took my satchel and organised my books for the morning.

'We have French, History and Maths before morning tea,' she informed me. 'And please, please, please answer as many questions as you can for Sister Augustine. We're doing something that's simply awful. Some tree thing. What is it again, Mary? For the life of me, I can't remember.'

'Trigonometry, Della,' Mary Byrne replied as she watched me fall, straight-legged into my chair. 'You have an accident?' she asked.

'My right leg's poorly,' I regretfully explained.

I pulled up the rings that locked the joints of my callipers and moved my now bent legs into a more conventional position.

'Do those braces hurt?' she asked.

I shook my head and nervously glanced at her. 'Not exactly,' I replied. Did she really want to know the truth? 'They're heavy is all.'

'Would you mind if I had a turn of your crutches?' Mary maintained her niceness.

'Aye, you can,' I answered, and hoped she would not run off with them and leave them somewhere.

'My brother had to use crutches once when he broke his ankle,' Mary tried to work out how to hold them. 'But they were different. They went under his arms. How do these work?'

To my surprise, I found myself explaining to Mary how to slip her hands through the cuffs at the top and grab hold of the supports. She tried to walk.

After that, everyone wanted a turn – except Frances and Kathleen who stared and whispered – some with very comical results. They had no idea how to use cane-crutches. When Sister Magdalene arrived to teach History, my crutches were in Elizabeth Fitzgerald's hands. The class pretended Beth had sprained her ankle. Tender-hearted Sister Magdalene oozed sympathy as she listened while Beth fabricated the tale of her misfortune, and assured Beth she would pray a novena for her recovery. Beth gratefully accepted Sister's kindness before crumpling onto her desk and silently venting her mirth.

'And a thousand welcomes to you, Lucy,' said Sister Magdalene as she looked at me with a steady gaze, her mouth twitching a smile. 'I hope you're feeling better.'

Sister had not been fooled at all.

At recess, I discovered that someone had locked my cloakroom and impounded the possessions I stowed there. These I had to retrieve: a candle and matches, a notebook, a bag of barley sugar, a crocheted throw rug and a cushion. It cost me three pence ha'penny and a chiding. I was now obliged to roam the grounds and deal as best I could with any looks, taunts and comments.

Over the next couple of days, however, the 'Spastic! Spastic!' jeer I used to hear so frequently began to diminish. Della's cheerful influence had a great deal to do with it. But there was also another force at work: Pim Connolly.

Pim happened to be St Dominic's head prefect, and as head prefect she had the authority to issue a detention to anyone she caught misbehaving. Misbehaviour, in Pim's eyes, seemed to include unkind remarks about me, and if ever she chanced upon anyone making comments about me or my legs, she did not hesitate to stride over to the girls in question, loudly chastise them and issue them their punishment. For the embarrassed offenders there was no escape, for Pim reported directly to Sister Bellarmine and Pim took her role seriously. After a few such incidents – the last involving Leila Sotheby and her cronies – no one dared speak disparagingly about my legs, at least within Pim's earshot. And somehow, Pim was ubiquitous.

And there was an added bonus: Pim was genuinely friendly. My journeys around school invariably encountered her dominating the hockey field, rolling on the grass in mirth over a joke, or, garlanded with daisy chains, lustily singing popular songs arm in arm with her comrades. She yelled and waved whenever she saw me, regardless of whether she was nearby or on the other side of the grounds. Stout, well-flanked, big of bone and brawn, she banged and barged her way up and down the stairs and along the corridors, and if she ever passed me, I was sure to be greeted with a vigorous whack on the back and a loud 'G'day Lucy'. Della found her behaviour brash and took whatever measures she could to avoid it. But I liked it. It was a welcome change from the sterile politeness I tended to receive from other girls. More than anything else, Pim's rough and ready comraderie made me feel as though I belonged.

Being fond, it seemed, of any occasion to celebrate with food, Pim suggested we enjoy some refreshment before our lesson at Mrs Epstein's on Thursday afternoon. We met at the soda fountain in Petersham. Pim ordered two sodas which she drank in the time it took for Della and me to consume our more modest treats.

'Have you always played the viola, Pim?' Della asked.

'Nah,' Pim replied. 'Started on the violin. Played it for a few years but I ended up hating it.'

'How could you hate the violin?'

'All right, maybe hate is a bit strong. I didn't want to play it any more. Mrs Ep wouldn't let me give up so she started me on the viola. Learning from Mr Ep now.'

'Do you mean at the Conservatorium? I say!' remarked an impressed Della.

Mr Epstein only taught at the Conservatorium.

Pim did not dwell on the circumstance. 'See Mrs Ep from time to time but, which is why she roped me into this. What about you?' she turned to me and gestured with her spoon. 'You ever play the violin?'

'Aye, I did.'

'So when did you take up the 'cello?' Pim continued.

'Five years ago.'

'Before or after you had polio?'

I returned to my soda.

'After, it was.'

'So, what made you take up the 'cello, Luighseach?' asked Della. 'Why didn't you stay with the violin?'

I tightened my hold on the straw and glowered. Levering a deliberate spoonful of ice cream into my mouth, I confronted her face to face. Della wore one of her determined looks. Her lips had tightened, her nose had become more beak-like, and her eyes assumed an affectionate intensity as the rim of her glasses caught the afternoon sun.

'Anyone would think polio was a mortal sin the way you carry on,' she teased. 'I bet you've a story and a half hidden away.'

The three of us drew sips. Pim's warm brown eyes were ready to take in every word that followed, and Della's were only too keen to push out any words I had to offer.

'I'll have you to know I left my violin in Ireland, and after the Polio I was not of a mind to play it besides for I used to play and dance with it.'

'Dance? You?' interrupted Pim. I blushed, knowing how absurd it seemed given my present condition. 'What sort? Ballet?'

I shook my head. ''Twas sean nós—' I checked myself and searched for a more understandable explanation. 'Irish dancing: jigs and reels and the like. Well, after the polio I couldn't do all that any more.'

'So why the 'cello? Why not the flute, or the piano or something else?' Pim asked.

The light caught Della's glasses again and she silently echoed Pim's question.

'Well…' I began, 'I loved it. When I came out from the hospital, I wasn't very well, you know. I'd been in plaster for months and I had to wear callipers and I couldn't walk and didn't want to try. The callipers were stiff and heavy and I felt all caged up. So I used to sit in the wheelchair in the parlour all day long. All day I used to sit. Hardly a thing would I do and not a soul would I see.

'Well, 'twas Daid used to worry about me not being able to get about, so he made a point of taking me out every Sunday. He'd hitch up Mrs Murphy's horse and cart and we'd go exploring. At times we'd stop to look at a garden, or the tiles on a front step, or chat with a mother and her baby. And one day when we stopped, coming from one of the houses there, we chanced upon the most beautiful music I ever heard in my life. It flowed, you know, lilted over notes like water trickling down a stony slope. Such graceful music it was, and powerful too the way the notes built upon each another. Well, after that, I didn't want to explore any other street. I'd make Daid take me again and again, and I'd make him stop at that house, in case the music was playing; and when it was, I'd listen, and I wouldn't go until the music finished.

'So one such day, Daid put it into his head to find out a little more. Up to the door he went and knocked: a rat-a-tat-tat like that. Someone opened and they spoke a little. Daid told me after that it was a 'cello making the music.

'And that was when I asked my Daid what a 'cello was. Since Daid didn't know, he went to Mr Thomas' store and found me a book. All about the orchestra it was. Well, I didn't bother with the other instruments, I only read about the 'cellos, and I told Daid that it was a 'cello I wanted to play. My Da thought it a good idea. He decided that if he found a 'cello for a reasonable price, he would see what he could do for to have me to learn. So day after day I asked him whether he'd found a 'cello. He hadn't, and he made me read the paper for to see if any 'cellos were for sale. There were some but they were dear as diamonds. Not a one could we afford.

'But one evening Mr Birstall came to visit – Mr Birstall works with my Daid, you see. Well, Mr Birstall came with his son, Mr David Birstall, and they brought with them a great fat case done up with a wide green ribbon. Mr David gave it me and helped me open it. And, wouldn't you know, inside was a 'cello especially for myself! It belonged to Mr David who couldn't play it any more 'cause he'd lost an arm in the War. 'Twas a Turkish cricket ball blew it off, you see. Then Mr David told Daid about Mrs Epstein, who was a friend he used to play 'cello with, and Daid set about arranging some lessons. Then Mrs Murphy's horse had to be knackered. That was when my Da bought a motorcycle and Mr David taught him to drive.

'Well, to get to my first lesson, we had to drive down that very same street we used to walk, and we parked outside that very house with the music. And it turned out that it was Mrs Epstein herself I used to hear on those Sunday afternoons. So, when I met her the first time, I told her I wanted to play the tune she played. Mrs Epstein didn't know which one I meant, but after I sang a few bars she knew which piece it was and she played it for me. The Prelude from Bach's first 'cello suite it was. She said she would teach it me one day but I would have to learn many other things before that.

'And so we started. 'Twas hard in the beginning 'cause at the time I wasn't much bigger than the 'cello and I had to move my legs for to fit it and I used to fall off the chair when I tried. And 'twas a right stretch to get my fingers to reach the notes and I couldn't read music for I'd learnt to play the fiddle by ear. Mrs Epstein and I used to fight nearly every lesson because all I wanted to do was to play the Bach and all Mrs Epstein wanted to do was teach me Piatti. Aye, she was strict with me! In the end she gave in and would play the Bach for me at the end of my lesson, provided I made an effort with the Piatti. When she played that Bach, I'd listen as quiet as a mouse and glean as many notes as I could. Then I'd go home and try to learn it for myself. I'd play and play and the only time I'd stop was because I was too tired to play any more. And Mr David used to come from time to time to help me tune and show me how to crack eggs with one hand.

'And it was when I started going to lessons that I started to walk again because Daid and I had to walk to Mrs Epstein's house. And as the weeks passed we'd park the motorcycle further away so I'd get more practice walking. I can do it all now, you know.'

'Do what?' asked Della.

'I can play the Bach— and crack eggs with one hand. Everything, save walk properly.'

I sought relief in polishing off what remained of my soda.

'You will one day,' Della gave my arm a squeeze.

I glanced tentatively at Pim.

'You certainly know how to spin a yarn,' she said with a smile.

It was well and truly time to head to Mrs Epstein's.

We set off at a brisk pace. Pim strode out ahead. To keep up, I swung my crutches vigorously and swung my legs through in turn. Della half danced and half hopped from pavement to street to pavement and twirled around every pole she came to.

'And now 'tis your turn, Della Sotheby,' I prompted her. 'Did you always play the violin?'

Della nodded. 'I didn't really have a say in the matter. I wanted to learn the piano, like Wally. Wally plays the piano and the trumpet, and both rather well, too, when he bothers to practise. But Mummy and Daddy decided my hands were too small and wouldn't let me. So they said that if I had to play something, I ought to play violin. It was more of an appeasement, really. I don't think anyone expected much to come of it. Anyway, I persevered and took it all quite seriously. Now, I think, they wished they'd never made such a decision. They're always complaining I practise too much.'

'No one's ever complained about that from me,' remarked Pim.

'Which is why you play viola, I suppose,' Della teased.

'Hey!' Pim protested.

'What about Phoebe?' Della quickly resumed before Pim could retort further. 'Have you heard her play at all?'

Pim shook her head. 'She wasn't at Mrs Ep's Christmas concert. Were you there?'

'No, unfortunately.'

'How come?'

'Mummy didn't approve.'

'Come to think of it, I didn't see you at the concert either, Lucy. In fact, I've never seen you at a concert.'

'I—I cannot play in front of people,' I explained.

'Poor old thing gets frightfully nervous,' Della gently explained. 'But we're going to fix that,' she added. 'It's much easier playing in a group. You'll see. Dear me,' she sighed. 'Whatever are we going to do with Phoebe?'

'We can try putting the little brat into Lucy's calliper things to start with,' remarked Pim.

'Oh Pim, do be serious.'

'I am,' Pim replied. 'Otherwise she'll be nothing but trouble.'

'Why do you say that?'

'She was nothing but trouble last week. She was nothing but trouble at the boarding house—'

'Boarding house?' echoed Della. 'She doesn't look like a boarder. Phoebe doesn't board at school, does she?'

'Did at first. And she was trouble: wouldn't do jobs, wouldn't wear her uniform properly and wouldn't follow the schedule. In the end she ran away. They sent her home after that.'

'She sounds as if she's very unhappy,' Della replied. 'Surely it must have been something happened. Was she teased at all?'

'Probably, and little wonder if she was. She gave as much as she got. Anyway, it was a lower school problem.'

'And you know what class she's in?' I was a little surprised to hear Phoebe connected with the lower school. She seemed older.

'Second form, I think,' replied Pim. 'Maybe the third. Not really sure.'

'Well, girls that age can be frightfully catty,' observed Della.

'I think we got a taste of that last week,' scoffed Pim. 'Beats me why she was boarding anyway if she lives close by. They probably couldn't stand her at home either.'

'Pim!'

'It's about time you three arrived,' remarked Mrs Epstein as she opened the door. 'What did I say about punctuality last week?'

Mrs Epstein's welcome did not disturb Pim in the least.

'G'day Mrs Ep. Stopped for sodas and Lucy wouldn't shut up.'

Mrs Epstein gave me one of her looks.

'And I hope you've exhausted your tongue, young lady, because I am in no mood for verbal polemics this week. Phoebe's in the music room. Tune up please. I'll be with you in a minute.'

Sure enough the little Maja was there, semi-reclined in the lounge and languidly polishing her violin. As usual, she was clad in her personal variant of the school uniform, a fact only enhanced by the way she wore her hair piled high in an elaborate bun with soft curls toppling round her face.

'Hello Phoebe, how are you?' Della chirped as she took off her hat and gloves and attended to her instrument.

'So-so,' came Phoebe's off-hand reply as she stroked her violin and kissed it. She then tucked it under her chin, closed her eyes and started to play softly to herself.

'Oh you haven't!' Della exclaimed.

'What's up?' asked Pim.

'A Stradivarius!' Della was in raptures. Laying her own instrument aside, she drifted to Phoebe and knelt down beside her. 'May I please have a look?'

Now aware of the homage paid to her instrument, Phoebe opened her eyes and paused. Della repeated her request and, trembling with excitement, was gratified to find violin and bow placed in her hands. She took them lovingly, played a few dreamy bars and a smile of delight glowed over her face and fingers.

Della sent Phoebe another longing look as she handed the violin back.

'It's beautiful! Is it really a Strad? Where did you get it?'

'I found it in the attic.'

'You're joking! You could pay a fortune for something like this!'

'Well, I didn't. When I found it, some strings had broken and the bridge had collapsed. Poor violin! Mr Hunt set it up for me.'

'So how did you know it was a good violin?' I ventured a question.

For the first time, Phoebe bothered to look in my direction— or rather the direction of my 'cello, which with Pim's help I had wedged between my legs. There was no hiding the callipers when I played the 'cello in my school uniform, for my tunic, already short, was pushed back in order to fit the instrument. Everything was exposed: long skinny legs, irons, knee pads, even the bottom of the thigh straps, and there was nothing I could do to cover them. I felt in my pocket for some rosin and desperately hoped that Phoebe would not say anything about what she saw. She didn't say anything. She stared.

'So is it really a Stradivarius?' Della asked.

'No,' Phoebe replied, still staring vacantly at my legs. 'It's a Guarneri.'

'Strewth!' Pim exclaimed with a wink in my direction. 'You gotta a Ga-wanee-airee?'

'The Guarneri is quite different from the Stradivari,' Phoebe pronounced the Italian names with even greater precision than before. '*Your* violin is a Stradivari model.'

'Really?' there was a thrill of excitement in Della's voice. 'How do you know?'

'See? It's more streamlined. Its shoulders are more squared.'

Both violins were held up for comparison.

'I say!' remarked Della. 'They're quite different, aren't they? Why, yours is far more round than mine. Look at it! It's rather curvaceous, almost pear-shaped.'

Pim gave out a wolf-whistle as she slowly traced her hands in the shape of an imaginary hour-glass.

'Pim, don't be vulgar,' Della snapped. 'Phoebe, has it a label inside? Mine does. See? "Hart and Son": in there. May I have another look? I say! There doesn't seem to be a mark in yours. Are you sure it's a Guarneri?'

'Only the shape indicates that. Mr Hunt thought it might be a copy. It's old, though. More than a century.'

Della turned the violin around. 'It's very pretty. What lovely wood!' Then she stopped and rubbed her thumb along the neck of the instrument. 'I don't believe it!' she exclaimed. 'Someone's actually burned a hole in it! Have you seen what's been done to Phoebe's violin?' Della inquired of Mrs Epstein who now entered the room.

'I only know one person who used to perform that sort of abberation,' Mrs Epstein remarked, and she shook her head and uttered a brisk 'tut tut' at the thought. 'And he did it to an Amati to mark third position of all things. Heaven only knows why for he was the best violinist I ever played with. Now girls, it is about time we sat down and rehearsed.'

Chairs were drawn and music was gathered and dumped on stands. In haste we began to tune to Phoebe, who had already tuned before we came.

'Are you going to sit like that?' asked Mrs Epstein

Bewildered, with instruments and bows poised in query, we looked at each other and then at our teacher.

'Well, either you're afraid to catch cold from one another or else you're about to start a war. Bring yourselves together. Come on. You have to be in a position where you can hear each other and watch each other very closely. Phoebe, could you put your chair next to Luighseach?'

Phoebe did as exactly as bidden and no more. Mrs Epstein silently indicated for her to sit in the chair, but she simply looked the other way.

'Hmmph!' Mrs Epstein shrugged. 'Now Della, could you please bring your chair to the far left? No, not Luighseach's left, the other left, next to that other chair. Very good. Sit down, thank you.'

There was a cry of protest from Phoebe. 'She can't sit there!'

'I beg your pardon?'

'That's the first violinist's position. *I* am first violin!'

'And when did this come about?' Mrs Epstein looked first to Phoebe and then rapidly across to Della.

'*I* am first violin,' Phoebe repeated.

'Well, I regret to tell you, madamoiselle, that *you* are second violin. Della, don't tell me you took the second violin part home last week?'

'Of course, Mrs Epstein. Phoebe took the first and I didn't think to question her. I'm not nearly good enough to be first violin.'

'The recipient of the school music prize not good enough to be first violin?' questioned Mrs Epstein. 'Nonsense, Della. Besides, you are nearly two years older and have just a little more sense than Madamoiselle Phoebe, who at this very moment is demonstrating precisely why she cannot possibly be first violin. And would you mind telling me what is wrong with second violin, young lady?'

'It's boring!' Phoebe stamped her foot and angrily shook her curls. 'It has no real part to play. It's bits here and bits there.' At this, Della and I dodged her bow as it lashed from one side to the other. 'It's a fill in and a fetch-all. It's—'

'Yes, yes, you're quite right. It's all that. But what are you interested in, Phoebe? Are you interested in yourself or the music? Hmmm?'

Phoebe swung her bow even more vigorously.

'Well, if you're interested in yourself, that is exactly how you will see your role – boring, as you say – a copying act, a supplier of extra notes, a part without distinction. But Phoebe, you're interested in the music, aren't you?'

'I might be,' she snapped.

'Well, if perhaps you *are* interested in the music, you will find your part in many ways the most challenging because often it will be you who has to show the greatest degree of sensitivity. It will be up to you to show how well you enhance the harmony, how you build the drama, and, when you have a chance to shine, how you can do so in perfect unity with what has gone before and what comes after you. This part is going to demand every ounce of your musical talent in a way you have never applied it, and I am convinced you can do it in a noble and artistic fashion. Now do you understand?'

It was clear that however indifferent, however haughty, however eccentric she might be, music meant much to Phoebe Raye. While Mrs Epstein spoke, she gradually slowed the swishing of her bow and stood calmly again with her violin hanging loosely by her side. Mrs Epstein she acknowledged with a slight upwards tilt of the chin and a downward sweep of her eyes.

'Good,' Mrs Epstein gave her one of those rare smiles that was reserved solely for the accomplishment of difficult things.

'But I won't sit next to *her*!' Phoebe spat as she flashed her eyes and lashed her bow in my face.

'Pim, you sit down at Luighseach's right. Phoebe, sit in that empty chair between Della and Pim, this instant!' There was no escaping Mrs Epstein's gritty command.

'Finally,' our teacher sighed, 'we have something that looks like an ensemble. You might like to alter the arrangement later, depending on how effective you find it. Remember: First violinist and 'cellist must be able to communicate closely, second violin and viola likewise. Let's begin. Phoebe, sight-read second for now. Della, try first. When you're ready, lead them in. A slight gesture will do. The rest of you, watch and listen.'

Della, her eyes fixed on the music, nodded her violin. We plunged into a deluge of sound, sank beneath the weight of notes and rests, and in repeated attempts to save ourselves, clutched at what we could of our parts, only to have them swept away by the force of someone else's phrase.

Pim was the first to drown.

'I'm lost!' she groaned as she leant back in her chair. 'Cello and first violin died away, leaving second violin trickling a few solo notes before she realised she was on her own. Totally helpless, we turned to Mrs Epstein. She shook her head as she raised her hands and let them fall into her lap.

'I cannot believe what I have heard. Can it be that the four of you are the same capable players I thought I knew? I have never listened to such a drunken cacophony in my life! Luighseach, you have succeeded in turning a minuet into a gallop. The way you are thundering your instrument you would have us think we were at the Galway races, and this is not a competition to see who reaches the finish line first. There is no need to prove your might by playing loudly and fast. Quieten down. You are to be an anchoring force, a good strong support for this flighty character,' here she indicated Della, 'who is doing a brave job but has her wings caked with mud at the moment. Della, you can read better than that. If you learnt the second's part you should be able to see how yours fits in with it. For the minor section all you are doing is working with Phoebe an octave higher. Pim, have you even looked at your music?'

'A bit,' Pim sheepishly replied.

'A bit, my foot! We are not going to get anywhere if you don't make a solid effort to get your part under your belt. And concentrate! You won't lose your place if you count carefully and listen. Now let's try again.'

A marginally better effort followed, occasionally salvaged by Mrs Epstein calling the bar numbers or indicating an entry with an emphatic gesture. At the third attempt, phrases and harmonies started to surface, and in doing so, began to charm us. Upon reaching the end of the section, we lowered our bows.

I ventured a glance at Della. She nodded and smiled. There was a nudge in my side from Pim. 'Good work,' she whispered. Finally, I sought out Phoebe.

No sooner had she caught my gaze than she wrinkled her nose at me and poked out her tongue.

10

At the end of our lesson, Mrs Epstein suggested that if we wanted we could organise a rehearsal of our own. The idea seemed to have some appeal. Della, ever obliging, invited us to her place on Saturday afternoon.

Being occupied with the usual run of weddings, the only chance Daid had to drop me round was in the morning. This arrangement did not bother Della in the least when she telephoned with details. We could spend the morning studying and I could stay for lunch.

With a special 'Dia dhuit' which touched my father considerably, she greeted us and showed us into the large drawing room. All was neatly prepared: a vase of young, white roses stood on the piano, and four chairs and four wooden stands waited in expectation for the afternoon's music.

Daid installed my 'cello in its designated spot, and after a brief and overly polite encounter with Mrs Sotheby in the hall, took his leave. Della and I began our ascent of the mountain of trigonometry that lay in store for us in her room.

No matter how much I explained the function of sin, cos and tan and the use of logarithmic tables, nothing seemed to provide the rope, pick axe or helping hand she needed to climb the Everest she saw before her. Again and again I made her repeat the Pythagoras Theorem, explain its operation and work through the problems step by step. Yet when it came time for her to try by herself, she could not do it, and as much as I endeavoured to tell her that she had to find the answer in her own head, she still attempted a fruitless search of my face for a less treacherous path. Crying and fiddling did not make her journey any easier. So after an hour of struggle through a fog of numbers, with minimal progress made none the easier by her tears, we agreed that enough was enough. Croton was abandoned in favour of the more favourable terrains of Venice and Cyprus. Accompanied by Othello, Desdemona, Iago and Emilia, we recovered the intellectual energy needed before sailing with Aenaeus through Virgil's craftily charted waters.

A sudden gust of wind blew us off course when Leila burst into the bedroom with the announcement that lunch had been waiting for nearly ten minutes and that if we didn't come now we wouldn't get any.

'What have you been doing? Were you not aware it was past half past twelve?'

She may have been unaware of the hour, but Della was perfectly aware that her step-father did not want to know what she had been doing.

'I'm sorry, Daddy,' she blushed and pressed her hands anxiously together. 'We simply lost track of the time. It won't happen again.' Della then channelled her courtesies in my direction. 'Luighseach, you remember Wally, don't you?'

Wally nodded hello. Della and I served ourselves from the sideboard.

'I say, Dell. How's the study going?' he asked while Della helped me with my chair.

'Well, English is fine and Latin's passable,' Della replied as she placed my plate in front of me. 'But I don't understand Trig. Luighseach's been helping me, but—'

'You?' Wally looked straight at me. I perused my plate of ham and salad.

'She's an absolute wiz at Maths, Wally,' Della explained.

'I scored a summa in the last Maths test,' Leila interrupted.

'Wait a minute,' Wally didn't pay any attention to Leila who then proceeded to repeat her triumph for the benefit of her parents. 'Are you the one who lent Della that Canterbury Puzzle book?'

'Awful book!' moaned Della. 'Kind thought, old thing, but an awful book all the same. How anyone can butcher literature with ghastly logical problems and numbers is quite beyond me.'

'I thought it was tops,' Wally replied.

'You would,' retorted his sister.

'Have you done all the problems?' Wally asked me.

'I done most of them,' I eventually admitted. 'But 'tis some have the devil in them, I'm telling you.'

Wally agreed. 'I tried the broken chessboard one. Have you done that?'

'Aye, I done that one.'

'Della,' interrupted Mrs Sotheby. 'Could you tell me how many of you are playing in the quartet this afternoon?'

At this, Wally smirked and managed to hide his grimace in his serviette. I smiled at my salad.

'Four, Mummy,' Della patiently replied. 'There are four of us in the quartet.'

'And would you mind telling me *who* is playing?' she inquired.

'Well, Luighseach's playing the 'cello,' Della began. 'That's the big one.'

'What? Between the legs? With leg irons?' Mrs Sotheby cast a distasteful look in my direction. 'What on earth does your mother say about that?'

'Mummy,' Della cautioned in a softer voice. 'I thought I told you. Luighseach's mother passed away.'

'Oh yes, of course,' her mother brushed the reminder aside. 'Well, it's no wonder then, although I don't understand how someone as elegant and artistic as your father could allow you to be so unladylike.'

'My Daid lets me do as I please,' I rallied to Daid's defence. Daid had never ever made any negative remark about my playing the 'cello.

'So I see,' Mrs Sotheby was far from impressed.

'Anyway, Mummy. It really doesn't matter. Once Luighseach starts playing you hardly even notice the callipers, she's that good. Besides, many women play the 'cello. Mrs Epstein does.'

'That German woman,' tersely replied Mrs Sotheby, 'is hardly a model of what is ladylike.'

'She's not German, Mummy. She's Australian. Mr Epstein's German. Actually, I think he's Austrian.'

'Austrians, Germans, they're all the same,' her mother complained. 'War-hungry monsters.'

'And who else is playing, Della?' Mr Sotheby redirected the conversation.

'Pim Connolly's playing viola.'

'Pim?' repeated Mrs Sotheby. 'Pim! What sort of a name is that?'

'I don't know what her full name is. Do you, Wally?'

'Always been Pim to me,' Wally shrugged.

'Where do *you* know her from?' asked his mother.

'Oh, around, I suppose,' answered Wally.

'Around?' To Mrs Sotheby this did not augur well.

'Pim's from the country, Mummy,' Della explained, trying to restore Pim's reputation. 'At least she was. She's Head Prefect. She boards at school during the week, I know that much.'

'Oh? Then her parents have property?'

'Oh yes,' replied Della, hoping in earnest she wasn't telling a fib.

'Pim lives in Mosman,' Wally provided further details.

'Mosman? Why that's a nice suburb,' remarked Mrs Sotheby. 'Do you know which part?'

'Could be the zoo for all I care,' Wally answered curtly as he helped himself to a soft bread roll.

'Anyway, Phoebe Raye is the second violinist,' concluded Della.

'Phoebe Raye?' Leila giggled, 'Are you in a group with Phoebe Raye?'

'What's so funny about that?' asked Della.

'Nothing, except that she's the strangest girl in the whole school.'

'Well, I warrant you, Leila, she is a little odd,' acknowledged her sister. 'But she's a very good violinist. How do you know her, anyway? She's much older than you.'

'Yes, but she's in the Third Form, which is Cecily Mahony's class. Sissy told Angela and me everything about her.'

'So who is she, Leila?' inquired Mrs Sotheby.

'You mean, what is she? She's illegitimate. That's what she is.'

'Nonsense, Leila,' Della remonstrated. 'And I bet you don't even know what that means.'

'Yes I do. Sissy told me. It's when you're born—'

'Thank you, Leila,' Mr Sotheby intervened, 'I think everyone here is sufficiently knowledgeable as to the meaning of the word.'

'They certainly are,' muttered Wally under his breath.

'Besides,' Della asserted. 'What does it matter?'

'Della!' Mrs Sotheby exclaimed.

'Well, what does it matter, Mummy? Why, Phoebe might be the daughter of a beautiful ballerina who died of consumption. Or of a famous general who died heroically in battle. Or—' and she took a cue from the bare-breasted harem girl in the picture above the sideboard, 'Or a Persian Princess in disguise.'

'You read too much,' Wally remarked.

'And since when has art failed to imitate life?' Della retorted. 'The trouble with you, Wally, is that you don't read enough.'

'I don't need to,' he replied. 'I witness life's pageant parading past me on a daily basis.'

'Cynic.'

'Dreamer.'

'Anyway, whoever she is and however strange she is, I for one am going to welcome Phoebe Raye with open arms,' concluded Della in a tone that dared every other member of her family to challenge her. Nobody did. Like me, they all knew that when Della had made up her mind, no one was going to get the better of her.

'Shall we adjourn to the verandah for tea?' suggested Mr Sotheby.

'Not for me, thanks,' said Wally, 'for I'll be 'elpin' 'Ammond with the Rolls Canardly.'

'It's a Bentley,' corrected Mr Sotheby who seemed a little miffed.

'Well, you can 'ardly call it a Rolls,' Wally replied.

'Wally, don't drop your haitches,' scolded Mrs Sotheby. 'It's frightfully common.'

'Right-ho, Mater,' replied her son who now took pains to speak very properly indeed. 'Just off to give H-ammond a h-and with the old motor. Toodle-pip.'

'Meaning,' Della scornfully whispered to me as we left the dining room. 'He's just going out to smoke a fag.'

Nellie brought out the tea. Mrs Sotheby fussed over sugar and milk and commenced her counter-attack as she filled and passed the cups.

'Now Della, you are still friends with Frances, aren't you?'

'Of course, Mummy.'

'*Such* a lovely girl and *such* a nice family,' she remarked with a nod in my direction. 'You do know, Desmond, they've recently bought a magnificent property in Bowral?'

'Who has had this pleasure, Letty dear?' asked Mr Sotheby as he stirred his sugar.

'The Mahonys. From what Julia tells me the house is simply marvellous. Maybe Frances might invite you one day, Della. Now *that* would be very proper.'

Sensing another of his wife's indulgent descriptions of interior details, fabrics and decoration, Mr Sotheby decided, somewhat abruptly but pleasantly, to change the topic of conversation.

'So how is your father's work these days, Lucy? Has he had any more commissions for portraits?'

'Not lately, sir,' I replied. 'But his studio work's been keeping him busy and some photos he's had published in journals the last few months.'

'Really? Which ones?'

I listed some titles which Mr Sotheby verified with a slight incline of the head and a stroke of his beard. Della, by this time, had taken her tea and was sitting nearby.

'But Luighseach,' she remarked, 'I was looking at some of those last night. I didn't see your father's name anywhere. I would have picked it a mile away.'

'You wouldn't, Della Sotheby. My father does be anglicising his name for business, so 'tis not spelt the way I spell it. In future, when you see Morgan Straughan spelt like you English sound it and not Murchadh Ó Sruitheáin the way it should be, well you'll know that's himself.'

'Why I must have a look! Daddy, may I get the magazines?'

Mr Sotheby gave a nod and Della was off in an instant.

'Della! Must you run?' called Mrs Sotheby. 'My, Lucy, they're very well regarded publications,' she observed as she stroked the cat. 'I've always known your father's a rather fashionable photographer, but I didn't realise he's *that* fashionable.'

I smiled to think of Daid, with his solitary, prayerful ways and quiet, defined brogue as being 'fashionable' and nurtured the thought on a good warm sip of well-brewed tea.

'Aye, he's fashionable, Ma'am,' I replied. 'But I think he'd prefer to be thought of as an artist.'

Della returned with an armful of magazines and eagerly began to leaf through them.

'I say, Luighseach, show me some.'

I soon found a photo Daid had taken of some horses.

''Tis this one my father did, Della Sotheby.'

Della hopped to my side and poured over name and photograph.

Up she jumped and brought the magazine to her mother who nodded and sipped her tea. Mr Sotheby was next to view and immediately wanted to know how it was done.

'Well, to tell you true, sir, 'tis several photos in one,' I explained. 'I was with Daid when he worked on it last year. Early one morning, we drove to the track for to see the racehorses. Daid knows 'tis horses I like, so he left me to watch while he photographed. He took lots of pictures, getting up as close as he could and well nigh trampled. Daid was wanting pictures of the horses all angry and full of spirit, and when he finished, it was mud on him from head to foot. Then back in the studio, he cut the negatives and pieced them together.'

'I see,' Mr Sotheby studied the picture more carefully.

'You won't see any joins, sir,' I told him. 'My Daid's too good. But 'tis made from about four photographs. Daid printed it and printed it again on a larger sheet of paper and exposed it far longer than he should. After that he placed it on a dish with a solution in it. Phryo-something it was with a bit of soda sulphate. Well, would you believe the picture turned black as night. Then he washed it and rinsed it and dipped it in another solution. He placed the print on a piece of glass and rubbed it over with ferricyanide. Magic it was happened next. The horses stormed through the darkness and Daid played with the lights and shadows for to make them do what he wanted. And after that he built up the details even more.'

'So it wasn't like this when he photographed it the first time?'

'It was not, sir. He put together parts of pictures and developed it a special way for to produce the right effect. Them horses nearly jump from the page they're so angry, with their eyes aglimmering white and their hooves all thick with clay.'

'Stunning work! I gather your father would make quite a sum from a piece like this.'

'There bees bread on our table so we're not wanting.'

'I say, Luighseach,' said Della. 'It has a curious title: *The Horses of Disaster*. What does he mean by that?'

''Tis from a poem, Delleen, I know that much. Daid's always been one for poems.'

The doorbell rang. Leila, who had been trying to coax Ming the cat away from Mrs Sotheby, sprang to action. She was beaten by Della, who being slight, darted nimbly through a crack between Leila and the back door and entered the house first. Mrs Sotheby made a passing comment about decorum, settled the cat, picked up a magazine and turned to the social pages.

The girls returned, Della the vanquished and Leila the victor with her prize in tow.

'Good afternoon, Mrs Sotheby.'

'Why, hello Angela,' smiled Mrs Sotheby from the social pages. 'How are you?'

'Very well, thank you. Good afternoon, Mr Sotheby.'

'Your mother told me yesterday that her youngest sister, Violet, is engaged, Angela,' Mrs Sotheby interposed. 'When will the wedding be?'

'Aunty Vi's getting married in October, Mrs Sotheby. *I'm* going to be flower girl and Fanny and Celie will be bridesmaids.'

'Oh how lovely!'

Della was now at my side.

'Angela's one of the Mahony girls. Fanny has five younger sisters,' she whispered. Then she said in a louder voice, 'Angela, I don't think you've met my friend, Luighseach.'

Angela looked at me, looked at Leila and giggled as I bid her good afternoon. A titter that sounded like 'Lucia Spastica' ended Angela's greeting and the two girls ran back into the house.

The doorbell rang again. This time Pim made her bright and breezy entrance. She thudded her viola down, vigorously shook Mr Sotheby's hand, strode over to Mrs Sotheby, beamed 'g'day', and gave the cat such a heavy scrub on the head that the animal had to keep its balance by digging its claws into its mistress' silk skirt and stockings.

This salutation and its reception indicated that it was clearly time for us to begin our rehearsal. We paid the necessary respects for the hospitality and retired to the drawing room.

'You got anything to eat, Dell?' Pim inquired.

'Cook will be furious if I ask now, Pim. We've just finished lunch. But don't worry, I've organised a scrummy afternoon tea.'

Again the doorbell rang, and in anticipation of Phoebe's arrival we took off into the hall.

And we were not the only ones. Leila and Angela beat Della to the front door and opened it. Sure enough, Phoebe was there, quaintly dressed in a long duster, holding her violin and a parasol. Her appearance threw Leila and Angela into convulsions. Smirking and scuffling, they raced up the stairs where they perched near the top and indulged in whispers and giggles. Phoebe disdainfully cast her eyes over the vestibule before lighting them upon us.

'Did you have trouble finding the house, Phoebe?' Della asked as she offered to take Phoebe's things.

'Why should I?' Phoebe, removed her boater and lace gloves, squinted a little and sneered at the two on the stairs.

More giggles and whispers from the peanut gallery.

'What a pretty parasol!' Della mused over the tattered, dirty item as she placed it in the hat stand. 'May I take your coat, Phoebe?'

Phoebe took off her coat to reveal a longish lace-trimmed dress. It was neatly fitted at the waist and had an elaborate lace collar and leg of mutton sleeves. Upon seeing her attire, which was so very different to their own, Leila and Angela broke into peals of laughter, ran to the top of the stairs and into one of the rooms, slamming the door behind them.

'Phoebe, come and tune,' Della ignored her sister's silliness and steered us all into the drawing room. 'We've an awful lot to do. I think we should concentrate on getting through it and playing in unison. Let's start from the beginning and work slowly. When we come to a part where we're not together, let's stop, go over it and work at it until we are. Does that sound practical?'

Miss Sotheby was determined. Down we sat, finalised tuning, music and positions, and with a slight tilt of the first violin, we began.

We had barely played a phrase when Phoebe stopped.

'*You're* not in time!'

'Here we go,' Pim sighed as she lay back in her chair.

'Who wasn't in time, Phoebe?' Della asked.

'*She* wasn't.'

I was the victim.

'Phoebe Raye, I'm letting you know I was in time.'

'You were late. I heard it.'

'Well maybe you heard it wrong,' Pim interposed. 'That is possible, you know.'

'It is not! She was late! She didn't play on time!'

'You were a bit late, old thing,' Della whispered. 'Very good, Phoebe,' she added in a more chirpy voice. 'Try again, everyone?'

We repeated our endeavour and again Phoebe stopped.

'Why don't you watch and count?'

'I was watching! And counting! 'Twas on time that I played the note. 'Tis your—'

'Luighseach, please don't lose your temper,' Della implored. 'We've barely played two bars and there's so much more to do.'

'Della Sotheby, I am not losing my temper! I started with Pim, I did!'

'You did not! You were late. I heard it perfectly clearly.' Phoebe opened fire again.

'Can't we get on with it?' Pim interjected. 'I'm hungry. Dell, when are you serving tea?'

'Later, Pim,' snapped Della. 'Phoebe, perhaps Luighseach sounds late because she's playing on her low strings. They vibrate more slowly, don't they Luighseach? So even though she began on time, she came in late when she didn't intend to. Luighseach, try attacking the string a little earlier. Now, let's begin again.'

After two more false starts, we managed to play through the minor section quite happily and decided to repeat it. As we began, two figures appeared in the window and performed an apish dance. Leila was wearing Phoebe's coat and Angela had her parasol.

Phoebe seethed into her strings. Her tempestuous playing pushed the tempo beyond the stately allegretto that had begun the piece. Instead of stopping to correct her or take measures to slow her down, Della followed her lead.

Pim, meanwhile, took a sideways glance at the grimacing, dancing figures and began to shake with laughter.

With an exasperated stamp of her foot, Della shot from her seat and upset the music stand. Violin in one hand and bow in the other, she chased her sister away. She returned, flushed with annoyance and quite out of breath.

Pim was beyond control.

'Oh Pim! Pull yourself together.'

At Della's annoyed plea, Pim feebly attempted to gather her senses. Some minutes passed before the rehearsal could progress.

Leila and Angela reappeared for more capering and Pim could no longer contain herself. Shaking and swaying with silent laughter, she lost her count.

Della nearly got out of her seat but was prevented by a quick poke in the knee from Phoebe. She tried to resume her part but lapsed into a fit of coughing. Pim, now totally convulsed, had abandoned all efforts to continue. Phoebe muttered a 'keep playing' in my direction, then she rose, and, still playing, slowly walked to the windows, loosened the heavy drapes and allowed the curtains to close on the two characters bumbling around outside. She moved to the door, switched on the light and returned to her seat. Her glare prevented me from showing my amazement with anything more than a brief gaze.

'Keep playing!' she ordered me. 'Major section!'

Somehow we reached the end, with Pim inserting the occasional note between chuckles and coming to her senses for the last few bars.

'Our turns are messy in the Menuetto,' Phoebe commented. 'But I suggest we work on the Trio. Second violin, viola and 'cello need to concentrate on the accompaniment.'

'Do we now?' Pim queried. 'And since when have you decided to tell us what to do?'

'Have you any better suggestion?' Phoebe retorted.

'Della?' Pim ignored Phoebe.

Della managed to shake her head between coughs. 'It's a good idea,' she eventually spluttered.

Several experiments using different bowing actions ensued.

'First violin, you play your part,' Phoebe had assumed the lead. 'Follow the same bowing movements until you take the tune.'

Della wearily complied.

We were permitted a few minutes of solid work before the hissing of a cat and the canary's shrill chirrup was heard outside.

'Oh no! No! Stop it! Stop it!'

Della flung her instrument down, pushed the stand over and stumbled out, attempting to shout after her sister as she did and coughing instead. The three of us watched the canary stand angrily dumped inside. Della returned to the verandah and struggled in with Kismet in his cage.

'It is one thing for them to fool around with your coat and parasol but they are not going to torment my little bird!' she declared as she laboured to replace the cage on its stand.

We resumed the practice until Della's sweet, spiralling melody was drowned by a reveille from a trumpet in the adjacent room. It was all too much for her. Sighing and cringing from the noise, she walked over and opened the sliding doors that separated the large drawing room from the small.

'Wally!'

No response. Della tried again.

And again.

'Wally!' The music finally stopped. 'You know you're not to play that thing inside,' she implored. 'Besides, we're trying to rehearse and we can't concentrate with your noise.'

Trumpet in hand, Della's brother sauntered over.

'The spotty dog quartet,' he grinned as he viewed the ensemble of bodies, instruments and stands in the darkened drawing room. 'Hey, Pim! Haven't seen you for ages! How are you?'

'Beaut,' Pim slung herself over the back of her chair. 'Didn't see you last Saturday.'

'What's that?'

'Match between St Allo's and Trinity.'

Wally laughed. 'We took those tykes down with three wickets in hand. Not too good, eh, Pim?'

'Stop gloating, Toffee.'

'Oh, do be quiet, Pim!' Della intervened before her brother had a chance to open his mouth again. 'As for you, Wally, please, please, please either find something else to do or practise your trumpet in the summerhouse. Please!'

Fortunately Wally was more co-operative than Leila. He agreed with a smile, pushed his hand through his hair and waved goodbye to everyone in general and another good-bye to Pim in particular. Della nearly reached her seat when a knock was heard and Mrs Sotheby glided in.

'Della, Leila and Angela wish to play the piano.'

'Oh, Mummy, no! We're practising and we keep getting interrupted. No!'

'I'm not asking you to stop practising, darling, but to move.'

'Why should we? We were here first!'

'But they've been there all afternoon,' came Leila's whining voice. 'It's only fair they should give us a go.'

'Mummy! Leila knew I was going to be here. She's being annoying.'

'I am not,' Leila positioned herself at the doorway with Angela in the rear. 'Angela and I want to do some duets. We can't exactly move the piano.'

'Now girls, I don't want any fighting. Della you've had your fair share of the drawing room this afternoon. Do be gracious and allow your sister to have a turn, thank you.'

'Then may we practise in the parlour, Mummy?'

'No, darling. I'm listening to the wireless. Use the small drawing room.'

'But we can't play there if Leila's playing the piano,' Della was exasperated. 'We won't be able to hear ourselves.'

'Then go to your room, dear,' replied Mrs Sotheby. 'That's where you normally practise.'

'We won't fit! It's too cluttered for everyone!' Della was near tears.

'Then find somewhere else,' responded her mother as she left the room. 'I've made some suggestions.'

'Come on, Dell, let's get some tea and practise later,' Pim suggested.

Della meekly acquiesced. She invited us into the smaller drawing room and rang the bell. Nellie soon appeared.

'Yes, Miss Della?'

'Nellie, could you bring us some refreshments? I think something cool would be best. Does anyone wish for tea?'

While 'Chopsticks' was carelessly hammered out on the piano in the adjacent room and 'The Last Post' solemnly trumpeted in the garden, Della wearily tried to maintain a friendly conversation. All was lost on Phoebe who, unmoved and uninterested, found the glass-globed chandelier more stimulating. Pim's attention drifted between Della and the door and concluded that her preferences lay in the latter which, she hoped, would soon open to welcome the trayful of edibles.

The sight of my father's signature on Mrs Sotheby's portrait bade me to the mantelpiece. I studied the picture. Little wonder Mrs Sotheby was pleased with it, for with its lively, fruity tones, it was a very flattering, delightfully gay piece. Daid had taken great pains with Mrs Sotheby's beloved kimono, and I well knew the hours he would have spent with fine brush in hand spindling all the butterflies that must have been worked in delicate crewelwork. As to the subject herself, it was difficult to believe that she was the mother of four children for she had a coy, blithe expression. Her face, which peeped up over her fan, was firmly yet gracefully modelled and seemed to whirl you into a fanciful world of parties and pleasure. But it puzzled me. Ordinarily, Daid was very choosy about his subjects. Mrs Sotheby was a silly woman. What had possessed my father to take the time to paint her?

'I need a cigarette. Do you mind?' Phoebe took a small silver box from the bag she had brought with her.

Pim's face swung away from the door and Della could hardly hide her horror. 'Not at all,' the little hostess managed to say.

The maid entered.

'Nellie, would it be possible for you to bring an ashtray?'

The refreshments did not quite reach the coffee table. 'An ashtray, Miss Della?'

'Yes, Nellie. For Miss Phoebe Raye.'

The requested object was duly obtained.

'Would anyone else like a cigarette?' Phoebe offered her box.

Nobody dared.

Phoebe was a picture of contentment, alternating thoughtful exhalations with sips of lemonade and barely taking her fine eyes away from the ceiling. One only needed to loosen her hair, dress her in billowy trousers and serve her sherbet and she would have made a perfect rival to the Persian princess hanging in the Sotheby's dining room.

'And just how long have you been smoking like that?' Pim was stunned.

'Ages,' came the drawn out reply.

The door opened. Mr Sotheby swelled his chest and stood erect. From under their bushy browed eyrie his eyes surveyed all below and came to rest upon the beautiful girl in the old-fashioned frock. Phoebe noticed nothing and sent the chandelier a smoky serenade.

Della rose to attention, anxiously smoothed her dress and looked up at her step-father. Unable to bear the silence, she coughed and clasped her hands together.

'Daddy, I would like you to meet Phoebe Raye. Phoebe, this is my father, Mr Sotheby.'

11

'Young lady,' Mr Sotheby began. 'Would you kindly extinguish that cigarette.'

Phoebe did not look up. Two more languid, luxurious exhalations followed before she stubbed her cigarette in the tray. And she did so in a very precise manner, as if to make the point that she extinguished the cigarette because *she*, in fact, had finished it, not because Mr Sotheby had asked her to put it out.

But Mr Sotheby was above such distinctions. He had discharged his duty with elegant economy, eschewing any unnecessary drama or emotion. His business completed, he left the drawing room in the same assured manner as he had entered it.

Phoebe returned her silver cigarette case to her little drawstring purse.

'I've had enough,' she announced. 'I'm leaving now.'

'You mean you're not going to stay for more practice?' Pim queried, astonished. 'But they've stopped playing in there.'

'I don't think anything more is going to be achieved by staying,' Phoebe shrugged as she rose from the sofa. 'Furthermore, I have a business engagement at half-past four and I can't be late.'

'Business engagement?' echoed Pim. 'What's that supposed to mean?'

'It must be something very important, Phoebe,' asserted Della. 'I'll fetch your coat and parasol. Will you come into the hall?'

Della showed Phoebe out the drawing room door. As she did, she glared at Pim and me.

'Well, are you coming to say good-bye or not?' she asked and waited for us to follow.

Mrs Sotheby came down the stairs as Della waved Phoebe farewell.

'Della,' she called. Della looked up and watched her mother arrange the bracelets on her wrists.

'What is it, Mummy?' asked Della as she shut the front door.

'Did I see Nellie take an ashtray to the drawing room?'

'Yes, Mummy.'

'Were you smoking?'

'Of course not, Mummy.'

'*Somebody* was,' said Mrs Sotheby as she surveyed Pim and me in turn. But she was incapable of discerning the guilty party.

'It's no matter, Mummy,' Della replied. 'The cigarette was put out. It won't happen again.'

'But you haven't told me *who* was smoking,' persisted her mother, indicating her daughter to please step into the parlour.

Pim and I then overheard a discussion which became more hysterical and tearful with every accusation and defence. Pim said she had a ferry to catch and decided to leave and I alone witnessed Della emerge, crying helplessly, and fly up the stairs to her room. I was not, however, permitted to follow, for Mrs Sotheby, upon seeing me still loitering in the vestibule, coldly requested that I wait for my father outside.

I was only too relieved when Daid finally arrived.

I did not see Della again until Monday. She arrived at school in the middle of Latin not sick, as the class had presumed when the roll was called, but worried and restless. Sister Bellarmine, who taught us, kept a watchful eye on her throughout the lesson but refrained from involving her in any parsing. In Maths, Sister Augustine took the opposite approach. Fully aware that Della was one of her weakest students, she was determined to have her make the most of a lesson dedicated entirely to revision. Sister Augustine's interrogation reduced poor Della to tears and she ended up excused from class, being told in exasperation to 'clean herself up'. No escorts were permitted, for Sister clamped down on the offers of help that accompanied the sobbing Della from the classroom, an action which confirmed for Fanny, Kate and Beth that the tiny nun was the meanest mistress in Christendom. Later, however, when Della still had not returned, there was much concern in Sister Augustine's astute face. Perhaps Sister caught a similar expression in my own face for she requested me, of all people, to go and fetch her.

I did not find Della in the washroom as I expected. I had to look further afield. I spotted her coming out of the school chapel.

'Hello, Luighseach,' she smiled as she came towards me. 'You're very bold venturing all this way on your own.'

'You're looking pale, Delleen,' I observed.

Della sighed. 'It's horrible, horrible trigonometry!' she replied. 'It may be all very well for you, old thing, but for me it's a ghastly jumble of letters and symbols and words and tables full of nasty numbers and I can make neither head nor tail of those stupid problems! And then Sister Augustine questions me and questions me and I feel like such an imbecile, especially when the class starts to murmur and fidget. Furthermore, there's the test tomorrow and I'm going to fail again. I know I'm going to fail and if I do, Daddy will take me away from school.'

'Nonsense, Delleen. You've fretted yourself sick is all.'

'No, Luighseach,' she corrected me. 'Daddy even tried to help me with trigonometry last night and was furious with me by the end of it. He said he refused to see exhorbitant sums of money handed over to the Catholic Church to educate me in the stupidities of Spanish Holy Week customs when I can't even comprehend fundamental mathematics. But it's not the school's fault that

I can remember so-called stupidities about Holy Week and not stupidities about mathematics. What am I going to do? I don't want to spend the rest of my life giving garden parties!'

'Well, I'm thinking you'll be needing to pass your test.'

'Easier said than done, old thing.'

'Aye, but I think I know how to help. Will you not come to my house this afternoon? We can study and I'll show you a trick or two.'

'I—I don't know, Luighseach.'

'Delleen, what's the matter? I been trying to telephone you about it since Saturday night.'

'It's no use, Luighseach. Mummy will never let me!'

She hung her head and cried.

'She's furious about the smoking,' she explained amidst sniffles. 'And because I wouldn't tell her who smoked the cigarette, she's convinced I was the guilty one all along. She's seen the cigarette butts Wally sometimes leaves around.'

'Then why did you not tell who it was?'

'And defame Phoebe more than needs be?' Della replied. 'I couldn't do that to her, it wouldn't be fair. And I'm not going to get Wally into more trouble than he is already. I suppose I should have exercised a little fortitude and not have allowed Phoebe to smoke in the first place, but she's such a strange girl and I wanted her to feel at home. After all, that is what you are supposed to do when you have visitors. Now, Mummy's forbidden me to play in the quartet.'

'Faith! So you mean to say you won't be playing at Mrs Epstein's on Thursday?'

'Not exactly,' Della replied. 'When Mummy telephoned Mrs Epstein to complain, all Mrs Epstein did was to reschedule my lesson for the time of the rehearsal.'

I couldn't help a slight laugh. It was typical of Mrs Epstein to do something like that.

'But it's lying, Luighseach!' Della protested.

'And so is not saying who was smoking when you were asked.'

'Well, what could I do?' she grew more upset. 'Anyway, I can't go behind Mummy's back.'

I decided to return to our original subject, for to me it seemed that mathematics could solve at least part of the predicament.

'Will you come with me this afternoon, Delleen?' I asked again.

'Luighseach, did you hear anything of what I said?' Della tearfully replied.

'Aye, I did. But I don't think talking about it all is going to make much difference.'

After school, we walked to Della's house with the intention of asking permission to spend the evening at my place. Della requested I remain outside while she sought out her mother. She eventually returned, ecstatic and relieved.

'The dressmaker ordered the wrong fabric!' she announced.

I raised an eyebrow in request for further explanation.

'Mummy's beside herself for the garden party's only a few days after Easter,' was the answer I received. 'Collette will never have the costume made in time if she doesn't fix it now. Nellie says Mummy's been on the telephone all afternoon.'

'Is it herself speaking in the parlour there?' I asked, indicating the tirade of English-sounding French I could hear from the window.

'It certainly is. Mummy was raised by French nuns,' Della explained, 'so she speaks fluent French and there's absolutely no point in interrupting her when she does. All I could do was leave a message and tell Cook. Come on, quick! Let's go!'

We caught the train home. Upon fortifying ourselves with a cup of tea, we sat at the dining table and prepared once more to tackle the rudiments of trigonometry.

Della took out her maths book.

'Anois, Delleen,' I began. 'If you look here you'll find Bert Hinkler in Rome.' I pulled the book closer to myself and made a sketch of Hinkler in the Avro.

'What has Bert Hinkler to do with it?' Della eyed me dubiously.

'Let you wait a little.'

'You've got to put GE BOV on the side.'

I marked the letters on the side of his 'plane and made a small sketch of Della in the back. She was delighted.

'Well now, Delleen. Mr Hinkler, with the grace of God and a bit of help from yourself, is going for to take off from Rome to Malta. And the take off point is where I've drawn the 'plane and here's the runway.'

I drew in the runway and followed it with another drawing.

'What's that?'

''Tis the Colosseum. 'Twas where they fed the Christians to the lions and staged naval battles.'

'Oh. But Luighseach, you can't have that in the middle of the runway. He'll crash into it.'

'He will not. He's taking off from here, and you'll be working out how far he needs to travel in order not to crash.'

Della wriggled with interest.

'Now, Della Sotheby, the distance between the take off point here and the Colosseum there is four hundred and thirty three feet, and the— What is it you're giggling at?'

'Teerty tree,' she tittered.

That was when it dawned on me why everyone laughed so much in Maths class.

'Delleen Sotheby,' I probed. 'You'll be telling me now, what it is that's so funny about thirty-three?'

'Don't you know?'

'I might.'

'Well, Luighseach, if Mary Byrne were here now, she'd chalk up one hundred and forty four times you've said "tree" for "three" this term. I think that puts you in the lead.'

I was dumbfounded.

'We've been keeping tally, old thing, to see who would say it most: you or Sister Augustine.'

'And that's what makes you laugh so?'

Della nodded and continued to giggle, and I began to suspect there was even more to it than that.

'Well, then, it seems I'm going to win,' I remarked. 'Now, the line we've drawn is four hundred and teeer-ty tr-eee feet. And the height of the Colosseum— Anois! Stop your laughing! – is one hundred and sixty one feet.'

Height and distance were duly recorded. Then a line was drawn, thereby connecting the 'plane with the top of the building.

'And you'll be finding out what the distance is between the Avro and the top of the Colosseum. That's the hypotenuse. Do you see it now? Do you see the triangle there?'

'Yes.'

'Then you'll be telling me how to find the distance.'

The familiar shadow of doubt clouded over her eyes.

'Arrah! Delleen, do you still not know Pythagoras' theorem? Tell it me now.'

It was a while before $a^2 + b^2 = c^2$ emerged from her troubled countenance. I took her arm to reassure her.

'Look here, I'll make it easy for you. If you cannot remember the formula like that, remember it like this: Distance of take-off by Hinkler squared equals distance between take-off point and obstacle squared plus height of obstacle squared. In fact, you could say T^2 for distance between take-off point and obstacle squared + O^2 for height of obstacle squared = D^2 for distance of take-off squared instead of $a^2 + b^2 = c^2$ if you want for they're only symbols are they not?'

My substitutions, however, only served to confuse her. So I recorded the formula with its interpretation. Together we repeated the two versions until she could say them by heart. Then, with considerable effort on the part of fingers as well as pencil, Della made the appropriate calculations. Now it was time to explain square roots.

'So, Della Sotheby, the answer you've put there is the *area* of this squared hypotenuse here. But that doesn't tell you how *far* Mr Hinkler's to travel. If you want to find the distance so, you need to work out the *length* of the hypotenuse and you do that by finding the square root.'

Della nodded.

'And how is it you find the square root?' I asked.

'Do you look it up in the tables book?'

'You do.'

Her fingers scampered through the trigonometric tables and soon found the answer. At last the clouds of doubt were blown away by a smile.

'Dia go deo leat! 'Tis Mr Hinkler won't be crashing his 'plane with yourself in the back, Delleen.'

'Oh Luighseach, it's wonderful! Do another one!'

Over the course of an hour, we flew Bert Hinkler all over the world and Della's maths book became filled with tiny drawings of the Avro encountering all the landmarks we could think of. Before proceeding with more complicated issues of Mr Hinkler in relation to sin, cos and tan and angles of take off, I made a sketch of Pythagoras awarding Della with a prize for navigation and trigonometry.

While we were in the midst of slightly more complex theorem, the front door opened.

It was Daid.

I followed the familiar path of his footsteps. First he removed his jacket and hung it with his hat on its hook. Then he entered the parlour and paused in front of his wedding photograph. The footsteps crept across the rug to kiss the Sacred and Immaculate Hearts, and a creak on the floorboards and the squeak of his shiny shoes were heard when he came down the corridor. He caught sight of the two of us at work in the dining room and knocked gently on the open door.

'Dia dhuit, a Luighseach,' he lilted as he entered. He made the sign of the cross on my forehead and kissed it as was his habit.

'Dia is Muire dhuit, a Dhaidí.'

'Dia is Muire dhuit, Mr Ní Sruitheáin,' Della peeped up from the trigonometry. My father smiled and slowly shook his head. I began to smile too.

'What is it? Why are you laughing like that?' she urged.

'You do be using "Ní" for unmarried women only, Delleen. My father is Ó Sruitheáin.'

'Well, I didn't know.'

'Let your troubles, you know it now. Whisht! 'Tis this angle here we need to find.'

Della drifted back to her work and Daid resumed his trek to the kitchen sink. He filled his jug and creaked back up the hallway into his room. I propped my chin on my hands and traced my father's passage.

The only reason I ever had for entering Daid's room was to steal a look at the photograph on the bureau next to his St Joseph picture. It featured the three of us enclosed in an oval frame: my father in his Sunday best, my mother in her dress with the lace bodice and me, with one front tooth missing and the other half-way down, in my First Holy Communion guernsey. I would take that photograph and sit on Daid's bed. Then I would take up the battered little blue book he kept at his bedside and try and make sense of the poetry it contained. Invariably, I would give up reading the poems, lie on the bed and hug the photograph instead.

From the shifting sounds and small silences, I knew that Daid also gazed at the photograph and whispered a prayer while he unbuttoned his waistcoat and removed his bow tie. He took off his collar, rolled it and stowed it in the top drawer with its companions. Cuff links were then unfastened and shirt sleeves folded back. Water was poured into the washstand, glasses laid aside and Daid performed his ablutions. Then the water was taken outside and poured over the front garden. The basin came inside, was dried with the towel and returned to the stand. The towel was neatly hung at the side, exactly as before. Another creak announced Daid's return to the kitchen, and with that, the end of our mathematics session.

'Tis time we put that all away now and took some tea, Delleen. There'll be potatoes for to peel and I'll be asking you to help if you please.'

The prospect of peeling potatoes afforded her an adventure for which she was only too keen to relinquish her trigonometry.

We helped Daid gather potatoes and leeks from the back garden, and sat together to make our preparations. Della took a potato and eagerly began to wedge the skin off. After a few attempts I made her stop, for if she kept up her efforts, we would have had no potato left. She then tried to help Daid chop and wash the leeks.

We cooked the potatoes and leeks in butter, and Daid, despite his shyness, found himself answering all sorts of questions. What were we having for tea? It was porridge we were having. Did we always have porridge for tea? We did eat it only in Lent. Did we like porridge? It was wholesome. The Sothebys had porridge for breakfast with brown sugar. Did we serve it with sugar for tea? It was salt that we put and leeks and potatoes. Della had never eaten porridge like that before.

'An féidir leat an scaraoid bhán a chuir ar an mbord, a Luighseach?'

Daid was right. It was a special occasion, so I exchanged our everyday blue cloth for the white and set the table with our bits and pieces of second-hand china. We blessed ourselves, said grace in Irish as was our custom, and began our meal.

The silence my father and I usually maintained during tea did not last long. Our respective private worlds, made moreso by the fact that we both took off our glasses while we ate, were invaded by Della and her light-hearted chatter. To her evident relief, our porridge was not really porridge at all: it was a sort of potato and leek soup, with oatmeal added for nourishment. Why did we call it porridge? She then scouted through her favourite topics and tried to pull Daid's tongue about photography with a moderate degree of success. The conversation continued after our final grace, flowed through the washing up and did not cease until we began the Rosary.

The only time Della ever prayed a Rosary was at school. The nuns had taught her for her family did not pray the Rosary at home. She said she tried to say it before going to bed but usually fell asleep in the process.

That evening, she knelt beside Daid at the foot of the Immaculate Heart, closed her eyes, bowed her head and remained that way for the duration of the Sorrowful Mysteries, which were the mysteries we always prayed during Lent. She knew her prayers, and from their quiet intensity it was clear her Paters and Aves were filled with tiny pleas which she placed at the Virgin's feet. With every decade,

I caught a glimpse of mouthed intentions – 'Maths', 'Mummy and Daddy', 'Wally', 'Leila', 'Henry'.

What intentions did I have?

That God would make me walk properly again. That was a prayer half-answered. There I was, back on crutches, with braces on both my legs. Why, oh why was it so hard? Many a time I had been told that being crippled was God's will and that I should accept it. So, the polio was the result of some divine prank was it? Well, if it was God's will and God was all-powerful, why couldn't He will it some other way? Would it matter to God that much if I could walk? But God did not seem to care whether I could walk or not.

That Mam would come back. Mam would never, ever come back. Mam had gone to God, or so I was told. But of what use was Mam to God when I needed her? I wanted her to hold me, I wanted to tell her everything that had happened; I wanted her to care for me. But God had taken her away and all that was left of Mam was locked up in the photographs and paintings that adorned our parlour walls.

I swung my beads all the harder.

God was not fair.

We finished. Daid blessed himself, kissed his beads, and upon rising from the kneeler under the Sacred Heart, took his watch from his waistcoat pocket.

''Tis time for to go, Luighseach. I'll fetch your 'cello, and Della you'll fetch your books now. We'll take you home.'

Everything was organised onto the motorcycle and we rattled away to the Sotheby's. I sat in the sidecar with my 'cello, while Della sat behind Daid, clinging tightly to him and squealing for all she was worth.

****

Poor Della. Any hope she had for passing Mathematics was promptly crushed when she received her results on Thursday morning. To compound the situation, Sister Augustine saw her Maths book. Upon seeing the Hinkler drawings, she gave Della a detention for defacing her book. That decision annoyed me considerably and I told Sister Augustine that I did the drawings. Furthermore, because the drawings were intended to help Della understand trigonometry, they did not deface her book. Della, in consequence, should not be punished. Sister Augustine replied by giving me a detention for defacing Della's book and for rudeness.

'And have ye anything more to say, Lucy Straughan?'

If Sister expected an apology from me, she did not get one.

'Aye, I do, Sister Augustine. For 'tis an answer of my own you marked incorrectly.'

'I beg yer pardon?'

'The answer to question number five it is,' and I showed my paper.

'Aye, a decimal point ye put in the wrong place,' remarked Sister as she perused my work. 'Do ye not see that, Lucy?'

'Aye, I do, Sister Augustine. But 'twas but a slip of my pen for the numbers be correct and the working besides.'

'Aye, that's so and I credited ye for it. But the place is not. The answer is wrong and ye lost a mark.'

'But I didn't mean—'

'And to be sure every other girl in the class didn't "mean" to make the mistakes she made. Praise be to God that Mathematics is the one subject that cannot be tainted by human folly. An answer is either right or wrong and in this case it's wrong. To even think of quibbling over the matter, yerself of all people, Lucy. '

Although I knew there was no point in arguing, I remained rooted to my spot.

'Well, ye won't make that mistake again, will ye now? Let ye check yer work in future. That will be all, Lucy. May God go with you,' Sister dismissed me.

'Anyway, Luighseach, why won't you tell me your mark?' Della asked as we journeyed down the road towards Mrs Epstein's house that afternoon. It was the fifth time, at least, that she had asked me. Once again I refused to answer.

'You topped the class as usual,' Della persevered, 'I know that much. Your paper was the first to be handed back. I had to wait till last,' she lamented. 'What was your mark?'

'I'll not be telling.'

'Luighseach, that's not fair! I told you mine. It couldn't nearly be as bad as forty per cent.'

'And I'm still not telling, Delleen.'

'You don't seem at all happy about it, whatever it was,' she continued. 'What was all that fuss with Sister Augustine?'

'None of your business that is, and you're right, I'm *not* happy about my mark,' I replied, recalling the shock of seeing the mark on the top of my page and realising my mistake. I swung my crutches angrily in an attempt to erase the thought.

'But how could it possibly have been bad?' Della complained.

I stopped to open Mrs Epstein's gate and sighed as I did. 'Whatever it was, I'll not be telling, Delleen.'

'That's not fair!' she repeated and angrily rang the doorbell.

'Late again!' Mrs Epstein scolded.

''Twas—'

'Don't try and explain, Luighseach. Really, I would expect a little more responsibility from both you girls. Twenty minutes late! Go inside at once and get ready. Your 'cello's tuned— I wasn't going to wait any longer. Hurry up, Della! Stop moping! We've work to do! Quick! Inside!'

A rehearsal of sorts was already in progress. Stationed at one end of the room, Pim was carving into her strings like a butcher preparing a knife. Phoebe was pedestalled in the bay window opposite, performing a cadenza from a concerto.

Mrs Epstein slammed the music room door.

The playing ceased.

'Phoebe, get down from the window this instant and sit in your chair!' commanded Mrs Epstein, 'Now!' She had to enforce the command with a lunge before Phoebe jumped from the window seat and sought her place.

'We haven't much time left,' our teacher brusquely continued, 'which is unfortunate since I was hoping to start work on one of the other movements today. But that will have to wait. We'll revise the Minuet. I'm pleased you managed a rehearsal—'

'Rehearsal?' Pim interjected. 'Ha! Some rehearsal!'

Our teacher's strangely magnified eyes examined one face after another and paused at Della's hanging head. 'I'll determine whether or not the rehearsal was fruitful, Pim. Play.'

Della limply raised her violin. Her lips began to tremble as she endeavoured to concentrate on the tempo and lead us in.

Her efforts were in vain. Not quite three bars into the piece and Mrs Epstein shouted for us to stop.

'And what do you think you are playing, Phoebe Raye?'

'The Mendelssohn concerto. Third movement,' Phoebe snapped as she rose from her seat and walked away. 'I don't want to play quartets!'

'You sit down here this minute, young lady, and don't you move an inch.'

Phoebe was without say in the matter. Mrs Epstein laid her hand on her shoulder and marched her back to her seat.

'If you want to play the Mendelssohn concerto, you are going to have to learn an awful lot about ensemble playing if you are going to do it properly. There will be no playing with an orchestra for you until you can play well in a quartet. And that is that. Della, what on earth is the matter with you?'

At Mrs Epstein's exasperated inquiry, Della burst into tears.

''Tis her maths test that she failed, Mrs Epstein,' I began.

'Oh shut up about the stupid test, Luighseach!' Della sobbed. 'I can't play the quartet! I'm not good enough to lead! I'm hopeless!'

'Dear oh dear!' Mrs Epstein's manner began to soften. She drew a chair towards Della and put her arm round her. 'There, there. You've had a terrible time. I'm sorry. What happened?'

'And I can't tell a lie, Mrs Epstein!' Della cried as she pulled herself away. 'You shouldn't have made me come like this!'

'Della!' there was no small amount of annoyance in Mrs Epstein's voice. 'Are you always going to be ruled by your mother's whims and social mores?'

'No, Mrs Epstein,' Della replied with a sniff. 'I simply can't have her believe one thing while I do another.'

'Would somebody mind telling me exactly what happened on Saturday? All I managed to construe from Mrs Sotheby was that somehow I was responsible for defiling her house with riff-raff. What happened?'

''Twas Mrs Sotheby was upset about the smoking, Mrs Epstein,' I began.

'Smoking?' echoed an astonished Mrs Epstein, 'Who?'

'Phoebe,' answered Pim, her teeth gritted.

'Smoking?' Mrs Epstein turned to Phoebe, 'You?'

'She has a whole case full of cigarettes,' Pim explained.

'You were smoking cigarettes?' Mrs Epstein inquired again.

'Of course,' Phoebe was quite matter-of-fact. 'I always smoke cigarettes.'

Mrs Epstein turned her back on her. 'So that's what happened?' she remarked as she studied Della. 'But, for you to say you're hopeless, I gather that wasn't the only thing to go wrong.'

'Everyone kept interrupting us,' Della sniffed. 'We tried to practise, but first Leila started to annoy us, then Wally, then Leila again. Then we had to move and Mummy wouldn't let us play in the parlour. After that we had nowhere to go.'

'And Phoebe took over the rehearsal when she wasn't supposed to,' Pim added.

'Because *she* didn't know what to do,' Phoebe retorted, indicating Della as the accused. Della did not defend herself. 'And *you*,' she resumed, turning on Pim, 'You couldn't even concentrate for more than a phrase.'

'And you couldn't help bossing everyone about,' Pim interjected. 'Mrs Ep, I really don't think I can play with her. She's trouble.'

'She can be. So you don't want to play in the quartet, Pim?'

'Not with Miss Smarty-pants-second-violin, I don't,' Pim replied.

'It's never going to work,' Della forlornly hung her head.

'I don't want to play either!' Phoebe proclaimed. 'I never wanted to play!'

I looked from one to the other.

'What is it, Luighseach?' inquired Mrs Epstein.

'So there's not to be a quartet, Mrs Epstein?' I asked.

'Apparently not. Do *you* want to stay in the quartet?'

'Aye, I do.'

'I don't believe it! Two weeks ago, everyone except you wanted, to some greater or lesser degree, to try their hand at a quartet. Now, after barely three attempts everyone, except you, does not want to play. Luighseach, why, all of a sudden, do you now want to play?'

I hesitated somewhat before I answered. 'I—I don't want to be lonely any more, Mrs Epstein.'

'So it's the friendship you want?' asked Mrs Epstein.

'Aye,' I nodded.

'Friendship?' echoed Pim. 'Even with Phoebe?'

'Aye,' I replied, not wanting to look at anyone.

'But she's been downright mean to you,' Pim reasoned. 'Phoebe kept on picking on Lucy for coming in late,' she explained to Mrs Epstein.

'That's because she *was* coming in late!' protested Phoebe.

'And what about when you called her a spastic?' Pim turned angrily on Phoebe. 'What are you going to say about that? Are you going to say, "Because she *is* a spastic." Are you?'

''Twas Phoebe said that because I was mean to her,' I explained, thinking of the afternoon at Miss Bray's when I had snapped at her for spying on me. 'And I—I'm sorry for that,' I glanced tentatively in Phoebe's direction.

Phoebe looked away.

'Well, whatever happened, I'm relieved to see that one of you has her priorities straight, Luighseach,' Mrs Epstein observed. 'For this certainly puts an important matter in the limelight.' She walked to her sideboard and took something out. Placing an occasional table in our midst and seating herself before us, she opened the box she now carried and took out a pack of cards.

'You're probably wondering why I'm doing this,' she continued as she shuffled. 'Well, I'll explain.' Taking four cards, she balanced them against one another. She thumbed out some more cards and built them on top. A tower was in progress. 'I could keep doing this, and if I worked carefully enough, I could go up and up. Now, I know that in spite of yourselves each of you is very fond of music and you all wish to play well – perhaps play well together. Isn't that so?'

I nodded. Pim grimaced sceptically. Della refused to look up. I turned to Phoebe, and to my surprise was gratified by a glance of approval.

'Well,' Mrs Epstein did not take much notice of our mixed reactions. 'Your wanting to play well is like wanting to reach the ceiling by building a tower of cards. But being able to play like that is like being at the very top of the tower. There is a lot that has to go on before you get up there. And you won't even be able to dream of that until everything is right down here.'

She pointed to the carefully balanced base she had built.

'Now, these four cards here represent each of you. Let's see, what have we pulled out?' The tower collapsed. 'The Queen of Hearts, the Ace of Spades, the Knave of Diamonds and, hmmm, the Joker. I wonder who is who?'

Mrs Epstein smiled, but to no avail. No one smiled in return.

'But we won't worry about that,' she resumed. 'It was all chance, anyway. Still, it signifies that each of you is very different. You all have great strengths and weaknesses which can either make you or break you as a group. Now, you need to work out how you can put them to good use and for that you need to become *friends* – to understand and appreciate one another. Your friendship will be the finely balanced foundation upon which you build your music. It will be the basis for much of your musical interpretation, for in your music you will often find yourselves talking. You are, in a way, a little republic in which everyone gives their support and in doing so contributes to the good of the whole as well as to that of each one.

'In a quartet we're concentrating on a perfect unity of diverse elements. Now, when I speak of unity I don't mean uniformity – everyone the same as everyone

106

else. No. Differences of instrument and performer need to be respected. We can't expect the 'cello to be the first violin, nor the second violin to be the viola and so on. Della will not play exactly the same way as Phoebe, nor will Pim, Luighseach. Each will have to adjust so that we have a pleasing wholeness. It means a lot of give and take – both musically and personally – and that all depends on whether each of you is prepared to appreciate the other as she is. For you won't have the musical harmony you desire until you learn to live in harmony yourselves. Do I make myself clear?'

One by one, we nodded. But the dubious glances we exchanged indicated that while we may have understood our teacher's remarks, the extent to which we were prepared to abide by them remained more questionable. On one matter, at least, we were united.

'Hmmm,' Mrs Epstein resumed. 'At present, however, we seem to have some concerns which need sorting out. Who is going to speak first?'

Phoebe opened her mouth to speak but was quickly silenced by our teacher.

'Luighseach, I suggest you do. You're probably the most rational. Is Phoebe still giving you trouble?'

'Only a little more than most people, Mrs Epstein,' I replied, 'But 'tis Delleen Sotheby who worries me more. And now she's angry at myself.'

'Because you won't tell me your mark,' Della interjected. 'She topped the class in Trig, Mrs Epstein, and she won't tell me what she got.'

'Luighseach, what was your mark?' Mrs Epstein wearily inquired. 'Della wants to know.'

''Twas ninety-nine per cent,' I muttered, my jaw clenched.

'Oh! It's not fair!' wailed Della.

'You got ninety-nine per cent? Pim was incredulous, 'For Trig? And you're annoyed about it?'

'Aye, I am. For it should have been full marks!'

'Crikey! What on earth did you do wrong?'

'I accidentally put a decimal point in the wrong place,' I admitted, 'and Sister Augustine failed to see it like so and marked it incorrect.'

'Do you mean to say you were haggling all that time with Sister Augustine about one silly, little mark?' Della gave a very annoyed sniff. 'Really!'

I blushed at the thought, realising now how petty it all seemed given Della's failure.

'Never mind, Luighseach,' Mrs Epstein responded. 'Apart from you, I don't think anyone is going to think any less of your ability for misplacing a decimal point. As for Della, from what I gather she tried her best and probably could not have done it without your help. What's more, I know that there have been times when you've floundered hopelessly, Luighseach, and it's been Della who's picked you up. Isn't that right?'

There was no need for me to reply.

'Della, is the maths the only problem?' Mrs Epstein asked.

'It's everything, Mrs Epstein! And it's all because of the smoking.'

'Ah yes, the smoking,' Mrs Epstein replied with a glare at Phoebe. 'And what have you to say on the subject?'

'I can do as I please,' Phoebe instantly responded.

'Yes, that is so,' returned our teacher, 'To the extent that your pleasure does not interfere with that of the others. On this occasion, however, it did, quite considerably. Is that all you have to say?'

'Yes.'

'Not even an apology? Do you realise you've caused Della a lot of trouble?'

'She's most welcome to it. I've had enough!'

'See what I mean?' Pim interjected. 'She's impossible! You heartless, little—'

'And tell me, Pim,' Mrs Epstein cautioned. 'Have you even attempted to understand Phoebe?'

'Understand her, Mrs Ep? What is there to understand?'

'I'll leave that for you to find out. So far, however, I have heard nothing but disparaging comments from you and that is hardly constructive.'

'But—'

'It might be justifiable, but is it constructive, Pim? For Heaven's sake you're Head Prefect! Is that the sort of leadership you should show?'

'But she's not doing as she ought!'

'And nor are you!'

'But—!'

'Is it right that you should criticise and accuse Phoebe in that manner?'

'I've good reason to do it. She—'

'Granted. And how effective has it been? Hmmm?'

Pim scowled at Mrs Epstein.

'Would not a more gentle approach be more fruitful?'

'Looks as if it hasn't been so far,' retorted Pim, this time with a scowl at Phoebe. 'She's a spoiled, selfish little brat.'

'So what are you going to do to rectify it?' fired Mrs Epstein. 'Beat her into submission?'

Pim winced and shifted uncomfortably in her seat.

Mrs Epstein glanced at the clock. 'I have another student coming in a few minutes, so you will have to think about the situation at your leisure.'

'Mrs Epstein,' I asked. 'Could we not have another rehearsal? Perhaps if we started afresh we could try and put things right.'

'Certainly, Luighseach. But you cannot have it here. I'm too busy this week. Can you arrange it for somewhere else? What about your house?'

I was taken aback. I was in no way disposed for neither Pim nor Phoebe to inflict their curiosity on the wheelchair in the parlour, the walking frame, and all the other helpmates that lurked in the various nooks and crannies of my house. Then there were the pictures of my mother…

'I—I couldn't do that, Mrs Epstein,' I replied.

There was a pause.

'I suppose you could all come to my place,' Pim made a tentative offer. 'I live at Mosman so you'll have to come on the ferry. If mum lets me, maybe you could stay the night. That way we might have a chance to rehearse properly. School breaks for Easter on Tuesday, so I reckon we could have it then. Even Phoebe can come if she wants. Would you like to come, Phoebe?'

'I suppose so,' Phoebe haughtily replied.

'I suppose so?' echoed Mrs Epstein. 'A simple "Yes" or "No thank you" would be a little more courteous, Phoebe.'

Phoebe said yes.

'What about you, Lucy?' Pim asked.

I smiled at her, delighted at the prospect of spending a day and a night in her company.

'Della?'

'That's all very well, Pim,' said Della. 'But Mummy is not going to let me go.'

'Of course she will,' Pim confidently replied. 'Wait till my mum talks to her.'

Della shook her head.

'My mum's had twelve kids,' Pim explained. 'She can talk anyone into doing anything.'

****

Pim's mother lived up to her daughter's claims, at least as far as Della was concerned. The moment Della saw me at school on Friday morning she announced that her mother had indeed given her permission for the venture. Pim, it turned out, was not quite the untouchable Mrs Sotheby had originally imagined; for her family owned a very reputable guest house at Bradley's Head. Mrs Mahony herself had stayed there, so it had excellent credentials.

'Mummy's even allowed me to stay two nights!' Della chatted excitedly at morning tea. 'She decided that the sea air would do me good.'

'And I still cannot believe she's let you go even for one,' I remarked.

'Nor can I, old thing,' acknowledged Della. 'But Mummy found out about the guest house and how Mrs Mahony had stayed there and that Mrs Connolly knows Mrs Mahony. Then Mrs Connolly found out that Mrs Mahony was having an Easter party and that Mummy was having trouble with her dressmaker. So Mrs Connolly chatted to Mummy about her costume and assured Mummy that it was certain to be the most elegant of all. Mummy was so thrilled by the end of the conversation that she would have given me permission to go to Africa.'

'Told you,' observed Pim, her mouth full of apple.

'And your step-father?' I asked. ''Twas last week he was threatening to take you away from school for failing Trig and here you are back again. What has he to say on it all?'

'Oh, Daddy's gone sailing,' Della blithely explained. 'As he says, there's nothing better than messing about on a boat when the weather's as fine as this. So he's on the harbour for a week. I daresay we'll see him on our way to Pim's,' she giggled. 'Anyway, Luighseach, why are you so glum?'

Mrs Connolly may have kissed the Blarney, but there was absolutely nothing she could say to convince Daid to let me go; for that same Thursday evening I had been witness to a brief and polite telephone conversation in which Daid firmly refused his permission.

'You're not letting me go because you think I'm too crippled,' I bitterly remarked when he hung the receiver.

'Well, Luighseach, I wouldn't be putting it as bluntly as that,' answered Daid.

I stamped a crutch on the floor and went to my room, slamming the door behind me.

Later that evening, Daid came to massage my legs.

'You're ruining everything, Daid!' I began. I had never spoken so accusingly to my father.

'And you'll be ruining yourself if you go,' replied Daid as he worked my knee. ''Twas gadding about on the airfield was bad enough and I'll not be letting you wear yourself out like that again.'

'But you didn't even give me a choice, Daid!' I complained. 'How is it you let me go to school and you let me go to Delleen Sotheby's house and you cannot let me go to Pim's?'

''Tis overnight, Luighseach,' Daid reasoned. 'Can you do for yourself overnight? What will happen, lass, if you cannot move yourself? I'll not be there to see to your legs. And there'll be stairs, you know. What will you do if there be stairs you cannot climb? And the ferry now, will you be managing that? I'm not knowing where you're going, lassie. How in God's name will you fare?'

Daid had been known to make a reconnaissance of my every route with a yardstick in hand to make sure I could mount whatever step and curb came my way.

'Then I'm telling you I'm going to Pim's house, Daid, and I'll get there myself if needs be. I'm not going alone, you know. I'm going with friends. My friends will help me, Da. 'Tis Delleen Sotheby and Pim Connolly. They're always looking out for me.' I could not vouch for Phoebe. All she ever did was stare.

'And you'd let them help you?' Daid did not usually hear me speak of letting people help me.

'They're my friends, Daid,' I proudly emphasised the word 'friends'.

'And it means that much to you, does it?' asked Daid as he pulled the covers over me.

Daid said nothing more about the matter. But on Monday afternoon when I returned from school, Mrs Murphy came out to inform me that my father would be late home. When Daid arrived, some hours later, he reported that he had reconsidered the matter and had changed his mind. I could go to Pim's house after all. As a safeguard against getting over-tired, he decided that I was to have a half-day on Tuesday in order to rest before my journey across the harbour.

Della and Pim were already waiting at Circular Quay when Daid and I arrived. Pim waved her tennis racquet and ran up to us, grinning from ear to ear at the sight of the motorcycle and side-car, its goggled driver and passenger, and the assortment of luggage we had brought with us.

She introduced herself to Daid in her typical hale and hearty fashion, and jestingly volunteered to be my packhorse. I was happy to see Daid warm to her greeting. But he did not stay long. He signed the cross on my forehead, gave me his blessing and was soon heading homeward on his motorcycle.

'Crikey he's young,' Pim remarked as Daid drove away. 'How old is he?'

'Thirty-six he would be now,' I answered.

'Teerty-six,' giggled Della.

'What did he say to you then?' Pim ignored Della.

'Twas Irish: May God and His angels go with you,' I replied.

'Mum told me he popped in for a cuppa yesterday,' Pim continued.

'What was that?' I asked.

Pim repeated her remark.

'And did he bring a yardstick with him?'

'Yardstick?' queried Pim.

'Never you mind, Pimmy Connolly,' I replied. So Daid had made a reconnaissance after all. That was why he was so late last night.

'Thanks be to God!' I quietly sighed, knowing now that there would be nothing in my journey that would present any difficulty.

'I say!' exclaimed Della. 'There's Phoebe! Phoebe!' she called and waved to the distant hour-glass figure. Phoebe did not wave back. If Della had not run up to her, grab her violin and tuck a friendly hand in her free arm, Phoebe would have walked straight past.

'Where have you been, Phoebe?' Della attempted some amiable conversation as she guided her towards the ferry.

'Piano lesson.'

'Where do you learn?'

'Over there.'

'Where?' asked Della. 'Do you mean the Conservatorium?'

'That's over there, isn't it?'

Pim led us over the gang plank and onto the ferry. She was keen to secure a seat at the stern and used my 'cello to clear a passage. Occasionally she came across someone she knew and exchanged a brief but friendly greeting. We soon arrived at the designated spot, dumped our instruments and bags and took in

111

the harbour views. A few other people also sought outside seats, including a middle-aged gentleman who was well-known to Pim. He had an interest in violas, remarking in an aside to Della, who had taken a seat next to him, that he learnt the instrument when he was a boy. To my surprise, he asked Pim to play him something, and to my further surprise, Pim agreed.

'Any special requests, Dr Little?' she asked as she tuned.

'Will you play the Brahms for me again, Pim?' replied the doctor.

''Course I will.'

Accompanied by the rumble and drone of the ferry and the splash of the sea Pim launched into the second of the Hungarian Dances. The doctor was delighted and whispered his praises first to Della and then to the lady on his other side. I marvelled at Pim's confidence. How could she get up and play before people so easily? I would have liked to join in, to pull out my 'cello and pluck a harmony then and there. I could hear it all in my head. But it was impossible for me to reach my instrument. Even if I had been able, fear had already crippled my fingers.

Pim finished to smiles and applause and a heartfelt thank you from her doctor friend. No sooner had the cheers and clapping died down than a violin was heard, this time from Phoebe, who was seated cross-legged on a crate.

'And now,' she announced. '*Hungarian Dance Number Five.*'

And she proceeded to play to a polite and appreciative audience. In fact, her audience grew as men and women, curious to learn more about the spectacle on the stern, began to crowd around. As the crowd increased, so did Phoebe embellish her performance with brilliant runs and double-stops.

Somebody gave me a nudge.

'Who does she think she is?' Pim nodded in Phoebe's direction.

'You'll be agreeing she's a fine fiddler, Pim,' I answered, marvelling again at Phoebe's style and ability.

'She's showing off,' Pim criticised. 'I only played because I was asked. Wouldn't have done it at all except that he's a family friend and a bit lonely,' she indicated Dr Little.

'Maybe Phoebe's the same,' observed Della who had joined us. 'What I mean is maybe she needs people to listen to her because nobody does – if that makes any sense. Come on, Pim,' she urged. 'Please don't gripe. Let's dance instead. I simply cannot resist.'

Pim scowled in Phoebe's direction. Then, with a shrug of her shoulders, she gave in. Round and round they romped, Pim stomping and Della stepping out a merry polka.

I leaned more heavily against the side of the ferry, looked down at the water in search of fish, and lost my gaze in the slaten waves which splashed in rhythmic conflict against each other and the rocks nearby.

I longed to dance – to reel and jig – to swing my legs up high and step and hop in mad delight to the tune of a fiddle. Yet brimful with desire though I might have been, I was totally at odds with myself as to its accomplishment and mourned over the metal, leather and scrawny limbs that scarred my desires. I could not even tap my feet.

The ferry turned and I took a final look at the iron girders of that grandiose callipered construction which, gripped forcibly by muscular pylons, was soon to stride out from the two opposing shores.

'I say, what are you staring at?' Della, breathless and dizzy, put her hand on my arm and followed my gaze.

'Them harbour bridge pylons there,' I replied. 'Do you think the bridge will meet in the middle, Delleen?'

'I've never thought about it. Of course they will. Why? Don't you think so?'

'I'm not sure. And I'm after wondering how they're going to keep it together if they do. And how will it meet in the middle without sagging? And them pylons there: 'tis the same they look, but considering the load they'll be carrying and that they're on different shores and all, do you think they're really the same now? What calculations would they have made to get it all to work do you think?'

'You're asking *me* a question like that?' Della wryly replied. 'Don't worry, old thing, you're bound to figure it out sooner or later.'

And, with a friendly squeeze, she let me ponder alone.

12

A young man met us when we disembarked at the Mosman wharf. Stocky, moon-faced and freckled, with a curly top of carroty hair, he was, without mistake, one of Pim's brothers.

Pim introduced him as Benny and he helped us into an enormous touring vehicle, which fortunately was able to accommodate our instruments and luggage. The tourer wound its way up the hill, cruised past the zoological gardens and down an elegant avenue before purring into a driveway.

Della may have lived in a mansion; but on the grand scale, the Connolly's house with its three storeys, turrets, wide verandahs and vast, park like grounds, way outclassed the Sotheby's.

'Now don't get any fancy ideas into your heads,' Pim warned us as the car came to a stop. 'It's a guest house,' she emphasised her last words.

The front door opened and a large, flaccid young fellow came out. The moment he saw Pim he grinned, opened his arms wide, gave her a huge bear hug and rocked her from side to side as he did.

'Pim! Pim!' he kept on saying. 'I missed you, Pim. I missed you!'

'Spotty dogs are here!' announced Benny as he carried a few bags inside.

A voice was heard in the hall:

'Is that Philomena and the girls?' And an older woman, wearing a full, white apron, walked quickly towards us. There was no doubt that she was Pim's mother for she too had red hair, albeit faded and mixed with grey, which she wore in a serviceable bob.

Della and I glanced at each other and then at Pim who was still being hugged.

'Did I hear her say Philomena?' whispered Della.

'That's enough, Bertie,' the woman ordered Pim's other brother. 'Help the girls with their things. I'm Mrs Connolly. Now, it's Della, Phoebe and Lucy. Who's who? Philomena!'

Pim gave her mother a hug hello and introduced us. Mrs Connolly welcomed us inside.

'Tea's ready,' she said as she led us down the hall, 'so freshen up and come to the dining room. Philomena will show you where everything is.'

'My, my, Philomena Connolly,' Della mused. 'In all the time I've known you, I've never heard your real name.'

'Mum ran out of names by the time she had me,' Pim sighed. 'Get called Pim because my sister Gracie couldn't say Philomena. Used to say Pimeena. So everyone calls me Pim. Except Mum,' she loudly complained.

It may have been Holy Week, but the Connolly's dining table was laid out more for a feast than a fast. There were baskets of freshly baked bread and tureens piled high with bulbous heads of cauliflower, bright carrots and beans glistening with melted butter. My eyes widened in delight at the appearance of an enormous fish pie. Busy with final table preparations were other family members, all variations on the stout, freckled, red-headed theme. The moment they saw Pim there were more bear hugs and welcomes. Aside from Mr and Mrs Connolly, who presided over the head and foot of the table, and Bertie and Benny, whom we had already met, there was Lily, Leo and Gracie.

'Of course that's not all of us,' Pim concluded her introductions. 'The rest of the family's on the sideboard. All in all, it's Paddy, Leo, Lily, Rosie, Polly, Annie, Benny, Bobby, Johnny, Peggy, Bertie, Gracie and—'

'Phil-o-MEEN-a!' chorused her brothers and sisters.

'St Philomena, Virgin and Martyr. You ought to be proud of it,' scolded Mrs Connolly, unsuccessfully hiding her smile, 'instead of insisting upon being named after an aperitif.'

Grace was said and concluded with a loud 'And God bless the cooks', and the dining room exploded with gastronomic energy. Knives and forks clanked against crockery, plates were passed in response to friendly requests for food and returned mounded with creamy mashed potato, steamy seafood and buttery veggies. Tea was poured, and milk jugs and sugar progressed from one hand to the next, up and down each side of the table.

'When did you get back, Gracie?' asked Pim of her sister who was a year older.

'This afternoon,' replied Gracie.

'How's Annie?'

'Doing beautifully and the baby's a darling – a bonny, gay, chubby little fellow.'

'Annie's just had number five so Gracie's been up the last couple of months to help out,' explained Pim.

'Cut my carrots, Pim,' Bertie requested.

'All right, Bertie,' Pim sighed. 'Pass your plate.'

'By the way, Gracie,' said Lily, 'Billy Bailey called last night.'

'Billy?' Gracie blushed.

'Said he'd call by tonight.'

'So is he going to pop the question?' asked Benny.

'None of your business, Benny.'

'If he doesn't, the Bachelor Tax will get him.'

'Ridiculous thing. They'll never pass it.'

'You better look out too, Benny,' commented Lily. 'How long have you been walking out with Daphne? Two years?'

'Carrots are tasty,' remarked Bertie, loudly.

'You grow 'em?' asked Pim.

'Yep. Me and Dad. Me and Dad grew the carrots.'

'Well they're about the tastiest carrots I've tried. Beats soggy school carrots,'

Pim replied.

'Pim, how's Polly?' asked Gracie.

'Played tennis with her yesterday. She thrashed me.'

'She's well then,' commented Mrs Connolly. 'She enjoying teaching?'

'Pretty much,' more explanations were required. 'My sister Polly teaches the fourth grade at school.'

'Faith!' I exclaimed. 'Pimmy Connolly, do you mean to say your sister's Sister Scholastica?'

'That's right,' Pim replied with a smile which was quickly replaced with a more cautioning look. 'And I know what you're thinking, Lucy Straughan.'

I tried to look blank, but to no avail. Pim knew exactly what I was thinking. She picked up her napkin and wrapped it round her head in imitation of the nuns' wimples. 'Sister Scholastica. And just because I look like my sister doesn't mean I'm going to be a nun,' she warned, partly in jest and partly in earnest. 'Anyway, you can talk, Sister Augustine,' she jibed.

At this, Della burst out laughing. Gracie, who was seated opposite me, also began to laugh. Even Phoebe, who had not spoken a word, let slip a smile.

'I'm sorry, I knew you reminded me of someone,' remarked Gracie with a kindly gesture in my direction. 'Sister Augustine. Remember Sister Augustine, Lily?'

'The Dragon of St Dominic's? How could I forget? She's not still teaching, is she?'

'She most certainly is,' said Della. '*And* she has a prodigy.' Here she nudged me.

'Not a jot am I like Sister Augustine!' I retorted.

'Come on, Lucy,' said Pim. 'You're a carbon copy.'

'I amn't,' I tersely replied. 'For one, I'm nearly a foot taller than herself.'

'Which is what makes it so very funny,' giggled Della.

'And you're both as skinny as rakes and you wear the same glasses,' continued Pim. 'You even talk the same.'

'I do not talk the same as Sister Augustine!' I protested.

'You're both Irish.'

'Aye, indeed we are. But Sister Augustine's from the north and I'm from the west. There bees a difference, you know.'

'Sounds all the same to me,' goaded Pim. 'All right, if there is such a difference, how does Sister Augustine talk?'

'Different from myself,' I declined the challenge to imitate Sister.

'Go on,' urged Della. 'Do what happened this morning,' and she began to giggle again. 'Sister Augustine was trying to correct our homework,' Della explained, 'and, as usual, she was firing questions at us left, right and centre. Anyway, every time she asked dear old Luighseach, who's by far the best in the class, Luighseach replied with another equation.'

'Aye,' I acknowledged with a smile. 'For, as usual, Delleen Sotheby, everyone

116

was refusing to answer any question with the number three in it and this time, I wasn't about obliging Mary Byrne and her tallies. So I said "half six" or "the square root of nine hundred" or the like.'

'Oh, is that why you did it?' Della really was a dunce at maths. 'Anyway,' she proceeded, 'when Luighseach came up with the most preposterous answer I ever heard, Sister Augustine completely lost her composure. "Mercy me," she said—' But then Della's mirth got the better of her.

'Mercy me! Lu-cee Strau-ghan!' I continued the narrative, turning my own napkin into a wimple, and emphatically rolling my 'R' and heavily aspirating the 'gh' the way Sister Augustine did whenever she said my surname. 'Will ye lewk in yer bewk and tell me 'tis nat t'answer ye've written there? Mathematics, as ken ye might, is the language of simplicity, is it nat? And t'answer tree hundred and fifty tree. What put it into yer head—?'

Fortunately, I did not need to say any more. Pim and her sisters, along with Della and Phoebe, were laughing so much they were shaking. Della had tears rolling down her face. Even Pim's father and brothers were enjoying the caricature. Evidently they were familiar with Sister Augustine tales. Only Mrs Connolly was aware that I, too, had begun to shake. But it was not from laughter. In my attempt to mimic Sister Augustine, I had succeeded in sounding exactly like my mother.

'Would you like some more pie, love?' whispered Mrs Connolly.

I shook my head and wiped my eyes with my serviette.

'Come on, pass your plate,' Mrs Connolly did not heed my refusal and held her hand out to receive my dish which I then willingly handed to her. 'Heaven knows you could do with more.'

Quinces and custard were served for dessert. More tea was offered and then the table was rapidly cleared. A statue of the Blessed Virgin was placed in the centre. Two candles were lit, beads were passed around, and chairs were turned away from the table or shunted towards the wall.

'We pray the Rosary after tea,' explained Mrs Connolly, speaking above the commotion. It appeared that Della, Phoebe and I were expected to join them. 'But you don't have to kneel,' she continued as the Connolly family knelt to pray. Della instantly knelt beside Gracie. Phoebe, on the other hand, refused the offer of a pair of beads and looked for a path of escape. Finding the dining room door blocked by Leo, who was kneeling directly in front, she had no alternative but to seek a corner and kneel and fidget for the duration of the prayer. Pim's oldest sister Lily solved my own predicament by beckoning to me and patting the seat of the chair next to her.

'I've got housemaid's knee,' she whispered to me as I sat. 'Can't kneel to save myself.'

Immediately the Rosary finished the family sprang to action, extinguishing candles with dampened fingers, returning the statue, collecting beads, shifting chairs and ordering each other about.

'It's feeding time at the zoo,' Pim called out from the doorway. 'Guests' dinner time. Gotta help serve. I'll see you later in the lounge room. It's the big room next on your right towards the front door. Make yourselves at home.'

We easily found the lounge room. Although very spacious and generously proportioned, it was rendered homely by soft lighting, a crackling fire and an abundance of very comfortable looking armchairs and settees. Clusters of books could be found on tables and shelves, and there was a wooden chess set laid ready on a card table.

Phoebe was immediately attracted to the piano, a grand piano with a beautiful, warm oak finish. She lifted the lid. 'Mmm, a Broadwood,' she dreamed as she stroked the keys.

'Phoebe, do you think you ought?' queried Della.

'Why not? Pim said to make ourselves at home, so that's what I'm doing.'

And she sat at the piano and launched into what turned out to be a spectacular collection of pieces.

'My!' Della exclaimed quietly to me. 'You said Phoebe was a good pianist, Luighseach, but I didn't imagine she would be this good. Gracious!'

'Do you know what she's playing there, Delleen?' I whispered.

Della nodded and whispered back. 'It's Schumann's *Carnival*. I heard Padrewski play it last year at the Town Hall. I say, Phoebe,' Della took advantage of a small pause. 'Did you see Padrewski?'

Phoebe nodded and recommenced playing. 'Mrs Epstein took me.'

'Mrs Epstein?'

Phoebe nodded again. 'She often takes me to concerts. I met Padrewski afterwards and played for him.'

The remark made the same impression on Della as it did on me. In our rehearsals we had only observed Mrs Epstein taking a very firm hand with Phoebe. But Phoebe's comment revealed that she also had a share in the deeply generous heart which we regarded as a trademark of our teacher.

We compared experiences. Della confided to me that Mrs Epstein was very much behind the acquisition of her full size violin. She had spent hours hunting for a suitable instrument; and having found one, spent further hours convincing her parents of Della's need.

'It was the first time in my life anyone had said I was actually good at something,' Della commented, 'and that I deserved to have a decent instrument. Up until then I suppose my parents regarded the violin as a toy. They still do in many ways. They cannot come to terms with my playing anything advanced, let alone performing.'

'And what is the matter with performing?' I asked.

'It's not the done thing,' Della replied. 'I mean it's perfectly proper to play in private company, but certainly not in public. As for earning a living from it— well, as far as Mummy and Daddy are concerned, it's akin to being little more than a servant. So you can imagine how Mummy views Mrs Epstein. Of course, Mrs

Epstein pays no attention whatsoever. I gather you don't have those sorts of predicaments, old thing.'

''Tis myself's the one with the problem of performing, in private and in public,' I sighed.

Pim came in wearing a full apron similar to her mother's. 'Hey Phoebe!' she called, her voice booming through the Schumann. 'There's been a request for some Chopin.'

Phoebe brought her performance to an end with a series of spectacular chords. 'Which Chopin?' she asked.

'Dunno,' replied Pim, much to Phoebe's annoyance. 'Play anything.'

'What about a nocturne, Phoebe?' Della was more helpful. 'I like the E flat major one. Wally used to play it. Do you know the E flat major one?'

Phoebe knew it and began.

Gradually, as if drawn by the beauty of the music, guests wandered into the lounge. An elderly lady, Mrs Macgregor, thanked Phoebe profusely, asked to see her hands, marvelled at them and told her how much she had loved to hear her husband play that very same piece. More Chopin was requested. Phoebe obliged with a waltz and old Mrs Macgregor was in raptures.

Pim, her dining room duties finished, sat with Della and me and pointed out some of the other guests. Over near the fire sat Miss Glass, a rather stiff and proper person who preferred books to people. Major Barton, a retired army officer, took his place at the chess board with his off-sider, Corporal Stevenson, and opened combat. A young married couple, whom Pim had not met before, and who had not yet laid claim to any of the room's settees, hovered nervously around the piano and ended up under Mrs Macgregor's protection. The doorbell rang and Billy Bailey joined Gracie near the fire. Lily and Benny entered, still discussing the prospective Bachelor Tax.

'Are you going to play for us tonight, Lily?' asked Mrs Macgregor.

'No, Mrs Macgregor,' declined Lily. 'I think I've been well and truly outshone.'

'But you will sing for us, won't you?'

'Of course I will. Pim! Benny! Come on, let's sing. Phoebe, can you play "I'm looking over a four-leafed clover"?'

Phoebe queried the request, a snatch was sung and the music organised on the stand. A quick glance at the notes on the page and Phoebe began the song.

'If she's using music, you can be sure she's reading by sight,' I remarked to Della.

'My!' Della exclaimed. 'She's absolutely faultless!'

The Connollys all possessed good voices. Next, they were singing and laughing over 'Yes, we have no bananas'; Gracie and Billy joined in for 'Baby Face' and the married couple lost their shyness with 'Pack up your troubles in your old kit bag'. Mrs Macgregor asked for 'Daisy, Daisy'; Leo entered requesting 'Bless This House', and with that, everybody was singing. Even the reserved Miss Glass was singing for it was impossible to concentrate on a book with the Connolly clan at large.

'Supper's made,' announced Mrs Connolly as she brought in the tea trolley.

'Let's hear it for the piano player!' applauded Benny, and an exhausted and radiant Phoebe curtsied to claps and cheers.

'Whew!' she said quietly as she sat beside me. 'Do I need a cigarette!'

'Well 'tis the corporal there you can ask for one,' I nodded in the corporal's direction. 'Or you'll be asking the major for a puff of his pipe.'

Phoebe looked at me, a little shocked that I should suggest such a thing.

''Tis many an old woman in Galway I seen puffing her pipe of an evening,' I remarked, shrugging my shoulders.

Phoebe huffed in disgust and left me for the cocoa Mrs Connolly had poured for her.

One by one, guests and family members returned their cups and saucers to the trolley and bid good night.

'I've put you girls in the Royal Room,' said Lily. 'Pim will take you. God bless and don't hesitate to ask if you need anything.'

'The Royal Room?' queried Della as we followed Pim up the stairs. 'Why is it the Royal Room?'

'You'll see why when we get there,' was all Pim said in reply.

Pim opened the door and showed us into a richly wallpapered room that was as large as the one we had left. Its main feature was an oversized four poster bed with a great velvet canopy and opulent swags.

'Bed came with the house,' explained Pim. 'Must have been built in the room 'cause there's no way we could get it out. Mum refused to have it chopped for firewood, so we kept it. Use it for guests we want to impress,' she added drily. 'I'm going to get my stuff from my room. You lot sort yourselves out. Bathroom's down the end of the hallway. Washstand's over there and there are coat hangers in the wardrobe if you need to hang anything.'

Della volunteered to use the bathroom to do her toilette. Phoebe picked up her bag and disappeared behind the embroidered silk screen.

I surveyed the room and wondered how I was going to organise myself without Daid. Thankfully the sheets had already been turned down, which meant there was one less complication involved in making ready for the night. But I hesitated over any further preparations. The last thing I wanted was to be seen removing the callipers. So I found my hairbrush, sat on the edge of the bed and began to undo my braids instead.

Pim was the first to return. 'Aren't any of you in bed yet?' she said.

'A long time they're taking,' I replied.

'You all right?' Pim asked. 'You look a bit worried.'

'What is it you've put on your face there?' I inquired, for Pim had smothered her face with a strange, green cream.

'Beauty cream,' she answered. 'Supposed to fade freckles and make your skin smooth. Want some?' And she dabbed a little on my nose. I wrinkled my nose and wiped the cream off with my finger. 'Don't worry, Lucy. You don't need it. With skin like yours, you look as if you've bathed in ass's milk. Hey, is there a draught? You're shivering. Shouldn't be a window open.'

Pim made sure the double doors opening onto the verandah were secure. Then she noticed that the curtain covering the window behind the screen had been pushed aside.

'A-ha!' she concluded.

She strode over, moved the screen and exposed Phoebe clad in her nightdress, leaning out the window.

'Caught in the act!'

Cigarette in hand, Phoebe turned round.

'Put that thing out! Now!' commanded the green-faced Pim.

'I'll do no such thing.'

'Guest house rules: no smoking in the bedrooms.'

'I wasn't smoking in the bedroom,' retorted Phoebe. 'I had my head outside.'

'Outside or inside, you're not smoking anywhere,' Pim resolved. 'You're not going to ruin things like you did at Della's. My mum would have a fit if she saw you smoking.'

'So are you going to tell her?' challenged Phoebe.

'No. But I'm going to make you stop.' Pim snatched Phoebe's cigarette and tossed it out the window. Phoebe made for the chair nearby but was beaten to her destination. Pim grabbed Phoebe's drawstring bag and held it out of her reach. Around the room they ran, with Phoebe leaping like a cat in repeated attempts to reclaim the forbidden goods. I kept well out of their way, found my nightclothes which Daid had thoughtfully packed in a pillowcase to make them easier to carry, and went to undress behind the screen. Meanwhile, the fight continued:

'Give me back my cigarettes! I want my cigarettes! Give them back!'

'You can have them when you leave. Don't you have parents?'

'What has that to do with it?'

'It's a wonder your mother lets you smoke. What's the matter with her? No mother in her right mind would let you get away with smoking at your age.'

'Don't you talk about my mother like that!'

'Well? How is it that she lets you? Hmmm?'

'I told you, it's none of your business! And I can do as I please!'

'Not in my house you can!'

'Give me back my cigarettes!'

But the rumpus ceased the moment I emerged. Both Pim and Phoebe had noticed I was only wearing a slipper on my right foot. Without the built-up shoe, my left foot hung uselessly from beneath my nightdress and was covered with a sock.

'Please, let yous not look at me,' I begged.

'You're all right, Lucy,' Pim gently remarked as I pulled myself along on my

121

crutches. 'So you don't have to wear those braces at night?'

I shook my head. 'Not any more, thanks be to God. I used to be wearing splints to bed for to keep my legs straight. But I'm not needing them now I've stopped growing,' I added, much relieved, as I laid my crutches beside the bed and yawned. My tired response served as the cue for Phoebe to follow me into bed. She crept over the covers and settled down next to me, bringing with her a small, stuffed toy.

'Do you remember being able to walk?' she asked.

Her question took me by surprise. Usually people tended to draw attention to my inability to walk by remarking about my legs or my crutches or callipers and completely eschewed the idea that I may at one time have walked exactly like themselves. And the fact that the question came from the self-centred Phoebe further astonished me.

'Do you remember before you had polio?' she asked.

How did she know I had polio? I had never told her. I rolled my eyes. Della must have told her, for Della made it her duty to tell everyone.

'Aye, I do,' I eventually replied. 'I used to be able to run and jump and dance and play like yourself.' Phoebe looked at me with a curious, penetrating look and nodded. It was as if she had actually envisioned such a scene. Her empathy was strangely consoling. 'But it feels like a long time ago now,' I added. ''Tis as if something's been broken inside and I've lost the pieces.' Phoebe nodded again, slowly, thoughtfully.

Della burst into the room, nervous and frightened.

'What's the matter with you?' asked Pim.

'Pim! It's awful!' Della spoke hastily. 'Someone's in trouble! They're shouting and calling for help and moaning. I tried to open the door to see what was wrong but it was locked and they wouldn't open when I called. It's terrible! Whatever should we do?'

'Don't worry, Dell. It's only the Major,' replied Pim as she continued to wash the cream off her face.

'But there's something the matter!'

'He's having a nightmare,' Pim patted her face dry. 'Used to scare the living daylights out of me too. It's the War.'

'Oh dear. Do you know what happened?'

'Apparently he lost all his men at Passchendaele or something like that. That's what Mum said. Doesn't usually sleep in his bed.'

'But—he was in his room. What do you mean?'

'I mean he doesn't sleep in his bed. He sleeps under his bed. Been in his room to clean it dozens of times and you can tell. Don't ask me why and there's nothing you can do about it.'

'Poor man,' lamented Della who then dropped to her knees to say her night prayers. She blessed herself, clambered up on the bed and sat next to Phoebe.

Pim squeezed herself in next to Della. 'Say, Dell. Was it your father or your step-father who was in the War?' she asked.

'My father,' Della replied. 'He flew a 'plane. He was shot down in France a few months before the War ended. He was awarded a lot of medals for bravery.'

'Really?' Pim was very impressed.

'Yes. Wally knows all about it. Anyway, his valour cost him his life. I suppose it was for the best that it did,' she sighed.

'And do you be meaning that, Della Sotheby?' I asked.

'Yes I do. When I see some of the men who came back maimed or blind or disfigured, I think that that could have happened to my father and I'm very relieved it didn't,' Della replied. 'Did any of your family fight in the War, Pim?'

'My brother Paddy,' said Pim.

'Did he come back?'

Pim shook her head. 'Got gassed at Wipers.'

'Oh, I am sorry.'

'Funny thing is,' Pim continued, 'he would be a bit older than your dad is now, Lucy, if he had come back. His photo's on the sideboard in the dining room. Frankly, I find it hard to believe that he shot people. All he ever shot at home was rabbits and a few 'roos.'

Della nodded. 'I think the same when I look at my father's photo. He looks an awful lot like Wally. Then I look at Wally and try to imagine him harming someone, not to mention killing them, and I'm absolutely baffled.'

'I once asked my Uncle Ted about that,' replied Pim. 'He fought at Beersheba. Said that if he didn't he would have been killed himself. As far as he was concerned, he had too much to live for to let that happen. Ted got shot but: bullet in the shoulder. Would have got another in the heart but he had his Missal in his pocket. Bullet got stuck in his Missal instead. Talk about lucky.'

''Twas luck was it?' I queried.

'Mum reckons it was Providence. 'Specially since it was the Missal that stopped the bullet.'

It always irked me when people attributed good fortune to divine intervention, particularly when missals, medals and rosary beads were involved.

'So was it Providence got your brother killed?' I asked.

'Hell, I dunno, Lucy. Gas got Paddy. Guess it's like Della said and it was better he died. We've all gotta go sometime. Anyway, what about you? Your father fight?'

I firmly shook my head and felt the force of Pim's critical gaze.

''Twas an English war, was it not, Pim Connolly?'

'Suppose so. Didn't stop Paddy but.'

'Or my father,' chimed in Della. 'He was Irish and he fought.'

'Aye, but your father's not Irish the way my Daid is.'

'What do you mean by that?'

'Was he a Catholic, your daid?'

'Yes—well, at least I think so,' Della added, doubtfully. 'I—I really don't know. I assume— What does it matter? I simply don't understand why you're always bent on making such distinctions.'

'Never you mind,' I sighed. Della had absolutely no idea about the Ascendancy. 'But I know for a fact there's nothing would make my father fight in any war. Not a thing. Not even an Irish war.'

'My brother Leo's a bit like that,' Pim acquiesced. 'He was in the seminary when the War broke out. Then he decided to go to France himself and help Paddy. Refused to fight but. Drove an ambulance instead so he still did his bit.'

'And he never became a priest after?' Della asked.

'Couldn't,' Pim replied. 'The War really rattled him. He lost a lot of mates besides Paddy. Anyway, he had to help keep the farm going afterwards, but even that was too much. Leo never cared for farming.'

'I thought you came from the country,' remarked Della. 'Don't you have the farm any more?'

'Had to sell. We couldn't get anyone reliable enough to help out after the War, and it didn't get any easier when Dad had a stroke. You probably noticed my dad didn't talk at tea time.'

'He was very quiet,' Della observed.

'Well that's why. Can't get the words out and when they do come out they're all mixed up. He's all right but. What about you, Phoebe?'

'What about me?' asked Phoebe in a very subdued manner.

'You have anyone in the War?' asked Pim.

'What?'

'Did you have anyone who fought in the War?' Pim asked again, this time more insistently.

'What war?'

'You know, silly, the Great War,' Pim's insistence gave way to impatience. 'What we've been talking about.'

'I don't know of any Great Wars.'

Phoebe frowned as she drew her hands round her legs and sucked her knees.

'Well, did you?' Pim pressed her for more.

'Why should *I* tell *you*?' was the moody reply. Phoebe sniffed, but her sniff came too late.

A tear dropped to the coverlet.

****

Toast, stewed prunes and pots of tea awaited Della, Pim and me the following morning; and before we even had a chance to greet her, Mrs Connolly saw that we helped ourselves to a hearty serving of lamb's fry and gravy. Pim's mother's cooking was magnificent there was no doubt about that.

After breakfast, we brought our instruments to the lounge room.

Phoebe entered as we were tuning. She had been the last one to rise that morning and did not come down until after we had finished eating. Although immaculately groomed in her old-fashioned attire, she looked jaded. Her eyes were swollen and she seemed to lack the energy to be as defiant as she usually was.

'Come on, Phoebe,' Della welcomed her with a smile. 'Come and tell me what you think about this plan. Did you know we're not going to see Mrs Epstein for two weeks?' she excitedly began. 'There's no lesson on Thursday because of Easter and Mrs Epstein's away after that. So I propose we learn the whole quartet to surprise her. If we practise hard, I'm sure we can do it or at least get some of the way. We could do the first movement this morning. What do you say?'

'I'm all for it,' Pim's reply was delivered more speedily than my protest. 'Anything's better than the Epstein Evil Eye.'

'The what is it?' I asked.

'You know,' and Pim turned her head towards me, imitating the oblique way Mrs Epstein would stare when she asked a question. 'And precisely how much practice have you done this week, Lucy Straughan?' she mimicked.

My laugh briefly quietened my nerves. I had succeeded in memorising the minuet for the rehearsal and had come downstairs feeling quite keen and confident about playing. Now Della had put forward a plan which relied on the skill I lacked most: sight-reading. I reached for my music, pushed my glasses onto my forehead and anxiously began to study my part.

'What on earth are you doing?' asked Phoebe. I returned my glasses to my nose. She was staring at me in a very scornful way.

'Here we go again!' sighed Pim.

'Pim,' Della cautioned.

''Tis learning my music I am,' I explained.

'Do you have to be so gauche about it? Why don't you sight-read for Heaven's sake.'

'I—I don't sight-read well,' I hated having to admit my weakness to Phoebe, particularly when she was so adept. 'I—I have trouble reading the notes.'

'We're not all as clever as you, Phoebe,' said Della, sensing as I did a torrent of criticism coming my way.

'You don't have to read every single note, silly,' remarked Phoebe. 'You can improvise, can't you?'

Phoebe knew full well that I could. She had heard me do so in the music store. I nodded.

'And you've studied harmony?'

Of course I had. Many a bedridden day had been spent mulling over chord progressions and counterpoint.

'Well, what key are we in?'

'D Minor it would be,' I replied, and I hurriedly checked the key signature and the first line of notes.

There followed a series of rapid-fire questions. Phoebe ignored Della and Pim who started to complain about her treatment of me.

'Then what's the Dominant?'

'A major.'

'Sub-dominant?'

'G minor.'

'Relative major?'

'F major.'

'Raised seventh?'

'C sharp.'

'Then it should be easy. Don't worry so much about the notes. All you have to do is listen to the harmonies, look for the patterns and count like blazes.' And with a shrug of her shoulders and a toss of her curls, Phoebe sat down and began tuning her violin.

'Crikey, Phoebe,' complained Pim. 'Of all the ways to say something, why do you always have to choose the more unpleasant?'

'You can talk,' retorted Phoebe.

'Let her alone,' I interrupted Pim who was ready to answer back. At least this time Phoebe had only called me silly. Besides, Pim had only heard the tone of Phoebe's voice which had been hard and demanding. I, on the other hand, had looked her in the face and had seen a softer expression in her eyes, tired as they were. It was an expression which seemed to say, 'Please don't give up. Please play. I want you to play.'

'Shall we start?' asked Della.

It turned out that Phoebe had given me very sage advice. I found that if I listened carefully to the harmonies, I could quickly anticipate the notes I had to play. With that in place, I could attend to the rhythms and sequences, which were far more easy to read than individual notes; and once I discovered the unifying pattern, my mistakes began to subside.

What was particularly consoling was the fact that I was not alone in error.

'Oh help!' Della cringed when we were some way through. 'What was that?'

'Sorry, my fault,' replied Pim, 'wrong clef. I forget sometimes.'

'Let's pick it up from bar thirty-two. I must say, Luighseach old thing, you're playing awfully well!'

Pim warmly agreed and Phoebe sat a little straighter and smiled to herself.

'I found the secret code,' I replied with a gleam of pleasure. ''Tis not called the *Fifths* quartet for nothing, you know, for the whole movement's built around fifths.'

'Is it really?' replied Della. 'I haven't had much chance to notice, I've been so busy concentrating on my part. Why Mrs Epstein made me first violin, I don't know.'

'Well, there are fifths everywhere: sequences, running passages, upside down and right way up,' I continued. ''Tis as if Haydn's plucked a piece of music from the spheres!' I added, beaming.

'I was wondering why this string crossing was driving me round the bend!'

remarked Pim.

'Then let you try it on a 'cello, Pimmy Connolly,' I replied, wriggling my left index finger which frequently had been flattened across two strings.

'I think I'll leave you to enjoy the torture,' said Pim.

'Bar thirty two?' suggested Della.

We had nearly finished the first movement when Lily popped her head in at the door.

'That's sounding great! Hope you're going to play for us later on. Pim, Benny's meeting Daphne down at Balmoral. He's offered to drive you all there if you want a break. Should do you good. I've battered some fish and you can take it with you for lunch. The fish is fresh this morning. Leo and Bertie made a terrific catch.'

Balmoral was a friendly alcove with waves that delighted in whispering secrets to the sand. Benny greeted his lady friend on the promenade and left us to set up our own picnic which we chose to do on the beach. Lily had packed us each a newspaper shell of fish and chips. Pim returned the greeting of a group of boys who were playing shuttlecock nearby. 'St Allos boys,' she explained. 'I'll see them at Mass tomorrow.' Children were building sandcastles or drawing with sticks. A little girl was being tossed over the waves by her mother and father.

'I've never been to the beach before,' remarked Phoebe as she licked the oil and salt off her fingers.

'You mean to say you can play la-di-da piano pieces and you've never been to the beach?' queried Pim with a critical edge.

'That's right,' Phoebe replied. Of course it was perfectly logical to play fancy piano pieces and not to have been to the beach.

Pim sighed and shook her head.

'Can we play in the water?' Phoebe asked, undaunted.

''Course you can,' came Pim's disinterested response.

Phoebe smiled and began to remove her shoes and stockings.

'What are you doing?'

'I'm going to paddle. Do you mean to say you've been to the beach and you've never been for a paddle?' Phoebe tucked her frock into her knickers and curled her lip in mock disgust. 'Talk about la-di-da.'

Not at all. Pim grinned and also began to pull off her shoes and stockings.

'Heavens above! You'll catch your death!' Paddling was not quite to Della's taste.

'No we won't, silly! It's a warm day,' Pim replied. 'You coming, Lucy?' she added as she ran down to join Phoebe who had already reached the water.

'I must say, the water does look rather inviting,' Della confessed and then glanced anxiously at me.

'You can go if you want. I'll not mind if you do,' I lied and looked away.

Della placed her shoes and stockings at my side. 'I'll be back soon, old thing.

Promise,' she whispered.

I watched her bare feet tip-toeing over the sand before returning my attention to the scene which had occupied me since we arrived.

The little girl was no longer being swung over the waves. She was walking along the shore, hand in hand with her mother, on a quest for shells. She picked up as many as she could and dropped them into her father's hat, which now served as a basket. Occasionally she found a shell that intrigued her. When she did, she would study it with her mother and then proudly show her father. Those special shells she put in the pocket of her pinafore.

There was a shout. One of the boys playing shuttlecock lost his balance and fell, comically, into the sand. His mates applauded him and he grinned, somersaulted and bowed before retrieving the shuttlecock and merrily buffeting it through the air with his racquet.

Pim and Phoebe, meanwhile, were romping through the water. They were watched by Della who shrieked with a mixture of fear and delight every time the waves rushed round her knees.

I lay back and tried to imagine the water trickling around my toes. But it was not enough to imagine, especially when my feet were trapped in a cumbersome pair of boots.

How I wanted to play in the sea!

Cautiously I drew up my legs and began to undo my laces. I glanced around. Everyone else was far too engrossed with seaside pleasures to notice anything ugly. So I began to undo my callipers as well. I rolled down my stockings and let my feet feel the sand. It was velvet soft. Now, all that remained was to crawl down to the water. I consoled myself with the fact that I could always stop and pretend to look for shells if anyone chanced to spy me.

I set out, reaching my arms forward then pulling my body along behind, with my legs crumpled underneath.

Pim was the first to notice, but it was not until I had neared the water's edge. She nudged Della and nodded in my direction. The two of them waved and called before wading towards me, the tucked up ends of their frocks now soaking wet.

'I win,' claimed Pim. 'Cough up, Dell.'

Della pulled a bon bon from her pocket and passed it across. Pim immediately pressed the sweet into her mouth.

'Didn't think it'd be long before we'd see you down here,' she remarked as she watched me stretch out my legs into a more comfortable sitting position. 'Della said you wouldn't even dare.'

'What on earth possessed you, Luighseach?' asked Della.

I didn't bother to answer. I simply smiled and fondled the wet sand. A wave swept up, spreading a cool, wet coverlet over my legs.

As far as I was concerned, that was explanation enough.

13

The next day, however, I was confined to bed.

'I can do it myself,' I informed Mrs Murphy with a sneeze as I pulled myself up on my crutches. 'I'm not needing your help.'

'And I suppose you're not needing my help to empty your commode either now?' Mrs Murphy replied.

I scowled at her and edged back to my bed. Mrs Murphy became busy with my sheets and coverlet.

'Did you not hear what I said? I told you, I'm not needing your help!'

Mrs Murphy paid no attention whatsoever. The moment I sat on my bed she took my crutches from me and placed them against the wall.

''Tis too far you put them,' I complained. Mrs Murphy handed my crutches back and I repositioned them half an inch closer to my bed. 'I told you I could do it,' I remarked as I set them in their place. 'Every night I do as much without the like of yourself to fuss.'

At least Mrs Murphy had the decency to let me sort my legs into bed. I reached over to pull the covers but they had been pulled too far back. So I had to put up with Mrs Murphy fussing over my bedding.

'And did you get wet all on your own?' she questioned while she smoothed and tucked the sheet and blankets. 'Did anyone help you take a dip in the sea? You didn't mind a bit of help then, did you?' Mrs Murphy then launched an assault on my pillows, pommelling them into shape and verbally pommelling me in the process. 'Madness! That's what it is. To even think of it, in your condition, going into the water and getting soaked. Why, it's April already! What's more you put sand and salt through your boots and leg irons and didn't they cost a pretty penny? As if your dear father hasn't enough on his plate without spending hours cleaning them up. The things you do when you're out of his sight! I'd like to know what company you're keeping in that school. Wild young things! That's what they must be.'

They were wild. They were wild and fun. There we all sat with waves washing round our toes, our knees and occasionally up to our waists. We swished our hands in the water. We splashed. We splashed each other and laughed and wet our hair. Pim carried me pick a back up the sand and let me fall on the picnic rug. We put another rug over my callipers, and by arranging picnic items and placing a hat on top, made it look as if someone was having a rest, with their boots sticking out from underneath. Never before had I laughed at my leg braces. We all laughed and licked ice cream and lay in the sun.

But then the boys' shuttlecock landed in our midst.

'You'd be that much happier if you offered your sufferings for the Holy Souls instead of hosting a pity party,' continued Mrs Murphy. 'You should take more advantage and use your sickness as a time of reparation, it being Holy Week and all.'

'Reparation? Reparation?' I repeated, even more irate. 'And why should I be always saying sorry to God? Why, for Heaven's sake does God not say sorry to myself now?'

'Mercy!' Mrs Murphy exclaimed.

'Well, if God sent the polio, He's not apologised for it. Not to my knowledge He hasn't. 'Tis God should be making reparation, not myself.'

'Proud as Lucifer, that's what you are!'

'Will you not shut your gob you ugly old cow!'

'Well! I—'

There was a knock at the door and Mrs Murphy trudged off to answer it. I listened for the visitor who was brought in without a word.

'Hope I haven't come at a bad time,' Pim remarked with a glance in Mrs Murphy's direction. 'You sick?'

'I am,' I replied, crossing my arms. 'I'm sick of Mrs Murphy, I'm sick of you and I'm sick of everyone!'

'You're sick of yourself more like.'

'Listen, if you come here to sport—'

Pim groaned. 'Don't tell me you're still brooding over what happened yesterday.'

I kept my arms crossed and glared at her.

'Honestly, Lucy!'

'You don't understand, do you?' I protested.

'Oh, I understand all right. You wanted to get up with Della and me and play shuttlecock and talk with those boys and you couldn't or, more likely, you wouldn't. So you got angry and spent the rest of the afternoon sulking. You wouldn't even do any more practice— you sat moping on the verandah instead!'

'But yous all went off with them boys and left me behind!'

'No,' Pim admonished, wagging her finger at me as if I were a naughty child. 'No you are not going to make me or Della or anyone else feel guilty for something you could have changed. You left yourself behind. You could have made things happen differently.'

'And how would that be?' I furiously interjected.

'You could have watched us play. You could have dragged yourself over. You dragged yourself to the water all right.'

'Aye, I did. All the way, and what's more across sand it was. And I was tired. I'm still tired. Look at yourself: you're strong and able with legs like a pair of hams. You've no idea what it's like to pull the dead weight of your body like that, do you now?'

Pim reddened, but she was not going to relent. 'Anyway, if you hadn't bitten his head off when he offered you some help up, I reckon Ambrose O'Connor – he was the one who came to get the shuttlecock – he would have sat and chatted with you. He wanted to, but you, you—! What did you do? Get your fur up and spit like a cat at a dog.'

'He was looking at my legs!' I shouted.

'So what?' Pim shouted back. 'All right, you've got legs like a newborn foal. You've got one foot smaller than the other. One leg's shorter than the other. Your feet hang. You can't wiggle your toes. You've got one hell of a scar running down your left leg and two on your right. I looked at your legs, too. So what? Why be rude to someone who only wanted to be friendly?'

I looked down at the covers and bit my lip hard to stop the blush I could feel sweeping over my face. It didn't work so I squeezed my eyes shut.

'Listen, Lucy,' Pim's tone softened and I felt her hand lean on one of my legs. I could not move my leg away. 'Listen. I didn't come all the way here to get caught up in some wretched argument about your precious polio.'

'Get off my leg! Let you not talk about that for I'm fed up with it!'

'For Pete's sake, I said I wasn't going to talk about it! I came to ask you something. Do you want to know what it is or not?'

I shrugged my shoulders and looked over at the fireplace.

'Fine,' Pim stood up. 'Then I'll go.'

The prospect of being left alone again was, at this point, unbearable.

'Don't, Pim. Will you not stay a little more?'

'And argue with you? No thank you.'

'Please?'

'Oh, so you do want to know?' Pim leant against the doorpost and folded her arms.

I nodded. If that meant more of her company and less of Mrs Murphy's, so be it. But I was not at all prepared for what she had to say.

'I'm going to the country for a few days after Easter to stay with my Aunt Rose and Uncle Ted,' Pim explained as she sat on my bed again. 'Rose wrote the other day to ask if I wanted to bring a friend. I don't usually, but I thought you might like to come.'

'Myself?' I sent a wary glance in her direction for I had not left Pim's house in the best of moods. Pim smiled at the reaction she had caused.

'Same as the maths test when all you could think about was that decimal point in the wrong place,' she remarked. 'Apart from the shuttlecock we had good fun on the beach, didn't we?'

'Aye, we did.' The thought of the water made me smile again.

'And the morning's rehearsal was terrific.'

'Indeed it was.'

'So would you like to come to the country?' she asked.

'Myself? How can I? What am I going to do? I can't!' I lamented. 'I can't walk! I can't ride a pony! I can't— And I'll never be allowed! Not after yesterday! You should have heard my da when he found out—'

'Calm down and forget about your legs for a minute will you? Mum's written a letter to your folks. Would *you* like to come?'

****

Whatever Pim's mother had written in that letter to my father worked a miracle. Daid and I met Pim, Benny her brother and Mrs Connolly under the big clock at Central Railway Station. Pim's mother was determined to have a few words with my father and pulled him aside. Stooping slightly, with one hand on his chin, he listened to all she had to say, which seemed to have something to do with my polio. When he did chance to speak, Mrs Connolly had difficulty in hearing him. This forced him to bend a little more and raise his voice, something he never ever did.

We loaded our compartment. 'Cello, viola, bags, chrysanthemums picked from our front garden and a basket packed with a Connolly style lunch were placed inside, and Daid double-checked everything to make sure all was safe. He gave me his blessing and smiled in a rather worried way. Waving a last farewell, he carefully closed the door behind him.

The train passed through Strathfield. I bid a silent good-bye to all I had known of the world for the last few years and sighed as the train pulled across that private boundary. Pim became busy with our meal and the two of us dined upon an abundance of sandwiches, fruit and chocolate, and washed it all down with tea packed in a thermos.

Pim pulled out her knitting.

'You're knitting something, Pimmy Connolly?'

'Certainly looks that way.'

'What is it you're knitting?'

'Footy scarf. For Bertie. Bertie goes for the Shoremen. Gotta get it finished.'

'A long scarf it is.'

Pim nodded and clicked away.

'You got brothers?' she asked.

I shook my head.

'Sisters?'

'Only myself.'

'Crikey.'

I pulled out *Amusements in Mathematics* and began another puzzle.

'Say, do you normally read like that?'

'I do.'

'You'll ruin your eyes if you're not careful.'

'You've a right to know I see perfectly well up close.'

Pim clicked and clicked away. The afternoon sun made itself at home, stretched out its legs and, hushed by a chugged lullaby, nodded its head against my shoulder. Dudeney disappeared down celadon hills, a blanket of darkness descended and dim forms steamed far, far into the distance...

'Wake up, sleepy-head! We're here and we've gotta to get out quick smart. Station Master's holding the train for you.'

Pim pulled two bags along with her and bashed her way down the corridor. A yell brought in a broad man – taller than Daid – clad in jodhpurs, long boots and an old, tweed jacket. He ducked his head as he entered, held out a huge, sausage fingered hand, introduced himself as Mr Pearse and ducked out again with my 'cello. Pim returned full of vigour, grabbed her viola, stuffed her knitting in the basket and pummelled me outside. A splash of crispy freshness welcomed me to Moss Vale.

'Have a good trip?' asked Mr Pearse.

'Fine, Uncle Ted. By the way, this is Lucy.'

'Bit slow, Pim, we've already met. You forgotten something?' Mr Pearse made a cursory glance of the luggage he had loaded into the buggy.

'No. What?'

'Kitchen sink?'

'Go on, Uncle Ted.'

Our remaining items were loaded. Pim, after lavishing attention on the horse, sprang up and encouraged me to do the same. But I could not climb up. Her uncle lit his pipe and took advantage of that operation to assess my predicament.

'Just a minute,' he mumbled as he put his pipe in his mouth. Then he walked back down to the station.

With the assistance of a step stool borrowed from the station master, he helped me over to a surprised Pim, jumped up, clicked the reins and we set off at an easy trot.

'You're from the Emerald Isle I hear, Lucy.'

'I am, Mr Pearse.'

'Then you should find yourself quite at home. I imagine it's not as lush as you're used to but we had some rain ordered before you came. Hope it's to your liking.'

It was. Oh it was! We clopped away through the township and out into a wide green world wrapped with sunshine and tied with ribboned hedges. Hidden inside were rare treasures: cottages with chimney smoke, horses in paddocks, thickets, roads of stone, tall pines and leaves of flame and gold. And an old wooden bridge and elm-lined drive undid the strings of the most beautiful parcel of all.

It was laced with lavender, rough-hewn and Georgian. There were rose bushes too, and an amiable clump of cypresses conversing in a corner. Small paned windows blinked shyly in the sunlight, and the front porch with its modest pediment, smart straight columns and double door introduced itself with friendly formality.

The door opened. A little boy with feathery blonde hair scrambled down the steps and ran up the path. Pim leapt out and ran towards him, picked him up, swung him round, tickled him and smothered the him with loud blowy kisses. Two more children romped out and were soon tossed and tickled and kissed to their hearts' content.

'Lucy, you able to climb down by yourself?' It was Mr Pearse.

The step was too low.

'Never mind. I'll lift you off. There you go.'

He set me down and passed me my crutches before calling Pim and the children to help him with our things. He was met by a host of eager hands which tugged our luggage inside. Taking custody of my 'cello, Mr Pearse invited me to follow. We were barely half-way down the path when Pim gave a whoop of delight.

'Aunty Rose!'

And she dumped her viola and ran and hugged the tall, sandy-haired woman who had come out onto the porch. Warm exchanges followed before Pim brought her to me and beamed an introduction. Pim's aunt did not seem to mind my callipers and crutches. There was an affectionate embrace and I found myself the recipient of two kisses, one on either cheek.

'Lucy! Welcome! I'm glad you could come. I'm Mrs Pearse. You've had a long trip.'

I nodded and endeavoured to say something about the flowers I now handed her. Unfortunately they had arrived in a somewhat wilted state despite Daid's efforts to wrap them well.

'Why, they're lovely! And they'll revive once we put them in water. You'll see. They're home grown, aren't they? What a pretty garden you must have!' remarked Mrs Pearse as she escorted me down the path. Before I even realised it, she was helping me with the front steps. 'Pim,' she continued. 'Your room's ready. I'll let you show Lucy where it is. Have a wash and come and get some tea. I'll get a vase right away.'

Pim's aunt left with the flowers; and her uncle, after storing my 'cello in a safe place, wandered back to see to the horse and cart. Pim bounded up the stairs, yelling out for me to follow.

One look at those stairs and I knew I was not going to get up the way I would have liked. Fortunately no one was around. I lowered myself onto the second step and began to pull myself up backwards.

A door was wrenched open, an impatient call to hurry followed and Pim thundered down again.

'What the dickens are you doing?' she stopped in her tracks

I could not look at her and felt all too acutely the painful presence of that old torture: that slow, studied stare. Why did she have to come out then? I heard

Della's voice inside and I tried to smile but to no avail. No smile could rise above the nervous paralysis that had seized my heart. I continued to climb in silence.

'I've never seen you go up stairs like this,' she squatted next to me and moved up in the same way.

'You haven't, but these are steep steps and this is the way I climb steep steps.'

Once at the top, she helped me onto my crutches, pushed me into the bathroom and ordered me to tidy myself.

A pot of tea and a plate of hot scones with jam and fresh cream awaited us at the kitchen table. Pim and her aunt exchanged family news in a manner which seemed, from its intimate jollity, more sisterly than anything else. As always with Pim, there was an explanation. Aunt Rose was Mrs Connolly's youngest sister and had been raised with the Connolly family since she was a baby. 'In fact, she didn't really become my aunt till after the War,' remarked Pim. Aunt Rose laughed in agreement and offered more scones.

'There time for a ride before tea?' Pim asked as she finished her fourth scone.

'Just a short one, Pim,' replied Aunt Rose.

'C'mon Lucy, I'll show you around,' Pim rose from the table and took another scone.

Aunt Rose watched me reach for my crutches. I coloured and muttered a tentative 'Excuse me', and followed Pim out of the kitchen.

Pim pulled a couple of apples from a barrel and took me out the back door.

'You'll need this,' she said as she passed me one.

'But 'twas a plateful of scones I've eaten already,' I replied.

'Not for you, silly, for Jezebel. She always likes an apple before she goes for a ride.'

'Your horse is it?'

'Nah, Captain Thunderbolt's mine. Couldn't bring him to Mosman so I keep him here. You're riding Jezebel.'

I halted. 'Myself, you're saying?'

'Of course,' Pim answered. 'Don't know how else I'm going to show you around.'

'But—!' I protested.

'Your calliper things?' said Pim. 'Take 'em off.'

'How can I?' I began to panic. 'What about my boots? 'Tis a spanner I'll need for to take my boots off my callipers. I've not a spanner in my pocket!'

'Don't worry, Lucy,' Pim confidently replied as she continued to walk towards the stables. 'Hughie'll have a spanner. Hey! Hughie!' she called.

A young man with a well-baked face came out as we neared the stables.

'Pim!' he called back as he leant against the doorpost. 'Thought I heard you. How're you going?'

'Great. Got a spanner on you? Lucy here needs a spanner to get her leg braces off.'

135

Such was my introduction. Hughie knelt down and studied my boots and callipers as if he were examining a fetlock. Had I been an able bodied horse, I would have kicked him or at least given him a good whisk with my tail.

'Should have something that'll do the job,' he remarked as he inspected the calliper.

'Why did you have to do that now?' I complained to Pim as Hughie ambled inside to find the tool.

'You and your polio,' Pim sighed. 'Didn't matter to Hughie. You could tell him the sky was falling and he'd work out how to fix it. He's that sort of bloke. Look, you go plonk yourself on those bales of hay over there and get your braces off. I'll saddle up.'

Hughie reappeared with a spanner.

'This do?' he asked as he passed it to me.

I took it and fitted it over the nut of the calliper. 'Aye,' I whispered.

'Beaut. I'll saddle Jezzie for you.'

Pim and Hughie conversed in their lazy drawl while they prepared the horses and brought them to where I was sitting. Soon I came face to face with Jezebel, a stately old mare whose name was a humorous mismatch for what was undoubtedly a placid temperament. She let me pat her and I pulled the apple from my pocket and fed it to her.

'You lead her out,' said Hughie. 'That way she'll know who's riding her. You can mount her from the fence. You're tall enough and you look strong enough. Reckon you can pull yourself up?'

Somehow, with a bit of a push from Pim, I managed to climb the fence in question and somehow, with more pushing and pulling and tugging and fumbling, I was able to climb on top of the poor mare which did not flinch, despite the clumsy operation. I gasped in pain as I stretched my right leg over the saddle.

'You all right?' asked Pim as she mounted her horse.

I nodded, still not quite recovered.

'Wanna get down?'

I shook my head.

Hughie, meanwhile, fitted my boots in the stirrups and passed me the reins.

'You're sitting well,' he observed. 'Give her a flick when you're ready,' he said. 'She'll know what to do.'

And off we set.

'Crikey!' exclaimed Pim with a smile as she looked across at me. 'You know how to ride! How did you know to hold the reins like that?'

''Twas my Uncail Eachan, my Daid's eldest brother, taught me.'

'In Ireland?'

'Aye, it was.'

'Did you have a horse of your own?'

'I did. 'Twas a white pony called Peigeasus. My uncle taught me to ride her bareback, you know, and without using my hands. Not a chance there'd be of doing that now with my legs all gammy.'

'Well, you're doing all right. And don't worry. I'm not going to make you rise to a trot. How do you like it?'

We rode across a paddock and up a small hill. From our knoll, Pim pointed out the neighbouring farms, the boundaries of her Uncle's property, some kangaroos bounding towards the creek, the Goulbourn road and the direction of the town, and I feasted for an age upon that rich, verdant meal with its piquant sauce of chill air, its flavour enhanced by the golden liqueur of the setting sun.

****

But I paid for my pleasure. The horse-riding expedition left my thighs so badly bruised that I could not put the callipers on when I dismounted. There was nothing I could do to make the pain go away. To make matters worse, the night turned cold and frosty. I fell asleep from exhaustion, and when I woke the next morning, the result was what I dreaded most: stiff, frozen, aching legs.

I could not move.

And there was no Daid to help me: no Daid to warm and ease my limbs, no Daid to tell how much it hurt, no Daid make everything right again. There was not even a Mrs Murphy.

Pim's bed was already made. She was nowhere in the room. There was no noise to indicate that she might be upstairs, either, and it was always easy to tell where Pim was. I laid my glasses aside and sucked my pillow.

A distant clatter of hooves, a bold push of the front door and a loud query as to my whereabouts confirmed her presence. Her heavy thud up the stairs was soon heard, the door was thrust open and a sponge was thrown in my face.

'Wakey, wakey! Rise and shine! Sun's up!'

Pim pulled off my bedclothes. Too occupied with removing the sponge to resist, I let her do as she pleased.

'Up we get!'

I tightened my hold on my pillow and closed my eyes. Suddenly, savagely, my feet were wrenched.

'Mo Dhia! Cuir stop leis! Cuir—'

'What the devil's the matter with you?' Pim stopped dragging me off. My feet were thrown back on the bed and Pim thumped down beside me. I buried my head in the pillow.

One foot was raised. I winced. It was lowered again. A hand pressed the other.

'Blimey! They're blue with cold, Lucy. I'm getting Aunt Rose. She used to be a nurse. She'll know what to do.'

Out she dashed before I could protest, trumpeting my predicament as she went.

That was news indeed. Pim's aunt may have been a kindly soul but she was a

137

nurse. And I knew that no matter how kind they were, nurses could inflict a great deal of pain: especially the ones who knew what to do. I stopped sucking my pillow for fear I would get into trouble if I was discovered. Nurses did not like pillows being sucked. There I lay, listening in dread for voices and footsteps. Sure enough I heard them, faint murmurs and thuds which became more distinct as they approached, to the point that words could be heard. Pim was describing my blue legs to her nurse-aunt.

The door opened.

'Lucy,' Aunt Rose came and sat beside me. I could not move away. She placed her hand on my shoulder. Her hand was soft and warm. 'You're not well. Are you in pain? Did you sleep at all?' My back was slowly rubbed, round and round, and my hair was gathered and smoothed. 'Now let's have a look at those legs.' I clutched at what I had managed to salvage of the blanket. I did not want her to see my legs and feet in their weak, raw state. I did not want her to touch them. 'Show me,' she persevered. 'Don't be frightened. I'll try not to hurt you, darling.'

Usually when people said that, torture was sure to follow. I prepared myself for the worst. The blanket was coaxed away from my fingers. Aunt Rose's hands wended their way over my spindly lower limbs and nursed and stroked my dropped feet.

'Pim,' she whispered. 'Go and get me a good jug of warm water, a few towels and a sponge, Uncle Ted's goanna oil and some sulphur. Emily will show you where to find everything. And do it quietly.'

The door was banged shut before that last word was uttered. Still stroking my feet, Aunt Rose continued.

'It was a cold night last night. Did you have enough blankets? I'll get an eiderdown out for you. It's nice and light and it should keep you warm as toast. In the meantime, we're going to have to try and get you on your pins again. We can't have you spoiling your holiday with your legs all stiff. What a shame that would be. We'll have an easy day today, though: a good massage, a nice hot breakfast, a little rest and maybe a short trip in the cart this afternoon. Somehow I don't think we'll be doing any riding today,' she laughed a little. That was as close as I came to a scolding. 'It's a lovely morning outside – very cool at the moment, but it'll warm up. Emily and Jack will be eager to play with you so you needn't be shy of them. They're very keen to make friends and they would love to show you their pets. Ah! That sounds like Pim.'

Aunt Rose opened the door for her niece who entered carrying a tray of supplies. Pim watched while her aunt sponged my legs.

'I noticed you play the 'cello. Have you been learning long?'

She talked about music while she worked. They had recently bought a player piano which was a favourite entertainment, and she listed some of the rolls they had and sang a few tunes to see if I recognised them.

'My, your legs are looking better already and I need to make your breakfast. Lucy, the most important thing is to keep warm. Sprinkle some sulphur in your socks. Put on a couple of layers – you'll feel cosier that way. When you're ready, put your braces on and come and get something to eat. Pim will stay to help you.'

'Did I hurt you before?' Pim took charge.

'Aye.'

'I'm sorry. I forgot. What do you need?'

Upon my request, she threw socks, stockings and clothes in my direction.

'You want help with those leg braces?' she asked.

I sighed at the callipers which had been placed out of my reach near the wardrobe.

'What's up?'

'I don't want to wear them for 'tis too heavy they be and I'm bruised right where they do up.'

'You don't have to wear them, do you? You *are* on holiday, you know.'

'But I can barely walk without them.'

'And by the look of you, I don't think you can walk with them either. Don't worry, Lucy, we'll look after you.'

'But what about the stairs?' I asked. 'I cannot get down the stairs, Pim.'

'Never mind the stairs,' Pim replied. 'I'll get Ted. You finish getting ready and wait there.'

There was no chance to object. Pim dashed down and charged outside sending the news of my difficulties to the four winds. In due time there was movement back on the staircase, a knock on the door and Mr Pearse entered with his niece at his heels.

'Gotta bit of a problem here? You'll be right. We'll carry you down. Ready?'

He deftly scooped me up and took me from the room. As we departed, I cast an anxious look after my crutches which had been left abandoned next to my bed.

Down to the dining room we went.

'Well done!' welcomed Aunt Rose as I was lowered into my chair. 'Right on time. I've just put the tea on the table.'

She returned to the kitchen and came out with a plate.

'Here you are, Lucy,' she said gently as she laid my breakfast before me. 'A nice, hot breakfast. Enjoy it!'

With an affectionate hug of my shoulders, she left me to my meal. Try as I might, however, I could not touch it. There on the plate sat a plump potato cake coated with oats, cooked on the griddle and cut into four. And there were two goodly rashers of bacon with large, ruddy heads and well-streaked tails. My soul swelled with the waves of salt tinged memories that crashed hard upon the rocks of my heart. All the ugly, unsightly, uncomely things of seven years past broke and splintered and scattered their debris across its shore. And deep beneath the waters was a face that looked up and smiled at me – the face of a fiery-haired fairy with eyes of glistening green, a fairy who had once filled our home and hearth with laughter and love – and who now lay cold and dead in a deep dark grave in Galway.

14

'Lucy? You awake?'

The voice was all wrong. It was friendly enough, but it should have been light and crisp with a pretty Scots lilt.

I shivered and pulled the rug closer to my chin. The rug was wrong, too. It was knitted in bright coloured squares. Where was Mam's cashmere that she used to coddle me on a winter's afternoon? Where was my red flannel blanket?

'Lucy? You all right?'

'Who— who are you?' I made an effort to speak in English.

'It's Pim, silly. You know, Pim from school. Pim who plays the viola. Pim who took you riding yesterday. Philomena?'

'Why do you be here?' I asked.

'What do you mean?' she replied. 'Where do you think you are? Heaven?'

All the green began to make sense. 'For a minute I thought I was Home again is all,' I sighed. And before I could stop them, I felt the tears well in my eyes.

'I don't believe it!' said Pim. 'We've already bailed out the dining room, you cried so much. You'll flood the garden too if you're not careful. Crikey.'

She wrapped her strong arms about me.

'I thought you'd gone stark raving mad,' she continued. 'You sat at the table, staring at your bacon, with tears streaming down your face and none of us could make sense of a word you said. In fact, it took us a while to get anything out of you that sounded like the King's English. Then you held on to Aunt Rose for dear life and wouldn't let go until you fell asleep. You've been asleep ever since.'

'Asleep? Arrah!' I muttered. 'And what time is it now?'

''Bout four-ish. Just a minute.'

Pim excused herself and left me puzzling over the sinister deadness that seemed to trouble my legs. I leant over and tried to rub some life into them.

There were voices. I looked up but I could only make out the blurred forms of two figures coming towards me.

'Lucy, darling, it's Mrs Pearse,' began Pim's aunt as she sat. She took my hand and guided my fingers around what turned out to be a pair of eyeglasses.

'I'm short-sighted, you know,' I murmured as I peered at the black frames. 'Mam says I'm short-sighted, like my Da.' I put them on but they did not help much. Salt had crusted over the lenses and they were greatly in need of cleaning.

'Dear me,' remarked Aunt Rose, 'they're not much good, are they? I'll go and wash them for you. And what about something to eat? You must be hungry.'

She left me with Pim who had sat down at the far end of the wicker settee.

'Pim,' I whispered. 'I cannot move my legs.'

'Have you gone that barmy?' she replied. 'Lucy, you had polio. Your boots and crutches are down here.'

It was reminder enough. Memories torrented in – of falling, of long months in a plaster coffin, of endless days with my legs fixed in splints, of being unable to move or do a thing for myself – and with them, another wash of tears.

'Oh dear!' exclaimed Aunt Rose. 'Pim, would you mind taking the tray?' I felt myself cradled in Aunt Rose's arms. 'You've had a very sad time,' she said as she stroked my hair. 'Well, darling, you can cry all you like, provided you don't miss any more meals. Will you do that for me?'

Somehow I managed to laugh, sniff and sob simultaneously.

'Good,' replied Aunt Rose. 'Now Lucy, hold on to me and I'll sit you up and fix your pillows.'

She made her final comforting touches, smoothing out the rug and wiping my eyes with her handkerchief. 'Your specs are nice and clean now. Put them on and have something to eat.'

Aunt Rose placed before me a bowl of Colcannon.

'Here we go again,' said Pim as she watched more tears fall.

I sniffed and wiped them away.

'Another favourite?' observed Aunt Rose.

'Aye,' I replied.

'Then honour your dear mother's memory and eat it all up. What would she say if she saw you push it away?'

I wiped my eyes and reluctantly began to eat. Then I realised I was very hungry.

'Good?'

'Aye.'

And she continued to sit by me, her warm, freckled face with its wide-spaced, hazel eyes content to follow the passage of every mouthful.

'Do you look like your mother, Lucy?' she asked as I finished.

I shook my head.

'Spitting image of her dad she is,' commented Pim.

'Do you remember her?'

'She was like a Botticelli, only real,' I closed my eyes and pictured Mam's face before me. 'Mam had soft hair – spun from silk of the finest copper-gold – and skin like alabaster and emeralds for eyes. They used to laugh, her eyes. You'd look at her and she'd laugh them at you, and her mouth would twitch before it smiled and while you talked as well.'

'Like you do?'

'I do that now?'

'You're doing it right this very moment,' smiled Aunt Rose. 'Save that your eyes are not laughing quite as much as I imagine they might.'

'Aye, well she was always scolding and teasing and laughing and telling all in one breath was Mam. But she was gentle, too, and of an evening when I'd snuggle close to her by the fire or when she put me to bed, she'd listen to all my sayings and doings and we'd read together – she loved poetry my Mam did – and we'd say a prayer for this and that.'

'You have lovely memories of her, Lucy.'

'Aye. Only— well, that's all they are,' I sighed. 'Memories.'

'No,' corrected Aunt Rose, 'they're more than mere memories. They're *your* memories. They're part of you, and you are part of your mother, darling. How lucky you are to have those memories! Now, it's getting chilly and I need to check the roast. Pim, can you find out from Ted when he plans to be in?'

Pim strode off towards the sheds. Aunt Rose, meanwhile, picked up my boots and fitted them on my feet.

'Aunt Rose?' I asked.

'What is it, Lucy?' she answered with a smile.

'Would it be putting you out if I called you Aunt Rose?'

'Not at all, Lucy.'

'You see, you're as close as I've come to a real mother in years. I'd forgotten what it was like.'

Aunt Rose gave me another hug and passed me my crutches. Together we walked back to the house.

'Did your mother nurse you through the polio, Lucy?'

I shook my head. ''Twas the nuns did. Mam died before that. The polio happened around Easter time and Mam died before Christmas the previous year. During the Troubles it was she died.'

A concerned look passed over Aunt Rose's face. 'The Troubles? In Ireland you mean? Was she killed, Lucy?'

I nodded slowly. 'Aye, she was.' And then I spoke of something I had never spoken of before. ''Twas the Goddam Black and Tans shot Mam.'

Aunt Rose opened the back door and studied me very carefully.

'You didn't see it happen did you, darling?'

Again I looked into her trusting face and nodded.

This time, however, there were no more tears left to cry.

''Twas the day I got my glasses,' I began. The delicate smell of roast lamb and rosemary wafted through the kitchen. Aunt Rose bade me continue while she tended to the meal. Her youngest little one, Angus, ran in and she gave him a hug hello. He helped her collect some potatoes, piling them into her apron. These they brought to the table. Aunt Rose put her son on her lap, passed me a knife, took up another for herself and we began to peel.

''Twas a half day from school that day, it being the feast of the Immaculate Conception, you know,' I resumed as I peeled. Somehow, peeling potatoes helped the words come out. 'I walked home for lunch and then Mam and I we walked to the occulist for to collect my speclaí. After that we had a pot of tea and some apple cake at Mrs O'Malley's tea shop. That was when Mam told me we were going to have another baby. She was so happy about it, you know. Then Mam decided to show me how bright and beautiful the world looked now I could see properly, so we visited all our favourite places. To the Claddagh we walked, and we stopped on the bridge to watch the swans on the river. We made a visit to the Blessed Sacrament at St Mary's church, which has fine mosaics of fish in the sanctuary, and I said a prayer for the new baby and counted the fish. After that, we set off for home. 'Twas getting colder, so we stopped for to buy some chestnuts. We were near the college when we heard the lorries. That was when Mam remembered the curfew. Well, we kept close to the wall and one lorry rolled by. Full of soldiers it was and they shouted things at us that didn't sound very nice. Mam blessed herself and pushed me behind her. Another lorry drove past. Then some shots were fired. A soldier on the truck fell down as they fired shots from that truck. Mam dropped the chestnuts and fell back on top of myself. I remember her looking up at me and trying to smile or tell me something, and then it was as if the world stopped still. Not a word I said for a long time after that. Not for months did I speak.'

I raised my glasses and studied the potato to make sure I had not missed any skin or eyes. I took up another potato, and in an effort to stop my hand from shaking, began again to peel.

'You know, I've never told anyone how it happened,' I said as I looked across at Aunt Rose. Now it was Aunt Rose whose eyes had become wet.

'Not even your father?' Aunt Rose kissed and stroked the top of Angus' head.

'Not even my Daid.'

'And so your father has looked after you all these years?'

'Aye.'

'All by himself?' Aunt Rose queried in a very puzzled way.

'Aye. After I fell sick there was talk of putting me in a home but my Daid wouldn't hear of that. He did everything for me when I came out of hospital. I used to beg him to make my legs work again, so he'd rub them the way my Uncail Eachann used to do to the horses and he'd wrap them in the warmest, softest wool he could find. Every morning he'd do it, and again at noon when he came for lunch, and then some more before I went to sleep at night. He wore himself out with it. Some mornings I'd wake up and find him asleep in a chair next to my bed, still in his clothes. But he got me walking again. He found me some crutches and taught me to use them. And then he helped me walk without them. He's never given up on me, Aunt Rose.'

'But he couldn't have done all that alone, Lucy. Doesn't anyone else help out?'

''Tis an old cow comes to help from time to time,' I admitted, reluctant to disclose that piece of information.

'Oh. And does the old cow have a name?' Aunt Rose arched her brows. 'Is it Buttercup?'

''Tis Mrs Murphy,' I smiled. Buttercup was hardly the name to give Mrs Murphy. 'And she doses me on martyrs, miracles and castor oil every chance she gets.'

'I see,' mused Aunt Rose with a knowing smile. 'Well, I'm sure she tries her best.'

'Well, 'tis a poor best,' I mourned. 'And it's not the same as having a real mother.'

'No it isn't,' Aunt Rose agreed. 'But I gather you haven't been the best of patients either?'

How did Aunt Rose know that?

'It's not easy to nurse someone whose sorrow is greater than their sickness, darling,' she observed. 'You can help their ailments but many a time you cannot help their hearts. And there are times when it seems you can do nothing right. I was in a war, too, you know.'

'You were?'

'I was twenty-two and I went to France to do my bit for the boys on the front. I nursed. I had to tend young men with the most horrific injuries. Some had lost their sight, others had lost limbs, still others were badly burned and all were terribly disturbed by what had happened. I did what I could – we all did – but mostly it was the girlfriend who remained true, the wife who was strong and faithful, the family that stood by that really brought them through.

'I remember there was one such fellow,' Aunt Rose took up another potato, 'a trooper who'd been thrown from his horse. The poor lad had lost both his legs and things were looking pretty bleak for one arm. He was in tremendous pain and we had to keep him heavily sedated. But he was so very gallant – deeply courageous – particularly given his injuries. We used to call him Romeo because when he was conscious he was always talking about going home to his Juliet,' she smiled. 'It was the one thing that mattered to him. I wrote her in the end: one of those difficult letters breaking the news and offering encouragement. She took the trouble to write and thank me. It was a lovely letter, and the look on that trooper's face when I read him her reply, assuring him she would keep the home fires burning, was a joy to behold. I always hoped it worked out for Romeo and Juliet. For others, unfortunately, such loving support wasn't there at all, poor fellows, and it was very hard indeed,' she sighed, 'for everyone.'

'Aye,' I agreed. 'I've given Mrs Murphy a rough time, you know. Would you believe that when I was in a wheelchair I used to prefer wetting my pants to having her help me? And that was all because I wanted Mam. It upset my Da when I did that. But I'm telling you that if it ever occurred to Mrs Murphy to make fatai cakes, then things might have been a little different.'

'I dare say,' Aunt Rose's eyes twinkled. 'And what if there had been no Mrs Murphy?'

While I had often wished that the cat had eaten Mrs Murphy and the Devil eaten the cat, I had never considered the implications as seriously as I did now. I bit my lip in thought.

'We'd better get those potatoes on or they'll never be done in time,' Aunt Rose interrupted my speculations.

Angus gave a shout when Pim galloped in with Jack on her back and Emily prancing alongside her shouting for her turn. It was the children's tea time. But before the kitchen was turned into a corral, Aunt Rose intervened with firm indications that there were to be no horsy hands at the table. Contention arose over this for Aunt Rose and Jack had very different standards regarding cleanliness. Oblivious to dirty fingernails and patches overlooked, Jack insisted his hands were clean. His mother was not going to be contradicted and gave him marching directions under my supervision to make sure he did the job properly before he took his tea. While Aunt Rose, Pim and I prepared the rest of the vegetables, Emily and Jack chatted about their day around the farm. Squeals of delight followed when Pim galloped them upstairs and saw to baths and bed.

During my long sleep, the Pearse family apparently had taken the initiative to move all my things down to the parlour. There I went, to find that the room had been transformed into a very charming albeit makeshift bedroom, with clean white sheets, a pretty quilt and piles of pillows on the day-bed. On the little table beside it was a vase of flowers and a lamp. *Amusements in Mathematics* had even been found and placed beside the vase, ready for me to read. I also noticed my nightgown neatly folded and tucked under the pillows, and my callipers propped against the end of the bed.

I did my best to dress for dinner, found ribbons and pins for my hair, re-braided it and tried to put it up.

Whoever had been responsible for arranging the room had decided that I could do with some literature, for another book lay underneath my Dudeney. I picked up what turned out to be *Pride and Prejudice*, read the first two lines and dismissed it with a sneer.

Pim appeared.

'Hey look at you,' she said. 'Nice hair.'

'And you really think that now?' I asked as I returned my glasses to my nose. Pim had thrown on a velvet frock in place of her jodhpurs.

'Of course. A bit old-fashioned, but nice. C'mon. Dinner's ready.'

Uncle Ted and Hughie, scrubbed up and ready to dine, rose from their chairs when we entered. Aunt Rose had prepared a splendid roast and it was followed by treacle pudding. Conversation flowed around the Easter Show, the polo and the farm; around the children's escapades and family memories. Then we gathered round the player piano and sang song after song from Gilbert and Sullivan.

But there were other songs which were had that night: songs which had no sound; songs which were sung with the eyes and heart. Aunt Rose had a special message for everyone, but when she sang, she sang for Uncle Ted, and when he sang, he sang for her. Hughie and Pim sang as they shared the pedals on the pianola, and I sang my own songs for the mother and father and home I had loved so much.

15

The light rattle of teacups and a dainty plate of bread and butter brought a welcome bedside visit from Aunt Rose the following morning.

'How are you today? Were you warm enough?' she whispered as she handed me my tea.

'Much better I am thank you, Aunt Rose.'

Aunt Rose smiled and sat beside me while I drank.

'We thought it would be easier if you slept here in the parlour,' she maintained her soothing *pianissimo*. 'That way, you can come and go as you please. No one told us you had that much trouble with stairs. We never would have put you upstairs in the first place if we had known. Did you sleep comfortably?'

'Aye, I did.'

'Good. Now let me take your cup and I'll see to your legs. Are they still stiff?'

'A little stiff they are.'

'Well, lie down again and I'll give them a quick rub. Then get ready for breakfast. I've something to show you I think you might like. Pim's already had hers. She's been out fixing fences with Hughie this morning. She should be back soon.'

Aunt Rose, gentle as ever, began to massage my legs.

'Lucy?' she asked.

'What is it, Aunt Rose?'

'I think Pim would appreciate knowing what happened to your mother.'

I sighed. 'I don't know that I could tell it all over again, Aunt Rose.'

'Pim's a big-hearted girl but she can be a bit dogmatic,' Aunt Rose continued. 'It does her good to know others' stories. What's more, she thinks the world of you.'

'She does?'

'Yesterday, she hardly left your side while you were asleep she was so worried about you.'

'She's becoming a grand friend to me, you know.'

'And I think you're becoming a good friend to her, too.'

'Well, I cannot think how that could be for I cannot do all the things she can do.'

'Perhaps not, Lucy,' replied Aunt Rose. 'But there are a good many things you can do. More to the point, though, it's who you are that matters.'

My massage over, I prepared myself and ventured to the kitchen on my crutches, brimful with curiosity as to what Aunt Rose had in store for me.

'That was quick,' she smiled. 'Come here. I thought you might like to learn how to make potato cakes. Then you can cook them when you go home. Maybe you could even show Mrs Murphy how to make them.'

I did not know whether to laugh or cry.

'How did your mother make them?'

'The same as yourself there,' I sniffed. 'And they were seasoned with songs. Boxty she called them. "Boxty on the griddle, boxty in the pan. If you can't make boxty, sure you'll never get your man."'

'Well, you'll be sure to get your man now, Lucy,' Aunt Rose laughed.

'Boxty or no, I don't stand a chance,' I sighed as we mixed the flour, potato, milk and eggs. 'Look at me: I'm tall and I'm thin, with a big mouth, a long, pointy nose and a jutting chin. I wear thick glasses and I limp. I'm as ugly as sin, Aunt Rose. What man could ever want the like of me?'

'The man who thinks your nose is fine and straight instead of long and pointy. The man who thinks your chin fits very well with the rest of you. The man who also happens to notice that you have beautiful fair skin, a pretty voice, elegant hands and a very endearing smile when you choose to show it,' she quickly replied, looking me square in the face. 'And perhaps if you wore your hair in a more modern style instead of those plaits, you would not be quite as plain as you think. Now shape the mixture into balls and roll them in the oatmeal.'

'But what about my legs? All boys ever do is stare at them.'

'Well, maybe something more could be done to help you to walk better. After all, your right leg is quite a lot stronger than your left. You shouldn't have to brace it so heavily. Perhaps—' Aunt Rose caught sight of my face and decided not to pursue that matter. 'Never mind, Lucy. I'm sure there's a young man out there who can see there's more to you than crutches and callipers. And if not, well they're not worth knowing.'

We cooked the boxty golden brown. Bacon was fried and Aunt Rose sat me down at the kitchen table.

She continued to work and talk while I ate. Already she had been up since dawn to milk the family cow and see to Uncle Ted, the children, Hughie and Pim.

'What would you like to do now?' she asked me as she took my plate. 'Some 'cello practice?'

I did not want to go and sit in a room all by myself.

'May I stay and help you, Aunt Rose?'

Aunt Rose glanced over her kitchen. 'I'm nearly done here, Lucy.'

'Please?' I implored.

'Very well,' she smiled. 'You can cut the apples for tonight's apple pie,' and she laughed as she caught my eye. 'Another favourite?'

'Aye. With lots of cream. Will there be cream with it, Aunt Rose?'

'Of course, Lucy. And farm fresh, too.'

I commenced my job of peeling and coring and chopping. Aunt Rose eventually came over and began making the pastry.

'Did your mother make apple pie, Lucy?' she asked.

'She did,' I smiled as I looked over at Aunt Rose and remembered the way the dough stuck to Mam's fingers, 'except she used potatoes as well as wheat flour for the pastry.'

'Potatoes?'

'Aye. We use fatai for everything in Ireland.'

'Hey there, sleepy-head,' Pim strode into the kitchen, leant over the table and helped herself to a slice of apple. 'Hughie and I hitched up the pony cart. Wanna come for a ride, Lucy?'

'Another ride, Pim?'

'What a good idea,' enjoined Aunt Rose. 'Can the two of you go to the post office and pick up a parcel for me? I'll make some sandwiches and you can take a picnic. Lucy, could you turn on the tap so I can wash my hands? Then run and get ready.'

I came outside and found Scruffy, a pony much loved by the Pearse children, harnessed to a cart. Thankfully, the opening of the cart was low to the ground so I was able to get in and out without much help. Aunt Rose passed us some baskets and provided us with instructions.

'When you collect the parcel, make sure you post these letters,' she tucked a couple of envelopes into our picnic basket. 'Now this other basket contains the altar linen, and whatever else you might do, please don't put anything on top of it. The altar linen needs to be taken to Father at the presbytery and the third basket has a few provisions for Father and some preserves and pies for old Mrs Cox. Do you remember where Mrs Cox lives, Pim?'

Pim said she remembered and we were soon on our way.

'Would you like to drive?' asked Pim as we turned onto the road.

'Indeed I would,' I replied, 'if you're not minding.'

Pim passed me the reins and we set off towards the station at a leisurely pace.

There was ample time to talk and Pim wanted to know all about Ireland. So I began to tell her bits and pieces about the little four-roomed cottage where we lived, about the Claddagh and the fishing boats, about the wild, grey Atlantic and the farms and fields with their crumbly stone walls and the remains of homes that fell to ruin after the Hunger.

'So how do the horses fit in?' asked Pim.

'They've been part of my Da's family since olden times. My Daid's da managed the stables on one of the estates and his daid did that before him. My Uncail Eachann trains horses, you know, and so does his son. That's my cousin Liam who's a fair bit older than myself.'

'Racehorses?'

'Aye. All my Daid's family had something to do with them: Uncail Eachann trained them, Uncail Breandán shoed them, Uncail Ciarán rode them, Daid drew them and, well, Uncail Ruaidhrí drank their health.'

Pim chuckled. 'So your dad's from a large family?'

'Aye, he is. Daid had four brothers and three sisters grown up. But 'tis only my Uncail Eachann and my aunts alive now. My Daid's other brothers were all killed.'

'What? In the War? But you said nothing about that the other night.'

I shook my head. 'Not that war. 'Twas when us Irish fought the English for to rule ourselves.'

'Oh,' Pim grew thoughtful.

''Twas my Mam died the same way, you know,' I ventured, and little by little I began to tell Pim what happened.

'Crikey,' Pim quietly responded. 'You know, Lucy,' she began after a pause, 'I always thought that sad look you have was because of the polio. I had no idea that happened to your family. I'm sorry, really sorry. Crikey.' And she grew quiet again.

'So it's your dad,' Pim resumed, 'and your cousins and your uncle— What's his name?'

'Uncail Eachann.'

'Him,' she gestured, 'and your aunts still alive?'

'Aye. All my aunts are nuns,' I continued. 'Would you know I've three aunts and five girl cousins – they're Uncail Eachann's daughters – and they're all nuns?'

'Looks like there's not much hope for you, Sister Augustine,' Pim wryly remarked.

'Well, here's hoping against hope, Sister Scholastica,' I replied. 'I'd sooner die than become a nun.'

'Me too,' Pim agreed. 'Gosh it's good to see you smile. Any other cousins?'

'A few in Belfast there be on my Mam's side, and some in New York, and probably some second cousins by now, for I think my cousin Liam took a bride a year or two ago. But I don't know my Belfast cousins very well and my New York cousins not at all. We've not any family out here, though, save my Daid and myself.'

Pim nodded thoughtfully.

'Wanna sandwich?' she presently asked.

''Tis a grand family you have, Pimmy Connolly,' I began as we ate. 'Will you tell me some more of them?'

Pim obliged. 'I'll start at the top. Mum and Dad: best parents you could ever want. Paddy – he's my oldest brother – left for the War when I was about four as you know, so I've only a few memories of him. Things like him coming home with rabbits over his shoulder, a gun in his hand and a dog at his side. He used to give me horse rides, too, on his back. Lily and Leo are twins. Lily's like my second mother. She lost her fiancé in the War but and never married. Leo should have been a priest but he ended up studying accountancy when he came back from France. He never married either. It was Lily, Leo and Mum's idea to sell the farm and start the guest house after Dad got sick. When they bought it, the place was going to rack and ruin. Anyway, they worked like Trojans and did it up. I was boarding at school by that stage. Every time I came home for holidays they'd have done something new: a room decorated – Lil even stencilled a wall to make it look like wallpaper – an old piece of furniture restored or the garden replanted. They run that place like a ship now.'

''Tis a fine job they've done,' I acknowledged. 'And who's next in line?'

'Polly – Sister Scholastica – you know her, I believe.'

'Aye. 'Tis some of her class that I help with reading,' I replied.

'How'd you ever get roped into that?'

''Twas sport that I mitched one afternoon.'

'Truanted?'

'Aye. But I don't mind helping out like that. I quite like it, in fact. And 'tis far better than being forced to do sport, I'm telling you.'

'Bet it is,' remarked Pim. 'Anyway, Annie's after Polly. She and my brother Bobby are both married. Annie's got five children, Bobby's got four. Benny, whom you also know, looks after the car and the grounds. He's a mechanic and a bit of a handyman. Bertie looks after the vegetable patch and the chickens. He was born with a few 'roos loose in the top paddock. He's all right but. Leo looks after him. Gracie left school last year and helps with the house. Johnny you're going to meet in a little while.'

'He lives in Moss Vale?'

Pim nodded. 'He's curate here. He was ordained last year.'

'A blessing for your mum and dad, that was.'

Pim nodded. 'They've always prayed for a priest in the family. Well, they finally got one.'

'Did you not leave someone out? 'Twas only ten brothers and sisters you mentioned then. There's yourself of course, but are you not an even dozen?'

'Well, we're a baker's dozen if you count Rose. You don't miss much, do you?' replied Pim. But she did not come forward with any more details.

We entered the township and became occupied with finding the post-office, posting the letters and collecting the parcel. We did not return to our conversation until we were on our way to the presbytery.

'My sister Peggy doesn't live at home any more,' Pim explained with a sigh.

'Is she not well?' I asked.

'Who knows.'

'Peggy hated leaving the farm,' Pim eventually resumed. 'She hated the guest house; and whenever she came home from school, she'd spend her time complaining that no one ever paid her any attention. Then she left school. Wouldn't go back. Mum tried to get her to help out but she wouldn't pull her weight at all. Got a job in the city instead and started mixing with a loose crowd. Then one holiday, when Gracie and I came home from school, we found out Peggy had left for good. She hasn't been back since. That was five years ago.'

''Twas a shock for you, Pimmy Connolly?'

Pim looked at me. She seemed very upset indeed, even angry.

'She didn't even say good-bye, Lucy.'

''Tis hurt she must have been losing your brother and seeing your dad get sick and your older sister and brother suffering.'

'It's been hard for all of us, Lucy. But you don't jump ship because of it. Peggy did the wrong thing. Now she's got a kid, which makes it even more wrong.'

'Maybe she's not as strong as yourself.'

'Maybe she's selfish,' retorted Pim. 'Listen, Lucy, I really don't want to talk any more about it.'

'Well, at least she isn't dead,' I quietly replied.

Pim heard me but did not retaliate. She flicked the reins and we set off at a trot.

We passed the church and Pim slowed the pony to a walk. Coming towards us further down the road was a dark figure on a black horse with a black and white dog at his side.

'That's him,' said Pim. 'Hey, Johnny!' she yelled and waved.

Pim's brother raised his broad-brimmed hat in reply.

Presently we came face to face with Father John Connolly. He was dressed in clerical garb over which he wore a long, black riding coat and long, black riding boots. At first he seemed very preoccupied, but he brightened a little when Pim greeted him again and made her usual introductions. He responded with another raise of his hat and nodded a 'Pleased to meet you' as he did.

As with the other Connollys, Father Connolly was red-headed and freckled and had the same merry brown eyes. But his hair was more russet than carroty in colour, and was closer-cropped than his siblings. He also appeared taller and thereby a little less stocky, a fact which was confirmed when he dismounted.

We walked down the drive together.

'Where've you been?' began Pim.

'Robertson's farm,' her brother replied. 'Sick baby.'

He grew quiet again.

'Getting better?'

Father Connolly wearily shook his head.

'Doesn't look good,' he drawled and walked a little further in silence.

Pim waited for his next remark.

'The mother's not taking it too well.'

There was another pause. 'It's hard when they're young like that.'

More silence.

'Don't think I'll ever get used to it.'

He looked across at the two of us and sighed.

'Just gotta trust, don't you? C'mon Snow,' he called to the dog and headed towards the stable.

'You wanna cuppa?' Pim called after him.

'Be great. Thanks,' called back Father. He stopped at the stable door. 'Back door's open,' he said. 'Father Dwyer's on retreat so there's no one home. You can go inside. I'll be with you in a minute.'

Pim was familiar with the presbytery. She led me through to the drawing room and picked up a large black kettle from a stool next to the fireplace. Then she pulled a canister of tea from the mantelpiece and ordered me to spoon the tea into the kettle. She filled the kettle with water from the kitchen, hooked it over the fire and began to stoke a hearty blaze.

Father Connolly soon reappeared, a cassock and leather pumps replacing his riding gear.

'Tea's nearly ready,' said Pim.

'Ah, good,' Father smiled. 'Afraid I haven't got anything to wash it down with, apart from a bit of bread and butter.'

'Don't worry, Johnny, Rose baked you a cake. Altar linen's here too.'

A grateful smile lit up his face and he rubbed his hands together.

'I'll get some plates,' he said.

We sat at the fireside and enjoyed a hearty cup of tea accompanied with thick slices of buttered brack.

'How's the folks?' inquired Father.

Pim readily provided details and anecdotes, and her brother gradually relaxed in his enjoyment of family stories. More brackbread was sliced and buttered and brother and sister chatted and argued, joked and reminisced.

Father Connolly evidently was of a literary bent, for several classics were stacked on the side table next to the armchair where I was sitting. I picked up the one that was already open. It was poetry. Apart from Daid's volume of poems and what I was obliged to study, I did not read much poetry; but the book with its worn pages, the cosiness of the chair and the blaze of the fire made reading poetry seem quite a pleasing way to pass the time.

And so I commenced, rather casually, to read the verses there on the open page. At first I glossed over the lines. It was not a lyric piece of the kind my father occasionally liked to read, but was instead an essay in rhyme. I had to acknowledge it had a certain appeal. It was measured and orderly, pithy and precise, and it explored a favourite topic of mine: the ways of God and man. Before long, I was immersed in an argument that was as compelling as it was witty. I slowed my pace, carefully mouthed each line and began to attend to the finer points of punctuation and phrase. By the end of the poem, I was whispering the lines to myself:

> Cease then, nor order imperfection name:
> Our proper bliss depends on what we blame.
> Know thy own point: this kind, this due degree
> Of blindness, weakness, Heav'n bestows on thee.
> Submit. In this, or any other sphere,
> Secure to be as blest as thou canst bear:
> Safe in the hand of one disposing pow'r,
> Or in the natal, or the mortal hour.
> All nature is but art, unknown to thee;

All chance, direction, which thou canst not see;
All discord, harmony not understood;
All partial evil, universal good.
And, spite of pride, in erring reason's spite,
One truth is clear, 'Whatever is, is right.'

The fire cracked and cackled. I read that verse again. A log fell and the flames burst bright. At the same time, it seemed as if another fire had risen inside me as I riled against the line that now clamoured through the chambers of my mind and heart:

'One truth is clear, "Whatever is, is right."'

I glanced across at the argumentative, forthright Pim and her more studious brother-priest. They were immersed in a discussion which seemed to centre on their sister, Peggy.

'You're only saying that because you're a priest,' contended Pim.

'Yes, I am,' answered Father Connolly. 'A priest who also happens to be your brother. So I believe I have twice the authority. Listen, the way you shunned her at my ordination was disgraceful. It was hard enough getting her to come, only to have *you* turn your back on her.'

'She shouldn't have been there. She only does things to please herself.'

'*I* invited her. Do you honestly think it was easy for her? Come on, Pim. How do you expect her to return to the sacraments if members of her own family treat her so harshly?'

'So that puts *me* in the wrong, does it?'

'It certainly doesn't put you in the right. Hear me out, Pim. I'm not condoning Peggy's actions either. But at least she had the little girl— and quite frankly, she's doing a darn good job bringing her up. She needs forgiveness, Pim, not retribution.'

Silence.

'So what are you going to do about it?' Father Connolly demanded of his sister.

I turned back to the book.

'"Whatever is, is right."' How could that be? As far as I was concerned, 'Right', like it clearly was for Pim, was the Ten Commandments. 'Right' was doing what I was told. Not eating meat on Fridays was 'Right'. Wearing callipers, however heavy and horrible they might be, was 'Right'. Geometric proofs were 'Right'. Bach was 'Right'. Wait, I corrected myself, Bach was not 'Right': Bach was perfect. But 'Right' did not explain Mam's untimely death. 'Right' did not explain the polio. 'Right' did not explain wrong or bad or ugly or painful. Yet the phrase seemed to imply precisely that.

Who wrote such a thing?

I turned to the front cover and read: *The Complete Poetry of Alexander Pope.*

'Well, Mr Pope,' I remarked quietly. 'An armchair philosopher you be now?' And I began to flip through the pages. Presently I came across some biographical information.

It appeared Mr Pope had some credentials. He was twelve when he was struck with tuberculosis of the spine. It left him a hunchback and stunted his growth. I turned to the frontispiece and studied the picture of the poet. So this was a man who knew what it was to be sick. He did not speak from the comfortable position of health or wealth or fortune. I returned to the beginning of the poem and read it slowly, thoughtfully, and stopped from time to time to consider a few points by the firelight.

'Proud as Lucifer, that's what you are,' flickered the fire.

Those had been Mrs Murphy's words and I had to admit they contained a good measure of truth. I was proud. I had indeed set myself up as 'the god of God', bringing it upon myself to decree how life should be and resenting the fact that it was, in reality, otherwise. Now I began to think that perhaps my own predicament was not the application of a formula to a problem; it was not a cruel and logical equation with a single solution but instead was part of a great scheme way bigger than myself. And that scheme was not a wicked enterprise bent on making my life a misery. There was goodness hidden there. There was beauty and order and truth, and in some peculiar way I was rightfully bound within it.

All I had to do was to seek it out.

Suddenly I felt my foot touched. One of my crutches moved.

Who did that?

I found the culprit on the floor next to my chair: a black and white puppy. He was gnawing away on my sticks.

'Hoigh, a mhaidrín,' I whispered as I softly clicked my fingers. Soon my hand fell into the grip of tiny, pointed teeth. My efforts to remove my fingers resulted in more chewing and toying with my hand. Eventually I was able to free myself and pat the little fellow. I picked him up and put him on my lap. There he chewed and played to his heart's content.

'What a bonny lad you be,' I stroked his soft fur. 'Look at those eyes of yours. Why, they're bright as buttons!'

'You've made a friend,' remarked Father Connolly. Apparently he and Pim had finished their conversation on a positive note for they were both smiling at the sight of the puppy on my lap.

'He's a lovely puppy,' I replied.

'He belongs to Snow,' said Father. 'He's the last of his litter.'

''Tis as if he's put on his evening dress and spats, you know.'

'Border collie. Would you like him? All his brothers and sisters have been given away and I have an ultimatum from Father Dwyer: No more puppies in the presbytery when he returns from retreat. That's tomorrow.'

'I'd like very much to keep him, Father,' I replied.

'And what's your dad going to say to that?' Pim interjected.

'My Daid bees fond of animals. He'll not turn him away, you can be sure of that. You're not minding I take him, Father?'

'You'll be doing me a favour.'

'Guess we better get going,' said Pim as she gathered the plates.

'Leave those,' said her brother. 'I'll fix them.' He pulled his watch from his pocket, 'Time for me to prepare Sunday's homily. I'll see you out. C'mon Snow.'

So saying, he and his dog walked out with us to the cart. Father bid farewell to the puppy, patted the pony and gave his sister a consoling hug.

'All I have is a post box address,' he said as he passed her a slip of paper. 'I hope it's still current. I haven't heard from Peggy for a while. You'll try and get in touch with her, won't you? She'd appreciate it.'

'I'll try, Johnny,' sighed Pim.

'Good,' he replied. 'God bless.'

He stayed at the gate and waved us good-bye and did not return to the presbytery until we were well on our way down the road.

Our arrival at the Pearse farm was brought to Aunt Rose's attention by the jubilant shouts of her children:

'Mummy, Mummy! Come and see! Lucy's got a puppy!'

Aunt Rose, pulled out of the house by an excited Emily and Jack, exclaimed in dismay when she saw the little fellow who was being carried by Pim.

'Oh no! Not another dog!'

'Don't worry, Aunt Rose,' Pim reassured her. 'Lucy's taking him home with her.'

'Thank goodness!' she sighed as she wiped her hands on her apron. 'Where did you find him— Don't tell me: Johnny. Father Johnny and his dogs!' she laughed fondly. 'Well, bring him inside and he can have some milk in the kitchen.'

'There must be at least a hundred stories about Johnny and his dogs,' remarked Pim.

I called the puppy Danny Boy after Mam's favourite song. So Danny Boy he became, and that night while we sat round the hearth, building and rebuilding ivory walls as we rivalled each other for chows and pungs and kongs, he lay at my feet and happily worked his teeth on my boots.

16

If there was one thing that had to be done it was to make a sketch of the farm. I could not allow myself to leave without a faithful record of the home which had breathed new life into the dearest of memories. On our last afternoon we took the cart up the hill. There, with sketchbook in hand and an old set of watercolours beside me, I busily worked while Pim and Aunt Rose gathered mushrooms and Angus and Danny hunted for lizards and rabbits.

It had been some time since I had drawn a landscape, let alone painted one – not since those special times in Galway, in fact, when I used to go sketching with Daid. The confinement of the last few years instead had restricted me to detailed botanical drawings, carefully drawn still lifes and copies of Old Masters.

Had I been able to exercise more freedom of choice I would not have elected to use watercolour as my medium. Daid was a masterful watercolourist and there was no way I could emulate his skill. But there was nothing else available and I did not want to restrict myself to ink or pencil.

Painting in watercolour, however, meant that I was denied the luxury of an eraser to correct and refine my work. Once I overcame my initial dread of making a mistake, I made a rough notation of forms and then plunged into the paint. Oddly enough I found that process easier to execute without my glasses. Over the course of a golden afternoon, I played with the colour on the paper and worked in detail after detail: Aunt Rose and her little boy tramping across the field, the farmhouse cosily nestled among the cypresses, cows wending their way to the milking shed. The activity was very refreshing indeed. It was as if I were fashioning my world anew.

But I was a bit surprised with the result. In my enjoyment I had completely neglected perspective. Cows and cypresses, shed and stable, Aunt Rose and Angus, farmhouse and fields all seemed to float happily across my picture with total disregard for correct proportion, placement or depth. Blues and golds, greens and pinks and oranges splashed over the paper as one would romp in a puddle after the rain. And for once I did not care that it was not precise. In fact, I quite liked my uncalibrated, colourful composition, for every line and every shape seemed to sing with the sheer joy of the loves I cradled in the deeps of my heart.

Morning came and it was time to go.

There was a quick tap on the parlour door and Aunt Rose peeped in.
'Are you rea— Pim, what are you doing?'
'I'm cutting Lucy's hair.'

'Dear me! We must get going. Ted's waiting. Why did you have to start that now?'

Pim kept on snipping.

'Don't blame me! Lucy talked me into it! Don't worry Rosie, we're nearly finished.'

'Well be quick. I don't want Ted getting irritable.'

Snip, snip, snip, and more locks of jet black hair fell to the ground.

'You're hurrying, Pim Connolly, for I'm asickening keeping my head down.'

'You wanted it cut, so shut up and don't move.'

Aunt Rose called again.

'Let you be finishing *now*!' I tried to stand and was pressed back down again.

'Hold your horses. Two more snips.'

Snip. Snip. This time Pim let me get up. She passed me a mirror, handed my glasses back and told me to look.

The same old thin face found its hair cropped and parted to the side, sharply cut over the left ear and flopped over the right eye. Proud of her achievement, Pim declared I had the Eton look which, she said, was the latest style.

'Do you like it?'

''Tis short like a boy that you made it.'

'Of course it's short! What d'you think I've been doing for the last half hour?'

'Not short has it been since I was sick. 'Twas all my hair they cut off—'

'You said you wanted it short. So do you like it? *Yes* or *no*?'

There was an impatient bellow from Uncle Ted. Newspaper scattered with hair was frantically crumpled off the floor and scissors were snatched. Pim thundered out, yelling the fact that we were coming. I gave Danny a whistle and ventured a smile at the face in the mirror.

'My, that is smart. It makes you look brand new!' Aunt Rose thought my hair was splendid. 'Now have you remembered everything? Toothbrush?'

With a firm look in Uncle Ted's direction and without heeding a testy puff of his pipe, Aunt Rose ran through her checklist and proceeded to add a few more items.

'I have this basket for Danny. He can ride in it on the train. It should keep him out of sight. Pim, here's your basket to take home again. I've put in a rabbit pie, a few jars of pickles, some marmalade and a bottle of apple liqueur. Lucy, this basket has a few things for you and your father: two little rabbit pies, some mushrooms, a loaf of brack-bread, a bottle of goanna oil and some sulphur. There's an envelope inside which has the potato cake recipe, guidelines for cooking mushrooms, and a few surprises I thought you might like. You can return the baskets through Pim. Now be good the two of you and come again soon.'

She gave us each a hug and saw us into the cart with Angus. Uncle Ted was about to help me in when she gave a cry to stop.

'What is it now, Rose?' Uncle Ted did not hide his exasperation.

'Hold on a minute,' Aunt Rose had already turned and dashed back to the

157

house. She reappeared with the scissors in hand. 'Stay still, Lucy. Pim missed a bit.'

'For Heaven's sake, Rose, they'll miss their train.'

'All done now, Ted. Dear me, we couldn't send you back to your father with a few stray ends like that. All right, off you go.'

Waving good-bye, we set off down the drive. The house disappeared from sight as the cart rumbled across the bridge and I closed my eyes to fix it fast in my memory. To anyone else that bridge, wooden, rickety and shaded by elms, was a means to cross a tiny creek. To me, however, it spanned an ocean.

It was easy to spot Daid there on the platform when our train steamed in, and it was not merely his height that made him so identifiable. That afternoon he was wearing his Donegal tweed and the vest Mam had knitted the year she died. A natty bow tie, checked shirt, two-toned shoes and a jauntily fitted cap completed his ensemble. The soft, smoky blue of his jacket and trousers, the play of pattern, and the muted, moorland colours of his vest marked him as an artist, but any thought of dismissing him as a dandy was abolished by the cut of his suit which dated from well over a decade ago.

But five days' absence also brought to my attention what a solitary figure he looked as he waited on an otherwise busy station. Usually when I saw my father he was very close to me, not at the opposite end of a railway platform. I could not bear to see him alone that way, fingering the rosary in his pocket.

I gave a shout. Daid looked up. A zephyr of surprise lifted his features when he saw me coming towards him as fast as my crutches could carry me, with the porter and Pim, holding Danny, pacing along behind.

'Daidí!' I called again. Daid smiled and quickened his pace. Within seconds I was back in my father's arms.

Daid took off my hat, smoothed my hair and fondled my shorter locks. He studied my face and smiled and gave me another hug. I introduced him to Danny.

'Danny Boy you're calling him, Luighseach?' Daid subjected his fingers to a toothy introduction. He shook his head gently and smiled. 'We'll not turn him away. 'Tis in the washroom he can sleep. Anois, Pim,' Pim gave him a cautious glance. Clearly she was worried about what my father had to say about my hair, let alone the dog. 'Your mother's not come yet?'

'Don't worry, Mr Straughan. She'll be here soon,' she replied with evident relief.

'Then we'll wait here with you till she arrives. A grand time it's been for yous?'

I decided we were not going to have sausages for tea. Danny could have the sausages. So, while Daid went to Confession, I lit the oven ready for the rabbit pies and studied Aunt Rose's mushroom recipe while I shelled the peas and Danny chewed my boots. Daid returned with his customary creak and pause and knock on my door. This time he could not hide his astonishment when, jug in hand, he entered the dining room to find a meal already underway and a very different

158

smell wafting through the air. He did not say anything but continued with his usual routine now joined by Danny who was eager to learn the procedure. Daid took a little longer to get back to his room that evening.

There was a lot to tell him as we supped, and after our Rosary I fetched my painting and used it to show him round the farm as Pim had done me. What my father would say about the picture itself, I had no idea.

''Tis a fine painting you made, Luighseach,' he said. 'A wonderful palette of colour you used there.'

'There was no black in the paintbox, Daid, so I didn't know what I was going to do about putting in shadows. In the end, I didn't bother.'

'And if even if you did, lass, since when was a shadow ever pure black?' Daid replied with a smile. 'Will you be mounting and framing your painting now?'

I beamed with delight. 'I'm thinking to frame it in gold, Daidí.'

'A gold frame is it?'

I nodded.

'Then some gold frames I'll bring from the studio for you to choose. Would that give you pleasure?'

'It would.'

'And you'll be signing your painting, Luighseach. We'll not frame it unsigned.'

I wandered to my room, sat at my desk and took up my pen. In the corner of my painting I proudly signed my full name: Luighseach Meidhbhín Ní Sruitheáin. And I had good reason to do so, for bound together in that name was my own name, Mam's Christian name and Daid's family name, and I vowed I would sign it that way forever more.

Upon my return to the dining room, I encountered an unusual sight: Daid was writing a letter. Daid rarely wrote. When he did, the process was awkward and painstaking, partly because he was left-handed and seemed to hold his pen in a strange manner, partly because his labour presented such a stark contrast to his drawing which was so supple, so fluent and so expressive. There were faint gnawing sounds emanating from underneath where Danny was acquainting himself with his shoes.

'Luighseach, is it grateful's spelt "A-I-T" or "A-T-E"?' he asked.

'"A-T-E", Daidí.'

'And two "O's" after the "F" is it?'

'A "U", Daid.'

'And do you put the one "L" at the end, or two?'

'Only the one you put, Da.'

Daid had always been terrible with spelling.

''Tis a letter I'm writing to the Pearses for to say thank you,' he said. 'Will you be adding some lines of your own?'

I shook my head.

Daid looked up and tried to make me out without his glasses.

''Tis my own letter I'll write, Daid,' I reassured him. 'Tomorrow I'll do it.'

'Will you be going to bed now, lassie?' he asked.

'Aye.'

'And will you be needing me to rub your legs?'

'There's no needing, Daid,' I replied. The last thing I wanted Daid to see was the bruises for I had not told him of the horse-riding.

'Oíche mhaith, a Luighseach,' he said as he rose from his chair and gave me a kiss. ''Tis grand to have you back again, lass.'

I gave him a hug in return. 'Oíche mhaith dhuit, a Dhaidí.'

17

The next day, after Mass and breakfast, I sat at my desk and composed my thank you letter to Aunt Rose and Uncle Ted. While I wrote, I recalled some of the conversations I had had with Aunt Rose; and not only did I come to the conclusion that there was someone else I needed to thank, but also that she deserved more than a letter.

Since that particular thank you was not going to be easy, I decided to solicit Della's help. Della always knew how to say such things in the most pleasant way.

I quickly finished my letter, found a stamp, and after informing Daid of my intention to visit the Sothebys, took Danny on the train to Strathfield. We reached the Sotheby house and journeyed down the drive only to stop several feet short of the front steps.

Wally Sotheby was sitting there, with sunglasses on, smoking a cigarette.

I hid amidst the camellias and watched him and wondered how I was ever to get up the steps with him in the way.

Wally, however, had not noticed me. He could not help but notice Danny for the little puppy trotted straight to him and started to lick and nibble his hand.

'Hey!' he exclaimed at Danny's introductory bite. 'Hello there! Where did you come from?' And he stubbed out his cigarette and began to play with him.

Danny, of course, brought his attention to the crutches, sensible brown boots and metal braces hiding in the camellias.

Wally took off his sunglasses.

I blushed and bit my lip.

'Hello. It's Laura, isn't it?' he greeted me.

I shook my head.

'Louise?'

'Lucy,' I corrected him, assuming that if he hadn't yet remembered my name, he was not going to have much success if I gave it in Irish.

'That's right! Lucy Fibonacci!' he grinned, recalling the agnomen bantered about by the flirtatious clique on the station platform.

'Would Della Sotheby be home now?' I inquired.

Wally confirmed that she was. 'Would you like to come inside?' he asked as he gazed intently at me.

I shifted from one crutch to another and tried to spot Danny who had since raced off to investigate the lawn and shrubbery. I wanted very much to come inside but I wanted to enter alone.

But that was not to be the case.

'Allow me to show you in,' Wally smiled and held out his hand.

He escorted me towards the house. 'Dell's up in her room,' he informed me. 'I'm afraid she hasn't been too well the last couple of days.'

I stopped. 'And do you be sure I'll be able to visit, Wally Sotheby?'

'Of course you can,' he replied. 'She'll be glad to see you, I bet. I say, don't look so worried. She's much better. All she needed was rest.'

We reached the front steps and Wally immediately realised the impending difficulty.

'Do you need some help?' he asked.

'I can do for myself, you know,' I replied and demonstrated as much by planting a crutch on the step and levering one leg, then the other, and finally pulling up the other crutch. Danny, meanwhile, dashed up to the verandah and had a good sniff of the door mat and pot plants.

When I finally reached Della's room, I opened the door and let Danny push his way in. I remained on the landing and waited for the squeal. Then I edged inside and watched Della's honied enticements to 'come' followed by her motherly reproach against 'biteys'.

'Luighseach!' she gasped the moment she saw me. 'You're back! Goodness gracious! Look at you! You cut your hair! Whatever possessed you?'

'Do you like it, Delleen?'

'Dear me, yes,' she smiled as she rearranged the bedding. 'You don't look nearly so dour. Now tell me, what have you been doing? Your father said something about you being away when I telephoned. I didn't quite grasp the details because he's a little difficult to understand on the phone. It's like holding a shell to your ear and listening to the sea when he speaks.'

'Aye,' I agreed.

I told her of my week in the country. 'You know, Delleen, I nearly thought it would be the worst week of my life for my legs were troublesome and I could hardly walk. But Pim and her aunt and uncle took grand care of me.'

'I'm so pleased. And is he yours?' she asked, indicating Danny who had returned to his investigations.

'Aye.'

'Why, he's adorable.'

'And what of yourself, Delleen? You don't be well now?'

'Only terribly tired, that's all. I must be anaemic. Don't worry, old thing. I'll be right for school on Tuesday. What are you doing here on a Sunday afternoon anyway?'

'I wasn't going to telephone in case your mother answered, so I decided to come myself. 'Tis something important I'm needing to ask you.'

'What is it?'

''Tis no matter now, yourself being unwell.'

'Come on. You've come all this way to tell me something and now you're not going to breathe a word?'

162

'Delleen, I'm needing to visit Mrs Murphy this afternoon.'

'But Luighseach, she lives next door to you. What are you doing here?'

'I was wanting to ask you to come with me to visit her for I'm needing to see her and I cannot go alone.'

Della laughed. 'Nonsense. Don't be such a nervous nelly. Oh, I'm so glad you're here! I haven't seen anyone all weekend. So if you can spare a moment, may I tell you a few things? I've got some super news.'

'Have you now?'

'Absolutely. Best of all is Mummy is completely approving of our quartet and we have Mrs Mahony and Phoebe to thank for it.'

I completely failed to see what connection lay between Phoebe and Mrs Sotheby's best friend. Della noticed my puzzlement.

'Let me explain,' she began with a giggle. 'Now, you do remember that Mrs Mahony was hosting a garden party, don't you?'

I nodded compliantly but again was unable to see the connection.

'Well,' continued Della, 'it was a terrific success and Mummy's costume was simply superb. Now Mummy, as usual, was full of news when she came home from the party. Piffle mostly, but apparently Mrs Mahony had engaged a string trio for the occasion.

'Anyway, the next day I had made arrangements to do some practice with Phoebe. The problem with that was that I didn't know how I was going to convince Mummy to let Phoebe visit. I didn't want to tell a fib but I had no idea how else I was going to manage it. Well, old thing, no fibs were necessary. Mummy was surprisingly amenable to Phoebe visiting and to our doing some practice. In fact, she asked again how many people were in our quartet. Don't snigger, Luighseach!

'Really it was quite odd, but who was I to complain? Now it turned out that while Phoebe and I were practising together that afternoon, Mummy was discussing with Hammond how the garden was to be laid out for Spring. You see, that's when Mummy will be giving *her* garden party.'

'Now Delleen, will you be telling me what all this has to do with our quartet?'

'Be patient. I'm getting to that. Phoebe and I did an awful amount of work on the quartet, then Phoebe accompanied me for my Mozart sonata. Luighseach, she's positively amazing! Do you know that when she learns a violin piece, she learns the piano accompaniment at the same time? She knew my Mozart perfectly! *Both* parts! Oh, it was a dream playing with her! Phoebe admitted, though, that she doesn't really have a Mozart touch but I think she was being modest.'

I pursed my lips as I took in that observation. To me, Phoebe was more likely to be blatantly truthful than modest. But then, I thought, how could one be modest if one was not truthful?

'I say, are you listening?' asked Della.

'Aye.'

'Well, then we began to play the *Spring Sonata* which Phoebe also knew how to play because she learnt it last year. After that, Phoebe played the piano by herself. That was when Mummy, who had been listening to everything, decided to invite her to afternoon tea. So Phoebe joined Mummy and me for Devonshire tea on the back verandah. I must say Mummy's frightfully taken with Phoebe, which is little wonder, I suppose, given how pretty Phoebe is. Well, that day she was wearing one of her old-fashioned dresses. Mummy noticed that its collar was made from a very fine piece of lace. Phoebe explained that it was made by her grandmother. Of course Mummy then had to find out *who* her grandmother was. You know what Mummy's like. Phoebe said she was French. Her name was Fleurdelys Volcot and that she was a concert pianist.

"'Oh,' said Mummy. "No wonder you play so very well. What piece were you playing?"'

'Phoebe said it was Beethoven, which it was. According to Phoebe, old thing, we have a Beethoven style piano. Then Phoebe said the most preposterous thing I have ever heard her say in my life. She said, "I'm related to Beethoven."'

Della, by this stage, was engrossed in her narrative, and as was typical of her in these situations, she lapsed into pure dramatisation, imitating her mother and Phoebe drinking cups of tea and conversing politely:

"'Really?" said Mummy who, as you can imagine, was very, very impressed.

"'Oh yes," replied Phoebe. "You see, Ludwig van Beethoven taught Carl Czerny piano. Czerny was a famous pianist and teacher. He taught the great Franz Liszt. Liszt taught my grandmother, my grandmother taught my mother and my mother taught me. That's why *I* am related to Beethoven."

'Luighseach old thing, I had to try so hard not to laugh, for Phoebe was perfectly serious. As for Mummy, there she was, nodding her head in agreement.

'Anyway, at dinner that night, Mummy informed Daddy that Phoebe had been taught by Beethoven which, of course, was far from true as Daddy pointed out. So Mummy told Daddy about Phoebe's grandmother. Now, would you believe Daddy had seen Phoebe's grandmother perform years and years ago? What's even more intriguing is that her grandmother married a very old friend of Daddy's, a Mr Digby Devereaux. Daddy said he was an "Or-stralian" – you know how he talks. He and Daddy met when Daddy made the Grand Tour as a young man.'

'But Delleen, what has all this to do with our quartet?'

'Well,' Della resumed, 'the next day, Phoebe came over and we did more practice together. That day, Mummy had some friends for Bridge. They were playing in the small drawing room and we were practising in the large drawing room. Apparently Mummy's friends thought someone was playing a gramophone recording. They didn't realise we were only practising. They came in rather full of praise which was very nice. Mrs Mahony was particularly charming. She always is. Mummy then told them all about our quartet and how we were going to play at *her* garden party in September. She was very emphatic that she would have four musicians providing entertainment. I tried to stop her but Phoebe then interrupted and said we were going to play Haydn and told everyone how she was related to Haydn because Haydn taught Beethoven. So, my dear Luighseach, I'm

164

afraid I have to tell you that we are going to perform.'

I swallowed hard.

'I thought you said your mother didn't approve of playing in public.'

'She doesn't. But *this* is at *her* garden party. Besides, if it means creating a show, Mummy's more than prepared to bend a few rules. She's determined to outdo Mrs Mahony, and as far as Mummy is concerned a quartet outdoes a trio by one.'

'Mother of God,' I muttered. 'And you're letting her have her way?'

'Nothing will stop Mummy now, old thing. Phoebe and I had a big argument about it afterwards. I told her she was very naughty agreeing like that without considering what you or Pim had to say. I won't repeat what Phoebe said about that. How do you think I feel? I'm first violin and I have to think through a whole quartet in order to master it and lead everyone else. Mrs Epstein even made me copy out the entire score over Easter to help me learn all the parts. Now I have to learn more than one quartet! How will we ever have the repertoire for an entire afternoon? I'm sure it will work out very well and I'm quite excited about it but I don't know how I'm going to do it all!'

Della had exhausted herself. She began to cough and wearily laid her head back on the pillows.

'Don't fret yourself so. Will you be needing a drink, Delleen? You're looking a wee pale.'

'Would you fill my glass for me?' she indicated a jug of water at her bedside table.

'Well, you can be sure I'll be giving Phoebe Raye a piece of my mind when I see her next.'

'Don't be too hard on her, old thing. She's so keen to perform. She really can't help it. Frankly, I think she needs to perform. In fact, there's something more I must tell you.'

How much more did Della have to say? One look at her pensive little face told me that she had quite a bit more.

'I went to visit Phoebe on Friday. I felt I ought to apologise for the argument. Luighseach, you wouldn't believe what I saw. I knocked at the door and a man answered. I nearly screamed when I saw him because, I tell you, all he was wearing was a *bathrobe*. And he had vine leaves in his hair. You should have seen the hairs on his chest! Sure as I'm lying here, he had absolutely nothing on underneath. Luighseach, I was scared out of my wits. I couldn't even bring myself to say "Mr Raye" or introduce myself or anything. And he was not at all embarrassed. Then, the smell when I walked in! The hall was filled with the most peculiar sweet smell. I thought I was going to fall under a spell.

'He told me where Phoebe's room was. I went there as fast as I could and do you know what? Phoebe had actually locked herself inside. I had to knock and call several times before she would open it. She'd been smoking again and her room stank of cigarettes.

'We managed to make up, thank goodness, but I really couldn't stay very long.

I was beginning to feel frightfully ill. And as I left, her mother came out. My, she was strange. She was— well, floating— as if she were in a trance. I don't know how I managed to get home. I felt quite intoxicated really. Not that I've ever been intoxicated before, and I haven't been able to breathe a word to a single soul till now. Poor Phoebe, it doesn't seem as if anyone really cares for her. I know my parents have their peculiarities, but imagine living in a house like that with a father who dresses like Bacchus and a mother who cooks flowers!'

'And you're sure it was her father you saw, Delleen?'

'Well, I—I assumed it was,' Della was more perplexed than ever. 'He certainly wasn't the butler, although I cannot imagine how anyone's father could possibly— Oh it doesn't bear thinking about! I say,' she whispered, 'you don't believe what Leila said about Phoebe, do you? You know, about being born out of wedlock?'

I shook my head. 'I'm thinking her dad was in the War, Delleen.'

'Oh!' Della put her hand to her mouth, 'Dear me! Do you mean he might be a bit—?' and she put a finger to the side of her head and spun it in circles. 'Do you? But she *was* awfully quiet that night at Pim's when we were talking about the War, wasn't she? Oh dear! How terribly thoughtless of me to chatter! But she didn't *say* anything, Luighseach.'

'Aye, she's a queer one there's no doubting that, Delleen. Would that be the clock chiming?'

'Two o'clock,' remarked Della. 'I suppose you have to go?'

'Aye, I do. I'd best be on my way. 'Twas grand seeing you again, Della Sotheby. And you'll be well enough for to go to school?'

'I'm sure I will be. So I'll see you on Tuesday, old thing. Good luck.'

Danny eventually trotted out of Della's room, but he did not follow me to the staircase. Nose to the ground, he made his way into another bedroom.

He gave a delighted yap.

'Danny!' I called softly but urgently, hoping desperately someone was not napping inside.

More yaps. Then came low, curdling growls and a hiss. Danny had awoken someone but that someone was not human. Ming, the Sotheby cat, dashed out of the room, eagerly chased by my puppy. Neither animal heeded my crutches as they darted across the landing. To the floor I fell. The cat leapt down the stairs, with Danny scrambling and tumbling behind.

There was only one place of refuge for Ming. He sprang to the hall table, only narrowly escaping Danny who skidded recklessly over the tiles.

'Merciful Jesus, Mary and—!'

'The vase!' yelled Wally Sotheby who dived after the Majolica urn as it toppled from the table. Wally Sotheby may have missed a season of cricket, but that catch was first class.

'What on earth is going on?' I heard Mrs Sotheby's voice in the vestibule. 'A dog!' she screamed when Danny dashed past her, barking after the cat. 'My urn!' she screamed again and snatched it away from her son. 'Wally, what on earth do you think you're doing? Get off the floor!'

She restored her treasure to the table.

'Heavens!' she exclaimed, her hand to her breast.

Then she saw me, flat on the landing, with my crutches having slid half-way down the stairs.

'You again! Do you always visit impromptu?' she demanded.

'Only when I'm not invited, ma'am,' I replied as politely as I could.

Mrs Sotheby glared at me.

'Actually, *I* invited Lucy,' her son casually remarked, his face inscrutable.

'Take your hands out of your pockets,' scolded Mrs Sotheby.

Wally watched his mother leave. Then he climbed the stairs and picked up my crutches on his way.

'The like of yourself inviting me,' I remarked while I busily organised my legs. ''Twas nothing of the sort you did.'

'But I did invite you,' he smoothly corrected as he passed my crutches to me. 'I invited you inside. I say, Lucy,' his tone changed from jest to more serious inquiry. 'One thing is to get up the stairs the way you did. How on earth do you get down?'

I did not bother to explain. I gripped the banister, balanced myself on my crutches and swung my legs to the step below. Wally remained at my side and seemed to respect my silence.

'To tell you the truth,' I admitted between breaths when we were a good way down, 'I wouldn't mind throwing myself the rest of the way.'

'Ever fallen?' he asked.

'Aye, many a time,' I replied. 'I even dream about falling down stairs, and oddly enough 'tis always the same stairs – a timber staircase with blue carpet – can you credit that?'

'Hey! Careful! Don't do it again!' he steadied me, and in doing so prevented another fall.

'Thank you,' I said quietly and completed my descent without saying more.

Wally saw me to the door. 'Lucy,' he began, 'Nellie will be bringing afternoon tea soon. Would you like to stay? We could take it on the front verandah.'

'I— I can't for 'tis a train I need to catch. They don't be regular on a Sunday, you know.'

'Can't you take the next train? There'll be cake.'

'I was planning to visit someone else this afternoon,' I answered, now feeling the urgency to get to Mrs Murphy's house before dark.

'Uninvited?'

I looked up and saw a mischievous twinkle in his eye.

'Aye.'

And I found myself unable to withhold a smile.

'Well, you mustn't be late for your appointment,' he advised.

I had the feeling he was not mocking me as much as he was mocking members of his own family. Still, I could not help adding a remark in my defence.

'It's important,' I replied.

'Then I'll walk you to the gate. I say, where's your puppy?'

It took a little time to locate Danny who had long since dashed out in the direction of the back garden. Wally eventually found him and brought him round the front.

'Do you still catch the train to school?' he asked while we walked down the drive.

'Sometimes I do. It depends—' I halted. Wally did not need to know any more about the problems I had with my legs, he had witnessed enough already.

He opened the gate for me.

'Then I guess I'll see you soon,' he smiled. 'Cheerio.'

I resumed my journey with Danny trotting along, ever intrigued by the swing of my crutches.

So, we were going to perform at a garden party. Even the thought of it made me nervous. The devil with Mrs Sotheby! The devil with Phoebe for consenting and the devil with Della for not being more forceful! So what if Phoebe 'needed' to perform! I certainly did not. I did not need to play in front of others. My music was a private affair. It was my way of putting the world right again. My legs did not matter when I played the 'cello. I could fill my room with phrase after phrase, memory after memory, sing out whatever was filling my heart and the result was hardly ever a clumsy, awkward, stumbling mess. I did not like the idea of the world intruding on my sanctum of sound, let alone staring at me while I played.

On the other hand, I had to admit that playing quartets was proving more enjoyable than I expected. Perhaps if it had not been for the Polio I would not have minded so much.

'Stupid Polio!' I exclaimed in annoyance as I took a seat in the carriage. 'Stupid legs, stupid callipers, stupid crutches!' I exclaimed as I bent my knees and planted my crutches beside me.

If I were back in Galway I would not have minded performing, for music was a part of life there. If ever you wanted to learn a tune on the fiddle, you took yourself down to the pub to visit blind old Daniel Burke, and amidst the cheer you would fiddle away till you mastered it. Provided you paid with a pint, blind old Dan would always oblige a reel, a jig or an air. At any family gathering, someone – Daid, Liam, Uncail Breandán – was sure to pick up a fiddle and play. Quick as a wink, Uncail Ciarán would fetch his concertina, Uncail Ruaidhrí would grab a couple of spoons, Uncail Eachann would stamp in time and our family would burst into song and dance. On those occasions I had no hesitation of joining in. Then an argument would erupt. The argument would be appeased with a joke. Another song would follow, a story perhaps, then more songs and a dance or two. How many times had I fallen asleep amidst such a lively hullabaloo! But dancing and singing by the fireside was a far cry from playing quartets in the Sotheby summerhouse surrounded by snooty ladies in hats. And being able to leap and

168

kick and twirl and stamp at the drop of a hat was vastly different from being dependent on crutches and callipers to move about.

'Stupid Polio!' I exclaimed again. 'Stupid legs, stupid callipers, stupid crutches! And I'll be damned if I'll perform!'

I stared out the window and wiped my eyes. What would Pim say? I wondered, and I hoped desperately that she would take my side in the matter.

The train pulled in to Newtown station. I whistled to Danny and we alighted, climbed the stairs and wandered back up King Street.

By this time, I was not in any mood to see Mrs Murphy and my resolve was hardly strenghtened by the fact that we were not on very good terms, particularly after my last bout of cold.

Since that time I had done my utmost to avoid her. I did not speak to her during any of the Easter services, and today I remained in my pew after Mass and did not come out of the church until Daid came in to fetch me. The one occasion I did glance across the aisle to where she knelt, she glared at me and indicated with her rosary the direction of the altar.

Danny and I finally turned down Watkin Street. I stood for a while outside Mrs Murphy's house and deliberated over what to do. With a sigh, I opened the gate and walked up Mrs Murphy's path. I took a deep breath and knocked at her door, half hoping she would not be there and half hoping she would in order to get the whole business over and done with.

The door opened.

'Lucy Straughan. Well I never! What brings you here?'

I bit my lip and sent my eyes down to my boots. I ventured to look upwards and reached as far as the enormous safety pin that fastened her cardigan.

'Good afternoon, Mrs Murphy. I— I'm come to visit. I was after wanting to say thank you for caring for me while I was sick the other week and to apologise for my rudeness towards you. I been rude and I want you to know that I'm sorry for that. 'Tis much you done for me these years past and I've only ever been rude in return.'

To my utter surprise, Mrs Murphy was delighted. Danny was pronounced a lovely little doggy and I was welcomed inside for a cup of tea. Mrs Murphy made sure Tiger the cat was not around. Danny was then permitted inside. He found that a great treat for there was another feline smell to investigate upon admittance.

I had never been inside Mrs Murphy's house. Being a terrace house, it was darker than our cottage, but like our cottage it had floorboards which creaked. Mrs Murphy took herself into the kitchen and left me to wait in her parlour.

The parlour was a forest of cloth covered tables, battered chairs, pictures and statues. The Sacred and Immaculate Hearts greeted me upon entry, and their welcome was extended by St Joseph and St Patrick who had taken residence in opposite corners. None of these venerable inhabitants seemed to mind the dust as much as I did. Saints for all occasions adorned the four walls, photographs littered the mantelpiece and the largest rosary I had ever seen, with great wooden globes for beads, hung over the chimney piece and served as a second frame for a family portrait. Down at my feet was spread a rag rug which was very like the rug in my bedroom. Danny was especially taken by one armchair and it was easy to understand why – it was full of cat hair – and the presence of cobwebs in the upper corners was clear indication that Mrs Murphy kept more than cats in her house. The entire place made me shudder. However plain our house might have been, Daid and I were scrupulous about keeping it clean and tidy.

Mrs Murphy appeared with a tray, placed it on a side table and eased her person into her armchair. She invited me to sit down.

'Now Lucy, I know you take your tea strong and black. Would you like some bread and jam to go with it?'

'I would, Mrs Murphy.'

Mrs Murphy performed the required duties, offered me some bread and jam and we stirred our tea in expectation. The initiative was taken by the lady of the house.

'I was speaking to your dear father on Friday after Mass— such a good man,' she indicated to me with a firm nod of her head. 'He was telling me you'd been to the country for a few days and wasn't I pleased to hear that. It's a pity you didn't go for longer, I told him. It would have done you good to get some fresh air with your legs the way they are.'

It had to come up. Mrs Murphy never failed to mention my legs every time she saw me.

'And what is the air to do with my legs, Mrs Murphy?'

'Dear Lord,' Mrs Murphy continued, 'it would be nice to see you strong. It breaks my heart to watch you struggle when your father's so straight and tall. What a gentleman he is. He takes good care of you, Lucy. You look a lot like him and to see you stagger beside him with your legs in braces and those crutches— Child, you should be up and running around,' and before I could say a word, she was off again. 'Our Lord sends these things to test us, you know. We all have our crosses to bear and I pray that one day He makes you well, Lucy. You're still saying your prayers aren't you, dear?'

By this point, I had abandoned my tea and directed my attention to the photo that stood on the side table next to my chair.

I replied without looking up. 'You know very well I do, Mrs Murphy, and that I tell my beads of a night with my Da.'

'Good girl. The Blessed Virgin always listens to the sick. And even if there's no cure, she'll give you the grace to bear your suffering well. But make sure you're generous with your prayers. Have you still the devotion to St Jude?'

'I do, and to be sure I pray it from time to time: "O good St Jude—"'

'Then make the effort to pray it every day. That way there's bound to be a miracle. Did I ever tell you about Mrs Quinn?'

Mrs Murphy had told me about Mrs Quinn at least a hundred times. I removed my glasses to study the family photo more closely. Three hefty young men, two of whom were dressed in military uniform, stood around Mrs Murphy and her late husband. The photograph had been taken in front of the house.

I then realised that the usual rattle about Mrs Quinn had ceased. I put my glasses on. Mrs Murphy was looking directly at me. Embarrassed, I returned the photograph to the table.

'It's a lovely photo, isn't it, Lucy?' Mrs Murphy remarked as she offered me another slice of bread and jam.

I accepted.

'Is it your lads there, Mrs Murphy? I've not seen your lads around. I didn't know you had lads of your own.'

'Yes, Lucy. Them's my boys: Peter Murphy, Paul Murphy and Patrick Murphy.'

I picked up the photograph again. 'Will you be telling me who's who, Mrs Murphy?'

'Well, bring the photo here, Lucy, and I'll show you.'

I passed her the photo, struggled out of my chair, staggered across and leant against the arm of Mrs Murphy's chair. She pointed out each of her sons.

'They look fine fellows, Mrs Murphy. In the War were they?'

'Yes, Lucy. They all joined up. It was the two eldest first. Oh, they were keen! All ready for an adventure. And my, they looked smart in their uniforms – the smartest of them all. Wasn't I proud to see them off! Then Peter, God rest his soul, was shot down at Gallipoli. I remember when we got the news. A letter came telling how he went. He was a brave boy and died in the midst of a charge. We never heard more than that. Then young Pat said it was his turn to do his bit. Barely nineteen he was and off he went to France. I never saw him again. Our Paul was the only one to make it through. How overjoyed we were when he came back. It was only a limp he had – a slight one, not heavy like yours – 'cause he'd copped a bullet in the leg.

'But there was a lot more wrong. He'd lost his brothers and most of his mates, poor lad. He'd put on a brave face but you could see he was hurt inside. He started to drink a bit more than he ought. And the dreams he had! He couldn't talk about it. "You don't want to know, Ma," he'd say. "You don't want to know."'

'Aye,' I observed. ''Twas a bad war that, was it not? A few friends of mine have folk they lost or were hurt because of that war. Della Sotheby, whom you've met, she lost her dad, you know. And my other friend, Pim, who came to visit before Easter, her uncle was shot and her brother too was killed. So what happened to your Paul, Mrs Murphy?'

'The Influenza took him in the end, Lucy. At least that's what the doctor said. But my boy didn't die of influenza. My boy died in France with the rest of them. It was a broken spirit killed my lad and there was nothing I could do, nothing at all for my poor boy.'

Then I saw tears channel along the wrinkles of her face and fall over the photograph that shook in her hands, and at that moment I learned that Mrs Murphy saw me in a very different way to the way I saw Mrs Murphy. Even though Daid used to say she was a good woman, she was not my mother. She was a nuisance and I had no need of her. But strangely enough Mrs Murphy had need of me. She needed to care for me. To see me well was consolation that her efforts and counsels were not in vain. And Mrs Murphy and I had something in common. We both had lost those whom we had loved so much. But Mrs Murphy had lost much more than me. I had lost Mam and three of my uncles. That was much. But I still had Daid. Mrs Murphy, however, had lost her entire family. She had no one.

I took her hand.

'But you did a lot, Mrs Murphy. You were his mam. You can't be more than be a mother.'

Mrs Murphy was still for a long while and she kept holding my hand.

'God bless you for that, Lucy. God bless you.'

'He had so much to live for,' she continued. 'He had a sweetheart waiting for him. Such a lovely girl, too: Jeanie Riley. You've seen her at Mass, haven't you? You know, it's a wonder your father doesn't court her.'

'Too big and bossy,' I thought to myself as I recalled the various times I had seen Miss Riley pour tea and offer cakes at First Holy Communion breakfasts.

'But Paul wouldn't marry her,' Mrs Murphy resumed. 'He said she'd be marrying a dead man. How could he say such a thing, Lucy? He was alive! He'd come back alive!'

She began to sob again. Again I took her hand.

'Aye, but let you remember something, Mrs Murphy. Your lad was in pain and 'tis pain does strange things to a person. It twists your soul, you know.'

'But that's no reason to give up hoping, is it child?' Mrs Murphy gazed at me. 'Is it?'

Some months ago, I would have said it was. Now, however, I knew differently. I shook my head.

'And God will never test us beyond our strength. You know that, child, don't you?'

'Well, if that's the case, Mrs Murphy, do you not think God's opinion of how much we can handle is a wee too high?'

'Maybe it is, Lucy. You miss your mother very much, don't you, dear?'

Mrs Murphy had never spoken to me about Mam.

I nodded.

'I'm sure she's in Heaven, Lucy.'

'Aye, Mrs Murphy. And I know for sure she's still looking out for me. She's doing it from far away is all. Sometimes, though, even thinking that makes me pine for her the more,' I sighed.

Mrs Murphy squeezed my hand.

'But 'tis no point wishing for something that cannot happen,' I continued. 'And what of your lads, Mrs Murphy?' I asked. 'Let you tell me some grand things about them instead. I'm thinking there's a few tall tales tied up in your heart.'

'They're Paul's crutches you're using, you know, dear,' she remarked. 'The ones he had when he came back from France.'

'Is it the truth? Well, Mrs Murphy, I'll be telling you they're the best crutches I've had. I like them much more than the ones that go under your arms.'

'You'd be about the same height as my Paul. I never thought you'd grow tall as that. Ah, my sons were always healthy young fellows. Never had a complaint from them. All stout and hearty like their father. Sometimes I thought they'd eat us out of house and home. But the merciful Lord saw we never went without. They used to play cricket all day long in the summer time— Down in the side streets where it's flatter. Lots of boys used to play from dawn to dusk, and they'd come back for breakfast and back for lunch and back again for tea and they'd keep on playing until they couldn't see the ball. They did a few windows in but they paid for the damage. Only poor Arthur Harrison's left now. They all went to the front. They all thought it was a big adventure. How young they were!

'Oh and I remember when our Paul was in a Christmas play. He was a generous soul but his generosity went a bit far that time. Sister Agnes made him the innkeeper and dear Paul took such pity on poor Mary and Joseph out in the cold with nowhere to go that he invited them inside instead of turning them away. I laughed and laughed when it happened but I had to scold him afterwards for not doing what he was told. And do you know what he said to me? He said, "But Mum, wouldn't you have done the same?" Well, I daresay I would have. That's exactly what I would have done. Mr Murphy and I we always taught them to look out for those who were weak or needy, that God had given them strength and they had to use it right, not waste it on bullying and showing off. They had a few fights, but on the whole they kept clean my boys…'

She talked and laughed about old times. From out of the dusty box of memory came stories of Christmases past, of turns to serve at the altar, first girl friends, picnics and St Patrick's Day processions. I was not sure how I was going to leave until Mrs Murphy herself realised the time.

'Dear me, what a talker I've been! And look at you so patient. I'm sure you've plenty to do without listening to an old sod like me carry on like this. You're usually mulling over a puzzle of some sort or playing away on that fiddle of yours.'

''Cello it is, Mrs Murphy,' I interrupted.

Mrs Murphy did not hear. 'Lucy, your dear father'll be wondering what's become of you. Help me load the tray.'

I did as bidden. Mrs Murphy then asked me if I would not mind walking ahead and opening the kitchen door for her. I washed the teacups and pot while she attended to her stew.

'Thank you for the cup of tea, Mrs Murphy,' I said as she showed me to the front door. 'And I'm truly sorry for all the trouble I've caused you.'

'Think nothing of it, dear. I've always known you were a good girl.'

There must have been quite a perplexed look on my face for Mrs Murphy quickly continued:

'Oh, I've seen you many a time sitting under the orange tree in your back garden stroking old Tiger and going out of your way to give him a saucer of milk. And the effort you make to water the plants despite your poor legs. No love, you're a good girl who's had a bad time, that's all,' she smiled.

I had to force back the tears.

'There, there now, Lucy,' she said as she gave me a hug. 'You run along home to your dad. Good-bye, dear.'

And so saying, she waved me off, shooed Danny along after me and watched me from her doorstep. I opened our front door, saw Danny into the house and waved a last good-bye.

Daid and I sat at the table and quietly set about peeling and slicing onions and potatoes.

Mrs Murphy was a bit like an onion. Outside she was brown and flaky like an onion's skin, and the tangled tuft of roots that stood on the bottom of the onion was like the clump of hairs that grew from the mole on her cheek. I fingered the onion's roots and peeled away its delicate brown shell. As I did, I recalled the Christmas play incident and smiled.

'And did today go well with you, Luighseach?' I glanced up and saw that Daid was smiling too.

'Aye,' I replied as I chopped the onion in half. I angled my knife at thirty degrees and began dissecting the onion into equal sixths.

18

Daid promised he would have my picture framed by Tuesday. Rather than wait for him to bring it home, I resolved to collect it on my way back from school that afternoon. The bell tinkled as the studio door smiled open and I braced myself for the jovial welcome which awaited me whenever I dared venture inside.

Gingered and spruced in his suit and spats, Mr Birstall bowed under the counter and opened his arms out wide.

'Well, well, well, if it isn't young Lucy! Haven't seen you around for months! Where've you been hiding?'

'At school it is, Mr Birstall.'

'So I see, so I see. *And* don't you look smart. Come and have a look, Mrs Birstall. What do you think of our Morgan's Lucy in her uniform? Doesn't she look well?'

Mrs Birstall bustled into view. Taking a few admiring paces back to the counter, Mr Birstall joined his wife in a proud perusal of my person.

'Got roses blooming in her cheeks, hasn't she, Mr Birstall?'

I began to feel roses blooming all over and tried to bury them in my boots. Still, I could not help warming to their sunbeam praises and sent a quick glance through my hair in their direction.

'Good of you to say, Mrs Birstall.'

'Why you do, honey,' Mr Birstall bent down and tried to meet my eye. 'You've two fair posies in that puckish face of yours. You shouldn't be so hard on yourself, Lucy Straughan.' A sudden dash of his hand on the bench caused me to look into his twinkling tom-cat eyes with their whiskery brows and laughter lines. 'Now I know what you're here for. You're here for that painting of yours.'

'I am.'

A grin of Cheshire pleasure met my reply. Mr Birstall ducked under the counter and strolled out to the back room.

'Young Morgan had it finished for you this morning, Lucy.'

'Did he, Mrs Birstall?'

It always intrigued me that the Birstalls referred to Daid as 'our Morgan' or 'young Morgan' as if he were another son, particularly when Daid was considerably taller than Mr Birstall who was short and tubby.

'Here it is!' Mr Birstall placed my picture on the easel. 'Our Morgan was very pleased with it wasn't he, Mrs Birstall? Didn't it come up well? What do you think, Lucy?'

'I made a mess of the perspective you know, Mr Birstall. But I was wanting to put everything in – the house, Aunt—I mean Mrs Pearse, the hills and trees – I forgot about making the perspective correct. How could I forget the perspective, Mr Birstall?'

'Leave the perspective for the camera, Lucy. It's the colour I like. It dances.' And he rested one elbow on the counter and continued to view it.

'David,' Mr Birstall greeted his son who had come in from the solicitors' office across the road. 'Take a look at this.'

Mr David Birstall stopped to look at my picture. 'Unusual piece of work,' he remarked. 'That's not one of Morgan's is it?'

Mr Birstall shook his head and raised his brows in my direction.

'Crikey!' Mr David exclaimed with a smile. 'Is that Lucy?'

'Grown quite a young lady, hasn't she, son?'

'I forget how tall you are when you're not in your chair. Strike me a light, will you?' he reached into his pocket and tossed me a box of matches. 'So what's it like being a spotty dog?'

'A spotty dog, Mr David?'

'Didn't you know that's what everyone calls St Dominic's girls?' I shook my head. 'Because of the dalmation holding a torch on your school shield,' he explained as he indicated with his cigarette the embroidered emblem on my blazer pocket.

Mr David Birstall had only one arm, his right, having lost the other to a grenade at Gallipoli. He was about my father's age and was a very good friend. I did not tell him much about school while I helped him light up, for my first day back after Easter had not been the happy event I hoped it would be. Everyone in my class had much to say about their own holidays, but no one had asked me about mine. All that drifted my way were plenty of stares and a few snide comments about my new haircut:

'She looks like my cousin Robert,' whispered Fanny to Kate.

'No,' giggled Kate, 'she looks like Sister Augustine without her wimple'.

As for meeting up again with Della, Pim and Phoebe, news of the garden party performance had caused our friendship to take a very different turn indeed.

'And how's my Mavis?' Mr David asked, affectionately referring to his 'cello which he so kindly let me play.

'Mavis 'cello is fine,' I answered.

'Had a beer with your dad a few days ago. He told me you'd started playing in a quartet. Now if I know your teacher, you're playing Haydn.'

'Aye,' I smiled. It was always good to hear a jibe at Mrs Epstein's expense.

'So are we going to hear you play?'

I grimaced. Why, upon hearing about a string quartet, did everyone expect a performance of some sort?

'We are going to hear you play sometime, aren't we?' he repeated as he leant back on the counter.

If there was one person who ought to hear me play it was Mr David. I owed it to him.

'Aye,' I sighed.

'What's up?'

I told him about the argument I had had at school that day.

'And the only one who doesn't want to perform at the garden party is myself, for Pim sided with Della and Phoebe,' I explained. 'So Della Sotheby said she'd ask Kathleen Doherty to play instead, for Kathleen used to learn the 'cello, although she's not very good, Della Sotheby says. Then Pim said that if Della and Phoebe didn't mind having a boy as part of the quartet she'd ask Ambrose O'Connor who also plays a little. They left me out of it all,' I sniffed. 'Now I'll never have any friends!'

'Oh,' nodded Mr David and gave a thoughtful puff. 'Seems to me as if someone's going to have to give in a bit.'

'But—!'

'Just what are you afraid of, Lucy? Making a mistake or being stared at? Or both?' he eyed me as he tapped the ash off his cigarette.

If there was anyone who understood exactly how I felt about such things, it was Mr David Birstall.

'I cannot play in front of people, Mr David! Not with the callipers and all. Everyone stares at me and then my fingers don't know what to do and I can't hold my bow. Playing in front of Mrs Epstein's bad enough!'

'So you're going to spend the rest of your life playing Bach in your bedroom?' he stopped me. 'Lucy, I don't know a single musician who hasn't felt the same way. It's nerves, that's all it is. You know what I used to do to get rid of them?'

I shook my head.

Mr David gave me a nudge and whispered: 'I used to imagine the audience were all wearing their pyjamas. I still do, you know – new clients who can't seem to cope with the fact that their solicitor's a one-armed digger.'

It was not the answer I expected at all.

'Anyway, kid, if you're really worried about your legs, a longer skirt would work wonders. You'd hardly notice there was a problem,' he smiled gently. 'Go on, give yourself a chance, Lucy. You might be surprised. I think you know how you'll feel if you don't.'

'I couldn't bear giving it away now, Mr David,' I replied.

'Then there's only one way to go, isn't there?' he said. 'Forward. Cheer up! You can do it. You want me to get your father? Morgan's in isn't he, Dad?' he called out to Mr Birstall.

'Up top,' Mr Birstall called as he re-emerged from one of the back rooms. 'Had his nose to the grindstone all day. Want me to fetch him, Lucy?'

I shook my head. 'I'll go up my way, thank you all the same, Mr Birstall.'

Curious to find out who was making such an unusual ascent of the studio stairs, Danny clattered across and gave several barked encouragements from the landing. I hugged him hello, submitted my fingers to the usual treatment and continued to drag myself along the floor into the studio.

Daid shifted his posture in acknowledgment and proceeded with his job amidst Danny's continued skirmish of pattering and gnawing and my several attempts to pull myself up onto a chair. He sat on a hard stool, hunched over his retouching desk, peering through his magnifier, with his glasses laid beside him. Pencil in hand, its long lead shaved to a needle-like point, he was applying a series of meticulous downstrokes to a negative with all the assiduity of a monk at a manuscript. Shadowed by his lamp was the usual congregation of brushes, compounds, varnishes, gums and turpentine he had at his disposal. The rest of the room, however, was not as orderly as it usually was. A well chewed slipper now lay abandoned in the middle of the floor, and a fruit crate lined with an old blanket had been installed under the table for Danny's benefit. Not liking to leave him at home while we were both out, Daid had resolved to take Danny with him to work.

Daid's portfolio lay on the small table next to me. I leafed through it and introduced myself to the married couples who served as a sepia testament to my father's skill. Picture after picture depicted a perfect pair, smiling and flawless. Every portrait contained details that could only be admired: wisps of veil captured with delicate pencil touches, hands deftly modelled, gloves and petals softly formed. Set against a plain background, they did not really belong to this world at all.

Another of Daid's pieces was fastened to the easel in the corner. This was no photograph, however. It was a watercolour. Daid must have worked on it while I was away. It depicted a moonlit scene in which a jewelled landscape was set against a night sky of brilliant ultramarine. Glimmering gemlike tones and silver touches gave form to the fruit and leaves and branches of apple trees, and to the mythical robes of a pair of lovers in fond embrace.

Those figures troubled me. The man, with his tousled black hair, bore some resemblance to Daid himself. As for the woman, those burnished tresses were very much Mam's. But that was not how I knew Mam. Mam's hair was always braided, not long and flowing. And Mam was always busy. Even when she was quiet she was busy reading or sewing or making lace. When she listened, her lips would move as she followed what I was saying and her eyes were always bright and probing. My father was always so sensible, shy and pious. What business did he have in painting my mother – let alone himself – that way? The title disturbed me, too. 'The silver apples of the moon', which Daid had scripted in his distinctive Celtic hand, had an uncanny familiarity. I felt I had no right to be privy to that intimate, passionate world. Curiously, though, I felt entwined within it.

Danny's attention was alerted by a yawn. Daid stretched, blinked his eyes hard, groped for his glasses and looked at his watch. Then he began the methodical process of packing up. The negative was stowed away, the desk was folded down, a knife was applied to the pencil which then joined its companions in their box, and the box, along with the bottles and brushes, was stacked on the shelf. Daid removed his sleeve guards, laid them on the table and pulled his waistcoat straight.

'Dia dhuit, a Dhaidí.'

'Dia is Muire dhuit, a Luighseach.'

'A busy day was it, Daidí?'

'A good day, Luighseach. Your picture's framed.'

'It is indeed. 'Twas Mr Birstall showed me.'

'And it pleases you?'

'It does.'

'Where will you hang it now?'

'In my room, I'm thinking. Will it be well with you if I hang it there?'

'Aye it will. Are you ready for to go downstairs now?'

'I am.'

With a kiss and the sign of the cross on my forehead, Daid picked me up and carried me over to the stairs. Not having witnessed this operation before, Danny became excited by the fact that I was in my father's arms. He picked up the slipper and began to caper round Daid's feet.

'Cuir stop leis, a mhaidrín. Ná bí dána. Luighseach, I'll be putting you down.'

He eased me to the ground, saw to it that I was standing safely, and gave a soft whistle to the troublemaker.

'Danny, tar liom.'

Daid and dog disappeared downstairs. Issuing an Irish command to 'stay', Daid hurried up again, returned the slipper to its box and took me in his arms once more.

Danny witnessed our descent from below, his front paws on the bottom step, his eyes bright as onyx studs, his head cocked to one side, one ear pricked up and the other flopped over. Unable to contain himself any longer, he lowered his nose and prepared for a charge. A firm 'Fan thos ansin' from the two of us put an end to the attempt and he darted out of sight, announced our passage to Mr Birstall and scurried back to check on our progress. Happy to see me finally restored to a chair, he pawed over my boots and enjoyed a bout of finger play while Daid returned to collect his things.

'Lucy,' Mr Birstall ducked underneath the counter leant back against it and signalled Danny over. 'I was wondering if you could do me a favour?'

'What is it, Mr Birstall?' I was curious but pleased to be asked.

'Well it's like this,' he continued. 'I've bought me a new camera and I need some help with a subject. Now a string quartet I thought would be tip-top. Would you and your group like your photograph taken?'

I did not know which was worse: performing or being photographed.

'I— I'm not so sure, Mr Birstall,' I hesitated.

'Come on,' he coaxed. 'Young Morgan's been telling me some snippets about you and that 'cello. You've made a few friends, I hear?'

I nodded.

'Well then, what about it? I need a subject and I reckon you might like a photo to put on your wall next to that painting. What do you say?'

Mr Birstall's idea had a certain appeal. Undoubtedly the invitation would be well-received by the others. In fact, I thought it could be used as a way of reinstating myself after what had happened at school. I could not bear the loneliness I knew I was going to feel if I did not resign myself to the garden party performance.

I gave my consent. Mr Birstall's eyes gleamed and his laughter lines deepened.

'So when can you all come?' he asked.

'Now you know I'll need to ask the time of the others, Mr Birstall, but Saturday morning would be proper. I'll be letting you know if it isn't. Will Saturday morning be fine with you, Mr Birstall?'

'Shall we say half past ten?'

'We shall.'

'And how are you going to package your masterpiece?'

'I'm thinking to box it. Is there a box on you as will fit my picture, Mr Birstall?'

'I think we can manage a box of some sort, Lucy. Let me have a look.'

Sending the query to his wife, Mr Birstall returned to the other side of the counter and began to rummage underneath for the desired item while Danny and I listened to his rhythmic musings:

'A box, a box, a box, where can we find a box?'

His rummaging lured Danny into the back room, and the lines could still be heard when Daid, hatted and jacketed and armed with my crutches, came down the stairs.

'Danny's not gone abroad is he, Luighseach?' he queried as he laid my crutches next to my chair.

'He's not, Daidí. 'Tis to the back room with Mr Birstall that he's gone.'

Daid lifted the counter hinge and walked out. Presently he returned, with Mr Birstall declaring victory at having found a suitable box, and informing my father of our planned photography session while they packaged my picture. Daid and I made our farewells and set off for home with Danny at our heels.

As we passed the street lamp on the corner, I looked up at my father. There was always something silvery about him. There were slivers of silver in his teeth and sparkles in his eyes. His wedding ring, with its two hands holding a crowned heart, was silver; and silver was the watch chain which scalloped from his waistcoat pocket. Silver shimmered at his cuffs, studded his collar and pinned his tie.

And I ate silver, thought silver and prayed silver until the time came to make ready for bed.

I looked at myself in my nightgown. How could I possibly have consented to be photographed? I had not been photographed in years. I shuddered at the thought of seeing myself permanently bromoiled on a surface: a gangly vignette from the Book of Kells conceived in chemicals as a reminder of the peculiar fact that I actually lived and moved in the twentieth century. I began to unfasten the callipers. No amount of touching up would ever hide the truth about my limbs.

What was I going to do?

I folded and unfolded my legs into bed, pulled up the sheets and coverlet, prayed my three Aves and sighed into my pillow.

****

I returned to school the following day with the news that I now agreed to the garden party performance. When I mentioned Mr Birstall's proposal, Della became thrilled at the thought of a photograph and immediately seized the opportunity to schedule a much-needed rehearsal at my place. To a certain extent that was all very well. Della was familiar with my house and its peculiar contents. As for Pim, she and I had become very good friends despite our many differences. I was quite willing for them to visit. But the critical, scathing Phoebe was another matter altogether.

So, on Saturday morning, I found myself faced with the task of organising the house and providing my companions with a suitable meal. Such a challenge could only be met if my hands were free, not grappling with crutches. That meant resorting to my old limping gait with only my flail left leg braced and hoping that my right knee would hold out.

Lunch was not going to be easy. While Della was quite obliging about what was placed before her, she was accustomed to silver service and Cordon-bleu. And I knew all too well that Pim relished the fine home-cooked meals that were the specialty of her mother and Aunt Rose, and detested the sub-standard mess she was dished out at school. Phoebe's preferences were sure to lie outside the bounds of our pantry's peasant fare. Mashed potato and butter was not going to do.

It was an agonising decision.

Daid departed for work, leaving me to mull over the complexities of Aunt Rose's cheese pudding recipe. Ignorant of what constituted 'stock', I took a trip to Mrs Murphy for an explanation. I returned with a horrid soupy concoction and Mrs Murphy's assurance that it was exactly what I needed. Then there was the matter of a baking dish. We did not have a baking dish. Once again, Mrs Murphy provided the answer and advised me to pray to St Martha.

As for the house, it had to be completely expunged of anything associated with the polio. I wheeled the wheelchair into Daid's room and pushed the walking frame out the back door. On no condition was I prepared to provide Phoebe Raye with a single opportunity for comment on that aspect of my persona.

The parlour presented a different problem. It was the only room large enough to play in and the photos, paintings and statues were sacrosanct. That room had to remain intact at all costs. Besides, I dearly wanted to further acquaint Pim with Mam. But Phoebe's observations and conclusions posed a constant threat.

Finally, there was the job of disguising my legs for the photograph.

I knew that Daid had in his wardrobe a pair of trousers that he rarely wore. They were a heavy tweed, perfect for an Irish winter but far too warm for Sydney's more temperate clime. They would suit my purpose exactly, however. It may have been a mild April day, but my legs were cold despite my woollen stockings. I snuck into his room, pulled out the trousers and set about altering them.

Since Daid and I possessed the same thin build, the small problem of width was easily solved with the aid of suspenders. Length was a more complex issue. At six foot two, Daid was nearly five inches taller than me. Furthermore, there was the discrepancy between the lengths of my own legs to consider. I made some measurements as best I could, found the kitchen scissors and cut and stitched the hems. I wrestled my way into the trousers only to realise that I could not get them over my boots. That meant removing the calliper, unscrewing my boot from the brace, refitting the calliper on my leg, pulling on the trousers and then finally screwing the boot back in place. It was an exhausting process but well worth the effort, for when I viewed my achievement in the mirror I was happy to see that the trousers disguised my legs perfectly.

Now, I could be photographed!

A knock put a stop to my self-congratulations. I went to the front door and opened it. It was Pim.

'G'day, Lucy.'

'And a good morning to yourself, Pimmy Connolly. Was it not at the studio we were supposed to meet?'

'I've been there already. No one around so I thought I better come down to your place seeing it's close by. Need a hand? It's just gone half past ten.'

'Faith! Is it the time? Mother of God I'm late!'

'Can I help you with anything?' she called after me as I hurried down the hall. The trousers may have hidden my legs but my limp was as pronounced as ever.

'I'll be putting the pudding in now,' I called back. 'And 'tis my 'cello I need to take. Muise! Will you be taking my 'cello, Pim?'

Pim followed me to the kitchen, helped me put the pudding in the oven and moved aside to let me pass to my room. Fearing my leg would not manage the walk to the studio, I grabbed my crutches. Pim picked up my 'cello and we left together.

'You're game, wearing trousers like that,' she remarked as we hiked up the street.

'Anything's better than having my legs photographed,' I replied.

'What about a long skirt?'

'Aye, someone suggested that, but it makes me feel like a grandmother.'

'Well, you certainly don't look like a grandmother in trousers. By the way, they suit you. Personally, *I* wouldn't do it, but I think you can get away with it. Where did you get them?'

'From my Da.'

'Crikey! What did he say?'

'Not a word did he say for he wasn't there to ask.'

'You mean—?' Pim whistled. 'Gosh you're game.'

Della was waiting outside the studio.

'Don't tell me Phoebe's not with you,' Pim groaned. 'Where is she?'

'Dear me, I don't know. I was hoping she would be with you. She had all the details. Oh, I do hope she's not going to be difficult!'

'Difficult? Phoebe?' Pim rolled her eyes skyward and sighed.

'I suppose we better go in regardless,' resolved Della. 'We're a bit late. Luighseach, what in Heaven are you wearing?'

Mr Birstall did not seem to mind that he was missing one of his subjects; he was much too excited about his camera. He busied us about a very modern set of cylinders, tables, stools and ladders, and even had us playing some of our music. It did not sound at all right without a second violin but, as Mr Birstall assured us, what was a camera to know about that? After a few shots, we lost some of our apprehension and experimented with combinations of our own.

'Lucy,' Mrs Birstall appeared at the door. 'I'm sorry to interrupt but there's a young girl waiting outside who seems to be part of your group. Would you mind coming?'

I excused myself and accompanied Mrs Birstall.

'She seems to be very shy, dear,' Mrs Birstall explained with some concern. I looked at her and raised my brows. Shy was hardly the word I would have used to describe Phoebe Raye. Besides, who could possibly be shy of the Birstalls? 'I invited her in,' Mrs Birstall continued, 'but she refused. Oh dear,' she glanced out the shopfront window. 'She's not there. Go outside, Lucy, and see if you can see her.'

Out I went and just in time to glimpse what could only be Phoebe heading in the direction of the station. I called after her and she turned round.

I was accustomed to seeing Phoebe in outmoded clothes and the swashbuckling coat and immense plumed hat she wore that morning were no exception. Phoebe, on the other hand, clearly expected a very different Luighseach to the one she saw. She began to walk back, scrutinising me in her usual fashion as she did.

'Will you not be having your photograph taken, Phoebe Raye?' I asked. 'We're all inside there – Pim, Della and myself – and, to tell you the truth, we're having a bit of fun. 'Twas Mr Birstall took a photograph of us with our instruments all swapped around. Aye, a treat it was indeed to see the like of Delleen Sotheby playing a 'cello, herself being so small! Why did you walk away?'

'I don't want to be photographed,' was the stubborn reply.

'Arrah, Phoebe, you've nothing to be worried about. A bit nervous myself I was about it all for I didn't want any photo to show the callipers,' I noticed Phoebe glancing once more at the trousers. 'But let you not worry about anything like that – not yourself – for you're pretty as a picture. Besides, would it not be a fine thing to have a photograph of us all together? I'm thinking I'd like to put a photo on my bedside table that I could see while I'm in bed and think of my friends that I play with in a string quartet. Would you not like that, Phoebe Raye?'

'Are we going to practise?'

'Aye, to be sure we are at my house after the photographs. I made some lunch and you're more than welcome, Phoebe Raye,' I added, knowing full well that I had now placed myself under the obligation of extending my hospitality to the person I least wanted in my home. 'Will you be coming in now?' I showed her the door to the shop.

Phoebe silently assented and I brought her to the studio.

'Ahoy, me hearty!' called Pim. 'Where did you come from? The pantomime?'

'How are you, Phoebe?' asked Della, more by way of correcting Pim than by inquiring after Phoebe's health. 'You're just in time for one more photograph. There is time isn't there, Mr Birstall?'

'One more, Della,' Mr Birstall replied. 'Let's line you up, with instruments, shortest to tallest and I'll take the four of you together. Now, what's your name, lassie?' he asked of Phoebe.

''Tis Phoebe, Mr Birstall,' I answered. 'Phoebe Raye.' Phoebe seemed to have lost her tongue.

'Phoebe Raye, eh?' Mr Birstall committed her name to memory. 'Now then, Phoebe, take off your hat and I'll have you stand between Della and Pim. There's no need to be afraid. I'm a photographer, not a dentist.'

He tried to escort her but Phoebe would not let him. She joined us of her own accord.

It took three attempts and a very corny joke to get Phoebe to smile before we finally had a photograph of the four of us together.

'What do you call yourselves?' asked Mr Birstall as we left.

'And what are you meaning by that, Mr Birstall?' I asked.

'Well, most quartets have a name, Lucy,' he replied. 'What's yours?'

I made a silent appeal to the others and received a blank response.

'We've not a name, Mr Birstall,' I confessed.

'No,' echoed Della. Pim shook her head.

'Better do something about that,' Mr Birstall smiled. 'Hoo roo. I'll let you know when the photos are ready.'

****

Our house was quiet as ever, but warm on account of the oven being lit, and there was a pleasant cheesy smell wafting through the air when we entered. Never, since coming into our service, had our modest hallstand been given charge of such a supply of hats, coats and gloves, and my friends left it to deal with the situation as best it could. As for our instruments, the only place to leave them was the parlour. I gave the appropriate indications, opened the parlour door and took a deep breath.

'Is this a convent?'

Phoebe barely entered the room before she simply dropped her violin and turned to me.

I felt myself colour.

'Convent my foot,' I replied. ''Tis our parlour.'

'Then what are these doing here?' she gestured in the direction of the Sacred and Immaculate Hearts.

'It's to remind us that God is close by, Phoebe,' Della patiently explained.

Phoebe sought verification from me by raising an eyebrow in my direction. I excused myself and hastened to the kitchen. There was the cheese pudding to take out of the oven, and the task, although brief, offered me welcome respite from any further interrogation, let alone catechesis.

I eventually returned, dreading whatever questions I knew Phoebe was going to ask. I found her sitting in my armchair, surveying the pictures above our hearth.

Pim smiled knowingly at me.

'So that's your mother, Lucy?' she asked, indicating the wedding portrait.

'Aye.'

'She's very pretty, like you said. She doesn't look very old.'

I thought briefly. 'She would be sixteen there,' I replied, surprised to realise that my mother in that photograph was only a year older than me.

'And your dad's so handsome! He doesn't look a shade over twenty.'

'He would have been nineteen when that photo was taken. 'Tis a fine picture that one.'

'And that's you?' Pim wandered down to my pictures. 'What an imp! You know, Lucy,' Pim observed as she leant against Daid's armchair, 'you really do look a lot like your mother.'

'Whisht, I don't,' I said. 'Like my Da, I am.'

'Didn't you say she had green eyes?'

'Aye she did.'

'Well, so do you,' Pim continued. 'You've got green eyes. You might be tall and thin and have black hair like your father, but you have your mum's eyes. That's for sure. Doesn't she, Dell?'

'I'd never really looked closely enough,' Della replied, perusing the wedding photo and then taking in certain details of my own face. 'You know, I think you're right, Pim. Take off your glasses, Luighseach, and let me see more closely.'

I obliged.

'Definitely your mother's eyes,' Della concluded. 'Beautiful, bright, green eyes shaped just like almonds. What a lovely, lively person she must have been!'

'Aye, she was,' and I thought of the times when I was tucked in my bed, when through the darkness I would hear Mam laugh — a delightful, musical laugh — at Daid's gentle teasing. I used to love hearing that laugh for it always made me feel so content.

'You know, Pim, I could spend hours in this room,' Della continued, putting her arm around me. 'It's such a happy place. Luighseach, old thing, you are so lucky. All I can remember of my father is sitting on his lap and looking at the

185

statue of Peter Pan in Kensington Gardens, and the only photograph I have of him is tucked away in my violin case.'

'*I* don't have a mother either,' blurted Phoebe.

We all looked across at her. She tossed her curls over her shoulders.

'So the stork brought you? Might have guessed,' Pim scoffed.

'No,' corrected Phoebe. 'I was found in a cabbage patch. Are we going to practise or not? I have a business engagement at half-past four.'

'In a minute, Phoebe,' Della responded quickly but calmly and with a cautioning look at Pim. 'Whenever Luighseach says. Are you ready, old thing?'

'Aye,' I sighed. 'But we'll be having some lunch first if you care for it. Do you like cheese pudding now?'

****

Since we had not practised together for some weeks, we had much to do. Della suggested we tackle the last movement of the quartet which we had not yet tried.

Our rendition revealed marked differences in our playing. Della had taken her role as leader very seriously indeed. She knew that any decisions about phrasing fell on her shoulders, and from the outset it was clear that she had practised long and hard so as to address the matter with conviction. In addition, there was the demand of having to play at least as well as Phoebe if she was going to have any credibility in the eyes of her younger and talented second.

On first impression, Della would not have been classed as a strong violinist. Her manner of playing was neither vigorous nor flamboyant. Instead, she possessed an elegant effortlessness. Her bowing was very pared and pure, and this at first made her easy to follow. Above all, she had a deeply lyrical sense. She knew instinctively how to shape every passage; or else she had worked and worked to make the music sing. Della's strength lay not so much in Della, who seemed to disappear into her instrument, but in the sheer beauty of the music she produced.

Della had earned Phoebe's respect. The compelling charm of her phrasing had led Phoebe, to my utter surprise, to abide by her lead, although in some passages, where it was the second violinist's turn to shine, Phoebe would break into her showy, slightly aggressive style. But she was quick to restrain herself. In fact, on such occasions, she seemed embarrassed by the comparative harshness of her playing.

There was, however, a serious problem. Della's playing may have been musical, but she took liberties with the tempo. Again and again, speed was sacrificed to mood and I became annoyed by it. Dancing had made me very attuned to rhythm and time, and while my legs could no longer carry out the complex steps I once knew so well, the ability to divide and subdivide while maintaining a consistent pulse had not left me. I began to tap my bow on the body of my 'cello in an effort to bring Della into line.

'Mother of God! Delleen Sotheby!' I finally exclaimed. 'You do be hurrying again.'

'Am I?' queried Della. 'I had no idea. I'm very sorry.'

'You're playing well, though,' Pim interjected. 'Really well.'

'Why did you have to interrupt anyway?' complained Phoebe. 'You've spoilt the flow of it.'

'Because I couldn't keep track of it,' I replied.

'You mean you haven't practised enough,' Phoebe shot back. 'If you'd practised more, you'd follow better.'

I felt myself redden.

'I'm getting my metronome,' I announced.

'Come on, Lucy,' Pim stopped me with her bow. 'Admit it. You've got to do more practise.'

'Well, if that's not the pot calling the kettle black, Pimmy Connolly. And I'll be getting my metronome.'

'Oh, please no!' implored Della. 'Not the metronome! I simply cannot play with the metronome! I hate that thing!'

'All right,' Pim took hold of the matter. 'No metronome. No metronome, Lucy,' she repeated with a glare at me. 'We'll fix the problem another way. Della, what you've done is terrific. Isn't it, Lucy?'

'Aye,' I acknowledged. 'Delleen, you done a fine job there, only you're not—'

'Lucy, get off your soap box,' reprimanded Pim. 'Look, I've got practise to do too and I don't think we're going to solve the tempo problem till you and I have learnt the notes better. If tempo's such a thorn in the side, why don't we try a less demanding section? What about the Minuet? We're all more familiar with that.'

'Oh, no!' protested Phoebe. 'It's too boring for words!'

'Come Phoebe, it isn't,' soothed Della. 'Actually, it rather reminds me of a witches' dance,' and she cackled as she played the opening phrase. '"Double, double toil and trouble, fire burn and cauldron bubble."'

Phoebe giggled but still refused.

'Well, have you a better suggestion, missy?' answered Pim.

'The second movement,' Phoebe resolved. 'I know we haven't done it yet, but it's slower, so everyone should be able to keep apace. And, since you and I and Lucy are mainly accompanying, Della has to play in time with us.'

'Good idea,' Pim responded. 'Della, how slow will you be taking it?'

'Dear me,' Della fumbled with her music and instrument. '*Andante piuttosto allegretto.* How fast is that?'

'Twould be about seventy-six beats per—'

'Lucy, cut it out. Play the opening how you think it should go, Dell,' encouraged Pim.

Della began, but I could not help tapping the beat with my bow. This time, instead of stopping me, Pim and Phoebe joined in and gently tapped their bows in time with mine. Although she was a little tense at first, Della soon gained confidence and began to work with the pulse instead of against it. The phrase mastered, we substituted percussion with pizzicato.

The result was very pleasing.

We had no idea how long Daid had been listening there, leaning against the door.

'Daidí,' I beckoned him, 'Come in and sit.' Daid did not make a move. 'Come on, Da, come and sit.'

Echoed pleas eventually brought him inside. Daid sat on the arm of his chair and we played for him. He smiled shyly as we finished and began to polish his glasses with his handkerchief.

'Tis a grand sound you're making there. Ar é Haydn an ceol sin, a Luighseach?'

'It is, Daid.'

'You'll let your tiredness now and I'll make a cupán tae. Will there be tea for yous all?'

It was indeed time for a break. Daid whistled to Danny and strolled to the kitchen. I excused myself and went out to help.

I was soon followed. Phoebe appeared at the kitchen door and was watching my father and me as we prepared kettle, tray and tea things. She seemed very perplexed.

'What language are you speaking?' she asked.

'Tis Irish that we're speaking,' I replied as I counted the cups.

'What were you saying?'

'Me Daid's chiding me about the trousers,' I explained.

'Aye,' continued Daid. 'And what were you thinking, Luighseach, pulling trousers from your da's closet and cutting the legs?'

'I was thinking I wasn't about being photographed with the callipers.'

'Tis unwomanly, I'm saying. And you walked into town so?'

'Twas only to the studio that I walked. Besides, Daid, wearing callipers is unwomanly,' I retorted.

'I think trousers look very modern,' Phoebe ventured a contribution in my defence.

'And that doesn't make it right,' Daid tersely replied. 'Tis father's hearing confession now at chapel, Luighseach. You'll be going after tea.'

'Confession is it, Daid?' I was indignant. 'And what is there to confess I'm asking?'

'Them trousers there for one thing,' remarked Daid.

'A sin to wear trousers is it now?' I complained.

Daid replied in Irish that we would discuss the matter later. That answer infuriated me.

'Da—!'

'Luighseach,' Daid interrupted me in a quieter, sing-song brogue. 'Let you put on a frock so and come and take some tea. We'll talk some more after that on the way to the chapel.'

'I'll not be going to Confession!'

Daid calmly repeated his request for me to change and emphasised his point by indicating the direction of my room.

When I returned to the parlour I found my father, with Phoebe's assistance, pouring tea and passing round a plate of bread and jam. He handed me my cup, poured some tea for himself and sat and sipped with us. Little by little he began to ask questions about the music and about our instruments. Della and Phoebe's violins he took up in turn. He smoothed his hands over the wood and marvelled at their craftsmanship before fiddling a reel himself. Pim's viola particularly intrigued him. He played an air and delighted in its deeper tones.

It had been a long time since I had heard Daid play the fiddle.

****

There was a pressing need to have our quartet in shape for Mrs Epstein and we practised hard in order to play the work in its entirety. Solemn declarations were made not to breathe a word about what we had planned.

We converged on our teacher the following Thursday and she was eager to hear how we had progressed with the Menuetto and Trio.

Della led us into the Allegro. All eyes were cast simultaneously in her direction and in Mrs Epstein's just to spy the reaction.

We played through the entire quartet.

Some moments passed before Mrs Epstein spoke. With instruments at rest and bows politely pointing towards her, we awaited what she had to say. Her eyes had watered and she smiled gently.

'Did you enjoy doing that?' she asked.

We did not need to reply.

'I could tell you did. And you're playing like a quartet. To be frank, there were a lot of rough spots, and yes I know the fourth movement was mainly sight-reading. Still, you managed to stay together. What is more important, however, is that you're talking. You have a sense of each other. Do you know why?'

Her question was rhetorical.

'Because you listened,' she concluded. 'You *really* listened— not only with your ears but also with your hearts.'

Mrs Epstein beamed her special smile to each of us.

'I think the time has come to let you try another work,' she resumed.

'Beethoven?' Phoebe asked with enthusiasm.

'Mendelssohn,' suggested Della. 'I adore Mendelssohn!'

'Schubert for me,' Pim cast her vote. 'Dad likes Schubert.'

'No, no, no,' replied our teacher. 'It's the *Sunrise* quartet. I have it ready for you.'

Della obliged by locating the music on top of the grand piano and passing it round.

'Oh no!' protested Phoebe. 'Not more Haydn!'

'If you can't play Haydn, you can't play quartets,' argued Mrs Epstein.

'But—!'

'Oh, you can bluff, but you can't play.'

'Mrs Epstein!'

'Forget Beethoven. Forget Mendelssohn. Forget Schubert. Forget the lot of them!' decreed Mrs Epstein. 'Master the Master and I might reward you with something more.'

'I'm thinking I like Haydn,' I remarked as I looked over my music.

'Oh, Lucy!' groaned my friends in unison.

19

Spurred by Mrs Epstein's words of encouragement, we resolved that we would practise together more frequently. Pim proposed we meet up at school and she procured a music room for the purpose.

Of course, practices at school meant bringing my 'cello. On the morning of the day appointed for our next rehearsal, amidst the stately procession of cars and the occasional carriage, Daid drove up the school driveway on his motorcycle. He wove in and out of the other vehicles, parked directly before the front steps, helped me out of the sidecar, took charge of the 'cello and escorted me to the classroom.

The appearance of my tall and youthful father in the fourth form room caused considerable titillation. Daid was dressed for work as usual in his pinstripe suit, candy-cane shirt, starched white collar and flamboyant bow tie; and as he passed the various groups of girls, he politely tipped his cap. His greeting sent them giggling to the far corners of the room.

'Was that your brother?' asked big Kathleen the moment my father left the room.

'Brother you're saying? Nothing of brother! 'Twas my da,' I replied, incredulous.

Upon overhearing this piece of information, Fanny Mahony blushed. Kathleen even looked a little envious.

Fanny's embarrassment quickly turned to scorn. 'You're crippled. You can't possibly play that thing,' she said, pointing to my 'cello.

'Fanny!' admonished Elizabeth Fitzgerald.

'So you can play the 'cello, Fanny Mahony?' I asked.

'No, of course not,' sneered Fanny.

'Well then, you must be crippled,' I concluded.

There was a laugh from Mary Byrne and Fanny turned away, a little puzzled at my reply.

'Luighseach would have to be the best cellist with callipers I know,' Della spoke in my defence.

'I'm probably the only cellist with callipers you know,' I muttered.

'I still don't believe you can play,' sneered Fanny as she turned round again.

'Nor do I,' echoed big Kathleen.

'Then why don't you play something for us, Lucy?' Mary asked in a far kinder voice.

I hesitated.

'Would you?' repeated Mary.

'I say, Mary! What a wonderful idea!' agreed Della who immediately took the initiative to fetch my 'cello.

'Delleen Sotheby, what do you think you're doing?' I protested.

Della continued unbuckling the straps on my 'cello case. 'Go on, old thing, play something you love. You can do it.'

She pulled out my 'cello and showed it to Mary.

'It's handsome isn't it, Mary?' she said. 'Look at the flaming on the back. It's like a tiger.'

Mary was very appreciative. 'Wish I could play. I never got to learn an instrument,' and she tentatively plucked one of the strings.

''Tis not in tune,' I complained and, in resignation, I fell into a nearby chair, placed my crutches on the floor, adjusted my legs and held out my arms for the 'cello. Della passed it over and fetched my bow. I tested my fifths and harmonics, and was soon busy shifting pegs and tuning pins. My preparations instantly caught the attention of the rest of the class.

'So, are you really going to play something?' Mary asked again.

I surveyed the group that had clustered around me. Mary appeared genuinely interested and encouraging. Beth seemed intrigued. Della smiled at me, eager and hopeful. Kathleen, who apparently also played the 'cello, was curious. Fanny remained aloof and disbelieving. I remembered what Mr David Birstall had said about pyjamas and smiled to myself. But it was not enough. My fingers seemed to liquefy. I took off my glasses and sighed.

I could not do it.

'Told you she can't play,' remarked Fanny.

'She plays very, very—' began Della, but I had had enough of Fanny Mahony.

'Indeed I can, Frances Mahony,' I announced. 'And 'tis the minuet from Bach's third 'cello suite in C major that I'll perform.'

Fanny began to giggle. 'Turd,' she tittered.

'Oh shoosh up, Fanny!' scolded Mary.

It was my 'cello that finally shut her up. At first it was daunting, being stuck in front of my peers like that, and I had never played in as open a space as a classroom. But after the surprise of hearing my first triple stop, I began to warm to the acoustic. There was a lovely resonance and I decided to repeat the first section, just so I could enjoy it. I closed my eyes, forgot about my listeners and lost myself in a tune I loved to whistle almost as much as I loved to play. And I could easily imagine Mr Bach strolling down the street whistling it, too.

The class did not break its silence until I finished. Then they cheered and clapped. Della jumped up and down, clapping and shouting 'You did it! You did it! I knew you could do it and you did it!' Overjoyed and overwhelmed, I started to laugh. Never before had I ever received applause like that for my 'cello. I put my glasses back on. Nearly everyone was smiling.

'Lucy my child, why that was beautiful!' exclaimed Sister Mary Magdalene.

I blushed. When had Sister Magdalene come into the room?

'I had no idea you played the 'cello so well.'

'She's like a spider, don't you think?' observed an excited Della. 'A spider weaving a web of sound the way her fingers move across the fingerboard.'

'Can she play something more, Sister Magdalene?' pleaded Elizabeth Fitzgerald. Beth's request was very quickly taken up by the rest of the class. I laughed at them. If ever there was an opportunity for missing lessons, they would spare nothing to take it.

Sister Magdalene made her own assessment of the situation. 'Very well,' she smiled. 'Since the Council of Trent has waited three centuries for us so far, I don't think a day is going to make too much difference.'

'Come on, Lucy. What else do you know?' encouraged Mary.

'Can you play something a little more modern?' suggested Beth. 'What about "Tea for Two"?'

I gave the request some consideration. It was a song that Daid liked to sing while working in the garden. I had also heard the song on the wireless and there had been a few times when someone had played it on the piano at Miss Bray's store. As I result, I was quite familiar with it. It would not be difficult to play.

'I think I can do it,' I pondered out loud while I worked out where to place the tune on the fingerboard.

And I began to do what I did best on the 'cello: I began to improvise. The only way to deal with the rhythmic interludes in the chorus, I decided, was to make a quick, light bow of the final note of the phrase and then tap the rhythm with both hands on the body of my 'cello. This delighted the class and they joined in the tapping the next time round. After that, I could not resist double stopping or playing the tune as high up my 'cello as I possibly could, then playing the second phrase on my lowest string. It was always fun to make use of my 'cello's many voices and stage the appropriate faces to go with them: anything from a grumpy old man, to a lover sick with melancholy to a half-crazed madman; or otherwise to delight in the sheer athleticism involved in making those sounds: rapid bow movements and dexterous fingerings, or else wallow in vibrato. In the end, the class could not resist singing along. I could not resist singing. Even Sister Magdalene was singing.

'You're really funny!' Mary was beaming with pleasure. 'I had no idea you were so funny! That was absolutely fabulous!'

'Bet you can't play a jig,' sneered Fanny.

Fanny's remark silenced the class. No one could believe she was still being mean.

'Indeed I can, Fanny Mahony,' I replied. 'And I bet, for the love of God, you cannot dance one.'

There were a few nervous laughs.

'Well, *you* certainly can't,' retorted Fanny.

'Hoigh! Well if that isn't clear as day!' I angrily replied.

'Now girls,' Sister Magdalene cautioned.

'So are you going to dance now, Fanny Mahony?'

No one in the class could resist my challenge.

'Go on, Fanny! Dance!' they began to call.

Fanny tightened her lips with annoyance.

'I haven't the right shoes,' she complained.

''Tis not a thing the matter with them brogues,' I remarked as I eyed her feet. I had always danced in heavy shoes.

'They're not my dancing shoes!' Fanny protested.

'Come on, Fanny,' urged Mary Byrne. 'Lucy's well and truly proven her point. You prove yours.'

'Well, *she* had to. She's the crippled one,' argued Fanny.

'Girls,' interposed Sister Magdalene, 'I think we—'

'You know, Fanny Mahony,' I interrupted, ''Tis yourself who's the crippled one.'

'I am not! How dare you!'

'Aye you are,' I replied, leaning on my 'cello and pointing my bow at her. 'You don't be wearing callipers on your legs and using crutches to get from here to there like myself. You're pretty and graceful and I bet you've a home that's fine where you've everything you've ever asked for, but you've nothing in your heart to accept anyone who might be a wee bit different from yourself.'

'Good for you, old thing,' Della whispered. Other than that, the class remained hushed and looked to Sister Magdalene for guidance.

'Well, dear child,' said Sister Magdalene to Fanny. 'Is Lucy right? Have you a crippled heart?'

Fanny shifted from one foot to another and bit her nails as she looked at Sister Magdalene and then at me.

'Do you know "The Jolly Foxhunters"?' she asked.

'Indeed I do,' I replied. 'A slip jig is it not?'

Desks were rapidly and noisily moved aside. I played an introduction. Fanny bowed and began. She was a very good dancer indeed: neat and nimble on her feet, her chin held high, her body straight and her hands loosely at her side. Her steps and posture were more contrived than mine would ever have been, but it was beautiful to watch all the same. The rest of the class clapped and cheered in time.

'Sister Magdalene!' called a shrill, Scots-Irish voice.

The clapping and cheering, 'cello and dancing ceased. Everyone stared at Sister Augustine. The only sound that could be heard was Fanny panting.

'And what is the meaning of this rumpus? Why are the girls not studying history?'

'My dear Sister Augustine,' began Sister Magdalene. 'There was something far more important than history to be studied this morning.'

'Well whatever it is, it's not more important than mathematics. Kindly straighten the room and prepare for class. Hail Mary full of grace the Lord is with Thee. Blessed art Thou among women and blessed is the Fruit of Thy Womb, Jesus.'

A subdued response followed and the desks were put in order again.

'I hope you don't mind me asking,' I said to Fanny, 'but would you mind passing me my 'cello case on the floor there near yourself?'

Fanny spotted the case, picked it up and passed it to me without as much as a word or smile.

'You know, you danced it well that jig,' I ventured a compliment. ''Twas as if you danced on a penny.'

'Thank you,' she replied.

'I used to dance it myself, you know.'

'But—' she looked at me in disbelief.

'I wasn't always like this. My legs, I mean. I used to be able—' I stopped and swallowed hard. 'Now I dance it with my fingers instead.'

'I—I had no idea—I—'

'Never you mind about that, Fanny Mahony. We'll be friends now?'

'Friends?' Fanny hesitated as she looked at the hand I held out.

'Lucy Straughan and Frances Mahony!' called Sister Augustine as she rapped with her ruler.

Fanny and I looked at each other and rolled our eyes.

'Ma-hony,' I mimicked in a whisper.

Fanny giggled. 'Strau-ghan' she mimicked in reply and, still giggling, we returned to our seats.

20

The two remaining weeks that passed between Easter and the May holidays were busy ones indeed. Nearly every day at lunch, and sometimes even after school, we practised our quartet. There were also end of term tests to sit and essays to submit. Had I been more astute, I could have made quite a lucrative business out of the mathematics tutoring I supplied to nearly every member of the fourth form. Instead I had to accept payment in laughter as classmate after classmate heard my Sister Augustine impersonations during the course of a coaching session. I did not mind at all, particularly when they reciprocated by working out ways to accommodate me in their games at recess, be it Hide-and-Seek, French cricket or rounders. I was officially one of the class and the result was that I finished my first term at St Dominic's very tired and very, very happy.

Still, by the Monday of the first week of the holidays, I was relieved to have a day entirely to myself. I whiled away the morning cosy in trousers, with a brace only on one leg, playing Bach. I needed pure 'cello and Bach's first 'cello suite was the purest 'cello music I knew.

In a way it was an unusual choice, for a year ago, following an agonising struggle and countless arguments with Mrs Epstein over bowing and fingering, I had abandoned my study of the first suite in a fit of rage. Time, however, had proved my ally. That morning, to my delight and satisfaction, I found the suite much easier to play than I anticipated.

By early afternoon I was brimful of Bach and, feeling rather confident, I decided to play the music for Mam. I glanced up at the wedding picture.

'Not ever have I played the 'cello for you,' I told her. 'Well, I'm playing it now, I am. 'Tis a collection of dances called a suite by Bach and I'll be doing my best for you and I hope you're listening.'

Giving the right impetus to the bow in the opening bar of the Prelude was always a challenge. On this occasion, however, it simply happened. My fingers thudded onto the fingerboard, my bow swept and dipped, and I was immersed in a rich, buoyant sound. Allemande, Courante, stately Sarabande, Minuet and Gigue followed.

I decided to end the Gigue by triumphantly double stopping the final note. It was satisfying to see the strings vibrate and hear the deeper, more resonant sound that was produced.

It was all over. I wiped the sweat off my forehead and leant back in the chair, exhausted, content and surprised to hear a distant patter of applause. I peeked out the window.

It was the postman.

'Beg your pardon, miss,' he tipped his cap as I opened the door. 'There's a letter and a parcel for you.'

'Thank you,' I replied.

I tucked my bow under my arm to receive the items. The postman tipped his cap again, bid me good afternoon and went on his way.

While I walked back to the parlour, I deliberated as to which to open first. The package was from Aunt Rose, the other letter from someone unknown for it did not provide a return address.

I decided upon the anonymous letter. All credit had to be given to the Postmaster General's Department for delivering it. It was addressed in an ornate hand in which the letters looped into one another making it nearly impossible to read. As for the address itself, it was an embarrassment: 'Lucy the lame girl who lives in a small, white house in Newtown'. The letter was no epistle. It was a summons from none other than Phoebe Raye to present myself at her house on Saturday.

Why did Phoebe not ask me in person? We had seen enough of each other at school so she had had ample opportunity to ask me. Why should she be so secretive?

I shrugged my shoulders and opened Aunt Rose's parcel. I gave a whoop of joy when out of the brown paper came *The Complete Works of Alexander Pope*. Tucked inside was a letter which I eagerly began to read.

It was a motherly treat full of homely news and gentle observations. Aunt Rose was 'so glad' I was fitting into school now, for a week ago I had written and told her everything that had happened, particularly about Fanny and the 'cello. Then she proceeded to give me news of her family and the farm. In detail she described the early morning mists and frosts, told of the busy time she had spent gathering and drying the last of her herbs, pickling the remaining summer vegetables and planting anew for winter and spring. Emily and Jack had both come down with colds. Uncle Ted and Hughie had taken the calves to market and the cows were keeping everyone awake at night with their mournful lowing. Toward the end of May the family would be attending the Bong Bong picnic races, an event which Aunt Rose was looking forward to immensely. It was always a lovely chance to meet and talk and have a flutter on the ponies:

> Now, dear Lucy, it seems my little Angus has woken from his afternoon nap. I can hear him coming down the stairs. How delighted he'll be tomorrow when we take a trip into town to post this letter. So I must finish and make his tea.
>
> By the way, the book comes from Father Connolly. He mentioned you seemed quite taken with it when you visited and decided to pass it your way. Send it back when you've finished with it. I think it's a favourite with him, too.
>
> I conclude with a hug for you, darling, and do send my regards to your father.
> With love from your Aunt Rose.

Oh how I wanted that hug!

Aunt Rose's letter, simple, sincere and full of warmth, made me miss Mam more than ever. I looked up at the girl in the wedding picture and wished once more that she would come to life. But there was only silence, stillness.

'In ainm Dé, cén fáth nach bhfuil tú ag caint liom!' I blurted at the picture and began to sob. In desperation, I made for my father's room, took the small photograph from his bureau, flung myself on his bed and hugged it tight.

'Mam!' I called and called. 'Mam!'

For how long I lay there I had no idea, but there was a slight chill in the air and the room had darkened. I sat up and rubbed my eyes.

That was when I noticed the battered little book of poems on my father's bedside table. I picked it up and stroked it fondly. It was bound in magical blue and the binding was falling apart now from overuse. The title on the front was lettered in gold and the gilt was slightly smeared. I opened the book and studied the signature on the fly leaf. Mam's maiden name, 'Maeve Dunne' and a date, '1910' was penned in her tidy copperplate. Beneath it was a poor attempt on my part to copy her signature and underneath that I had pencilled 'Luighseach' in Irish letters and also in my neat but awkward script. Then I began to read the poems. Page after page I turned and desperately tried to make sense of the words my mother loved to read by the fire late on chill nights.

Marking one poem was a small sheet of paper on which had been sketched a young girl. It was a competent drawing, far better than anything I could ever do. It must have been one of Daid's for the linework bore close resemblance to the fluid, linear style that characterised his drawings. There was no signature, however, and Daid always signed his work. I studied it closely. It revealed a very strong likeness to myself at about the time I was stricken with polio. But strangely I had no recollection of that picture being made and I was usually good at remembering such details. Besides, the hair was wrong. When long, my hair was always plaited in two neat braids, it was never untidy the way it was in that picture. I sighed and wished that I could remember more clearly what happened between Mam's death and the polio. But it was all a terrible blur punctuated here and there with vivid impressions, some of which I was unsure as to whether they actually occurred at all. So I sought consolation in reading the poem which had been bookmarked by the drawing. As I read, I could vaguely recall Mam's voice.

Then I began to recall a picture I had only recently seen. It was Daid's watercolour – the strange and beautiful watercolour of the embracing couple that I had come across in the studio a few weeks ago.

I read the final verse again:

> Though I am old with wandering
> Through hollow lands and hilly lands,
> I will find out where she has gone,

And kiss her lips and take her hands;
And walk among long dappled grass,
And pluck till time and times are done
The silver apples of the moon,
The golden apples of the sun.

And I realised something more about my father that I had never before
considered. Until now I believed that Daid's chief purpose in life was to look
after me or, more particularly, to look after my legs. Daid was the one who made
sure everything was as it should be. And, when things went wrong, Daid was the
one who tried to make everything right again. The idea that my father actually
had thoughts and feelings that extended beyond me and my legs had never really
entered my head.

But who did look after Daid: Daid who rarely said a word about himself, who
cared for me and carried me, who shared with me all that he had? Who looked
after him? Mrs Murphy? Mrs Murphy washed and ironed his shirts. But who cared
for him? Who loved him?

And I realised that my father missed my mother as much and possibly even
more than me.

A nuzzle and lick of my hand from Danny alerted me to the fact that my
father had arrived home.

'What do you be doing in here, lass? Would everything be well with you,
Luighseach?' I put my glasses on and saw Daid in the doorway.

'Aye Daidí,' I sniffed.

'Well, there's a couple of letters you thrown down in the hallway, a book lying
open on the floor, your 'cello you left in the parlour and your music,' he replied
as he fetched his jug. 'You'll be putting it all away before tea now. And you'll be
changing out of them trousers too,' he advised as walked back down the hall.

'Aye,' I sighed as I closed the book.

'Daid?' I called.

But Daid had already gone to the kitchen.

That night we sat together by the fire. I began to reread Mr Pope's 'Essay on
Man'. I glanced across at my father. He was sitting, quiet as ever, working on a
plan for our back garden in his sketchbook. I resumed my reading and could not
resist the occasional chuckle at the poet's observations.

It soon became apparent that my amusement did not pass unnoticed. With
every chortle or smile on my part, there was a pause in the scratching of Daid's
pencil. The last thing I wanted, however, was to make eye contact with my father.
I had avoided his gaze all evening. I did not want to look into his eyes and see the
sadness there.

'A book you're reading there is it, Luighseach?' Daid presently asked.

'Aye, Da,' I replied.

'And what would be the book about?'

I held up the book for Daid to read the title.

Daid resumed his sketching.

'You know, Da,' I began a little while later. 'Mam would have liked this book.'

The pencil stopped. Daid stiffened. Up until then neither of us had ever spoken of Mam.

'Do you remember how she used to read us, Daid?'

I waited for a verbal response.

None came.

But the pencil had stopped sketching.

'It was *A Midsummer Night's Dream* Mam was reading to us before—' I could not bring myself to say 'she died'. 'She could do all the voices could Mam. Aye, 'twas a funny play that, and I didn't realise it was as funny as it was until Bottom turned into an Ass. I remember asking Mam about that. "Mam," I said. "Is it true that when Bottom turns into an ass that Shakespeare means— you know, Mam, like— well, you know, Da?" And Mam she smiled and laughed and put her arm around me and said, "Aye, Luighseach." And we both laughed and laughed and you laughed too, Daid. Do you remember that, Da?'

Still no reply. I looked across at my father and saw him looking at me.

His eyes had filled with tears.

'You needn't be ashamed of crying, Daid,' I reassured him as I put my hand out to him. 'It bees good to cry. I'm missing Mam too, you know.'

'Oh, 'tis not so much missing Mam, Luighseach,' he replied and took my hand in his. 'I cried my heart out for her many a time. And while you were away, I missed you both so much not a wink could I sleep. But I don't cry that your Mam's gone, mo mhuirnín. I cry because my little girl's come back. You've come back, lassie. You've come back at last.'

We looked at each other. Daid smiled through his tears. His eyes – gentle, intense, with their kind lines – gazed into mine. He walked over and stroked my cheek. I took off my glasses and began to wipe the tears that now filled my own eyes.

'So sick you been and sad for so long, Luighseach,' he said as picked me up and hugged me close. 'I'd almost given up hope. You had a good cry for your Mam now?'

'Aye Daid. At Aunt Rose's. You don't mind if I call her that, do you, Da? Like a mother she's been to me, you know.'

Daid smiled and shook his head, sat in my chair and hugged me close again.

I told him all about that morning with the potato cakes.

'The next day, Aunt Rose showed me how to make them,' I concluded. 'And the recipe she gave me too, but I cannot bring myself to make them for fear of crying all over again.'

'Never you fear about that,' smiled Daid. 'We'll make them tomorrow for breakfast shall we?'

'Aye.'

Together we warmed our thoughts on the flames.

'Do you remember the manor house back home, Luighseach?' Daid began.

I nodded. 'The squire's house is it?'

'Not the squire's house, lass, but the grand, grey, stone place along the road. Do you remember riding there?'

'Aye. 'Twas Mam said she used to live there, Da.'

'Aye. 'Twas where I first met your Mam, you know.'

'You'll be telling me, Da.'

'Well, we'd be going back many years now. 'Twas eleven summers I'd seen at the time and it so happened one August morning that a gentleman arrived at the estate and met your Uncail Eachann. His horse he brought with him. Would a farrier be nearby he asked, for his horse had lost a shoe. A farrier indeed there was and Eachann called Breandán who set about making a shoe and fitting it so. Well, while Breandán was hammering the shoe into shape, the gentleman he was telling a little about himself. From up north he came, and it turned out he was spending part of the summer here with his family. Did they find everything to their liking? They were settling in well, thank you, to be sure, but they could do with a little more of help about the place. Help is it? Eachann knew how to fix that, and so it fell to myself to ride to the manor each morning with a basket of brown bread and eggs and whatever was fresh from the farm and make myself useful, be it chop some wood or work in the garden or fetch and carry whatever the family needed.

'The family kindly gave me my dinner in return and I took it under an apple tree. And it came about that one day I decided to make a sketch of the place. Busy drawing I was there when I heard a crunch up above. I looked up, and in the tree was a pretty little lass with copper-coloured hair. Munching an apple she was, and not more than eight or nine years old if that, I'm telling you.'

''Twas Mam was it, Da?'

'Aye, lass, 'twas your Mam.'

'"You're an artist, are you not?" she said. Well, Luighseach, 'twas no one ever called me an artist before. Now young Meidhbhín, for that was her name, knew all there was to know about artists for an artist had come to her home to paint a portrait of her da. Could I paint portraits? Well, I liked drawing people more than anything else, so I said I could. Could I draw herself? Aye I could. So down she came out of the tree and sat quiet for me and I made a sketch. She asked to see and, when I finished I passed it to her. Well, never was there a lass so happy. "Will you not sign it for me?" she asked.

'Now Luighseach, never was there a lad ashamed as myself when she asked me to sign her picture for at the time I could neither read nor write. It wasn't through want of trying, Luighseach, but somehow I couldn't make head or tail of letters and figures; and as for writing, the nuns at school would tie my left hand behind my back for to make me write with my right hand and I couldn't do it, lass,' he sighed.

'"I can read and write," she replied. "But I cannot draw like yourself. You don't need to read and write, you draw so well, but I can teach you all the same. 'Twas my brother, Sean, I taught to read this Christmas past. Sean's five, you know, and if he can read then you can too. I'll teach you if you want."

'And so she did. Every day she sat with me under that apple tree, with a great fat bible and a stick for to write letters in the dirt. Meidhbh didn't mind me making letters with my left hand. Well, Luighseach, somehow I managed to read a good way through the Book of Genesis and write my name. But, you know,' Daid added with a smile which only partially shielded a look of deep regret, 'try as she might, she never managed to teach me to spell.'

All I could do was to give him a hug.

'You know, lass,' he continued. 'You might think them legs of yours troublesome. But equally as troublesome is not knowing from one day to the next how you're going to write your words.'

'I can always understand what you write, Daid,' I apologised for him. 'You get the sounds, you know, and you copy well.'

'Aye, if I think of words as pictures, I do a little better.'

'Then perhaps you ought to write in hieroglyphics like the Egyptians, Da,' I teased.

'Like King Tut, Luighseach?'

'Aye.'

'Well now,' he replied with a smile. 'Can you imagine Sister Bellarmine's face if I wrote her a note of absence in hieroglyphics?'

We both enjoyed that idea.

'Will you tell me some more, Da?'

'Well, as I said, Mam taught me to read and I taught her a few things in return: about the fields and the flowers, the birds and animals, how to ride her pony and to speak some Irish. And so it was that we'd meet every summer. We'd ride together and walk together and talk on all manner of things. She'd read me stories and try to teach me a little more. A whole year she stayed once. But after that she stopped coming. Her family came but not my Meidhbhín. In Scotland with relatives she was they said, then off at school, then visiting friends. For three summers she didn't come. How I missed her, Luighseach!'

'Did you love her even then, Daid?'

'Aye, lass, though I didn't know it at the time. Well, the year I turned seventeen, her da asked me to make a painting of the house. He paid me handsomely for it, would you believe, much more than he ought. But I think he did it to prove to me what I could do if I applied myself. There was a living to be made from painting and drawing as well as that, he said, and a little training wouldn't go astray. A reference he gave me too, and with that and the money I'd made from that painting, I took myself to Belfast. I found me a job with a photographer and took some classes at the School of Art in the evenings. And every day I'd look out for Meidhbh. I used to wonder how she'd grown and if she'd recognise me if she saw me for I'd grown tall, and by then I was wearing glasses and I wasn't dressed in my farm clothes.

'Well, one day I was walking out from Half Bap, looking out for her as usual, when I bumped into two young ladies near St Anne's. One of the ladies dropped her parcel. I picked it up for her and raised my cap and made my apologies, quite forgetting to speak in English. I was about to go on my way when she stopped me. "It's Morgan, is it not?" she said. "Old Patrick's Morgan?" she asked, saying the name I was always known by back home. "Aye, it is," I replied.'

''Twas Mam, was it Da?'

'Indeed it was and she was all grown up and pretty as ever. Well, after that I began to court her. She was from a fine family, I can tell you, Luighseach, but her da gave his permission nonetheless. He'd started from nothing himself, you know. All a lad needs is a chance, he used to say, and I'd already proved what I could do when a chance came my way. "Besides," he told me, "You'll do for her what many lads with their pockets full will never be able to do: you'll make her happy". And we were happy, Luighseach, we were very happy indeed. It wasn't always easy, lass. Your mam's health wasn't always good. 'Twas a little trouble she had with her lungs, you know. Still, with God's good grace, we had a beautiful little lass. And then—'

But Daid could not talk about Mam's death.

'Well, I'll tell you one thing more,' Daid continued. 'When I was packing our suitcase for to come here, Luighseach, I picked up that little blue book you were reading this afternoon.'

'The book of Yeats' poems?'

'Aye. A fine poet is Mr Yeats.'

'I don't know, Daid. They puzzle me, them poems.'

'Well, your Mam used to like them very much, and do you know what I found inside? 'Twas the picture I drew of her way back when we met under the apple tree those years ago. Fancy that! To think she'd kept it all that time.'

'So 'twas Mam in that picture?' I echoed. 'I thought it was myself but it didn't make any sense, Da.'

'Well, you know, there bees a lot of your mam in you, Luighseach Meidhbhín.'

'Truth be told, Da?'

'Truth be told, Luighseach.'

21

'Luighseach, I don't know what's gotten into you,' said Mrs Epstein during my lesson the following morning.

'What is it you're meaning, Mrs Epstein?' I asked.

'Well, for a start, you're playing better than ever,' Mrs Epstein's strange, dark eyes lost their probing glare and warmed. 'I think the Beethoven's even better than the Bach.'

'Bail ó Dhia ort. A pleasure it is to hear that, Mrs Epstein. You've a right to know I been hard at it of late.'

'You don't need to tell me that. Besides, it's more than practice,' she smiled again. 'Now, how's the quartet going? What are you all up to these holidays?'

I sighed. 'Mrs Epstein, I'm missing them already. For 'tis Della Sotheby's in Bowral with the Mahonys and Pim Connolly's helping her family run the guesthouse. Only Phoebe Raye and myself it is still here. Would you know Phoebe's asked me to her house, Mrs Epstein?'

'Really? She's invited you?' Mrs Epstein seemed quite surprised.

'Aye. She's a strange one to be sure. She sent me a letter you know instead of asking me to my face. She might as well have sent a telegram it was so brief, Mrs Epstein. All it said was: "Lucy stop Come to my house stop Saturday stop 10 o'clock stop Bring 'cello stop Phoebe stop". No more, no less, save she had sense enough to include her address.'

'I suppose she wants you to play the Beethoven with her,' observed Mrs Epstein.

I looked at her quizzically.

'Some time ago I gave Phoebe the accompaniment to the sonata you've just finished,' my teacher explained.

'Faith! You did that, did you?'

'Well, you need an accompanist and Phoebe seemed the perfect person to do it,' Mrs Epstein casually responded. 'She's an exceptionally talented pianist, Luighseach.'

'I've never heard anyone play like that before, Mrs Epstein.' Phoebe never ceased to impress me.

'I have met only two people in my time who are capable of performing with equal proficiency on more than one instrument: Mr Epstein's one, Phoebe is the other. She's probably more a pianist than a violinist but her talent on either instrument is indisputable. Besides, I believe the admiration's mutual,' replied my teacher. 'Phoebe thinks you're a terrific cellist.'

'Whisht! All I get from Phoebe Raye is, "You're coming in late", "You don't do enough practice", and she does be always staring at my legs. And now she tells yourself she thinks I play well. Not a bit do I understand Phoebe Raye.'

'I suppose in time you will. Come on, next piece.'

'And what do you want me to play now?' I queried.

'I think you know,' came the shrewd remark. 'You've been avoiding it all morning.'

'The *Sunrise* quartet is it you want?' I asked tentatively, hoping that Mrs Epstein would request I play her some of the more difficult bars in my part.

She shook her head.

'Not the Dotzhauer,' I grumbled.

'Come on, come on. Out with it,' goaded Mrs Epstein. 'You'll only be as good as your technique.'

I pulled the music from my bag, found the appropriate page, checked my tuning and began to play. It was a study I had been given a week ago. Mrs Epstein stopped me half way through.

'Mistakes everywhere!' she gave me the evil eye. 'Exactly how much work have you done on this?'

''Twas more time I spent on other things, Mrs Epstein. The Beethoven, you know,' I replied and bit my lip.

'So you're sight-reading?' Mrs Epstein studied me even more carefully and watched me nod. 'Luighseach,' she began in a more cautious tone. 'I know sight-reading is not your forte, but can you even *see* the music?'

Embarrassed, I looked down at my fingerboard and absently plucked the strings. I was having a lot of trouble reading the notes.

'I think a trip to the eye doctor wouldn't go astray,' suggested Mrs Epstein.

I groaned.

'Will you speak to your father or will I?' Mrs Epstein persisted.

'I'll speak to my Daid myself, Mrs Epstein.'

'Well be quick about it. The last time you said you would, it was months before anything happened. How you think you can get through life without seeing properly is a total mystery to me. Actually,' Mrs Epstein stopped scolding, 'it reminds me of when you first started coming to 'cello lessons. Do you remember?' she asked me with a fond smile.

'Aye,' I replied.

'What a scrawny little ragamuffin you were, struggling on crutches. To be quite frank with you, I didn't know how I was ever going to teach you. Getting you to learn Piatti was like pulling hen's teeth, you were that bloody-minded about learning the Bach prelude.'

'Aye,' I agreed as I stroked my 'cello.

'You know, it was Mr Epstein who realised what you were up to.'

'What do you mean?'

'Do you remember how I used to play the Bach for you at the end of your lesson?'

'Aye, I do. 'Twas my reward for complying with Piatti.'

'Complying my foot,' retorted Mrs Epstein, smiling. 'Well, Mr Epstein suspected you were learning the Bach on the sly. I didn't believe him at the time so we decided to leave you alone one lesson to see what you would get up to. Do you remember?'

I nodded.

'You scamp! You played the first half of that prelude by heart! And it wasn't a bad effort by any means. After that, I discovered the reason why you simply wouldn't learn the Piatti was because you were so short-sighted you couldn't see to save yourself!'

'You know, you said you didn't want to see me back for lessons ever again unless I had a pair of speclaí atop my nose. So upset was I when you said that, Mrs Epstein, I barely ate for a week.'

'Well, don't do that again. You're wiry enough as it is,' Mrs Epstein drily replied as she scrawled a note on my music and passed it to me.

Above the tempo indication she had written, 'New Eyeglasses Obligato'.

****

Saturday finally arrived. After a lengthy appointment with the optician, Daid drove me to Phoebe's place in Stanmore. We were both surprised with what we saw.

Phoebe, it appeared, lived in a large, ramshackle Italianate villa, set amidst an equally large, overgrown garden. We pushed open a rusted wrought iron gate which hung from its hinges in a drunken stupor. Piano music could be faintly heard as we contended with a rioting crowd of shrubs and weeds. Daid dodged the corpse of a swing which dangled, broken and useless, from the gibbet of a great white poplar, and helped me up the steps. He rang the bell and we waited amidst a cluster of statues, the kind that usually filled a fine arts academy, which had taken shelter on the verandah.

The door was opened by a plump woman with green eyes, heavily rouged cheeks, and a mass of dark hair piled higgledy-piggledy on top of her head. Evidently she was in the middle of some artistic production for she wore a paint-smattered smock over an exotic, flowing, mauve garment, and held a spatula in her left hand, which also balanced a palette thick with brightly coloured paint.

Daid tipped his hat and began his introduction.

'A good morning to you, Mrs R—'

'Devereaux. Ailine Devereaux,' the woman interrupted.

Daid was baffled. Nevertheless, he tipped his hat again and introduced himself, taking great pains with her name and meticulously anglicising the pronunciation of his own name and, to my annoyance, mine.

'Yes…'

With that single lingering word a mysterious wealth of information was somehow conveyed and Ailine Devereaux nodded slowly as, leaning back a little, she looked us up and down.

'I'll not stay longer, Luighseach,' whispered Daid while he apologetically handed Ailine Devereaux my 'cello. ''Tis a wedding I'm needing to be on time for now but I'll come by and take you home about half three.'

Daid politely tipped his hat a third time, kissed me on the forehead, thumbed that spot with his usual sign of the cross and whispered a quick 'Dia Dhuit'. Giving a soft whistle to Danny, who had made a thoroughly doggy inspection of the statues, he departed.

'I suppose *you* want to see the child,' the woman remarked as she stood aside to make entrance possible.

Assuming she meant Phoebe, I nodded.

'Well, she's the one responsible for all the cacophony in here.' Ailine Devereaux certainly was not going to trouble herself any more than necessary and leant my 'cello against the wall to indicate as much before she disappeared into another room and shut the door.

I removed my hat and gloves and deposited them with a particularly grotesque hallstand. The sounds of the piano became louder as I made my way across a tattered Persian rug and groaning floorboards. I stopped outside the room where the music was coming from and listened. It was a mighty, uplifting piece – youthful, mountainous and vibrant – a welcome contrast to the mournful shreds of wallpaper and the cobweb veils that hung from the ceiling in the hall. Then there was that sickly, sweet smell that Della had described…

Some final chords sounded and I decided to enter.

'You're late,' scolded Phoebe from the piano.

''Twas an appointment I had with the eye doctor,' I apologised and blinked hard. The doctor had put drops in my eyes and I was having trouble focussing.

'You should have come *last* Saturday.'

'And how was I supposed to know that I'd like to ask? 'Twas no date you put in the letter, which, I might add, I only received on Monday.'

'But *I* sent it a week ago!'

'Well, the way you addressed it, 'twas a miracle it arrived at all. Anyway, I'm here and my da's not coming for me till the afternoon.'

'So I'm stuck with you?' Phoebe was exasperated. 'But *I* was practising Chopin!'

'And that's what you were playing there?'

'A flat major Ballade,' Phoebe answered proudly. 'Now I suppose you want *me* to play with *you*?'

'I'm thinking 'tis *yourself* who wants to play with *me*.'

'Beethoven,' she huffed as she put her own music away and angrily searched for my sonata. 'Go and sit over there,' she absently instructed, impervious to the fact that it was not easy for me to manoeuvre myself around the grand piano to the designated chair. 'I can't give you much time. I have a business engagement later today. You can use my music stand.'

'I—I haven't got my 'cello.'

'What?'

'I mean—I left it in the hallway. I—I can't—'

'So you want *me* to fetch it?' she complained as she rose from the piano and pushed passed me.

'I'm—'

'Don't say "sorry"!' she ordered me and opened the door. Then she stopped. 'I—I wish— Oh, it doesn't matter!' she added in a softer but still frustrated tone.

She soon returned with my 'cello, passed it to me and resumed her seat at the piano.

Phoebe was impatient to tune and did not appreciate what she regarded as an intolerable wait. To her mind, I always seemed to take too long to do anything. I, meanwhile, wrestled with an eccentrically engineered music stand, sorted out my music, pulled out my bow, unbuckled my case, pulled out my 'cello, fixed its endpin, and finally started to work on my tuning pegs.

'Are you ready now?' she sighed. 'Then play the opening phrase. I'll come in after that.'

So I began the A major 'cello sonata. I first thought through the opening tune in my head, which I liked to do before I started playing. Its simple, friendly melody was made rich and warm by my low strings. Then came that long, low 'E'. How I loved to bow that note and build that crescendo!

This time, however, my performance was disrupted by the piano. Phoebe made her own brilliant and equally warm entrance.

All I had heard in the past was Mrs Epstein's very sketchy rendition which was coupled with emphatic counting and bowing instructions. Phoebe's version was completely different. I stopped.

'Why are you playing all them notes for?' I asked her.

'Because that's what's written here,' she replied with an abrupt tap of her music.

I eyed her sceptically.

'Look, if you don't believe me, come and see for yourself,' Phoebe then decided it was too much of an agony to watch me try and get out of my seat. She raised her hand to stop me. 'Stay there,' she instructed and thrust the music under my nose.

I followed my part, which was printed above the piano music, and saw that what she had played was indeed correct. I looked up at her.

''Tis two staves you're reading,' I commented with some awe. 'As well as my own part.'

'How can you be so gauche!' Phoebe could not believe what she had heard. 'That's how piano music is written, silly. One stave for the right hand and one for the left,' she explained. 'Now can we go on?'

'Aye. We'll play from the beginning. Is that fine with you? It's a beautiful sound you make and I want to hear it all over again.'

'Oh, all right,' she sighed. But I could tell that Phoebe wanted to hear it all over again, too, for there was considerably less annoyance in the tone of her voice.

We played and we played. Gradually the music bound us together. No longer was it a cantankerous pianist arguing with a self-conscious cellist. It grew into a conversation between two curiously like-minded souls.

'Arrah! I cannot believe how wonderful it is!' I marvelled after my final note could be heard no more. 'I've always enjoyed that piece, but I never thought what a difference the piano would make. Will you play some more with me?'

'Of course,' Phoebe replied. She was radiant. She always was when she was absorbed in her music.

'I've the Saint Saens here,' I began as I looked through the rest of my music. 'The *Allegro Appasionata* it is. And there's some Schumann which I learnt last year, and a sonata by Romberg but I don't like that half as much. But I've only the 'cello parts with me,' I lamented. 'I don't have any piano music.'

'Don't worry,' Phoebe replied with a smile and held up a pile of music. 'Mrs Epstein gave me the accompaniments.'

I could not hide my surprise and delight.

'She said you wouldn't want to stop once you discovered how beautiful it is,' Phoebe explained.

'Jesus, Mary and Joseph! Can you credit that?' I laughed.

'What about the Saint Saens?' she suggested. 'That looks like fun.'

'Aye, indeed it is. Let's go!'

No sooner had we finished than Phoebe shut her music and rose from her seat. 'I'm famished!' she announced. 'Put that 'cello down and come and get something to eat.'

I followed her to the kitchen where she immediately ran to the larder and pulled out a platter.

'Faith, is it chicken that is in it?' I was incredulous.

Judging from the look I received, my remark was clearly 'gauche', but this time Phoebe refrained from comment. Instead, she dumped the chicken on the kitchen table, wrenched off a drumstick and passed it to me. She yanked the other one off for herself and furiously began to eat. The last time I had eaten chicken was the Christmas in Galway before the Troubles.

'Are you still hungry?' she asked as she sucked on the bone. Phoebe evidently was and she began to search the cupboards.

''Tis a cup of tea that I'd like,' I made my request.

'Ailine only drinks coffee,' Phoebe replied as she continued her search, opening and shutting cupboards with increasing vigour and frustration. 'Bother, Ailine! Where's the chocolate?'

Apparently I was to go without any tea. The chocolate was hunted down and stuffed in the pocket of Phoebe's pinafore.

'Leave all that and come up to my room,' she instructed as she passed me. For me, it was unthinkable to abandon the kitchen without cleaning up. 'Come on!' she urged. 'I've something that belongs to you that you need to see.'

Together we climbed the stairs, and as we did I pondered what possession of mine Phoebe possibly could have acquired. To my knowledge I had not lost anything, and during the times we had been together, I could not think of a single opportunity for Phoebe to take something that belonged to me. Besides, no matter how rude or eccentric she was, I did not believe Phoebe to be dishonest.

She would not permit a single question, and while she searched the contents of her armoire, I sat on the bed and mused over the contents of her room. Originally it must have been a nursery for there was a cradle in the corner. The bed itself was a child's bed and it was well that Phoebe was not too tall for that bed certainly would not have accommodated me. The walls were papered with old-fashioned wallpaper. Its satin finish was very worn and faded, but the original design of dainty pink rosebuds could still be seen. Hanging from the picture rail were several nursery prints now washed out and spotted. An old, ragged horse made of brown velvet sat on the pillow, and a very elaborate dolls' house stood opposite the cradle.

Phoebe produced a box which she placed on her bedside table and opened with a key. From the box, she handed me what she wished me to see.

It was a small, hard case covered in green leather, and on the lid was embossed the name and address of the eye doctor in Galway. I opened it and inside lay a pair of spectacles, almost identical to the ones I was wearing, save that the lenses were considerably thinner.

I was speechless. Not only did those glasses remind me of those final, terrible days in Ireland; they also evoked memories of another place nearly forgotten.

'They're yours, aren't they?' Phoebe remarked, looking steadily at me.

She knew they were. Her pinafore swelled slightly as she acknowledged my reaction with a deep breath.

'Aye, they are indeed... How— How did you come by them?'

'I saw you bury them,' she explained. 'You didn't think anyone was watching you, but I saw you do it. You buried them—'

'I did I did. Underneath the pink rose bush at the back of the garden near the Sacred Heart. The garden where the nuns sometimes sat. The garden at the back of the orphanage. The orphanage...' I was dumbfounded.

'It's not far from here,' Phoebe began to supply me with the answers to the questions I wanted to ask.

'Do you mean on the hill in Ashfield there?' I asked, thinking of the large building topped with crosses that could be seen from that station.

'No. That's a convent. The orphanage is in Leichhardt, across the busy road from Mrs Epstein's. Don't you remember?'

'Aye, I do a little,' I replied, still baffled by the idea that something so remote in my own memory could be so astonishingly close to where I lived.

'Don't you remember me?' inquired Phoebe.

I looked at her and slowly shook my head.

'Well, I remember you,' she replied, her confidence balancing my own bewilderment. 'You were very shy and quiet and didn't want to play with the other children. But you were very kind to me.'

'I was, was I? I'm sorry, I don't remember very much at all you know, with my Mam dying and the polio.'

'Well, I'll tell you then. I had not been there long when you found me crying one day. You didn't say anything – you never did – but you sat beside me and put your arm around me and let me cry. I must have told you about my piano because the next day you showed me how to get into where the nuns lived, where there was a room with a piano that I could go and play. After that, we would run away to that room nearly every day and I would play for you. You loved to hear me play. Then one day a nun came towards the room and we hid in a cupboard. She came in and she didn't find us. You were very good at hiding and finding secret places and hidden ways. You were always doing it. The nuns were always looking for you.'

'Were they now? Well, apart from getting sick, the one thing I remember is standing at the gate and looking down the street.'

'Sister Anne always had to drag you away.'

'Aye,' I sighed and shuddered. 'I used to wait for Daid. He put me there, you know, after we arrived from Ireland, for to keep me safe and sound while he found us a house where to live and a job for himself and a school for me to go. I'd wait and wait and wish he'd come back and that Mam would come back too. But only Daid would ever come. On Sundays for Holy Mass he would come, and he'd take me out and bring me back by evening. I'd cling to him hard when it was time for him to go. Daid would say clinging wasn't a way to solve problems, but he'd let me cling to him all the same. 'Twas the nuns would have to stop me from clinging. Then …'

I looked down at my spindly legs in their callipers and tried in vain to block out the recollection of the polio.

'I know,' declared Phoebe. 'You caught cold. Then you were sick. I asked you what the matter was and you said you had a headache. Don't you remember me asking you what was wrong? It was the only time I ever heard you talk.'

'I don't,' I replied. ''Twas the headache I remember. 'Twas the worst headache ever was put on me. And my legs were aching too – as if a thousand iron spokes were pressing and scraping. 'Twas hard to walk so. And I remember trying to eat my porridge and I could barely hold the spoon. A nun asked me what was wrong and when I told her it was a headache come upon me she said it was no wonder since I wouldn't wear my glasses and she ordered me to go upstairs and find them quick smart.'

'That was Sister Mary Paul. She was always making you wear your glasses. And whenever she saw you taking them off she'd pounce on you. No wonder you buried them.'

'Now tell me something, Phoebe Raye. Would there be a staircase there at the orphanage? A wide timber staircase with ten steps up and a landing and fifteen steps more and blue carpet in the middle?'

'Of course. That's the front staircase.'

'And there's a statue of the Holy Family on the landing is there not?'

Phoebe nodded.

'So it is real! I used to dream about that staircase when I was sick. I still dream about that staircase, about falling down the stairs.'

'You fell on those stairs.'

'Aye,' I nodded. 'I couldn't climb them for I couldn't lift my legs at all, at all.'

'And the nuns picked you up and took you to the infirmary. Then they took you to the hospital. They told us you were very sick and made us pray a Rosary every day for you. Another girl also fell sick.'

'She did?'

Phoebe nodded. 'But she died. I used to think a lot about what happened to you and whether I would ever see you again. I knew you were still alive. Your father told me.'

'My Daid? How do you know my Daid?'

'He used to do painting and gardening and odd jobs for the nuns while you were in the hospital. I used to watch him and he let me help. Afterwards he'd give me a sweet and I'd ask him if you were going to come back and play with me. But he would only smile and ask me to pray that one day you would be able to. So I did. But you never came back.

'I didn't see you again until that day in the music store. I knew it was you the moment I saw you. Then I saw what had happened to you. They lied.'

'Who lied?'

'The nuns lied. They told me you got better. But you didn't! You couldn't walk. And that's why you never came back to play!'

Phoebe was visibly upset. She looked at me and pouted, her eyes doleful and puddling with tears. She wasn't heartless. She wasn't insensitive. On the contrary. She was deeply affected by what had happened to me. She could not bear to see me crippled and I knew then that the reason she stared at me in that annoying way was because she was desperately trying to make sense of it all.

Poor Phoebe. Her hopes and dreams, childlike as they were, had seemingly been shattered. And instead of giving voice to her devastation, she had behaved in a way that could only be described as 'gauche', to use one of her own favourite words. I put my arm around her to comfort her and wondered how I could help her to see the rightness of it all. For in the situation I could see a glimmer of rightness, and I took it close to my heart and held it tightly there.

'But I did get better, Phoebe,' I said, giving her another hug.

'You didn't!' she lamented. 'Look at you! Why did that have to happen to you?'

'And I cannot tell you how many times I've asked that very same question. But you're wrong about my not getting better. I did get better. Aye, I know my legs are useless, but *I* got better. *I* got better! I'm well now! And look, you silly goose, I *did* come back to play. See? I'm here, sitting right next to yourself! Have we not been playing all morning? To be sure 'tisn't children's games we been playing. 'Tis something far more grand. Whoever thought we would come together and make music like that?'

Phoebe sniffed and smiled a little. 'I'm very glad you play the 'cello,' she said.

'And so am I,' I answered with a smile. 'And if it wasn't for the polio, I doubt I'd ever have played it at all.'

And we began to talk about everything that had happened. Phoebe wanted to know all about my illness and slow, halting recovery, about trying to walk and what it was like to wear callipers, about learning the 'cello and how I felt starting school again.

'So, all that time you were in the orphanage?' I asked her. 'Seven years was it now?'

Phoebe nodded. 'But I was safe there,' she said. 'The nuns took good care of me. Sometimes I even miss being there,' she sighed.

'The like of you to miss being in an orphanage!' I exclaimed. 'And was it the lady downstairs took you out?'

Phoebe nodded again.

'That's Ailine. She's my aunt.'

'An artist is she not?'

'She thinks she is. She came back from France last year and took me home.'

'And were you not glad of that?'

'At first I was, but she was too busy painting to bother with me. Then she put me to board at school. She didn't want me here,' Phoebe sniffed. 'But I ran away.'

'And did you go back to the orphanage?'

'Yes. But the nuns wouldn't take me. So I went to Mrs Epstein.'

'Mrs Epstein?' I echoed.

'But Mrs Epstein took me back to Ailine and made Ailine keep me.'

Mrs Epstein never ceased to surprise me.

'And how did she do that?'

'I don't know exactly, but they had a very big argument about it. Mrs Epstein even threatened to go to the police.'

'And are you not happy here with your aunt?'

Perhaps not many people asked that question of Phoebe, for it had a curious effect on her. She shifted to the corner of her bed. Her lips trembled a little and she swallowed hard.

'I can play the piano whenever I want. After all, it's my house so I can do as I please,' she replied, a hint of defiance creeping into her voice. 'She doesn't care what I do. This was my room when I was small. I like this room.'

''Tis a pretty room indeed. That horse on the pillow there looks special,' I gestured at the bedraggled stuffed creature which Phoebe was absently stroking.

'It's Gregory Allegri,' she replied.

'Is it really?' I smiled. What an odd name for a horse, I thought.

'He was the finest and noblest horse who ever lived,' Phoebe added.

'He looks a little worn out to me.'

'That's because he's lived a long time,' Phoebe nodded in justification and smiled a small, rare smile. 'My mother made him for me the Christmas before—' she suddenly broke off.

'So you knew your mother?' I asked.

Phoebe nodded.

'She made that house too,' and she indicated the dolls' house. 'That is, she made all the things inside it. She made them when she was as old as I am now. Her father, my grandfather, made the house. You can look if you like.'

She opened up the dolls' house to reveal an intricately painted interior filled with miniatures.

'It's this house, is it not?' I marvelled. 'There's even a piano here! A beautiful house it is! Your mam's very clever to do all that. But what happened, Phoebe? What happened to her that you should be put in the orphanage?'

Phoebe shrugged her shoulders.

'What happened to your mother and father? What happened to them?'

No response.

'Have you not a photograph of your family?' I had not seen any photographs anywhere in the house.

'No I don't,' she tersely replied. 'Ailine burnt all the photographs.'

'She burnt—?' I was horrified.

'They're only *pictures*! They're not *people*!' Phoebe retorted.

I sensed that if I replied to that particular remark I was going to be ensnared in pointless argument. I changed tack.

'Your father was in the War was he not, Phoebe?'

'That's none of your business!' she replied angrily as she hugged the poor, stuffed horse. Then she looked away.

'You weren't wanting to talk about it that night at Pim's place when we were discussing the War,' I observed gently, recalling the silent tears Phoebe had shed whilst holding out against Pim's inquisition. 'Upset you were about it all,' I continued. 'Is it true your dad was in the War?'

Phoebe held on to her horse and would not look at me.

'I told you,' she said, her voice subdued and dangerously quiet. 'It's none of your business.'

She leant across and opened the little silver box on her bedside table, pulled out her cigarette holder, fitted it with a cigarette, and lit up. There she sat in the corner of her bed, hugging her toy and smoking. The only link between that little girl dressed in a simple navy frock and white pinafore, and the girl who had played the piano with such joy and warmth, was her muscular hands. For a brief moment she looked at me. Her eyes grew sorrowful, and her pursed lips were pregnant with some strange, silent story. I smiled at her and she looked away.

So it was that I was quite relieved when Daid finally arrived. He met me in the hall with Ailine. She uttered no more than a single 'Yes…' while her green eyes attempted to leech my own of their colour. Determined to maintain their full pigmentation, I kept my gaze until Daid guided me outside. We nearly reached the gate when I heard Phoebe call my name. I turned and saw her holding fast to the rope of the broken swing, swaying a little one way and then another.

22

'Miss Devereaux's an interesting lady,' Daid remarked as we began our tea.

I looked up from my meal and arched an eyebrow. Over the course of the afternoon, I had amassed quite a different collection of adjectives to describe Phoebe's aunt.

'She paints, you know,' Daid continued.

'Aye,' I was more preoccupied with Phoebe and the roast chicken.

''Tis interesting pictures that she paints, I'm saying. Did you her pictures see, Luighseach?'

I shook my head and wondered whether or not Phoebe would eat more chicken for tea, all by herself, picking at the carcass on the kitchen table.

'I'm liking her palette,' Daid was inspired. ''Tis many a trick with her colours she plays that give good form and harmony. Some paintings she showed me while I was waiting for you to come. You'd do well to see her paintings. Luighseach?'

'Aye?'

'What's troubling you?'

'I'm thinking 'tis all very well for Miss Devereaux to paint as she does, but she doesn't be caring for Phoebe Raye the way she ought.'

I explained what happened that day, told Daid about the chicken, the nursery, my old glasses, the orphanage, the cigarettes…

'Phoebe's aunt doesn't care for her, Daid. Nobody cares for Phoebe Raye.'

'Aye, a hard thing indeed it is to be on your own like that,' Daid remarked and I knew it was an observation which had roots in experience. Daid's mother died when he was born and his father when he was very young.

'But 'twas Uncail Eachann and Aintín Maire reared you as their own, Daid.'

'And plenty of brothers and sisters besides. Aye, Luighseach, Our Good Lord gave me a big family with a big heart.' There was a bark from Danny who then clattered down the hall. Daid put down his knife and fork and listened. 'Was it the door knocking now?'

A knock was heard.

Daid rose to answer and I followed him into the hall.

No sooner was the door opened than Phoebe, her violin and her carpet bag pushed their way inside.

'Ailine's having an orgy,' she announced. 'Can I stay?'

Daid and I silently queried each other.

'An orgy is it, Phoebe?' That was the last thing I expected to hear. 'And what do you mean by an orgy?'

'Precisely that.'

'You're not telling the truth.'

'I am too. They all come in togas and robes with wreaths on their heads and they lie on cushions in the studio and gorge themselves. There are hundreds of people there. May I stay, please?' She was desperate.

Fancy! After all the tensions of the afternoon, Phoebe wanted to spend the evening in my company. I looked to Daid for the response.

'Aye, Phoebe,' he replied. 'You're more than welcome. And is it tea you taken?' She shook her head.

'Well, for the love of God let you share some with us,' Daid escorted her to our dining room. 'There'll be plenty to spare, lassie.'

'Aye,' I added. 'But 'tis not the like of roast chicken, I'm telling you.'

Daid offered to make more tea and took our teapot back to the kitchen. I proceeded to set another place at our table and pile Phoebe's plate with mashed potato and cabbage and apple.

'And who is it is come for the orgy, Phoebe Raye?' I asked.

'Ailine's friends,' she answered. 'What's that?'

'Black pudding it is,' I replied as I placed some on her plate.

Phoebe seemed a little puzzled.

''Tis made from pig's blood,' I made my eyes big and smiled when she dropped her fork in horror.

'It's not!' she protested.

'Aye,' I continued to jest. 'I seen my mam do it. You get the pig's inners and—'

Phoebe pushed her plate away in disgust.

'Oh, come now, Phoebe Raye. Eat your supper. 'Tis good food there on your plate. I was but pulling your leg.'

I helped myself to some more black pudding. Phoebe watched me eat the pudding and decided, somewhat hesitantly, to copy.

'And does Ailine often hold orgies?' I asked her.

She nodded.

'The last time she had one there were people I didn't know sleeping all over the floor and someone had been sick on the stairs. There were even people in my room—' she shuddered. 'There was nowhere for me to go. The next day there was an awful mess which Ailine didn't bother to clean up. I had to do it, seeing it was my house. This time I locked my door,' and she dangled a bunch of keys which she had round her neck.

Daid came in with the tea and we finished our meal together. We prayed our final grace and began to clear the plates.

'It really was pig's blood you ate,' I teased.

'Luighseach...' cautioned Daid.

During the washing up, Daid assumed responsibility for preparing Phoebe for the next part of our evening.

'We'll be praying our Rosary in the parlour now, Phoebe,' he informed her as

217

he passed her a plate.

Phoebe took the plate without comment.

'Do you pray the Rosary, Phoebe?' asked Daid.

She shook her head.

'But you said you did when we were talking this afternoon,' I commented from my seat at the kitchen table.

'I said the nuns made me pray it,' Phoebe retorted. 'I don't now.'

'And why would that be?' I questioned.

Daid seemed to think it better not to probe. 'Well, perhaps you'd like to make yourself at home another way,' he said. 'Luighseach can show you her room.'

But Phoebe did not stay in my room for long. During the third glorious mystery she dawdled into the parlour, sat on the hearthrug and leant back on my chair. She contributed a few fragmented Hail Marys before pulling out a cigarette and lighting up. And so she sat in moody silence, brooding over the photos and pictures that covered our wall and mantelpiece.

By the time we finished she was ready to fire with questions. Before she could launch any large-scale attack, however, Daid went to his room and presently returned with his pipe and pouch.

''Tis tobacco I do be giving up for Lent,' he remarked as he filled his pipe. 'And come Easter time I forget how good it is to smoke some. Moladh le Dia!' He relaxed back in his chair and took his first puff.

Phoebe began her inquisition.

'Who are they?' she asked, indicating a photo on the mantelpiece.

'They're the Jesuits,' replied Daid.

'They are not,' contended Phoebe. 'They're school nuns. Who are they?'

''Tis Sister Mary Loyola, Sister Mary Gonzaga and Sister Mary Francis Xavier,' I added. 'They're my aunts.'

'We've always called them the Jesuits, lass,' Daid explained with a smile, 'despite them being Dominicans.'

'And who's he?' Phoebe demanded, pointing to another sketch.

'That's my Uncail Eachann. And the sketch next to it that looks like my Daid without his glasses is my Uncail Ciarán, who's a pint-sized version of himself there,' I nodded in my father's direction. 'Uncail Ciarán was a jockey, you know. And that watercolour there's Uncail Breandán at his forge. I like that painting.'

'And what about him?' Phoebe giggled as she scrutinised a tiny pen and ink drawing that was more a caricature than a portrait.

'That's my brother Ruaidhrí,' answered Daid. 'Do you remember your Uncail Ruaidhrí and the farm, Luighseach?'

'Aye, how could I forget Uncail Ruaidhrí, Daid?' I smiled at the thought and then related my memory to Phoebe. ''Twas Uncail Ruaidhrí used to sing "Tim Finnegan's Wake" at the top of his voice while he blacked his boots of a Saturday night. Do you remember that, Da?'

Daid took leave of his pipe and began to sing in his light and musical voice:

Oh, whack fol' the dah now dance to your partner
Round the flure your trotter's shake
Isn't it the truth I told 'ya
Lots o' fun at Finnegan's wake

I joined in with the two last lines and we both began to laugh.

'You know, 'twas Uncail Ruaidhrí would be going to daily Mass if there was whiskey instead of water for the blessing,' I added.

'Was it Ruaidhrí who told you that, Luighseach?'

''Twas Mam who used to say it, Da.'

Daid smiled softly at the wedding portrait. 'Aye, and she was right, you know. A little whiskey in the font would have done our Ruaidhrí no harm at all.'

'Where are they all now?' asked Phoebe. 'Do they live here?'

I looked at Daid and we silently agreed that he should do the explaining. This he did, gently but somewhat sparsely. Phoebe listened carefully, her back to the fire, her cigarette long forgotten, and her chin on her knees. From time to time her brow rippled with concern or she fiddled with the buckles on her shoes. It was clear that she was moved, even disturbed by the account.

'This room isn't a parlour,' she sneered when Daid finished. 'It's a mausoleum.'

'Is that how you see it?' replied Daid and he slowly shook his head. 'Well, for myself 'tis a corner of Heaven.'

Phoebe angrily pursed her lips. Then she blinked hard.

The fire chilled and flickered and a blackened log spilled into the silence.

'Why are there wars?' she asked.

Since her question did not appear to reach Daid, she repeated it. Daid puffed his pipe and smoked a consideration to the statue of the Sacred Heart before resting his elbow on the arm of his chair and leaning his head on his hand.

'I'm as much at a loss about it as yourself, Phoebe,' he sighed. 'I suppose some people think a war's a good way of solving problems.'

'Do you?' she asked.

Daid shook his head. 'And a few white feathers I been handed on account of it.'

'What do you mean, Da?' I asked.

''Twas partly why we moved from Belfast back to Galway, Luighseach,' Daid informed me. 'When the English went for to fight the Germans 'twas some folk there thought we ought to join them and didn't think much of any lad who didn't sign up. As for the Black and Tans and ourselves, well let's say we forget about all the trouble we make when we war. After treading the earth so long you'd think we'd have learned that by now.' I could hear the emotion tighten its hold on Daid's voice. 'But I'm thinking maybe God in His goodness wants each of us to learn for himself,' he added and fondled Danny between the ears.

'I don't believe in God,' Phoebe declared as she lit another cigarette.

Daid looked at her and gave a thoughtful puff of his pipe.

'He's let you down, has He?' was all he said.

It was not the reaction Phoebe had intended. She tossed her curls and exhaled a stream of smoke.

'Can we see the sunrise tomorrow?' she asked, almost daring my father to refuse.

Daid, in turn, did not expect such a reply. But Phoebe's request did not ruffle him as much as his question had annoyed her.

'Aye, we can,' he said. 'To the seaside we can go for that. Luighseach, what of yourself now? Will you manage rising early in the cold and walking on the sand?'

'Aye,' I shrugged my shoulders.

'Then we best be off to bed,' he concluded. 'We'll put you here in the parlour, Phoebe. A cosy bed we can make by the fire and we'll see what blankets we can find.'

We put together a bed as best we could and Phoebe settled down for the night. I went to my room and set about my own bedtime preparations. There was a soft tap on the door.

'Luighseach, an bhfuil cead agam teacht isteach?'

'Tar isteach, a Dhaidí.'

Goanna oil in hand, Daid edged inside.

'Phoebe's asleep is she not, Da?' I asked.

'Aye. As silent as the stars she bees by the fire, curled in a blanket and cuddling a wee pony.'

'Well, she doesn't seem to mind sleeping in a mausoleum,' I joked.

'Come on, lass,' Daid smiled as he helped me with the callipers. 'I'll do your legs now.'

He sat at my bedside, and with his lithe fingers began to soothe and ease my limbs.

'Daid?' I asked as he gently worked my knee. 'If God is good as you say, why is it that bad things happen?'

'Well lass, God may be good, but we've faults aplenty. He can't stop our sins, Luighseach.'

'And is that why Mam died?'

'Aye, I suppose it is. And a terrible thing it was indeed. But it wasn't as if God deliberately set out to take her away, Luighseach, because she'd done something wrong. Nor did He take her away to spite yourself. You don't think that, do you?'

'Sometimes I do, Da, and I get all angry and upset.'

'Don't I know it,' Daid seconded. ''Twas a soldier killed Mam, Luighseach,' he continued. ''Twas a poor, crazed lad with a gun in his hands. And, like yourself, God saw it happen. So He took Mam to Heaven for to look after her until we're ready to see her again. One day, lass, you'll see your Mam and I'll see my darling wife and dearest friend.'

I looked up at my father and swallowed hard.

'Then why did I get polio, Da?'

'Well lass, that wasn't a punishment either. Don't you ever think that.'

'Then why did it happen so?'

'Well, funnily enough, sometimes bad or sad things happen that good may come of them. Do you think you'd play the 'cello as well as you do if it was not for the polio?'

'I might. I mightn't,' I shrugged.

'Well,' Daid paused from his massaging, pulled up a chair and sat at my bedside, 'before you start getting clever on me, Luighseach, I'll tell you something important: your polio saved my life.'

How could that be? Of the two of us it was Daid who was the stronger. Daid was the one who had saved my life. How could I have possibly saved his?

'Do you remember how hard it was after Mam died?' he began. 'How sad we both were and yourself, poor lass, you couldn't speak for shock. As for myself, all I wanted to do was to run to the end of the world.'

'Is that why we came here, Da?'

'Aye. In part it was. We talked about it years ago, you know. Your Mam's health being what it was we thought a warm and sunny place would do her good. And then came the war and there was little hope of travelling to foreign parts and— Well, you know what happened next. I couldn't bear it back home without your Mam. As for the like of yourself growing up less than a mile from where you saw her shot, 'twas unthinkable.

'Well, not long after we arrived here it seemed as if the end of the world wasn't far enough. 'Twas hard to find work and when I did I couldn't keep a job for tiredness and worry, and there was hardly money for food, let alone a place to sleep. I didn't know how I was ever to provide for you. And so I began to give up, lass. God forgive me, I decided to put an end to it all. Luighseach, I was going to take my own life.'

'Daid?' I could not believe what I had heard.

'We're none of us perfect, lass,' he gently remarked. 'And God knows it all too well, He does, for the day I came to the orphanage for to tell you good-bye was the day there was no little girl waiting for me at the gate. You'd fallen ill. The nuns they brought me to see you and there you were, all alone, unable to move and fighting for your very life. You put me to shame, lass. To think I despised my life so much I wanted throw myself over a cliff, while yourself, weak and sick as you were, you were clutching at a mere thread. I remember for the rest of that day walking till I could walk no more, and having no place to go I found a church and there I knelt and poured out my heart. I prayed that if Our Lord took you to Himself, would He take me too and if it was His will you should live that He would help me to live to take care of you. And would you know, lass, that very evening my prayers were answered.'

'How, Da?' I asked.

'Well, while I was praying there, I felt a tap on my shoulder, just like that,' and he tapped my own shoulder three times. 'Around I turned and there was a woman, an older woman with her hair all graying so and her face creased with care. "'Tis three candles I light every evening," she said. "Three candles for my three lads gone to Heaven. Well, tonight I lit a fourth. That fourth candle's for you, young man. Now, you look as if you could do with some dinner."

'Luighseach, never was a truer word spoken, and that night she took me to her home and fed me and gave me a bed and not a penny would she take for her trouble until I found myself a steady job. I think you know who it is I'm talking of.'

I shook my head.

"'Twas Mrs Murphy, lass, and all those months you were in hospital, 'twas herself and Mr Murphy, God rest his soul, looked after me as if I were one of their own. And then, slowly but surely, 'twas yourself became well again.'

'Except for my legs,' I added with regret.

'Aye, them poor legs of yours,' he sighed as he covered them with sheet and coverlet. But I'm telling you it's been a deep pleasure and a privilege to look after them legs and get you well. I'm not saying it's been easy. Not at all. And I know how much you like your independence, lass, but them legs of yours have done much good to many souls.'

'Like Mrs Murphy?'

'Aye, like Mrs Murphy,' echoed Daid in a very knowing way. 'And Mr David Birstall – a hard time was it for him trying to live without an arm – and then along comes yourself, hardly able to walk and that keen to play his 'cello. Do you remember the eggs, Luighseach?' he finished with a smile.

I began to laugh, thinking back to the time when Mr David had spent an afternoon in the kitchen showing me how to crack eggs with one hand. 'How many was it we'd broken, Daid?'

"'Twas a dozen to be sure, lass,' Daid replied and chuckled at the memory. 'And let you not forget the eggs that slipped to the floor. Dear Mother of God, never was there a Friday penance as that plateful of scrambled eggs we ate that night for tea.'

'You know, Da, I've not been able to eat scrambled eggs ever since.'

'Aye,' Daid agreed. 'And Mr David neither. Oiche maith, a Luighseach,' and he bent over and gave me a kiss.

'I love you, Daidí.'

'I love you too, lassie,' Daid smiled in return. 'And let you not think that God loves you any less for what has happened, Luighseach,' he said as he signed the cross on my forehead. 'Perhaps He loves you all the more. Did you ever think of it like that?

23

Phoebe's determination to watch the sunrise fully impressed itself upon me the following morning. She shook me from my dreams, pillaged my bed of its blankets and covers and repeatedly switched the light on and off, forcing me to make agonised sense of time and place.

'Hurry and get up, Lucy!' she ordered. 'The sun's coming and I've been shaking and calling for ages and ages and you don't move!'

I leaned over to my bedside table and fumbled for my glasses. Phoebe stood back and watched me with a mixture of wonder and concern as I manoeuvred my legs over the side of the bed. I reached for my crutches and hoisted myself up. She stepped aside to allow me passage.

Already shaved smooth and dressed in his Sunday best, Daid was adjusting one of my callipers when I entered the dining room. He stood, smiled a good morning, gave me a kiss and pulled out a chair.

'And how do you be today, Luighseach?'

I scowled at him as he helped me to my seat. As far as I was concerned, morning was not the most pleasant time of day. I yawned, laid my arms on the table, and rested my head.

'Your callipers are looking the worse for wear, lass,' Daid remarked. 'The leather's nearly worn through in parts now and the metal's been badly knocked about. What is it you been doing to make them so?'

'French cricket,' I mumbled into my arms. The right calliper had frequently been removed for the purpose of playing games and the left calliper had taken a beating from the consequent spills and falls.

'What was that?' Daid asked.

I raised my head. 'French cricket,' I repeated. 'Besides, I'm not wearing them today. I'm too tired,' I protested and I put my head back down on the table.

'Will you be needing your wheelchair, Luighseach?' asked Daid.

I shook my head. 'I'll use my crutches.'

'And you'll manage fine at Coogee?'

Phoebe quickly detected Daid's doubtful tone. 'We *are* going to see the sunrise, aren't we?' she queried.

'Aye, Phoebe,' I blearily replied as I staggered from my chair. 'I'll get myself ready now. Faith, it's cold.'

When I finally ventured outside, I found Phoebe waiting near the back shed, busily tucking one of Daid's scarves into her coat.

'I've never been on a motorcycle before,' she called gleefully, rubbing her gloved hands together. 'In fact, I hadn't even been in a motorcar until I went to Pim's place.'

We walked out the back gate together and met Daid in the lane. Daid helped us into the sidecar and gave Danny Irish instructions to stay. Then he hopped on the motorcycle. After a few false starts, we puttered down the deserted Sunday streets to Coogee.

Soon we were sailing and bumping up and down hills.

'Wheee!' squealed Phoebe in delight. 'It's so much fun!' she shouted.

But she grew more subdued as the journey progressed.

'Do you be all right there?' I called as we turned into Anzac Parade.

'I— think— I'm— going— to— be— sick!'

Daid pulled over to the curb.

By the time we arrived at Coogee, Phoebe was quite recovered. She discarded her shoes and stockings the moment we reached the beach. Down to the water she ran. The waves tickled her toes and she squealed and ran back again, beaming and gasping with joyful surprise.

'Brrrrrrr! It's so cold!' she frantically rubbed her legs. Upon noticing my smile she looked at me a little harder, twinkled and shook her curls in my face, 'Brrrrrrrrrrr!'

'Brrrrrrrrrrrr yourself,' and I shook my head back at her. 'What put it into your head to do this?'

'I wanted to get inspired, silly. For our quartet. It's got to be called the *Sunrise* quartet for a reason, doesn't it?'

'Aye. But did we need to get up at four o'clock in the morning to find out?'

'Well, I don't know how else you're going to see the sunrise. Is that the sun?' she asked as she pointed to the glow that crowned the horizon.

'No sun yet, Phoebe,' replied Daid who was busy organising his paints.

'Oh! Look at the colour! The sun's playing peek-a-boo!'

Phoebe's innocent enjoyment made me cast aside my own discomforts. Sitting on the promenade steps with a blanket over my legs for warmth, I could not help sharing her delight.

The sun, meanwhile, continued to trick her by donning a rainbow of disguises. But there was no mistaking the tyrien fanfare that proclaimed its arrival, and wild applause followed from the hands of an ecstatic Phoebe when it finally slipped into the sky.

'It's here! It's here!' she shouted, and down to the water she ran.

'I like to have a picture in my head or a story to tell while I play, don't you?' she asked me the moment she returned.

'Sometimes I do,' I replied while I considered the idea.

'You had a picture in your head when you played that piece in Miss Bray's workroom,' remarked Phoebe.

'Which one was that?'

Phoebe hesitated before she began to sing. Perplexed, I tried to make out the melody, but I had little more than the rhythm to go by, for despite her other musical gifts, Phoebe could hardly sing a note in tune. I eventually took up 'Danny Boy' myself. Pleased that I was able to make sense of her efforts, Phoebe smiled in appreciation.

''Twas a song my Mam used to sing me, that one,' I explained.

'It was beautiful,' Phoebe sighed a little wistfully.

'Which song was that, Luighseach?' asked Daid as he tinkled his brush in a cup of water.

''Twas "Danny Boy", Da. The "Derry Air" it was.'

Phoebe giggled.

'The Derrière,' she tittered and began to blow raspberries to the tune.

This was not a side of Phoebe I had seen before.

While Daid was busy painting, Phoebe and I decided to explore the new pier.

'Delleen Sotheby told me 'twas your grandmother taught you piano, Phoebe Raye,' I asked her as we walked together.

'That's right,' Phoebe proudly replied. 'Bobeshi taught me. That was what I called my grandmother. But she died when I was five. My mother taught me after that.'

'And what about when you went to the orphanage. Who taught you then? Was it the nuns?'

'Oh no,' Phoebe replied. 'The nuns never taught me. They certainly encouraged it, though. Not to practise would be a waste of God-given talent, so they insisted I practise. I studied at the Conservatorium. I still do. Mrs Epstein arranged for me to have lessons there.'

Here, the mention of Mrs Epstein had me a little perplexed.

'Mrs Epstein?' I queried.

'Yes.'

'Mrs Epstein?' I asked again. I could not reconcile Mrs Epstein and the orphanage.

'Mrs Epstein began to teach the violin at the orphanage not long after you fell sick,' Phoebe explained. 'She taught anyone who wanted to learn and soon began giving me special lessons. Then she took me to Mr Hutchens at the Conservatorium for piano tuition.'

The only conclusion I could reach regarding Mrs Epstein and the orphanage was that my teacher's generosity knew no bounds.

'So you've known Mrs Epstein all that time?'

'Yes. She gave me violin lessons twice a week. She used to take me to my piano lessons and afterwards she always made a point of treating me to tea. I've even stayed the night at her house.'

'Which one?' During my five years of study with Mrs Epstein, I had had my
'cello lessons in as many houses.

'All of them.'

'You stayed the night indeed?' In every instance, I had never been beyond the
boundary of Mrs Epstein's music room. 'What's it like there?' I asked.

'Quiet,' replied Phoebe. 'Or maybe I should say it's studious, because it's only
quiet when there's no music, which isn't very often because if Mrs Epstein's not
giving lessons she and Mr Epstein are usually practising or playing together. They
speak German when they're on their own or when they don't want me to know
what they're talking about; they don't have any children, and they bake bread that's
been braided and eat goulash.'

'Goulash is it?'

'It's a stew with meat and tomatoes and paprika and funny seeds in it. It's
probably the only thing Mrs Epstein doesn't burn. It's what makes that smell
when you go her house.'

'I've always wondered about that smell.'

'It's the paprika. I like it. I like the bread, too. It's sweet and moist and soft. Mr
Epstein makes it every Friday. Is that your father over there?'

I looked up from the water and could vaguely make out Daid standing on the
promenade, waving. I waved in reply.

'It must be time for to go to Mass,' I concluded, and tried to deduce what time
it might be from the position of the sun.

'Mass?' questioned Phoebe. 'I'm not going to Mass.'

Phoebe had pronounced the unthinkable. The only time I had missed Sunday
Mass was when I had been too sick to attend. Even then Daid had made sure I
received Holy Communion.

'But you have to go to Mass,' I replied.

'*I* don't *have* to do anything. And *I* don't go to Mass. I don't go and I won't go.'

'Does your aunt not take you?'

'Ailine? You've got to be joking! Ailine wouldn't be paid to set foot in a church.
Mrs Epstein tried—'

'Mrs Epstein?' I echoed again. This was too incredible. 'But— Mrs Epstein's
Jewish is she not?'

'Jewish? Mrs Epstein? No!' replied Phoebe in a very informed manner. 'Mr
Epstein's Jewish. Mrs Epstein's a Catholic, or she was a Catholic.'

'And how do you know that?'

'How else? She told me so.'

'Luighseach! Phoebe!' Daid's voice floated over the waves.

'She started taking me to Mass after I went to live with Ailine,' Phoebe
explained as we walked back down the pier, 'but it was embarrassing going with
her because she didn't know when to sit or kneel or stand, nor did she go to
Communion. I asked her why and she told me she'd been raised a Catholic but

she hadn't been to church for years. Then I asked her why not but she wouldn't say. So I asked whether it was because she'd done something bad and she said no it was because she did something good.'

There was a shout from Daid who now began to run towards us.

'Mrs Epstein doesn't go to Mass because she did something good?' I repeated, and tried in vain to see the logic in the statement.

'That's what she said, Lucy. After that she wouldn't talk about it. You know how she is when she's annoyed. I didn't like going with her anyway. It made me sad. A lot of people who go to church are not very kind to Mrs Epstein.'

It seemed odd that anyone could be unkind to one of the kindest people I ever knew.

'And why is that?' I asked, my concerns mounting.

'Because of the War, silly. Because Mr Epstein's Austrian. We were at the butcher's once, and the butcher's wife, who sat in front of us at Mass the Sunday before, wouldn't serve us even though we were third in line. Silly Mrs Epstein didn't do or say anything so I stepped in and made her serve us. And it was all because the butcher's wife lost her son at Messines. Honestly! It wasn't Mr Epstein's fault he went missing at Messines, let alone Mrs Epstein's. If that's the way Catholics behave I'd prefer to be Jewish than Catholic any day.'

'But you can't stop being a Catholic. You're not allowed to do that.'

'Says who? If Mrs Epstein can stop being a Catholic then I can too. Besides, Bobeshi was Jewish. She only became a Catholic because she grew up in France. That's what Ailine told me. So I'd prefer to be Jewish, like Bobeshi, thank you very much. And if I'm going to be Jewish I don't have to go to Mass.'

In my time I had employed many an argument for not going to Mass, but no argument of mine came anywhere near Phoebe's for sheer ingenuity.

'Well, you're not Jewish yet,' I concluded, 'so you ought to go. She's not going to Mass,' I informed my father who joined us on the pier, 'for she wants to be Jewish.' And I delivered the explanation with a roll of my eyes. Daid pursed his lips slightly as he glanced at Phoebe.

'Anyway, that would be hypocritical,' Phoebe continued to argue, 'to go without wanting to.'

'You're already being hypocritical,' I replied.

'I am not!'

'Aye you are. For you're doing the opposite of what you know to be right.'

'But——!'

'Come, Phoebe Raye. Don't you go telling me now that after seven years of living with nuns in an orphanage you don't be knowing it's a sin to miss Holy Mass.'

'Nuns! Why do I need nuns to tell me when I've got you? You're as bad as any nun ever was. Put you in a habit and no one could tell the difference between you and the nuns in that photograph on your mantelpiece.'

It was all perfectly true. Phoebe had noted the similarity between me and my aunt, Sister Gonzaga, who was also tall and thin with black-rimmed glasses.

While I fumed over the comparison, Daid, who had not yet said a word, quietly but firmly remarked, ''Tis better to do right and be ridiculed than do wrong and be praised.'

Daid may have intended his maxim to be a defence of my ground and I was grateful for his words. But as a repudiation of Phoebe's position it had little impact.

'You don't mean to say you actually like going to Mass,' she continued, pursuing another course of attack.

'Not particularly,' I replied, still anxious to dissociate myself from any connection with nuns.

'So you go to Mass because you have to, just because it's the right thing to do and it would be a sin if you didn't?' she scornfully questioned.

'Aye, sometimes I do.'

'That's not very good.'

'Indeed it isn't,' I agreed. 'But sometimes I can't do much better.'

'So you're going to leave the beach on a glorious sunny morning to go to Mass because some ridiculous rule says you ought to go?'

I stopped, shook my head and looked Phoebe firmly in the eye. 'Not today, Phoebe Raye. Today I'm going because I want to.'

And it was true. For once, I did want to go to Holy Mass.

Since Phoebe did not have any money for a tram ride home, she had to submit to riding back with us. Reluctantly she climbed into the sidecar and we drove to St Joseph's. She refused to go into the church, so Daid and I left her with the motorcycle. By the time we reached the top of the steps she was smoking a cigarette, quite unmindful of the raised eyebrows and surprised remarks of the other parishioners who were at that time arriving.

We were early for Mass that morning and so comfortably took our preferred place, two pews from the front. Daid passed me his Missal and left me to organise the ribbons at the appropriate points for the readings and prayers of the day. Meanwhile, he knelt, removed his glasses, blessed himself and closed his eyes in prayer.

Mrs Murphy entered, made an arthritic half-genuflection, and took her place in the pew opposite ours. As she did, she caught sight of me. Ordinarily she would have scowled me back to attention on the tabernacle. Today, however, she smiled and nodded good morning before pulling out her beads.

Once upon a time, the pew Mrs Murphy occupied alone would have been filled with her husband and three well-grown lads. Now she was obliged to move aside for the sake of the Geraghty family. Mr Geraghty, scrubbed until ruddy, stood in the aisle and ushered into the pew Hilda Geraghty, who was about my age, and seven more children ranging from an energetic boy of twelve, to a little lad of two who was clutching a piece of toast. Mrs Geraghty, heavy with child, came last of all. Mrs Murphy stood to let her through and she sat with a weary nod of thanks. Mr Geraghty sat too, and again Mrs Murphy took her post. She resumed her prayers which were now disrupted by shifting, wriggling children, and by intensifying demands for more toast from the two-year old who was subsequently taken out of the church by one of his sisters.

More families entered: fathers and mothers with troops of children; young couples not yet with family; courting pairs; elderly men and women whose sons and daughters had all grown up; war veterans, widows, all took their seats. Miss Jean Riley, who would have married Mrs Murphy's Paul, sat alone in the front pew. They were all people I had known by sight for years now, but I had never really spoken to any of them. Why had they all come? I wondered. Was it just to fulfil their Sunday obligation?

'Well, they're certainly not here because they've new hats,' I remarked to myself as I continued to survey the congregation. Daid, I knew, wore the suit he was married in, and I had seen those clean, white frocks pass down the ranks of the five Geraghty girls. As for Mrs Geraghty, she wore the same Sunday dress whether she was expecting a child or not.

'I wonder what story she has to tell,' and I resolved that, should the opportunity arise after Mass, I would say hello. 'She looks a kind mother,' I mused.

As for stories, my thoughts wandered back to what Daid had told me last night. Well, Daid certainly did not go to Mass because he ought. And he didn't go because life was easy, either. Life had been hard, cruel, had driven him to the brink of despair, and yet there he was, kneeling, prayerfully absorbed and peaceful. Like my father, I too closed my eyes, and as I did I recalled the worn-out face of Father Connolly and the words he spoke as we walked down the driveway of the presbytery in Moss Vale:

'You've just gotta trust, don't you?'

That morning, those words became my prayer. It wasn't really much of a prayer. They weren't fancy words at all – nothing elaborate or poetic – certainly not prayer book material, and they sent my thoughts along another trail. I recalled my first staggering, locked-legged steps after the Polio, when I held onto my father for dear life and collapsed exhausted into his arms after traversing barely a yard. Those steps had marked the beginning of a gritty reliance on my own scant resources, a foolhardy determination to succeed at all costs. There had been very little room for trust ever since, only ample space for resentment of anyone or anything that stood in my way – particularly God Whom I believed lay behind all my problems. Now, here I was considering that embracing all that had happened was a God who loved me more than I could ever imagine. All I had to do was trust.

And trust I did.

I began to trust.

The bell sounded for Mass. I gave Daid a poke and we stood while Father

Callaghan and the altar servers processed up the aisle. Behind gold cross and candles, altar boys and priest, a light, quick footstep sounded and in came Phoebe. She made a hasty genuflection and pushed her way in next to me.

'Guilty conscience is it?' I whispered as I sat.

'Not at all,' she replied. 'I was getting too hot.'

'Hot as hell, I'm thinking.'

Daid turned and put a warning finger to his lips.

We said no more. Daid went back to his missal and lovingly mulled his way through the liturgy. Phoebe rested her head on my shoulder and within minutes was asleep. And she wasn't the only one. Having succeeded in ferrying his family to Mass on time, Mr Geraghty had also nodded off and was quietly snoring.

'Better than not going at all,' I thought and wondered what God thought of sleeping through the Holy Sacrifice. Did God know Mr Geraghty did shift work? And I rested easy in knowledge of the fact that God probably did.

But what of those who did not go to Mass at all? That Phoebe's aunt did not attend came as little surprise. I did not have a high regard for Ailine Devereaux, and it seemed quite understandable that anyone who was as neglectful of their own flesh and blood as Ailine was toward Phoebe would be equally indifferent as to their Sunday obligations.

Mrs Epstein, however, was quite another matter. How could you not go to Mass because you had done something good? That did not make sense. In my limited experience, people who prayed, people who attended Church were people who tried to do good. They had their faults, certainly, but they meant well nonetheless. The nuns, on the whole, were good people; Mrs Murphy was a kindly soul; and in my eyes there was no one better than Daid. Now, another of my syllogisms concerning life was being torn asunder. To wilfully not hear Sunday Mass was a mortal sin. If you died in mortal sin, you went to Hell. But I could not come to terms with the idea that my beloved 'cello teacher, who did not go to Mass because she did something good, could end up in the inferno.

I sighed.

Already my trust was under siege.

After Mass, Daid and I bid good morning to Father Callaghan and introduced him to a suddenly shy Phoebe. I smiled and greeted Mrs Geraghty, but received little more than a brief hello in return for she was too busy with her youngest charge to talk. Behind her came Hilda Geraghty and our eyes chanced to meet.

'Hello Hilda,' I made an effort to smile.

'Why hello, Lucy,' Hilda replied in a surprised but friendly manner.

'How are you?' she attempted a conversation.

'I'm well, thank you,' I answered and quickly deflected the conversation away from the unpleasant topic of my health by introducing Phoebe. Hilda eyed Phoebe curiously as she said hello and continued her study while I told her of our morning's excursion. But I had to resign myself to the fact that it was little wonder Hilda found Phoebe more interesting than anything I had to say. With her beautiful complexion, exotic curls and outmoded clothes, Phoebe was indeed a curiosity. Phoebe, in response, said and did very little. I could see her fingers drumming a pattern on her skirt, however, and this was a clear indication that she had music on her mind.

'Saints alive!' Hilda suddenly exclaimed, with an excited smile at my young friend. 'I know where I've seen you! You're the piano player at the Picture Palace!'

Phoebe suspended her fingering activity and nodded.

'Oh, I think you're the bee's knees!' continued Hilda. 'You do the nicest music and you make it fit the scene perfectly. I always like it when you play.'

'You play for the pictures, Phoebe Raye?' This was news. 'And how long is it you been doing that?'

'Only this year,' replied Phoebe in her usual matter-of-fact manner. 'I do Saturday afternoons and evenings mostly and a matinee or two during the week. I don't go to school on those days,' she added proudly. School was beneath Phoebe.

'So that's your business engagement now? Piano player at the Picture Palace?' I questioned.

'Yes.'

'Hope you don't mind me asking, but does it pay well?' asked Hilda.

'I buy food and cigarettes,' informed Phoebe.

'Food you buy?' I questioned. 'And does not your aintín feed you?'

'Why should she?' answered Phoebe. 'I can feed myself.'

'You didn't play yesterday, did you?' Hilda inquired.

Phoebe nodded.

'What did they show?'

Phoebe informed her and conversation galloped away at a very lively pace indeed, for Phoebe had seen every film that Hilda had seen at least twice over, much to Hilda's amazement and delight. All I could do was listen and try my best to make what I could of the latest picture palace entertainment.

Daid, who had been chatting on the steps below, came to inform me that he was going to give Mrs Murphy a ride home.

'Do you mind waiting while I take her, Luighseach?' he asked, knowing full well that I would not mind given that I was occupied with a conversation of my own. ''Tis her hip's giving her some trouble,' he explained.

I consented, and, while simultaneously attempting to follow the news of next week's picture (which Phoebe had already seen), watched my father graciously assist Mrs Murphy into our sidecar.

'Hilda, we're going!' called Mr Geraghty, who with his family was sitting ready in their cart. Hilda's shoulders sagged in disappointment.

'Do you mind if I walk?' she called.

'Don't be too long,' called Mrs Geraghty.

'Do you mind walking?' Hilda asked us, looking eagerly at Phoebe and more worriedly at me. 'I don't live too much further than you, Lucy.'

Phoebe and I looked at each other and nodded.

'Can you walk that far?' Hilda glanced at my legs and crutches.

'Don't mind Lucy,' Phoebe confidently advised. 'She's strong as an ox.'

I smiled. Coming from Phoebe, that was praise indeed.

'But how are you going to get down the steps?' asked Hilda who knew full well that Daid usually carried me up and down the church steps, which were irregular, steep and without a handrail. I answered by lowering myself to sitting position and levering my way down, scrambling and unscrambling my legs in the process.

'What to talk about now?' I wondered. But there turned out to be plenty to talk about. As we walked up King Street, Hilda readily chatted about the exploits of her younger siblings, the last lot of scrag chops she had purchased at the butcher's, which ribbons she liked in the haberdashery and the best place to buy cream buns.

'Do you like going to the pictures, Lucy?' she asked me when we reached my house.

'I don't be going too often,' I had to own.

'Well, what about coming with me on Saturday? Are you playing then, Phoebe?'

Phoebe said she was.

'It would be nice to go with you,' continued Hilda. 'I don't get much of a chance to see anyone now that I'm home all the time. Most of my old school friends are working at the factories or have city jobs. We occasionally see each other, but nowadays we don't seem to have as much to talk about. Would you come with me?' she seemed genuinely eager for the friendship.

'Aye,' I smiled. 'I'll come. Next Saturday is it?'

We waved each other off. Phoebe and I crossed the road to my house. As was to be expected, Mrs Murphy appeared on her front steps.

'Yoohoo! Lucy!' she called. 'I'm bringing down a roast, dear. Make sure your father's set the oven to the right temperature. You know what he's like.'

'Aye, Mrs Murphy!' I yelled back and waved.

'Not too hot, mind you,' warned Mrs Murphy. 'Just enough to keep everything warm while I do the greens.'

Daid had already made porridge and we ate hungrily before disappearing to opposite corners of the house: Phoebe to practise, and me, exhausted, to the comfort of my bed. Mrs Murphy arrived towards noon carrying a roasting pan sizzling with beef and onions, potatoes and pumpkin, which she placed on a plate and popped into our oven. Much to my delight, she then set about teaching me how to make gravy and had me stirring away while she prepared the Brussels sprouts.

Phoebe, meanwhile, continued to practise and practise. I found myself stirring the gravy in time to gruelling double stopped scales. Then followed a study featuring hook strokes, and while I set the table I could not refrain from imitating the stroke with knives and forks and spoons. Finally our dinner was dished up to fragments of our quartet. But Phoebe did not restrict herself to practising her own part. She was also practising Della's.

Daid treated Mrs Murphy with a mixture of respect and humour that could only be described as filial. He showed her to her seat and carved the meat for her, praised her for the meal and talked to her of all the things he knew interested her. Mrs Murphy, in her turn, regarded Daid with warm admiration, as if he were her oldest and dearest son.

I smiled at them and shifted a little in my seat.

'Everything all right with you, Luighseach?' Daid asked.

'Can you stop being a Catholic?' I asked, at last giving voice to the subject which had most troubled me that morning.

'Stop being a Catholic? The questions you come up with!' exclaimed Mrs Murphy.

'Come now, Mrs Murphy,' soothed Daid. 'If you don't ask questions you don't get answers. Aye, Luighseach, you can stop being a Catholic.'

'And if you do,' cautioned Mrs Murphy, 'you'll find yourself on the high road to the hot place.'

'For not going to church?' I questioned. 'And what if you're a good person? 'Tis not merely about going to church is it? What if you're good at heart? Is it not more important to be good at heart?'

'Well what does the catechism tell us now?' Daid calmly responded and immediately began to supply the answer. ''Tis that we must know, love and serve God in this world...'

'And love Him forever in Heaven,' I dutifully replied. Like my father, I knew every word of my catechism.

'Aye, that's it,' accorded Daid. 'And ought we to judge, Luighseach?'

Mrs Murphy answered for me. 'Judge not lest ye yourselves be judged,' she said with a firm nod of her chin.

'You ought to—'

'Take your own medicine,' I was about to add, when Daid cut me short.

'Well then, Luighseach,' he said, 'let's leave the knowing and loving up to ourselves and the judging up to God.'

Phoebe arrived, took one look at the Brussels sprouts and wrinkled her nose in disgust.

'What beautiful music you play, dear,' commented Mrs Murphy.

'Franck sonata,' Phoebe absently replied as she sat down. 'Exhausting.'

She did not say much more after that, she was far too preoccupied. But she revived with the roast beef to the extent that she answered any questions that came her way with some measure of civility.

After dinner, Daid suggested a game of cribbage and fetched the board and cards from the living room. Cribbage was an old favourite with us, dating from the time I was in hospital when we devoted entire afternoons to the game. Mrs Murphy was also a keen cribbage player and apparently had been responsible for showing Daid how to play.

The only card games Phoebe knew were children's games like 'Old Maid' and 'Beg o' my neighbour', but she seemed willing, if not eager to learn cribbage. Daid arranged that we play in partnership so that he could show her how to play. Mrs Murphy was a solid ally and she and I easily won the first two games. Phoebe resented being skunked twice in a row and resolved she and Daid would win the third. Through the luck of good cards and improved strategy they did, and Phoebe clapped and cheered at the victory.

I had never seen her so utterly normal. Gone were the coquettish mannerisms, no cigarettes were smoked, no smart remarks were made. The only time I had seen her as happy as that was when she was playing the piano. She gathered the cards and passed them to me, and as she did she gave me a rare smile. I smiled in return, took the cards, shuffled them and dealt another hand, and we played long into the afternoon.

By the following morning, however, Phoebe had disappeared without as much as a word or note.

24

Although it was a cold and windy Autumn afternoon, I was determined that the weather was not going to stop me from missing a lesson with Mrs Epstein. For this time it was to be a session on our quartet – the first after too many weeks. I stood on Newtown station and watched the train as it hissed and chugged and finally steamed to a stop. The carriage doors rumbled open and a few people alighted. I boarded the train and took my seat, as I usually did, near the guard's compartment.

I was not alone in my choice. A middle-aged woman, who was a rather stout and sensible person with a handbag, came down the carriage and sat opposite me.

She did so with an annoyed 'Humph!'

'I don't know what it is with young people nowadays,' she began with a brief glance at my legs. 'Hoodlums in there,' she continued and nodded in the direction of the main part of the carriage. 'I've told them that many times to quieten down. You'd think they owned the train the way they're carrying on.'

An outburst of raucous laughter underscored her remark. The two of us looked at the band of youths which occupied a bay of seats and the neighbouring section of the aisle. From the shouts and gestures that followed, they seemed to be engaged in a very lively debate. My travel companion tightened her hold on her handbag and 'Humphed' again. I tried to refrain from smiling and managed to prevent the smile from escaping by pulling out Mr Pope and finding my place.

The journey proceeded relatively smoothly. I continued to read, the larrikins continued to banter and argue, and the woman continued to 'Humph' and shift with every laugh and shout.

That was, until the train arrived at Petersham.

I did not realise I had reached my destination until I glimpsed a capital 'P' in a station sign. How long the train had already stopped at the station I had no idea. I hastily pushed my book into my satchel, slung my satchel over my shoulder, grabbed my crutches and pulled myself up.

The next thing I knew I was flat on my face on the carriage floor. A whistle blew, there was a toot of steam, and with a jolt the train began to pull out from the station.

'Oh my Jesus!' I called. 'Help!'

'A girl like you shouldn't be using public transport,' declared the handbag woman as she used her foot to push one of my crutches towards me. 'You'll get yourself killed.'

'Lucy!' called a voice from the direction of the hoodlums.

I looked up and saw Wally Sotheby striding towards me.

'Lucy!' he said again as he bent down next to me. 'I thought it was you. Are you all right?'

'Does the guard know? Did you call the guard?' he rapidly questioned the handbag woman before I could answer.

'Is that the way to address a lady? You mind your manners, boy!' the woman cautioned.

Wally didn't bother to mind his manners. He walked to the guard's compartment and banged loudly on the door. The guard entered, took one look at the situation and applied the emergency brake. The train ground to a halt.

'I'll tell the driver,' said the guard. 'Were you getting off at Petersham, miss?'

I dragged myself back against a seat and nodded helplessly. The guard left the carriage and made his way to the front of the train.

'I say, Lucy, you're shaking,' Wally gently observed. 'Here, take my jacket,' and he placed his jacket over my shoulders. I pulled it close around me. 'What happened?' he asked as he knelt beside me.

'I—I don't know, Wally Sotheby,' I replied. 'My leg collapsed.'

'Let's have a look. Which leg was it?' And he pulled from his waistcoat pocket a pair of gold-rimmed spectacles and began to examine my legs and callipers.

'Hey, Toffee! How's your patient?' The remaining half-dozen rogues converged on the scene.

'Get on, you lot!' replied Wally with a grin. 'Can't you see she's in shock?' he added more seriously. After that, Wally paid no more attention to his mates and continued to look over my legs. 'I think I've found the problem,' he commented and indicated my left calliper. I leant forward to look. One of the rivets at the knee joint had popped out, and the ring which locked the joint had fallen off. On the other side, which was already bent, the ring had jammed and as a result had failed to slide and lock the joint. Little wonder my leg had collapsed.

'Jesus, Mary and Joseph!' I muttered.

'What's up?' he asked.

''Tis broken,' I sighed. 'It must have come apart when I fell.'

Wally put his hand on my shoulder and gazed at me in a kindly way, his blue eyes a little magnified like his sister's. 'Don't worry. I'll see if I can find the pieces. What am I looking for?'

And he commenced what turned out to be a fruitless search for the missing parts. The search extended to the territory staked out by the handbag lady who furiously began to object. Meanwhile, the guard returned.

'Driver's taking the train back to Petersham, miss,' he announced over the top of the handbag lady's complaints about Wally. 'We're not too far out as it is.'

As he spoke, the train slowly started to reverse. Soon we were again at the station. The guard opened the door.

'You all right to get out?' he asked me.

Wally, his waistcoat filthy from lying prostrate under the seats in his quest for the missing rivet and ring, stood and took it upon himself to answer in my place.

'She's pretty shaken. And her leg's not right. She can't walk.'

He then began to converse more quietly with the guard and between them they made a decision.

'Come on, miss,' said the guard, who was a short and burly man. 'I'll carry you.'

The guard picked me up and took me to the station master who escorted us to his office. Wally followed carrying my crutches and satchel, and was cheered by his mates who were all leaning out of the carriage windows and banging the side of the train with their fists. Mr Hogan the station master, who knew me from Mass at St Joseph's, made us a cup of tea.

'Where are you going, Lucy?' Wally asked as he sipped.

I told him.

'Of course,' he replied. 'Della mentioned something about her quartet practice last night.'

'And yourself?' I asked him.

'I've been down at the bridge,' he answered. 'We went early this morning to have a bit of a snoop around.'

It so happened that Wally and his mates had been out and about on the bridge site since dawn. They had inspected one side and then caught a ferry across to the north shore where they had explored the other side.

'We managed to climb the approaches before we were chased off,' he told me. 'Spectacular view,' he added. 'Then we had a look at the tunnels for the underground and took off to the pictures after that. Now we're going to Archie's for tennis.'

'And do you think the bridge will meet in the middle?' I asked him.

'Of course,' Wally confidently replied. 'It's absolutely brilliant.'

Wally had quite a detailed knowledge of the endeavour, having closely followed the bridge's progress. His experience was supplemented with facts gleaned from building and engineering articles. Along with the Station Master, the Porter and the Ticket Master, I listened happily, fascinated by his explanation.

A distant toot was heard.

'You catching this train, young man?' asked Mr Hogan as he left to see to his duties.

Wally looked at me and smiled warmly. 'You seem much better now. How are you getting to your lesson?' he asked. 'I—I could walk you there if you'd like.'

'But are you not playing tennis this afternoon?' I asked.

'I've a whole afternoon to play tennis.'

'Then 'twould be very kind of you to walk me if you don't mind my—'

I was going to say callipers and stopped myself. I did not want to draw any more attention to them.

''Twould be very kind of you indeed, Wally Sotheby,' I repeated.

The train steamed in and the Ticket Master went to collect the tickets. Presently he returned with a recalcitrant in tow.

'What do you think you're doing?' protested the offender. 'I've got a valid ticket! You can't do this to me! I haven't done anything wrong!'

The voice became more familiar as it neared. Sure enough, it was Pim.

'So you're the problem!' she exclaimed, her indignation disappearing the instant she saw me. 'You been holding up trains now? Might have known!' she added with a smile.

'Hello Pim,' said Wally.

'What are you doing here?'

'Station Master's holding the train for you, lad, if you want to catch it,' interrupted the Ticket Master.

Wally quickly assessed the situation and decided to go. He picked up his jacket, put on his cap and tipped us good bye.

Pim gave me a very curious look but said nothing.

'I thought you'd be catching the tram to Mrs Epstein's, Pim. Did you not come from the Quay?'

'Not exactly,' she answered. 'I popped in at your place to see if you needed a hand. You weren't there so I walked to the station and caught a train. You all right?'

I explained what happened and showed her the broken calliper.

'So what are you going to do now?' Pim asked.

Mr Hogan made some suggestions and offered to convey a message to Daid. In the end, we left the callipers at the station for Daid to collect. The Porter carried me up and down the steps to the street, and Pim and I set off to see our teacher.

'Actually, I've been with Peggy,' Pim explained after we had walked awhile. 'You remember I told you about my sister Peggy?'

'She's the one you've not seen for some time, is that right?'

Pim nodded. 'I wrote her a few weeks ago and right when I was about to give up on her I got a letter. She suggested we have lunch together.'

'''Twas good to see her again was it not?'

'It wasn't too bad. Nearly had an argument but I managed to keep my lid on.'

'Well, it seems I'm not the only one with an Irish temper.'

'Nah,' Pim agreed with a smile. 'You know, she lives in your neck of the woods.'

'Does she indeed?'

'Teaches violin and works in a music shop in Erskinville. Turned out to be not too far from your place.'

'You've a lot in common then with your music?'

'Suppose so. And you're right. Peggy was the one who first taught me violin. We used to play a lot together – duets and stuff.'

'Do you miss her?' I missed those happy times making music with my own family.

'Well, it all stopped when she left home, didn't it? You seen anyone lately?' she asked, changing the subject.

'Only Phoebe it is I've seen. She stayed a couple of days at our house, you know.'

Pim whistled. 'How'd you survive that?'

''Twas a grand time we had. She arrived out of the blue one Saturday evening and stayed a night and a day. Then she left without as much as a word and I've not seen her since.'

'Well, she's already at Mrs Ep's. Can you hear the piano? It's got to be Phoebe. Not even Mr Ep plays like that.'

We rang the bell, listened to the distant Chopin Ballade, and looked at each other as we waited, knowing full well the reprimand we were about to get for being late.

Mrs Epstein ushered us inside. She was too annoyed that Della was not with us to give us much of a scolding.

'What are you staring at?' she asked me.

'Yourself,' I replied.

'Well, stop gawping and go into the music room where it's warm. Your 'cello's there. What was your father doing to drop it off so early?'

'Photographing the quality on the North Shore he is today,' I explained.

'Not painting?'

'Not at the moment, although he's keen to do some more.'

'I imagine he would be. If I were in his shoes, I'd be itching to enter the Archibald. I hear he's exhibiting, though.'

'Aye he is. With Mr Cazneaux. A photograph of a steam train he's showing and you should see the way he's done the smoke.'

'Make sure you give him my congratulations.'

'He'll be happy to hear that, Mrs Epstein. For I let my temper on him when he said I'd have to catch the train today on account of himself being too busy to take me.'

'Luighseach! After all—'

'I'm knowing, Mrs Epstein. A talking to I received already about the fact that God in His goodness and mercy made the world revolve around the sun and not around myself.'

'And will continue to do so for some time to come, I believe,' replied my teacher. 'Cocoa?'

We readily agreed.

The piano stopped the moment we entered. Phoebe ran over and gave me a hug hello. We sat down together and exchanged news.

'You left without even a note, Phoebe Raye. Where did you go?' I asked her. 'Did you go home?'

She shook her head. 'Not for long. I came here instead,' she answered.

'You've been staying with Mrs Ep?' queried Pim.

Phoebe nodded. 'I had to play the piano somewhere! Ailine's still having an orgy.'

'A what?' Pim was incredulous.

The doorbell rang. We listened for the expected upbraiding. Sure enough it came, followed by an equally predictable apology:

'I'm so very sorry, Mrs Epstein. Mummy insisted I play something for her luncheon guests. I simply couldn't get away any earlier.'

Della entered, as dainty and delicate as ever.

'I say, it is good to see you all again,' she beamed.

'And a grand time was it you spent with Fanny Mahony?' I asked.

'Super,' Della replied. 'Actually, I met someone you both know. "Aunt Rose" sends her very warm regards.'

'How'd you meet Rose?' asked Pim.

'At the picnic races. Your aunt knows the Mahonys very well – I think she and Mrs Mahony were at school together. Anyway, we picnicked with her family. It was a lovely day. And what have you been up to, Pim?' asked Della.

'Mangling sheets and making lemon meringue pies,' answered Pim as she helped herself to a scone and took the cup of cocoa Mrs Epstein poured for her. 'Swear I've made at least fifty over the last couple of weeks. If I see any more meringue, I'll throw up.'

'And if you eat any more, you're going to burst,' observed Della with a giggle.

'In your mouth for a minute, on your hips for a life time,' remarked Mrs Epstein as she sat with us.

'Oh, come on, Mrs Ep,' Pim complained, her mouth full of scone.

'Now,' Mrs Epstein had decided there was no more time to waste. 'I thought you might like to listen to a recording before we start playing. Della, have you a copy of the score?'

'I'm sorry, Mrs Epstein,' answered Della with a very guilty look. 'I—'

'I do,' Phoebe came to Della's rescue. She dusted the crumbs from her fingers and began to look for the requested item in her music bag.

'What are *you* doing with a score?' asked Pim.

'I found it,' retorted Phoebe who brandished a little book and passed it to Mrs Epstein.

'Where did you get this?' Mrs Epstein inquired as she took it. The book itself was clearly very familiar to her.

'I found it in the bookcase upstairs,' Phoebe explained. 'Is it yours? It doesn't look like your writing.'

'No, it's not,' our teacher fondly flicked through the pages. We all leant over to have a better look. The score was crawling with bowing indications. These were coupled with annotations in English, written in a neat but florid hand, as well as what must have been German, if the gothic script was any gauge. A skull and crossbones marked the occasional problematic section.

'You should find this very useful,' Mrs Epstein passed the score to Della. 'First violinist's responsibility: know the score. You all need to be familiar with it, but Della needs to know it inside out. Now for the recording,' she announced.

Mrs Epstein pulled a record from a large album. She passed the album to us before setting the record carefully on the gramophone.

'I say, Mrs Epstein,' Della excitedly exclaimed as she studied the handwritten label on the front. 'The Klimt Quartet. That's not your quartet, is it?'

'Yes, that was my quartet,' Mrs Epstein replied.

'"Haydn, *Sunrise*, Klimt Quartet, Vienna, 1910",' Della read. 'Did you live in Vienna?'

'I studied there.'

'In 1910, Mrs Epstein?' I remarked with a smile. 'Faith, you must be old. I wasn't even born then.'

'Enough of your cheek, Luighseach Straughan,' Mrs Epstein smiled back. 'Anyway, the recording was a bit of an experiment, but a worthwhile one nevertheless. Listen.'

Gradually the music ground its way out of the shell-like speaker and, before long, none of us could resist accompanying the musicians by fingering through our respective parts. It was the quality of the first violinist's playing, however, that had us most captivated.

'You don't expect me to play like that, do you, Mrs Epstein?' inquired Della.

Mrs Epstein smiled. 'It's good, isn't it?'

'Is it you?' asked Pim.

'Heavens no,' answered our teacher. 'I'm playing second violin.'

We all looked at her for further explanation. Mrs Epstein obliged. 'Mr Epstein,' she continued, 'is playing viola of course, and two very dear friends are playing first violin and 'cello.'

'Do you still play together?' asked Della.

Mrs Epstein shook her head. 'The War, among other things, put a stop to all that, I'm afraid.'

As she spoke, there was an edge in her tone which warned us that further questions on the matter were not necessarily going to be warmly received. Mrs Epstein clarified her position by removing the record from the gramophone the moment it finished and bustling us into action.

'You can listen to the rest of it another time,' she said in response to our protests that we had heard only half the first movement. 'We've an hour before I'm expecting another student and you'll be better off doing some playing yourselves. Tune up, please. Luighseach, it's a 'cello lead, so could you count us in?'

'Myself?'

'First violin enters after the opening chord,' Mrs Epstein explained. ''Cello takes the lowest note so it will be your bow that dictates when the others should play.'

'And how fast will we be playing it?' I asked.

'*Allegro con spirito*: lively, with spirit. Quite fast. Della's semiquavers will give you an idea. Della, could you play from bar twenty-two, please?'

Della complied with a nervous, but nonetheless competent, rendition.

''Twould be a hundred and twenty four beats a minute,' I observed, only to hear a groan from Della, Pim and Phoebe. 'Arrah!' I protested. ''Tis how fast she's playing it!'

Mrs Epstein confirmed my estimate with her metronome and a suppressed chuckle. 'Yes, Luighseach. One hundred and twenty four beats will be fine.'

'How on earth did you know that?' asked Pim.

'When I was sick, sometimes I—I would fiddle with the metronome and play at guessing the different speeds. I ended up memorising them,' I confessed and sheepishly looked at the others.

'Well, count us in, you old pedant,' laughed Della as she raised her violin.

Della, however, could not reconcile the tempo of her more languid opening bars with the excitement of her faster passages. Mrs Epstein repeatedly stopped her, warning her that if she began that quickly she would have us shipwrecked in no time.

The constant interruptions and corrections drove Della to teary frustration.

'I can't do it!' she lamented.

'This whole quartet is about tempo and keeping in time. Think of your semiquavers and fit your quavers accordingly,' Mrs Epstein advised. 'Take a deep breath and think it through. Let's do it together.'

Matters improved with Mrs Epstein playing alongside; but as soon as she withdrew, Della was helpless.

'You're going to have to do some metronome practice,' remarked our teacher.

'No! Please!' Della wailed.

'No, I don't mean that ticking thing there. I quite agree. It's awful,' Mrs Epstein replied. 'But you're fortunate enough to have a human metronome in your 'cellist friend. Take advantage, Della. Do a bit of practice with Luighseach. She'll sort you out. First violin and 'cello have a lot of work to do together in this quartet. For now, however, let's take it up from bar twenty-two. Della, listen to the 'cello. That's your pulse.'

Mrs Epstein drilled us and drilled us through the section at a variety of tempi, fast and slow, to make sure we understood, intimately, how to play rhythmically and in time. Finally we had the satisfaction of playing together at the correct tempo without error. We were rewarded with a much-needed break when the telephone and the doorbell sounded simultaneously.

Mr Epstein popped his head into the music room.

'Luighseach,' he said. 'Your father telephoned to let you know he'll come for you in half an hour.'

Mrs Epstein's next student entered and we were required to pack up. Phoebe and I waved Pim and Della down the street and returned to the music room.

'And the orgy's still underway is it, Phoebe?' I asked quietly.

Phoebe took the remaining scone. 'Cedric, Harry and Arthur have taken over the house,' she whispered in a fervid and urgent tone, her eyes wide. 'Ailine is painting Arthur and he spends the entire day in nothing more than a dressing gown. He and Cedric are fairies.'

242

'Aye, and I'm one of the little people,' I laughed. Mrs Epstein stopped her student and gave me a deadly look.

'Don't be silly, Lucy!' scolded Phoebe, 'They— Oh, never mind! And Harry kept on coming into the music room to talk to me about some libi-thingummy which he says generates creative activity.'

'A what is it?'

'A libido thing. He said everyone has it inside them and that they have to release it because it gets suppressed. I kept on telling him to go away because it has nothing to do with Chopin and he ignored me. And Cedric writes poetry – awful stuff which makes absolutely no sense – and he thinks he's a genius. Worst of all, the house stinks of opium.'

'Is that what that smell is? Opium? What is it?'

'It's something they smoke. They smoke opium and you get no sense out of them for days when they do.'

'And of yourself—?'

'Luighseach and Phoebe!' Mrs Epstein interrupted with considerable exasperation. 'If you two cannot be quiet, you're going to have to go somewhere else. Phoebe, haven't you anything better to do?'

Phoebe refrained from action until Mrs Epstein began again to insist she go elsewhere. Then she sighed, curled her lip, picked up her violin, propped it under her chin and dawdled out, testing her strings the while. I remained on the couch and waited for Daid, and tried not to groan every time Mrs Epstein's student played out of tune.

25

More than a week had now passed since our rehearsal at Mrs Epstein's. Winter, by this time, was well on its way, and with the cold came red, swollen toes, blisters, itchy feet and chilblains. It was Friday, and I awoke as usual to Daid's familiar creak across the floorboards and Danny's cheery clatter which always indicated their return from early Mass. A series of 'good morning' scratches on my door followed by 'Hoigh! Danny! Ná bí dána!' preceded Daid's knock.

'Do you be awake now, Luighseach?'

'Aye, Daidí,' I replied from my cocoon of eiderdowns and flannel sheets.

Daid entered with a basin, Friar's balsam, towels and fresh dressings which he placed on my bedside table. He undid the bandages on my feet and removed the towels and the potato poultices he had bound on them the night before.

''Tis better they're feeling, Daidí.'

'And they're looking better too, Luighseach, despite the blisters. But I'm thinking 'twill be a few more days of rest for you.' Daid would not let me say anything in reply. 'We're needing to get you well before school goes back, Luighseach, for there'll be no classes for you till them chilblains be healed. Doctor's orders they be and you're knowing that.'

I conceded with a sigh while Daid, his every movement studied by his doggy disciple, handled my feet as if they were vessels made óf the finest crystal rather than misshapen clay. Carefully he washed them, dabbed them dry, gently painted them with Friar's Balsam and re-packaged them in bandages, socks and knitted slippers. What would I be wearing today? He asked, and quietly gathered my requests before waiting outside while I changed. Then, with a kiss on my forehead, he picked me up, took me out to the chair and wheeled me into the dining room. The next piece of news was good indeed and Daid delivered it with an appropriate morning twinkle.

''Twas extra fatai I cooked last night, Luighseach. Will you be eating some boxty for breakfast?'

Daid knew only too well that I would and before long we were happily partaking of one of our favourite meals.

Once again he had a busy day ahead. There was an important photographic session up north that morning, followed by an afternoon of bread and butter by which he meant his ordinary studio work.

'And is it anything you're needing while I'm out now, Luighseach Ní Sruitheáin?' Daid asked me as he passed me a washed plate.

''Tis a book I'm needing, Daidí, for Mr Pope I finished this night past.'

'Well, 'tis on the sideboard I'll leave some money for Mrs Murphy—'

I crashed the plate to the table. 'You'll not be letting Mrs Murphy buy the book, Da! For 'tis holy books she'll buy. I'll not be reading holy books.'

'Nothing wrong there bees with holy books,' Daid remained perfectly calm and passed the second plate. 'And the Lord God knows it does be good for you to read the like from time to time for 'tis much wisdom in them to be sure.'

'Aye, Daid. Like there's soot in a fireplace. 'Tis enough I've had of holy books.' I sent the second plate to the table.

'Enough is it? And when were you reading holy books, Luighseach? Never did I see you reading holy books.'

'Mrs Murphy's reading me *Lives of the Saints.*'

'And a blessing on her for doing so. Here's a cup. 'Tis the saints do help many a soul to devotion.'

'The devil with them I'm saying.' Down went the cup.

'And I'm saying that's not possible. I'm thinking you're afeard of them.'

'I amn't.'

'So you are, so you are I can see it.' Dish mop in hand, Daid turned round and bent over a little. He looked sharply inside me, sparkled and proceeded with a slight joust. ''Tis fear lurking in your eyes, skulking like a fox through the snow. Fear that our Good Lord might ask a little more of you.'

'I'll not be like the Jesuits, Daidí,' I was in earnest.

Daid jerked the plug chain, wiped his hands on my tea towel and hung it for me.

'Is it nuns the problem now?' He laughed as he removed his apron, hung it and restored me to the wheelchair in the dining room. 'Well, maybe God in His mercy decided to spare the convent of yourself and your noising, and yourself of the convent by sending you the polio. You'll not be fretting on that, Luighseach Meidhbhín. Let you love Our Good Lord in the little things He sends you from one day to the next, come what may.' He wheeled me into the parlour. With a final check to see I was warm enough and our morning prayers concluded, Daid donned jacket and hat and prepared to leave.

''Tis Danny will stay home for to keep you company and Mrs Murphy will be down soon to help you along and see to lunch. I'll not return till tea. And let you remember – you'll not be sitting on top of the fire now.'

'Aye, Da. Maith an lá dhuit, a Dhaidí.'

'Go ngnóthaí Dia dhuit, a Luighseach.'

****

'May the Divine Assistance remain always with us.'

'And may the souls of the faithful departed through the mercy of God, rest in peace. Amen, Father, Son, Ghost.' I made a speedy sign of the cross and quickly kissed and pocketed my beads. 'Mrs Murphy.'

How many more prayers could Mrs Murphy say? She indicated for me to wait while several more petitions were lodged with the Immaculate Heart. The medals dangling from her own rosary she kissed one, two, three and four times over. Then, at last, she laboured up from the kneeler and hobbled towards me.

'What is it, child?'

''Tis the third Rosary you made me pray today. I done my fair share of mysteries, Mrs Murphy. Would it not be putting it out of you too much to buy me a book in return?'

Mrs Murphy began to rearrange my blanket. 'Day in, day out: books and violins! Books and—'

''Cello it is! 'Cello, 'cello, 'cello! You're forget—'

'Doesn't anything else fill your head?' she rested her arms on either arm of my wheelchair and gave me a good opportunity to study her safety pin closely. It was fastened in the wrong buttonhole. Then she smiled a creased, zinc, toothy smile which showed up all the crows' feet round her eyes.

'Very well,' she conceded. 'You've been a good girl today. I can't complain. What sort of book would you like?'

I was not prepared to allow Mrs Murphy neither an ounce of her own initiative nor trust her with an ounce of her memory. 'I'll none of saint books, Mrs Murphy. Mr Thomas up at the bookshop knows what I've read and what I've not so let you ask himself for advice.'

For that I had a finger wagged in my face and my blanket arranged a second time. 'If only you knew what was good for you, Lucy.'

'And you think I don't, Mrs Murphy? 'Tis the like of holy books and castor oil and rosaries and beef broth and may St Jude have mercy on me for putting up with it all.'

'Indeed he will. And your dear father's already given me firm instructions – no holy books.' Mrs Murphy left me with another smile.

She had barely gone from the house when I heard coming from the street the chatter of three very familiar voices.

Our gate swung open. I tapped on the glass and made indications to come inside. Danny escorted my visitors to the parlour and introduced them with a bark. The moment she saw me, Phoebe froze.

'Wh—what are you doing in that?' she asked.

'It's only a wheelchair, Phoebe,' Della tried to appease her to no avail. Phoebe continued to stare at me and shake her head slightly.

'You can't sit in it,' she said.

'There's not a choice for me with my feet all swollen, and what's more, Daid took the callipers for to be fixed,' I explained. 'You'll not be fearing a wheelchair, Phoebe Raye. I'm still myself here.' I began to wheel myself towards her but she backed away.

'You need a licence for that contraption?' Pim asked with a grin.

I smiled back. 'Well I've not a one, so let you mind. I'm dangerous.'

'Care for a barley sugar?' Della produced a brown paper bag full of my favourite treat and passed it to me. I eagerly took one and offered the bag to my friends. After considerable encouragement even Phoebe decided to accept.

'A fine surprise this is! And what brings yous all here?' I enquired. ''Tis grand to see you! I been couped up in here for nearly a week now.'

'We had to see how you were doing, especially since I'm going to the mountains tomorrow. I won't see you again till school goes back,' Della informed me. 'What's more, we have the recording!'

'Recording?'

'The *Sunrise*! Mrs Epstein's gramophone records!' explained Della. 'It was Phoebe's idea. Phoebe managed to get them, didn't you, Phoebe? And for the life of me, I don't know how you did it. Mrs Epstein has been so guarded about them.'

'I borrowed them,' Phoebe replied with some importance as she produced the coveted box.

'Borrowed?' queried Pim. 'Pinched more like, I bet.'

Pim was right. Phoebe blushed.

'I'm going to return them!' she retorted. 'Stingy Mrs Epstein! Only letting us listen to a little bit the other day.'

'I still don't know how you managed to get your hands on them,' Della repeated.

'Mrs Epstein lets me listen to them as much as I want,' Phoebe added nonchalantly.

'Oh! It's not fair!' Della usually curbed any annoyance she had with Phoebe, but this time she gave vent.

'But I'm staying with her at the moment,' Phoebe retorted with equal indignation. 'She can't exactly tell me no. Come on, let's put them on quick before Mrs Epstein misses them. We can sit down by the fire and listen together.' Then, looking at the wheelchair, she realised that what she had envisaged was not going to be achieved. Again there was that puzzled, pitying, frustrated, almost angry look in my direction.

'I'm thinking 'twill be easier in the dining room,' I suggested. 'And we can enjoy a cup of tea. You can move the gramophone there if you want.'

'So how does this contraption work?' Pim asked as we prepared to shift to our chosen venue.

'Like any other wheelchair, Pim,' I replied.

'Well, do you wheel yourself or does someone wheel you?'

'Either it is. But 'twill be quicker if you push. Only let you take care of the door there.'

Through to the dining room we went, an awkward procession featuring a rather ungainly gramophone, followed by the wheelchair which met with several collisions with doorposts and hallstand along the way.

Phoebe took charge.

'Lucy, how do you work it? Show me,' she demanded as she brought the record to the machine and mulled over the mechanics. I could not manoeuvre myself to do so. But before Pim decided to come to her aid, she positioned the record and determinedly set about winding the crank. Then she lowered the needle and succeeded in starting the record with little more than a few crackles.

'Voilà!' she exclaimed, at the same time listening carefully to the music. 'There's a complete story in this. Here the sun is yawning and stretching. The sun bids hello to everyone and smiles. All the birds and trees sing in chorus and welcome him. First violin and 'cello represent birds, second violin represents the sea which is very still and the viola represents the wind stirring in the trees. Soon, all of creation is wide awake. They are very glad to see the sun after such a long, dark night.'

Pim looked at her curiously. 'Do you always think of music like that?' she asked.

'Yes, I do,' Phoebe curtly replied. 'Don't you?'

'Oh, I just like doing it,' answered Pim. 'I like moving that bow over those strings, and I love the sound: rich, round notes.'

'My, you can be quite poetic when it suits you, Pim,' Della observed. 'Rather odd, though, since the viola only ever plays two or three notes in a piece.'

'So?' Pim retorted. 'They happen to be the *best* notes,' she added haughtily and turned to Phoebe. 'Anyway, it's interesting hearing what you have to say.'

'Ah, ha! 'cello part,' Phoebe announced. 'Sleepy old 'cello; doesn't want to get up. Just like Lucy,' she teased.

'You're telling me,' remarked Pim. 'What time do you normally wake up? Eleven o'clock?'

'I get tired!' I protested.

'So we have to pester you,' continued Phoebe. '"Merde alors! Lucy! Get up!" she called into my ear. 'That's the sforzando section there,' she tapped at the appropriate place on the score which Della was intently studying. 'Eventually you do get up, but because you've missed the sunrise we have to do it all over again. Hence, repeat the first section.'

'Anyone wanna cuppa?' Pim drawled as she made her way to the kitchen.

'Kettle's on the stove there,' I called after her. 'And tea's in the chest in the dresser with the tea pot.'

'Any cake?'

''Tis bread and jam is all. Jam will be in the dresser near the tea and the bread in the cupboard below.'

'Now for the development,' Phoebe turned the record over and redirected our attention to the music. 'Here the wicked storm clouds come and they threaten to cover the sun and cast shadows over the sea and banish all the jollity. There's a fight and then the wind and the birds come to chase the clouds away.'

'Would that be the E flat major bit now, Phoebe?' I asked.

'How did you know that was E flat major?' Della interjected. 'You're not looking at the score.'

'I can hear it,' I answered. 'It's the green bit.'

'Green?' Pim was incredulous.

'Do you not see music in colour?' I always saw music in colour. ''Tis green's full of life and hope like E flat major. And then the music turns gold and red—'

'Yes,' Phoebe added excitedly. 'Because the sun emerges triumphant and begins a mighty ascent of the sky to proclaim his glory. That's where the second movement begins. Quick, pass me the next record!'

'I say,' commented Della. 'It does rather sound like a procession.'

'Yes,' answered Phoebe. 'A royal procession of the sun into the sky. It's very dignified. The sun acknowledges his subjects and they bow venerably.' Phoebe was completely immersed in her own imaginative music world. She nodded as a king would nod to his subjects, and followed the nod with a deep curtsey. 'The loyal clouds are introduced and the sun surveys creation. He contemplates his reflection in the ocean and the ocean dances for the sun.'

'That will be the 'cello part there,' I remarked.

'Yes. And then the sun reaches the summit and is enthroned in majesty.' Phoebe climbed on top of the chair and sat on the table.

'What do you think you're doing?' Pim made to stop her but Della intervened.

'Have a heart, Pim' she said. 'This is fun. He's given attributes of power,' Della made her own contribution and pulled out our tablecloth and draped it around Phoebe, who giggled at the idea before reassuming her role as the sun. 'Here's a mantle, an orb, a sceptre, and a crown.' Phoebe was duly invested with an egg cup and spoon in each hand, and an overturned porridge bowl on her head. 'Then he sits on his throne to watch a dance in his honour.'

'That's the Minuet,' informed Phoebe. 'Bother! Pim, put on the next record!'

'I say, it's a dance performed by peasants in folkloric costume!' announced Della as she listened to the opening bars. Phoebe immediately abandoned her majestic pose and transformed herself accordingly.

'The first violin,' Della had taken up the narrative, 'is a pretty girl who likes to dance but she has careful parents who keep reminding her about how to behave – that's the 'cello. And there are others who like to gossip – viola and second violin.'

'But *I* want to dance too!' Phoebe continued to frolic round the table.

'You can in the Trio,' replied Della. 'For here the bagpipes are introduced and everyone joins in.' At this point Phoebe grabbed hold of Della and began to dance her round the table. 'Don't you think it sounds like bagpipes?' called Della as she whirled around.

Their caper caused the needle to jump. The dancers abruptly halted and ran over to inspect the record.

'Is it all right?' gasped Della, out of breath and anxious. 'Dear me! Mrs Epstein will kill us if we've broken it!'

'Doesn't seem to be a scratch,' Pim reassured her as she watched the record turn round and round.

'Take it off and check!' ordered Phoebe.

'Phew! It looks fine,' Della sighed. 'Have you the recording of the fourth movement?'

'That's the banquet scene,' Phoebe panted while Pim organised the next record. 'There is a lot of polite conversation.'

'Frightfully proper?' asked Della in her most well-spoken English.

'Frightfully,' Phoebe mimicked, arranging the tablecloth over her lap as though it were a large linen napkin. 'Exquisite dishes are being served.'

'I say, I can see it now,' add Della. 'Camembert, quail's eggs, canard à l'orange, jelly and a towering croque-en-bouche.'

'A what is it?' I asked.

'Croque en bouche? Pastry balls filled with custard and piled together with toffee. It's magnificent! Mummy had one at her last garden party.'

'Can you make sure she has one at her next garden party?' requested Pim, her mouth full of bread and jam.

'Then, the Master of Ceremonies proposes a toast,' explained Phoebe.

'"Ladies, His Most Royal Majesty the glorious Sun!"' Della proclaimed as she took up the egg cup.

'Hear! Hear!' shouted Pim and I.

'But the guests become inebriated,' Phoebe ran back to the score on the table and turned to the final pages. 'Near the end, everyone (particularly the first violin) gets rowdy. Only a little at first. Then someone squeals because another guest drops a piece of camembert down her bodice. The first violinist is accused and runs away. There is a chase, with calling out, from the "Più allegro" onwards. Come the "Più presto" all the furniture is upset. The banquet becomes a bacchanal!'

'What a rumpus!' said Mrs Murphy who was standing in the doorway.

I felt myself redden.

'Can't leave you alone for a minute, Lucy Straughan,' she continued with a gleam as she put down her basket and collected the tea things. 'Would you like another cup?'

I extended the offer to my friends and we all agreed.

'I thought your dear father wouldn't have time to do any shopping so I bought you some food for the weekend,' Mrs Murphy explained as she lumbered into the kitchen. 'That'll save him going out tomorrow and he can have a good rest. Hasn't he been busy, Lucy?'

'Indeed he has, Mrs Murphy,' I called after her.

From the kitchen sallied forth a litany of praise for Daid's photographic accomplishments and virtues:

'Such a good man. And he's had that many photos published as of late. Wasn't it a beautiful one he did of the steam engine, Lucy?'

'Aye, Mrs Murphy,' I agreed before describing the photograph to my friends. 'Twas Daid put such a shine on the engine and made the steam swirl round it like—'

'And, do you know, he manages to get to Holy Mass nearly every day? It all goes to show when we give Our Lord His due He's bound to reward us.'

Mrs Murphy undoubtedly saw that Daid's recent successes were due to his attendance at the Holy Sacrifice. I thought otherwise.

''Tis no prayer's ever put a penny in one's purse, Mrs Murphy.'

Mrs Murphy appeared at the kitchen entrance 'Ah, Lucy,' she scolded me gently. 'If you only knew—'

'What was good for you! 'Tis books be good for me, Mrs Murphy,' I glared back with a smile. 'Is it my book—?'

She put her hands to her ears. 'Books! Books! Books! Books and vio—'

''Cellos! Well, is my book in that basket there or not?'

'Yes, child,' she returned to the dining room with a small parcel. 'Here it is, a life of Saint Therese.'

'Mrs Murphy!' It was not possible. Despite my suspicions I did not believe Mrs Murphy would really go so far as to buy me one of her books. I scowled as I undid the brown paper and string.

Della was the first to laugh. She had been watching over my shoulder while I pulled out a cloth-bound volume.

'"*Poems*, Lord Byron,"' she read. 'I say, Mrs Murphy, jolly good joke.'

Mrs Murphy smiled as she sat at the table with us.

'After all the talking to your father gave me this morning about it, and your carrying on this afternoon, to think I'd have the hide to go against either of you.'

I stroked the cover and flicked through the pages to glimpse some of the titles.

'Aye, 'tis a fine book you bought me, Mrs Murphy. Thank you,' I smiled back at her.

'Although what all the fuss is about holy books, I don't know,' Mrs Murphy continued. 'What have you been reading lately? Some Pope or other: Pope Alexander, that's who.'

'Heavens, Luighseach! Wasn't he one of the bad ones?' asked Della.

By this time, however, I had abandoned my examination of the poems and had turned to the fly leaf. It was always interesting to find out if a book had a prior owner. This one had, for a decorative *ex libris* had been pasted over part of the illustration.

'Phoebe,' I asked. 'What was your dad's name?'

'Roderick Raye,' she replied without much interest. She had started to scribble on the score. 'Why?'

''Tis his book,' was all I said.

26

That evening, convincing Daid to take me to see Phoebe was no easy matter.

'Can it not wait until school goes back, Luighseach?' he replied after yet another attempt on my part to persuade him.

''Tis important, Da,' I insisted. 'I'm needing to go tomorrow.'

'Lass, you cannot walk.'

'My feet be much better, Daid. The swelling's gone down now and my callipers are fixed. I can get my boots on.'

'And what of the blisters still there? I'm not wanting them feet getting infected.' Infection was what Daid dreaded most.

'Please Daid. Please...'

Finally, Daid gave in. He would take me on Saturday morning, but I was not to prolong the visit and I was to spend the remainder of the day in the wheelchair.

****

We were not far from Mrs Epstein's when we saw my teacher walking down the street with her shopping. Daid tooted his horn. Mrs Epstein waved and he pulled up nearby.

'Phoebe's not here,' she replied in answer to my explanation. 'She went home last night.'

'She's gone back to her aintín now? I was wanting to give her this.' I showed her the book of poems. 'It belongs to her dad, you know.'

'So *that's* what she was so choked up about,' Mrs Epstein mused. 'I couldn't work out what the matter was,' she sighed as she returned the book to me. 'Well, good luck. I have to get back and clean her room. She's left an absolute pig sty.'

We turned and headed for Phoebe's house.

'She's upstairs,' was all the welcome we received from Phoebe's aunt when she opened the door. Daid said he would wait while I paid my visit.

'Will you need any help with them stairs there, Luighseach?' he asked.

'I won't, Daid,' I replied. Daid smiled a little, took a seat next to the hallstand and pulled out his rosary. I, meanwhile, pulled myself up the stairs to Phoebe's room.

The door was shut.

I knocked.

'Go away, Ailine!' Phoebe called.

''Tis not Ailine,' I called back. ''Tis Luighseach here.'

The door opened and Phoebe stood defiantly, cigarette in hand. I coughed.

She allowed me inside. I came in and sat on her bed. The sheets were very dirty.

'I think 'tis yourself might want this,' I choked on the stuffy, smoke-filled air, and produced the book from my satchel.

'I told you,' Phoebe retorted as she extinguished her cigarette. 'I don't want it. It's not mine.'

'Indeed it isn't. 'Tis your da's.'

'No it's not.'

'But you said it yourself it was the same name.'

'But I told you already, that's not his handwriting. My father doesn't write like that. He—'

Her eyes grew large with fear.

'Doesn't?' I echoed. 'And what do you mean "doesn't"? I thought he was killed in the War, which is why I thought you might like the book. At least you'd have a memento of him, considering—'

'Well, I don't want it! I don't want it! I don't—'

'Phoebe. Phoebe,' I repeated. 'Listen to me. If you don't want it, that's fine. I only thought you might. And if you don't want to talk about your da, well that's fine too. It took myself years to talk about my mam 'cause I was so upset about it all. But if ever you do want to tell, I don't mind listening. Anyway,' I continued, 'although you mightn't want the book, you might want this.'

I passed her a photograph of a young woman which I had discovered marking one of the pages.

''Tis your mother, is it not?' I asked. 'It looks a bit like yourself. And you said you no longer had a photo of your mam.'

Phoebe shook her head in disbelief.

'No,' she whispered. 'No. That's not my mother. My mother had fair hair. That's— That's— That's *Ailine*.'

'And you're sure of that?'

She did not reply. She sat on her bed, shaking her head and saying 'No, no, no' over and over again. Then she began to whimper and cry. I shifted a little further up the bed and put my arm round her to comfort her.

'No!' she shouted as she sprung away. 'No! You leave me alone, do you hear! Leave me alone! Go!'

I remained where I was, but to no avail. Phoebe demanded I get out. As I closed the door, I heard thud against it what must have been the book I had deliberately left behind. But that was only the first missile to be heard. Many others followed and they became more muffled as I neared the stairs.

'Daid!' I called.

A door creaked open and Daid walked down the hall.

'Will you help me, Da?'

'Everything well, Luighseach?' Daid picked me up and glanced anxiously in the direction of Phoebe's room. Phoebe was wailing.

'Upset she is, Daid. And she won't tell why.'

'Never mind,' he replied and hugged me close. 'When the apple is ripe it will fall. Come and see something.'

He set me down and brought me to Ailine's studio.

'So much for not prolonging the visit,' I thought as we entered. Where art was concerned, Daid had a weakness. He bade me greet Ailine and introduced me to the infamous Arthur who was still in his dressing gown. Arthur took the hand I held out and pressed it to his lips.

'Enchanted,' he gushed, eyeing the while my legs and crutches.

''Tis Phoebe Raye says you're a fairy,' I remarked as I wiped my hand on my skirt. 'Now why would she be saying that?'

Daid cringed as he faintly muttered, 'Luighseach'. Ailine smirked, glanced at Arthur and raised her deftly pencilled brows at me.

'It's because I live at the bottom of the garden, darling,' he languidly replied.

'Would you be minding if I showed Luighseach the portrait there?' Daid asked Ailine in a tone that was more suited to 'I do beg your pardon' than the request he actually made.

'Not at all,' Ailine casually replied as she rose and showed us to her easel.

'What do you think?' Daid whispered. I looked up at him. Clearly, he was very impressed with the work. It was a portrait of Arthur, but it was Arthur with purple cheekbones and a green stripe down his nose, with bold black outlines and a storm of colours that had been lashed about the canvas with a knife.

'Do you see how she's used the colour to build her forms, Luighseach?' Daid continued in a hushed voice, his eyes bright with enthusiasm. 'Look how that green makes the nose project, all because it's placed side by side with those softer strokes of pink and orange. Clever it is. All carefully worked out.'

Daid straightened himself and continued to peer down at me to make sure I had followed his explanation. I looked again at the portrait and then I turned and looked at the artist. Ailine was observing her masterpiece with a gleam which suggested that she was relishing every ounce of my father's praise.

'Have you ever been to Dresden?' she asked.

Daid replied that he had not.

'I was there after the War,' she continued while my father accompanied her to the settee. 'Interesting art in Dresden.'

Regardless of what Daid had to say, I did not like that portrait at all. It was harsh and angry. So I cast my eye round the studio to see if there was something more pleasant to look at. Some copies, mostly of Italian masterpieces, were hung on the longest wall, but as far as original works were concerned, not a one was there that pleased me. There was a landscape, such as it was, but what might have been pastures, copses and cottages was instead a bleak expanse featuring only the blackened remains of trees, a ruined church, a village crumbled and fields muddied with toil.

Near the landscape was what I thought was a still life. It turned out, however, to be the portrait of a man wearing a hat. But this was not the faithful replication of a face; it was an experiment in minimal colour and heavy line. The face itself could hardly be described as human. It was composed of a violin which had been fragmented and rearranged into odd-shaped blocks of olive green, brown, grey and white, all strongly outlined and occasionally patterned in black. Some music had even been torn and pasted to form part of the man's forehead, and there was more coming out of his mouth. The assortment of shapes and colours, lines and designs made the picture curiously animated. In fact, it had quite a humorous quality for the f holes of the violin had been used to denote a moustache and violin pegs had been painted in place of ears. The delineation of eyes, nose and lips were eccentric to say the least.

"'Tis very odd,' I thought to myself as I tried to fathom how anyone could conceive such an idea. Not finding any immediate answer, I studied the painting next to it.

It was a mother and child. Once again it featured thick, heavy, dark lines – hardly the means, one would think, to represent such a tender subject. But this was not a tender subject. The child appeared dead, the mother thin and hollow-eyed. The name 'Devereaux', written with an enormous 'D', gestural horizontals and an emphatically crossed 'x' strode across the bottom of the work.

How could anyone ever paint something like that?

I watched Ailine as she conversed with my father and her latest subject. Her eyes and lips were heavily made up and outlined almost as if she had applied her painting style to her own face. She noticed me watching her and glinted at me. I turned back to the paintings before glancing again at Ailine, then Arthur, and finally at Daid who was revelling in the discussion. They were talking about art and were passing sketches across a coffee table littered with demi tasses, paper, ash trays and books. I resumed my study of Arthur's portrait and slowly shook my head at my father.

'Daid better not be too inspired,' I thought. 'If he begins to paint like that…'

'Are you wanting for to go now, Luighseach?' asked Daid.

'I'm not minding, Daidí.'

But Daid noticed me leaning against the wall in an attempt to rest my feet.

'We're best being off,' he decided. 'An enjoyable time it's been talking with you. And thank you for the coffee.' To my knowledge Daid only drank tea and the occasional Guinness. He polished his farewells with two polite bows and warm handshakes, paused to let me bid my leave and guided me out.

27

Late that night I lay in bed, huddled and helpless, listening to the dogs whose barking had broken the chill stillness. Danny soon joined his voice to the chorus which gradually faded, leaving our puppy performing a solo of excited yaps while he trotted out of the shed where he slept and into the back garden. Danny was investigating something. Whatever it was, however, did not appear to upset him. That being the case, I decided it was not going to worry me. I snuggled into my covers and settled down to sleep.

Again I was roused, this time by a soft but persistent tapping at my window. There was no wind that night and there were no branches nearby that could have created the sound. What could it be? A possum perhaps? Not likely. Danny would still be barking if it were a possum. Instead I could faintly hear him sniffing and prancing about. I put on my bedside light. The tapping ceased. I fumbled for my glasses but could see nothing. So I shrugged my shoulders, turned out the light, placed my glasses back on the table and lay back on the soft pillow.

All became quiet once again.

'Deaf, blind and lame!' sounded Phoebe's voice as I was angrily shaken awake. 'I have been knocking and calling for ages out there. Didn't you hear me?'

'I—'

'It's freezing outside! Just as well you left your back door unlocked. You might have said something.'

The hall light came on and I heard Daid's footsteps on the floorboards.

'Luighseach?' he called, his voice tinged with worry.

I groped for my glasses. How was I ever going to explain Phoebe?

'Let you hide under the bed!' I advised her. I would have preferred to postpone any explanation of Phoebe's appearance at least until daybreak.

Too late. The door opened and I stared at my father's dressing-gowned figure.

'Faith!' he exclaimed as he caught sight of Phoebe. ''Tis two o'clock in the morning! What do you be doing here, lass?'

'I couldn't sleep,' explained Phoebe.

'So you decided to noise the fact to the neighbourhood did you now?' Daid turned on my light.

'I—I'm sorry,' she stammered and blinked.

'But how did you come here, lass?' Daid's annoyance rapidly gave way to concern. ''Tis no train running these wee hours for you to catch. Were you walking the streets in the dead of night, Phoebe? Were you walking alone with no one to guard you?'

All Phoebe could do was nod. Daid looked her up and down and noted the broderie on her nightdress peeping out from under her coat, her long locks wrapped in curling rags, and the stuffed animal she was clutching. He studied her face, which was sad and anxious, shook his head and sighed.

''Tis no bed we have to spare,' he continued as he made his way to my wardrobe in search of an extra quilt. 'But we can put you down by the fire as before. If you're thinking about going to sleep, that is.'

'Let you not worry about a bed, Da. 'Tis Phoebe can sleep with myself.'

'You're not minding that, with your feet all bandaged, Luighseach?'

'There'll be plenty of room, Daid, for 'tis a good sized bed I sleep in.'

Daid eyed Phoebe. She seemed quite receptive of my idea.

'Then let you remember, lass,' he instructed. ''Tis Luighseach needs to rest. You'll not be chatting idly keeping her awake and causing her trouble now.'

Phoebe silently gave her assent, sat on my bed, took out a button hook from her coat pocket and undid her boot buttons. Daid sent me a cautionary look, reminded me in Irish that we would be hearing Holy Mass in a few hours, and returned to his room.

'In you come, Phoebe Raye,' I moved aside a little to allow her more space. 'But let you mind my legs.'

'Have you got another pillow?'

'In my cupboard there'll be an extra one.'

Phoebe found the pillow, hugged it tight and brought it over to my bed. She clambered up and wriggled in beside me.

'Do you be snug and warm there?' I asked her.

She nodded and gave me a grateful half-smile. I turned out the light and set about getting back to sleep.

'Lucy?'

Now what was it?

'Is your mother in Heaven?'

'I like to think she is, Phoebe Raye,' I answered with a sigh. How many times, when preparing for Confession, had I ended up examining Mam's conscience rather than my own for mortal sins? It was a means I had of reassuring myself that my darling mother could only be in Heaven, for as far as I was aware she had done nothing wrong.

'But do you know she is?'

'Well, 'tis not as if she's written me a picture postcard – "Dear Luighseach. I'm having a wonderful time. Wish you were here. Clouds a delight. Love Mam." – but deep in my heart of hearts I know she's there. She saved my life, you know.'

'She must have been very brave and very clever.'

'Oh, I never would describe her as clever. She was my mam is all.'

'From what I've seen in those pictures on your wall, I'm certain she must have been clever. In fact, if I ever went for a walk with your mother, I'm convinced she would know every flower in every garden, and every tree in every park and every person in every house. The world would be like a book for her and she would read me chapter after chapter from it.'

'Is that what you think?' Phoebe's description pleased me very much indeed. I reached over and, for a third time that night, switched on the bedside light.

'I often imagine what it would be like to have someone else's mother for my mother. Don't you ever do that?'

I had to own that I had often done precisely that.

'For example,' resumed Phoebe who was warming to her topic. 'If Pim's mother were my mother, I would end up very fat and jolly. I don't think I would ever want for anything if Mrs Connolly loved me as one of her own. And I would eat roast dinners swimming in gravy every night, and pudding, too, and Mrs Connolly would always be there especially for me. She would put me to bed and tuck in my sheets, and everything would be lovely and crisp and clean.'

'And she'd make sure you did your fair share of the work, I'm thinking.'

'But I wouldn't mind, she would love me so.'

'And what about Mrs Sotheby? What sort of mother would she be?' I put on my glasses, intrigued to find out in what light Phoebe saw Della's mother.

'Oh, she would be my gay and pretty mother. She would dress me in beautiful clothes and take me to plays and concerts. We would visit kings and queens and I would play the piano for them and they would applaud me and cheer for more, and Mrs Sotheby would be so proud of me she would dress me more finely than ever.'

'And spoil you rotten.'

'And I would love it.'

'And so what of your own mother?' I ventured. 'How would she be? Do you remember her at all?'

'Oh yes, very well.' Phoebe was obliging but not forthcoming.

'And what was she like?'

'She was like an angel guarding a tomb.'

'She was a sad person?'

'Sometimes, yes. Sometimes she was very sad. But it was more that she was calm and quiet, very thoughtful and peaceful – the way your father is if you really want to know. I suppose you could call her prayerful. She went to church a lot. She used to sing, too. She had a beautiful voice,' Phoebe added after a pause.

'Did she?'

'I can still hear her. When she sang low it was lush and rich, and yet when she sang high it was delicate and playful. Sometimes a song would mean so much to her that she could not sing it for crying. She used to practise with Bobeshi at the piano. Bobeshi was wonderful. She told stories when she played and my mother and I would act them out. Bobeshi and my mother gave concerts, lots and lots of concerts. I grew up with concerts. It must have been to help the War because

I seem to remember flags everywhere. I played in the concerts, too, once I was old enough.'

'You cannot have been very old.'

'I was four.'

'Were you now? Well, that explains why you were so at home at Pim's place that night playing all them songs.'

'It used to happen all the time when I was little.'

''Tis odd, though,' I observed.

'Why?'

'Well, you play the piano like I never heard anyone play before, but— and I'm not wanting to be mean when I say it, but you don't sing very well yourself. You cannot even sing in tune.'

'I can't sing,' she lamented. 'I can hear the notes in my head but when I try nothing seems to come out right. I can't do it. I don't have any voice.'

'And all the time your mam was giving concerts, your da was in the war?' I prompted.

Phoebe nodded.

'And he came back?'

'Yes,' she whispered.

'When did he come back?'

'When I was five. It was before I started school and I cannot remember whether he came back before Bobeshi died or after. Bobeshi died of the Influenza, you see. It must have been after for I don't ever remember them at home together. But everything became so very busy all of a sudden that it's difficult to say.'

'Was your da badly hurt?'

Phoebe looked at me and from her eyes I could tell it was so.

'My mother arranged a special room for him downstairs and she spent hours in the garden making it pretty,' she said. 'A nurse came to live with us. She was a very big lady. I'm sure she was at least three times as big as Pim. We used to call her The Troll, but she was quite kind in a very gruff sort of way. She and my mother looked after my father. They had to help him with everything at first. He began to get better, though. It made my mother so happy to see him get better. She used to tell me he was the bravest man who ever lived. But she didn't mean he was brave because he went to war, she meant he was brave because he came back. I didn't know who he was when he arrived and I was a bit afraid of him, but we became good friends. He used to let me ride with him in his chair.'

'He was in a wheelchair?'

Again she nodded. 'He was trying to walk, but he was in a lot of pain. It used to make him cry. Sometimes my mother would cradle him in her arms as if he was a baby and he would weep.'

'I'm so sorry, Phoebe,' when pain sliced your limbs like that, short of beating yourself black and blue, the only thing left to do was to cry.

'But I liked sitting with him. Even though he was very sick he was always there for me. We did lots of things together. He loved hearing me play the piano. He would sit, ever so still, and listen while I played or while my mother taught me. Even now when I play, I like to think of him sitting, listening to me.'

'Could he play himself?'

'No,' she smiled. 'He would ask me to teach him the tunes I was learning, but he would make a terrible mess of them. It's funny. Thinking back now, I have the feeling he did it on purpose. He'd always end up singing my tunes instead and making up nonsense rhymes to fit. He had quite a good voice. He and my mother loved to sing together.

'He used to paint, too. My mother found him an easel and some paints and brushes and he taught himself. He sat outside and painted in the garden. Sometimes he gave me my own paper or canvas and let me paint with him. He also helped me learn to read, and we used to practise together writing letters and words on slates.

'By the time I started school he was walking quite well and he came with my mother every afternoon to collect me. I was the luckiest child in the class because, when everyone else had only one parent or none at all to walk home with, I had both. Eventually he was able to take me to school and take me home. And he told good stories. They were always about a horse. I liked those stories so much my mother ended up making this for me,' and she showed me her little stuffed horse.

'Aye, I've met him before,' I acknowledged. 'And what was his name again?'

'Gregory Allegri. My father called him that and said that he had a Christian name and a surname because he was such a brave and honourable creature. I still tell myself those stories to help me go to sleep but I couldn't do it tonight.'

'Will you tell myself then? I like stories.'

'I learned my first history lessons from my father's tales,' she continued. 'He used to say that Gregory Allegri was born from the wooden horse the Greeks made when they defeated the Trojans. That was why he was so smart. He was ridden by Alexander and Alfred and Charlemagne, and Richard the Lionheart rode him into Jerusalem. He was so noble that at the Battle of Bosworth when Richard of York cried "A horse, my kingdom for a horse!" Gregory Allegri galloped up to him and told him he would not be that horse for he was the mount of just and righteous kings not murderous usurpers. After Bosworth Field, however, Gregory Allegri changed his mind about kings and became a freethinker instead. He carried Paul Revere at full pace on his midnight ride from Lexington to Concord to warn the colonists the British were coming.

'Not only did Gregory Allegri have a noble spirit, he also had a fine pair of legs. Gregory Allegri could jump so far he could fly across chasms forty feet wide and he could jump so high he could clear church steeples. He was so sure-footed that he could walk on a tightrope that stretched from one end of France to the other and he did it with fireworks exploding to right and left and crocodiles and pallid monsters beneath him waiting in the mire to gobble him up if he fell.'

'They sound like stories my uncles used to tell,' I smiled at the memory.

'My mother would laugh when he told them. He knew exactly how to make her laugh. It was always good when she laughed because I knew everything would be all right. But she stopped laughing, Lucy.'

'What happened?'

'She died.'

'All of a sudden? How?'

Phoebe choked on the words and sniffed. It was up to me to work out what she was trying to say.

'She killed herself?'

There was a slight nod and a stifled sob.

'My Aunt Sara said she committed the sin of despair.'

'Another aunt you have?'

'She's my father's sister. She was the one who put me in the orphanage.'

'And why could she not look after you herself?'

'She didn't want me,' Phoebe cried. 'She said the orphanage was where a child like me belonged. She hated my mother and my father. She said my mother was little more than a glorified harlot and my father was a prodigal who only married my mother to save what little honour she had; that the wounds he received were just punishment for the profligate life he had led and that my mother's suicide was proof of her weak character and her disregard for godly ways.'

'Well,' I remarked, 'perhaps it was a blessing you were put in an orphanage and didn't live with the like of your Aunt Sara.'

'Aunt Sara said that because my mother took her own life she was denied Christian burial and would forever burn in Hell. And it's true, Lucy,' Phoebe stopped me from saying what I wanted to say. 'My mother's not buried with my grandparents. I've been to the cemetery hundreds of times to look for her and she's not there. But why would she do something like that? How could she lose hope? She had *me*. *I* was her hope.'

'Aye, you were,' I tried to console her. 'And you are still.'

'My mother used to say I was her joy and her little ray of hope. That's my name, you know: Phoebe Joy Raye,' she sniffed. 'All she wanted was for my father to come back and she was so happy when he did. She could never have taken her own life. She was happy the night she died. My father had to have special medicine for the pain. They said she took some of his medicine and it killed her, but I don't believe them. She wouldn't do that. She would never do that. She never touched his medicine. She was afraid of it.'

Again I tried to give her comfort.

'Don't fret yourself so, Phoebe. Don't fret. 'Twill not make anything better. I know 'tis hard but you cannot keep thinking about how she died. My mam was shot by an English soldier and for years I used to think of her lying there in the street with her life draining out of her body and all the love she had trickling out of her eyes. I'll never forget that last sweet, pained look she gave me. But I'd go mad if that's all I thought of. And if I don't hold fast to all the other treasured memories of her, well, they'll die too.'

'I didn't mention my mother but I once asked Sister Magdalene about it and all she said was that we should pray for the dead. But, Lucy, what good is that going to do if she's burning in Hell?'

'Well, I'm thinking Sister Magdalene's right for you don't know your dear mam's burning in Hell. You need to trust that God knows her better than your Aunt Sara. So what happened to your da with your poor, wee mother gone to God?'

'He became very sick, Lucy. Not sick in his body. He was already sick there. It was a different sort of sick. Sick here,' Phoebe indicated her head, 'and here,' she put her hand over her heart. 'He was so terribly sad. They took him away. They took him away from me and put him in a home. My Aunt Sara used to take me to see him but he didn't want to see me,' she faltered. 'I made him upset. He became angry and— In the end they forbade me from seeing him. I haven't seen him since. I miss my daddy! I miss him, and I want him back!'

Phoebe could halt the tears no longer. I pulled my handkerchief from under my pillow and dabbed her eyes.

'The nuns in the orphanage said I should pray for him to get better. And I have. I've prayed and I've prayed and I've prayed and I've prayed. But for what purpose? Nothing! Absolutely nothing! I've given up praying. I can't pray any more, it makes me sick to pray.'

'And so all you have to remember your da is that dirty old horse you're holding?'

'And this,' and she produced a key from round her neck. 'He gave it to me before they took him away. He told me to look after it very carefully and never ever lose it. I kept it in my special box for years. I didn't know what it was for until I came back home. It turned out to be the key to the attic.'

'And why did he give you that?'

'I don't know, but it was very important whatever it was.'

'You poor lassie for losing him so; and I don't care what your aunt says, your da sounds like a fine man and your mam sounds fine, too.'

'Not according to Ailine.'

'The aunt you live with?'

'She's my mother's sister. She hates my mother, Lucy. If ever she speaks of her, it's only to curse. She said my father never loved my mother.'

'Nonsense. He must have loved her for you to tell about him the way you do.'

'Then why was there a picture of Ailine in his book? Why?' Now, amidst the tears, there was anger.

'I—'

'Because he loved Ailine, not my mother,' she declared. 'He never wanted me, Ailine said. After you left my place I went to the studio and showed Ailine the picture. I asked her what it was doing in my father's poetry book. She told me it must be because he loved her and not the slut that was my mother— That's what she said, Lucy, only she added even worse words. Ailine told me the only reason my father went to war was to get away from me and my mother and the only reason he came back was because he was injured, otherwise he would never have bothered. He would have stayed in France with Ailine.'

'But you don't know that for certain.'

'That's what she said. She said he stayed with her in Paris and was going to stay with her when the War was over. She said he never loved my mother and he never loved me and the reason why I'm not allowed to see him is because he doesn't want to have anything to do with me. My mother couldn't cope with the truth, Ailine said, let alone his injuries. That's why she committed suicide. Then I began to think that what Aunt Sara said and what they said at school was true.'

'And what did they say at school?' I suspected that Phoebe, like me, had been a victim of teasing.

'Ailine brought me to school on the first day,' she sniffed.

''Twould be like a pheasant among magpies and sparrows,' I observed while I imagined Phoebe's colourful, artistic aunt amidst crowds of sensibly dressed parents, nuns in habits, and black and white schoolgirls.

Phoebe nodded and continued her story. 'She left me there all by myself. She didn't want me either. She was mean to me. She only cares about herself. "Who was *that?*" asked one of the girls. "My aunt," I answered. "Where's your mother?" "She's dead." "How did she die?" "I'm not telling." "Where's your father?" "Why should I tell you?" Well, why should I tell, Lucy? Why should I? It's none of their business!'

'Aye, you're right. It's none of their business.'

'So, to shut them up, I said he was in the War. Then one of the girls smiled strangely and whispered something to her friend. They giggled and whispered some more. No matter where I went, all they did was whisper. Then they started to tease. "War baby, war baby, wa, wa, war baby!" they used to call. And they did nasty things. They filled my shoes with mud and put a frog in my pencil box and smeared my desk with marmite, and they took Gregory Allegri and threw him round the dormitory and hid him in the coal chute.'

Exhausted, confused and hysterical, Phoebe began to cry.

'It's not true! It can't be true!' she sobbed. 'But I don't know what to believe. All anyone wants to do is to poison my mind, to ruin my memories, to hurt and harm me. Why should they want to do that? What have I done that people should hate me so? Why, oh why doesn't anybody love me?'

'Why indeed?' I thought as I put my arms around her and let her cry. 'How could anyone not love you? You've such a fire inside, Phoebeen, so much passion and power. And there's goodness and warmth there too. Aye, but when that fire goes out, 'tis a bleak, black hearth indeed. Little wonder you play your music so well for you've that much to say. Perhaps that's where the rightness is,' I sighed.

'But it still doesn't make sense!' I protested as Phoebe's sobs were subdued by sleep. 'Your mother took her own life; your father's sick; your aunts don't want you; girls at school are mean to you. Where's the rightness there? Where's the rightness in all that? Where? Where?'

'Perhaps the rightness lies with you, Luighseach,' lilted a voice.

'Mam?'

I looked around. Save for Phoebe's sniffs and whimpers all was still and quiet and cold.

Mam was not there, although I could have sworn that she was.

How very odd! It was but one short, sweet moment: so fleeting and yet so intensely metaphysical, and what comfort did it bring!

'I'll do what I can,' I resolved. 'I don't know how but I'll do what I can.'

28

Phoebe stayed with us three more days. She came to Mass without a protest and seemed content to participate in all our daily doings, be it gathering oranges from the tree near our back gate, helping Daid in the garden, or giving Mrs Murphy a hand with the laundry – a task which kept her busy most of Monday morning. In the process, my wheelchair became almost a comfort to her to the point that she took it upon herself to wheel me from one place to another and see to my every need. She even had the initiative to take me to visit Hilda Geraghty, who lived round the corner, and we spent a happy Monday afternoon on the front steps of the Geraghty house having a chat. Then on Tuesday, after visiting the eye doctor, we went together to the picture palace where I was treated to Mary Pickford in *Sparrows* while Phoebe played the piano.

But, just as she had done before, she disappeared. Again there was no note, no word, not even an indication that she even intended to go.

'She'll come back, Luighseach,' Daid assured me when I appeared at breakfast on Wednesday with the news. 'Now, what about coming to the studio today? I could do with a bit of help from yourself with the books.'

'Aye,' I sighed. I knew what that meant, and I also knew that Daid's mild request was as close as he would come to a plea.

****

'Luighseach! Over here!'

Della continued to call until finally I saw her waving on the other side of the road.

My reply was drowned by the clang of a passing tram. When at last I was able to wave and shout back, she had disappeared.

The next thing I knew she was at my side.

'My, it is good to see you on your pins again! I thought you would still be sitting in that wheelchair in the parlour. I didn't expect to see you coming out of the studio at all.'

'I been doing a bit of work for Daid, Delleen,' I explained. 'Accounts,' I groaned.

'It's not like you to be so dismal over sums,' remarked my friend.

'You'll not believe it, Della Sotheby. A fine artist my Da might be, but may the Lord have mercy on him for the way he keeps his books. 'Tis a drawer in his studio, you know, and whenever someone pays him for the work he's done, he puts the money in the drawer. If it's something he needs to buy, he takes money out of the drawer. And when the drawer's full, then it falls to myself to sort it all out. Wouldn't you know it, 'tis pounds here, shillings there, pennies everywhere, and piles of receipts put in without rhyme or reason.'

'How very strange. Your father always strikes me as a most orderly person.'

'Indeed, indeed he is, only when it comes to letters and numbers it all goes to pieces. All mixed up he gets and puts it all back to front so you're needing to sort out his mistakes on top of all the mess. I'd prefer to deal with the mess without the mistakes.'

'Well, I'm glad it's you sorting it out and not me. I think I would be as bad as your father. I say, you look a bit different. What is it?'

Della studied me carefully. Then she smiled and clicked her fingers.

'New specs! That's what it is! When did you get them?'

'Yesterday it was. And I'm feeling like a fish in a fishbowl, I can tell you that,' I sucked in my cheeks and made a fish face.

Della laughed. 'Stop it, silly. They look very smart – much better than those thick, black frames. Mind you, those glasses were such a trademark of yours, it's going to take some getting used to seeing you without them.'

'Aye, a bit of a time it's been getting used to seeing myself without them, you know. I been wearing them black specs for years. But Daid suggested I get a new pair so I chose silver rims instead so I wouldn't look like Sister Augustine. Do you think they make the lenses look too thick, Delleen? They're that much stronger.'

'Not at all. In fact, they show your eyes up more. How could I ever have thought you had blue eyes? They're deliciously green!'

I beamed at her. I was glad I had Mam's eyes.

'You know, Luighseach,' observed Della. 'You *are* rather good-looking in a clever sort of way.'

'Whisht!' The memory of Mary Pickford instantly caused me to dismiss that compliment. 'You're talking through your hat, you are. Now, Delleen Sotheby, I took a break from work to put the fatai on for lunch, but I could do with a cup of tea before I begin. Would a cup of tea be good with you?'

'A cup of tea would be very nice indeed.'

We resumed our walk up King Street and paused occasionally to look at the window displays. It was Empire Week and the Union Jack was unfurled in every shop. Bold maps boasted Britain's dominions and hailed the Albion triumph of the seven seas. 'Land of Hope and Glory' was the only tune to be heard in Bray's music, while Shakespeare, Tennyson and a whole host of English literary greats were wreathed and Jacked in the bookshop window. 'Buy British' was the order of the day and British goods and British slogans were brandished far and wide to make sure everyone did. Much to my annoyance, even the studio had contributed more than its tuppenceworth of flags and photographs. But, as Daid explained, that was Mr Birstall's idea and it was Mr Birstall's shop after all. We would have our turn come St Patrick's Day, and what a window display we would put up then! My reply to that was 'Erin go braugh' and I would say it every time I saw a Union

Jack.

'What are you muttering about?' asked Della as we passed yet another flag.

'Erin go braugh: Ireland forever,' I replied. 'Ireland forever!' I repeated more loudly. One passer-by turned her head. 'Erin go braugh!' I shouted at her, waving a crutch as I did.

'Troublemaker,' Della laughed and gave my sleeve a tug. 'Take me home.'

We sat at the kitchen table with a cup of tea each, and half a cabbage and a bowl of potatoes between us. Cabbage was sliced and potato peelings wound their way to the newspaper on the table as we talked.

'Now what would you be doing coming here, Delleen?' I asked her. 'Were you not to be holidaying in the mountains till school returns?'

'That certainly was the plan,' Della replied, 'but it all went awry.'

'What happened? Would everything be well with yourself and your folk now?'

'Luighseach, old thing, I can tell you in one word.' Here Della paused and looked at me with a very serious face:

'Wally.'

'Would you mind putting the fatai on the stove, Delleen?' I was still hampered by callipers and crutches.

'Fatty?'

'Fah-tee: potatoes.'

'Not at all, old thing,' she replied. 'It will be quite a pleasant relief to sit in a kitchen watching potatoes cooking in a pot with all that's going on at home. May I mash them as well?'

'Aye, you may.'

'I was so looking forward to it,' Della continued as she filled the pot and placed it on the stove. We left the potatoes to come to the boil and wandered off to my room.

'The mountains are beautiful this time of year,' she proceeded with her narrative while I took off my right calliper. 'The leaves are the most glorious gold and red and there is nothing more delightful of a morning than to watch the mist floating over the valley.

'Anyway, on Saturday we started out early for our long drive. Cook packed a splendid picnic and we arrived at Medlow Bath in time for the tea dance. It turned out that our visit coincided with that of a very lively party. Would you believe they were all friends of Wally from the aerodrome? Most of them were aviators and ex-servicemen with their lady friends and all were quite a bit older than my brother. They were quite charming though. Anyway, I danced two foxtrots with Wally and a waltz with Daddy. Then, before I retired, I watched Mummy and Daddy dance the tango, which was a delight since they are both very good dancers. Wally was supposed to go to bed too, but I didn't see him until very late that night when the manager brought him up. Luighseach, he was frightfully drunk— drunk would you believe, and making a terrible racket. May I get your shoe for you?'

'Aye, you may, thank you.'

Della fetched my other boot from my wardrobe, helped me fit it over my foot and began to lace it for me, chatting the while. 'As you can imagine, Mummy was beside herself and Daddy was furious. He had words with the proprietor; then he got stuck into Wally's friends. That was when he found out that Wally had lied about his age. Daddy was going to call the police, just to teach Wally a lesson, except that Wally was so sick that Daddy reckoned a hangover was sufficient punishment for the moment. In the end, we decided to leave early, so we packed up and travelled home on Monday. Wally is in disgrace and, apart from school, is not allowed out for a whole month. Serves him right, I say, and I hope he's learnt his lesson. Have I laced it tight enough?'

''Tis grand what you done there. Will you come back to the kitchen now for there's the cabbage to cook.'

'Daddy's all right,' Della remarked as she watched the potatoes come to the boil. 'Today he's out playing golf. Mummy, however, sits and smoulders behind magazines. If I try to talk to her about it, all she ever says is "He's just like his father". Wally feigns indifference and, if he's not sneaking off somewhere to have a smoke, spends most of his time bowling a cricket ball at a set of stumps in the back garden. That only makes Mummy even more furious because the grass is getting worn from all his running, the stumps put holes in the lawn and the cricket ball keeps rolling into the garden beds and damaging the plants. Leila and Henry are staying with friends. Mummy simply cannot cope with them at the moment. So that leaves me in the middle. But the worst of it is that Wally won't talk to me, and I know there's something terribly wrong. I know it!'

Della was fighting tears.

'It's not like him,' she sniffed. 'We've always shared our thoughts. Even when he was at boarding school he'd write me.'

'Your brother was at boarding school, Delleen?'

'Back Home in England. Wally went to the Duke of York's.'

'The Duke of York's is it?'

'Take that silly scowl off your face. It's not quite as posh as you think. I mean, it's not like Eton or Harrow or any of those public schools. It's a military school in Dover. Wally went there because our real father, the Captain, was an officer, and the fact that he was as well as the fact that he was killed in the War entitled my brother to a very, very good education and a prospective military career. So, from the age of nine, Wally boarded at the Duke of York's while I attended day school in London.

'But everything changed when we moved to Australia. The intention was that Wally should stay behind. He had some important final exams to sit and after that he was expected to prepare for Sandhurst.'

'Do you mean to say you left the country without him? Mother of God! And how did your brother feel about that?'

'I don't think he was all that pleased,' Della remarked as she vigorously mashed the potatoes. 'The next thing that happened was that Wally got the sack. I don't know what he did, but the school is very, very strict. So out he came to Australia and was sent to grammar school. To everyone's relief, he seemed to settle in quite well. Then he began behaving strangely. Fancy missing a season of cricket! That's completely out of character. He loves his cricket. He could play county cricket – even represent his country – he's that talented. Anyway, Wally's always been a bit naughty, but it's not like him to be bad. Not like this. Smoking is one thing, but drinking is quite another. He's sixteen years old, Luighseach! As for lying, well! I say, old thing, are you really going to put in that much butter?'

'Indeed I am, Delleen and let you mix it in with the cabbage there.'

Daid arrived and the three of us sat down to bowls of Colcannon.

'And will your folk be doing a little something special tomorrow for Empire Day, Della?' he asked as he passed her the butter.

'Oh yes,' she replied as she silently declined the offer and watched in amazement as Daid and I each topped our meal with a large lump of butter which melted and trickled down our mountain of mashed potato and cabbage. 'We always have a celebration dinner that day,' she said. 'And a fireworks display. Which reminds me, I was wondering if Luighseach would be able come?'

'To celebrate Empire Day is it?' Daid asked as he raised an eyebrow at me. 'Well, now what do you say to that, Luighseach Ní Sruitheáin?'

I was speechless.

'You will come, won't you?' Della pleaded. 'It would mean an awful lot to me. Mummy thought it would be nicer if I invited Fanny, but if I did I know Fanny would spend the entire evening flirting with Wally. I don't think I could bear that. It will only make him more cynical. Fortunately, Fanny's back in Bowral. So please come, old thing. You can stay the night and we could do some practice together the following morning. Heaven knows we need to work on the *Sunrise* before we see Mrs Epstein again.'

I looked at Della's anxious little face, then looked at Daid who nodded slightly in Della's direction as if to say, 'Go on, lass.'

'Aye, Delleen,' I sighed. 'I'll come, for your sake.'

****

The following evening, after our Rosary, Daid drove me to the Sotheby's. Nellie opened the door and puzzled over what to do with the bag and the 'cello we passed in her direction. Daid bid a quick farewell as Della, dressed in creamy silk and lace, darted down the stairs and waved hello and goodbye.

'You're just in time,' she said with a smile. 'We've only now gone into dinner.'

'You're looking pretty, Delleen,' I noted as I continued to admire her frock and the gold clip she wore in her hair, which, as always, was immaculate.

'And you're looking smart as ever,' Della returned a compliment. 'Is that your best?'

''Tis what I wear to Sunday Mass,' I replied.

'Then that's best indeed. Come and have dinner.'

A kilt and cabled guernsey, dark woollen stockings and brown orthopaedic boots may have been good enough for Sunday Mass; they may have been good enough for Della; but they were most certainly not good enough for Mrs Sotheby, and she glared at me when I entered the dining room.

Indeed, I was a very poor addition to the tableau. Standing around the table, which itself was laid with candelabra, china and silverware, were Mr Sotheby and Wally. They were each wearing tailcoats, white bow ties, waistcoats, and starched white dinner shirts with stiff white collars. As for the hostess, she was attired in perfect accordance with the Arabian inspired decor of her surroundings. Her evening dress was a deep tangerine, sequined with intricate motifs in black and cream and gold. It stood out beautifully against the glowing walnut furniture, the rich teal walls and the billowing cream and gold and orange drapes with their heavy cords and tassels. Her titian hair was adorned with a jewelled head-band which, like her necklace, evoked the mysterious world of King Tut's tomb.

Greetings were all too briefly made. Then Mr Sotheby raised his wineglass. Mrs Sotheby, Della and Wally did the same. I fumbled with a crutch and managed to reach my own glass in time.

'His Majesty, the King,' toasted Mr Sotheby.

'The King,' echoed Della, Wally and Mrs Sotheby.

'So much for a hearty "Sláinte!" and downing a pint,' I said to myself as I raised my glass. 'Besides, the king doesn't deserve a pint,' I added in silent justification.

Wally, it seemed, was on his best behaviour that night. No sooner than the toast was made, he walked round to the other side of the table, where Della and I were to sit, and helped us with our chairs. He pulled my chair out for me and waited while I sat and fixed my knees.

'Would you like me to put your crutches against the wall for you?' he whispered. Wally genuinely wanted to know the best place for crutches.

I shook my head. ''Tis close by on the floor I prefer them,' I whispered in reply.

He let me put them where I wanted and did not return to his place until I was properly set in mine. Nor did he seem to mind the extra time all this trouble seemed to take. Curiously, his parents did not know whether to be pleased with their errant son's display of chivalry or annoyed that it considerably delayed proceedings.

Lobster bisque was served. No one spoke. Little more than quiet sips of the velvety soup could be heard. Not a spoon chinked against the side of the plate and certainly no plates were tipped to scrape any soup that still lined bottom and sides. The shame of it, I thought as I refrained from helping myself to a piece of bread to mop up, and I sat on my hands to avoid succumbing to the temptation.

The soup was withdrawn and a tiny circle of what turned out to be chicken was served in its place. Once again, the meal was consumed with more than considerable restraint. Come the advent of main course, however, I could endure the pomp no longer. So, after busying myself with the silver service and tucking into my meal, I endeavoured to make some conversation.

'A wonderful sauce it is, Mrs Sotheby. I not ever tasted the like before. Would you be calling it anything special now?'

Mrs Sotheby signalled to Nellie.

'Yes, ma'am?'

'Nellie, Miss Lucy wishes to know about the sauce.'

'I'll ask Cook, ma'am,' Nellie politely obliged, at the same time sending me a very merry glance.

She soon returned. 'Miss Lucy, Cook says it's Bearnaise sauce and you make it with a good white wine vinegar, egg yolk, butter and tarragon.'

'Thank you, Nellie,' I replied.

'You're very welcome, miss,' answered Nellie with a wink.

'You will find it is commonly served with steak,' added Mrs Sotheby.

'Common is it?' I queried.

Mrs Sotheby sealed her lips with her serviette, stabbed her peas onto her fork and pushed a deliberate selection of carrot and potato onto its prongs.

I began to cut my potatoes. The Sotheby's potatoes were very different to the potatoes Daid and I ate. No hearty mashed fatai here. These were tiny and round and lightly tossed in parsley and butter.

'Luighseach enjoys cooking, don't you, old thing?' Della continued the conversation.

'I suppose you make stew,' remarked Mrs Sotheby. 'After all, stew is quite common in Ireland, isn't it?'

''Tis right you are there, ma'am,' I acknowledged. 'A lot of stew we eat – and potatoes. Fatai galore. I'm thinking 'tis potatoes we eat even more than stew. We boil them and fry them and mash them, we put them in soups and even make pastry with them, you know.'

'I see.' Potatoes clearly did not rank as highly on Mrs Sotheby's bill of fare as they did on mine. She shifted uncomfortably and tightened her mouth. Then she smiled more sweetly. 'But how do you manage to cook with your legs like that?' she asked.

'Oh, difficult it is indeed,' I sighed and slowly shook my head. 'I'm not finding my legs very useful for cooking at all at all, especially when I wear both my callipers, so I use my hands instead. 'Tis good with my hands I am.'

I popped a potato into my mouth and dabbed my lips with my serviette. Wally Sotheby coughed on his water.

Mrs Sotheby smoothed her front and resumed her meal. Della toyed with her food. Wally cut his meat and smiled a half-smile in my direction. I used some of my potato to sponge the Bearnaise sauce.

'We didn't expect to see you here tonight, Lucy.' I looked up in the direction of the voice. Mr Sotheby stroked his wineglass as he spoke.

'Well, to tell the honest truth sir, I didn't expect to see myself here either,' I replied.

'Your father didn't mind you coming?' Mr Sotheby questioned tentatively over a sip of wine.

'He encouraged it, sir.'

'To celebrate Empire Day?' queried Mrs Sotheby. 'I find that rather unusual.'

'My Daid's a little unusual, ma'am,' I apologised.

'You do realise it's Empire Day, don't you?'

'I do indeed, ma'am. I'm very, very well aware of it. There's been a lot in the papers about it you know, and all over the streets. Everywhere you look the British Empire stares you back in the face.'

'But, you *are* Irish aren't you, Lucy? And a Catholic?'

My reply in the affirmative had her most perplexed.

'So are you in support of the Empire?'

'I'm thinking the British Empire will last as long as it will regardless of what I've to say on the matter, ma'am. Besides, with my legs the way they are I'm having enough trouble supporting myself. I don't know I've the strength to support the Empire.'

'You haven't answered my question,' Mrs Sotheby replied with some frustration. '*I* am aware there are many in Ireland who *are* in favour of British rule. Did you know there's been trouble there because some people won't accept that? Now, what did I read in the paper the other day? Something horridly heathen. That's right: they were burning bibles at Galway railway station. Now what have you to say about that?'

'Well, if *I* was to burn bibles, ma'am, I wouldn't do it on Galway railway station for it's a little too windy, you see.'

Mrs Sotheby concluded that she was not going to get anywhere by asking me what I thought. So she tried a different approach. 'And what of your father?' she asked. 'I really cannot imagine an Irish Catholic like your father affiliated with the Empire in any way.'

'And nor can I, ma'am,' I firmly agreed.

'But your father would be a British subject,' suggested Mr Sotheby. 'In fact, both of you would have come to Australia on British passports. Therefore, regardless of what has happened with the Irish Free State, you would still be British subjects.'

I had never considered the matter in that light before. As far as I was concerned, we were Irish. Irish we always had been and Irish we would always be, British passports or not.

'So what does your father have to say about the Empire?' asked Mrs Sotheby.

'He doesn't say much at all, ma'am, about things he doesn't like. But I can tell you 'twas Daid lost two of his brothers at the hands of the Goddam Black and Tans, you know, during the Troubles.' I did not mention Mam.

'Black and Tans, you mean,' corrected Mr Sotheby.

'My Uncail Eachaan always called them the Goddam Black and Tans, sir,' I replied, feeling the need to correct Mr Sotheby. 'And for good reason too, I might add.'

'I see.'

'Your uncles were shot?' asked Wally.

'Shot you say? 'Twas more than that. Beaten they were and bound and dragged along the road and beaten some more. Then they were shot, and after they were shot they were burned and letters were carved into their charred flesh.'

'By British soldiers?' he added with much concern.

'Aye, by British soldiers.'

'Did your uncles belong to the Irish Republican Army?' inquired Mr Sotheby.

'Aye, they did, sir. 'Twas my uncails Ruaidhrí and Breandán, you see, they were all for independence and took arms against the English to prove it.'

'See?' asserted Mrs Sotheby. 'I could have told you she was a revolutionary.'

'What about the rest of your family?' Wally asked.

'Well, you know how it is, if there be two Irishmen, you can be sure there'll be three opinions. My Uncail Eachann, unlike Ruaidhrí and Breandán, he was against independence for he didn't trust the lads in the lead and he didn't like their methods. As for my Uncail Ciarán, well, he was killed by his own countrymen before he was able to speak his mind on account of the fact that he rode an English horse for an English lord.'

'What about your father? Did he fight?' he inquired.

I slowly shook my head.

'My Da didn't fight at all. Against the fighting he was and there were arguments aplenty about it at home, I can tell you that.'

'So your father *is* in support of the Empire?' Mrs Sotheby questioned yet again.

'Well, if it means making a show with flags and the like, I guess he is, ma'am,' Della's mother was exasperating. ''Twas just the other day he was helping Mr Birstall hang Union Jacks in the shop window.'

'I see,' Mrs Sotheby gave a nod of approval.

'Aye, I bet you do,' I replied. 'But, if you want to know the truth, I think my Da did that because he happens to be a wee bit taller than Mr Birstall, you see, so it's easier for him to reach up high. And if you really want to know, I'll tell you a little something more: we speak Irish between ourselves at home, for my Da won't let me forget where I'm from. Daid prays harder in one day than most monks would do in a lifetime and he's a friend to everyone he meets. It wouldn't matter what they believed in or what they thought or where they came from or what colour their skin was or how well or badly they behaved. My Daid doesn't see the world like that. Aye, he's Irish and he's a Catholic as you said, ma'am. But he's more Catholic than Irish and I'm thinking that's why he's so accepting of it all.'

Mrs Sotheby realigned the cutlery she had already set straight on her plate.

'Well then, I suppose it's wise that your father conforms,' she remarked and smiled tritely at me. 'After all, when in Rome do as the Romans do.'

But I had had enough.

'You really don't understand, do you now? Do you know what it is to watch a war tear your world apart? Do you know what it is to leave behind everything you hold deep in your heart? Do you know what it is to lose the people you love? Do you know what it is to see someone shot and bleeding to death in your arms? Well, when that's happened to yourself, and when the person who was shot was your own dear mother and five months pregnant, and whose only fault was to get caught in crossfire, you'll know what's important in life. And 'tis more than a silly Empire it is! Or Ireland itself, I might add. So, if you really want to know, I don't have much time for the British Empire, but I do have time for Delleen Sotheby who happens to be a very dear friend indeed and if Empire Day means a lot to Della, then so be it, 'twill mean a bit more to myself than I might otherwise prefer.'

If I expected sympathy, the only sympathy that came my way was a small sniff from my little friend who put her hand on mine and squeezed it gently. Mr Sotheby sat silently at the head of the table. Wally was about to speak, but he was cut short by his mother.

'Oh, you Irish are all the same,' she said. 'You poor, downtrodden lot: you think you're the only ones to have suffered. I'm not saying you haven't suffered,' she added, swiftly preventing my protest. 'One look at you and it's perfectly obvious to anyone that you have.'

How could she be so scornful? Incredulous, I looked across at her. But if I was angry, she was also. She was angry and upset and struggling to hide the fact that she was, and I began quickly to amass the snippets I had learned from Della. If I had lost my mother, Mrs Sotheby had lost a husband. But I had had the privilege to hold my mother and stroke and kiss her as she lay there lifeless. Not so Mrs Sotheby. Her husband had been shot down in flames over France, never to be seen again. Beneath the immaculately done hair and nails, the carefully painted face and beautiful eyes, the fine jewellery and elegant costume was a woman who once was tragically widowed. I glanced at Della and her brother. How old would they have been at the time? Not very old at all. Six or seven at the very most.

'Aye 'tis true, ma'am,' I acknowledged, controlling my own temper as best I could. 'Indeed I'm not the only one to have suffered. 'Twas yourself lost your hus—'

'*You* have no idea *what* I have suffered,' was the carefully measured reply.

'We didn't only lose our father, old thing,' Della explained quietly. 'We lost our home too.'

'Zep raids on London back in sixteen,' Wally added.

'Bombed,' elaborated Della.

'Bombed was it?' I echoed. 'But you've never said anything about that, Delleen.'

'It's not something you really talk about is it, old thing?' Della replied, and I suddenly realised why she had been so accepting of my reluctance to talk about

Mam. 'Well, we were bombed, and had we not been at the theatre that night we most certainly would have perished.'

'Faith! You don't say!' I was amazed. 'And you remember what happened?' I asked.

'I don't remember terribly much. After all, I was only very little. But I do remember being at the theatre. What was the performance?'

'*Chu Chin Chow*,' inserted Mr Sotheby. 'All about Ali Baba and the Forty Thieves. It was a sensational show, by Jove.'

'Mummy used to be a dancer, you see,' Della began excitedly. 'Letty Lowell was her name.'

'I don't think you need to go into too much detail, Della,' advised Mrs Sotheby with an air of polite caution.

Again I looked across at Della's mother and saw another reason behind the face paint, the poise and natural grace, the petite features and expressive eyes, now aflame with wary rage. It all made perfect sense: Mrs Sotheby was a dancer. She was every inch a dancer.

'But it's such a good story, Mummy,' responded Della, who seemed oblivious to her mother's mood. 'As I said, Mummy used to be a dancer and on some nights she would bring Wally and me to the theatre. We'd have to stay backstage but it was awfully fun, wasn't it, Wally?'

Wally quietly agreed and Della immediately resumed her account.

'That night we were backstage as always. I fell asleep in one of the dressing rooms.'

Mr Sotheby continued. Like Della, he relished any chance to tell a story. 'The show ended. I don't think anyone really wanted to go home. There were lots of chaps on leave from the front and I think they all wanted the Arabian Nights to last a hundred years. So we drifted around the bars and lounges without much care for time or place. Then word got round there was a zeppelin in town. There was an explosion in the East End. Some people went out on the streets to see what it was all about, while others took refuge in the theatre. As for me, I soon found myself in a room with a sizeable portion of the Royal Navy and a deucedly beautiful houri,' here he winked at Mrs Sotheby. 'She was still in her costume, which was rather like the jewels and trousers that young lady is wearing in that painting over there only even more splendid,' and he nodded in the direction of the picture above the sideboard.

'What were you still doing in your costume, Mummy?' asked Della.

'I had been detained,' Mrs Sotheby replied, a little uncomfortably.

'Well,' resumed Mr Sotheby, 'upon seeing the houri, the gentlemen began passing the time singing "Any-time's kissing time". Do you remember, Letty?'

'Desmond, please—' Mrs Sotheby protested.

But Mr Sotheby was warming to his story. He began to sing, looking fondly across the table at his wife:

Youth is the time for loving,
So poets always say,

The contrary we're proving,
Look at us two to-day.
Love has no charm, no meaning,
Till man has reached his prime.
Surely 'tis so,
You ought to know.
Any time's kissing time.

'Needless to say,' he explained, looking at Della, Wally and myself in turn, 'our houri here needed some protection.'

'Mr Sotheby very kindly lent me his cape,' added Mrs Sotheby who, to this day, seemed grateful for the gesture.

'Now you can imagine we were all in a bit of a state,' continued her husband. 'We didn't know what was going to happen, did we, Letty?'

'The theatres had been bombed before,' explained Mrs Sotheby.

'Well, we waited and waited, and in the end everyone decided to call it a night. My beautiful houri, however, had lost her two children. Eventually we found her little girl fast asleep under a dressing table and her little boy out in the street.'

'What were you doing out there, Wally?' asked Della.

'Looking out for the zep of course,' explained her brother.

'Now it turned out that the houri and her little ones lived in the direction of the explosion,' resumed Mr Sotheby. 'She was rather worried, so I offered to escort her home. With two sleeping children in our arms, we took a cab to Bromley. But when we finally arrived, we were unable to get through. The entire place was a mass of rubble and smouldering beams. The poor houri was homeless. What to do now? Well, I decided to bring them back with me to Piccadilly.'

'We were looked after a treat,' contributed Della. 'Do you remember, Wally? Lots of lovely afternoon teas, hot baths, a cosy bed with the fluffiest eiderdown, and smooth white sheets. Daddy bought me a china doll and pretty dresses and took us for walks in the park. And all those stairs! How we loved to play on those stairs!'

'It was rather nice to have children running around that old place,' reminisced Mr Sotheby. 'As for their pretty mother, why, she turned it into a paradise! It made me think of very happy times which I thought had been closed to me forever.'

'Daddy's first wife and daughter had died years ago in India, you see,' Della inserted. 'Cholera, wasn't it, Daddy?'

'Typhoid,' corrected Mr Sotheby. 'So,' he continued, 'I decided that, all being well, I would rather like to marry that houri. And marry her I did.'

Mr Sotheby finished his story with a smile and began to sing 'Youth is the time for loving' all over again. This time Mrs Sotheby joined in.

'Meanwhile,' here Wally calmly took up the story and looked directly at me, 'my father was fighting for his life in a military hospital in France.'

'Ah yes,' Mrs Sotheby stopped singing. 'Lest we forget: the great, gallant war hero.'

'But—' I began.

'And pray, what medal did he win that time?' prompted Mrs Sotheby.

'Distinguished Service Order,' Wally curtly replied. 'He nearly lost his leg on the Somme.'

'Well,' coolly continued Mrs Sotheby, 'it didn't stop him getting into an aeroplane and going back for more, did it? It didn't matter to him that he had a wife, not to mention a mistress, and two children. Oh no! He was far too busy fighting for King and Country wasn't he?'

'He gave his life!' Wally protested. 'And what do you care, you heartless whore?'

'Wally!' exclaimed Della.

'You care for nothing save your own comfort!' he continued, standing and glaring angrily at his mother.

'Wally, son, that will do!' admonished Mr Sotheby

'Son? I'm not your son!' Wally turned on his step-father. 'Besides, what did you do in the War? Get rich from shares in a munitions factory?'

'That is enough, boy.'

'And what did you do?' Wally again turned on his mother. 'Make yourself—'

'And what was I to do with two children to provide for?' seethed Mrs Sotheby.

'You could have waited for him,' replied her son, and he quietly left the room.

'Waited for him?' she called after him. 'Waited for him? If I had waited for him, *you* would have starved! And why should I wait when he left me with nothing? Nothing do you hear?' Mrs Sotheby was an actress as much as she was a dancer and she began to imitate The Captain: '"For Heavens' sake, Letty, do you not realise there's a war that must be won?" That's what he said. He had no time for love. He had battles to fight, didn't he? Of course it would all be over by Christmas. He would see to that. But it wasn't over by Christmas, was it? Bothersome, bloody business! It seemed as if it would never end. But I couldn't worry, I couldn't cry, I couldn't mourn when he went missing. That was for the loyal wife. Loyal wife!' she scoffed. '*She* wasn't loyal! *He* didn't love her. But the mistress has to pretend. Years and years of pretence that no one she loved had gone to war. And what did he care anyway? He left me! He left me!'

And finally she began to sob.

'There, there Letty,' Mr Sotheby rose and lovingly attended to her. 'What's done is done. Put it all behind you, dear. Della, Lucy,' he advised, 'I think it would be best if you went upstairs.'

'I— I'm sorry—' I ventured an apology.

'Never mind, young lady,' he replied. 'You're not to blame. Run along now.'

29

Without a word, Della and I climbed the stairs to her room.

Wally was there on the landing, leaning over the banister. He was a formidable sight with his strong, athletic figure still in dinner dress, his bow tie undone, his wing collar unbuttoned and darting out at odd angles. A heavy scowl clouded his features and smoke curled and drifted from the cigarette that drooped from his fingers.

'Della,' he began.

'Put that wretched cigarette out, Wally,' scolded his sister.

'Della,' he began again as we reached the landing.

'Don't you "Della" me,' she angrily replied.

'Come on, Dell,' he urged.

Della pushed past him and opened her bedroom door. 'No, Wally, I'm not going to "Come on". First you ruined what promised to be a lovely holiday and now you ruin a special family dinner, this time in the presence of my best friend. Come on, Luighseach.'

'I need to talk to you,' her brother persisted.

'Well, *I* don't need to talk to *you*,' and she shut the door in his face.

Wally's muffled voice continued from the other side. 'Then if you don't want to talk you might want to read.'

A note was pushed under the door.

Della picked it up. Curious, she unfolded it. Judging from the stained creases and the limpness of the yellowed paper, it appeared very worn.

'It's a letter,' she mused as she studied the envelope.

'"By Hand. Master Ralph Walsingham Ponsonby",' Della read in a quiet, puzzled voice. Then she mumbled the London address. She turned the envelope over and, upon reading what was written there, immediately opened the door.

'Wally!'

Evidently, Della's reaction was precisely the one her brother was expecting for he was waiting just outside.

'What is this?' she demanded. 'Where did you get it?'

'It's from The Captain.'

'I don't understand. Is he still alive? What is it all about?'

'Read the letter and you'll find out.'

'I'm thinking I'll make myself ready for bed now,' I excused myself.

'No!' they simultaneously replied.

'Please stay, old thing,' added Della, now very anxious. Wally echoed Della's request but did so with more gravity.

Della sat on the edge of her bed and nervously opened the letter. I sat beside her and she handed me the envelope.

''Tis yourself there?' I tapped the address and looked across at Wally. He pulled up a chair and nodded. 'Walsingham is it?' I could not stop my lips from twitching. That Wally was short for Walsingham and not Walter or Wallace was too much.

'It's a family name, on my father's side,' he replied somewhat defensively. 'Anyway, at least most people can pronounce Walsingham,' he added with a wry smile. 'Not like some Irish names I've heard recently.'

'Aye, well, 'tis ourselves do be simplifying our names on account of you English not having a hope in Heaven of learning a language other than your own,' I answered as I perused the back of the envelope. It read, 'Maj. R. W. Ponsonby, Esq., D.S.O., M.C., R.F.C. Barracks, Upavon.'

Della began to read out loud:

October, 1917.

My dear Son,

Should you receive this letter you will know that I am gone to my Valhalla and will return no more to this green and pleasant land I have been proud to call my Home. Perhaps History will tell the death I am to die and my hope is that, if ever you chance to read of it, it will be one worthy of a man who has endeavoured to serve his country faithfully and well.

In writing this epistle, I have made it my purpose to tell you what manner of man is he whom you so fondly call "The Captain", he who also has the fortune to be your father. Since I will not see you grow to manhood, I regard it as my duty to provide you, in my own words, details which, if left to History, may be misrepresented and, in being misrepresented, be misjudged.

'He goes into some family background,' she commented as she continued to scan the letter. 'He was born in 1883 in Kilkenny. Where's that, Luighseach?'

''Tis down south and to the east,' I replied after drawing a map of Ireland in my head and mentally marking out the counties.

'The third son of the Earl of— Goodness, gracious! It reads like something out of *Burke's Peerage*!' Della exclaimed. 'Heavens above! There are lords and barons everywhere, all the way back to Charles II! I say, Wally, he sounds frightfully proud.'

Wally raised his brows but said nothing.

'He was educated at Harrow, then— oh my!' Della started to read out loud again:

I did not excel at school, nor did I care for it; so, the moment the opportunity presented itself, I pursued a military career. I joined the Royal Dublin Fusiliers as a bugler. In that capacity, at age fifteen, I served in the Boer War. I was wounded at Colenso and invalided home.

'He fought? At fifteen years of age?'

Not exactly,' answered her brother. 'He played the bugle. He had to give signals for troops to advance and retreat and so on. This sort of thing,' and he began to demonstrate the different types of calls by holding a pretend bugle to his mouth and imitating the sound, comically getting red in the face and adding false notes, odd spits and splutters in the process.

'Do you play the bugle?' I asked, impressed by his mimicry. It was very easy to imagine Wally Sotheby in military attire.

'I used to play it at school,' he replied. 'A bugle was used instead of a bell to mark out the time. You know, morning call: "I can't get 'em up, I can't get 'em up, I can't get 'em up this morning",' he tooted.

But I was the only one to laugh. Della had completely withdrawn into reading the letter. She sat, biting her lip and slowly shaking her head.

'Is everything well with you now, Delleen?' I asked.

Della silently passed me the page she had just finished. I took it but hesitated to read and looked to Wally for permission. He had become serious again and nodded his consent. Why did he want me to read it? Probably for the one reason that prompted me to do so: he was very concerned for his sister. I read without a word:

> Upon recovery, during which time I devoted attention to my studies, I entered the Military Academy at Woolwich. I was commissioned as Lieutenant with the Royal Engineers and was subsequently promoted to the rank of Captain with the newly-formed Royal Signals Service.
>
> Not long after my promotion, I married. The union was not a happy one and soon resulted in separation. Preferring the company of dogs and horses, my wife remained on the country estate. I, on the other hand, enjoyed the occasional game of polo, frequented the Royal Aero Club, played cricket for Surrey and moved in military circles amidst London's many pleasures. It was while in London that I met your mother. She was then eighteen years old and a dancer at the West End theatres.
>
> What I intended to be a passing liaison, however, was quickly complicated by the fact that she conceived a child. Since she had had no prior relationships she knew I was the father. Now, your mother, as probably you are aware, is of the Roman Catholic faith. She was also a foundling. Undoubtedly, it was these two factors that induced her to insist upon having the baby and upon caring for it herself. I am ashamed to say that both decisions were against my wishes. Nevertheless, I performed my duty as a gentleman and saw that she was well provided. Little did I realise that what I considered at the time to be my greatest curse soon became my deepest joy: she bore me a son. I bestowed on you my name. I also continued the affair and a year later a daughter was born: your sister, Mary Arondelle.

Again I looked across at Wally.

''Tis the truth?' I whispered.

He nodded.

'Wally, it's terrible!' Della lamented. 'How could he? I had no idea he was that much older than Mummy.' She began to work out the difference on her fingers. 'Nine years!'

'Well, our step-father's at least twenty years older,' Wally retorted.

'Yes, I know, but he married her. This is quite different. I don't think I want to read any more.'

'You need to read it, Dell.'

Della shook her head.

'If you don't,' her brother persisted, 'you'll end up doing precisely what he feared would happen: you'll misjudge him. Please read it.'

'You read it,' and she thrust the letter in his direction.

'You'll listen, won't you?'

Wally put on his glasses and continued:

They were happy occasions, those visits I used to pay your mother and my little family, but they were not to last, for, in August, 1914, war was declared. Now Son, you must understand what I am about to say. I am first and foremost a commissioned officer in the Corps of the Royal Engineers of the British Army. It is my duty to serve His Majesty the King and I must go wherever the cause of right and glory lead. I was given orders and I departed for France a few weeks later.

The events of the ensuing months I will leave for the history books. What soon became apparent was that the war was not going to be the brief interlude I hoped it would be. The likelihood of surviving the ordeal became increasingly remote, the possibility of returning home ill or incapacitated very real indeed. Fearing the worst, I resolved to break off relations with your mother for the duration and took advantage of a brief spate of leave to inform her of my decision.

'The cad!' Della was fuming.

'Let me read,' Wally persevered with the letter:

It was not an easy decision, but it was made with your mother's best interests at heart. She is such a naïve, sweet-natured little person and I did not want to burden her with the dreadful undertaking which had befallen me. Being young, she had every promise of rebuilding her life. I failed, however, to appreciate the depth of her passion. She would not agree. Dry with rage and extreme toil, weighed down by the abysmal loss of life and limb and frustrated by her stubbornness, I resorted to violence, and, to make my point, severed all communication with her. It was with a heavy heart that I returned to the trenches. What acts of valour, what battle honours I received were poor compensation for the cruelty I displayed towards that young and beautiful woman.

'Can you imagine what he must have been going through?' he asked her.

'But he left us! He left Mummy helpless! The brute! I never realised. Just think of what *she* must have been going through!'

'Will you let me read? It gets better.'

'It better get better,' Della sighed.

Perhaps Providence had a part to play in what happened next. At least, I thought so at the time. I was wounded in the July of 1916. I made a full recovery, but I was no longer fit for active duty on the battlefield. The thought of a desk job, however, was abhorrent to me and I requested a transfer to the Royal Flying Corps.

My transfer was granted and I was posted to Farnborough where I commenced duties as a wireless instructor. I was also given leave to attend to my affairs. Foremost in this matter was the need to re-establish communication with your mother. Whilst in hospital, I received news of the death of my wife. Her passing opened the possibility of marriage to your mother. This was something I previously had not contemplated. Since my wife and I were both High Church, divorce had been out of the question. Even if I had entered into such proceedings (which, believe you me, I had been tempted many times to do), the idea of marrying your mother was equally impermissible. Social differences aside, your mother's religion made marriage with her impossible. Our family does not marry Catholics and such an act on my part would have sorely tried the already strained family relations which had arisen from the separation.

'Well, I like that!' it was unusual for Della to be sarcastic. 'So it was all very well to have Mummy for his mistress, wasn't it?'
Wally ignored the remark and read on:

But my experience in a war in which an illiterate miner is capable of more intelligence and gallantry than a public school popinjay, now rendered me indifferent to such distinctions. My greatest curse, which had become my deepest joy and most heartfelt sorrow, had now become my one true hope. I was determined to marry your mother. That way, in the event of my death, at least she would have the dignity of being a war widow and my children would have a worthy legacy. The probability of surviving the war, which I regard as remote, I would consign to Providence.

'See?' he said.
Della huffed with annoyance and tightened her lips.
Wally continued:

Finding your mother, however, proved no easy matter. To my dismay, her last known address had been razed by German bombs. She no longer worked in the theatre. Inquiries at the fashion house where I knew she was once employed yielded no clues. Eventually I learned what I had begun to suspect: your mother had married another man and I had only my choler to blame.

'Now,' he broke off and challenged his sister. 'Can you tell me why she did that?'
Della did not hesitate. 'Of course I can. He brutally rejected her. She was left to fend for herself. She met Daddy. They fell in love and they married. It's as simple as that.'

'But he came back.'

'Too late, dear brother, too late,' insisted Della. 'And, as he says, he had only his anger to blame. Listen, Wally, I know you adored The Captain, I did too. I still do, in spite of it all. But you've got to accept the way things are, tragic as they may seem. The Captain did,' she tried to encourage him, and sat on the arm of his chair and put her arm round his shoulder. 'Come on, read some more. Please.'

So, with Della looking on, Wally resumed:

Still, I deemed it imperative to make contact with her and one day I followed her to the park.

'Why, I think I remember that day,' his sister interrupted in another attempt to lift her brother's spirits. 'It must have been about Easter time. I remember because the daffodils were out. Do you remember, Wally?'

'I don't remember the daffodils.'

'You wouldn't. He was always racing off,' she explained for my benefit. 'Racing off and getting into trouble. That day was no exception, only that you began shouting, "It's the Captain! The Captain!" And sure enough, you came back with him, still shouting. He was in uniform and he had a stick. I didn't realise he had the stick because he'd been injured. Dear me! Anyway, Mummy was absolutely silent. I have never forgotten that silence. It's simply not like Mummy to be so quiet.'

'He writes of it here,' Wally remarked, turning back to the letter. '"Heaven has no rage like love to hatred turned, nor hell a fury like a woman scorned".'

Your mother refused to have anything to do with me. Fortunately, your step-father was more amenable. I will have to admit that, had the incident occurred a decade ago, I would have put a bullet through the man's head, but I had seen and done too much of that lately and did not have the inclination. Far better was it to have the matter sorted out over a decent meal within the comfort of a gentleman's club. Should you wish more information, your step-father, whom I have since come to regard as a sensible and liberal man, is fully informed of the particulars of my estate, as is my lawyer,

'He gives a name. Apparently it's a cousin. It gets a bit business-like here.' Wally turned the page and recommenced reading:

There remained now the issue of my children. Arrangements were made for me to spend time with you and your sister before I was due to leave for France. My son, for a man who has seen for the last months – nay years – of his life, nothing but the vilest carnage, I cannot tell you what it means to be embraced by a child. And when that child, that innocent, wholesome child, is his own flesh and blood, his own dear boy, the emotion is indescribable. It will be these cherished memories and these alone that I take with me when I cross the Channel. I hope that you, too, will always hold dear the happy times we spent together.

'Do you remember them, Wally?' I asked.

He nodded. 'He took me everywhere: museums, parks, galleries, pantomimes, and best of all he took me out to see the 'planes. We'd watch them together and he'd tell me all about them. The last time he saw me he gave me his medals and photographs.'

'It was like being out with a prince, wasn't it?' added Della as she took up the page Wally had just read. 'I remember him being quite tall. Mind you, everyone looks tall to me. And he used to swagger a bit when he walked.'

'I think he did it to disguise the fact that he limped. There was no way he'd let on that he'd been wounded,' remarked her brother.

'Everyone would doff their hats and nod and smile at him,' Della fondly recalled the scene. 'Some would even come to him and offer words of congratulation or gratitude. Given the chance, I think they would have touched the hem of his garment. I say, where's the ring?'

'What's that?' asked Wally.

'It says here: "You should find enclosed a ring. It was intended for your mother. I will leave it for you to do as you wish with it. Hopefully, you will put it to better use than me. I remain your father and beloved 'Captain', Ralph William Ponsonby." Where's the ring?'

Wally brandished his watch chain. To it he had coupled a plain gold band.

'What are you going to do with it?' asked his sister. 'Are you going to give it to Mummy?'

'Are you mad?'

'But it was intended for her.'

There was a large explosion outside and the three of us went to the window. A magnificent display of fireworks puffed into the night sky. Down below, in the Sotheby's garden, there was laughter and a gleeful clapping of hands. 'Whee! Desmond, dear, do another!' giggled the musical, girlish voice. A rocket whistled through the air and burst into stars. Catherine Wheels whirled and 'Land of Hope and Glory' was lustily sung by the gentleman and lady of the house.

'Oh my!' Della blushed. 'She's sounds as if she's tipsy. No, Wally, don't show her the ring, she won't know what to do, poor thing.'

'Can you imagine how she'd behave?' Wally cringed at the thought. 'No, I mean to do right by this ring,' he added solemnly, 'and the woman who wears it I will serve as nobly as my father did his country.'

'Well, my dear brother,' Della began to chastise, 'if that's what you aspire to, you're going to have to mend your ways. Anyway,' she quickly added, 'how did you come by the letter? When did you come by it?'

'Last November. If you turn the page over and read the other side, you'll find out how I came by it. He must have run short of paper.'

Della instantly obliged. '"P.S. Should Fortune favour me, the bearer of this letter will be Private George Hammond". George Hammond? Good heavens! I say, that's not Hammond, is it?'

Wally nodded.

'The gardener? Mummy's chauffeur?'

''Ammond 'imself,' he replied, folding his arms and leaning back against the wall just as Hammond was wont to do while waiting with the car.

'What on earth was he doing with it?' demanded Della.

'He was our father's batman.'

'What?'

'Read.'

Della read:

He was with me in the field and proved himself not only a trustworthy servant, but a brave soldier and loyal companion. He saved my life in '14 and I have every confidence that he will do what he can for you, my son.

'How long has he been with us?' she asked. 'It must be at least seven years. Why, Hammond's never said a word about that.'

'It's not his business to, Della.'

'No, I suppose it isn't. But do you mean to say he'd been holding on to this letter all that time? He had no right to do that! How dare he!'

'Calm down. How could he give it sooner? He couldn't exactly give it to an eight year old boy, could he? What would Henry do with something like this? Make a paper dart?'

'I suppose you're right.'

'Listen, I was as flabbergasted as you when I found out. I didn't have any idea that Hammond had anything to do with our father until the chaps at the airfield mentioned him.'

'Is that why you've been spending all that time out there?'

'Of course, silly! Most of those fellows knew our father, either through flying with him or through wireless operations. That was his specialty: wireless telegraphy. The flying came later. He was training as a pilot about the time this letter was written. Hammond worked with him on his 'plane.'

'I see. Wally, how absolutely fascinating! But what about Daddy? Does Daddy know?'

Wally shrugged his shoulders.

'You've got to tell him, Wally. He must know something. For Heaven's sake, he even met The Captain. The letter says so.'

'But how am I going to tell him? What am I going to tell him?' he questioned, frustrated for the first time that evening. 'What would be the point?'

'Really, Wally, you're as bad as Hamlet,' scolded his sister.

'We've hardly ever spoken about anything, let alone about my father. I can't talk to him, Dell. No. I'm not going to talk to him.'

'Well, if *you* don't, Wally. *I* will.'

30

I was the only one to appear in the dining room for breakfast the following morning.

'And how are you today, Miss Lucy?' asked Nellie in reply to my greeting. 'Now, don't you go trying to serve yourself. You sit at the table and I'll bring your breakfast to you. Cook's made kippers this morning. How would that be?'

"Twould be grand indeed, thank you, Nellie,' and I sat down to a very stately breakfast all on my own.

'Where is everyone, Nellie?' I asked as she served me my tea and toast.

'Well, miss, I haven't seen Miss Della yet and goodness knows where Master Wally is, although it's not like him to miss a meal. Mr Sotheby breakfasted bright and early as he always does and Mrs Sotheby prefers to take breakfast in her room. So it's only yourself at the moment and don't you hesitate to ask for anything more if you need it.'

My breakfast finished, I decided to do some 'cello practice and went in search of my instrument. It was not in the large drawing room where I expected it to be. Eventually I found it in the smaller room, which was a bother because now I was not able to set myself up to play. Not only was I unable to carry my 'cello, but there was no suitable chair. I decided to wait in the vestibule. Someone would pass by sooner or later and I could ask for help.

And sooner, rather than later, someone did. Heading down the stairs, two at a time, came Wally.

'Halloa there, Lucy,' he said with a smile. 'What's up?'

I could feel my cheeks redden as I explained my predicament. Of all people, why was it always Wally who discovered me in such dilemmas?

'I think Della used some of the dining room chairs last time you all came to practise,' he replied. 'I'll fetch one for you. Where would you like to play?'

Wally returned with the chair and showed me through to the large drawing room. Again he helped me sit and then he brought me my instrument.

'I say, that is a handsome piece of wood,' he remarked as I pulled the 'cello from its case. 'Where did you get it?'

"Tis not really mine,' I explained, 'for it belongs to a very good friend who cannot play it any more.' And I told him about Mr David. "Twas a very kind gesture, you know, lending it me, and I'll always be grateful to him.'

Wally nodded. 'But it's not the same as having one of your own,' he said, as he looked me carefully in the eye.

I had to admit that he was right.

"Tis a goodly enough 'cello, is Mavis 'cello. But I'm telling you there's a 'cello at

Miss Bray's music shop that's a dream to play. 'Tis not a pretty 'cello. 'Tis dark and drab-looking for it doesn't have the fancy flaming you see on most instruments. In fact, the way it's been put together it makes you wonder how anyone made such a thing in the first place. But you'd not believe the sound it makes, Wally Sotheby. Such beautiful colours and silken tones, why 'tis like the very cloths of Heaven! If cloth could be woven in sound, that is,' I added, realising the stupidity of my analogy. I had never told anyone about the 'cello in Miss Bray's shop.

'They're a bit like people, aren't they? Instruments, I mean,' he observed. 'It's quite surprising what's hidden inside, isn't it?'

'Aye,' I agreed. 'And you don't really know what they're like until you've played them a bit. But there's a difference, you know.'

'Which is?'

''Tis a person has feelings. An instrument, as much as you'd like it to have feelings, is but an instrument. You can play an instrument. You cannot play a person.'

'I reckon you can,' he smirked. 'Well, there's plenty of it going on around here at any rate. Whether you ought: now that's another matter altogether. Anyway, speaking of playing, I suppose you want to practise and I'm going to miss out on breakfast if I don't get to the dining room on the double. I'll see you later,' he gave me a wave and opened the door. 'Ma'am,' he addressed his mother and clicked his heels together as Mrs Sotheby entered.

I nearly smiled. That someone could be so very kind and friendly one moment, so annoyingly smug and so mockingly regimental the next was almost comical and I might have laughed outright had it not been for the chill of Mrs Sotheby's reception. If mother and son were not on good terms prior to last night's events, their relationship had markedly worsened. Wally's salute was cruel and there was such a mixture of hurt and horror on Mrs Sotheby's face that I was compelled to remove any trace of emotion from my own and busy myself with tuning my 'cello.

Aside from Wally, I was probably the last person Mrs Sotheby wanted to have anything to do with. She was bent on looking for her cat and minced out to the verandah, calling for Ming in a tinkling, bell-like voice. I acknowledged her indifference by launching into a perfectly proportioned C major scale. Such a sparkling, sunny morning, with the sky bright blue and the lawn glistening, was a fitting occasion for Bach's C major 'cello suite. As for what happened last night, playing the 'cello suite was a blessed relief.

Mrs Sotheby's cat, however, happened not to be outside; he was in the drawing room itself. Before long, the lithe, sleek creature made a lunge for my bow and swiped it off the strings with a deft pat of his paw. Ming had been stalking the 'cello and had decided to attack before mewing plaintively and proudly trotting across to his mistress who picked him up and caressed him.

'Who gave you permission to move that chair in here?' she asked.

'Permission to move the chair, ma'am?' I echoed while I nursed my hand; for the cat had succeeded not only in dislodging my bow, but also in giving me a nasty scratch.

'Yes,' she replied, very annoyed that I did not seem to comprehend her question. 'Who gave you permission to move the chair?'

'This chair?' and I looked at the chair I was sitting on. ''Twas no one gave me permission to move it, ma'am.'

'Oh? So you took the liberty of moving it yourself?'

'I didn't move the chair, ma'am,' I replied truthfully.

'It didn't get here by itself.'

'Indeed, it did not, ma'am,' I agreed.

'So who moved the chair?'

'Mrs Sotheby,' I was not going to implicate Wally if I could help it. 'I'm thinking I should apologise for some of the things I said last night. 'Tis my tongue, you see, has a habit of running away and I've a bit of a temper, I'm afraid.'

'Yes, you certainly have,' she acknowledged. 'In fact, I don't think I've met a more arrogant and bumptious girl as you in all my life. I suppose being crippled has something to do with it. Or else it's because you haven't a mother to teach you any sense of propriety,' she added as she looked with disgust at my legs which were wrapped around my 'cello. 'Why your father doesn't remarry I don't know. He's such an elegant, attractive man and I simply cannot imagine him marrying a woman who was not in any way the same. What was your mother like?'

Did she really want to know? If she did, I was not prepared to provide her with details.

'Like a sunbeam dancing on water she was,' I replied.

'Well, if by that you mean she was in any way pretty, *that* quality certainly wasn't inherited,' returned Mrs Sotheby. 'Nevertheless,' she sighed, 'I suppose you have been a very kind friend to Della, although what Wally sees in you is quite beyond me. But then he has grown tall – taller than his father – and you are rather statuesque even with your legs in those horrid irons. At least you can be thankful they're straight. Are you able to see without your glasses?'

'I beg your pardon, ma'am?'

'Are you able to see without your glasses?' she repeated.

Now why would I be wearing glasses if I could see without them? I asked myself.

I held my tongue.

'Only for to read, ma'am,' I replied. 'For I'm very short-sighted, you see.'

'Yes, so it seems. Still, you have improved since I first met you. You seem to be growing out of that frightful gawky phase that some girls go through. Thank heavens Della never went through that awful stage. Ah, Della dear,' she smiled at her daughter who at that moment entered the room. 'Lucy and I were having a little chat.'

'Good morning, Mummy,' smiled Della. 'How nice. Mummy, Mrs Mahony's on the telephone. It's a trunk call.'

Della waited until her mother was out of earshot before she began her next piece of news.

'Luighseach, old thing, you won't believe what's happened!'

'What is it, Delleen?'

'Wally has actually gone upstairs to talk to Daddy! Can you believe it? Isn't it wonderful? Now, come on,' she continued excitedly as she took my 'cello and passed me my crutches, 'you must come out to the garden.'

'But, 'twas some practice I was doing, Della Sotheby,' I protested.

'On a beautiful morning like this? Practice can wait, don't you think? Come on, just for a few minutes. I say, you look a bit upset. You're not too troubled by what happened last night, are you?' she asked as we walked outside.

'Delleen Sotheby, I'm telling you that no fishwife in Galway could come anywhere close to your mother for idle talk.'

'What on earth happened?'

I told her.

'It sounds as if she's getting to know you in a Mummy sort of way. You know she has a habit of saying whatever comes into her head, and she can't help but dwell on appearances. That's how she thinks.'

'She even had the gall to hint that your brother was keen on me,' I added with a sniff.

'But he is, old thing,' Della replied and smiled gently. 'He likes you. As for confiding in you the way he did last night, well, I've never ever known Wally to do such a thing. Besides, what's really rather nice is that I think you like him.'

'I do n—'

'Luighseach, don't be such a prude! There's nothing wrong with your liking a boy or a boy liking you.'

'But, why would he ever—'

'You silly girl, there's a lot to like! Poor old Wally, to think he'd been hiding all that about The Captain. I had absolutely no idea and I can tell you it is far more upsetting not being able to explain all the tensions than learning the truth, however unpleasant it might be. I say, there's Hammond.'

She brought me down to the back of the garden where the gardener was planting seedlings.

'Just puttin' in some pansies, Miss Della,' he said as he raised his hat in greeting.

'Oh how lovely, Hammond! You know they're my favourites. Are these snapdragons?'

'Yes, Miss, and 'olly'ocks along the wall. As for them roses over there, I'll prune 'em back when it gets a little colder and they'll be bloomin' all right come Spring. We're needin' everything picture perfect for your mother's party, eh?'

'It will be splendid, Hammond, I'm certain. It always is. A thoroughly English garden. Mr Hammond,' she began again.

'Yes, Miss Della?' the gardener smiled kindly. 'What can I do you for?'

'I—I want to say "thank you". Thank you for saving my father's life.'

'Ah, so Master Wally 'e finally gave you the letter, eh?'

Della nodded and sniffed a little.

'Don't know what was in it, Miss. It was only my job to deliver it. I'd do anything for your father. He was a good man, Miss Della.'

'Was he?' Della sniffed again.

'Make no mistake about it,' he reassured her. 'Mind you, 'e wasn't the most likeable fellow – at least, not at first. Upper class, you know, and tough as old boots. But we were lucky to have 'im. Unlike most of the other lads, you see, we 'ad a captain who'd seen battle before. Some of the other officers, why they were as green as the men they were leadin'. They all fell like flies, poor souls. Not your father, 'e was different. I reckon 'e could smell Fritz. We soon learnt to trust 'im and 'e got us through Hell and back again. As a pilot, miss, 'e was one of the best, a right brave, true fellow. You've every reason to be proud of 'im, Miss Della.'

'Thank you, Hammond. Thank you very, very much.'

'It's a pleasure, young lady. And you enjoy your day, Miss Della.'

'I will, thank you, Hammond. Now what about some practice, Luighseach? I could do with some help on the *Sunrise*.'

31

School resumed for Trinity Term. I alighted from the train at Strathfield and was hailed by Fanny Mahony of all people. In response, I crossed the busy platform to the lively group of black box-pleated tunics, blazers, bags and boaters, bid my good morning to Fanny, Kate, Beth and Mary. I was introduced in turn to a trio of Lewisham beaux, and a fourth individual whom Fanny coyly presented as 'Toffee' Sotheby. Wally Sotheby responded with a tip of his boater and a slight bow. His formality contrasted markedly not only with Fanny's flirtatious introduction but also with the more casual manners of the Lewisham boys. The tone of his greeting, however, was very cordial and nearly elicited a reply on my part, had not Fanny interrupted with news of her recent holiday in Bowral.

Fanny was brimful of details regarding her highland vacation, as was everyone else by the time the city-bound train arrived to take the boys to their destination. Fanny, Kate, Mary, Beth and I left the platform and began our walk to school.

'I didn't realise you knew my aunt,' Fanny remarked to me.

'What is it?' I asked, a little astonished that Fanny should initiate a conversation with me, of all people, on the first day back at school. As for knowing any of her family, the idea was ridiculous.

'My Aunt Rose,' Fanny elaborated. 'I didn't realise you knew her.'

'Oh,' I smiled. 'Your aunt is she?' But I was still perplexed. That someone as frivolous and thoughtless as Frances Mahony could be closely associated with the likes of the Pearse family did not make sense.

'Actually, she's my godmother. So she's not really my aunt but I've always called her Aunt. She went to school with my mother. How do you know her?'

'Let's say she's my fairy godmother,' I replied as I fondly recalled my own holiday at the farm and the many letters I had sent and received. 'She writes me, you know.'

There was a pause. Fanny clearly did not wish to pursue that line of conversation.

'So how do you know Toffee?' she asked.

''Tis Wally Sotheby you mean now?'

'All his *friends* call him Toffee,' she replied. 'How do you know him?'

'Why, he's Delleen Sotheby's brother is he not?' How else would I know Wally Sotheby?

'Yes, but you don't know him just because of that. You *know* him and *he* certainly knows *you*. For your information, *he* was the one who suggested you come over just then. If I had had my way, I wouldn't have dreamed of inviting you, you can be certain of that.'

Fanny quickly walked on ahead with big Kathleen Doherty lumbering alongside her. The two girls began to giggle. Then there was some mention of my leg braces.

'He probably felt sorry for her,' was Fanny's next remark, which she obviously intended me to hear.

'Lucy, don't worry about Fan,' Mary caught me up. 'It's not worth it.'

'I thought we'd become friends,' I replied.

'Friends? With Frances Mahony?' Mary almost laughed. 'That's a very exclusive set to belong to, Lucy. In fact,' she nudged me playfully, 'I think there's only one member.'

'Kate is it?'

'No, silly! It's Fanny! Did you have a good holiday?'

****

I could not bear to watch Della. Like the rest of the class, she was decked out in her sports tunic. Unlike the class, which easily winged its way through the absurdities of eurythmics, Della's efforts were more like those of a chicken trying to fly. She flapped her arms quite out of time and could not work out what to do with her feet. When the class stepped right, Della stepped left, collided, and dizzily attempted to reorient herself. Sister Catherine Bernard shouted at her. Della briefly jumped into synchronization with her peers, coughed, promptly fell out of step, and spent her energies rectifying the error before being shouted at again.

In fact, Della had not been herself all week. To be sure, she was quite vivacious in company and happily partook of everyone's holiday news; but she was not particularly forthcoming with news of her own. Nor did she display much of her usual zest for her favourite subjects. Ordinarily, Della was a ready and able contributor to literary and historical discussions and her insights made her a great favourite with Sister Magdalene. Trinity Term, however, saw Della Sotheby not quite so eager to share her thoughts. She participated in the usual games at recess and lunch, but her involvement was preceded by a sojourn in the school chapel. And it was coming from the school chapel that I usually encountered her in the mornings before the bell rang for class.

I could not decide which was worse: seeing Della tortured over trigonometry by Sister Augustine, or bullied through Thursday afternoon sport by Sister Bernard. Whatever the case, enough was enough. Since Sister Bernard's back was permanently turned in my direction, I laid *Amusements in Mathematics* aside and presented a mock version of the exercises being performed. Della convulsed in a fit of coughing and was duly escorted from the field by Mary and Beth who were more than keen to avoid further physical exertion. They were not going to be given such licence if I could help it, and I took charge.

'You're very lucky Sister Bernard didn't catch you out, old thing,' Della gathered her breath. 'She would have made you do it in front of everyone.'

'And wouldn't I give her something to write home about if she did?' I replied. ''Tis the lot of you be lunacy incarnate.'

'Well I'm afraid some of us aren't so fortunate as to have callipers on our legs and be exempted from sport,' she replied with a gleam, but her attempt at a giggle failed miserably.

''Tis a bad cough that, Delleen.'

'I've always had it,' she continued to cough and tried to talk at the same time, 'and it always seems to worsen when I do a little too much. It will pass. I simply need to sit down. What are you doing here anyway? You're usually helping with Sister Scholastica's class on Thursday afternoons.'

'Aye, but the lassies I help with reading are all in bed with colds. What's troubling you, Delleen?' I was not going to have Della deflect attention away from herself.

Della sighed. She knew she had no choice but to talk. This time, however, she seemed to welcome the opportunity.

'Oh Luighseach, old thing, I cannot stop thinking about my father.'

'The Captain, you mean?'

She nodded. 'I suppose it's frightfully selfish of me but I wonder if he ever loved me. I know it sounds awful but I cannot help feeling that Wally was the only one he cared for. Wally was the one he wrote before he died and I barely get mentioned in that letter. He gave Wally his medals and he gave Wally his photographs. I only have a picture of him because Wally gave me one. I know I was very little when he died, but should a year make so much difference? After all, Wally is only a year older. Do you think that's selfish?'

''Tis nothing of selfish, Delleen, 'tis only natural you should wonder. I'd say he loved you as a daughter and Wally as a son. I suppose I'm not a one to talk for I've no brothers to speak of but I remember my Uncail Eachann and my cousin Liam, who's Uncail Eachann's only son, the other five being all girls. They've always lived and worked together. Eachann passed on to Liam all he knew about horses, which was what his da passed on to him and his da passed on before that. 'Tis what a father does for his son. It doesn't mean my uncail loves his lasses any less. He's that proud of them all being nuns you know. 'Tis different is all. So you can be sure your father loved you, Delleen.'

'You know, Luighseach, it's funny,' Della looked at me and smiled. 'I remember when you first called me that name. I had a strange feeling I'd heard it before. I've been wondering ever since and the only person who could possibly have called me Delleen is The Captain. He mostly called me by my full name. "And how's my Mary Arondelle?" he used to say and swing me high into the air. The only other person who ever calls me Mary Arondelle is Sister Bellarmine when she's annoyed with me for not conjugating properly. Even then it's Mary Arondelle Sotheby, never Mary Arondelle. But occasionally I'm certain The Captain also called me Delleen. It must have been The Captain. I mean no servant we've had has ever called me that and I've always been Della to the rest of my family. It's an Irishism, isn't it?'

'Aye, we do be adding a bit at the end of the name of someone we're fond of.'

'Then it could only be The Captain. Apart from you, he's the only Irish person I've ever known – not that you'd agree with his being Irish.'

'Well, Irish or not, he surely loved you to use a pet name like that. And he took you to Kensington Gardens did he not?' I added to avoid any further argument on that subject.

'Yes, and I sat on his knee looking at that statue of Peter Pan. He told me the whole story and very well, too, I might add. I remember being quite transfixed by it all. I suppose he did it to try and tell me he was probably going to die. He said he was going to fly away, just like Peter Pan. I read the book again last weekend and I could barely get through it for crying, Luighseach.'

And at that recollection, Della burst into tears. 'I feel so sorry for him!' she sobbed. 'I was talking to Daddy about it all. He met The Captain on several occasions. Daddy said he couldn't help but have the deepest respect for him. He had a horrible job to do and it had taken its toll. And to think of what happened with Mummy. Poor man! To die so sad! I wish— Oh! I wish I could give him comfort! I wish I could tell him that I loved him! I wish I could thank him!'

'Thank him, Delleen?'

'Yes, thank him,' she sniffed. 'As you can imagine, we've never wanted for anything, but, as far as Wally and I am concerned, that's mostly due to The Captain. That's what Daddy told me. I always thought my step-father provided everything; but apparently, before he returned to France, The Captain put his affairs in order and made arrangements for his estate to be left in trust for Wally and me. So all my schooling, my violin, my music lessons, everything I've ever needed, has been The Captain's doing. All these years he's looked after us. Can you believe it, old thing?'

'It sounds like a fairy tale.'

'It feels like a fairy tale.'

'Well, I'm thinking 'tis as your gardener says. Your da was a good man.'

'Maybe he was, although I have the impression he was a bit of a Harry Hotspur. You can't deny it: he made some ghastly mistakes, Luighseach.'

'We all make mistakes, do we not? Some of us even put decimal points in the wrong place,' I gave her a wink. 'You don't think of yourself as a mistake now, do you?'

'I don't know what else to call it.'

'Well, Delleen, I'll be letting you know I'm very glad of the mishap. Was that the bell ringing for change of class?'

'I think so. Where are you off to?'

'To Sister Comgall in the chapel I'm going for to help lay the vestments for Holy Mass tomorrow. Do you be feeling better now?'

Della smiled and waved me off.

We resumed our conversation that afternoon on the way to Mrs Epstein's.

'And does everything be well at home?' I asked, still concerned for my little friend.

'In some ways it's better and in other ways it couldn't be worse,' Della replied. 'The good thing is that Daddy and Wally are actually talking. We have you to thank for that. Wally's always been very stand-off-ish with Daddy but now things couldn't be more different. Daddy's awfully pleased about it. As he says, it's about time Wally realised the War ended a decade ago. He relaxed Wally's curfew a little and took him sailing last weekend. He's never done that before. They even spent the night on the boat. You probably noticed my brother was a little wind burnt.'

'And why would I have noticed that?'

'Why you saw him the other day didn't you? Wally said he saw you.'

'Well, I didn't notice he was wind burnt.'

'Anyway, they had a splendid time and the outing gave Mummy a bit of respite; for if things have improved between Daddy and Wally, they've only worsened between Wally and Mummy.'

'And I suppose 'tis myself you'll be thanking for that, too.'

'It's a battle that's been ongoing for more than a decade, old thing, and Heaven only knows when or how it will ever come to an end. Now Wally and Mummy are barely on speaking terms. If either one comes into a room, the other invariably leaves. Wally at least is civil, so I suppose that's a slight improvement. We haven't had to put up with his boorish cynicism as much lately.'

'And your mother?'

'Well, Mummy copes the way she always does. She's designing her garden party costume at the moment. Luighseach don't grimace like that.'

'I didn't grimace.'

'Yes you did, you groaned and you grimaced the way you do when you're annoyed. Why? What on earth did I say to provoke that?'

'Garden parties and costumes!' I scorned. 'Does your mother think of nothing else?'

'It's simply the way she is, Luighseach. Can't you understand that?'

I must have grimaced again, for my response, however silent it may have been, earned me an outburst from Della.

'Listen,' she began, her anger brewing. 'When you're sad and upset how do you behave? You become horribly morose and sullen and get into a complete funk from which it's almost impossible to pull you out. When Mummy's upset, she holds garden parties. And to be quite frank, I know whose company I would prefer in those situations, and it isn't yours.'

'The devil with your garden parties! If you're sad is it not logical you should show it?'

'You and your logic! Luighseach, not everyone is logical.'

'Well, logical or not, you cannot say 'tis normal not to show any sort of sadness or regret or sorrow and fritter your time and cares away on costumes and parties and niceness and hoighty-toighty what-not to the point of total disregard for others' feelings, let alone your own.'

'Then if it's not normal, as you say,' she retorted, 'it's deserving of greater sympathy, not less. Think of poor Mummy, imagine what it would be like to be eighteen years old, without any family and expecting a baby by a man who is not your husband, and who, to all effect, has no intention of becoming your husband. Then imagine being brutally cast out by the same so-called gentleman and having to provide for two little children during a war of all things. Imagine having to live every day of your life in the company of the ghost of my father that is my brother. How would you cope? I know my mother isn't as clever as you, but all you ever do is snigger when she says something foolish, or make smart-alecky comments for which she hasn't a hope of repartee. Why? Because all you ever see is her weakness. You ought to take a leaf from your father's book.'

'And precisely what has my da to do with all this?'

'Because he sees what I see. He sees how strong she is. In that picture he painted I think it's marvellous the way he's captured her fetish for beauty. At the same time there's true determination in her expression, yet it's been portrayed with such delicacy. Little wonder Mummy loves it. So the next time you dare criticise my mother, you think before you speak, because I won't stand for any more from you or anyone!'

'Della, Luighseach!' Mrs Epstein stood on her doorstep. 'What on earth is going on? We could hear the two of you arguing half-way up the street! Is everything all right?' she added as she saw us up the front steps.

'Quite all right, thank you, Mrs Epstein,' replied Della, her cheerfulness immediately returning. 'After all, what is an argument between friends?'

'Yes indeed,' agreed our teacher as she gave me the eye and raised a brow for verification.

The moment we entered the music room, Pim greeted us both with a hearty hug.

'Beaut to see you two again!' she said.

'And yourself, Pimmy Connolly,' I replied. 'Heaven only knows how I've missed you.' And, given all that had happened with Della and Phoebe, I was very pleased indeed to see Pim.

'Sorry I haven't been in touch,' she apologised. 'Lil went down to Rose's for a bit of a break, so we've been working hammer and tongs keeping things going at the guest house. When Lil's away, the mice don't play, I can tell you,' she smiled. 'I'm glad to get back to school for a holiday!'

Phoebe's reception, however, was one of wide-eyed reserve. Clearly, she was worried by whatever she had overheard.

'Now, it's time we all sat down to some business,' Mrs Epstein clapped her hands and rubbed them together as she took a seat amongst us. 'First, I should inform you that Mrs Sotheby telephoned this afternoon.'

That announcement sounded like the proclamation of a national event. Della, in response, sent me a cautionary glare.

'Apparently, she's arranged for you lot to provide the entertainment for her garden party,' continued Mrs Epstein.

'Mercy,' I muttered, and again was glared at by Della.

'Are you aware of this, Della?' our teacher asked.

'Yes, Mrs Epstein,' Della instantly replied. 'Do you mind?'

'No, no, not at all,' said Mrs Epstein, dismissing any of Della's concern with a wave of her hand. 'I think it's an excellent idea. And you've all agreed to it?'

'Absolutely,' said Della.

'Even Luighseach?' Mrs Epstein looked at me.

I nodded.

'You've agreed to perform? At a garden party?' she slowly questioned and arched an eyebrow. 'That's a bit of a turn-around.'

'Aye, it is.'

'Well, this is good news. Mind you, I would have appreciated being consulted in the process. You're going to have to get some more repertoire under your belt otherwise you won't have nearly enough for an afternoon's entertainment. Now, let me see…'

Mrs Epstein searched her bureau for her calendar and her reading glasses.

'Apparently the garden party is in September,' she remarked as she flicked through the months. 'That's perfect timing for it will be a month before the competition.'

'Competition?' echoed Phoebe.

'Didn't I mention a chamber music competition at the Conservatorium earlier this year?' We all shook our heads. 'Oh well,' Mrs Epstein shrugged, 'if you're going to perform at a garden party, I don't see why you can't play in a competition. Admittedly, a competition is not the ideal performance opportunity but it will do you good to hear others play and get some critical feedback for your own playing. You might be pleasantly surprised. Would you like to enter? I can see that Phoebe is more than keen,' she smiled. 'What about you, Pim? You've probably heard about it already.'

Pim nodded. 'Mr Ep mentioned it last lesson. It'd be great to enter.'

'Della?'

'Will we be playing in public, Mrs Epstein?'

'Yes, of course we will,' Mrs Epstein replied. 'And if your mother puts forward any opposition to public performances, I will merely inform her that you won't be playing for her garden party. What about you, Luighseach? You won't be opting out, will you?'

'Don't worry, Mrs Epstein,' Della answered for me. 'If she does, we'll ask Kathleen Doherty to play instead.'

'You will not!' my teacher and I replied simultaneously; and upon realising we'd been had, began to laugh.

'In the meantime,' smiled Mrs Epstein, 'I suggest you find as many performance opportunities as possible. Playing by yourselves is fine, but nothing brings a quartet together better than playing for an audience. Besides, I think you'll give a lot of people a lot of pleasure.'

It was agreed that we should each organise a concert. Phoebe, surprisingly, was the one most reluctant to undertake the responsibility.

'Never mind, Phoebe,' resolved Mrs Epstein. 'I will handle your concert myself. Now let's have some fun.'

The remainder of the afternoon we spent playing happily through string quartets. Mrs Epstein brought out a few simple pieces which she suggested we keep up purely for enjoyment. Then we embarked on her stockpile of Haydn: first the *Lark*, then the *Joke* and finally the *Kaiser*.

'However much you might like it, I suggest you refrain from giving the *Kaiser* priority,' she advised.

'Why not?' asked Della. 'It's wonderful.'

'Somehow, Della,' replied Mrs Epstein, 'I don't think playing the German national anthem, however wonderful a piece of music it might be, is going to go down terribly well with an audience here.'

'Can't we play anything other than Haydn?' complained Phoebe.

'Come on, Phoebe, we're doomed to play nothing but Haydn,' groaned Pim.

'Here's something you might like,' Mrs Epstein passed out some more music. 'The second Borodin quartet. It has quite a bit of work for the cellist, but I think Luighseach can handle it. Have a try. We'll do the Nocturne now. It's the third movement.'

Mrs Epstein brought out her 'cello and played with me. Della, Pim and Phoebe eventually found their places.

'Why, it's charming, Mrs Epstein!' Della was in raptures.

'I thought it might appeal. There is one caveat, however.'

'What?'

'I can't let you take the music out of this room, so if you want to learn it, you are going to have to write your part out by hand. It's the only copy of the entire quartet I have and it will be virtually impossible to replace if you lose it. Admittedly, it's not quite as precious as a certain gramophone recording that disappeared one afternoon,' Mrs Epstein paused and eyed Phoebe who could not hide her guilt.

'And just as well it was returned without a scratch, or you, Phoebe Raye, would have been far more upset than me,' was all our teacher said.

32

Later that night, as we finished our Rosary, the telephone rang. Daid answered, and for the best part of half an hour was taken up with making the appropriate polite remarks:

'To be sure she'll be happy to come, ma'am,' I heard him say. 'I see … Aye … Aye … Whatever you think is best, ma'am … Aye … She'll not mind, ma'am, for she bees more than used to it and a kind offer it is indeed … Aye … Sunday week you're saying? … Aye, well, I'll be doing the photographs for First Holy Communion that Sunday and there'll be a special breakfast after Holy Mass but I can take her when it's all finished. Will that be well with you now? … Aye … Aye … Very well, ma'am. Thank you for telephoning, ma'am. Good-bye, ma'am.'

'I'll not mind for I'm quite used to what?' I asked the moment he hung the receiver.

'To being measured,' replied Daid.

'And what is it I'm to be measured for?' I questioned warily. Daid certainly had not been on the telephone to the orthopaedic man and the only occasion I was acquainted with being measured was when new boots and callipers were concerned.

''Tis for a new frock that you'll be measured,' Daid informed me.

Never before had I been measured for a new frock. The closest my clothes ever came to being tailor-made was in the form of the extra pieces of fabric, cut from other garments, that I was wont to add to give more length to my frocks and skirts. As for the frocks and skirts themselves, they were usually acquired from diverse sources, mostly connected with well-meaning ladies from the parish.

''Tis Mrs Sotheby's wanting you to come on Sunday for to be measured for a costume to wear to her garden party.'

'Is that so? And what made you think I'd agree to come for that?'

''Tis a friendly gesture is it not and would it not please you to wear a pretty dress?'

'It would not,' and I folded my arms tight.

'Now I've not known it to be engraved on a tablet of stone that it's forbidden for a lass to look comely. Or did you decide of late to improve on God's Commandments?' inquired Daid.

'I don't see what's wrong with wearing the clothes I own.'

'And to be sure there's not a thing wrong with wearing the clothes you own.'

'Well, they're the clothes I'll be wearing to the garden party.'

'Oh? And so 'tis yourself who's giving the garden party is it?'

'Indeed it is not.'

'Well, when you give a party of your own, you can wear the clothes you please. But 'tis Mrs Sotheby's party you're playing at and you'll be decent enough to dress how Mrs Sotheby sees fit.'

'Aye indeed, for she thinks I'm ugly and awkward and not good enough for her quality ways,' I scornfully retorted.

'Is that so?'

'Aye it is. To my face she said it. Gawky and plain I am, so she thinks.'

'And so is that why she's kindly asked you to lunch and generously offered to make you a frock?'

I did not reply.

'Well, regardless of what she thinks of yourself and what you think of her you'll go and you'll do whatever the lady asks with God's good grace, a smile on your face and your own good will. Do I make myself clear now?'

****

I had never seen Mrs Sotheby as busy as on that particular day. She even opened the front door.

'Why, good morning, Mr Straughan,' she gushed. 'How nice to see you again. Good morning, Lucy. Do come in.'

Daid and I obliged.

'Begging your pardon, ma'am, for being late,' Daid apologised as he removed his cap.

'Collette is in the parlour getting everything ready,' Mrs Sotheby continued. 'In the meantime, I thought Lucy could do some practice.' Della, of course, had taken advantage of the event and had scheduled a rehearsal around the dressmaker's session. 'The others are already waiting for you, Lucy. I will call you in turn to come and be measured,' she instructed.

She showed us into the large drawing room before neatly tripping away, a tidy yet casual mixture of cashmere, pearls and fitted tweed, silk stockings and high heeled shoes.

Daid bid everyone good morning, helped me with the 'cello, and took his leave.

'No crutches today?' observed Pim.

'Not today,' I replied as I sat. I did not like the idea of having to contend with crutches and callipers in addition to a dressmaker, so I had braced only my left leg. 'I'll manage fine for I'll not be doing much walking. 'Tis quiet here today, Delleen.'

'Everyone's gone to Mascot to see Smithy fly in,' Della explained.

'Why didn't you go?' asked Pim. 'You're usually wild about that sort of thing.'

'I wasn't in the mood for it,' Della shrugged. 'Anyway, Mummy needed company so I chose to stay home. What do you say to doing the Borodin first? Has everyone copied it out?'

'Ugh!' Phoebe exclaimed at the mention. 'Boring old Borodin! It took me two hours to copy out one whole movement! Then horrid Mrs Epstein spotted a mistake in my manuscript and made me redo it.'

'I'm sure it won't be nearly so boring once we start playing, Phoebe,' Della smiled. 'Luighseach, how are you with the 'cello part?'

I grinned as I pulled out my music. It was very much to my liking.

'Would you mind if we start with the Nocturne?' I asked.

We decided to concentrate on the motifs, playing them over and over in a variety of ways. Then a game ensued. Della played a running passage which was then echoed, note for note, by Phoebe. Then Phoebe played the passage and altered her bowing slightly for Pim to copy. Finally, it fell to me to copy Pim's phrase before playing my own variation which became Della's lot to copy.

Whoever failed to imitate the passage exactly would be the first to get measured.

'Luighseach, you're going to have to make a mistake sooner or later. Everyone else has had their turn,' remarked Della as Pim was ferried to the parlour by Mrs Sotheby.

'I don't want to be measured,' I replied.

In the end, I was forced to take my turn and I found myself limping alongside Della's mother.

Collette, Mrs Sotheby's dressmaker, was, like the lady of the house, a very petite person. She, too, was exceedingly well-dressed in a simple tailored suit which was offset by an abundance of necklaces. Save for a delicate fringe, her hair was pulled into a chignon and she had very lively, probing brown eyes. Upon greeting her, I had the impression she spoke English for the same reason I did – as a concession to anyone who couldn't understand her native tongue – and I felt an odd sense of rapport because of it.

She advised me to undress to my slip and did not seem at all embarrassed by my appearance.

'Vous êtes un poliomyélite, n'est-ce pas?' she bluntly inquired while she pulled her dressmaker's tape from my shoulder to my knee.

The only word I really caught was 'polio'.

'Oui,' was all I could say and I began to regret that I had not made more of an effort in my years of French lessons.

'Quel dommage! Mais,' she paused and poked me in a way that I was forced to meet her gaze. 'You don't let that stop you looking your best, no?'

And she left me puzzling as to whether her remark was intended as a caution, a piece of advice or an acknowledgement.

Presently, I was released from the parlour.

'There you are!' exclaimed Della when she saw me. 'That wasn't too painful, was it?'

'Aye it was. Oh! Oh!' I began to exaggerate my limp and stagger back to my seat. 'To be sure she tried to strangle me with her tape! Oh! May God preserve me and may the Angels and Saints deliver me!'

'Stop it, silly!' Della laughed.

'Lucy, stop!' cautioned Phoebe as she indicated the door. I looked behind me and saw that Mrs Sotheby and Collette had also entered the room. They were talking in French.

'You know what they're saying?' whispered Pim to Phoebe.

Phoebe shook her head.

'Didn't you have a French grandmother?'

'That doesn't mean *I* speak French.'

We continued to listen to Mrs Sotheby's English sounding French and Collette's French sounding French. From their accompanying gestures they seemed to be having a very intense discussion about frocks.

Della giggled. Clearly her French was better than anyone else's.

'Collette's in an absolute state,' she commented as she cocked her head, listening intently. 'She cannot work out how to design a dress that will suit us all. Dear me, I'm afraid none of our figures seem quite right. Luighseach's too tall, I'm too short, Phoebe has too many curves, and Pim, well, you're too, well, too—' she hesitated and blushed.

'What?' questioned Pim, 'Buxom? Well if that isn't bleedingly obvious.'

'Della, dear,' interposed Mrs Sotheby. 'Why don't you play something? Collette is simply dying to hear you.'

'Of course, Mummy,' Della obliged. 'What about the *Joke*, everyone? We haven't really tried that one yet.'

That Collette was 'simply dying' to hear us was an exaggeration for she and Mrs Sotheby did not refrain from talking while we played. Then they started pulling out fabrics, and at very awkward moments one of us would find a sample of what seemed innumerable shades of 'ivoire', thrust against her face. This was accompanied by a discussion, still in French, which was carried out from opposite ends of the room. Finally they departed, and the emphatic French-French and equally emphatic English-French did not diminish until they crossed the hall and closed the parlour door behind them.

We had the remainder of the morning to practise as we pleased.

****

'What lovely music!' Mrs Sotheby exclaimed when she returned to the drawing room. 'Ordinarily, we only hear Della playing by herself. How nice it is to hear you all together. Now, luncheon is ready and you are most welcome to help yourselves. I will join you after I have finished with the designs. Della, will you show the girls to the dining room?'

'Certainly, Mummy,' replied Della. 'I say, are you really going to design our costumes?' she added.

'Of course,' her mother answered, her eyebrows arched.

'Goody! You see,' she explained to Phoebe, Pim and myself as we followed her into the hall, 'Mummy trained as a seamstress before she became a dancer. You know, Mummy, you ought to start a business designing clothes.'

'Really, Della, the ideas you come up with!'

'But you should, Mummy. You could own a shop or a studio.'

'What a frightfully common idea!'

'Nonsense, Mummy. I don't think there's anything common about outfitting the ladies of Sydney in beautiful costumes.'

'Della, dear,' Mrs Sotheby opened the parlour door and smiled, 'you sound like a nun.'

'I say! Croquettes! Super!' Della clapped her hands when she spotted the lunch laid out on the table. 'Come on, everyone, grab a plate and serviette. What else have we? Devilled eggs, veal terrine, fresh beetroot, salad, and fruit tarts with custard. What a spread!'

Phoebe and I happily began to serve ourselves. Pim, however, was distracted by the painting of the bare-breasted Turkish girl in the billowy trousers which hung above the sideboard.

'Crikey,' she eventually said.

'Frankly Pim, I don't know what possessed my parents to hang that painting there,' Della remarked as she piled her plate with salad. 'I think they became a little too carried away with the decor.'

Pim continued to stare at the painting.

'You know, it looks a bit like you, Phoebe.'

'What does?' asked Phoebe, her mouth already full of croquette.

'That painting.'

'What painting?'

'Didn't you see it? You can't miss it.' Pim was incredulous. But Phoebe did have a way of being completely unobservant when she was preoccupied with music, and since she was usually preoccupied with music, she was usually quite oblivious to her surroundings.

Phoebe looked up and squinted a little at the picture.

'It is you, isn't it?' Pim watched Phoebe's reaction.

'No it isn't.'

'Don't lie.'

'I wasn't lying,' Phoebe retorted. 'It's not me. It's a picture of me.'

'Don't be so smart. That's disgusting. Do you mean to say you actually took off your clothes and had yourself painted?'

'Well, it's even more disgusting to hang it in a dining room for every Tom, Dick and Harry to stare at,' Phoebe blurted back.

'It's not really that bad. After all, I mean she's not completely naked,' Della intervened, trying desperately to keep everything calm. 'In fact, it's quite an interesting painting in an exotic, modern sort of way. I rather enjoy imagining who the girl is and I'm sure that's what Mummy and Daddy thought when they bought it. No one had any idea it was you, Phoebe, I assure you.'

'It shouldn't be there!' Phoebe protested.

'You're right about that,' agreed Pim. 'Who painted it, anyway?'

'What does it matter who painted it?' contested Phoebe.

'You lay there like that with half your clothes off while a man sat and painted you and you say what does it matter? Of course it matters.'

'Well, a man didn't paint me. A woman did. My aunt, if you really want to know.'

I walked up to the painting and studied it closely. Sure enough, striding across the bottom of the canvas, was Ailine Devereaux's signature.

'It's still disgusting,' sneered Pim. 'You ought to be ashamed of yourself.'

'Of course I'm ashamed!' Phoebe cried. 'Do you think *I* wanted to do it? I didn't want to do it. She made me do it. She wanted me to have nothing on at all but I refused. So she made me wear harem pants with nothing on top and she had me drink something that made me feel sleepy and sick. She said she wouldn't sell the painting but she did. She sold it and now it's hanging here. Why did it have to come here? Why couldn't it go far away? Why did you have to buy it?' she turned on Della. 'It shouldn't be here! It shouldn't! You should take it down and throw it away! It has to go away! It can't stay here!'

'Phoebe! Don't!' Della shrieked.

But it was too late. Phoebe picked up the plate of terrine and hurled it at the painting. The terrine hit the painting full square in the harem girl's face and the plate smashed on the sideboard. Before either Della or Pim could restrain her, Phoebe picked up the fruit tarts and the jug of custard and threw those at the painting, too.

'Girls! What on earth is going on?' Mrs Sotheby exclaimed.

'You take it away!' yelled Phoebe as she pushed past Della's mother and ran out of the house.

33

Pim and I decided it was best to leave Della to handle her mother on her own, so we bid our good-byes and hastened in search of Phoebe.

She could not be seen in either direction along the street so we looked in the park opposite the Sotheby house.

Phoebe was nowhere to be found.

'You have any idea where she could have gone?' asked Pim.

'As many as I have fingers,' I replied, 'but I'm thinking 'tis best we first tell Mrs Epstein. She knows Phoebe inside out. She'll know what to do. Will you go and tell her, Pim?'

'What are you going to do?'

'I'll be going to Phoebe's house.'

'You be all right by yourself?'

'Aye. I been there a few times.'

'I mean without your crutches?'

'Aye. Only one station away from my house it is and a short walk besides.'

'You sure? Look, why don't you go to Mrs Epstein's and I'll go to Phoebe's house?'

'Did you go there before, Pimmy Connolly?'

Pim shook her head.

'Well, you're not going there now, I can tell you that.'

We caught the train together and I waved Pim off at Petersham. I alighted from the train at Stanmore and proceeded in the direction of Phoebe's house. But I was completely mistaken as to how far away it was. After several wrong turns and a few inquiries, I arrived at the dilapidated old house, trudged through the overgrown garden, pushed past the broken swing, climbed the stairs, rang the bell and waited amidst the statuary that still congregated on the veranda.

No one answered, so I rang the bell again.

Five times I had to ring the bell before the door finally opened.

'Oh, it's you,' Phoebe's aunt was barefoot. 'The child is not here.'

'I don't want to see Phoebe Raye,' I replied. 'For 'tis yourself I want to see.'

'And what on earth made you think I would want to see you?' Ailine began to shut the door.

'Why did you do it?' I immediately asked.

'Why did I do what?' she stopped the door's progress.

'You painted Phoebe Raye with half her clothes off when she didn't want to be painted like that and you sold the painting when you said you wouldn't. Why did you do it?'

'I needed the money,' Ailine shrugged. 'That's why you usually sell paintings, isn't it? Your father's an artist. You should know that.'

'Aye, but he wouldn't sell such a painting, let alone paint such a one, not for all the tea in China.'

'Oh no, of course not,' agreed Ailine in a very smooth tone of voice. 'Your father's far too conservative, isn't he? Tell me was it wrong to paint her in that way?'

'Aye it was, for you shamed her. You caused her shame. How could you do that? What did she ever do to yourself for you to do that to her?'

'She could try being born for a start,' was the indifferent reply.

'But—but she's your niece. She's your clan, your family.'

'Of course, she's my niece! I see,' Ailine smiled at the connection I had made. 'She's the child of my sister so therefore I should love her. Is that right?'

'Aye it is.'

'You've got a lot to learn,' she smirked.

'Aye, I do,' I nodded. 'And, what's more, I'd like to learn what it was happened between yourself and Phoebe's da that made little Phoebe so sad.'

'The hide!' she exclaimed, feigning shock. 'Well my dear, you might want to learn a thing or two but I'm not prepared to teach you, so you can run along back home where you belong. Oh, forgive me,' she added, glancing at my legs. 'You can't run, can you? You're crippled.'

'Lina darling, what's going on?' A man appeared in the hallway. He walked up and stood behind Ailine. It was not Arthur, whom I had met before. It was a different man entirely and he was wearing only a dressing gown.

I could feel myself blush and I turned away. The door closed behind me. As I struggled down the steps, I heard them laugh.

It was dark by the time I reached Watkin Street. Danny barked a greeting and I looked up and saw Daid waiting at the gate.

'Buíochas le Dia, you're home safe and sound, Luighseach!' he said as he put his arm around me and helped me up the steps. 'Let's get you inside. I was after arriving home myself.'

''Twas Phoebe Raye's place I been, Da,' I explained, hoping I would not get into too much trouble.

'Aye, 'twas Mrs Epstein telephoned while I was at the Sotheby's and passed on that message. So I drove by Phoebe's place on my way home in case you were there. Let's light the fire in the parlour and make a cupán tae and toast some bread and cheese.'

Daid had quite a story to tell.

'Well, lass,' he announced as he stoked the fire. 'It looks like Phoebe Raye will be staying in our back shed for a little while.'

'What do you mean, Da?' Given its contents – the motorcycle, garden tools and painting paraphernalia – our shed was no place for a guest.

Daid shook his head. 'I drove to the Sotheby's for to pick you up, as you know, and Delleen Sotheby came running out. At first I thought 'twas something happened to yourself for the poor lass was that upset. "Oh Mr Ó Sruitheáin!" she cried. "Could you help us please? Something terrible has happened and Mummy's simply beside herself." Well, Luighseach, as you can imagine, I didn't know what she was talking about. "Where's Luighseach?" I asked, still thinking it was yourself come to harm. "I don't know where she is, Mr Ó Sruitheáin. Please come!" and she brought me to the dining room.'

'Did you see the painting, Da?'

'Aye, I did. A right mess was it not with bits of meat and fruit and jelly stuck to it and a great splodge of custard dripping down. If there's anything to be said, well, 'tis Phoebe Raye's a cracking shot.'

Daid, in his gentle way, was trying to make light of the situation, but I could muster little more than a slight smile.

'Well,' Daid proceeded, 'Delleen Sotheby asked me whether I could fix it. "To be sure," I replied, "for 'tis only a little cleaning up it needs and the frame's a wee bit damaged there." "Oh, Mr Ó Sruitheáin, you cannot clean it," said Delleen. "You need to do more than that. You need to completely fix it." She told me all about what happened, Luighseach. How old is Phoebe, lass?' he added as he again grew grave.

'Fourteen years old she would be, Da. She's younger than myself although she looks the same age. Sometimes, when she piles her hair on top of her head, she looks even older.'

'Sweet Jesus!' Daid muttered sadly.

'And did you see Mrs Sotheby, Da?' I asked.

'Aye,' Daid lingered wearily over his reply.

'And?'

'Well,' he began again, ''twas Delleen Sotheby asked me if I could paint them a picture. Indeed I could, I said, and I looked at her mam. All anxious she was about it. Could it be done in time for her garden party, she asked.'

'Garden party,' I scoffed. 'Why is it always about her garden party?'

''Tis important to the lady,' Daid replied.

'And is Phoebe Raye not more important?'

'To be sure she is, and very concerned Mrs Sotheby is about it all, I can tell you that,' Daid answered in a very knowing manner. 'As for the painting,' he continued, 'although I agreed, I wasn't quite sure what sort of picture to paint. Well, I needn't worry about that for Delleen Sotheby worked all that out. Could I not paint a scene from the *Arabian Nights*? "Aye," I replied, "if you can tell me a little more." Well, no sooner said than done for Delleen told me all about it and even lent me a book,' and he showed me the book that was on the table next to his chair. 'So, Luighseach, 'twill be Sinbad the Sailor or Ali Baba and the Forty Thieves there above the sideboard instead of poor Phoebe Raye. What about it,

Luighseach? 'Twill be all put right and quickly too, for I'll start work straight away.'

'But what about Phoebe, Da? No one knows where she is.'

'She'll come back surely. Try not to fret about it, lass. We'll put it in God's hands. You know, I got me a fine photograph today.'

'Did you?' It was much harder for me to put it in God's hands than it was for my father.

'After I took you to Delleen's house, I drove down to the harbour. Well, I waited and waited and sure enough the *Southern Cross* came flying past, right between them bridge pylons,' he couldn't hide his excitement. 'A grand photograph indeed it will be, that one.'

'Daid, did you ever paint someone without their clothes on?' I asked.

Daid looked at me and his concern instantly returned.

'Aye, Luighseach,' he replied. ''Tis many a painting and sketch of that sort I made. 'Tis what you do in art school. 'Twas mostly plaster models that we used, although a live model would come from time to time. But as you know I always paint without my glasses on, so I never really looked,' he added. 'Besides, 'tis the forms you're working on and they're beautiful, Luighseach, for 'tis all part of God's creation is it not?'

'And did you ever sell a painting like that?'

Daid shook his head. Then he rose from his chair and walked to his room.

He returned with a tiny sketchbook which he passed to me.

'Take a look inside there,' he said.

I opened it. It was filled with sketches, most of which featured a woman breastfeeding.

''Tis your mam and yourself as a wee one,' he explained. 'Luighseach, 'twas such a contented scene I wanted to be part of it, and I couldn't think of any better way than to draw it. It's beautiful is it not? There's nothing shameful in such a picture as that, for there's love there – wonderful, life-giving love. I can show yourself, for you're part of that, but 'tis no one else I'll show. Now, can you bring yourself to read a few stories to your Da? You know if I'm left to read on my own, that painting will never be finished in time for Mrs Sotheby's garden party,' he added with a smile.

'Aye,' I sighed and held out my hand for the book.

34

'Have you seen Phoebe?' asked Della of Pim at recess the following day.

'Just been to the third form room,' replied Pim. 'She's not at school.'

'And you didn't hear from her at all, old thing?' Della asked me. 'You look exhausted.'

'I hardly slept last night,' I explained, 'for I thought she might come. And how was Mrs Epstein when you told her, Pim?'

'She hit the flamin' roof. Mr Ep came in and she sounded off in German. I've never seen her so angry. Anyway, all I managed to get afterwards was that "it's the last straw" with Phoebe. Trust Phoebe to get mixed up in something like this.'

'And what are you meaning by that, Pimmy Connolly?' I asked.

'Why does she always create trouble?'

'And why do you always be running her down?'

'I don't!'

'Aye you do, you do be criticising her for everything she does or else you're implying that whatever she does is cause for criticism.'

'Because it usually is!' retorted Pim, 'Or haven't you noticed that?'

'And if you weren't so harsh with her yesterday, all this wouldn't have come about. Why did you grill her in that way? Could you not see she was upset?'

'I like that! So I'm more to blame now, am I? Well, if Phoebe hadn't put herself in such a situation in the first place, we would have been spared of the trouble!'

'Do you not see it? She's not anyone to look out for her!'

'She ought to look out for herself. She knew it was wrong.'

'Of course she knew it was wrong! Now let you tell me something, Pimmy Connolly.'

'What?'

'Will you be telling me how many people are in your family?'

'Fourteen. Why?'

'And you stick together, do you not? You help each other out?'

'Of course.'

'Through thick and thin?'

'It's what we do and shame on anyone who doesn't. What's that got to do with Phoebe?'

'Well, I'm telling you that Phoebe Raye's neither brothers nor sisters. Her mother died, and I don't know exactly what happened to her da but he was in the War and he was injured and he can't look after her, I know that much. She lives with her aunt, the aunt who painted her, the one person who ought to care for her and who abused her trust instead. So, Pimmy Connolly, before you say another word against little Phoebe, you can put that in your pipe and smoke it awhile.'

'Anyway, if Phoebe values her life she better not go anywhere near Mrs Ep,' Pim remarked.

'And I don't think you're right there either,' I replied, 'for 'twas Mrs Epstein telephoned our house early this morning to ask if Phoebe was there. I've never known her to be so worried. To the police she's going.'

The three of us sat and mulled over the situation. Della silently offered round some biscuits from her lunchbox.

'How's your mum?' asked Pim as she munched.

'Much better than she was yesterday afternoon, thank you,' said Della, who clearly was very relieved. 'You know,' she added with a slight giggle, 'I don't think she could decide what was worse: the mud all over Daddy, Wally, Leila and Henry when they came back from the airfield, or the terrine, tarts and custard all over the painting. Then Henry showed her the leech he peeled off his leg while he was waiting for Smithy. He's taking it to school today. Oh, I do hope Phoebe's safe,' she sighed.

'Hoigh! I think I know where she is!' I clicked my fingers.

'What?'

''Tis Phoebe's at the one place she knows she's safe.'

'Where?'

'Listen, will yous come with me after school today?'

'Of course, old thing, if you don't mind waiting while I ask my mother. Where are we going?'

'And yourself, Pim? Will you come?'

'Suppose I can sign myself out. You're on my list. Where are we going, Lucy?'

'You're better off seeing for yourselves rather than listening to myself explain it all. Faith! Why did I not think of it before?'

We arranged to meet after school and headed off together to the Sotheby house with the intention of informing Della's mother of our excursion.

'I say, Luighseach,' said Della as we reached her house. 'Isn't that your father's motorcycle?'

It was and we found Daid in the drawing room with Della's parents. They were discussing the painting. I took it upon myself to explain to my father in Irish what I had planned. Daid reacted with his usual concern but gave his permission all the same.

'What on earth is happening? Would somebody kindly tell me what is going on?' questioned Mrs Sotheby who seemed quite annoyed that people were speaking another language in her presence.

'We're going to see Phoebe,' Della explained.

'On the train?' queried her mother. 'You're not going on the train. Not at this hour! It will be dark by five.'

'Mummy! It's imperative! We simply *must* go!' pleaded Della.

'I don't think the train will be necessary, Letty,' Mr Sotheby intervened as he rang the servants' bell. Nellie appeared and he gave his instructions for Hammond to bring the car.

'Come on, Lucy, spill the beans. Where are we off to?' asked Pim as we were helped into the Bentley.

'You'll have to tell us now,' prompted Della, 'or Hammond won't know where to take us.'

'To the orphanage it is,' I replied. 'In Leichhardt.'

'Is there an orphanage in Leichhardt?' Della could hardly believe her ears. 'Whatever gave you the idea that Phoebe would want to go to an orphanage? How could anyone possibly want to go to an orphanage?'

''Tis the one place Phoebe knows she's safe.'

'How do you know that?' asked Pim.

'She told me so. Did you not know Phoebe Raye lived in an orphanage for seven years?'

'No,' Pim quietly replied. 'I didn't.'

****

The orphanage was a once stately home in the grand style of the Sotheby's house. Its heyday, however, had long passed, and while it seemed reasonably well-maintained, it was decidedly frugal in its absence of garden adornments and sparseness of blooms. I rang the bell. The door was opened by a young nun in a brown habit with a blue-braid insignia and a wimple that spread out across her shoulders and front like a great white napkin.

I made the necessary introductions.

'Would Sister Mary Paul be here?' I asked, giving the name of the only nun I could remember.

The young nun replied that she was, showed us to a sitting room and left us to wait.

'Sister Mary Paul?' slowly echoed Pim. 'How come you know so much?'

Presently the nun appeared with another, older nun. They were talking between themselves. The older nun was facing in our direction and it was clear from her expression that she recognised me. The only familiar thing about the nun that I could see was that she had bushy eyebrows.

'Lucy Straughan!' she said as she came towards us. 'We wondered what had become of you! How many years has it been?' she asked.

'Seven years it would be, Sister,' I replied.

'You did grow tall,' she remarked. She seemed pleased with the fact that I had. 'I can tell you, child, that not a day has passed that we haven't prayed for you. Are you managing all right?'

'I am.'

Sister sensed my reluctance to provide further details of my own situation, and, no doubt, she detected the defensiveness embedded in my reply. 'Child,' she said, 'we all have our crosses to carry. But what matters is not so much the cross that we carry as it is how we carry the cross,' she halted my attempt at combat with a slight wave of her hand. 'How may I help you?'

I asked after Phoebe.

'Yes, Phoebe Raye is here,' Sister Mary Paul made her own assessment of the possibility of my knowing Phoebe and her whereabouts. 'You go to the same school, don't you?'

'Aye, we do. We're friends,' I explained. 'All of us here and we play in a string quartet together.'

'I see. Lucy,' she continued in a deep and solemn voice, 'I am sorry to say that Phoebe is not at all well. We found her this morning on the front door step. Apparently she spent the night there. She's very shaken.'

'Does anyone know she's here?' I asked.

'The doctor has been to see her.'

'And her violin teacher? Does she know?'

'We managed to send word to her violin teacher, yes. We usually do when we cannot reach her family.'

'Could we see her, please?' asked Della.

'I don't see any harm in it,' considered Sister Mary Paul. 'Phoebe hasn't spoken to anyone, nor has she touched any food. Maybe a visit from friends might help.'

'You're a bit of a dark horse,' remarked Pim to me as we followed Sister into the vestibule. 'What were you doing here?'

I explained a little about my brief stay and then stopped when I saw the staircase which for years had been the subject of so many night wakings. There was the polished timber banister, the blue carpet running up the centre and the holy family statue on the landing. But it did not loom and spin the way it did in my dreams. Nor was it as big as I expected it to be. Furthermore, I knew I could climb those stairs. I began my ascent, my confidence increasing with every step.

And I needed every ounce of confidence when we arrived at the infirmary.

'You remember this place?' asked Pim. 'You look pale.'

''Twas where they put me when I fell sick, Pimmy,' I whispered. 'Before I went to the hospital. Yellow walls...'

Phoebe lay, curled up tight, in the bed at the very end of the long room. She did not stir as we came close and seemed not to react when Sister Mary Paul explained who it was had come to see her.

'You may stay a few minutes, girls,' said Sister.

Pim was the first to begin, and she tackled the matter in her usual head-on fashion.

'Listen Phoebe,' she said, 'I still think you were wrong to do it but it doesn't mean I'm not your friend or that I don't like you. I'm sorry about what happened but I'm not going to hold anything against you. I want you to know that.'

There was no response.

'Phoebe, your beautiful violin is still at my place,' added Della, hoping that an indirect approach would be more successful. 'I'll look after it, I promise. Would you like me to bring it here for you?'

A small shake of her curls and Phoebe wriggled more tightly into the blankets.

'Nobody's angry with you, Phoebe,' soothed Della. 'Not even my parents. Well, they were a bit angry at first,' she admitted, 'but once they understood, they were surprisingly sympathetic. They simply had no idea. In fact they liked that painting because it reminded them of the time they first met in the theatre, believe it or not, and because they liked the colours and how modern it is. So, in an odd sort of a way, the painting was more about Mummy than anyone. They never, ever meant any harm by it. It was bought on a whim. Do please try to understand.'

The huddled figure under the blankets gulped suddenly and sniffed. Della pushed back her own tears and continued in a desperate attempt to coax Phoebe out from her covers.

'We're going to get a new painting for the dining room, Phoebe,' she gently informed her. 'Luighseach's father's going to paint it for us and I have a feeling that Mummy and Daddy are going to pose for it themselves. We were talking about it last night. It was a bit of a joke at first but then it turned into rather a good idea. Mummy and Daddy love fancy dress. The only catch is that Daddy's leaving for England at the end of the month. I don't know what your father will think, Luighseach.'

It turned out that Daid thought it a very good idea indeed and the following afternoon I again visited Phoebe with the news that the painting was now in our shed, completely covered, and awaiting its new subject.

'Is he going to paint over me?' her voice was weak and hesitant.

'Aye, he is. And in the blink of an eye there'll be nothing left of that picture. So don't you worry yourself any more about it.

But Daid had different plans.

On Friday afternoon he came with me to the orphanage and persuaded Phoebe to travel home with us. He took her into our shed and invited her to help him remove the painting from its frame. He passed her a hammer and together they pulled out the tacks that fastened the canvas to its backing. Finally, he handed Phoebe a pair of scissors and they cut the painting to shreds. The cuttings they put on the fire.

'Never more will there be a chance for anyone to see yourself like that, Phoebe Raye,' said Daid.

Phoebe stared as if spellbound by the flames. She did not, however, seem encouraged by my father's words.

''Twas not the only time it happened then?' Daid questioned in his most gentle tone.

Phoebe dolefully shook her head.

'Your aintín painted you in that way many times?'

There was a slight nod.

'And anyone else? Did anyone else draw or paint you like that?'

Another nod.

'Friends of your aunt was it?'

A third nod, and no matter how much she grimaced, Phoebe could stifle her tears no more. She buried herself in my father's arms and cried and cried.

'There, there, little Phoebe, better out than in,' Daid tried to give her comfort. 'We're going to make sure it will never happen again.'

Once Phoebe had quietened, he settled her by the fire. The remainder of the evening he spent on the telephone.

'Do you all really care about me that much?' she asked me as we sat, squeezed side by side, arm in arm, in my chair.

'Aye, we do,' I replied. 'We all do. Each of us in our own way, you can be sure of that.'

35

Neither Mr nor Mrs Epstein opened the door when I arrived for my 'cello lesson the following Monday. Phoebe opened it instead. She welcomed Daid and me and showed us inside.

''Tis grand to see you well again and looking happy,' I smiled. 'But what do you be doing here? Do you be coming to your lesson on a Monday evening now?'

'No, I'm living with Mr and Mrs Epstein!' she replied, her eyes glowing with excitement and gratitude. 'They've given me a room of my own and they collected my things and brought them all here. Everything except the piano because there's one here already and there's not enough room for two.'

Mr and Mrs Epstein came into the hall and more greetings were made.

'Now Phoebe,' Mrs Epstein instructed, 'you're going to school tomorrow, so you can catch up with Luighseach then. Have you organised your books?'

There was a groan from Phoebe. Living with the Epsteins may have had high appeal but it also had its consequences.

'You would like a scotch and a game of chess, yes, Morgan?' asked Mr Epstein. Daid agreed and he and Mr Epstein retired to Mr Epstein's study. It was far too cold a night for a walk.

'I suppose Phoebe told you her news,' remarked Mrs Epstein as we prepared for my lesson.

'Aye, she did,' I replied, 'and I'm glad of it, too. She's not been happy living with her aunt, you know.'

'Yes,' Mrs Epstein looked me through. 'Tune up, please.'

'And 'tis fine with you, Mrs Epstein?' I asked as I fixed my pegs and tested my harmonics.

'It seems the best thing to do for the moment, Luighseach. I think we'd better tackle the Borodin first, don't you?' Mrs Epstein performed the honour of finding my music and placing it on the stand. 'How is it going?'

''Tis going very well indeed, Mrs Epstein,' I smiled. I loved the Borodin.

'Well, you've certainly earned it. Haydn has its appeal, I know, but the 'cello does little more than maintain the pulse and add depth to the harmony – an important role, but not without its limitations. In the Borodin, the 'cello shines. Did you know Borodin was a cellist?'

'I didn't, but it makes a lot of sense if he was, Mrs Epstein, for it sits just so under the fingers, you know.'

'He wrote the piece as a present for his wife for their wedding anniversary. It's very much a love song and it demands great warmth of tone from the 'cello – rather like something your father would sing, I imagine. He has quite a good voice, doesn't he?'

'Aye, he does. And he's already singing some of the tunes.'

'Well, better start at the top, for from the first bar you're going to be the one setting the mood.'

I obliged with my opening phrase. 'You're very fond of Phoebe Raye are you not, Mrs Epstein?' I asked the moment I finished.

Mrs Epstein owed me an explanation and I was inclined to think that she knew it.

'Yes, Luighseach, I'll have to say that I am,' she sighed.

'And why is that?'

Mrs Epstein wisely consented to suspend our lesson for a few minutes. 'I suppose it's primarily because Mr Epstein and I don't have any children of our own.'

I nodded.

'Well,' she added, 'that's not quite true. We did have a child, but he died not long after he was born. Joseph would have been twelve years old this year if he had lived.

'Anyway,' Mrs Epstein briskly changed tack, 'I don't know about you, but I firmly believe that everything happens for a reason. Since we were unable to have any more children, we dedicated ourselves to our teaching. As a result, we tend to consider our students as our own flesh and blood and try to give our best to each. Unlike sons and daughters, however, students come and go, but there have been some who seem to have valued us as much as we have valued them. Of those there's a certain pint-sized violinist who makes her instrument sing like a bird, a hot-headed violist, and a cellist whom I never thought would play as well as she does now.'

'And there's Phoebe Raye,' I prompted. Mrs Epstein had strayed from the point.

'And there's Phoebe Raye,' Mrs Epstein echoed. 'In a way I think we've especially needed each other, although I've always hoped that someone in her family would take her into their care. After such a long time it was so encouraging when her aunt finally offered to look after her. Unfortunately, things have not worked out in that regard and it has ended up doing more harm than good. Worst of all, it seems to have been malicious. How could anyone do that to a child?' she protested, briefly giving outlet to anger and sorrow. 'Some people don't know how lucky they are to have family, do they?'

I nodded and thoughtfully stroked the neck of my 'cello.

'I heard about your experience at the orphanage,' my teacher proceeded. 'I think "flabbergasted" was the word Della used to describe her response. I would have to second that.'

'And I'm thinking that's precisely how I felt when Phoebe Raye told me 'twas yourself taught there,' I replied. 'What was it brought yourself to the orphanage, Mrs Epstein?' Mrs Epstein had been so unusually forthcoming I decided to risk another question. It was a matter which had been on my mind for weeks.

'It's not that surprising, is it? All right,' she conceded, 'I suppose it is if you don't know my own circumstances. You see, my family was dirt poor, Luighseach. Irish Catholic like yourself.'

'You're Irish, Mrs Epstein?' I had always thought Mrs Epstein an intriguing mixture of the familiar and the foreign, but I never suspected the combination to include anything so close to Home.

'Well, I'm of Irish descent,' she added. 'McGillycuddy was my maiden name and I don't think you can get more Irish than McGillycuddy.'

'Indeed you can't,' I agreed with a smile.

'My father was a coal miner,' Mrs Epstein's seriousness returned. 'He could have provided for his family, but unfortunately he drank his wages and my mother had to do laundry at the hotel to pay for his beer and feed her six children. Then, when I was nine, my father died in a mine accident. My oldest brother took his place. My mother continued to work until she collapsed following the death of my brother in another mining accident a few months later. After that, my oldest sister went into service and homes were found for my youngest brother and sister; but as for me and my other brother, well, no one wanted a boy with a cleft palate or a girl who was half-blind. So we were put in orphanages.

'It was a strange turn of fate in a way. The nuns found the money for an operation and the glasses I needed to see properly. Then, assuming I would be no use in domestic work, they taught me violin. I'll have to say they were right on that account,' she smiled as she looked over her music room which was always a mess of music, instruments, pencils, papers, chairs and stands. 'Those nuns changed my life. Who would have thought a dim-sighted girl from Cessnock would end up studying music in Vienna? Yes, Luighseach, I owe them a lot.

'Anyway, many years later, after the war, Mr Epstein and I, like everyone else, were trying to piece our lives back together again. At that time we rented a house that turned out to be close to the orphanage in Leichhardt. I used to walk past that place every day and couldn't do so without thinking I had to do something to help those children, just as I had been helped when I was a child. In the end, I offered to teach. There were a lot of children there at the time and one of them happened to be Phoebe.'

'But how is it you know Phoebe's aunt?' I asked.

'Which one?' asked Mrs Epstein.

'Both.' I was feeling lucky.

'What? Only two?' Mrs Epstein sized me up with one of her looks.

'And are there more? 'Tis only Aunt Sara and Aunt Ailine I know of.'

'Well, of those two aunts,' she conceded a little more information, 'Sara Raye I know only slightly. She passed away a few years ago. Ailine Devereaux, on the other hand, I know very well indeed. We met in Vienna. Now, the Borodin.'

'So did you know Phoebe's mother?'

'You're very inquisitive this evening. Has Phoebe told you anything about her mother?'

'Aye, and quite a lot I might add.'

'Really?' reflected Mrs Epstein. But she said nothing more.

'What was she like?'

'Very like Phoebe in many ways, if you really must know.'

'And what of Phoebe's da? Do you know him?'

'Why do you want to know?'

''Tis Phoebe's my friend is why, Mrs Epstein, and she's upset about her da.'

And there followed a very slow, thoughtful smile from my teacher.

'Well, that is another story entirely and I will tell it when I am ready. Now, may I ask you one final question?'

'Aye, you may.'

'Could we get back to our lesson?'

36

After that, Phoebe started coming to school every day, instead of only when she felt like it. Once she knew which train and carriage I caught in the mornings, she made a point of joining me, and we would arrive together. Little by little, aspects of her very distinctive version of the St Dominic's uniform began to change. The pretty blouse with its lace-trimmed collar and puffed sleeves was replaced with a more standard, tailored style in keeping with the shirts worn by everyone else. Her button-up boots gave way to conventional school shoes with low heels and straps. She even wore a tie. But nothing and no one could induce her to shorten her hemline or wear her belt on her hips. She was convinced it was ugly and blatantly refused to comply. So her tunic remained below her calf and neatly cinched at her waist.

Most astonishing of all, though, was that she started to braid her hair.

Of course, for most girls with long hair, braids were the norm. Not so with Phoebe who had invented quite elaborate ways of showing off her beautiful dark curls. In the past, she had habitually arrived at school with her tresses arranged in a fanciful style à la Mary Pickford, had been scolded into plaits by a nun at recess, and had rearranged her hair, shaking her curls over her shoulders or piling them on top of her head the moment she was released from school. Now the braids were to be seen from Petersham, where she boarded the train, all the way to school and back again.

Phoebe hated those plaits. As it turned out, it was not because of the braids themselves, but because they exposed a scar that extended from her brow and out past the corner of her eye.

''Tis little more than a scratch, Phoebeen,' I remarked when she showed me. 'You can hardly see it.'

'Well, scratch or not, I wish it wasn't there,' she replied.

'How did you get it?' I asked.

'Not telling,' Phoebe shrugged off my question.

'Well, wishing it away will not make it disappear, so you'll be getting used to it if you know what's good for you.'

'You can talk.'

'Aye, I can, for I've scars on my legs worth writing home about.'

'Which you keep very well concealed.'

'Aye, I do, for 'tis nobody's business how I came by them. 'Tis the callipers are more than enough.'

'Sauce for the goose, sauce for the gander: if it's fine for you to hide yours, then I can hide mine. And I don't care how small a scratch it is: it's nobody's business neither.'

For all these amendments, Mrs Epstein was responsible, although Phoebe preferred to say 'to blame'. And there were more to come. Her piano playing activities at the picture palace were brought to an abrupt halt one Saturday afternoon. According to Hilda Geraghty, who reported the incident to me after Mass the following Sunday, there had been a commotion in the foyer after which 'a shorter, fat man with glasses and a beard and a tall woman with glasses' strode into the cinema in the middle of *Wings*.

'You wouldn't believe what happened, Lucy,' said Hilda. 'The woman pulled Phoebe out and the fat man sat down and played the piano in her place.' Stern words were then had with the manager, who, in Mrs Epstein's opinion (for the woman was none other than Mrs Epstein), should have known better than allow a child of fourteen to play the piano for films in which the content was well beyond her years, and as far as Mrs Epstein was concerned, it didn't matter how good a pianist Phoebe was.

The picture palace affair put Phoebe into a horrible mood which was further exacerbated by the abolition of her cigarettes.

'Nasty Mrs Epstein turned my room inside out and threw them all away! All of them! And the box!' Phoebe angrily announced during one of our many lunch-time rehearsals.

'Three cheers for Mrs Ep!' shouted Pim. 'Hip-hip-hooray!'

'She had no right to do that!' complained Phoebe. 'She went through my things, worse than a nun in a dormitory: my room, my bed, my clothes, my books, my violin case, my carpet bag! Everything!'

'Ah-ah!' corrected Pim, 'It might be your things in your room but your room's in her house. Her castle: Her rules.'

'But Phoebe, why did you even smoke them in the first place?' Della asked. 'It's an awful habit.'

'It was fun.'

'Fun?' repeated Della. 'Making yourself nearly sick on smoke? Fun?'

'The way we did it was fun,' Phoebe explained. 'It was fun at the orphanage. You see, one day a plumber came to fix the drain and he left behind his tobacco and cigarette papers. We found them. I said I knew how to roll cigarettes so I rolled some and we all had a go.'

'Who taught you to roll cigarettes?' asked Pim.

'My father,' replied Phoebe in her most matter-of-fact manner, 'When I was six. I used to roll them for him all the time.'

'Oh, so we've your old man to blame for your filthy habit?' It was odd to hear Pim jest on the subject, but it was equally odd to hear Phoebe mention her father so candidly in company.

'He only taught me to roll them. He didn't let me smoke them,' Phoebe was not quite so prepared to joke. 'And, for your information, Philomena Connolly, my mother didn't approve either. Anyway,' she continued, 'we used to hide behind the gardening shed and smoke them. Then the tobacco ran out. So we made a pact: whenever someone left the orphanage to get a position, they had to buy everyone else a cigarette out of their first pay. When that happened, we'd arrange to meet behind the shed and catch up. After that, it became a bit of a habit. That's all.'

'Well, I don't know how you've managed to keep it up for so long. I would be positively sick if I smoked like you do.' Della patted her breast. 'Even the smell of it makes me ill.'

'Oh, don't talk about it!' moaned Phoebe. 'I'm hanging for a cigarette as it is. Horrid Mrs Epstein for throwing them out and I've no money to buy any more.'

'She certainly has you under her thumb,' remarked Pim. 'Good for her, I say. And good for you for taking it pretty well,' she added. 'It can't be easy living under the Evil Eye.'

That comment took me by surprise. It was the first time there had been a conscious effort on Pim's part to say something encouraging to Phoebe.

'Speaking of the Evil Eye,' Pim added. 'I have a concert date: my place the day after the St Dominic's Day picnic.'

'Oh dear! Does it have to be then?' Della lamented. 'I'm performing in the dog show the night before.'

'Dog show is it?' I queried.

'It's what everyone calls the school concert, old thing. Didn't they ask you to play?'

'They didn't, thanks be to God.'

'Well, Sister Bellarmine's roped me into playing the *Spring Sonata* and Phoebe's accompanying, aren't you, Phoebe?'

'Yes,' groaned Phoebe. 'Silly school concert.'

'I know it's not the Town Hall, Phoebe, but I am not going to play with Sister Alberta accompanying me. You've got to do it!'

'I didn't say I wasn't going to! I only said it's a silly school concert, that's all. Besides, there's no way Mrs Epstein's going to let me get out of it.'

'I'm glad about that. It's been wonderful having you living at Mrs Epstein's and accompanying me during lessons. Mrs Epstein can't play the piano for toffee. But Pim, why does your concert have to be then? There's so much going on!'

'It's only going to be afternoon tea, Dell, nothing too fancy,' Pim tried to reassure her. Della was feeling the burden of mastering so much music. 'I thought it would be good to have it that weekend because Rose will be there. She's coming up for the picnic and will be busy catching up with friends then, but she'd like to see everyone on Sunday. Why not put on a concert? She hardly ever goes to concerts and she'd love it.'

'Very well, Pim,' Della sighed a tired smile. 'I suppose we ought to do some more work before the bell.'

St Dominic's Day fell on the fourth of August and was our school's feast day. Apparently it was traditionally celebrated with a school Mass, followed by a picnic to which students and ex-students, their families and friends were invited. On the evening before, there was a concert showcasing the best of St Dominic's talent. Throughout the entire month of July the entire school was abuzz with preparations: concert rehearsals, a pageant of saints from the lower school, choir practices, play presentations and sporting events. Pim, as head prefect, was absorbed with writing a speech and with numerous meetings with Sister Bellarmine in addition to her studies, hockey games and quartet work. Even Daid had been called upon, for Sister Bellarmine had engaged him as the photographer for the event.

As a result, my involvement on St Dominic's Day was in the capacity of my father's assistant. Following from the school Mass that Saturday morning, I had to accompany Daid on his rounds of various groups and activities, organise the plates for his camera, and make the necessary notes. And so I succeeded in seeing nearly everything there was to see: races and games on the sports field; Sister Augustine and Sister Magdalene enjoying chicken sandwiches; my young charges in the fourth grade dressed up for a jolly parade of saints; Leila Sotheby and her friends being denounced as Albigensian heretics in the Life of St Dominic pageant; Fanny Mahony forced to play St Catherine of Siena persuading the pope to return to Rome, and Pim crowning the statue of St Dominic in the school quadrangle during the singing of the school hymn. The day concluded with Benediction and a Rosary procession. Aunt Rose I only managed to glimpse sitting in the middle of what turned out to be a crowd of old girls, which included several nuns and most of Pim's sisters. We managed only a brief wave while I was pointing her out to Daid.

'Never mind, lassie,' said Daid when he heard me sigh. 'You'll see her tomorrow.'

Sunday could not come fast enough. Along with the Epsteins and Phoebe, Daid and I took the ferry across the harbour and were met at the wharf by Pim, her brother Benny, and their enormous touring car. Our arrival at the guest house coincided with that of Della and her mother in the Bentley. Greetings were made. Mrs Sotheby was introduced, having not met Mrs Connolly in person, and we were welcomed inside.

'Is Aunt Rose here, Pim?' I asked as I looked over the vestibule and up the stairs. The grand old house seemed unusually quiet.

'Upstairs having a nap,' Pim replied. 'Listen, we've got a bit of time to rehearse. We can't use the front room 'cause it's set up for the concert, so we'll go to the back parlour. Hey Dad,' she greeted her father who happened to be there, sitting in an old armchair.

Mr Connolly did not get up, nor did he greet us. At least, he did not greet us verbally. But he seemed to say hello with his eyes.

Eventually, however, as he watched us pull out our instruments, some words stumbled out:

'Bum, Pim. Bum.'

'Mum's out the front having a chin wag with the visitors,' replied Pim.

'Lil's tickin'?'

'Yeah, Lil's in the kitchen and Leo's taken Bertie fishing. You wanna come and meet everyone?'

'Mucky gum?'

'Beg yours?'

'Mucky gimmick?'

Pim shook her head, unable to work out what her father was trying to say. Mr Connolly, in response, became more emphatic and began to point to Della and repeated, 'Mucky, mucky, mucky!'

'Dear me! What have I done?' Della started to panic.

'It's all right, Dell.' Pim continued to study her father who had stopped talking and was gesticulating, first in Della's direction, then in Phoebe's. Phoebe took a few steps backwards and made a silent appeal.

''Tis not yourselves he's talking about,' I observed. ''Tis the violins, is it not?' I looked to Mr Connolly for confirmation. A terrible and terrifying thing it was have your thoughts imprisoned and no one to free them.

'Mucky!' acknowledged Mr Connolly.

'Mucky?' echoed Pim, still very puzzled. 'Mucky? Ah, Peggy! That's mucky all right. Is Peggy coming?' Mr Connolly's eyes watered. 'No, Dad. Peggy's not here,' she explained with a very guilty glance at me. 'You still want to come and meet everyone?'

'Dunno.'

'Come on, Dad. I can take you. Come on,' Pim helped her father out of the chair. 'But you gotta mind your language, all right?' she joked as she guided him out. 'Won't be long. Start without me,' she called.

But, in their respective ways, Della and Phoebe were too stunned to do little more than tune their instruments.

'Was he in the War?' asked Phoebe the moment Pim returned.

'Who? Dad?' answered Pim. 'Nah. Thought I told you he had a stroke.'

'I didn't realise he was so frail, Pim,' Della sadly observed.

Pim nodded and sighed. 'We're lucky to have him. He understands everything, just can't get the words out. You get used to it after a while. He's looking forward to this afternoon. Dad loves music.'

'Was your sister coming today?' I asked.

'Who? Peggy?' Pim replied in a way that made me feel that I was asking for trouble. 'No. Dad misses her, that's all. Listen, are we going to practise or not?'

Our rehearsal was interrupted by Lily. 'Time,' she announced. 'Everyone's here.'

'How are you going to carry your 'cello, Lucy?' asked Pim.

I looked at the 'cello and then at my crutches lying on the floor and bit my lip. It had never occurred to me that I would have to carry my 'cello into a performance.

'I'll carry it, Lucy,' Lily offered.

As we walked down the hall to the drawing room, we debated over who should enter first. Finally we decided on order of height. That meant I entered last, which was very much my preferred position.

Della halted at the door.

'Pim, I thought you said this was only afternoon tea,' she whispered.

'It is.'

'But—the room's packed. How many people did you ask?'

'Everyone. Guess they all ended up coming,' Pim shrugged. 'Nobody misses a Connolly afternoon tea.'

There was barely enough room for me to manage my crutches and I was very grateful that Pim's sister walked behind me. She waited for me to sit and whispered good luck as she handed me my 'cello and bow.

While Pim, Della and Phoebe acknowledged everyone's applause, I congratulated myself on the fact that I had chosen not to wear the callipers for the occasion. I organised my music and peered over the stand at the rows of faces: members of Pim's family, guest house lodgers, and friends. There was Daid, at the very back, well-pleased and eager. Aunt Rose was bending over, whispering snippets to her children who were all sitting in anticipation on the floor in front. Mr and Mrs Epstein had discreetly positioned themselves at the far side with Mr and Mrs Connolly, while Mrs Sotheby, as mother of the first violinist, had taken pride of place in the very centre.

'Lucy!' Phoebe jabbed me with her bow. 'Hurry and tune!'

I pushed my glasses back onto my nose, made a few final adjustments, gave my left hand a good shake from the wrist, took a deep breath and thought of my opening B flat. It was my job to lead. I raised my bow and we began.

I may have been nervous, but I was by no means prepared for what followed.

We had decided upon the *Sunrise* quartet as our performance piece. Of the several Haydn quartets we now knew, it was the one we had worked at hardest and the one we liked best. We should have played it well, but Della's usually winsome phrasing was surprisingly lacklustre. Nor did Phoebe play with her characteristic verve. She even missed an entry, something we had never known her to do. Pim, however, was in home territory. She was a competent, solid player who was quite in the habit of giving presentations. So it was in Pim's playing that I took refuge and from that safe retreat I found myself trying to make every note and phrase of mine an encouragement and support to poor Della who was struggling with her part.

Still, whatever our faults may have been, our audience was appreciative. Warm applause followed and everyone was invited to afternoon tea on the verandah. I was in the middle of pushing my endpin back inside my instrument when I heard someone clear their chest. I looked up and saw a boy about my own age.

'Hello,' he said. 'I just wanted to say I thought you were terrific.'

'Thank you,' I replied and could not stop a smile escaping.

'Have you been learning the 'cello long?' he asked.

'Nearly six years it would be now.'

'Six years? That's amazing! You could be professional you're so good. By the way, I'm Ambrose. Ambrose O'Connor. Do you mind if I sit down?'

'You can sit if you like.'

'You're not going to bite my head off if I do?' he hesitated.

I looked at him once again and realised he was the boy with the shuttlecock who had offered me his assistance those months ago on Balmoral Beach. I blushed.

'At least there's no sand for you to throw at me this time,' he smiled as he sat.

'I'm sorry,' I felt myself turn even more red, if that were at all possible. 'I would very much liked to have played that day but I'm afraid I— I don't walk very well.'

'It's all right. Your music makes up for it. I play too, but the 'cello doesn't get a look in during the cricket season, so I don't progress very much from one year to the next, unfortunately. I enjoy it, though, when I do play. We've an orchestra at school and that's good fun. You play in an orchestra?'

And on we talked about which composers we liked best, our favourite pieces and our instruments, where we went to school and our plans for when we left. We would have talked the afternoon away save that I glimpsed Aunt Rose standing quietly to one side.

I started.

Ambrose noticed my surprise.

'I'm going to grab a cuppa and some cake before it all disappears. Can I get you anything?' he asked.

'I'll come myself in a wee while.'

'Then I'll see you outside?'

'Aye.'

I watched him leave and then gazed wide-eyed and incredulous at Aunt Rose.

'Lucy,' she said warmly. 'How are you?'

'I—I'm fine, Aunt Rose,' I replied quietly. 'Are—are you expecting a baby?'

'Yes, darling. A new baby due in December.'

'You didn't say in your letters.'

'I didn't like to. I was hoping to see you and I thought it would be much nicer to tell you in person.'

'A hundred thousand blessings on you!' I didn't know whether my tears were of joy for Aunt Rose or sorrow for the loss of my own mother and my little unborn brother or sister. 'Did you meet my Da?'

'We've already been introduced and we had a lovely conversation. I can see where you get your good looks from,' she added with a smile.

'Whisht! Aunt Rose!' I scolded. 'They may sit well on himself but they don't sit right on me.'

'I don't think that young man thought so.'

'He's going into the seminary next year, Aunt Rose.'

'Is he really? Then he should make a very fine priest. Let's have a cup of tea. It's lovely outside and still quite warm. Haven't we been lucky with the weather?'

We walked out to the verandah and found some seats next to a table upon which stood a three-tiered plateful of sandwiches, cakes and slices. Aunt Rose brought me some tea and we chatted as we watched her children join in the croquet game that had started on the front lawn.

Eventually our conversation turned to our quartet. 'Now, that's Della over there isn't it?' Aunt Rose nodded at Della who was sitting further along the verandah attempting conversation with Pim's father. 'And the pretty, dark lass is Phoebe?' here she indicated Phoebe out on the lawn, swinging her mallet with vigour and delighting in her triumph at sending her ball through a hoop.

'Aye,' I smiled.

'What a beautiful dress she's wearing. I couldn't help admiring it the moment I saw it.'

'Isn't it exquisite?' interrupted Mrs Sotheby, who was conversing nearby with Lily, 'And so delightfully old-fashioned! I believe the collar is handmade French lace.'

'Is it really?' Aunt Rose seemed to share Mrs Sotheby's penchant for beautiful clothes. 'I bought a collar like that when I was in France during the War. I've always kept it for best. Goodness, Phoebe reminds me of someone! I suppose yesterday's trip down memory lane brought it on. Now, what was her name? Lucy, she was the most beautiful girl in the school. Come on, Lil, you should know. I'm certain she was in your class. She sang. She had a voice like an angel. Don't you remember, Lily? She wore a dress with a pretty lace collar like that and she sang the Rosary song at the concert while her mother accompanied.'

'I know who you mean, Rosie,' Lily nodded. 'No, it was her sister who was in my class. I'll get her name in a minute. Lydia? Lenora? No. That's it! Lina! Lina Devereaux!'

'My, my! Lina Devereaux!' enjoined Aunt Rose. 'How could I forget Lina Devereaux? Why! She played the cello like you, Lucy.'

'And how could we forget that cello?' Lily remarked. 'She was so possessive of it – a bit like a small child with a stuffed toy that's lost its eyes, its ears and most of its hair. Lina Devereaux and her cello,' Lily laughed a little at the memory.

'Lina Devereaux?' echoed Mrs Sotheby. 'You don't mean Ailine Devereaux the artist?'

'Artist?' repeated Lily.

'Why, she did have a French name, Lil,' Aunt Rose responded. 'It was Ailine. And she was good at drawing as well as music. It wouldn't surprise me in the least if she did become an artist.'

'She's frightfully modern,' added Mrs Sotheby. '*We* have a picture painted by her. Well, we had—'

'And were you friends?' I enquired, astonished to think of Lily Connolly, Pim's kind and homely oldest sister, ever having anything to do with Phoebe's aunt, and equally at pains to silence Mrs Sotheby on the unpleasant subject of the painting.

'Friends?' scoffed Lily. 'Heavens, no! I'm afraid I wasn't quite in her league. Bit too talented for the likes of me.'

'There you go again, Lil,' reproved Aunt Rose. 'Always running yourself down. Goodness! The Devereaux sisters! Now that really is going back! Why, I haven't seen them since school. Ailine and—and—'

'And fair Juliette,' concluded Lily.

'Juliette Devereaux! That's who it is! Pretty Juliette with the golden curls and the most beautiful brown eyes.'

'Just like a jersey cow,' Lily commented sardonically. 'Moo!'

'Well, I thought she was beautiful.'

'And you were friends with her?' I asked Aunt Rose.

'Lucy,' she sighed, 'I idolised her, rather like you with the paintings of that artist you like. Who is it again?'

'Botticelli.'

'Botticelli,' Aunt Rose seconded. 'But I wouldn't say we were friends although she was always very kind. She was a few years older than me: one of those still-waters-run-deep sorts. You never would have expected a girl who was so serious and so softly spoken to sing with so much strength and feeling.'

'And she went to St Dominic's?'

'Yes, we were all at school together. They were city girls, though, weren't they, Lil?'

'They were from the Big Smoke, all right. A pair of petted prima donnas the two of them.'

'They weren't,' remonstrated Aunt Rose. 'They were French, that's all. They'd been brought up differently.'

'French children do tend to be more petted,' accorded Mrs Sotheby.

'You can say that again,' remarked Lily.

'Well, Aunt Rose,' I resolved, ''tis little wonder you've déjà vu, for Phoebe Raye's Juliette Devereaux' daughter, and to be sure 'tis the very same dress with the very same collar she's wearing.'

'Phoebe Raye did you say, Lucy?'

'Aye, I did indeed. Why?'

'No matter, darling,' Aunt Rose looked fondly in the direction of the croquet game and smiled to herself. 'A happy thought, that's all. I suppose it's another case of déjà vu,' was all she said.

37

Daid was by nature a quiet and gentle man, but he was quieter than quiet during our ferry ride back home that evening.

'Did you speak to Aunt Rose, Da?' I ventured to ask.

'Aye,' he replied in a very soft voice. 'A fine lady she is and I'm glad she's a friend of yours, lass.'

The silence returned.

''Twas a good chat we enjoyed, Luighseach,' he resumed and then hesitated. 'She introduced me to a doctor she thinks might be able to help you.'

Now it was my turn to be silent.

'You could be walking better than you do, lass,' Daid tried to sound encouraging.

'I'm sick of doctors!'

'The doctor thinks he could fix your legs a little more.'

Daid retreated into his thoughts again, leaving me silently venting my anger on the polio, doctors, hospitals, operations, plasters, callipers, wheelchairs and crutches. I was about to give voice to my frustrations when I caught sight of the sad expression on my father's face.

I knew he was thinking of Mam and I took his hand instead.

''Twill be grand when that bridge is built, will it not, Luighseach?' he observed in his gentle way. 'They'll be building the arch soon. Think how easy it will be to cross the harbour after that. Do you know it took the Sothebys over an hour to travel today in that car of theirs? Well, soon there'll be a Jacob's ladder stretching from one shore to the other. If only we could get to Heaven the same way,' he sighed.

''Tis Heaven's but a prayer away is it not, Da?'

'Aye,' he nodded, and gave me a kiss on the forehead.

That weekend, with its gloriously sunny days, had been an early taste of Spring. Come Monday, however, it poured and with the rain came wind. Aside from the classroom the only place to go during the lunch hour was the library, and by the time Phoebe and I arrived there it was crammed with chatting, laughing groups of girls. Elderly Sister Comgall, who was in charge, was at her wits' end keeping the place quiet and orderly.

Phoebe and I walked up to the monitor's desk and I greeted Sister Comgall in Irish.

'Dia dhuit agus Damhnaic, a Luighseach,' she returned. Being the only other Irish speaker in the school, Sister enjoyed speaking Irish with me. As a result I knew I could get whatever I wanted from her and on that particular rainy day I had a mission.

Sister Comgall nodded when I finished my explanation and told us to wait at the desk while she fetched a few things.

'What did you say to her?' asked Phoebe.

'I told her that your mother went to St Dominic's and that you wanted to know whether there would be any photographs of her.'

'You did what?'

'You heard me right. Do you not want a picture of your mam?'

'Yes, but—'

'Well, Sister Comgall said there might be some and we're welcome to look, providing we put the photographs away as we do which would be a grand help to her since she's needing to put everything in order after the picnic day display.'

'You might as well start with the photographs already out,' advised Sister as she placed a box before us. 'They're mostly dated as you will see there on the back and you can group them by year. When you're done with those you can put them in the appropriate boxes and sort through some more.'

We took the box to a spare table and began our search.

'Hey, Lucy!' Pim bellowed as she entered the library with a few of her classmates. 'Thought you might be here. Where's Della?'

'Not at school she is today, Pimmy.'

'Weekend pretty well knocked her for six, I reckon. Ha! That's Polly,' and she pointed to one of the girls in a class photograph that we were about to file.

Having had all her five sisters as well as at least one aunt, not to mention cousins, pass through the school, Pim knew a lot about the photographs and was soon providing details. Between Pim's anecdotes and explanations, which were all delivered in her usual hearty manner, and my responses, we soon drew a crowd.

'We can't hear our own conversations the way you two are carrying on,' complained Mary Byrne with a smile. 'What are you doing?'

''Tis looking at photos is all,' I replied.

'Bet my mother's in one,' Mary remarked. 'What a hoot. Say, isn't that Sister Catherine Bernard? Look! Put your fingers around the face.'

'Kate, get some paper and scissors,' Fanny ordered. Fanny's offsider immediately obeyed. Upon her return, Fanny cut a hole in a piece of notepaper and put it round the face. We giggled at the discovery.

'I always wondered what her hair was like,' tittered Fanny. 'Who do you think that is?'

''Tis Sister Alberta is it not?'

The paper trick confirmed that it was.

'There's Sister Augustine. Honestly, some people never change. How long ago was this photograph taken?'

'Twenty-three years for 'tis dated nineteen hundred and five,' I commented.

'Are you quite sure you two aren't related?' Mary nudged me.

'Ha, ha! That's my mother!' Fanny snatched the photograph Phoebe had taken up.

She pointed out her mother standing next to another chubby, awkward girl with glasses who stood pigeon-toed next to her. I could not help feeling sorry for that girl.

'Do you want to know who that is?' Fanny noticed my concern.

'Do you know?' I asked.

'Of course I do. It's *your* fairy godmother,' she replied with a very knowing air.

'You're not serious,' it was hard to believe that that little girl was dear Aunt Rose.

'Well, I am. Mummy said she was the plainest girl in the school. Little wonder she has a soft spot for you. You're both ugly ducklings, save that in your case *you* didn't become a swan, except for your nose. Come on, Kate.' And with that, Fanny tossed the photograph back on the table and waltzed away.

'Hey! Frances Mahony!' Pim boomed, 'You come back here!'

Since Fanny did no such thing, Pim strode off to sort her out.

'Don't let it bother you. She's jealous, Lucy,' Mary remarked.

'But what in heaven's name is there to be jealous about?' I blinked as I put on my glasses.

'Fanny's jealous because she knows Della's brother is keen on you and not on her and there's absolutely nothing she can do about it.'

'You're not serious, Mary,' I could feel the colour rising in my cheeks.

'Didn't you know Wally waits on the station for you every day?' Mary informed me with a smile. 'Fanny can't get a look in edgewise. Listen, if you want my opinion, she needs bringing down a peg or two and I can't think of anyone better than you to do it.'

'Well, Mary Byrne, I'm letting you know I'm not a wee bit interested in bringing her down a peg or two. All I want is to be friends.'

'Lucy, it's her loss, not yours.'

Phoebe, meanwhile, was studying the discarded photograph.

'It's her!' she exclaimed quietly, and she pointed to the well-developed young woman with long, curly hair, who stood next to the St Dominic statue with Fanny's mother and Aunt Rose. 'That's my mother. She's wearing my dress. Look.'

''Tis the same dress indeed, Phoebe,' I agreed.

'Of course it is. After all, I found that dress in the attic. How else could it have got there if it didn't belong to my mother?'

'Aye, but more to the point, Phoebeen, 'tis her hair's like yours save that it's blonde and her eyes and lips are the very same shape as your own. Why Phoebe, it could be yourself there. So your dark looks you get from your da?'

Phoebe nodded.

'Well, you've been blessed with a lovely mother, if that picture is anything to go by. She's gracious and pretty and it would seem she's a tender sort the way she's looking after them two other lassies. Shall we ask Sister Comgall if we can take the photograph? To be sure she'll give it once she knows the reason why.'

And, to Phoebe's astonishment and pleasure, Sister Comgall obliged.

38

'It was a typical first performance, that's all,' Mrs Epstein tried to assuage us, 'a bit nervous; a bit self-conscious. It was nothing to write home about but it wasn't unmusical, not by any means.'

'It was terrible, Mrs Epstein!' Della lamented.

'Della, stop punishing yourself,' advised our teacher. 'You played the Beethoven beautifully on Friday night. Sunday afternoon's performance at Pim's was a little under the weather.'

'I was so tired, Mrs Epstein,' Della was forlorn.

'Are you getting enough sleep?'

'I'm trying. Really, I am.'

'But…' prompted Mrs Epstein.

'I cannot stop thinking about everything: the performance last Sunday, the competition, Mummy's garden party, rehearsals, and practice, practice, practice, practice. Music swirls around in my head and I toss and turn, and no sooner than I've fallen asleep I break into a sweat and it starts all over again.'

'Della, don't worry so much. You've holidays next week so make sure you get some rest. It's time to stop and see how much you've achieved in the last few months. You've learnt all the music and you've learnt it well. All you have to do is practise performing. Play for anyone who wants to listen. Play for anyone who doesn't want to listen. The more you do, you'll learn that some performances will be good and others will be even worse than Sunday.'

'Worse than Sunday, Mrs Epstein?'

'Much worse than Sunday. What concerns me more is your presentation. Della, I had an earful from your mother about it on Sunday evening, and for once I had to agree with her. Have you girls no idea at all about how to groom yourselves for a concert?'

'What do you mean?'

'First of all, you wandered in like Brown's cows. It was hardly the entry of a quartet of musicians proud to play music everyone will love to hear. As for acknowledging your audience, Luighseach here plonks herself down and gawps at everyone. Hasn't anyone taught you to curtsey?'

'I cannot curtsey, Mrs Epstein.'

'You could at least have nodded. Besides, I didn't mean you, I meant your compatriots. Hasn't anyone taught you girls to curtsey?'

'My mother taught me,' inserted Della.

'Yes, that was quite evident, which showed up all the more how Phoebe and Pim have no idea, bobbing up and down like a couple of barrels tossed on the sea. As for you, Luighseach, what are you going to do? How are you going to come on stage? On crutches with the latest ring-in to carry your 'cello and bow any old how?'

'I'll not be performing with callipers on my legs.'

'You're going to have to carry your 'cello and I don't see how you're going to do it without bracing your leg the way you usually do when you want to walk without crutches. So, like it or not, you're going to have to perform with at least one calliper. My dear girl, you, more than any of the others, are going to have to give this the most thought because, I hate to say it, there are people out there who are narrow-minded enough to think that a girl like you shouldn't be seen in public, let alone play a 'cello, and you are going to have to prove them wrong. What are you going to wear?'

'Clothes, I'm thinking, for I'll not be wearing my birthday suit now, will I?'

'And that sort of impertinent remark, young lady, shows how little respect you have for yourself, let alone anyone else. I've never seen such a motley lot. What are you all going to wear?'

'Mummy's having costumes made for the garden party, Mrs Epstein,' Della explained. We could wear those.'

'Garden party costumes!' Pim, Phoebe and I groaned in unison.

'What's the matter? Mummy's taken a lot of trouble over our costumes.'

At which point, Pim and Phoebe launched into what had become a well-rehearsed imitation of Mrs Sotheby and her dressmaker, fussing over an array of imaginary fabrics which they flung across my person:

'Young ghells look so nice in white,' Pim assumed an English accent. 'What shade of white will suit, Collette?'

'Do you like cette white, Madame?' Phoebe pretended to be Collette.

'Darling, it's a little too pink, don't you think? Non. Pas rose.'

'And the ivoire, Madame?'

'Dieu! Pas jaune! Cette ivoire ici. Qu'est-ce que tu pense?'

'Stop it! Both of you! Now! Mummy's put a lot of care into our costumes and you're all going to have to come for another fitting sometime soon, whether you like it or not.'

More groans.

'Well, it's either garden party frocks or your school uniform,' concluded Mrs Epstein. 'What is it to be?'

'Garden party frocks,' Phoebe answered in an instant. 'I will not wear that school uniform a single day more than I have to.'

'Very well. Now, I've entered you in the competition as the St Dominic's Quartet.'

'Mrs Epstein!' we all protested.

'Have you a name for yourselves yet?'

'What about Brown's Cows?' suggested Pim.

'I think you can do better than that, and you're going to have to do it by

333

October. Which brings me to the next matter. Have you managed to arrange any more concerts? Luighseach, I believe it's your turn, and, if you don't mind, I think you should perform the Borodin.'

As much as we liked the Borodin, the prospect of actually performing the piece was a daunting one indeed. Mindful of the fact that poor Della needed rest, not to mention that we could all use a few weeks to consolidate the hardest piece in our repertoire, I decided upon the Sunday after school returned for Michaelmas term as the date for my concert. It was only days before the Garden Party but Mrs Epstein insisted it be sooner rather than later.

Our holidays were spent in rehearsal either at Mrs Epstein's or at my house (the quietest), and in private practice. Most in need of work was the second movement. It was a scherzo which incorporated a very charming waltz, but never was such a light-hearted piece in need of such careful attention.

'It's like beating eggs for a soufflé,' Pim commented during one session at my house.

'Soufflé is it?' I asked.

'Listen, light the oven and I'll make you one when we've finished. You got eggs?'

'I say, scrummy!' Soufflé, it turned out, was on Della's favourite foods list. 'Would you, Pim?'

Pim nodded. 'Anyway,' she continued, 'you haven't a hope of the thing rising if you don't whisk those eggs for all they're worth and fold them in carefully as can be.'

Mrs Epstein and the metronome whisked us for all we were worth. It was imperative for us to be able to play series upon series of whirling passages perfectly in time with each note articulated precisely. And that was not the only challenge, for those very passages alternated with impish staccato sequences which demanded both lightness and accuracy.

For my part, hours were spent alone, practising segments in isolation and gradually joining them. To better learn the notes and fingerings I played those sequences forwards and backwards, transposed them, worked them over two and three octaves, and applied as many different bowings as I could think of until I could deliver them with the same ease and grace as any violin at six quavers to eighty-three beats per minute: no easy task for a 'cello. Privately I strove for six quavers to eighty-six beats, to make sure.

That task alone kept me occupied for most of the holidays.

A few days into term, Pim cornered me.

'Lucy, I need to ask you a favour,' she said.

'What is it, Pimmy Connolly?' I asked.

'Would you mind very much if I asked my sister, Peggy, to come on Sunday? She lives quite near you and it would mean a lot to her to come. It would mean a lot to me, too, and I'd like you to meet her. Do you mind?'

'Not at all, Pim,' I smiled.

'Thanks,' she answered. 'Thanks: Not only for letting her come but for helping me get back in touch with her.'

''Twas nothing I did, Pimmy Connolly.'

'Apart from Johnny, who makes a point of talking about it, you're the only person I've been able to talk to about Peggy, and if you hadn't said what you did that day, I would have refused to have anything more to do with her.'

'Which day? What did I say?'

'When we were at Rose's. All you said was, "At least she isn't dead". Coming from anyone else I would have brushed it off and told them to go jump. Coming from you—'

'Well, you couldn't exactly tell me to go jump now, could you?' I answered with a smile.

'Nah,' she grinned.

And she left me to ponder how I was going to accommodate yet another guest.

Since our parlour lacked the grand proportions of Pim's drawing room, I had been obliged to limit the size of our audience. So far, everyone had accepted my invitation. Mr and Mrs Epstein, of course, would be there. Mrs Murphy offered to bring a cake. Father Callaghan and Hilda Geraghty replied that they would be glad to come, as were Mr and Mrs Birstall. Mr David Birstall answered with a note:

Will come in pyjamas.

XXX

Mr David.

There was one last invitation pending: Miss Bray; and I made a point of calling in at the music shop after school that afternoon.

'Lucy, I thought you'd be more likely to invite the 'cello,' she teased. 'So, after all these years we're finally going to hear you perform? I'd be delighted to come, dear.'

My mission accomplished, I went to open the door, only to find that someone had opened it for me. I glanced up and to my surprise there stood a tall, athletic figure sporting a green and white striped blazer and a green school tie. Wally Sotheby tipped his boater and bowed slightly in his formal way, his mischievous sky blue eyes magnified a little by a pair of gold-rimmed glasses.

'Lucy!' he exclaimed. 'I say, fancy seeing you here!'

''Tis nothing fancy about seeing myself here for I do often come to this shop,' I replied.

'Can you spare a minute? Dell broke a string last night and the shop near our place doesn't carry the ones she likes. I had an appointment this end of town so I promised her I'd pop in here and buy one. I say, it is good to see you! You will wait, won't you?'

I had no choice but to wait. It was useless trying to escape because I knew I could not move fast enough. Besides, there was nowhere to disappear to. If I took refuge in another shop I would be faced with having to explain my presence to a shopkeeper, and I did not particularly like having to explain my presence to shopkeepers. For the entirety of last term I had gone out of my way to avoid any further contact with Della's brother. This had usually meant catching an earlier train or, when that failed, walking to the opposite end of the station platform, using Phoebe as a shield or else hiding until he caught his own train – anything but catch his eye, or, even worse, Fanny Mahony's.

'I haven't seen you for months,' he smiled as he pocketed his parcel. 'You're well, I hope?'

'Aye.'

'Are you on your way home?'

'Aye, I am.'

'Would you allow me to walk you?'

How could I refuse?

Wally immediately placed himself between me and the roadside. At first he began to stride out too quickly, but no sooner than he realised that I could not keep up, he checked himself and fell in step with the pace set by my crutches. Soon he was strolling beside me much in the way Daid was wont to do.

'Were you buying music today?' he asked.

I explained the purpose of my visit.

'Wait a minute, that's this Sunday isn't it?' he queried.

'Aye it is.'

'I remember because I'm playing my first match the day before.'

'Cricket is it?'

He nodded. 'Tell you the truth I'm a bit nervous. I missed a season, you see, so I've been working like mad to get my form up. Do you like cricket?'

It was not usual for anyone to ask me if I liked any sport. 'I'm afraid I know nothing about it,' I confessed. 'All I know is French cricket, for I play it at school. I like French cricket. Would it be like French cricket at all?'

'French cricket? Not exactly.'

'So how do you play?' I asked, thinking that since he raised the topic, he probably wanted more opportunity to talk about it.

He did.

'Well, you have two sides,' he explained, warming to his subject. 'One side's out in the field and the other's in.'

'Out of the field, you mean?'

'Yes,' he chuckled. 'Then each chap that's in the side that's in goes out.'

'Into the field?'

'Out into the field. Now, when a chap goes out to go in, the chaps who are out try to get him out, and when he's out he goes in and the next chap in goes out and goes back in when he's out. When both sides have been in and all the chaps have been out, and both sides have been out twice after all the chaps have been in, well, that's the end of the game. That's cricket in a nutshell.'

'Is that so?' I replied, amused and rather baffled by the summary.

'You'd like it,' he continued. 'If you want more of an account of the strategy, you could think of it as maths and physics played with a bat and ball: See, when you bowl, you try to outwit your opponent by the amount of pace and spin you put on the ball as well as how long or how short you pitch it,' and I was treated to a demonstration of bowling techniques which took us as far as Daid's studio. 'As far as batting is concerned, it's all about defending your wicket and scoring runs, who's on strike and who's not, and how well you judge the speed and bounce of the ball. How good you are depends on your average and your average determines your position in the batting line.'

'Your average?'

'The total number of runs you scored in a season divided by the number of games you played,' he elaborated.

'And what position do you bat?'

'Usually number four, sometimes number five. I like batting at the top of the middle order, but I don't think I'll be quite so high up this season, especially since I'll be playing club cricket instead of school cricket. The last season I played back Home, my average was fifty, which is pretty good. Scored a couple of centuries, too.'

'A century?'

'A hundred runs in a single innings without getting out. Anyway, I was stupid enough to boast about it when I started school out here. Chaps set me up. It was a house match. The first time I went in to bat I didn't expect the pitch to be as hard as it was. The pitches here are much harder than in England, you see. Anyway, they had me for lunch: I was out for a duck.'

'A duck you're saying?'

'Bowled clean on the first ball, and no runs to my name. Probably the most humiliating thing that can happen to a chap. When I was leaving the crease the wicket keeper said, "Pity about that century, mate". Well, I had my revenge next innings. Given my batting performance, the captain was reluctant to trust me with the ball. Finally, he gave me a chance. Turned out the pitch suited my bowling once I slowed my pace and started to use the seam. I bagged a fifer, with three maidens and a hat trick.'

Whatever did he mean? Evidently, it was impressive, but I had no idea what he was talking about.

'Sorry, Lu,' he apologised. 'I took five wickets for thirty-six runs. That is, I bowled five chaps out and they scored only thirty-six runs between them. A maiden is an over in which no runs are scored and a hat trick is where you bowl three chaps out on three successive balls.'

'I see,' I nodded as I tried to make sense of it all. ''Twas quite a triumph for you, was it not?'

'It most certainly was. I got to keep a stump for that. It's in my room. Regardless of the achievement, though, the nickname stuck.'

'And what would that be?'

'Toffee. You know, from Toff – what they call a stuck-up Pom out here. Well, with a name like Walsingham Ponsonby I've no hope, have I?' he joked and quickly became serious. 'Anyway, I've cricket on Saturday and I'm worried. I can't say I'm looking forward to facing one of my own balls with these,' and he indicated his glasses.

'Well, you cannot hit the ball if you cannot see it,' I remarked. 'Besides, they look well on you.'

'Do they?' he was eager for confirmation.

'Aye, they do. And there does be nothing wrong with wearing glasses if they help you see better for there's a lot of wonderful things to see.'

'I don't know my mother would agree with you. She wouldn't be seen dead with her specs. Matter of fact, we're all a bit long-sighted. Della's worst of all. She's worn glasses since she was four. I've always worn them for reading but I'm afraid everything was becoming a bit blurry and the headaches were getting the better of me. I've had my prescription changed and the doctor advised me to wear them all the time.'

'Well, that was what my Mam said to myself when I first got mine,' I replied. 'Not that I took her advice, I'm saying. In fact, after she died, I couldn't even bring myself to touch my speclaí so I didn't wear them until my eyesight became so bad I could scarcely see two feet in front of me.'

'Well, they look well on you too,' he said with a smile.

'Do you think so?'

He nodded. 'Have we much farther to go?'

'We'll be turning right at the pub there.'

We took the turn and walked down Watkin Street.

'Is this is your house?' he asked as we approached.

'Aye, it is. I'm afraid 'tisn't quite as grand as yours.'

'But it's home, isn't it?'

'Aye,' I sighed. 'It is now.'

'It hasn't always been so?'

I shook my head. 'For a long time it was a very strange house in a very strange land.'

'How old were you when you came here?'

'Eight I was. Well, I was nine by the time I came out of hospital and it was while I was in hospital that my da found this house. So, the first time I set foot inside was after I was sick. You know, Wally, I had absolutely no idea where I was.'

'That must have been terrifying.'

I nodded. 'It was it was. But I'm better now, thanks be to God.'

'So what was home before that?' he gently changed the subject.

'It was a little four room cottage with a thatched roof and a hearth. A kitchen there was in one room and a parlour and Daid's studio in another, and I slept in a bed in an alcove in my parents' room. I didn't even know what a bathroom was until I came out here. Can you credit that?' I laughed. 'And we had candles. Nothing fancy like electricity, let me tell you now. I couldn't believe my eyes when Daid flicked a switch for to make the light go on. And when I was finally able to get up and do it myself, I couldn't stop turning the lights on and off.'

'There are no lights on at the moment,' he observed. 'Is anyone home for you?'

'Not yet. If my da were home he'd be waiting out on the front step there with Danny. Thank you for walking me home.'

'It's my pleasure. Will you be all right on your own?'

'Aye, I will.'

'Then I suppose I best be going. I say, Lucy,' he added as he lingered and removed his boater. 'I was wondering— Well — Would you mind awfully if I came to your concert on Sunday? You see, I'm not going to be able to make it to the competition because of cricket, so Sunday will probably be the only chance I'll get and I'd really like to hear you play. Would you mind?'

'Aye, you can come,' I couldn't help but say. 'You're more than welcome.'

'I say, Lu! That's topping!' he beamed, tossed his hat and returned it to his head. 'Till Sunday then?'

'Aye,' I smiled.

And he tipped his boater, bowed and bid me good-bye.

I stood at the gate and watched him walk back up street. As he neared the pub he turned round and waved. I waved back before turning to climb the front steps. I halted as I opened the front door and looked again up the street.

'Lu was it he said? Fancy calling me that!' I laughed to myself.

For the first time in my life I had a nickname.

39

'How many people did you say were coming now, Luighseach?' Daid asked me on Saturday night.

''Twill be twelve, Da,' I answered. 'Will we fit everyone do you think?'

'There'll always be room on a pew, lass, and Mrs Murphy's offered some of her chairs if we need them.'

And need them we certainly did.

Daid and I arrived home from Mass the following morning to find Pim on our doorstep using her viola to stop Danny from sniffing the tin she was carrying.

'I thought you might like some help,' she said, 'so I'm here early. Lil baked you a cake.'

Mrs Murphy came down with a roast and we enjoyed our Sunday dinner together before setting about the task of reorganising the house. The wheelchair was pushed into the back yard, the walking frame hidden in Daid's room, every chair in the house was requisitioned for the concert, more chairs were brought from Mrs Murphy's and the parlour arranged accordingly.

There was a knock at our door and Danny barked his welcome. Judging from the flaming chestnut hair, freckles and deep brown eyes, our first guest was undoubtedly a Connolly.

'You must be Lucy,' she said as she confidently held out her hand. 'I'm Peggy and this is Caroline,' and she introduced her little girl of five. 'I brought some sandwiches.'

'Céad míle fáilte romhat! Come in, come in! Pimmy your sister's here!' I called. The two sisters met in the hall and hugged each other. Then, in true Connolly fashion, Peggy Connolly rolled up her sleeves and joined us in arranging the tea things, a task which included racing over to Mrs Murphy's to get more cups. The Epsteins arrived with Phoebe and another plate of sandwiches. Then along came Hilda who also had baked a cake for the occasion. Mr David came in his Sunday suit and presented me with the prettiest posy of spring bulbs. He was soon followed by Mr and Mrs Birstall with yet another plate and a parcel.

'Something to add to your gallery,' twinkled Mr Birstall as he handed me the parcel, and inside was none other than the pictures he had taken of the four of us so many months ago. Father Callaghan arrived and finally Miss Bray.

Only Della and Wally were yet to come.

At last there was a knock.

'We're frightfully sorry we're late. We missed the train!' Della was breathless.

'I nearly carried her up the hill,' explained Wally. 'Listen, is there somewhere for her to lie down to catch her breath?'

'I'm quite all right now, Wally. Truly,' panted Della.

'Go and lie on my bed, Delleen. There's plenty of time.'

Pim took charge of Della.

'I say, that's not Smithy is it?' Wally caught sight of Daid's latest photograph which occupied a solitary position in the hall, there being no free hanging space in our parlour.

'It is indeed,' I answered. Daid was introduced and had the pleasure of briefly recounting to a very impressed Wally Sotheby how he had come to take the picture.

With Della recovered, we made our way to the parlour.

'Where's your 'cello, Lucy?' asked Phoebe.

'In the parlour it is already,' I replied. I was still not prepared to wear any calliper while performing and so was unable to carry my 'cello with me. 'I've already tuned it.'

'Are you going to make an introduction, old thing?' Della asked.

'And you think I should do such a thing as that? Can we not simply play the music?'

'Mrs Epstein will skin us alive if we don't do things properly this time.'

'Don't forget: one-two-three, curtsey-two-three, stand-two-three, sit-two-three,' Phoebe reminded us of the drilling our teacher had put us through during our holiday rehearsals.

Our audience must have overheard our hallway conversation for a wave of laughter greeted us as we entered. One-two-three, curtsey-two-three and I was prodded by Pim who mouthed, 'Introduction.'

I took a deep breath, glanced up at Mam, smiled at Daid, shifted a little from one crutch to the other and began:

'Well, this hardly needs an introduction 'cause 'tis perfectly obvious what you're here for. But on behalf of my Da and Della and Pim and Phoebe, I'd like to say a hundred thousand welcomes and a warm thank you to everyone. Back in Ireland 'twas our family used to gather round the hearth of an evening, and to see our parlour filled with friends as it is now, well, 'tis a joy words cannot tell. Now, as for music, we're playing a quartet by Borodin this afternoon; and as for food, well, there'll be plenty of that once we're finished for there's a feast fit for a king on the table and a hot cup of tea for yous all in the kitchen.'

I sat, picked up my 'cello, we tuned and began. Sure enough, it was a far less nerve-ridden performance than the one at Pim's. But it was not without distractions, most of which were embodied in the person of Mrs Murphy. She sat in the front row, shaking her head slightly and smiling the entire time. After a little while she started to sniff and dabbed her eyes with her handkerchief. Then she leant across to Hilda, whispered and leant back; then she leant in the opposite direction and whispered to Miss Bray. We finished the first movement and she clapped.

'Shh!' I hissed.

And for the remainder of the quartet I had to contend with a repeat performance of shifting, head-shaking, whispering, sniffing and smiling. We dug into our final, triumphant note, and Mrs Murphy could contain herself no longer.

'It's a miracle!' she exclaimed, rising to her feet and applauding for all she was worth. 'Not the miracle I'd hoped for but it's a miracle for sure! Dear child, I've prayed and prayed for a cure and He's cured you in His own good way. He might not have made your legs strong again, but He put it all in your hands. My dear girl, He put it all in your hands!'

And before I had even lowered my bow, I found myself wrapped with Mrs Murphy amidst laughter, cheers and friendly applause.

'Will you help me stand, Mrs Murphy?' I stood and the applause grew all the warmer.

Everyone wanted to say something.

'Well done,' nodded Mrs Epstein, and from her look and that of Mr Epstein, she meant what she said.

'That was the most beautiful music I have ever heard in my entire life,' Hilda declared. 'Wasn't it beautiful?' she repeated to Miss Bray.

'It was perfectly lovely,' agreed Miss Bray. 'I cannot believe how athletic you are on that instrument, Lucy.'

'She's a champion,' remarked Mr David, who was standing nearby, his eyes glistening. 'Thanks, kid. Thanks,' was all he could say as he gave me a hearty slap on the back and a hug.

'Why, I believe I know that 'cello,' observed Miss Bray. 'It's Mavis, isn't it?'

'Aye it is,' I replied with a smile at Mr David. 'How did you know that?'

'I remember it very well,' replied Miss Bray. 'How are you, Mr Birstall?' she asked politely.

'Fighting fit. Thank you, Miss Bray.'

'And how *is* Mavis? I haven't seen her for years.'

'Married a Queenslander.'

'Oh! Oh, I didn't know. Dear me, I always thought—'

'Would you like a cuppa?'

Our little house was brimful with cheer that afternoon. Mrs Murphy and Mrs Birstall chatted away in the kitchen while they waited for the kettle to whistle. Mr Birstall, Mr Epstein and Father Callaghan struck up a conversation in the parlour. They were occasionally joined by Daid who otherwise strolled from group to group, offering plates and beaming a smile I had not seen for a very long time. Mr David perched his tea cup on the mantelpiece and engaged in a tête à tête with Miss Bray. Pim and Peggy chatted with Mrs Epstein. Hilda joined in with Phoebe and Della who were entertaining little Caroline with their violins. Only Wally remained alone, but he was not aloof by any means. He was busy studying the pictures on our wall, moving from one to the other and thoughtfully taking in the contents. He spotted me at the parlour door and smiled as he walked across.

'That's quite a rogues' gallery up there,' he remarked.

'Aye.'

'Come and tell me who's who.'

'Aye, I'll come.' And I introduced him to Mam and my aunts and uncles.

'And all this is your father's work?' he asked.

I nodded.

'I say, Lu,' he nudged me, his eyes sparkling as they seemed to have a habit of doing when he was formulating some scheme or other. 'Is the picture here? You know: the dining room painting?'

'In the shed abroad in the yard it is.'

'Would your father mind if I took a peek?'

'Not at all,' I replied and we walked out together.

''Twas only last week that he finished it,' I explained as we pulled away the cloth that covered the easel. 'It's Scheherazade telling one of her tales to the Sultan.'

I fully expected Wally to come out with another 'I say!' but he said nothing. Spellbound, and absently rolling up the cover sheet, he stood in front of the picture. Then he walked up close and poured over the details.

'Would you believe,' he eventually remarked, 'they came down to dinner dressed in those costumes.'

'They did?' I laughed at the idea of Mr Sotheby sitting at the head of the table dressed in a long embroidered robe and a turban and Mrs Sotheby sitting opposite, bejewelled with diamonds and veiled in sumptuous silk.

Wally grinned at the memory. 'And afterwards,' he continued, 'my step-father coaxed my mother into performing an Arabian dance. She did it, too, once she had a couple of brandies. You should have seen her swaying her hips and flinging her arms about.' And, unable to resist, he took off his glasses and gave a mock-performance using the cover sheet as a veil, fluttering his eyes and singing his own version of *In a Persian Market*. So entertained was I by his tomfoolery that I couldn't help picking up a paintbrush and joining in with my own musical accompaniment using the brush as a pretend pipe. In the end, we were both laughing so much we were in tears.

'Seriously, Lu,' he remarked as he wiped his eyes, 'sometimes I wonder who is supposed to be the parents in my family and who is supposed to be the children. Crikey, he's done them well!' he turned back to the painting.

'Aye,' I agreed. 'Daid might not be good with the like of sums and reading and writing, but he knows how to paint.'

'He certainly does. The colour's magnificent.'

'Aye, he wanted it to glitter like Aladdin's cave.'

'Well, he succeeded. He doesn't miss much, does he?'

Again I agreed. 'He's quiet, my Daid is, but he notices everything. What is it makes you say that?'

'The facial expressions. I've seen my mother and step-father look at each other like that thousands of times. There he is: sceptical, amused, fascinated, charmed even; and there she is – my mother to a tee – beautiful, vulnerable, determined. And there's a fire in both of them. You know, ever since I can remember I've been trying to convince myself that my mother and step-father don't love each other. One look at that painting and I know I'm wrong. I only wish she didn't hate my own father so much,' he sighed.

'He hurt her.'

Wally nodded sadly. 'Oh well,' he shrugged. 'At least I'll be able to eat my dinner in peace. You don't know what it was like to see a scantily clad maiden looking straight at you every time you glanced up from your plate.'

'Well, now you'll have your folks to contend with. You can look up and see your mother instead: "Wally dear, don't put your peas on your knife. It's not proper,"' I tried to imitate Mrs Sotheby.

'I think I know how to handle that,' he laughed. 'I say, that's quite a tree. Fancy an orange?'

I did, but before I could speak my mind, he had walked outside and had begun to climb our orange tree.

'There's a good view up here,' he called. 'You can see nearly every back yard in the street.'

'I know,' I called up.

'How so?'

'I climbed it.'

Down he came.

'How so?' he asked again and guided me over to our garden seat. Then he spotted my wheelchair and, to my astonishment, he sat in it.

'This yours?' he asked.

'Well, 'tisn't the cat's.'

'Do you use it much?'

'When I need to and if I didn't wear boots and use crutches or callipers, I'd be in it for good.'

'So, tell me about the tree,' he prompted as he began to peel the orange and hand me segments.

'I was twelve at the time. 'Twas four years passed since the polio and my legs were getting stronger, so much so that I was starting to walk with only one brace. Well, I used to like sitting out here of an afternoon and one day I decided to see if I could climb the tree. I took the brace off my left leg, and by using my arms and my good leg, I managed to climb it. So after that I began to spend a good part of the afternoon up in the tree, which I liked because I could pick the oranges and watch all the comings and goings in the neighbourhood – you know, things like chickens scratching for worms, and children playing and mothers taking in the washing. Even better, I could hide from Mrs Murphy. Mrs Murphy, you see, would come out looking for me for to come and take my tea and she'd not find me. So, once I was sure she'd gone inside again, I'd climb down and appear in the garden as if nothing had happened.

'Well, one day I decided to stay up in the tree. Mrs Murphy came out looking as usual and of course she couldn't find me. Again she came out and again. All worried she became and off she hurried to fetch Daid from the studio. Daid came out and he called for me in a way I'd not heard since the day Mam died. 'Twas so frightened he sounded, Wally, that I knew I must climb down. But by then voices were playing in my head, for I remembered back to that terrible day. I think I blacked out for I lost my hold and fell. I broke my left leg in two places, wouldn't you know it, which put me in hospital for four months with plaster to my hip. 'Tis partly the reason why it's shorter than my right. Aye, 'twas a heavy price indeed to pay for a wee bit of freedom and in the end even that was denied me.'

Wally nodded. 'I know what you mean. I stole an auto for the same reason.'

'You did what?'

'I stole a motorcar. I don't know how much Della has told you but I've received most of my education at military school.'

'Aye, she told me that. 'Twas some posh school you boarded at was it not?'

'Posh?' he echoed, and I felt the full force of his irony. 'You call a school for the orphaned sons of soldiers posh? I was a Dukie and by some mysterious decree, I was to have a career in the army regardless of whether I wanted to or not. I always thought it had been a scheme cooked up by my mother and step-father to get me out of the house. I learned recently, however, it was my own father who'd made the arrangements, but that's another story.

'As you know,' he resumed, 'we emigrated out here only a couple of years ago. That is, the rest of the family came out. I was left behind to finish school and prepare for Sandhurst.'

'You weren't to join your family?'

Wally shook his head. 'That was it for me. It was one matter to be separated from Della during term, but it was another matter altogether to be separated from her for good. So I ran away from school. My intention was to travel down to the port, stowaway on a boat to France, find my father's grave, then travel to Australia to fetch Della and take her back to France to show her. After that, I was going to make my own way and take care of my sister. When I look back it was quite stupid really, but I remember thinking it all perfectly logical at the time.'

'And where does the car come into it?' I asked.

'You see,' he was quite pragmatic about it, 'I didn't really fancy the walk from school to the docks. I happened upon a motor so I decided to drive down instead.'

'And did you know how to drive?'

'No,' he shrugged and smiled a little at his achievement, 'but I had a pretty good idea by the time I arrived.'

'And then what happened? How far did you get?' I couldn't help but be impressed.

'They caught me trying to get out at Calais. I was apprehended there but the charges were dropped because I was under age. I got the sack instead. I suppose the school decided I wasn't officer material after all and that it was better if I were transported out here instead of trying to run off to France. It was intended to be a disgrace, but I didn't care. I got what I wanted. Besides, I didn't fancy a career in the army.'

'And why was that? Your da was a soldier. Did you not want to follow in his footsteps?'

'Not a bit. And I don't care how much of a hero he was. I didn't love my father because of that. I loved him because he was my father. I might be a son of the brave, but I'm not a fool. You see, Lu, where I went to school, every single chap who was there was so because his father fought in the War and either had been killed, maimed or incapacitated. We'd all lost our fathers in some way and, I'll tell you now, I'm not going to let that happen to any son of mine if I can help it. As for killing or maiming— I couldn't do that. It's— it's not in me to do that,' he halted and looked anxiously at me.

'To top it all off,' he continued, 'I used to have to play the bugle at military funerals. Apparently certain people find some morbid sentimental appeal in having a boy in a red jacket with gold braid and brass buttons tootle "The Last Post" when their soldier son or husband or father finally kicks the bucket. They don't bother asking what the bugler might be thinking or how many funerals he's played at the last few months or that he's lost his own father and was never allowed to mourn him. You know, they never even bothered to tell me he died, Lucy—' he broke off.

'What do you mean?'

'They never told me. My mother and step-father never talked about it and I was never permitted to mention it. All I had to go on was what my own father said to me the last time I saw him: that if he didn't come back it was because he had gone from this world forever. I only found out what really happened to him when I was at school.'

'And so you know how he died?'

'I chanced to read about it in a Sunday paper a few weeks after Della left England. It was one of those articles reminiscing about the War – you know, "We Remember Our Heroes of the Air" – that sort of thing. Well, there was a story about him. As a reconnaissance pilot he was one of the hidden heroes of the War. His job was to fly across enemy territory and photograph or telegraph information about positions, troop movement and artillery fire, which he had to do from quite low altitude. It was frightfully dangerous because he often came under attack himself, but it was important because they used the information he gathered to develop strategies and maintain communication.

'He was also involved in front line activity. In battle, he had to drop grenades on enemy forces ahead of advancing soldiers. Apparently he had a habit of finishing his sorties by doing a loop around a church tower before returning to base. Fritz soon got wise to it and planted a sniper in the tower. The sniper succeeded in bringing him down. He crashed and broke his back and died a few hours later. He was awarded the Royal Flying Cross posthumously, but I haven't got that medal. I suppose it was sent to his real family,' he added bitterly.

'Anyway, if there was another war,' he continued, 'I'd be faced with the same obligations. I don't want to live my life under a shadow like that and I don't particularly fancy the idea of being blown apart or having to blow other chaps apart, regardless of how noble the cause. Call me a coward, but that's the truth. Do you think I'm a coward?'

'For wanting to take charge of your life? Not at all. Sometimes it takes a lot of courage to make a decision like that. You're lucky you could make such a choice at all.'

'I gather that hasn't been your lot?'

'Well, I didn't exactly choose to have polio and spend the rest of my life in and out of that chair you're sitting in, if that's what you mean. Besides, choice or circumstance, the outcome is still the same: you've still to live with the consequences and I'm inclined to think it's how you handle the consequences is what's more important. And what will you do with yourself now you'll not be a soldier?'

'I did consider engineering. My father trained as an engineer and I like machines and buildings and bridges. Oddly enough, however, my step-father suggested I do medicine. He isn't such a bad sort, really. Anyway, I've been giving it some thought lately and I have to admit it rather appeals although I don't know what I'm going to do about Latin. I was never taught any Latin. I say, what's the sour look for?'

'Doctors,' I sneered.

'Blimey, I thought you of all people would have something positive to say.'

'Myself of all people? And why is that?'

'Well, for one, you'd probably be either dead or bedridden without them. I imagine you've had quite a lot to do with doctors.'

'Indeed, indeed. I been poked and prodded more times than I'd like to count. I been discussed behind screens, been weighed and measured, put in plasters and put in splints, been told to do this and do that, and not to do this and not to do that. And in the course of it all there's been little regard for myself. I could have been a cow or a pig as far as any doctors were concerned. It wouldn't have made much difference. Would you know that when the doctor put callipers on me for the first time I was so confused and frightened. I thought they were going to help me and instead there I was, locked up in leather straps and great shafts of steel. They were so heavy and I was so terribly thin I could hardly move. I asked the doctor how would I be able to dance? He was a great, fat, tall Scotsman and it took me every ounce of courage to speak. And do you know what he did? He laughed at me. "Dance?" he said, "Dance? You'll be lucky if you ever walk you little tyke!" He thought it was funny—'

'Hey! Hey! I didn't mean to make you upset. Don't cry. Here.' He handed me his handkerchief.

'Daid's been talking about seeing another doctor,' I sniffed. 'And Aunt Rose keeps suggesting. 'Twas another letter I received about it a few days ago. She knows of a doctor who might be able to fix my legs a little better.'

'But wouldn't you like to have your legs fixed?'

'And another operation, and more plaster and months in hospital and another ugly scar, and not much more to show for it than a pair of skinny legs and a horrible limp that everyone makes fun of?'

'But imagine being able to walk, being able to run and jump, perhaps even climb the tree again,' he began to enthuse in a very kindly tone. 'Imagine not having to use crutches or wear those irons you usually wear. Don't you want that or do you really want to spend the rest of your life with braces on your legs and dependent on wheelchairs and crutches?'

'And what does it matter to you I'd like to ask?' I blurted. 'Why do you be so concerned? Because I'm a medical problem you'd like to solve 'cause you fancy yourself a doctor now? Or is it because you wish I wasn't crippled the way I am? For I am, Wally Sotheby, I'm crippled and I'll always be crippled! Or is it that you really care about me myself? And if you do, why should you care so? Why? Why? Why should you care?'

Wally did not reply. He looked me straight in the eye with an expression that did not meet my challenge. In fact, he seemed hurt by my outburst and I began to regret what I had said.

'Why do you think, Lu?' he asked.

40

'Yoohoo, Lucy!'

I was on my way home from school the following afternoon when Mrs Murphy beckoned me over to her front gate.

'What is it, Mrs Murphy?' I asked.

'A lady called to see you but a quarter of an hour ago.'

'Who was it, Mrs Murphy?'

'Ooh, she was very glamorous and well-to-do, I can tell you that, dear. A bit like one of those film stars your friend Hilda prattles about. She gave her name. Now, what was it? A Mrs S—'

'Sotheby was it?'

'That's it! Mrs Sotheby. Now I told her you'd not yet come home from school and she said she had some business in town and would call back in a little while.'

'Well, well, well, a visit from Mrs Sotheby and without invitation too,' I said to myself as I opened our gate. 'Did she not know we received visitors on Wednesdays between two and four o'clock?'

'What on earth could I have done to merit a visit?' was my next thought as I took off my collar and tie and set about my usual routine of removing my right calliper before heading to the kitchen to make a cup of tea.

I was in the middle of threading my bootlaces when there sounded the awaited knock at the front door.

'Arrah! Will you hold on now?' I called.

There was another knock. Then Mrs Murphy made an announcement over the back fence.

'Will you tell her I'm coming?' I yelled back.

Finally, I managed to open the door, and there was Mrs Sotheby in her town clothes, replete with hat and coat, gloves and handbag.

'Good afternoon, Mrs Sotheby,' I welcomed her.

'Good afternoon, Lucy,' she nodded.

'Will you be coming inside? I was about to put the kettle on. Would you care for a cup of tea?'

'No thank you, Lucy,' she said as she entered, looking to her right and left as she did. 'I don't intend to stay long.'

What a relief!

'Aye, very well, ma'am,' I replied. 'As my da would say, a short visit is usually best is it not, and that not too often.'

Mrs Sotheby tightened her lips.

I arched an eyebrow.

'I have your costume for Wednesday's garden party,' she informed me. 'Where would be a suitable place to leave it?' Perhaps she thought our parlour provided the appropriate location, for she kept looking past me to the photographs above the fireplace.

''Tis in my bedroom you can put it,' I advised her, and stood a little more squarely in front of the parlour doorway. Surely a bedroom was where one put clothes.

'Very well.' And she tap-tap-tapped in her high heels out to our front porch and gave a nod to Hammond.

And so I was witness to the passage of no less than five boxes into my room. Out of the Bentley they came, up the steps, down the hall, into my bedroom and onto my bed.

'You have quite a pretty little house,' remarked Mrs Sotheby as she supervised the procedure.

'Aye,' I responded absently as I noted the size and shape of each of the parcels.

'Is that everything, Hammond?' she asked.

'It is, ma'am,' Mr Hammond nodded.

'Very good. We'll not trespass any more on your time, Lucy. Good afternoon.'

I stared at the pile of boxes on my bed. How could there possibly have been any more? Sighing, I sat and untied the ribbon on the smallest package. Inside was a pair of pale silk stockings, soft and sheer, hardly the type of stocking to wear with callipers.

'What was the woman thinking?' I wondered.

I opened the second of the boxes and pulled out a pair of knickers, also of silk, and prettily trimmed with lace. They were a far cry from the plain woollen or cotton undergarments I usually wore.

The dress itself was simply and elegantly made, with short sleeves cut on the bias and a Peter Pan collar. The fabric – a delicate ivory and very nearly white – was voile, and fell with clean, soft lines over a silk chemise.

A large, round box was home to a hat, also ivory, and a very different number it was from my wide-brimmed old straw which had performed long and faithful service in keeping freckles at bay. This hat was one of those fashionable pudding basin styles.

I put it on.

I had to admit, that however impractical it was as a defence against freckles, I liked the hat.

The last box was heavier than the others. Surely, it could not contain what I thought. I undid the string and had my suspicions confirmed. Inside was a pair of orthopaedic boots. They were not a sturdy, sensible brown, for the leather had been dyed to match the dress. The laces were satin ribbons and the built-up heel had been disguised in such a way that the boots almost looked elegant.

I did not know whether to cry or to throw the whole lot at the mirror. I was about to do both when I noticed Daid standing in the doorway.

'Did you know about this?' I demanded and held up the boot.

'Aye, I did,' he replied. ''Twas Mrs Sotheby telephoned me about a month ago. She wanted to know what you did about your shoes and I told her.'

'You did what? And why did you not tell myself?'

'Well, one look at you the way you're behaving at the moment should tell you the reason why.'

'It would have cost her a fortune! All this for a garden party? For a silly afternoon of tea and cake and small talk? The woman's mad!'

'I offered to pay for them, but the lady insisted upon doing it all. Besides, Luighseach, whatever the case, you'll not let your rough and Spartan manners and notions interfere with her pleasure. Can you not accept the gesture with the same grace and generosity as was put into the giving?'

'Generosity?' I scoffed. ''Tis nothing but vanity! 'Tis self-indulgent pride and vanity!'

'I'm thinking 'tis a little like Alexander the Great and the beggar,' Daid calmly persisted. 'For Mrs Sotheby's given according to the person she is.'

'And that's where the analogy ends, Da,' I answered back, 'for I'm not a beggar.'

Nevertheless, come Wednesday, I was obliged to put on the outfit. I smoothed the stockings over my scrawny legs, and as I did, I knew I could not bring myself to wear the callipers. I fitted the boots on my feet and tied the ribbons in pretty bows. I pulled myself up on my crutches and ventured across to the mirror. I expected to look silly and was astonished to find that I did not look so— well, so crippled if the truth must be told.

Daid knocked.

'Aye, you can come in now, Da,' I replied.

My father entered and I watched his reflection in the mirror.

'Luighseach,' he whispered and paused. 'Dear Mother in Heaven, you're all grown up, lass.'

'Do you think it's pretty, Da?'

''Tis much more than pretty,' he smiled. 'Well, lassie, whatever her faults, you cannot deny the lady's done you a grand favour. I wish I had the money to do for you the same way.'

'You're no needing, Da. I'd prefer your love to her lavishness a hundred times over.'

'And I'm glad to hear it. Still, will you let your da lavish a little love on you now? For I'm thinking we can improve things a bit. Come with me, Luighseach.'

I followed him into his room. On his bureau sat a box in which he kept his tie pins and cuff links, and from that box he pulled out a pouch. From the pouch he produced a delicate pearl ring which he slipped on my finger. Then he fastened round my neck a simple gold chain on which hung a gold crucifix.

'They're Mam's!' I whispered.

'Aye they are. I been saving them for you all these years and till now I never thought you old enough to wear them.'

'Oh, Da! Thank you!'

'We best be off, lass,' he said, returning my hug. 'I'll fetch your 'cello.'

We arrived at the Sotheby house and rang the bell. There was a shout of 'I'll get it!' and someone thundered down the stairs. The front door was flung open to reveal none other than Wally.

For one brief moment, our eyes met.

'Oh, I—!' But Wally could say little more than that. Out came a tangle of words. 'Giving— hand— late— Invasion. Break a leg—Sorry! I mean—Well, you know— All best!' Then all of a sudden his military manners returned. He came to attention and tipped his boater. 'Morning, Mr Straughan,' he said, and ran down the steps and along the drive as fast as he could.

'Was that Wally?' inquired Mrs Sotheby. She knew perfectly well it was and shook her head disparagingly. 'Do come in. I thought you might like some refreshment, Lucy, before you begin.'

She escorted us to the dining room.

There were cheers when we entered.

'Oh Mr Straughan, it's beautiful!' squealed Della. Accompanying her exclamation was a glow of deep thanks from Phoebe and a nod of approval from Pim. 'Every evening we're transported to an Arabian paradise!'

Daid blushed a little and smiled to himself as he viewed his painting in its proper setting.

'I had the drapes changed,' Mrs Sotheby informed him. 'They simply had to complement the picture. After all, it's a little more purply than the other one.'

Nellie escorted us past the marquee, which had been erected on the back lawn for the occasion, to the summerhouse.

'I hope, Miss Della, it's been arranged to your liking,' she said. 'Master Wally insisted on setting it up himself before he left for school.'

'Wally did it?' asked Della. 'Oh dear. Watch out, everyone! Nellie, I do hope he wasn't up to one of his pranks.'

Nellie began to laugh.

'I'm sorry, miss, but the thought of that poor piglet running through all them ladies and Mr Hammond diving after it—'

'That was last year's trick,' explained Della. 'Wally truanted. Don't ask me how, but he managed to get his hands on a baby pig which he smeared with lard and set loose on the lawn. Needless to say, Mummy wasn't pleased.'

This time, however, there were no pranks. The four chairs and four wooden stands had all been perfectly positioned. On each of the stands lay a long-stemmed white rose. Pim immediately picked up hers, put it between her teeth and swept an unsuspecting Della into a tango. Round and round the summerhouse they paraded, with Pim singing 'Jalousie' and making silly dips and swift, smooth turns. Phoebe quickly took up the tune on her violin and I responded with an accompaniment on the 'cello, marvelled at the beauty of my rose and wished with all my heart that I could dance again.

'Della!' Mrs Sotheby appeared. 'I thought I had engaged a quartet, not a band. The guests are arriving. Really, darling! '

'Well, here we go! Play it all, and play it all again,' Della smiled, echoing Mrs Epstein's words of advice.

'Where is Mrs Ep, by the way?' asked Pim.

'She said she wasn't invited,' replied Phoebe.

Della blushed.

'She said she wouldn't have come anyway,' Phoebe added. 'Don't ask me why. What's so funny, Lucy?'

'I think I know the reason,' I could not stop smiling at the bright clusters of ladies now parading into the back garden. 'To be sure there would be nearly a hundred versions of your mother out there, Delleen.'

'And they all look splendid,' came Della's mild retort. 'Let's start with the *Lark*'.

We had every right to feel proud of ourselves. Since coming together we had succeeded in learning five Haydn quartets, the Borodin and sundry light arrangements (sight-reading pieces which Mrs Epstein deemed suitable for garden parties). All were played and played again. Ladies wearing fancy hats and costumed in rainbows of silks wandered past and occasionally paused from their conversations to listen. In the distance could be heard a rival performance, for Kismet, Della's canary, seemed to delight in pitting his song against Della's violin. All in all, it could not have been more idyllic: dappled sunshine, the garden in full bloom, the lawn soft and green, and the most comforting of breezes ensuring that pleasant did not become unendurably hot. It was perfect for playing quartets, not to mention enjoying a day off school.

'Beg your pardon, Miss Della,' said Nellie when we finished our second run through the *Kaiser*, 'but your mother asked me to tell you you're to finish up and come and have something to eat.'

'Hooray!' replied Della. 'I don't know about you lot, but I'm positively wrecked. How long have we been going?'

'Just shy of three hours,' answered Pim as she looked at her wrist watch.

'Have we really?'

We were in the middle of packing our instruments when there appeared an exceedingly well-dressed woman whose striking costume and jewellery seemed quite at odds with her mild bearing and manner.

'Why, hello Mrs Mahony,' beamed Della.

'Della, how are you, dear? It's been so lovely listening to you all play,' she lisped and smiled sweetly. 'How lucky your mother is! I wish Fanny could have learned to play like you. Celia tries but it seems none of my daughters have any aptitude for music, I'm afraid. And how are you, Pim? How nice it was to see Rose again in such a short time and isn't it exciting about the baby? How is Lily? Mr Mahony and I had a marvellous weekend at Balmoral last summer and I must remember to book another before you get too busy. Now, you must be Lucy. How do you do? Fanny has told me so much about you.'

I raised an eyebrow in reply. 'And none of it good, I bet,' I thought to myself.

'It seems you've settled very well into life at St Dom's. Are you enjoying school?' she nodded and smiled.

'Aye, I am,' I answered and smiled back. 'And no thanks to your daughter, I can tell you that,' I added silently.

'Have you met Phoebe, Mrs Mahony?' Della glanced at me and immediately decided it would be better to direct Mrs Mahony's interests elsewhere. Della knew very well what my smile meant.

'It's Phoebe Raye, isn't it? Well, Phoebe, it appears you play the violin as well as you play the piano. It was such a lovely concert, Della, before the picnic. How do you do, Phoebe,' she nodded at Phoebe and studied her thoughtfully. 'Phoebe Raye. Well I never!'

'Do I know you?' Phoebe stared hard at her.

Mrs Mahony gave a small laugh. 'Well, if you do, darling, you have a very good memory indeed. The last time I was introduced to you, you were a curly haired tot in the prettiest of pinafores who picked me a posy of daisies. How like your mother you are! And then again—'

'Did you know my mother?' Phoebe had no time for niceties.

'Yes dear, we're friends from way back. How is she? Is she here today?' Mrs Mahony looked around blithely and seemed a little puzzled that she had actually missed someone.

'No she isn't,' Phoebe's sharp retort put a halt to her survey. 'And you can't have been a very good friend of hers because otherwise you would have known she's dead.'

'Oh! Oh, my dear girl! I'm so terribly sorry,' Fanny's mother faltered. 'When did that happen? Oh, your poor father!'

'Do— do you know my father?'

'Why yes, dear,' Mrs Mahony smiled in a kind way. 'I met him many years ago. Oh, it must be terribly hard for him. How is he?'

'I *don't know*. Excuse me please.' And Phoebe pushed her way out of the summerhouse.

'Oh my goodness! I really had no idea! I didn't mean to upset her,' Mrs Mahony was genuinely troubled. 'Please excuse me, Della, and you, Pim. It was lovely to meet you, Lucy, and you must come and visit. I don't know why Fanny hasn't yet invited you – it's terribly remiss of her. And thank you for such lovely music.'

Della sadly shook her head as she watched Mrs Mahony walk back to the party. 'Something tells me we're not going to be doing any more playing this afternoon,' she sighed.

Pim, however, had other plans.

'Yes we are. I'm going to find Phoebe,' she announced, and headed out to the garden.

It was not long before she returned, racing across the lawn with Phoebe running behind her.

'Give it back! Give it back!' called Phoebe. 'You're a mean bully! You think that because you're head girl you can do anything you want. Give it back!'

'She was smoking behind the shed,' reported Pim.

'Oh Phoebe, I thought you'd stopped all that,' Della remonstrated.

'How'd you get your hands on them?' Pim demanded. 'Mrs Ep certainly didn't give them to you. Where'd you get the money?'

She had to repeat her questions before Phoebe answered.

'I bought them with my return train fare.'

'But Phoebe, how were you going to get home?' asked Della, her concerns taking a different course to Pim's.

'Walk, of course,' replied Phoebe. 'How else was I going to get home?'

'From Strathfield to Petersham?' Della was incredulous.

'I can walk if I want, can't I?'

'You got any more?' Pim remained distrustful and she opened Phoebe's violin case and began to search through it.

'What do you think you're doing?' Phoebe ran into the summerhouse and tried, unsuccessfully, to stop her. Pim, meanwhile, managed to locate three more cigarettes hidden in a compartment. 'And I bet you weren't going to tell Mrs Ep either,' she concluded. 'How could you? Mrs Ep has barely a brass razoo to rub together and you go pinching the money she gave you in good faith for the sake of your dirty habit.'

'Why can't I have a cigarette if I need one?' protested Phoebe.

'You don't need a cigarette. You need to face life, that's what you need.'

'Don't you think she's faced enough of life already, Pim?' Della objected.

'No I don't,' Pim argued back. 'And whatever more there is to face, she's going to do it without a cigarette between her fingers. You're coming with me.'

'W—What are you going to do?' Phoebe watched as Pim shoved violin and viola in their respective cases and gathered and stuffed music into bags.

'I'm going to take you home, that's what I'm going to do. And I'm not lending you the money for your fare because I can't be sure you'll go off and buy some more fags and abuse my trust as well.'

'You're not going to tell Mrs Epstein, are you?'

'I might if I think I have to,' Pim cautioned as she thrust upon Phoebe her battered case and the ribbon she used to bind it closed. 'But I'm not going to dob you in and abandon you either. It's bad enough you losing your parents. You're not going to lose your friends as well. Come on. We'll get something to eat on the way out. Guess you were right, Dell. See you two at school tomorrow.'

She grabbed Phoebe by the hand and pulled her out of the summerhouse. Della and I wearily watched them leave: Pim at full stride, Phoebe half running to keep up and simultaneously begging her to slow her pace.

'Hungry?' asked Della as we packed the last of our things.

'Like the wolf's at my door, Delleen.'

'Come on, then. Let's see what they've left us. Oh dear!'

'What is it, Delleen?' Della was unable to hide her pain.

'Oh, it's a funny ache in my back.'

'Do you need to lie down?'

'No, no,' she politely declined my advice and at the same time tried to alleviate her trouble by swinging her arms. 'It must have been all that sitting and playing. A little walk will do me good. I tell you what, let's pile up a plate, take it inside and have our own private feast.'

We wove through all the silks and hats, nodded and smiled at the compliments and did our best to avoid being detained from reaching our destination: the marquee where there was laid out platter upon platter of sandwiches, slices, cakes and pastries.

'Oh, I say! Scrummy! Cook's made choux pastry swans!' Della helped herself to a plate. 'What would you like, old thing?'

'One of everything, if you please, Delleen.'

'Luighseach, I don't know how you manage to eat so much and stay so thin. Listen, why don't you go up to the house and find us a spot and I'll follow with the food.'

The most secluded place turned out to be the front parlour. It was a charming, chintzy room, filled with flowers and other items selected for the exclusive entertainment of Della's mother: a wireless and gramophone, a bureau, a tea set and tea trolley, and a work basket in which, to my surprise, I found some very skilful embroidery. I took a seat on a large padded lounge, picked up the copy of *The Home* that lay on the coffee table, briefly tried on the spectacles used by the lady of the house to read the contents, then leant back and amused myself by pretending to be Mrs Sotheby enjoying a moment of solitude.

The door opened.

It was not, however, Della who entered.

I remained on the lounge and listened.

'I do hope I didn't upset her too much, but Letty, I really had no idea,' Mrs Mahony lisped and sniffed. 'And I can't understand why I wasn't told for we were friends and I should have liked to have gone to her funeral. But it was so very hard after the War, particularly once Pat came back. I thought I had it tough, but poor Juliette! Poor Roderick! You know, dear, it may sound callous, but it would have been better if some of them had never come back, although it must have been terribly hard for you, dear, when Ralph died.'

'Frankly, Julia, it was a relief,' I heard Mrs Sotheby reply. 'But everything usually happens for the best, doesn't it? One simply has to get on with one's life. In many ways, it's been harder on the children than it has been on me. Wally, in particular, has had a very difficult time of it.'

'I can imagine it would be hard for a son to lose his father. But daughters need their fathers, too. It hasn't been at all easy for Fanny and Sissy either. I suppose it's my fault. I was so busy with Pat trying to get things back to normal again I simply couldn't spend as much time with the girls as I should. Poor Fanny still resents the fact that her father's missing a leg, and Sissy and Angela always follow her lead. They can't abide the wooden one and yet they won't go near him when he doesn't wear it. The younger ones don't mind. They're rather amused that their father can take his leg off. Really, I think that little Kitty, Betty and Tessie have done more for Pat than anyone. He simply adores them.'

'He's done so well, dear. Why, he even plays tennis. If you had never told me, I never would have known.'

'It's been ten long years, Letty.'

'You've done wonders, darling.'

'But poor, dear Juliette! Oh Letty, they were such a handsome couple. And the wedding! Darling! Why I remember it as if it were yesterday, probably because it was the last wedding of any consequence before the War. I mean, when the War broke out, things became so frightfully austere.'

'I know, dear. We were terribly fortunate that Desmond had contacts in the East because I don't know what I would have done about a gown. And the lengths we had to go to get a cake! Do tell about the wedding.'

'It was something out of a fairy tale. Seriously, Letty, it could have been Oberon and Titania themselves being married. Juliette always had the most gorgeous curls and he was so dashing— rather slight for a man but so delightfully bohemian. Although I'm sure she was expecting. She had that glow about her. And she wore the Empire line which was so very fashionable at the time. Now when was the Baptism? Why, it was later than usual for little Phoebe was already toddling. But then Juliette was always quite blasé about church things— at least she was at the time— so it wouldn't surprise me if she *had* put the cart before the horse. And it was so different from the wedding! I suppose it was the War, but still one would expect the Christening to be the jewel in the crown of the first anniversary. Letty, she was frightfully moody. Roderick was in uniform and that was odd too. He did look stylish, though, in breeches and with that hat. They all wore it with such a tilt. But to me he didn't seem the type to join up. I mean, he wasn't the adventurous sort and he certainly wasn't political— at least not that way. He was probably more of a Socialist if anything. But then one never knows what some people are capable— Why Della dear!'

'Really, Della,' Mrs Sotheby scolded. 'Must you barge in like that? One should always knock before entering a room.'

'I do beg your pardon, Mrs Mahony. I beg your pardon, Mummy,' Della apologised. 'I thought—'

'And what are you doing with all that food?' demanded Mrs Sotheby.

'I—I thought Luighseach might be here.'

'Lucy!' Mrs Sotheby hissed. 'I might have known. No. Lucy is not here.'

I determined that if I did not own up where I was who knows how long it would be before I could sample a choux pastry swan.

I cleared my throat and peeped round the lounge.

Mrs Mahony nudged Mrs Sotheby and nodded in my direction. 'Heavens!' she giggled. 'A chiel's amang ye takin' notes! Oh dear, Letty, perhaps we were the ones who should have knocked.'

'Really, Julia!' Mrs Sotheby did not have quite the same sense of humour as her friend. 'And in my own house!'

41

'What else have you in there?' inquired Pim of Della's lunchbox at morning tea the next day.

'Let me see,' Della perused her box, 'A slice of Dundee cake, some petits fours and a few pieces of ginger shortbread. Care for any?'

'Dundee cake for me, thanks.'

'What about you, Luighseach?' Della offered me her box.

I helped myself to a piece of ginger shortbread.

'Do you mind, Delleen?'

'Not at all. You're saving me face. Cook won't be pleased if that lunch box comes home with food untouched.'

'You didn't eat much,' I observed. All Della had eaten was a cucumber sandwich, and a little potted salmon which she spread on Melba toast.

'To be quite honest,' she shrugged, 'I'm not very hungry. Besides, if I ate as much as the two of you, I would be a little round ball. By the way, Pim, Mrs Epstein telephoned this morning and asked me to pass you a message: No rehearsal this afternoon. Phoebe's sick.'

'I'm not surprised,' Pim commented.

'Poor little thing,' sighed Della. 'What happened? You got her home safely, didn't you?'

'Safe enough,' replied Pim, 'although I thought she might do something stupid on the train. She didn't, thank goodness. She was pretty quiet. Who knows what was going on in her head but. Anyway, I got her to Mrs Ep's. Mrs Ep took one look at her and asked her what the matter was. Oddly enough, Phoebe left it to me to explain.

'Well, I was in the middle of telling Mrs Ep what happened with Mrs Mahony when she started to mutter. She kept on saying the same thing over and over: "I'm not going back! I'm not going back!" Before we knew what had hit us, she was out of control, screaming and throwing whatever was in reach. It took the two of us to pin her down. Then I had to fetch the doctor. Didn't get back to school till tea.'

I received an updated account after my 'cello lesson the following Monday evening. Normally Phoebe opened the door for me when I arrived and she tended to appear later in my lesson to accompany me on the piano. That evening I saw her not at all and I missed her.

'She's asleep, Luighseach,' Mrs Epstein explained. 'The doctor gave her medicine to keep her calm.'

'Nearly a whole week she's been absent from school, Mrs Epstein.'

She's getting better, Luighseach, but she's terrified of going back. Mrs Sotheby made a few remarks concerning what happened which I won't bother you with at present, but all I can get out of Phoebe is that the mother of one of the girls in her class knows "everything" and now "everyone" will know and no one will leave her alone. Do you have any idea what she is carrying on about?'

''Tis something about her da, I'm thinking, Mrs Epstein. Nothing upsets Phoebe Raye more than talking about her da.'

'I see,' nodded Mrs Epstein. 'Has there been any nastiness at school? Towards Phoebe, I mean?'

'Not much of late,' I replied, 'but she's been teased badly in the past so she told me. She stays with Della and Pim and myself most lunch times – that is, when the nuns don't tell her off for not playing with girls her own age.'

'I see,' Mrs Epstein said again as she saw me out. 'Well, Luighseach, I think the time has finally come.'

'For what, Mrs Epstein?'

'For setting the cat among the pigeons. I'll see you on Thursday.'

I arrived at Mrs Epstein's on Thursday a little later than everyone else. Mrs Epstein showed me inside and I was pleased at last to see Phoebe sitting in her usual chair with Della and Pim.

'Ho, ho!' welcomed Pim. 'Two truants! She was practising piano,' she gestured in Phoebe's direction. 'What's your excuse?'

'Let you hold your tongue, Pimmy Connolly. 'Twas nothing of truanting, I'm saying, for 'twas a doctor's appointment in town I was at, if you're needing to know.'

'Everything all right, old thing?' asked Della after a tentative pause.

'Aye.'

'So what's he going to do? Put you on a rack and torture you?' Pim teased.

'And 'twould not be the first time, Pimmy Connolly. This one's a new doctor and 'twas but a few notes he was taking today and I'll be going back for an assessment next week.'

'Well, you sound unusually chipper about it,' Della remarked with some relief.

'To tell you the truth, he was very kind, and for once I wasn't a pair of polio legs,' I replied as I pulled my 'cello from its case. 'Would you know one of the first things he said to me was, "Now I reckon you'd like to walk as well as you can play your 'cello". Apparently he came to your concert, Pimmy.'

'Ah, you saw Dr Little,' responded Pim, who of course proceeded to add the necessary particulars. 'Noticed your dad having a bit of a yarn to him that afternoon. Aunt Rose worked with him during the War. He started courting her afterwards but she ended up marrying one of his patients instead. He's been a friend of the family ever since. So, what did he say?'

'Well, he wasn't going to promise anything but he'd see what he could do, and I'm telling you even that's better than "Circulation's poor", "Left leg's flail. Lucky she can walk at all". And 'tis always "she" you know, whether I'm in the room or not. You'd think I was the mother of the bleeding cat the way they talk.'

'And I do believe you always refer to doctors as "they" or "them",' teased Della.

'That's very encouraging news, Luighseach,' enjoined Mrs Epstein. 'And I have some more. Apart from one small incident, Mrs Sotheby was delighted with last Wednesday's entertainment. Well girls,' she rubbed her hands, 'I'm pleased to say I have another engagement for you. Are you all free on Sunday afternoon?'

We nodded. Mrs Epstein knew Phoebe was available, and, apart from a few minor alterations to Pim's commitments, Sunday afternoon was convenient for the rest of us.

'Good,' Mrs Epstein concluded in her most cut-and-dry fashion. 'I've arranged for you to play at the veteran's hospital in North Sydney. Not quite so appealing as a garden party, I dare say, but Mr Epstein and I play there on a regular basis and I know from first hand that your efforts will not go unappreciated.'

Silence followed.

'We'll need to take a ferry across the harbour and catch the tram from McMahon's Point,' Mrs Epstein proceeded to discuss travel arrangements. 'Now, Luighseach, I know you have a little trouble with the tram but I have assured your father we will give you whatever help you need…'

Tram? Who cared about the tram? We were going to play in a hospital. Why did Mrs Epstein have to ask me to do that?

I hated hospitals and anything remotely connected with them. But, despite my antipathy to the idea, I knew full well that I could have spent the rest of my days in such a place. And I also knew how much music mattered when my pains and sorrows were more than I could bear. As a result, much as I disliked my teacher's proposition, I could not in conscience utter the word she least liked to hear.

Neither, it seemed, could Della nor Pim. Pim gave ready and thoughtful assent, while Della nodded gravely. Phoebe sat in silence and did not move.

'Luighseach?' Mrs Epstein sought my attention. 'Are you coming?'

I glared my assent.

'Good,' continued Mrs Epstein. 'Now, can you arr—'

'No,' said Phoebe.

'I beg your pardon?' Mrs Epstein faced her.

'I said, no.'

'And I say you're going to play.'

'I am not.'

'He wants to see you, Phoebe.'

'How would you know?'

'Who wants to see her?' asked Pim.

'Phoebe's father resides in that home,' explained Mrs Epstein.

'Do you mean to say your—' Pim began, her temper rising.

'No, Pim, not now,' implored Della.

But Phoebe was more than prepared to take her on.

'Yes,' she snapped. 'I do mean to say that my father lives in *that* home.'

'What? Your father lives only a few miles away and you haven't seen him for how long?'

'Seven years. I haven't seen my father for seven—'

'You selfish little—'

'Brat,' concluded Phoebe. 'Yes, you're right. I am. I am a selfish little brat, aren't I? I must be, because all this time I haven't bothered to visit my father despite him living so close. But that's typical of you, isn't it, Pim? Always so quick to jump to conclusions and pass judgements about me you've no right to make! Did it ever occur to you that the reason why I haven't seen my father is because *he* doesn't want to see *me*? You see, I don't belong to a big family like you do and my father doesn't have the good fortune to have a family to care for him the way your father does, Pim. Your father might be sick and frail and hardly able to talk, but anyone can tell that he's spent his life for you and your mother and your brothers and your sisters, and you in turn will spend yourselves for him. The only person my father has left is me and he doesn't want me. And the only reason he married my mother was because she was expecting me. I'm a brat he wanted to be rid of so he used the War as a ticket to France. He left my mother for his mistress – yes, his mistress – who was none other than her sister, my aunt.'

'Phoebe—' Della pleaded.

'As for you, Della,' Phoebe turned on her. 'Your father was lucky. He met his death in that war. Just as well he was shot down. You yourself said how terrible it would have been if he'd returned maimed or blind or disfigured. Well, my father did come back and he hasn't got any legs, he's crippled in one arm and he has a horrible scar on his face. How would your mother have coped if your father had come back like that? My mother killed herself. My dear, sweet mother took her own life!

'And you, Lucy,' she continued, facing me, her face flushed and angry, 'you might have some idea what it is not to be able to do a thing for yourself, but at least you're not disfigured. You might be crippled but you can still get about, and you have both your hands. My father's life is a wheelchair wasteland. As for your father, a sweeter, kinder person could not be found this side of Heaven. What do you know of bitterness and hate when in spite of everything you've been surrounded by people who love you? What would you know of that? Your father would never shout at you, he would never throw things at you and hurt you and tell you never to set eyes on him again, would he? Would he? But my father, my father…'

And Phoebe crumpled into tears.

'He hit me!' she cried. 'My daddy threw a crucifix at me and it hit me. It hit me in the eye. It nearly blinded me!'

She wept and wept. Her curls convulsed as each sob heaved with grief.

'Hey,' Pim took her in her arms. 'Hey,' she soothed and stroked her curls. 'Hey,' she crooned and pressed her close.

'He told me to get out and they said I was not to come back,' Phoebe continued to sob. 'I'm the cause of his misery!'

'Phoebe,' Della spoke quietly, 'how could you possibly be the cause of his misery?'

'Because if I had never been born he would never have married my mother and if he had never married my mother he would never have gone to war and if he had never gone to war he would never have been wounded and if he—'

'Had never been wounded who knows what would have happened?' Mrs Epstein stopped her short. 'But it didn't happen like that did it? It is the way it is. And the way it is, is very different from the way you think. I don't know exactly what people have been saying, Phoebe, but you are very wrong about your father. Yes, he made his mistakes, we all have, but mistakes can be fixed, can't they? However things were at first, your father grew to love you. He loved you even when he hurt you. He was sick and he didn't know what he was doing. He loves you still, Phoebe, and he wants to see you.'

'How could you possibly know?' Phoebe angrily sniffed.

'He told me so,' Mrs Epstein replied.

'Wh—Why should he tell you?' she questioned.

'Because I have visited him week in and week out for the past seven years.'

'You what?' Phoebe rubbed her eyes in disbelief. 'Why should you do that? What business do you have with him?'

'No business, Phoebe,' answered Mrs Epstein. 'He's a friend. A very dear friend, if you really must know.'

Our teacher knelt in front of her and took her hands.

'Listen to me. Your father and I go back a long way,' she explained. 'I know him very well and I know that, whatever he may have done and whatever people have said about him, you are not to blame. Whatever part we have to play in the Great Fugue that is Life, we each of us are responsible for our own actions, and it is deeply unjust for anyone to make a scapegoat of another, especially when that person is only a child. Like the rest of us, your father has his faults, but he's a good man, Phoebe, a wonderful man.'

'And you wait till now to tell me this?' Phoebe queried. 'Why?'

'Because it's taken all this time to get him well again,' Mrs Epstein replied. 'He's been terribly sick. As for you, who knows how you would have coped had I told you earlier? You're so young and you've been so deeply hurt. But you can bear it now; you're ready now, for I know you are not alone,' and she looked at us one by one. 'He wants to see you.'

Pim was the first to speak.

'You know, Phoebe,' she began, awkwardly clearing her chest in the process, 'I made the mistake of shunning someone I loved – my own sister, in fact. And I shunned her not only because she did something wrong but because I loved her and admired her and she let me down. But I was most in the wrong because I did nothing to make things right. Instead I bore the grudge and rejected her when I should have helped her. We're reconciled now and we're both the happier for it. So, whatever your father's done or whatever's happened to him he has to live with, and he's lived with it a long time, but it doesn't mean he has to suffer alone, nor does it mean you can't forgive him. Believe you me, while you still breathe, there's always time to forgive.'

'I know my father died and he died a hero's death,' observed Della, 'but hero though he may have been, Phoebe, he treated my mother shamefully. He went to his grave with those sins, and although he tried to make amends, my poor mother shunned him. She will never hear from his own lips how sorry he was. What would her life have been if she had? Certainly, she seems to have a happy time of it and my step-father is very good to her, but it's a life that's buoyed up by parties and pretty things. Even to this day she's angry and hurt and she can barely live with my dear brother because of it. And how it has hurt him! But it doesn't have to be like that. Truly it doesn't. Please give him a chance to put things right.'

'Phoebe,' I remembered the time she called on me in the dead of night. 'You said to me once that you couldn't understand why your mother died without hope when she had yourself. Well, I'm thinking that perhaps the reason why your father still lives is because he has you. I said back then that you were still your mother's hope and I'm saying now 'tis yourself that is your father's. You need to be that hope, Phoebe.

'And you love your daid. All the snippets you've told me about him tell me you love him very much. You were upset when he was taken away from you and you said yourself he was very sick. You couldn't understand why people said horrible things about him or why your prayers for him were never answered. Well, perhaps your prayers were answered for it seems as if your da's coming back to you and you can love him all over again. Hopefully in the process you'll find out the truth, for the truth is what you need to know to make things right.

'That same night we were talking you asked me why it was that nobody loved you. Well, a lot of people love you, and I think you know that now. But you also know what it is not to be loved. Perhaps your father feels the same way. I've been horrible to people in my time, mainly because I was hurt and sad and lonely and crippled, but in spite of all that they kept on caring. You're one of those people, Phoebe, and I love you very much indeed. You helped me. I'll have to own you helped me in the oddest way, but help me you did. Perhaps your da feels like that too, and if that's so, then he needs you. Phoebe, you can help your father. We'll all help, will we not?'

'Of course we will,' resolved Della.

'But he told me to go away and they stopped me from seeing him,' Phoebe persisted.

'And now he's asking you to come back,' replied Mrs Epstein.

42

The recreation room at the hospital was filled with men. Some sat alone, others were accompanied by family or friends employed in cheery condolence. Faces cradling the last vestiges of youth were speared with pain, some pieced together by doctors of doubtful sanity so it appeared. There were lipless apertures for mouths, and what were once noses had been remade into misshapen projections for which 'nose' seemed an inappropriate term. There were men who were merely headed torsos, with eyes that questioned the future and retold the horrors and dim joys of the past without the aid of words. Others, sightless, trusted in the touch of comforting hands.

'Same as the garden party: an afternoon's light entertainment,' advised Mrs Epstein. 'Play everything. Once through will suffice. No repeats.'

We arranged our chairs and stands, organised our music and began to tune.

'Is your father here?' asked Della.

Phoebe studied her surrounds a little more carefully and shook her head. 'I don't think so. But I cannot make the faces out very well from here,' she sighed.

'What does he look like? Apart from missing a few bits,' asked Pim.

'Like a gypsy.'

'I suppose we should start,' Della suggested. 'What first?'

'Well, guess we're not playing the *Kaiser*,' Pim joked.

'Pim!' scolded Della. 'Let's do the light stuff. Once we're warmed up, what about the *Fifths*?'

Phoebe wrinkled her nose. She had never liked that piece.

'Very well. You win. *Sunrise* again,' Della sighed.

I had never played so badly. Crochet rugs kept catching my eye and the memories conjured by the smell of disinfectant and bleach made me sick. Led by headstrong nerves, my fingers were intent upon following a treacherous path of their own devising rather than that other well-paved way of notes which resulted, much to my embarrassment, in a horribly clumsy entrance in the first movement.

I could not continue.

'What's up, old thing?' asked Della.

'There are so many of them,' I replied as I wiped my eyes. 'I'm used to thinking of myself being the only one hard up like that, but—' and I shook my head and bit my lip as I watched a man younger than my father stagger and shake his way across the room. I never thought I would say I was lucky, but from that point I considered myself very lucky indeed.

'Would you be minding if we started again?' I asked.

We did not deserve the applause we received when we finished. We looked for Mrs Epstein and were relieved to find she was not in the room.

Our teacher did not reappear until we were half way through the *Fifths*. Phoebe immediately stiffened and lost her place.

'That him?' Pim whispered and made an indication with her viola.

Phoebe nodded.

Mrs Epstein was pushing a dark haired man in a wheelchair. She set the chair in a far corner, sat next to him and lit him a cigarette. They were obviously very well acquainted for there was between them a brevity of gesture and glance they each clearly understood. After the *Fifths* we began the Borodin. Occasionally they would pause from their conversation and listen, then he would make a remark and she would nod in her careful, thoughtful way. Then they would listen again, intently, and Mrs Epstein would lean across and ask him something. From the length and earnestness of his reply, I had the impression he knew what he was talking about.

Once we finished, Mrs Epstein stood and beckoned us to come over.

'Here goes,' said Pim. 'You ready?' she asked Phoebe.

'Do you think everything will be all right?'

'Don't you worry. We'll make it all right.'

'I'm warning you,' Mrs Epstein whispered before she introduced us. 'He can be caustic. Take him with a very large pinch of salt.'

Phoebe's father was a small, lean man. What was left of his legs was covered by a blanket, and his useless right arm had been carefully positioned on the arm of the chair. All that could be seen of his good left arm was his hand. It was finely formed, curiously well manicured, clean and capable, and it seemed to hold all the power in the world. I expected his face to be monstrous. Certainly, it was a little scarred down the right side, but the scars had faded with the years. The other side, however, was handsome and keen, and there was a hint of the orient in his bright eyes and high cheekbones.

We were introduced.

'I got mine at Bellicourt. Where'd you get yours?' he asked me when I shook his hand, and he indicated my legs with a raise of an eyebrow and a nod of his head.

'Luighseach had Polio when she was eight,' Della rallied to my defence.

'Well don't expect any sympathy from me however you got them,' he replied, looking straight at me, challenging me to reply.

'I don't,' I said.

Pim was presented.

'Viola player,' he scoffed. 'You don't only look like a tank. You play like one.'

'Consider it a compliment,' muttered Mrs Epstein to the surprised Pim.

He stroked his moustache, which was artfully shaped and pencil thin, and glanced at Della. Before Mrs Epstein could speak, he began a little more genially:

'Ah, the first violinist! Opus Seventy-six, Number Two, first movement: tell me, to which key do we modulate at the end of the exposition?'

Della hesitated. It was not the question she expected.

'F major,' she politely and cautiously replied.

'F major it is,' he agreed. 'It's not E sharp, nor is it G double flat; and B flat is B flat, not a flat B,' he added, picking on her intonation. 'And tell me something more: why are you so intent upon making every phrase sound beautiful?'

'Roddy—' Mrs Epstein cautioned.

'Bah, get her off that Haydn crap and give her some Schoenberg. Then we'll see what she's really made of. As for that romantic Russian garbage,' he snorted and gestured in my direction, 'too much limelight on the 'cello. So you think you're pretty good, do you?' he addressed his daughter for the first time.

Phoebe, shocked and nervous, was unable at first to speak.

'Well? Do you or not?'

Phoebe decided to be truthful and nodded.

'If you're any daughter of mine, you should,' he remarked. 'Bet you've learnt the first violin part too.'

He watched her blush.

'At least your instrument's good. I'll give you that.'

'A workman's only as good as his tools,' Phoebe managed a retort.

Her reply was met with a laconic smile.

'You know what they say about string quartets, don't you?' his manner softened somewhat.

We looked at each other. What trap was he setting us now? One by one we shook our heads and confessed that we did not know what they said, whoever 'they' were.

'Hasn't she taught you anything?' his teasing was now directed towards Mrs Epstein. 'A string quartet,' he sighed, and assumed the air of a professor on a final weary attempt to deliver a simple explanation to a class of backward students, 'A string quartet is comprised of four players. Three are violinists. There's a good violinist, who plays first violin,' and he nodded at Della and smiled in a very self-satisfied way. 'Then there's a mediocre violinist who plays second violin.'

'I'm not mediocre!' protested Phoebe.

'The jibe is at my expense, I assure you, Phoebe,' Mrs Epstein inserted.

'Thirdly, we have a very bad violinist,' Mr Raye continued. 'Viola,' he added, curling his lip and arching an eyebrow at Pim, who laughed at the truth of his statement. 'And finally there's a cellist who hates all violins,' and he gleamed at me, his eyes shimmering with delight and fury.

But I did not laugh with the others. In response, he looked away from me and instead turned his gaze towards Phoebe's violin. For a brief moment I saw his fingers move. At first I thought it was a nervous twitch. It wasn't. His fingers moved as they would if they were placed on a fingerboard.

'Do you play?' I asked him.

'Do I play?' he pounced on me. 'Ha! Do I play? Do *I* play?' he repeated, raising his voice enough to arouse attention and concern. 'What do you think? Give me that instrument,' he snapped at Phoebe.

'Wh—What are you going to do?' Phoebe's fears sprang into action.

'Give it to me!' he demanded.

'Please don't hurt it!' she passed him her violin. He grabbed it deftly round the neck, balanced it on his lap and rapidly plucked the strings.

'Do I play?' he mocked me as he fingered a passage. 'How can—'

He repositioned the instrument and ran his thumb up and down the back of the fingerboard. He spun it round and examined it, his dark eyes ablaze. He plucked the strings again and studied the neck.

'Where did you get this?' he asked his daughter.

'From the attic,' she replied.

'The attic?' he repeated. 'Which attic? This attic?'

'No.'

'Where did you get it?' he demanded. 'Paris? New York? Timbuctoo? The bloody moon?'

'I haven't been to Paris or New York or Timbuctoo or the bloody moon!' cried Phoebe. 'I found it in the attic of my house. Its strings were broken and I had it fixed.'

'The attic of your house?' he questioned in a milder, more cautious manner.

'Yes. My house. Our house. I found it in the attic.'

'You beautiful creature,' he kissed the instrument. 'Juliette,' he crooned to it and stroked the strings with his thumb. 'My beautiful, darling doe, how you could sing!'

'What's the matter, Roddy?' Mrs Epstein asked.

'It's mine,' he whispered.

'Yours? What do you mean yours? You used to play an Amati. What happened to the Amati?' our teacher queried.

'Had to pawn it,' he muttered.

Mrs Epstein seemed to scold him when she shook her head and sighed. 'So where did this come from?' she asked in a tired but patient tone.

'Cairo. Found it in a bazaar. I burned my cigarette into the back of it here. Look,' and he showed her the mark on the neck of the instrument.

'Same as your Amati,' Mrs Epstein peered at it and felt the mark in the neck. 'Third position. Roddy, that's very juvenile.'

'Took it to France with me and had it fixed,' he continued. 'Bridge needed work. Bought a new bow and lived on beans. What a little gem! Spent the entire week playing it. In the end I left it with her. Told her if I didn't come back, she'd know why. Didn't get a chance to explain till later. Asked her to sell it, but she didn't. She kept it. She kept it...'

'Who?' asked Mrs Epstein.

'Ailine,' he replied in a quiet, puzzled voice. 'She brought it back... Is she still here?'

'Hasn't she been to see you at all?'

'Only once… Last year…Very odd…'

He seemed to shrivel with sadness as he resigned the violin to Phoebe. 'Go will you?' he looked at no one. 'Look, just get out!' he ordered, and he thumped his fist on the arm of his chair.

'Come on, girls,' Mrs Epstein signalled to a nurse who promptly obeyed.

'I'm sorry,' he apologised, again growing sad. 'Please go.'

'I'll see you Tuesday, Roddy,' said Mrs Epstein.

She laid a hand on his shoulder and bade us take our leave.

43

We sat at the terminal, each one hugging her instrument, and waited for the ferry, which, true to the spirit of Sunday transport, seemed to take forever to come.

'Well, I never expected that,' Mrs Epstein was the first to break the silence.

No one replied.

'You know, he enjoyed hearing you play and meeting you,' our teacher began again.

'It didn't come across that way,' grumbled Pim.

'Quite frankly,' Mrs Epstein explained, 'I think he was as nervous about meeting you as you were about meeting him.'

'I really don't know what to make of him, Mrs Epstein,' sighed Della. 'On the one hand he was almost cruel, yet at the same time he was quite friendly. He's a bit like my mother's cat, really. Ming will wrap himself around your legs and purr and the next minute he digs his claws into your knees and makes you scream. Yet again, how tender he was with that violin. Poor man,' she sniffed.

'Listen,' Mrs Epstein advised. 'Roderick Raye is the master of making a single statement carry multiple meanings. He thrives on contradiction. He's always been like that.

'I remember when I first met him,' she continued, looking fondly out across the harbour. 'It was not long after I commenced my studies in Vienna. We had the same teacher at the time, only Roddy was studying at the conservatory and I was studying privately. He would frequently take additional lessons and they tended to be scheduled after mine. At the end of every lesson I would find him waiting outside, a sprite of a man, sitting with his legs neatly crossed, his violin in its case, his left hand busy drumming a passage on the arm of the chair and his eyes alert. He always had something to say to me and he said it in fluent German.

'At that stage my German was primitive so I never had any idea what he was talking about. After one such occasion I decided I would tell him so and I spent the entire week rehearsing what I was going to say. My accent must have given me away when I made the attempt for he grinned from ear to ear and began speaking to me in English and with a very broad Australian accent. I cannot tell you how surprised and relieved I was to meet someone from my own country.

'"By the way," he concluded and held out his hand, "Roderick Raye". "Mary-Anne McGillycuddy," I replied. "McGillycuddy?" he snorted just like he did with you lot. "Bet you're looking forward to walking down the aisle," was his next remark. Well, back then, I had no intention of marrying. After my studies I had planned on entering a convent and dedicating myself to teaching.'

'You were going to be a nun, Mrs Epstein?' asked Della.

'Oh, yes,' our teacher replied. 'But providence, fate, luck, call it what you will, has a way of turning our dreams on their heads. Anyway, at that point in time, Roddy had no way of knowing such a thing, but he was so shrewd. He was a larrikin with an uncanny knack of pinpointing your innermost concerns and toying with them. Yes, Della, he is a little like a cat that plays with its prey. But he's quite a nice pussy cat once you get to know him. I can tell you from long experience, with Roderick Raye your best form of defence is attack. And if you can't attack either you end up laughing at yourself or crying. If you cry, you lose.'

'Were you good friends?' asked Phoebe.

'Very. He was like a brother to me, Phoebe,' Mrs Epstein smiled. 'He took charge of me after that and I came to know him quite well. It turned out he was from Ballarat and he was in Vienna by virtue of a bequest of his grandfather, who had had much to do with his earlier musical exploits.

'His own father was a tea merchant who had made a considerable fortune during the Gold Rush, and who agreed to the venture provided Roddy returned to Australia when he finished his studies and work in the family business. I met him some years later. He was a stiff, stern man who believed in hard work and church on Sunday. Well, Roderick, being very much the black sheep of his family, was not the least bit interested in business, let alone darjeeling, but I can tell you that the discipline he learnt from his father he put into his music. Phoebe, your father was the most brilliant violinist I have ever known. He had the precision of Heifitz and the warmth of Kreisler. It was all there: wonderful, wonderful playing…

'I think in Vienna it was the first time he found himself among people with similar interests and inclinations. Well, girls, he and I were like Hansel and Gretel in a chocolate shop and that city was an indulgent grandmother who refused us nothing. Through him I met Mr Epstein. They were best friends. Tweedle-dum and Tweedle-dee I used to call them. They were constantly arguing about music: hair-splitters the two of them, and both superlative players. Ah, here's the ferry at last. Come on, it's high time you lot had some tea.'

The moment we arrived at Mrs Epstein's, Phoebe ran into the house and made straight for the music room. We found her frantically searching through the gramophone records. She set the one she wanted upon the player, wound the machine and waited for the music. We all stood, riveted to the floor, listening to the *Sunrise* quartet.

Mrs Epstein came in with the tea trolley.

'It's him, isn't it?' Phoebe demanded.

Mrs Epstein nodded and smiled. 'Yes, Phoebe, it's your father. He was the first violinist in our quartet.'

Phoebe's lower lip began to quiver. She wiped her eyes, but to no avail.

'There, there,' Mrs Epstein hugged her close. 'Cry all you like, little one. He played beautifully, didn't he?'

'Yes,' she sobbed. 'I—I had no idea.'

'We're very lucky to have a recording of him. It's for you to treasure.'

'Thank you, Mrs Epstein. Oh, thank you.'

'You've something very special to share with him. He is going to love sharing it with you. Now, I think you need a picture of him so you can match the music to the man. There's a photo of him somewhere. Help yourselves to some tea, girls, while I look.'

'Bakery certainly does well out of you, Mrs Ep,' said Pim as she served the tea and handed round a plate of cakes.

'Forget the bakery. You've Mr Epstein to thank. His father was a baker so he knows a thing or two,' replied Mrs Epstein as she wrestled with the bottom drawer of her bureau. The drawer was crammed with papers, some of which were wedged in the drawer above. Eventually she managed to free it and ended up pulling the entire drawer out and setting it on the coffee table. Then she began another search.

'Bother,' she muttered and walked out of the room. 'Reuben!' she called to Mr Epstein. 'Reuben! Have you seen my reading glasses?'

We were left to fossick through piles of newspaper clippings, letters, string, neatly folded scraps of brown paper, cards and photographs. A particularly large photograph was wrapped in tissue paper.

Della pulled it out.

'"Mazel tov! With apologies to Bellini, from A",' she read the inscription on the back. Then she turned the picture over and began to laugh. 'My goodness gracious! Look at this!'

It was a sort of picnic scene, a feast of the gods perhaps, for all the figures were dressed in tunics, robes or togas. Some had wreaths on their heads. Nearly all of them were people we knew.

'Spectacles and a chiton! Mrs Epstein!' Della screamed with laughter. 'Look! And that's Mr Epstein leaning over you.'

'Oh no, what have you found?' our teacher asked as she returned with her reading glasses in their case. It did not take her long to deduce what our discovery was. 'A little nonsense now and then...' she smiled. 'Just proves we were all young and silly once. It was a wedding present of sorts, and, given the people in it and what happened afterwards, a very cherished one. Do you recognise where it was taken?'

'It's not— It's not my front garden, is it?' said Phoebe. 'That's the big poplar tree, and look there, you can glimpse the gate. I remember when it was pretty like that.'

Mrs Epstein accorded that it was. 'We used to have some wild and happy times in that garden,' she mused. 'Can you see your father there, Phoebe? He's dressed as Pluto, sitting with—'

'Goodness, is that my mother?'

'Yes it is. I think she's Persephone.'

'Oh he was handsome, wasn't he?'

'Very. He still is, despite the scars. The photograph was your aunt's idea. She used to enjoy staging tableaux of well-known works which she then used for painting purposes. She was pursuing her art more seriously by that time. You can see her there sitting on the other side of your father with the crown of wheat in her hair making her petition to Apollo. His name escapes me now but he was one of her artist friends. As you know, Phoebe, your aunt has many artist friends.'

'And would that be Mr David Birstall in the front with the helmet?' I asked.

'That's right,' confirmed Mrs Epstein.

'And is that not Miss Bray there with the urn balanced on her head?' It was. 'And the other lady holding the dish?'

'Miss Mavis Travers. And that gentleman there holding the donkey is Mr George Hunt. You know old Mr Hunt at the music store?'

We all knew old Mr Hunt at the music store.

'Mr George Hunt was his son. He was engaged to Miss Bray and Mr Birstall was courting Miss Travers.'

'And my father?' Phoebe asked in a hopeful tone.

'Well, judging by that photograph, it looks as if he was very much engaged,' surmised our teacher. We all bent over to study the two figures: Phoebe's father, sporting a thin moustache and goatee, with a pitchfork laid beside him, had one hand on the lap of her mother, who was holding a piece of fruit. They were gazing fondly at each other.

'''Tis odd how you get used to a person, is it not?' I observed. 'I never think of Mr David as ever having two arms, and yet, there he is. And that's why he calls his 'cello Mavis? After that lady there?'

'They all did it. All the gentlemen, that is,' Mrs Epstein explained. 'They sat round one night after a show with a bottle of Scotch, christening their instruments with the names of the women they loved and drinking the health of those same ladies. Unfortunately, Luighseach, Miss Travers turned your Mr David down when he came back from Gallipoli. She didn't want to marry a man who wasn't whole. It broke his heart. And poor Miss Bray never married, for Mr Hunt was killed in action. As for your father, Phoebe, well, you saw what the war did to him. It did that to everyone in some way or other.'

Pim nodded. 'What about you, Mrs Ep?' she asked. 'What happened to you? Did Mr Epstein fight?'

'No. We'd been living in Australia nearly three years when war was declared. We were both classified as enemy aliens and sent to an internment camp, literally in the back of Bourke.'

'A what?' Della questioned.

'It was what happened to anyone who was German or Austrian regardless of how long they had lived in Australia or what their affiliations may have been. We spent most of the war years in a prison in the sticks. We buried our son there,'

Mrs Epstein paused.

'But Mrs Epstein, I don't understand,' Della quietly ventured another concern. 'If Phoebe's father was best friends with Mr Epstein and Mr Epstein's Austrian, why on earth did he go to fight? Surely he didn't have to. And didn't he have a wife and child? My father was an army man. He had to go, regardless of his family situation. Why would he have chosen to do something like that?'

Mrs Epstein suspended her thoughts. 'Well, for one, Roddy was viewed with suspicion. He'd lived in Austria, he spoke fluent German and he had German friends. What's more, with his wit and obvious talent he was considered a tall poppy. People were jealous of him. There was pressure on him to enlist or else face denunciation from other musicians, from authorities and even from his own family. But Roderick had reasons of his own. Still, it was a wonder they accepted him. He isn't a big man; he would have barely met the requirements. He was, however, extremely competent on horseback.'

'Horseback, Mrs Epstein?' repeated an astonished Phoebe. 'My father?'

'Apparently he was nearly as good a horseman as he was a musician, Phoebe. Believe you me, *I* had no idea until I saw him in uniform. When we were in Vienna he used to say in his typically cocksure manner that if he wasn't such a brilliant violinist he wouldn't mind riding a Lipizzaner but no one ever took him seriously. We did, though, when he joined the Light Horse. The last time we played together, he and David Birstall who played the 'cello with us then, were both wearing regimentals. Unfortunately, I haven't a picture of him in his colours but there's another photograph somewhere which is not quite as silly as the one you're looking at and which better serves my purpose. Where is it?'

Mrs Epstein rummaged through her collection. ''I'll sort it out one day,' she remarked.

She soon found what she was searching for.

'There you are,' she passed us the photograph. 'Our quartet: the Klimt Quartet.'

We crowded round it. 'You haven't changed much, Mrs Ep,' said Pim. 'Mr Ep's not quite as rotund as he is now.'

'Well, it's nearly twenty years since that photograph was taken,' replied Mrs Epstein.

'I don't know whether I prefer your father with a moustache and his hair slicked back or not, Phoebe,' observed Della as we studied the more boyish, clean-shaven figure of the first violinist dressed in a smartly cut tailcoat, waistcoat and trousers. 'He's quite the romantic with those curly locks falling forward like that. And do you see how he's holding his violin? Only this afternoon he held it that exact same way. How clever and accomplished he looks.'

'There's Ailine,' Phoebe's attention was on the woman opposite him.

'Didn't you know she played the 'cello?' Mrs Epstein asked.

'I had no idea,' Phoebe whispered.

'Well she did,' our teacher replied. 'And a very good cellist she was, too.'

'Was this taken in Vienna?' asked Della.

Mrs Epstein nodded. 'We were a piano trio at first: Mr Epstein, Roderick Raye and myself,' she explained. 'That was, until Ailine and Juliette Devereaux arrived. They were touring with their mother at the time, their father having passed away the year before. Originally they intended to spend a season in Vienna, but they ended up enjoying themselves so much they stayed a couple of years. The two sisters pursued their own studies: Ailine, the older of the two and the more unorthodox, drifted between painting and 'cello; Juliette, quiet and sensitive but equally gifted, gave her attention to voice and piano. Their mother, your grandmother, Phoebe, being a renowned concert pianist in her day, was immersed in the artistic life of the city. She chanced to hear your father perform and she invited him to her salon. Roderick, who was keen to further his musical career in any possible way, became very caught up in it all. Luckily for him, Madame Devereaux took him under her wing and he spent a lot of time with her family.

'By this stage your father was very keen to try his hand at the quartet repertoire, so he invited Ailine to join our little musical circle. As a result, we formed the Klimt Quartet. We named the quartet after an artist Ailine particularly admired. If that recording is anything to go by, I think we were rather good. We attracted quite a following, the least reason not being that we were two ladies and two gentlemen which was not the norm in Vienna, I can tell you. Your father, not to mention your aunt, Phoebe, delighted in the radicality of it.'

'And you, Mrs Epstein?' asked Phoebe.

'It was a treat to play with them, and yes, I'll have to own I have always liked throwing stones in ponds,' she smiled. 'At your father's insistence, Phoebe, we played mostly Haydn. He loves his Haydn.'

'Then why was he so critical of our choice?' asked Della.

'Didn't I tell you to take him with a large grain of salt?' replied Mrs Epstein. 'As for "that romantic Russian garbage", he gave that copy of the Borodin quartet to Mr Epstein and me for a wedding gift.

'Now, if I remember correctly, that photograph was taken a few weeks before Madame Devereaux and her daughters left Vienna to complete their tour. The recording was made about the same time. It was one of your father's many madcap ideas, Phoebe, and, looking back, it was just as well he did wheedle us into making it. By then he had finished his academic studies. He was supposed to return to Ballarat but he refused. He was determined to pursue his music career and continue studying privately, for by this stage he was working very closely with Meister Arnold Rosé.'

'Who is he?' asked Della.

'No less than the leader of the Vienna Philharmonic,' replied Mrs Epstein. 'Well, as you can imagine, neither Mr nor Mrs Raye had any idea of the significance of Meister Rosé and they demanded their son return. Again he refused, and in response his father cut off his income. Roddy had to fend for himself, which he did. Between a little teaching and quite a bit of performing he managed to do very well indeed.

'I departed for Australia the following year. Before I left, however, Mr Epstein proposed and I very happily accepted. We came out to Australia together where we again met up with Madame Devereaux and her family, who had returned to their home in Sydney. And who do you think came out several months later? Roderick Raye. That was another surprise. Roddy had every intention of staying in Vienna. But, as it happened, he had some business to attend to. "I thought I might get hitched myself," he explained when I questioned what on earth did he think he was doing travelling to the other side of the world. "To whom?" I asked, incredulous. "Ailine?" "Oh, I might," he replied. "Might even marry her sister. Her mother's not bad, neither. Tell you what, Annie, I'll marry the three of them and let you know which one I prefer." Well, marry he did.'

'He married my mother?' asked Phoebe.

'Barely a week after Mr Epstein and I were married, he announced his engagement. And it wasn't to whom we expected.'

'Was it to my mother?' Phoebe asked again.

'Yes, it was. But that announcement took us all by surprise. What business did our exuberant Roddy have with the shy and serious Juliette Devereaux? And we were even more astonished when he converted to Catholicism and walked her down the aisle in the grandest wedding you could possibly imagine. Your father never did anything by halves. As for his family, who are staunch Presbyterians, they were horrified. But it soon became clear why everything seemed to happen so suddenly. Juliette was expecting a child.'

'Was it me?'

'Yes it was, Phoebe. They didn't have an easy time of it after that, I'm afraid. I don't think your father realised there was actually a world outside his violin that demanded serious attention. Being only twenty-three, he was very young, both at heart and in years. Your mother was a couple of years younger, and neither of them was prepared for the kinds of hardships that marriage imposes.

'You see, your father was eager to return to Vienna where he had a series of concert engagements the following season. Your mother, however, did not want to go back right then and there, not with a baby on the way. She was not in the best of health, and, in the end, was advised not to make the voyage. So your father had to travel back alone. He did not see you until you were six months old when he came out to Australia a second time. Meanwhile, your mother had become very sick indeed. She was prone to terrible moods and your father ended up bearing the brunt of them.

'Unfortunately, he did not meet with much sympathy. Many people thought him rash and unprincipled. In their opinion, he had acted foolishly and had entered into a bad marriage as a result. As far as they were concerned, he had to live with the consequences.'

'What did you think, Mrs Epstein?' Phoebe wanted to know.

'Well, frankly, I've always thought him rash – a bit of a daredevil – it's part of his charm. But I have never considered him unprincipled. Admittedly, he fathered a child out of wedlock, which is both rash and unprincipled. But to marry your mother the way he did was imbued with the highest principles. He did everything in his power to protect her honour. He adopted her faith surprisingly willingly it seemed, in the face of enormous opposition and outright hostility, and in taking her hand he put his life on the altar. Living by those principles, however, posed its own set of problems and whether he had the moral fibre to solve them remained to be seen.

'To be quite honest, Phoebe, I ended up feeling very sorry for him. He was maligned by his family, by friends and associates. People were so quick to judge and so unwilling to accept. As for thinking he or your mother needed help, well, the idea never entered their heads. Roddy is impetuous, but he never intends any harm, and just because someone encounters difficulties – however they got into them – you don't leave them in the lurch. To see a dear and loyal friend, especially someone as lively and generous as your father, so down spirited, was heart wrenching.

'Sadly, of the few people he confided in, there was one who was probably the least equipped to offer sound advice: Ailine Devereaux. As you are probably aware, Phoebe, your aunt has always regarded institutions such as marriage as unnecessary social constrictions. She also knew your father's ambitions.

'Did they love each other, Mrs Epstein?' Phoebe anxiously asked.

'I can't answer that, Phoebe,' Mrs Epstein replied. 'What I do know is that your aunt sold her 'cello and left for France to pursue her painting. Your father, similarly, was planning to return again to Vienna where he had another season of performances. Your mother, however, was still unwilling to travel. Before your father was able to leave, though, war was declared. He was stranded instead, forced to cancel the season and faced with finding another means of providing for a sick wife and a child. To make matters worse, people accused him of harbouring German sympathies and refused to give him work. At the same time he had every finger pointing at him to do his bit.

'I never thought he would be so reckless but it came to pass that Christmas that he was visiting his parents in Ballarat. Apparently there was a huge family quarrel and before the week was out he packed you and your mother on a train back to Sydney and joined up. You're quite right, Phoebe. He used his enlistment as a ticket overseas and he intended to remain in Europe once the war was over. After all, the war would end soon. As for your mother, she was distraught.

'Well, your father's plans went horribly wrong. He was sent to Gallipoli, not France, to start off with. Somehow he managed to survive and was sent to the Western Front. However, it seems—'

'Didn't he ever care about me?' Phoebe's concerns remained.

'By that stage, I don't think he knew what he cared about, little one; but Phoebe, you've been a blessing in disguise,' replied Mrs Epstein, 'for life teaches us lessons in the strangest ways. Something happened during that war. Something happened that turned everything around.'

'But still, Mrs Epstein, how could he go over there and fight people he had actually lived with?' Della was equally perturbed.

'It puzzled me too,' acknowledged Mrs Epstein. 'Aside from Gallipoli, however, I have the impression he wasn't involved in much direct combat. Because he spoke German fluently he was given charge of prisoners or else put in the front line to investigate enemy activity. Other times he relayed messages. Regardless of what he might say to the contrary, I think whatever he did must have been pretty heroic and it cost him dearly. Miraculously, he survived. His survival has puzzled me more than anything else. How could someone endure so much injury? And why? Of all people, why Roderick: talented, charming, handsome Roddy?'

'That right may come of it perhaps?' I suggested.

'But what could possibly be right in all that?' Phoebe tearfully interposed.

'He came back to your mother, Phoebe,' Mrs Epstein replied.

'He came back because he was injured,' she retorted.

'No, no, no. Whatever your father's motivations were at the beginning of the war, they were very different by the time it ended. Injuries notwithstanding, his experience revealed depth of character no one thought he possessed. Your father was determined to come back and he came home in his heart long before he was invalided out. It's a pity wood and gut cannot talk,' Mrs Epstein sighed, 'for I have a feeling that violin of yours had quite a lot to do with it. Your father loved your mother, Phoebe, more than anyone realised. I think, deep down, you know that, don't you? Think back, little one. Do you remember when he returned? Do you remember how things were before your mother died? Try and remember, because you are the only one who truly knows how things were between them.'

'They were very happy, Mrs Epstein,' Phoebe slowly reflected. 'Sometimes I used to talk to my mother about my father, about what happened to his arm and his legs and whether they would grow again. She would try to explain and through the course of it she would always tell me my father was very special. And she meant it, Mrs Epstein. He was very special to her, not because of his injuries but because of who he was. And my father would say exactly the same thing to me about my mother: that she was a very special lady. He meant it, too. I knew I was very special to both of them. We were a family, Mrs Epstein, and we were all special.'

'That's good to hear,' it was odd to see Mrs Epstein cry. 'You see, it took Mr Epstein and me a while to get back to Sydney once we were released from the camp, so I didn't see your father again until after your mother died. Davy Birstall told us what had happened. When we first visited him, the poor man was emaciated, shell-shocked and completely shattered by your mother's death and what had happened to you. We did everything we could to get him better. For my part, I made it my business to look out for you. I sought you out and taught you and every week I talked to your father about you, what you were doing, how you were growing up. You gave him a purpose, and slowly he regained his health. In fact, I would go so far as to say that he has taught you as much as I have, particularly over the last couple of years. He's done it from afar, that's all.

'Where are you going now?' she asked, for all of a sudden, Phoebe, still wiping her eyes and sniffing, was gathering her things.

'To see Ailine,' Phoebe replied as she hurried away.

'Ailine? What on earth—? Now just a minute!' Mrs Epstein called after her.

'She certainly keeps you on your toes, Mrs Ep,' remarked Pim.

'Trotting over hot coals more like,' replied Mrs Epstein as she dumped a pile of papers back in the drawer, groped for her ordinary glasses and picked up her handbag. 'Can you girls let yourselves out? I'll see you all on Thursday. Luighseach, I'll see you tomorrow. Reuben!'

44

We did not see Phoebe again until the following Thursday after school when we chanced to coincide on Petersham station. Della, Pim and I had caught the city-bound train. Phoebe, who had not been at school for the entire week, alighted from the train headed in the opposite direction.

It was a hot afternoon. Everything had been baked dry, and the prospect of a southerly seemed very unlikely indeed. This being the case, we made a detour to the soda fountain before heading off to Mrs Epstein's. There, we caught up on Phoebe's news. The last few days she had spent almost exclusively in her father's company, and she was more than eager to pass on all she had learned.

'I've always wondered why your violin case was in such a sorry state,' Della remarked once Phoebe paused in her story. 'It's literally been in the wars. But how on earth did it get to Egypt in the first place?'

'Who knows?' replied an unusually talkative Phoebe. 'Anyway, my father couldn't believe what he saw inside. He said the violin reminded him of my mother the moment he laid eyes on it. You know how it's quite rounded and pear-shaped? Well, he joked about it to his mates and said it reminded him of a girl he knew, and when they prodded him for more he jokingly admitted it was his wife. Apparently all but one laughed and that man pulled my father aside and said that if he had a wife with a corker of a figure like that he would think twice before making light of it.

'My father said that that comment was as good as a kick in the pants. Apart from sending her money, he had turned his back on my mother. His one aim was to get to France and, as soon as the War was over, return to Vienna and resurrect his career. And once he did, only then would he invite my mother to come and join him if she wanted. Now, every time he took out the violin to play, the memory of my mother began to haunt him. But the poor violin worried him because it didn't sound right when he played it. The bridge was too thick and very badly made. He knew from the wood, though, that it was a good instrument. After that, he was determined to get to Paris to have it fixed.

'Well, eventually he was sent to France, and not long after he arrived my mother sent him a parcel of socks. They were the most clumsily knitted socks you could ever imagine. No two socks were the same length and no pairs could be made neither in colour nor stitch nor size. But they were a godsend. You see, my father has rather small, narrow feet.'

'Had, you mean,' corrected Pim.

'That's what I said. He still says "has" and insists I humour him on that one. Anyway, obtaining boots that fitted properly was a challenge and an extra pair of socks came in handy. My mother's socks probably saved his life for the winter was horribly cold and wet. You were as likely to die from disease as you were from shellfire, he said.'

'Sounds like your father's told you more in four days than my brother Leo or my Uncle Ted's told me in a decade,' Pim observed. 'Did he talk about where he fought?'

'He told me he lasted barely a day at Gallipoli. That's where he got the scars on his face. As for France, he says the only reason why he's still here is because the fellows in his regiment were some of the finest fellows you would ever meet. That was another kick in the pants, my father said. On the whole, those men had a very clear sense of what was most important, and it wasn't playing concertos in concert halls. All they wanted was to get back home to the people they loved, and because my father happened to be married, they often made decisions in his favour, even in the midst of heavy fighting, in order that he would have a chance to get back to his wife. In fact, the fellow who had pulled him aside back in Cairo pulled him aside at Bapaume and took a bullet which otherwise would have taken my father. He said if he had his time over he would willingly give an arm and a leg to get those fellows home.'

'But he did,' remarked Pim.

Phoebe nodded.

'So what happened about the violin?' Della was more interested in following the trail of Phoebe's instrument than any account of the battlefield. 'He made it to Paris, didn't he?'

'Yes. He did eventually, and he took the violin to a maker who was able to fit a proper bridge. The violin maker told him all about the instrument.'

'So, is it a Gawanee-airi?' asked Pim.

'No. It's a copy: a very, very good copy. It's a Vuillaume. It's about ninety years old and it was probably modelled on the violin Paganini owned. My father couldn't believe it when he played it. You know what it's like.'

'It has such a beautiful, dark tone,' added Della. 'I've always loved the richness of its low notes and yet it's so sweet and supple when you play up high.'

'According to my father,' Phoebe continued, 'it sounded like my mother when she sang. He couldn't put the violin down and in the course of it all he fell in love with my mother all over again. That was when he realised what a fool he'd been. My mother had been sick and she had needed him and he had been too caught up in his own ambitions to understand her trouble.

'My father said he was so filled with remorse that he made the first real confession he ever made in his life. After that, he was determined to make amends and he began to write to her. They wrote each other for the remainder of the war. He kept all her letters. I have them here.'

She pulled from the rosin compartment of her violin case a small packet. 'There's lots about me in them,' she proudly informed us. 'All sorts of bits and pieces; as well as songs my mother was singing to entertain returned troops, little things that reminded her of my father, memories from before the war, lots of things.'

'So when did he see your aunt?' asked Pim.

'Not until he went to Paris a second time, a few months before the war ended. He had some leave before he was sent to the front line. He was worried that he might not survive and he left the violin with her for safe keeping. He spent a day in her company and he asked her to take him to the places where she and my mother had spent part of their childhood. He insists there was nothing more to it than that, regardless of what my aunt might say. My aunt was never his mistress. There was a moment of weakness before the War, he told me, but, notwithstanding that incident, he has always been absolutely faithful to my mother.'

'But what of the poetry book?' I asked, 'The one with your aunt's photograph inside?'

'Oh!' Phoebe gave a small laugh. 'Dad said that must have been from years and years ago when they first met in Vienna. He can't think how else it could have got there. He did admit to being a bit keen on Ailine back then, but he hasn't read any Byron since he was eighteen!

'Anyway,' she resumed, 'if he managed to live through the war, my father had every intention of visiting my aunt again and making it clear to her that he was going home. Unfortunately, he was injured instead. In the end, he wrote my aunt a letter. It took him a couple of years because he first had to learn to write with his left hand.'

'What happened?'

'He was serving as a galloper, which means he had to take messages between brigade and battalion headquarters. He was relaying a message when he became caught in heavy fire. He managed to deliver it and return safely. Then an important order was called and the only way to send the message was by horse because all the telephone lines had been cut. My father offered to take the message and again encountered very heavy fire. He nearly reached his destination when his horse swerved and stumbled. My father was thrown and landed badly on his shoulder. He never saw his horse again for a shell exploded right near the poor animal. Even though he was injured, my father pressed ahead on foot and delivered the message. It was the worst barrage he'd experienced, but he wasn't going to leave those boys in the lurch, not by any means. He was taken to hospital after that, but when they finally came to treat him his feet were in a very bad way. He said his shoulder hurt him so much he hardly even noticed them. Anyway, what had started out as a few cuts and sores had turned nasty and they had to amputate. They managed to save his arm mainly because he was a musician and they hoped he might regain the use of it, but he never did.'

'Brave man,' Pim remarked.

'Did he win a medal?' asked Della.

'Apparently. He doesn't have it, though. He sent it to his parents. To put it my father's way: he got the guts, they got the glory. I didn't know I have grandparents still living. He hasn't seen them for years, which is very sad. They're both very old and they live in Ballarat. Can you believe it?'

'But my goodness, it must have been very hard for your mother when he returned,' Della observed, 'for you are quite right about my mother, Phoebe. Back Home she would hardly ever come with us to the park because she couldn't bear the sight of wounded soldiers. Had my father come back like that, I don't know how she would have managed.'

'Well, my father said my mother didn't flinch, not one bit. She was determined to get him walking again.'

'And is he able to walk?' I asked.

'We've been walking together every day. It's hard for him, but he can do it,' she replied with considerable admiration. 'He says he's lucky his legs came off below the knee. It would have been much harder otherwise. He has to wear wooden legs of course. He has names for them. My father has funny names for most things. One leg he calls Felix—'

'Felix?' echoed Pim. 'You're joking. Like Felix the Cat?'

Phoebe nodded and giggled a little. 'He started singing a very silly song about it. Oh! How did it go? Well, it was something about being blown up with dynamite and landing in Timbuctoo, however it went.'

'You're joking!'

'It gets worse, Pim,' Phoebe continued, now unable to restrain her laughter. Clearly she shared her father's sense of humour. 'The other one's called Culpa because when he first got it, it didn't work properly. Apparently it happened one time when he was walking in the garden with my mother. His leg jammed and he lost his balance and took her with him. Neither of them could help laughing, but the whole situation was beyond crying. They ended up laughing so much they didn't bother to get up, so they spent the rest of the morning lying on the lawn, talking of all that had happened. After that, they both knew everything would work out. They were going to make it work, come what may. And they did, too.'

'And yet you said your mother committed suicide,' Della remarked. 'That doesn't make sense.'

'Do you really think so?' Phoebe sipped the last of her soda and gazed hopefully at Della.

'From the way you talk about her, it doesn't seem at all right,' Della observed.

'It never made sense to me either, and my father never believed it. He gave me the note she wrote the night she died. Here it is,' and she pulled a letter from her pocket and passed it to Della.

'No, Phoebe, we can't look at that.' Della refused to take it.

'Please look at it,' Phoebe urged. 'My father says there's something wrong with that note and no one will believe him. I can't work out what it is, but according to my father, my mother never wrote that letter. She couldn't have.'

We all bent over the letter.

'What do you think, Luighseach?' asked Della. 'Your short sight is probably better than everyone else's.'

''Tis the handwriting's the same,' I noted as I compared the letter with the ones written during the war. 'I cannot tell them apart.'

'My father says not to look at what's the same but what's different,' Phoebe advised.

'Well then, let's see,' Della thoughtfully considered the respective letters. 'There's the paper for one,' she remarked. 'Those letters your mother wrote during the war are on her best writing paper. Phoebe, if your mother was anything like my mother, she had good paper she reserved especially for writing to your father and an ordinary pad for day-to-day matters. Why, only yesterday my mother wrote my step-father. She always uses scented paper when she writes him. This other note is written on plain bond. Now that's the sort of paper my mother would use to enclose a cheque for the doctor or the electrician for services rendered. Do you think you would use plain bond to write your last words to the person you loved most?'

'My mum would use whatever paper she could get her hands on. Maybe she'd run out of paper,' Pim was not convinced. 'After all, those other letters were written two years before at the latest. Who's to say she had any more left?'

'I don't think so,' Della replied. 'And even if she had run out, she would still have a supply of different best paper for special letters. Besides, those wartime letters feel emotional. The hand is not always steady. Look at the end of this one. The ink's smudged. Was your mother a passionate person?'

'Very,' acknowledged Phoebe. 'She cried a lot. There were some songs she couldn't sing for crying.'

'Perhaps those splodges are from tears,' suggested Della.

'Could be rain,' contradicted Pim. 'After all, they've been on the battlefield.'

'Whatever the case,' argued Della, 'it's quite clear from the handwriting that these letters have been written in haste either from emotion or urgency. If you were a passionate person and you were about to take your own life, wouldn't you be emotional? And yet this other letter has been written neatly. It's as if special measures have been taken to ensure everything's correct. Now that's how I write a history essay: carefully, precisely, making sure I've included all the dates and details. This letter is calculated. Quite frankly, it's the sort of suicide note you'd write, Luighseach.'

'The like of you suggesting such a thing, Delleen Sotheby. Never would I write such a letter, not in a month of Sundays.'

'Precisely,' Della gave the table a smart rap. 'In fact, you *couldn't* write a suicide note. Regardless of how intensely you might feel things, Luighseach, you're far too logical and sensible. Suicide would never enter your head. The writer of this note is the same. Whoever it is, they're in control of their emotions. And look at the way it's folded, into the middle in exact thirds. The letters written to your father, Phoebe, are carelessly folded: first roughly in half and then across in quarters. The folds are crooked for the corners don't meet. Funnily enough, your father's taken the trouble to fold them along those very same lines.'

'My mother was always in a rush to catch the post,' Phoebe recalled. 'She'd push the letter into the envelope and we'd race down the street to the pillar box. We'd give the letter a kiss for Daddy and she'd lift me up and I'd push it into the box.'

'She still could have died of natural causes,' Pim remained sceptical.

'And leave a suicide note?' Della was incredulous. 'Pim!'

'All right, Sherlock, there are discrepancies,' admitted Pim. 'But there's a lapse of a few years between those wartime letters and that note. They were written in different circumstances. The differences in the letters do not prove she didn't commit suicide.'

'Perhaps,' accorded Della. 'But what if you consider the possibility that someone else could have written the note?'

'Come on!' for Pim that possibility was out of the question. 'The handwriting's identical. How could you forge something like that?'

'Can you forge your mother's signature?' asked Della.

'Yes.'

'Well, perhaps this was someone clever enough to forge an entire letter, but who did not take into account a few little idiosyncrasies. It's not impossible, Pim. And if Phoebe's mother didn't suicide and she didn't die of natural causes, then it could only be one thing.'

Phoebe's troubled eyes wandered from one letter to the other. Slowly she shook her curls as she pondered the details. Then she looked up and silently implored us.

'But why would anyone want to kill my mother?' she queried.

We arrived at Mrs Epstein's to find our teacher waiting on her front doorstep.

'Where on earth have you been?' she was fuming. 'You were supposed to be home an hour ago,' she scolded Phoebe. 'I have been worried sick!'

'I—'

'And as for you lot, twenty minutes late for a rehearsal with only two weeks to go before the competition. Whatever the excuse is, it better be a good one. In fact, I don't think I want to hear an excuse.'

'We're dreadfully sorry, Mrs Epstein,' Della took the initiative to apologise. 'We've been in the middle of solving a murder.'

'You *what?*' our teacher exclaimed. 'Oh no!' she put her hand to her forehead and turned to Phoebe. 'Don't tell me he's conned you into that.'

'But—'

Mrs Epstein continued to lecture as she herded us inside. 'Phoebe, as much as I have a deep regard for your father, I am sorry to say that he is sadly paranoid about some things. Your mother's death is one of them.'

'No, Mrs Epstein,' protested Phoebe. 'I don't think you're right.'

'My dear girl, I am afraid there are certain facts you are going to have to accept about your father. Paranoia is one of them. It's the War and you're lucky he's only at Graythwaite. They could have locked him away in Callan Park years ago.'

'It's not the War and he's not paranoid because I know my mother didn't kill herself!' Phoebe was adamant.

'How could you possibly know that?' furiously questioned Mrs Epstein.

'Because she was happy, Mrs Epstein, that's why! All she wanted was for my father to come home and her prayers had been answered. She would never, ever have killed herself. There was someone in our house a few days before and there was someone in our house the night she died. My father heard them.'

'He was suffering from shell shock, Phoebe,' Mrs Epstein was very firm. 'Listen, he's had me take the matter to the police before. Given the opportunity, your father would wrangle anyone into talking to an inspector and they would get the same answer: your mother's death was a suicide and your father's notion that someone was in your house was yet another case of a poor, war-crazed digger imagining that Fritz had wormed his way into the attic. Besides, there was a note.'

'But it's not right!' Della added her protest to Phoebe's and quickly related her observations.

'Hmmm,' considered Mrs Epstein. 'I suppose it does depend from which angle you look at it. And I must say, from what you have been telling me about your mother, Phoebe, it seems she was made of stronger mettle than any of us gave her credit. I always thought your father's gilded accounts of her were part of his delusion for they painted a very different picture from the one I had of Juliette Raye the last time I saw her, which was before we were taken to the camp. Back in 1915, your mother was completely overwhelmed by the needs of her baby and quite unable to cope with what your father had done. She was anxious and depressed and required medicine to help her sleep. Yet it appears she handled your father's trauma extremely well. Everyone who knew her was surprised when she died but they all construed it in much the same way: try as she might to put on a good face for your father's and anyone else's sake, poor Juliette was finding it increasingly difficult to cope. She had had suicidal tendencies in the past, I'm afraid. Besides, who would possibly want to kill Juliette Raye?'

Phoebe stared absently at the floorboards.

'Ailine,' she whispered.

'Now this is getting preposterous!' Mrs Epstein's anger returned. 'Your aunt was in France when your mother passed away. She had been in France since before the war and she did not come back until a year ago. I corresponded with her on a regular basis and she never mentioned anything about travelling out here until she decided to return last year.'

'Then how did my violin get into the attic?' Phoebe challenged.

'Your aunt put it there!'

'And if she did she put it there in the February of 1921 when I was seven and my mother died! She couldn't have put it there any later because *I* had the key, Mrs Epstein! I still have it! See?' and she pulled out the keys she wore on the chain around her neck. 'My father gave it to me before they took him away and I kept it with me. It was with me when I was in the orphanage and when I came back to my house I found out which door the key opened. It was the attic. And when I opened the door the violin was already there, as if it was waiting for me. Ailine couldn't have put the violin there when she returned last year!'

'There could have been a spare key, or else your aunt could have had another key fashioned,' advised Mrs Epstein.

'There is no spare and she's *never* had another key fashioned!' argued Phoebe. 'She never goes anywhere near the attic. And you didn't see her face last Sunday when I told her that she was a liar, that I knew the truth about my parents and that I knew about the violin. I didn't know then what I know now, Mrs Epstein, but Ailine knew something, I'm sure of it.'

'And if that's the case, I am very glad I managed to intervene when I did. This is getting quite out of hand, young lady, and I will repeat what I said on Sunday and what I have said time and time again: You are not to go anywhere near your aunt. Do I make myself clear?'

'Yes, Mrs Epstein,' Phoebe meekly complied.

'And you – and this goes for all of you – will not go pointing the finger at anyone, accusing them of such a heinous crime without very substantial proof and without recourse to the law. Do I make myself clear?'

'Yes, Mrs Epstein,' we all replied.

'To accuse someone of murder is a very serious matter,' Mrs Epstein continued to urge. 'You are effectively sending them on the way to their death. To falsely accuse someone is equally serious and carries with it its own ramifications.'

'And to accuse someone of suicide and deny them a Christian burial, to blight their character and bring nothing but sorrow and shame and condemnation upon those who love them, is that not also equally serious, Mrs Epstein?' questioned a tearful Phoebe.

'You are quite right,' our teacher acknowledged gravely. 'It is equally serious. But I don't know how, so many years later, Phoebe, you are going to prove it otherwise. For proof you will have to have.'

45

Mrs Epstein should have known better. To even suggest that Phoebe Raye find proof to vindicate her mother's innocence was to throw the proverbial red rag before the bull. And sure enough, the moment the opportunity presented itself, Phoebe made her charge.

The opportunity came on Saturday. That morning, Mrs Epstein had scheduled a rehearsal at the Conservatorium so that we could acquaint ourselves with the acoustics of the hall. For the remainder of the day, both she and Mr Epstein were busy hearing music examinations, leaving Phoebe to her own devices. Arrangements were made for her to stay at my place, which she did, along with Della and Pim. Our sojourn, however, was brief: a passing stop to drop off instruments and down a sandwich and a cup of tea. Then we set off to Stanmore.

'We really shouldn't be doing this,' cautioned Della for at least the third time that afternoon.

'We have to,' insisted Phoebe.

'But Mrs Epstein said you're not to go anywhere near your aunt.'

'That's right. She said I was not to go anywhere near my aunt. She didn't say I was not to go anywhere near my house.'

'And what if your aunt's in your house?' asked Pim.

'She's not,' Phoebe contended.

'How do you know that?'

'Because I went to check yesterday after my piano lesson and there was no sign of her,' Phoebe was quite confident.

'But that doesn't mean she's not there today, Phoebe,' instructed Della.

Nevertheless, confident though she may have been, Phoebe took the precaution of using the tradesman's entrance, which was accessible via the rear lane. Like the once glorious front garden, the back of the house was an unkempt wilderness with sheds, outhouse, garden and wash house in a state of neglect.

Phoebe signalled for us to remain near the back door while she crept around to check if her aunt was in her studio.

The back door opened and Della screamed.

'It's only me,' said Phoebe. 'I climbed in through a side window.'

'Are you quite sure it's safe?' asked Della.

'No one's downstairs, so you can come in,' Phoebe assured us.

A hideous smell hit us the moment we entered the servants' quarters.

'Chicken!' exclaimed Pim as she put her hand to her nose.

'A rat!' Della screamed. 'I swear I saw a rat!'

'I'm going up to check in Ailine's room,' Phoebe informed us. 'If Ailine's smoking, she usually does it in her bedroom. And if she is, she won't even realise we're here,' she added as she ran up the stairs.

'Come up!' she presently called. 'It's quite safe.'

We decided to divide forces. Phoebe and Pim headed for the attic. Della and I were shown the direction of Phoebe's mother's room.

'To think someone was actually murdered here,' Della was chilled with nervous excitement and she lay on the bed and re-enacted her imagining of the scene.

'We cannot be sure till we're sure, Delleen. Can you think what we'd be looking for now?'

'A diary perhaps, or a copybook,' suggested Della, 'Anything written by Phoebe's mother.'

There was nothing to be found. The room had been cleared out long ago. All that remained inside drawers and robes were cobwebs and cockroach droppings.

Pim and Phoebe came to the same conclusion from their foray into the attic. It was full of odds and ends from decades past: trunks, scrapbooks, clothes, old toys, school books, a couple of violins, even a small 'cello. But there was no diary.

Down the stairs we went.

'Would your mother be one to write a diary do you think, Phoebe Raye?' I asked.

'She wrote a lot,' Phoebe replied. 'But I don't know that she kept a diary.'

'Well, my bet is that if she was a very sensitive, private sort of a person, she probably did,' concluded Della. 'And if she did, where would she hide it? Pim, your family's huge. Where would you hide something so that no one would find it? Especially something very personal.'

'Where would you hide a leaf?' asked Pim with a gleam.

'Why, in a forest, Father Brown,' smiled Della.

'Then I reckon if she was stupid enough to try and be private about something, she either put it with a whole lot of other books so as not to draw attention to it, or else she did the exact opposite and hid it in a very secret place.'

'My mother has a portable writing desk,' Della continued. 'Did your mother have one, Phoebe?'

'I don't know.'

'Where did she write her letters?'

Phoebe gave the question considerable thought. 'In the sitting room,' she concluded. 'My mother always wrote in the sitting room.'

'Where is it?'

'Later it became part of the room that was made over for my father. Originally, though, it was two separate rooms with partition doors; but when my father came home the doors were pushed back to make a big bedroom with a pleasant place for him to relax. It's this room here past the music room.'

She brought us down the hall and opened the door that was opposite Ailine's studio. The room, however, was no longer a large single room but had been converted to a formal lounge room. There were no books to speak of in any of the bookcases.

'Let's try the other room,' Phoebe opened the partition doors and in the smaller sitting room she found her mother's desk.

'It's completely empty,' she lamented as she frantically checked the various drawers and pigeon holes. 'There's nothing here!'

Pim's investigation focussed on a nearby display cabinet.

'Looks old,' she commented.

'It used to be filled with beautiful French porcelain,' recalled Phoebe. 'I wonder where it's all gone.'

'We found a cabinet like that in the Royal Room at the guest house,' continued Pim. 'Moved it down to the guests' dining room. Turned out it had a hidden drawer. You know – a compartment for important documents that doesn't look like a drawer. There was a catch at the back that you pressed.'

And she ran her hand up and down the back of the cabinet. It wasn't long before she paused and gave a triumphant cry. There was a small click and, sure enough, from underneath the carved plinth, out popped a drawer which would otherwise have passed unnoticed for it had no handles.

Della gasped. 'Is there anything inside?'

'Come on Lucy,' Pim beckoned me over. 'You've got a couple of inches on me, you have a sticky beak.'

I did and I glimpsed a dark shape at the back. I reached as far as I could and put my hand on a small, thick book.

It was a ledger.

'What on earth is a ledger doing in a secret drawer?' Della excitedly remarked. 'Quick, Phoebe! Open up!'

Ledger though it was, it had been used as a diary.

'It's my mother's!' exclaimed Phoebe. 'Nineteen fifteen! Oh, my!' she sat on sofa and flicked through the pages. 'Oh dear! What's happened here? A hole's been cut in some of the leaves. Look!' A rectangle had been cut out of the back third of the pages and in that hollow had been placed a number of letters.

'Are they from your father?'

Phoebe unfolded one and confirmed that it was; and a very entertaining letter it turned out to be.

'It's the same handwriting as in the score of the *Sunrise* quartet!' Della exclaimed. 'I would know that handwriting anywhere, it's so very flamboyant.'

But it was the drawings that impressed me. They were wonderful caricatures of soldiers going about their day to day business away from the line of battle. Prominently featured was a wiry figure, who was always drawn with a cigarette hanging from his mouth, and who was either on horseback or in close company with a horse. The horse also had been very humorously caricatured, its expressions sometimes in accordance with, but more often than not a foil for those of the rider who was, of course, none other than Roderick Raye.

'What a stupid name for a horse,' Pim drily remarked, shaking her head and smiling at the letter she was reading.

'What is it?' Phoebe had been too preoccupied with reading the diary to take more detailed note of her father's correspondence.

'Gregory Allegri. He actually calls his horse Gregory Allegri. I thought he was writing about a chum. Turns out to be his horse. The animal's almost human.'

'Show me,' Phoebe leant over to look at the letter Pim was reading. Again it was illustrated with a border of caricatures mostly featuring the horse, this time shaving, dining, saluting the colonel and undertaking an assortment of jobs as if it were a man.

'I don't believe it!' she cried.

'What?'

'When I was little my father used to tell me all sorts of silly stories about a horse called Gregory Allegri. It was his war horse he was telling me about, Pim! Lucy, it was the horse he rode in France!'

'I love the way the drawings depict what your father's doing while the letters, for the most part, tell what he's thinking,' commented Della who was engrossed in a third letter. 'At the bottom of the page he's on his horse following behind a line of German prisoners, and a very sorry lot they look, too. As far as the letter is concerned, however, he's not in France at all; he's ice-skating with your mother in Vienna. It's very sweet. Apparently they were learning the *Kreutzer* sonata together at the time. He describes it as "our musical Matterhorn". Fancy thinking of the *Kreutzer* while escorting prisoners! The discussion gets very involved and quite technical in some places. It's as if he's practising in his head. Oh Phoebe, it's so very romantic! He says he knew he was going to marry your mother after they performed the *Kreutzer*. Goodness! She was only eighteen.'

'Yes,' said Phoebe, looking up from the diary. 'But he told me my grandmother wouldn't give her permission. He had to wait until my mother turned twenty-one and Bobeshi took my mother to Paris to make sure he did. They were secretly betrothed before she left.'

'So, their marriage wasn't the hasty event Mrs Epstein assumed it to be. There was a romance! I say! Even thinking about it sends me into a flutter!' exclaimed a delighted Della and she returned to the letter to find out more. 'Now he's somehow managed to move onto literature. Hmmm, he doesn't entirely agree with Tolstoy. He can appreciate the moral sentiments and the moral predicament expressed by the author but he thinks Mr Tolstoy has failed to appreciate the depth and breadth of redemption. Well, he certainly has his opinions. Phoebe, you can tell he's utterly brilliant. How hard it must have been for your mother to see him come back so wounded.'

'She loved him all the more, it's as simple as that,' Phoebe fondly replied.

'I suppose it is. Finally he writes about what he's really faced with,' continued Della. 'Do you mind if I read this? It says rather a lot about him and he's no rogue. I'll go back a bit. Here we are: "My darling, you know as I do that whatever our sins may be there is always forgiveness, always grace. We only need ask for it.

Poor Pozdny—" it's some Russian name which I can't pronounce. It must be a character:

> had he been forgiven, he would not have been so depraved. Perhaps Tolstoy wants to instill in us the idea that the consequences of a corrupt life are dire indeed. We become so engulfed by our corruption that we cannot perceive a way out. We are bound to our doom, like a train rattling down a solitary track. There is a way, however, even if it is only the hope of one.
>
> For me at any rate, the delights of the drawing room are distant dreams. Here it is dank and squalid. Everywhere I look I see men whose souls have been beaten to a pulp. We go thin and hungry while the rats feast. And yet we press on. We must press on, miserable beings all of us. Hope is all we have left. Ah, hope! How precious it is!
>
> No, my dearest, beset as I am by the plight of friend and foe (if foe he can be called), I am not ashamed of my faults. I can't say I'm proud of them either, I simply know them for what they are. I cannot hide them and I cannot run from them. What I am certain of is that without them I would not know what it is to be sorry. I would not know what it is to be forgiven. Without them I could not kneel before what is beautiful, I could not yearn for what is good. I could not embrace my fiddle and weep and laugh and revel in all that life has offered me. Without my humanity, weak as it is, I could not truly love.

'After that it gets very, very personal. I won't read any more, it's definitely not for my eyes. Dear me, Phoebe, they're very special letters. To think he must have written that particular one only weeks before he was injured. Judging from the date it could have been the last letter he wrote. What have you found, old thing?' she asked me.

I looked up from the letter I had picked up. It had not been pulled out from the cavity which stored Phoebe's father's letters. Instead it had been used to mark one of the pages of the diary and had been absent-mindedly passed to me by Phoebe as she read.

'Pim, will you tell me something now?' I asked. 'Was your Aunt Rose's name Rose Connolly before she married?'

Pim nodded. 'She was brought up with us so she always used Connolly, even though she's Mum's sister. Why?'

'Well! Is it not a small world? For it seems as if your Aunt Rose, Pim, wrote a letter to your mam, Phoebe Raye.'

'You're joking! Let's have a look,' Pim began to read alongside me. 'Typical Aunt Rose all right.'

'Aye,' I agreed. 'She nursed your da in France, Phoebe, and she's telling your mam what's happened to him and how well he's doing and how much he's looking forward to coming home. 'Tis a fine letter: simple and sincere, encouraging your mam to cherish each day, to have faith that all will be well and not to be afraid to ask for help. If we take good care of the present, it says, the future will take care of itself. Your mam's underlined that bit.'

Della looked over my shoulder. 'She must have held on to that letter as a sailor would the flotsam from a sinking ship. It looks as if it's been read a hundred times. Did you meet Aunt Rose at Pim's place, Phoebe?'

'I was having too much fun playing croquet,' she replied. 'I wonder which page the letter marked. Silly me for pulling it out.'

'Have you found anything in your mother's diary?' asked Della.

Phoebe shook her head.

'Why don't you go to the last entry instead of reading through the whole thing?' advised Pim.

It took a little time to find the last entry for the book was not completely filled. Once she found it, Phoebe began to read.

'Oh!' she gasped.

'What is it, Phoebeen?' I asked.

Phoebe read quietly:

16th February, 1921. It is midnight. Have left R. sleeping peacefully. I told him my news today. Needless to say he was astonished and not a little delighted. True to form and bless him for it, he asked me whether I thought the little one would come out with its legs intact and I was compelled to remind him that as far as I can tell his condition cannot be inherited.

I assured him we could manage on his income if we're frugal and I have a few piano students which will help us along. He in turn assured me that he has every hope of obtaining a position before the year is out. I never thought I would end up married to a schoolmaster, but Roddy seems to have taken to the idea of teaching modern languages and he is certain to find a place at one of the colleges nearby. After all, he is fluent in both French and German and there appears to be a dire need for teachers. I am so proud of him!

In the meantime, a leg of lamb can be made to last a week, the garden yields a bounty and there is never any shortage of eggs. Phoebe has new shoes and there are clothes in the attic I can cut down for her. As for my needs, I still have garments from my earlier confinement. My precious little one will be so happy to have another brother or sister. To think, after so many years, so many trials, our family is growing.

We talked of names. We both like Mélisande for a girl. If a boy, I should like to name him Roderick. Roddy, however, would prefer to name him Gregory after his horse. Really, the esteem in which he holds that poor beast is beyond credibility, which reminds me I must ask Father tomorrow not to say another Mass for the repose of its soul.

'She was going to have another baby!' Phoebe was mystified and she held my arm tightly. 'Lucy, she could never have killed herself!'

'Shh!' warned Della. 'Did you hear something? I'm sure I heard a door open.'

Della heard right. One of the floorboards in the hall groaned and creaked. Someone was there.

'Don't make a sound!' whispered Phoebe.

We sat stock still, wondering who had come.

The door opened.

'Mr David!' I exclaimed.

'Lucy!' he was equally surprised.

'What are you doing here?' demanded Phoebe.

'I might ask the same of you,' he replied.

'It's my house,' she declared. 'I have every right to be here.'

'Ah, of course!' he clicked his fingers and smiled. 'Phoebe Raye! I might have known! Well, Phoebe Raye,' Mr David tipped his hat. 'As Lucy here would say, I am Mr David: Mr David Birstall to be precise and I'm here by order of the owner of your house who is, of course, none other than your father. He usually gets me to do his dirty work,' he explained. 'That aunt of yours has left a right mess, hasn't she?'

'It's awful what she's done,' and the tears pooled in Phoebe's eyes.

'Don't you worry, young lady,' Mr David reassured her 'That's what I'm here for. We'll get it all cleaned up again. Gotta get this place ship-shape before the new tenants move in.'

'Tenants?' Phoebe echoed. She was not the least bit pleased with that piece of news. 'But what about me? This is *my* house.'

'And you think your father doesn't know that?' he replied. 'My bet is that he's probably right this minute hatching some wild and woolly plan that'll take everyone else a few months to realise it wasn't quite so wild and woolly as they originally thought. Grand old place isn't it?' he tried to divert her concerns. 'Piano still here?'

'The next room along, where it's always been.'

'You used to be able to open all these doors,' Mr David indicated the partition doors connecting the sitting room to the front lounge and the ones leading to the piano room. 'Not to mention the doors opening outside. It all used to be opened up for balls and parties. Your grandmother entertained on the piano, of course. As for the duets your mother and father used to play—'

'My father played the piano?' Phoebe questioned.

'Still does,' Mr David replied with a smile and a show of his right hand. 'We're not a bad duo, he and I. Oh well, there's nothing here a lick of paint and a bit of elbow grease won't fix. And don't you worry about a thing, young lady. Your dad'll look after you, mark my words.'

'Where's my aunt?'

'Can't answer that one,' he shrugged. 'She cleared out a couple of days ago. No notice. No explanations. Dropped the keys in the letterbox and that was that. Don't know where she's gone. I'm pretty sure of one thing, though: she's not coming back.'

46

The next day, in company with Mrs Epstein, we again visited Phoebe's father. A very stern-faced priest raised his biretta as he passed us on our way to the cottage situated next to the grand old house that was the main convalescent home. It was in that cottage that Mr Raye had a private room.

As soon as he saw us he held up his hand in a deft, dramatic gesture which put an immediate halt to the torrent of excitement Phoebe otherwise would have unleashed. Phoebe's father was deep in thought. No conversation was permitted and we were left at liberty to acquaint ourselves with his abode. Della was quick to peruse a varied library and was soon sampling a collection of what turned out to be Dickens' novels. Pim and Mrs Epstein took in the garden views. For my part there was a painting to study: a newly completed, vibrant but intriguingly childlike work resting on an easel, and I followed the sinuous line formed by the branch of a tree as it reached down to the harbour. The bridge construction could be glimpsed at the side. The focal point, however, was a tiny boat dotted on a very distant horizon.

'Do you like it?'

Apparently the question was intended for me and I turned from my examination. Before me was a scene worthy of another painting. Phoebe's father sat in a red velvet grandfather chair. He was attired in his Sunday best which evidently included a pair of wooden legs. A sling made from Japanese brocade cradled his withered right arm. Phoebe crouched happily next to him and held his good left hand.

''Twas yourself painted this?'

'I asked first,' he replied.

'I like it very much,' I answered. 'And did you paint it?'

'Can't exactly weave baskets, can I?'

I shook my head and smiled. He smiled in return and in that smile could be seen the handsome, rakish fellow from the photographs.

'You weave baskets?' he asked.

'I do crochet.'

'That what they taught you, eh?'

'Aye, they did. But 'tis the 'cello I prefer to play.'

'Reckon that'll keep you out of a workshop,' he smiled again.

'Lucy's father's an artist,' whispered Phoebe.

'Bit of a connoisseur are we?' he continued the banter. 'Tell me then,' he again indicated the painting. 'Are you the boat or are you the tree?'

'I'm thinking I'm the tree, but I'd like to be the boat.'

'Riding the waves with the wind in your hair?' he shared my thoughts. 'Well, you make boats from trees. You like boats?'

'Aye,' I replied, fondly recalling the boats that were hauled onto stony shores by weather beaten fishermen up and down the Galway coast.

'And I reckon you've another name for them, too.'

'Curach, it is.'

'Curach, eh?' he replied, savouring the word as he imitated my pronunciation perfectly. 'And to what do I owe this pleasure?'

'Look what we found!' Phoebe announced as she passed him the diary she had pulled from the basket she brought with her.

'What's this, Possum?' There was no need for Phoebe to reply for he realised the moment she opened it and showed him the final entry. He held the book at arm's length to read but the book was too cumbersome for him to maintain in that position. Phoebe held it for him and he read silently. As he did, his eyes watered and he gave a slow and thoughtful nod. Then he began to chortle.

'Ha, ha, the padre did it!' he could not contain his delight and, for our further benefit, he put his finishing touches on the story. 'I slipped him a couple of bob to say a few Masses for Gregory Allegri. "He was a good mate of mine, Father, killed in action September 1918," I told him. Jules must have heard the Mass.'

'You actually had a Mass said for a horse?' slowly queried Mrs Epstein.

'You'd have a Mass said for a horse too if it had done for you what it did for me,' he replied. 'Gregory heard that shell and he saved my life. I've buried that poor horse in my dreams for years so I reckon I can pray for his soul if I want and I bet the Bloke upstairs won't mind if I do. Some animals you could swear they were nearly human, the way they seem to understand. Raggedy chestnut knew what he was about all right. I could trust him with anything. What the—?' he turned and came face to face with Phoebe's little stuffed toy which she had pulled out of the basket she brought with her and was using to tickle his cheek.

'You still got that old thing?'

'I would never let him go. Do you remember the stories you used to tell? How Gregory Allegri walked a tightrope that stretched the breadth of France, with—'

'Fireworks overhead and pallid monsters and crocodiles down below, ready to gobble him whole,' her father joined her, his face and voice rivalling hers for expression. 'Well, well, Gregory Allegri.'

He whinnied and snorted just as a father would when entertaining a small child.

'And I'm very pleased to meet you again, too. You know what to do with this, don't you?' he added in a more serious tone and indicated the diary.

'Phoebe and I are taking it to the police tomorrow,' informed Mrs Epstein. 'I should never have doubted you, Roddy.'

He drummed his fingers hard on the diary. '*That* was what Jules wrote the night she died. There *was* someone there that night,' he continued, his dark eyes intensifying. 'I heard footsteps overhead. I knew there was something amiss. I called the nurse and told her to check the attic, for the stairs to the attic were directly above my room. She told me no one was there. I told her to go back and lock the door and bring me the key, which she did under sufferance, convinced it was a delusional whim on my part. But I didn't imagine it. Juliette was murdered that night. Someone replaced her medicine with mine and wrote a note and put it in her room. You didn't know her the way I knew her, Anne,' he sighed. 'More to the point: never doubt the first violin!' he jibed. 'What about a walk?'

'We brought a small picnic with us: some ginger beer, sandwiches and a cake,' Mrs Epstein informed him.

'Sounds pretty good. Come on then, let's find a spot. Remember what to do, Possum?'

With Phoebe's help, he rose from his chair, took up his cane and donned a brightly trimmed boater. He was slightly bandy legged and walked by kicking his feet out from under him. Still, despite his gait and his injuries, he was a marvellously dapper little man and he ambled proudly alongside his daughter.

'I'd never quite thought of her like that before but Phoebe really is a bit of possum, isn't she?' Della remarked to me as we walked. 'She's soft and rounded, with clever hands and great big eyes, hair in ringlets like possums' tails—'

'And she scratches, bites and spits when annoyed,' added Pim. 'She's a possum all right.'

We were taken to a shady spot under a giant fig tree. Mr Raye sat on a park bench and lit a cigarette while we spread the cloth, laid the picnic and enjoyed the splendid view of the harbour.

'Gotta competition coming up, I hear?' he asked. 'What are you playing?'

'The competition requires one quartet by Haydn and one of contrasting mood and or style by another composer,' explained Mrs Epstein.

'Gather the Borodin's your other,' he immediately concluded. 'Which Haydn are you playing?'

'I thought you might like to make a suggestion,' our teacher offered.

'Which do you like best?'

'The *Sunrise*,' we were unanimous.

'Not with the Borodin,' he frowned as he tapped the ash from his cigarette. 'Wrong key for a start and too similar in mood. If I were you, I'd do the *Fifths*.'

'Oh no!' complained Phoebe. 'Why?'

'It's in the right key. If you're doing the Borodin you need the Haydn to be in a minor key. Lucky for you D minor's the perfect counterpart for D major. What's more the two pieces contrast in both mood and style. The *Fifths* is quintessentially Haydn. You pull off the *Fifths* and you will have the adjudicator eating out of the palm of your hand, see if I'm wrong.'

'I hate that piece!' Phoebe declared.

'You don't understand it, Possum,' few people could say that to Phoebe and get away with it. 'Now you go back to my room and see if you can find the score. It's there in the bookcase. And bring my fiddle, too,' he advised with another tap of his cigarette.

'But how can you still play?' Della anxiously asked him.

'Nothing wrong with my left hand. That teacher of yours keeps me busy thinking up exercises to keep you lot out of mischief.'

'So, from now on, if you ever complain about any of the torture *I* inflict on you, you can blame him instead,' added Mrs Epstein. 'He's diabolical when it comes to technique.'

'I'm not one of the Devil's Own for nothing,' he agreed with a grin as he took a puff and let out a stream of smoke. 'Got a name for yourselves?' he asked.

'Mrs Epstein's entered us as the St Dominic's Quartet,' Phoebe passed him the score and wrinkled her nose at the name.

'Ooh, St Dominic's Quartet,' he wrinkled his nose just as she did. 'Annie, you never did have any imagination.'

'Mind you, Roddy, not one of them has come up with a single alternative,' Mrs Epstein spoke in her own defence.

'It's so nunish!' groaned Phoebe.

'Well, what about the Cecilia Quartet?' suggested Della.

'Cecilia? Like Sissy Mahony?' queried Phoebe. 'Not on your life! Under no circumstance will I name a quartet after one of the nastiest girls in the world.'

'No silly,' replied Della, 'St Cecilia's the patron saint of music.'

'Delleen Sotheby, 'tis as nunish as the St Dominic's Quartet,' I complained.

'No more saints!' Phoebe declared. 'I don't believe in God.'

'Crikey, she's been brought up by nuns and she's an atheist! How'd they manage that?' remarked her father as he shook his head and lit another cigarette.

Phoebe heard his remark. Unsure as to whether or not he was jesting, she asked, 'You don't believe in God, do you?'

'Me?' he scoffed and puffed. 'Believe in God? Look at me! God's about the only thing left for me to believe in. No bleeding justice in this world, I can tell you that much,' he muttered.

'Very well,' fearing a sudden descent into morbidity, Mrs Epstein briskly intervened. 'No saints. What about favourite composers?'

'Bach,' I instantly replied.

'Mendelssohn,' Della chimed in.

'Schubert for me,' said Pim.

'Chopin,' added Phoebe.

'You can forget that one,' sighed her father. 'Favourite colours?' he suggested. 'Places? Food?'

There was no single answer to any of those questions.

'Really,' explained Della, 'apart from going to the same school, the only thing that unites us is that we're so different.'

'I still like Brown's Cows,' Pim observed.

'You are not calling yourselves Brown's Cows,' declared Mrs Epstein between her teeth while Mr Raye chuckled.

'The Motley Crew then,' suggested Della with a smile.

'Not bad,' Phoebe's father glanced at our teacher.

'It infers sloppiness, which I don't like,' said Mrs Epstein.

'What about the Piebald Quartet?' suggested Pim. 'That's motley.'

'Too horsy,' Della did not approve. 'The rest of you might like horses but I have absolutely no affinity for the creatures. They bite and kick.'

'The Dappled Quartet then,' Pim modified the horse theme and this time received a glare from Della. 'Well, I thought something spotty seemed to fit,' she shrugged.

Della began to giggle.

'What's so funny?' asked Pim.

'I can't believe I didn't think of it before,' replied Della. 'You know what Wally calls us, don't you?'

'No.'

'He calls us the Spotty Dog Quartet,' said Della. 'What about the Spotty Dog Quartet?' she suggested. 'After all, it just about encapsulates a motley crew from St Dominic's don't you think?'

Pim and Phoebe gave their approval but I did not agree.

'What's wrong with it?' Della sighed.

'I don't think it's a good name for us for it doesn't say enough,' I replied.

'Nonsense,' she argued. 'It's a perfectly good name. I bet you don't like it, Luighseach, because my brother thought it up.'

'That's not true.'

'Yes it is. You're blushing.'

'I amn't!'

'What is going on between the two of you? Wally's as bad. Every time I mention you he growls and ends up pelting cricket balls in the back garden. You should see what he's done to the lawn.'

'Wally, Wally, Wally, Wally,' gobbled Pim as she leant across, and for that she copped my elbow in her ribs. 'Ouch!'

'And 'tis a pity indeed I've not my 'cello with me, for my spike would be through your foot before you could say Jack Robinson!'

'Then you better think of another name quick sticks or Spotty Dog Quartet it will be, Luighseach Straughan!' Della threatened.

'Stop it!' Phoebe interrupted. 'What about The House of Cards?'

'The what?'

'The House of Cards,' Phoebe hastily repeated. 'I agree with Lucy. Spotty Dog doesn't say enough and even worse, it's schoolish. When we first began, Mrs Epstein, you said playing in a string quartet was like building a house of cards: that if we became friends we would build a tower to the stars and that our music would be the tower. Well, that's what we are. We're four flimsy playing cards who lean on each other and we've done it. We've built the tower. At least, I like to think we have,' she glowed with happy pride and beamed at each of us. 'For we have, haven't we? We've built a tower to the stars! We're The House of Cards Quartet!'

And The House of Cards Quartet we became.

'Out of the mouths of babes and sucklings,' smiled her father. 'They always this difficult?' he enquired of Mrs Epstein.

'You call this difficult?' she replied with a gleam. 'They're usually worse.'

'Better build that tower,' he resolved and prepared himself with a fourth cigarette. 'Come and have a look at the score. Pity Reuben and Davy aren't here. Nothing quite like a good old bicker over a quartet!'

For the remainder of the afternoon we were in the hands of a master craftsman. Phoebe's father knew that quartet note by note, phrase by phrase. All its nuances and intricacies of structure he understood as a watchmaker does the finely tuned workings of a watch. He gave Della charge of the violin and directed her through the entire work. In doing so, he discussed all our parts, questioned us, argued with us, challenged us. The same he did with the Borodin. In either case, it was not a dry and mechanical dissection. It was ornamented with little quips, amusing observations, stories of student days in his beloved Vienna, parodies of various teachers and composers, insights into art, architecture, literature, life, not to mention the smoking of at least a dozen cigarettes. But most endearing was the mood in which it was all conveyed. To see Mrs Epstein, usually plain and serious, relaxed and joyful; and the corresponding look of deep gratitude on the part of Phoebe's father, that lesson – for lesson it was – without doubt, was the best lesson we ever had.

47

Come Thursday, however, Mrs Epstein's gravity had returned with a vengeance. When we saw her that afternoon, her glasses seemed to rest more heavily on her cheekbones and her eyes appeared even more distorted and askew. Her face was shadowed with care; and her dark hair, which was always rolled and pinned, was pulled back more severely.

'Phoebe's not here,' she informed us in her most sober manner. 'Mr Esptein's taken her to an orchestral audition. They're late, which is probably just as well because I need to tell you a few things.'

We entered the music room and sat together on the lounge.

'I think you ought to know that Phoebe will not be returning to school,' our teacher announced. 'She is sitting for an audition because she has to find work. At the same time, she will be continuing her music studies with me and at the Conservatorium. Most importantly, though, she needs to be with her father. Given the way things are with regard to her mother's death it is probably better for her if she is removed from the school situation.'

'What happened, Mrs Epstein? What did the police say?' Della eagerly asked. Murder had been uppermost in Della's mind for the past week.

'We spoke to the police,' Mrs Epstein's leaden tone had a cauterizing effect. 'As you can imagine, the diary provides sufficient evidence to cast reasonable doubt on Phoebe's mother's suicide. And it's not merely the final entry. There is a pattern in the writing. It seems that Juliette Raye only wrote when she was happy. She suffered bouts of Melancholia during which she tended to withdraw and there are gaps in the dates of the diary entries which suggest that. One significant break coincides with a period during which she was hospitalised for her condition. It appears that the episodes diminished significantly after Roderick began writing, the exception being two occasions: one following the news of his injury, and another following the death of her mother. After that, she takes charge and the writing reveals a young woman of remarkable strength of character. It is highly unlikely that Juliette Raye committed suicide.'

'Will there be a murder investigation?' Della inquired.

Mrs Epstein ignored her.

'In due course, arrangements will be made for a proper burial,' our teacher continued. 'As you can imagine, this is going to be a very emotional time for Phoebe and her father. I think they would appreciate your support and understanding.'

'But what about the murder, Mrs Epstein?' Della again voiced her concern.

'Yes, Della, it would seem that there was a murder,' Mrs Epstein sighed. 'However, the possibility of it coming to trial, let alone any conviction, will be very remote given the years that have elapsed since the crime.'

'Do you think Phoebe's right in thinking her aunt did it?' Della persevered.

'Della,' Mrs Epstein paused and gave her a particularly saturnine look. 'Do you realise that what you are talking about involves two of my dearest friends?'

'I'm sorry, Mrs Epstein,' Della finally capitulated.

'Phoebe's aunt is a suspect,' our teacher resumed her more detached manner. 'So also is Roderick.'

'But that's impossible!'

'When a wife is murdered, the first suspect is invariably the husband.'

'Why, Mr Raye couldn't harm a single soul,' declared Della.

'No he couldn't,' our teacher agreed. 'Others, who were acquainted with Juliette Raye, are also being questioned, some of whom you know. Davy Birstall, for instance,' she added with a glance at me. 'Of course they will be quickly ruled out because they had no motive. Given the circumstances, Ailine Devereaux' sudden departure following Phoebe's impetuous visit the other day places her under a good deal of suspicion. The police are trying to find her. No one, however, knows where she has gone. Unfortunately, Phoebe's actions that Sunday may have prevented the matter from coming to justice. That is, if her aunt is guilty of such a crime. The violin in the attic is too ambiguous a clue. What the police must produce is substantial evidence that Ailine Devereaux was in the country at the time of her sister's death.'

'And what do *you* think, Mrs Epstein? Do you think she did it?' Della could not help herself.

Mrs Epstein looked away from us and gazed absently at the piano.

'Jealousy is a horrible thing, isn't it?' she remarked. 'And it's particularly inexcusable when it has its roots in one's own choices.'

I tried to follow her gaze. On top of the piano were the photographs she showed us two Sundays ago. They had been framed and were now arranged around the nine branched candlestick which once rested on the sideboard.

''Tis the photographs you put there, Mrs Epstein,' I began.

'That was Phoebe's doing,' she replied and smiled a little for the first time that afternoon. 'She keeps telling me that happiness shouldn't be locked away in bureau drawers. The problem is, the more I look at that photograph, the more I cannot help but forge the links in a chain of tragedy between the joys of the past and the sorrow surrounding the present situation.'

Mrs Epstein fetched the photograph of the feast of the gods.

'I told you it was a wedding gift, didn't I?' she asked.

We nodded.

'Well,' she explained, 'it was taken the day we were married. You see, Mr Epstein and I were not able to be legally married in Austria because Mr Epstein is Jewish and I am a Catholic. We did not have a wedding until two years after we came out to Australia, the reason being that, while a civil marriage was feasible, we could not be married in the Church unless the priest obtained a special dispensation. It was a very drawn out and difficult affair. Most priests we approached discouraged us from marrying and refused to take the matter any further. When we finally found a priest who was prepared to do so, we were not permitted a church wedding and were married in the presbytery instead.

'Reuben and I intended the wedding to be a discreet occasion but we made the mistake of asking Roderick Raye to be one of the witnesses. Now Roddy knew full well how hard it had been for us – in fact, it was he who found us a priest – the priest you met at the veterans' home the other day.

'What was he doing there?' asked Della.

'He's a very good friend of Roderick's. Father Moran is his name and, as well as presiding over our nuptials, he later received Roddy into the Church.

'Anyway, Roddy was determined to give us a wedding we wouldn't forget. Larrikin that he is he invited all our friends with the result that there was upwards of fifty people crammed into the parlour of that tiny presbytery.

'I don't think Father Moran could believe his eyes that morning. One look at Roderick with his dark curls, moustache and goatee, and Father could have sworn that Old Nick himself had come to play master of ceremonies. And Roddy, energetic and witty as ever, carried off his part with the most incredible panache. He was at his best that day.

'And the wedding was only the beginning, for that dear fellow had organised a breakfast at the Devereaux home. Part of the entertainment included an improvised staging of *Orpheus in the Underworld*. We'd all recently done the show so everyone was very well acquainted with it. We sang it through, doubling up roles as required. Madame Devereaux accompanied on the piano. George Hunt, who performed the role on stage, was Jupiter; Roderick, who can do quite a good falsetto, took the part of Pluto; Reuben was forced to play Orpheus, which demanded from him an appalling violin solo which he did appallingly well, and I was landed with Eurydice. We even performed the Can Can. That is, the Can Can was performed by Davy Birstall, Roderick, Reuben and George.'

Mrs Epstein paused from her telling to wipe her eyes. 'Honestly,' she said, 'Roddy couldn't have devised a better way to make fun of the whole situation. I don't think I have ever laughed so much in my life as when those boys appeared in all those petticoats and corsets.

'After that we gathered outside for the tableau. The donkey you can see there is real and no one could get it to budge from the vegetable garden. In the end it was Roddy himself who succeeded. Clad in a tunic, barefoot and with a pitchfork in hand, he ran off to the kitchen, and after scaring the living daylights out of the cook and housemaid, persuaded them to donate a sack of sugar for the purpose. He petted and coaxed the little creature, and in due course he mounted it and trotted it down to the front garden. It must have been the first inkling anyone had that he could actually ride.

'And that was when Ailine and Juliette had a fight. Ailine had managed to direct everyone to their positions. Juliette and Roderick, as Persephone and Pluto, were required to sit in the middle of the group. Ailine could not, however, get Juliette to comply. Against her sister's instructions, Juliette refused to avert her gaze from Roderick who, incidentally, was not making it easy for her to do otherwise. Never before had anyone seen little Juliette stand up for herself, declaring that she was free to look whosoever, howsoever and at whomsoever she chose. To make matters worse, she and Roddy had eaten most of the fruit in the cornucopia set before them. What they hadn't eaten they had passed to everyone else, including the donkey. All that was left were a few quinces, which couldn't be eaten because they're hard as rocks if they're not cooked. Of course, that provoked a ridiculous series of quince jokes on Roddy's part. Lina was furious and I don't know what angered her more: Juliette's coy defiance or Roderick's irrepressible *joie de vivre*. Now that was strange. Normally Ailine would have joined in the banter. When it came to repartee, she and Roddy were a veritable Beatrice and Benedick.

'Anyway, the result is what you see in the centre of that photograph: a picture of two young people who are deeply in love. It was taken in May 1913. A week later Roderick and Juliette announced their engagement. They married in September and Phoebe was born the following January. The odd thing about it all is that I never really noticed the expression on their faces until you girls were looking at it the other day. I cannot believe I was so blind.'

'But they had been courting for years, Mrs Epstein,' Della remarked.

'How do you know that?' asked our teacher.

'I—I read a few letters,' Della confessed. 'I didn't read everything!' she protested in the face of Mrs Epstein's scowl. 'Only enough to know, and Phoebe told me what her father told her. Did you hear them play the *Kreutzer Sonata*?'

Mrs Epstein looked incredulously at Della and came to her own conclusion as to how Della had acquired that piece of information.

'In Vienna? Yes, I did,' she replied, 'during one of those many soirees Madame Devereaux used to host. It was a brave effort by two young players. Juliette showed promise of being every bit as good as her mother and she held her ground with Roddy, which is no mean feat. As for Roddy, his technique has always been scintillating, but it was the conviction and intensity of his interpretation that was more remarkable. His teacher was very pleased. There are some works that are important to a musician not because of what they master but because of what they learn. The *Kreutzer* was that for Roddy. He crossed the Rubicon with that piece, and in more ways than one it seems. Little wonder,' she smiled to herself. 'He'd fallen in love. Well now, that makes tremendous sense.'

'He wanted to marry her, Mrs Epstein,' added Della. 'But her mother refused her permission so they had a secret engagement.'

'Which they managed to keep very well guarded,' Mrs Epstein concluded. 'I can understand why. He would never have permitted a private matter to interfere with his precious quartet. So, their marriage wasn't an impetuous folly after all?'

We shook our heads.

'Roddy can be exasperating,' our teacher sighed as she came to terms with this new consideration. 'He is so hard to keep up with. I think he forgets that when it comes to life we don't all have a copy of the score. He never explains his actions and yet he expects everyone else to be of one accord with himself. I could never understand why he rushed into something as serious as his own marriage with so much bravura, especially after what Reuben and I went through. As for being happy as a result of such a union— well, frankly their separation seemed inevitable. But he didn't rush into it, and what seemed rash was really the fruit of a deep and ardent love. Really, the man is a walking paradox! Mind you, it didn't make what he was faced with afterwards any easier – in fact it probably makes his subsequent misdoings all the more grave – but at least the marriage itself wasn't so foolhardy.

'How I've misjudged him! Roddy has always told me the two years he spent with Juliette and Phoebe after the War were the two best years of his life. Then he adds in his dry way that it must have been the morphine he was on at the time. I never believed him, partly because of how sick he was, partly because of the circumstances of his marriage, and primarily because I thought of him as a wonderful violinist, devoted only to his music, and never as a husband and father. But, as Phoebe pointed out to me the other day, she always thought of him as a wonderful father. She never knew him as a musician. When I see them together, I have to admit she's right. He is a wonderful father and it's beautiful to see.'

'Aye, Mrs Epstein, them two's thick as thieves,' I remarked.

'They certainly are,' she smiled. 'Anyway, Della, you asked me whether I think Ailine Devereaux murdered Juliette Raye and, yes, I would have to say I do. It's a question of motive, isn't it? And the more I think of it, the more I piece episodes and people together, the more I cannot help but conclude that she did. If Roddy and Juliette's romance had escaped everyone else's attention, Ailine knew what was going on, I'm certain of it. At least she knew what was going on at the time that photograph was taken. She's far more astute than me. She would have noticed the expression on their faces and gleaned the reason behind their high spirits: that Juliette was pregnant, that Roddy was the father and that the two of them were betrothed. She never turned that photograph into a painting and from that point she never played her 'cello with us again. She was jealous.

'The peculiar thing about it is that I cannot for the life of me understand why. The two sisters had their rivalries as sisters do, but on the whole they were close. As for Ailine and Roddy, they were very good friends and intellectually they were well matched. But there were no romantic attachments between them at all. He never paid her particular attention (which I now see why) and she never craved it. Besides, she entertained no shortage of admirers of her own. Nor was she remotely interested in marriage and children, whereas Juliette was. Ailine was married to her art. She still is. Why should she be jealous?'

'Did she secretly love him, do you think?' Della probed a little further.

'Maybe she did,' Mrs Epstein surmised, 'and Roddy rejected her. I shudder to think how she reacted to that letter he sent her after the War.'

'But why go to such extremes, Mrs Ep?' questioned Pim. 'Hadn't he suffered enough from his injuries?'

'You'd think it would suffice to let bygones be bygones, wouldn't you?' Mrs Epstein answered. 'It's incredibly cruel. Whatever Roddy's physical ailments may have been, Ailine couldn't have picked a better way to completely ruin him than to destroy the people he loves. As for the crime itself, only Ailine would have been clever enough and familiar enough with her sister's hand to forge a note like that, let alone have detailed knowledge of the house to be able to slip in and out so unobtrusively.'

'And if she did, Mrs Ep, she killed her own sister,' replied Pim. 'How could anyone kill their own sister?'

'It's very sad, Pim. But sometimes do we not hate more intensely the people we have most deeply loved?'

Pim regretfully acknowledged the possibility.

'Anyway, girls, what I might think has absolutely no bearing on the outcome of this horrible affair. Short of extracting a confession, the police will be lucky to find any substantial evidence to convict anyone. And if they can't find Ailine Devereaux, well, getting her confession is a lost cause, if any confession could be had. Having Lina admit to anything she doesn't want to would be like letting blood from a stone.'

'They'll find her surely, Mrs Epstein,' I tried to reassure her.

'Not if she's used another name. The police have asked us to suggest possibilities: her mother's name, anglicisations, even her Jewish roots. She could have passed as Adele Walkowicz, Adeline Volcot, Ailine Devereaux, any variation on the above or something entirely different.

'You know, girls, I feel like a pawn on a chessboard. I wrote to Ailine at Roddy's request to tell her of Juliette's death. I wrote frequently out of simple friendship to pass her news, particularly of the improvement in Roddy's health. Time and again I tried to persuade her to come and take care of Phoebe, only to find that put to destructive purpose. She neglected that little girl, degraded her, calumniated against her parents and vandalised the home she loves. She nearly drove that poor child to despair. I cannot comprehend that degree of vindictiveness. And to think I actually facilitated it.'

'But she didn't count with one thing, Mrs Ep,' Pim interrupted.

'What's that?'

'Phoebe has friends,' replied Pim.

'I think you girls probably saved her life,' remarked Mrs Epstein.

'And you too, Mrs Epstein,' added Della. 'It's wonderful what you've done for Phoebe. Anyway, you've told me a hundred times: you can only do your best, and yours has been a jolly good best.'

'I'm very worried,' Mrs Epstein sighed. 'I hate to think what an investigation, let alone a trial, is going to do to them. How Phoebe will cope, I don't know and I couldn't bear to see Roddy have another breakdown. He's come such a long way.

He cannot play the violin any more but you can tell he's a marvellous teacher. As for his painting well, you saw a landscape last Sunday. You should see the portraits. They're not quite as refined as the ones your father paints, Luighseach, but then Roddy's subjects are pretty quirky. You might have gathered that a lot of the men in that home are not the full quid, but they don't mind having their portraits done. Collectively, Roderick's paintings are one of the most poignant indictments concerning the War you will ever find.'

'Well, he has Phoebe now, thanks to you, and Phoebe has him,' concluded Pim. 'They'll look after each other. Besides, Mrs Ep, you can't solve everyone's problems. As my brother Johnny says, sometimes you've just gotta trust.'

'Speaking of Phoebe, I don't know what's keeping her. I'm sorry to waste your time, girls.'

'Nothing of that, Mrs Epstein,' I replied. 'There's still some time left for a lesson. In fact, I think you could do with a bit of Haydn yourself. Will you not play second violin with us this afternoon till your next student comes?'

'I say, Luighseach, that's a brilliant idea!' Della clapped her hands. 'What about it, Mrs Epstein?'

'Girls, I couldn't think of anything I'd like to do better.'

For us, Mrs Epstein had always been more than a teacher (although being a teacher is no small thing), and in many ways, for Mrs Epstein, we had always been more than mere students. During that afternoon, though, we became friends. From my point of view, my teacher had always been a friend to me. The difference now was that I knew I had become a friend to her.

Della and Pim said exactly the same.

48

Pim and I sat at the end of my bed and mulled over the problem before us. In the light of past events, it was not a very big problem, but it was a pressing one and it was as annoying as a fly on a summer's day.

The problem hung on a coat hanger that was hooked over my wardrobe door.

'I'll not be wearing that garden party frock, Pimmy Connolly,' I declared, 'not for to perform next Saturday.'

'What's wrong with it?'

''Tis too pretty, that's what's wrong with it.'

'What's wrong with that?' replied Pim. 'I thought you liked looking pretty.'

'Aye I do, I do indeed. But I'll not look pretty with a calliper, not with that frock. I'm needing to wear a calliper for to go on stage and carry my 'cello, you know, and if I do I'll be putting on thick stockings. 'Twill spoil everything. Can you imagine wearing such a frock as that with heavy brown boots and black woollen stockings?'

Pim smiled. 'Reckon it'll be enough to give Della's mother a heart attack.'

'Aye, and if I as much breathe a word about it to Delleen Sotheby a talking to will there be on how much time and trouble was taken over the making of it. I'll not be adding to her worries, Pimmy.'

And Della's worries were significant. All the excitement and intrigue that had been generated by Phoebe's situation collided head-long with her increasing anxiety over next weekend's competition. Della was exhausted. Her cough returned, as it frequently did when she was tired, and it became so bad that Mrs Epstein cut short our Saturday morning rehearsal at the Conservatorium and told her to go home and get some rest.

Della broke down in tears and took refuge in the washroom.

'I can't do any more!' she wept.

'Mrs Epstein's not asking you to do any more, Delleen,' I explained. 'All she's asking is for you to go home and rest some.'

'Yes, because I'm not playing well enough! I'm hopeless!'

'Nothing of that, Delleen. You're weary is all.'

But my efforts to calm her were fruitless.

'I'm not like the rest of you,' she continued, sniffing and wringing her hands. 'It's all so easy for you and Pim and Phoebe. You can hand anything to Pim and she plays it, it doesn't matter how difficult it is. As for Phoebe, she's holding herself back for my sake for I'm certain now she's every bit as good as her father. And you're no exception, Luighseach. You can tell what key a piece is in merely by listening; you improvise like I've never heard anyone before and your rhythmic sense is impeccable. You can do whatever you want on that 'cello of yours. But me? I have to work and work!'

'Aye you do, like the rest of us and look at what you've accomplished,' I tried again to give her some perspective.

'You're all so strong!' Della wailed another protest. 'You and Pim are born athletes and Phoebe has nerves of steel. I don't have any stamina at all. I'm weak, Luighseach! And Mrs Epstein made me— of all people, she made me lead!'

'Aye she did and she was right to do it,' I insisted. 'She made you lead so that we would learn how to follow. We couldn't have had a better leader. So kind and tender have you been with Phoebe and so patient with Pim and her temper. For myself, I cannot tell enough how much you mean to me, Delleen Sotheby. You've been a friend to each of us and you've won our hearts as much as you've earned our respect. 'Tis true indeed what you say. You're not strong: you're gentle, but there bees a lot of strength in gentleness, I'm thinking. Don't you be so cruel to yourself now. You said that to myself once and I'm saying it to you. Besides, you play beautifully, Delleen.'

'I can't compete with Phoebe, Luighseach.'

'Indeed, indeed, who can?' A fire had been lit inside Phoebe and her playing that morning had been as lively as Della's had been listless. 'But you're not being asked to compete with her,' I continued. 'Phoebe knows her job well enough and 'tis up to her to fit in with yourself. There'll be her da to answer to if she doesn't, as well as Mrs Epstein, and she'll be loath to disappoint either one. Which reminds me, Delleen, do you remember what happened with Mr Raye the other day?'

'The Sunday we spent talking about the quartets?'

'Aye, and do you remember how he treated you that day?'

'He made me do all the work,' even the memory of that afternoon seemed to exhaust her.

'Aye, he did. You were his voice, Delleen,' I reminded her, 'not Phoebe, and for good reason, too. 'Twas to yourself he passed the violin and he did so because you're first violinist and you're the leader of our quartet. Furthermore, everything you played that day was a joy to hear and not a word did he say in criticism. 'Twas high praise indeed. Mr Raye honoured you that day, not only because of your position but because of yourself and the way you play. Let you not forget that. You're tired now is all. Why do you be so tired? Are you not sleeping well?'

'Well enough,' she sniffed and dabbed her eyes with her handkerchief.

'Do you be in pain, Delleen?' I looked her through.

Della searched her purse for another handkerchief.

I passed her my own.

'Delleen?' I asked again.

'My back hurts,' she eventually admitted, and again she began to cry.

I hugged her close and in doing so I was in for an unpleasant surprise. So thin and fragile was she that there was almost nothing of her to hug.

Pim nodded at the memory of the morning's events.

'Dunno what we're going to do about Dell,' she said. 'Why don't you wear thick light coloured stockings?' she returned to the other problem.

'So that everyone will see the calliper, Pimmy?'

Pim crossed her arms and thought some more.

'Then you know what I would do if I were you?' she added.

'And what would you do?'

'Simple. Don't wear the dress.'

'And what will I wear instead?'

'Wear trousers.'

'You're pulling my leg.'

'You have a pair of trousers don't you?'

'Not any more,' I lamented, 'for my da gave them to charity. Can you credit that, Pimmy? For once 'twas myself passing clothes to charity and not charity passing clothes to myself!'

'First time for everything, Lucy. Anyway, I can get you a dinner suit. Ambrose will lend me one. He's about the same height and build as you and you can go on stage like that. All we'll have to do is fix the hem on the trousers. That way you can wear the brace and no one will see.'

'My da will kill me.'

'No he won't. It's not indecent,' Pim had arguments aplenty to justify her position.

'Indeed it isn't, but he doesn't like it all the same.'

'Listen, how did you learn to ride a horse? Side saddle or astride?' she asked me.

'Astride and bareback it was,' I replied.

'Did you wear breeches or jodhpurs?'

'Nothing of the sort for 'twas only skirts I ever wore.'

'But what if you were riding in a gymkhana? What about that?'

'Breeches indeed it would be to be sure.'

Pim nodded. 'Then think of it like this. Playing a 'cello is like riding a horse. You play with the darn thing between your legs; you don't play it side saddle. So you're going to dress appropriately, especially for a competition. Nowadays the only women who wear long skirts are grandmothers and nuns. You're neither and you're going to look silly in a short white dress with a leg brace and black stockings. Trousers are more suitable. I wouldn't suggest it if it was Phoebe or me playing the 'cello, but you haven't a curve in sight. Add to that being tall and broad-shouldered with cropped hair, you could pass as a boy any time. On a stage, who's going to know?'

'Anyone who knows my name.'

'The way you spell it? No one can pronounce your name at sight. It's as likely to be Louis as Lucy. We'll dress you up as a boy and you can be Louis Straughan for a day. What about it?'

I smiled. 'A grand plan it is. But not a word, mind you, to a single soul, not even Phoebe and especially not Delleen Sotheby.'

'Mum's the word,' grinned Pim. 'I'll see Ambrose at Mass tomorrow. I'll ask him then. By the way, how did you get that crack on your mirror?'

'I threw a boot at it.'

'Might have known. Speaking of boots, make sure you wear black ones for the performance. You got a pair of black boots?'

'Aye, I do. There'll be an old pair in my wardrobe from before I started school.'

'Beaut,' she concluded. 'Well, gotta go. Meeting Peggy for afternoon tea. I'll see you on Monday.'

Perhaps the best preparation Della could have made for next Saturday's performance was to take the week to recover her strength. And that was what she did. We did not see her until we came together at Mrs Epstein's for our usual Thursday lesson. Although pale, she seemed more relaxed and rested. We played both quartets through once and once only to replicate what we would do on Saturday.

Other than that, our respective preparations were private affairs. For my part, they involved practising walking with my 'cello. An earlier appointment with Dr Little had me undertaking some exercises designed to strengthen my right knee. I had to stand against the wall and keep my knee steady for the count of one hundred. It was holding quite well and I was feeling more optimistic than I had been for months about doing away with my right calliper.

As far as walking on stage was concerned, I set myself a course similar to what I would encounter at the Conservatorium. Every afternoon, with my 'cello in hand, I practised walking down the hall, out the front door, down the steps, along the path to the front gate and back again.

Through my little excursion, I discovered that the entire neighbourhood had been following my progress for some time. The hours I had spent practising in the parlour had been overheard by many a passer-by who now did not hesitate to chat with me if we chanced to coincide. And so I learned from the rabbitoh that he liked to park his cart outside our house of an afternoon to catch a bit of Bach, as did the milkman who also paused from his rounds. Children were intrigued by my 'big violin' and mothers were glad to see me 'doing so well'. 'We enjoy hearing you play, dear, and all the best for Saturday,' became the parting words of many a lady and gentleman, young and old.

I developed a technique for descending the front steps, using my 'cello almost as I would a crutch. Endpin extended, I planted the 'cello on the step below, eased my braced leg down and followed with my good leg. The day before the competition, I was about to engage in one such operation when Hilda Geraghty walked by.

'Hey there, Lucy!' she called. 'It's tomorrow, isn't it?'

'Aye it is!' I looked up and called back with a smile. I could no longer hide my excitement over the coming event.

'Good luck!' she called again and waved. 'I'll be thinking of you!'

I returned her wave by lifting the 'cello a little higher before lowering it to the next step. The spike hit the step with greater force than I anticipated. I lost my hold and then my balance.

'Lucy!' Hilda screamed.

Down onto the 'cello I fell. There sounded an almighty snap and crack before I rolled over the side of the step and crashed onto the petunias.

'What in Heaven's name was that?' I heard Mrs Murphy's voice. 'It sounded like a shot gun!'

'Lucy's hurt, Mrs Murphy!' exclaimed Hilda.

'Well, don't just stand there, dear! Run and fetch her father!'

I sat up in the middle of the petunias and peered at Mrs Murphy.

'I've broken my 'cello, Mrs Murphy!'

'Forget your violin, child. Are you hurt?'

Mrs Murphy brushed some of the dirt off my face, took out her handkerchief and dabbed my cheek.

'A nasty scratch that is,' she remarked as she passed me my glasses. 'How on earth did that happen?'

I knew full well. I had been lashed by a snapping string.

'I'll go and get a bit of steak in a minute to stop that bruise getting too bad. How are your hands, dear?'

My hands and wrists were fine. Years of experience with falls had led me instinctively to tuck them in close. With Mrs Murphy's help I pulled myself to standing position and stared in horror at the 'cello which lay on the lowest step.

Daid came running down the hill with Hilda not far behind him.

'Buíochas le Dia nach bhfuil tú gortaithe, a Luighseach!' he hugged me tight.

'I smashed it, Da!'

'Aye, lass,' Daid pulled his watch from his pocket and looked at the debris spread across the bottom step. 'And I'm thinking we'll be in time to catch Miss Bray before she closes her shop for the night and we'll see what she can do. I'll be getting the motorcycle now.'

Within minutes I was helped into the sidecar and I sat there cradling the poor, broken 'cello with one hand and pressing a small piece of steak against my chin with the other. Down King St we sped and parked in front of Miss Bray's store.

Miss Bray had just turned the key to the shop door. Accompanying her was the last person I wanted, at that moment, to see.

'Oh Mr David, I'm so very sorry!' I cried.

'What's up, kid?'

''Tis Mavis 'cello, Mr David. I've broken her!'

'Oh dear,' Miss Bray caught sight of the 'cello. 'I'll get Mr Hunt,' she said as she brought us inside. She bustled ahead of us and out the rear door.

We soon heard her calling over the back fence.

Old Mr Hunt presently shuffled in wearing his slippers and half moon glasses. He studied the injured 'cello which now lay in pieces on the table in the back room.

'Not the first time this 'cello's been to hospital, eh Davy?' he remarked.

'Poor old Mavis,' Mr David fondly shook his head at the 'cello. 'She's had her neck broken, been kicked in the ribs, her bridge collapsed and her pegs unstuck more times than I can count.'

'What between you and Dickie,' added Miss Bray.

'My brother,' Mr David gave me a nudge in explanation.

'Could have sworn you boys played cricket with that instrument,' continued Mr Hunt.

'I didn't know you had a brother, Mr David,' I remarked.

He nodded and quietly answered my silent question. 'Turks sniped him, Lucy.'

'Doesn't look good,' Mr Hunt finished his examination. 'We'll have to replace the neck and she's taken a beating in the belly. We'll need to patch her together and fit her with a new bridge and sound post.'

'Will I be able to play her again?' I asked.

'Can't say till I have a closer look, Lucy,' grimly replied Mr Hunt.

'I'm so very sorry!' I cried to Mr David.

'Doesn't worry me, kid,' replied Mr David. 'Mavis is a workhorse 'cello and I can't play her any more. More to the point, what are you going to do?'

'That 'cello's going to be in hospital for a few months, I'm afraid,' informed Mr Hunt.

'But I'm playing tomorrow afternoon in the competition! What am I going to do?'

'I have an idea, Lucy,' suggested Miss Bray. 'I'll lend you the old, dark 'cello. It's still here. Will you promise me you'll take special care of it?'

'Would you do that, Miss Bray?' To think I was going to play that 'cello!

'Of course. We can't have you without an instrument to play. Now, you'll probably want to warm up before you go on stage,' Miss Bray proceeded. 'I close the shop at noon tomorrow. I'll bring it straight round to the Conservatorium. We were planning to go the performance, weren't we, Mr Birstall? We'll come a little earlier and meet you there.'

Mr David smiled in his good-natured way. 'Well, Miss Bray,' he said, 'I think that calls for a picnic lunch in the gardens. What do you say?'

'What a splendid idea!' replied Miss Bray. 'I'll make some sandwiches and pack a thermos. Now the best thing you can do, Lucy, is have a good night's sleep. Don't worry! You're a perfect match for that instrument. It won't let you down and nor will we,' she reassured me.

We made a few final arrangements and parted company.

'They're not courting are they, Da?' I asked as I watched Mr David and Miss

413

Bray walk down the street together.

'I do believe he's been courting her since your concert, Luighseach,' Daid replied.

'She didn't smile at you the way she usually does, Da,' I observed.

Daid said nothing. He merely smiled.

And a very relieved smile it was, too.

49

As promised, Mr David and Miss Bray brought the old 'cello to the Conservatorium early on Saturday afternoon. We met in the corridor outside the room that had been allocated for our preparations. Mr David was carrying the 'cello in his right hand. Miss Bray had her arm tucked in to what remained of his left arm and brought with her a basket covered with a checked cloth.

'Here you are, Lucy, all safe and sound,' she smiled as Mr David handed me the 'cello. 'Mr Hunt played it a bit this morning to warm it up and your favourite bow's in the case. Best of luck! We'll be thinking of you.'

'Morgan here?' asked Mr David of Daid's whereabouts.

'To the Cathedral he's gone for to say a few prayers,' I informed him.

'They won't go astray. Knock 'em dead, kid,' he replied.

'Do you mean to say you're going to play that ugly old thing?' Phoebe wrinkled her nose when she saw the 'cello come out of his case. Since Mr and Mrs Epstein had a mid-morning commitment, she had come to the Conservatorium with Daid and me.

'I am indeed,' I replied. 'A fine 'cello he is and no mistake. 'Twas a long time ago you heard him yourself in the back room at the music store. Do you remember the time we met when you hid behind the cupboard there?'

'Oh yes,' she smiled. 'You were so angry with me. Can you play the Brahms *Double* yet?'

'A double concerto all by myself now?' I answered with a laugh.

Pim arrived with her oldest brother and sister.

'One dinner suit, and more lunch if we need it,' she announced as Leo and Lily offloaded a valise and a basket. 'Don't know about you but I can't play on an empty stomach.'

'Best of luck, little sis,' Leo made his departure.

'When did you say Peggy was coming?' asked Lily.

'Told her you'd meet her in the foyer at a quarter to two.'

'We'll be there,' Lily replied. 'Polly's coming, too. Good luck!'

'What – is – that?' Pim saw the 'cello.

'Faith, Pimmy Connolly, if you don't know how a 'cello looks by now—'

'Where's your 'cello?' she asked.

I told her.

'And not a word to Mrs Epstein will you say about it,' I cautioned.

'And not a word to Mrs Epstein will you say about what?' Mrs Epstein appeared at the door. 'What happened to you?' she asked the moment she saw the lash mark on my face.

''Twas but a string that I broke, Mrs Epstein,' I candidly explained.

'Really Luighseach, I thought you'd have a better understanding of the behaviour of 'cello strings by now. And that bruise on your chin, how did you get that?'

'A wee fall it was, Mrs Epstein, and not a bad one.'

'You certainly know how to pick your times. Where's Della?' Mrs Epstein anxiously glanced around the room and consulted her watch.

'Not here yet,' said Pim.

'Honestly! Given the opportunity, that family would institute its own calendar!' she scolded. 'Well, I hope she comes soon. You need to warm up.'

'I reckon you're more nervous than we are, Mrs Ep,' remarked Pim.

Mrs Epstein sighed in agreement.

'Now, I have a special something for the four of you,' she passed us a little cardboard box with a card marked 'To the House of Cards Quartet'.

We opened it and found four small corsages featuring the daintiest of pink rosebuds and a delicate spray of white.

'It's not my doing,' Mrs Epstein excused herself with a smile. 'You've Mr Raye to thank. Your father's here, Phoebe.'

'He's come to see me play?' Phoebe asked in astonishment and ran out before Mrs Epstein could reply.

'You don't call them Tweedle-dum and Tweedle-dee for nothing, Mrs Ep,' observed Pim when she saw Mr Epstein and Phoebe's father joking together a little further down the hallway.

'Ho, ho! Steady on!' warned Mr Raye with a laugh as he handed his stick to Mr Epstein. Phoebe nearly bowled him flat. Fortunately, she only knocked off his hat. Father and daughter fell into each other's arms and laughed and cried and laughed all over again.

'We brought him across,' explained Mrs Epstein. 'It was like taking a child to the zoo. You'd think the way he is he'd slow down but he was as lively as ever on the ferry. How he'll cope with the performance, though, I don't know.'

'As long as everyone plays in tune he'll be all right don't you think, Mrs Ep?'

'It's not guaranteed is it, Pim? Wish us luck. I'm already exhausted. As for you lot, enjoy yourselves and do your very best. I can't ask for more than that. You're well prepared and I couldn't be more proud of you.'

She parted with a hug to each of us and one to Phoebe. Along with Mr Epstein and Mr Raye, she gave us a final wave and walked back to the foyer.

Pim was pinning Phoebe's corsage when Della finally arrived with Mrs Sotheby. Mother and daughter were a pattern of each other: the epitome of embroidered elegance, petite and pert, hats and gloves perfectly fitted, shoes and stockings unsullied by dust and dirt, charm cultivated to a tee.

'Oh, how nice,' remarked Mrs Sotheby of the corsage.

'There's one for everyone,' Phoebe chatted excitedly. 'My father brought them especially.'

'How very thoughtful, dear,' Mrs Sotheby gushed her approval. 'What sweet buds! Della, did you see the corsages?'

'Yes, Mummy,' Della dutifully replied.

Oh, to be a fly on the wall when Mrs Sotheby meets Mr Raye, I thought.

'Why are you not dressed, Lucy?' Mrs Sotheby studied me with some consternation.

'I'll be changing soon to be sure, Mrs Sotheby,' I reassured her. 'I mean, to think of spoiling such a fine costume as that with a trip to town on a motorcycle and a performance to give. Imagine it! Walking on stage with my frock crushed and stockings laddered. 'Twould not be proper, I'm thinking, ma'am.'

'Yes indeed,' she agreed. 'How remarkably considerate of you.'

At that, Pim let out a guffaw and took a huge bite of apple to silence it.

'But what on earth have you done to your face, dear?' Mrs Sotheby pointedly ignored Pim's outburst.

''Tis but a scratch, ma'am,' I tried to dismiss it.

'Gracious, Lucy!' she exclaimed. 'To even think of walking on stage in that state!' Della's mother bade me sit. She opened her handbag and produced a dainty cloisonné box. Then she removed my glasses herself, and, to my horror, began to assault me with face powder.

'There! That's much better,' she declared with a final dab on my nose. 'Well, bon chance, girls, and we'll see you afterwards for supper,' Mrs Sotheby snapped shut the little box, graciously beamed good-bye and made her departure.

'Touché, Mummy!' Della giggled, gasped and coughed. She was certainly relaxed and rested, but by no means was she recovered. 'Oh, Luighseach! To see your face! Oh, it's priceless! Oh!'

'Wait till she sees the dinner suit,' I muttered as I examined the face powder I had wiped from my nose.

We began to warm up, each one working on passages of pleasure or concern. Our performance was to be the last of six ensembles and the competition had been spread across two sessions. Phoebe and I had sat in on the morning session during which we heard three different groups. They all were much older than we were, and to all impressions seemed far more experienced. Their repertoire included brooding and intense pieces by Schubert, Brahms and Beethoven in addition to the required Haydn, and the sheer power of the music left me a little in awe. Phoebe was not quite so perturbed for she knew some of the players from her studies at the Conservatorium and had heard them many times in recitals.

'I wouldn't worry,' she remarked as we left the auditorium.

'Did you not think that third group played well, Phoebe?' I asked.

'I liked the Brahms,' she replied with an air of authority, 'but not the Haydn. Dad says a Haydn quartet is the test par excellence of how good an ensemble is. That group played like four soloists and the Haydn exposed it. They're capable players, but they're not a good quartet.'

Thus spoke the virtuosic Phoebe.

'I suppose we ought to do some work together,' suggested Della. 'You know, I keep thinking of when we first started out. Remember when we played the minuet at my house and Leila and Angela clowned around in Phoebe's clothes? It wasn't so funny at the time, but I cannot help laughing now. Shall we try the minuet?'

I made my most grotesque face, crossed my eyes, stuck my tongue out and limped Quasimodo-like to the chair Della had set for me, dragging the 'cello and singing the minuet theme from the *Fifths* as I did.

I hunched my shoulders over my 'cello and stuck my tongue in my lower lip.

'Lucia Spastica,' I announced.

That was the cue. Hunchbacks all, we began to fool with the minuet until we could do no more through laughing.

'No more, please!' Della begged. 'Luighseach, old thing, please stop! Heavens! Anyone would think you were excited about going on stage.'

'Aye,' I agreed. 'I cannot help myself, Delleen.'

'We better do something serious,' she resolved. 'What about the slow movement from the *Kaiser*? A theme and variation would be just the ticket to play together, don't you think?'

And so we played until a lady came for our music and advised us to prepare to go on stage.

'I'm thinking I'll be getting dressed now,' I laid down the old 'cello.

'Need a hand?' offered Pim.

I nodded. Pim grabbed the case containing the dinner suit and we scuttled off to the washroom together.

Pim kept watch while I changed.

'Lucky no one else's here,' she commented when I emerged in trousers, shirt and waistcoat. 'You really do look like a boy. Did I fix the hem right?'

'Aye, you did.' A preliminary fitting at school during the week had resolved the problem of my shorter left leg. Pim tied my bow tie, I pulled on the jacket, Pim pinned my corsage and we returned to our rehearsal room.

'Oh my!' Della stopped playing the moment she saw me. 'Oh! Touché, old thing! Oh, I say, what a hoot! Luighseach!'

'Excuse me, Miss Sotheby,' interrupted Pim. 'May I introduce Master Louis Straughan?'

'I do beg your pardon, Master Straughan,' giggled Della.

'And a good afternoon to you, Miss Sotheby,' I bowed. 'Miss Raye,' I bowed again.

'So that's what you two were plotting!' remarked Phoebe. 'Mrs Epstein suspected something was afoot on Thursday, but neither of us could work out what it was.'

'Oh, I cannot wait to see the look on my mother's face!'

Della, however, could laugh no more. She coughed instead and she could not stop.

'You all right?' Pim asked.

Della gasped for her handkerchief. I immediately pulled mine from my pocket and passed it. She took it wordlessly and nodded her thanks. For a brief moment the coughing subsided and Della leant back in her chair, worn and pale.

'Here,' Pim offered her a flask from her lunch basket. Della declined the offer and began to cough all over again.

She grimaced, quickly put my handkerchief to her mouth, heaved and coughed some more.

We all looked on, stunned.

'You're sick,' remarked Pim.

'Please, I'm all right,' whispered Della as she wiped her mouth. 'Truly.'

'W—was that blood?' Phoebe anxiously questioned.

Pim and I nodded.

'Don't worry,' Della weakly attempted to reassure us, 'I'm quite all right. I feel much better now.'

'But you coughed up blood! You can't go on stage like that,' declared Pim.

'What do you mean?' Phoebe, wide-eyed and worried, could not believe what Pim had said.

'She's sick, Phoebe,' Pim firmly explained.

'Of course I'm going on stage, Phoebe,' Della again attempted reassurance.

'This happened before?' Pim demanded an answer.

'Last Sunday,' Della could not lie. 'Well, how could I say anything?' she protested. 'I thought I would get better and I did, too. I've been much better. I always get better if I rest. What else could I do? Listen, if I had said anything Mummy would have whisked me away to a sanatorium and we never would have played. I couldn't do that! I couldn't leave you!'

'But Delleen, you're badly sick,' I said, my own concerns brewing.

'I'm not as bad as you think, old thing, and I'm not going to disappoint you,' she resolved. 'Not now. Look at you, the three of you, fine musicians all of you and the best friends I ever had. How could I let you down? And Mrs Epstein's out there. Think of all the work she's put in. I couldn't disappoint her. We must go on. Who knows when we'll ever have this opportunity again?'

'There'll be opportunities aplenty to be sure, Delleen,' I tried to allay her fears, for, despite her efforts to comfort us, Della was scared. One brief look told me as much.

419

'Do you mean we're not going to play?' queried the troubled Phoebe.

'Crikey, Phoebe! Is performing all you ever think about?' Pim exploded. 'Can't you get it into your thick skull that Della's sick?'

'But my father's there!' she cried.

The lady who had come for our music appeared again.

'The last group has already finished,' she informed us in an annoyed and flustered manner. 'House of Cards Quartet, you should be backstage. Move along!'

'Excuse me—' Pim called.

'No Pim,' Della halted her. 'I am going to play. I mean, *we* are going to play.'

So saying, she smoothed her dress, tucked her violin under her arm and took her bow in hand. Della held her head high and slowly progressed down the hall to the stage.

The only thing to do was to follow.

50

Half-way down the corridor, I turned round. Pim was still standing in the doorway.

'We can't let her go on like that!' she remonstrated.

'She bees determined, Pimmy, and you know what she's like when she's made up her mind,' I replied.

'But what if she starts coughing on stage? What'll we do?' Pim could no longer conceal her worries.

'I'm thinking we'll be crossing that bridge when we come to it,' I sighed. 'And let's hope we'll not be crossing it at all.'

'But—' Pim objected.

''Tis what Delleen Sotheby wants, Pimmy. And if we never play together again, can we deny her this present pleasure and part happily?'

Pim stared at me dumbfounded. While she was fully aware of the potential seriousness of Della's condition, it seemed that the grim possibility of 'never' regarding our own situation had not occurred to her.

'And little Phoebe, with her da in the audience there,' I continued. 'How can we not go on stage and play? Delleen knows that, Pimmy, and we'll be giving them two fiddlers every support we can.'

All I received in response was a stubborn folding of the arms and a shake of the head.

'And if you don't come now, Pimmy Connolly,' I added more firmly, ''twill be yourself the one jumping ship.'

'Crikey, Lucy,' she scowled and disappeared into the room. I was about to walk back and fetch her when she re-emerged with her viola and strode moodily down the hall.

'Here,' she said, and she pushed into my free hand a couple of serviettes from the lunch basket. 'Put 'em in your trouser pocket. They might come in handy.'

We had no time to recollect. The moment Pim and I joined Della and Phoebe, we were hurried onstage.

'They've waited long enough,' whispered the woman responsible for organising us on and off. 'You're lucky you're allowed to perform at all.'

Into the glare of the concert platform we wandered.

There sounded an all too familiar titter. Once my eyes had adjusted to the light, I managed to make out Mary Byrne and Beth toward the back of the hall. Since my impromptu performance for the class all those months ago, Mary had taken a kindly interest in my 'cello activities. I must have mentioned Saturday's competition in passing for I had no idea how else she would have taken the initiative to come and see us play.

We acknowledged the audience's applause: Della, Phoebe and Pim with neat curtsies, me with a slight bow. In the process, I spotted Daid shrugging innocently at Mrs Sotheby's gestured indignation regarding my attire. I decided to turn my attention elsewhere and soon found the representatives of the Connolly clan a few rows behind near the opposite aisle. Prominent among them was the white habit of Sister Scholastica.

'Faith!' I muttered as we sat and finalised our tuning.

'What's up?' Pim nudged me.

With my bow I quickly indicated Sister Augustine and Sister Magdalene seated next to Pim's sister.

Pim smiled and checked her A string. 'Boy, are you in for it,' she whispered.

But at that moment I did not really care what trouble I was in for.

Della sat with her eyes closed and head bowed. Her violin she perched upright on her lap. From her demeanour, I knew she was praying.

'Whatever may happen, please help her,' I made my own prayer. 'And, dear God in Heaven, that I may help her as much as she needs.'

Somehow we had to get through this.

Not a sound could be heard. Della raised her head and turned to the adjudicator. He sat in the very centre in a row to himself and nodded obligingly. Della did not make a move. He had to nod again before she lifted her violin.

And, with that, we began Haydn's *Fifths*.

Della's opening rang out as clear and true as the unfailing toll of a church bell on a cold winter's morning. Those first notes stridently announced the dawn of another day and a descent of semiquavers seemed to protest the obligation of rising so early. Pim, Phoebe and I huddled together against her bleak, insistent clamour, shivered our accompanying chords and voiced our own mournful complaint:

Why did it have to happen this way?

Quietly, eerily, an icy octave higher, Della's plaintive motif sang through the stillness. With the same chill chords we responded, shared her lamentation, and in rueful chromatics questioned what had befallen us. By the time the phrase was finished, we reached the same inevitable conclusion:

Because it must be so, and that is that.

And, as a robin warbles over snow clad fields, his song and red breast both a winter's delight, so Della's second melody tried to brighten our downcast spirits. And still the knell of the descending fifth could be heard as the church bells themselves chime from one parish to another on an Irish Sunday morn.

What was it that took my mind back to Ireland? Perhaps it was the sight of blood on the handkerchief; perhaps it was Della's wan and fearful expression. For it was on one such mid-winter's morning that I had walked with my father through the snow to the new cemetery. How the church bell tolled that day, slow and solemn like the deep and sonorous notes of my 'cello, and a little robin sang indifferent to my plight. The faint December sun glowed through the cloudswept sky as Mam's coffin was lowered into the grave, and my grieving father carried me homewards, keening softly:

'Thou didst not fall off like a withered leaf, which hangs trembling and insecure: nay, it was a rude blast which brought thee to the dust, my darling Meidhbh.'

'Aye, Delleen, Delleen,' I moaned into my 'cello, 'You're bleeding and sick and still you sing.'

For she did sing. Della sang with all her heart. Passage after passage she played with delicate lilt and deft precision, despite being buffeted this way and that by the chiming clamour of violin, viola and 'cello. But even the hardiest of robins must find respite against snow and squalling winds. Perhaps my little robin found it in the church tower for her song gradually dwindled and she, too, began to chime in resignation amidst the icy chatter of softly repeated notes and my own low lamentations.

With the return of the opening theme, we again voiced our predicament. It was strange. We had played that first movement so many, many times, yet the emotions which now fuelled it were so very different. The phrase, 'because it must be so' was stamped out in staccato in each of our parts before a shrill squall swirled a snowfall of semiquavers and made me shiver. Still the church bell tolled the fifth and Della's robin's calls were echoed by Pim's as they each sought shelter. And my 'cello's winter wind howled through the jagged forms of trees and menaced the church bell, leaving behind glinting chords of ice.

Even the bleakest of winters, however, yield to Spring and Spring inevitably blossoms into Summer. And so it was with our second movement. Plucked strings broke the silence in the same way small shoots push through the cold earth; and high in the heavens above, like the March skylark chirruping his happy song, Della trilled her pretty melody. We took up our bows and our graceful phrases mirrored the ice melting into fresh mountain waters. Returning again to pizzicato, Phoebe, Pim and I transformed Della's theme into droplets of sweet rain, while Della changed those same drops into a trickle of notes that bubbled and babbled down the slopes, filling the lake anew. How I loved to visit the lake

423

in springtime and watch faithful swans venture from their reedy nests with a bevy of cygnets. In a way, the movement of my bow across my strings recalled the elegant length and curve of a swan's neck, and the tiny flutter of notes echoed between our upper and lower parts seemed to quiver like tail feathers. Finally, the cuckoo called, welcoming Summer's full fields and flowing streams, her long days and twilit nights.

Autumn is celebrated with the races and the harvest; and the harvest months at home were always spent on Uncail Ruaidhrí's farm. For me, Haydn's ungainly minuet brought to mind my father and my uncles' long, lean forms swinging through the oatfields, their bodies twisting slightly as they swept their scythes across the grass, and their legs bending and creeping slowly, steadily from end to end.

The minuet was a scythe dance.

Swish.

Swish.

Swish.

Our bows, too, were like scythes sweeping through notes, and our bodies and instruments swayed in alternating pairs to a steady plodding pulse.

And after a hard day of reaping and sheaving, everyone gathered for the harvest dinner, himself and the lads (as Mam invariably called my father and his brothers) threatening to burn their tools if the table wasn't spread with a hearty meal. It always was. Freshly churned butter and rounds of brown bread scored and blessed with a cross, a Michaelmas goose, fataí roasted in goose fat, and the best of summer vegetables followed by a pie made with the first of the apples and the last of the berries and served with plenty of cream. The Trio recalled those noisy, happy times: four instruments hungrily munching chords; and the conversation, not to mention the ale, flowing as freely as did Della's melody on that occasion. Then, following a good night's sleep, it was back to the fields for another day's reaping on a neighbouring farm. And likewise, with the minuet, we danced our peculiar scythe dance once again.

Come All Saints' Eve, the fields newly tilled and sown, the west wind rattles the doors and windows and whistles in the chimney flue. Winter, with its grey and darkening days, was announced in our fourth movement by softly moaning thirds, chattering staccato and frosty syncopation. Then Della's high descant sang out shrill as a banshee's warning on a stormy night.

'There's many say they saw the Banshee, and that if she heard you singing loud she'd be very apt to bring you away with her.' So said Mam on one such eve while we listened by the fireside to the wind howling and to the distant pounding of the wild Atlantic.

'And did you see her yourself, Mam?' I asked her.

'Not ever in my life did I see her. But let you remember this, that if perchance you do see the Banshee, be ye certain that she's not come for evil purpose. Aye, a dreadful sight she may be with her face like stone and her hair made as if from cobwebs, and well we might fear her, as we should fear death if death we meet with our souls unshriven. But the Banshee comes to tell us death is near, not for ourselves but for some other poor soul, that we might pray for their repose and that they not wander the world's rim like the ghosts I have seen.'

'You seen ghosts, Mam?'

'Aye, Luighseach, a ghost I did see once upon a time and all alone I was with yourself but a wee bairn asleep in your cradle by the fire. How it rattled the windows and pounded the door! Up I rose from my chair and lifted the latch and stepped outside into the cold to better see who it was.'

'Who was it that was there?'

'Not a one was there in body, Luighseach. But 'twas such a moaning could be heard methought it was indeed a ghost. "Who is it?" I called. But no answer sallied forth. Was it the poor man found dead in Little Patrick Street come to ask for prayers perchance? An Ave I prayed before closing the door and settling again by the fire. And the door she knocked again, and again I rose and stepped out into the cold. And what a moaning met me then! Was it one of the poor souls lost at sea in that great ship they never thought would sink? Another Ave did I pray as I took my seat by the fire. And a third time there was a knock. A third time did I rise and open. A third Ave did I pray. And when I turned back to the fire, there before me was the ghost himself.'

'And did he frighten you, Mam?'

'Aye he did, Luighseach, such a towering spectre was he with eyes like lakes and his face besmutted so. "Was it down the chimney that you came?" I asked him. "Nay Meidhbhín," he replied. "'Twas through the back door that I entered, and if it pleases you, I'll take my supper here by the fire." Aye, Luighseach, 'twas none but your da returned home late from his drawing class decided to play a few tricks!'

How we laughed that night and how many nights were similarly spent! For, no matter how cold and wild it might be without, there was always a welcoming fire and a pot of tea, a story and a hug within. And however long and bitter the winter, summer always followed.

The same assurance of sunny days came with our coda. Bright D major laughed at dark D minor. Triplets gambolled to the gay drone of my 'cello and our final happy chords set the stage for the summer that was the Borodin.

But no one clapped us when we finished. Instructions had been issued to refrain from applause until the conclusion of the second item. We waited in silence for the adjudicator to finish writing his comments.

Della began to cough

Instantly, I dived into my pocket for the serviette. She shook her head and smiled a little.

'Don't worry,' she mouthed.

How would she manage? Della had performed the Haydn beautifully. Every note had been perfectly executed. Her intonation was faultless, her bowing exquisite, her phrasing, as always, a joy. Would she have the strength to play another piece?

I closed my eyes and thought through the Borodin

'If ever there was a quartet about friendship,' Mr Raye had said to us under the fig tree that Sunday afternoon, 'this is it. Four friends leafing through memories: Ah, it was the best of times; it was the worst of times…'

'It was the age of wisdom,' Della added.

'It was the age of foolishness,' he nodded at her, impressed she knew he was quoting.

'It was the epoch of belief,' Della continued, fishing for the correct words.

'It was the epoch of incredulity,' he egged her on.

'It was the season of Light,' she supplied the next sentence.

'It was the season of Darkness,' he puffed his cigarette.

'It was the spring of hope.'

'It was the winter of despair.'

'We had everything before us!' Della was revelling in the exchange.

'We had nothing before us!' so was Phoebe's father.

'We were all going direct to Heaven,' Della smiled.

'We were all going direct the other way,' he added with a dark smile all his own. 'And whichever way we're going: we're going to play the Borodin!'

Perhaps Della was thinking of that same occasion, for when I looked at her again she had that same twinkle in her eye.

'Your turn old thing,' she whispered.

In opening our first movement, I remembered that first day of school when I met Della Sotheby. I was sick and lonely and scared and it was Della who stood alone in that class and welcomed me. She sought me out, bore my sullen moods, my fussy ways and my hostility with such loving kindness. Now it was Della who was sick and scared. She was not alone, though, for with my opening phrase, I held my hand out to her as she literally had held her hand out to me those many months before.

And how she responded! The warmth of her fiddle matched that of my 'cello, and she worked my theme to giddy heights with such delicate simplicity. As for the old 'cello, Miss Bray was right. It did not let me down. It had proved itself up to the task of the Haydn, its full, rich tone a perfect counterpart to Della's brightness and Phoebe's mystery. Now my instrument came into its own and filled the hall with sumptuous sound.

Pim and Phoebe were ever at my side. While Della and I conversed so amiably, they worked in harmony, their buoyant syncopation pulsing gently beneath our melody. The rapport they shared was all the more sweet given their opposite characters. Pim had pushed aside whatever differences stood between them and had given Phoebe what she so dearly needed: understanding and acceptance. Phoebe, in return, had affectionately opened her heart. Like Della and myself, they too had become firm friends. For the remainder of the movement the four of us romped through happy times – times spent splashing on the beach, hours and hours of practice, lunchtimes on the lawn at school – and troubled times too, but they were troubles that were not suffered alone. It was truly a conversation between the very best of friends.

With a playful pluck of my string we plunged into the scherzo. Della twirled into the limelight, ably supported by Phoebe's rapid accompaniment. Spiralling sequences, jesting accents and notes that wriggled with glee slowed into one of our favourite melodies. Now it was my turn to provide a rippling bass while Phoebe and Della joined each other in perfect partnership, and they swayed slightly as they played their pretty waltz.

Della need not be worried about being outshone by Phoebe for, as with the Haydn, Phoebe had proven how much she had taken to heart her father's observations of a fortnight ago:

'Listen Possum,' he commenced as he lit up a cigarette. 'Second violin is not second best. She's every bit as good as me,' he flicked his cigarette in Mrs Epstein's direction. Mrs Epstein looked at the ground and quietly denied his statement.

'Don't believe her,' he whispered to us.

'I don't like playing solo,' Mrs Epstein admitted.

'And that doesn't mean she's any less of a player,' he gave Phoebe a very firm look. 'She's a smart player, not a show off like me.'

'Don't believe him,' Mrs Epstein whispered to us.

'If she advertised,' he continued, 'she would write in letters as bold as could be: "No job too big; no job too small". Technically she's my equal; musically she's even better. She always knows exactly how to respond. In life as in art, eh, Annie?' he winked at Mrs Epstein.

Phoebe watched our teacher smile bashfully at his praise and knew, that however modest Mrs Epstein's reaction might have been, her father spoke no truer word.

'My father played second violin with the Rosé Quartet,' she proudly informed us during our rehearsal at the Conservatorium the following Saturday.

Somehow we were expected to understand the significance of this piece of news. Mrs Epstein provided the required details.

'The Rosé Quartet is probably the most renowned quartet in Europe,' she explained. 'Meister Arnold Rosé, Roddy's teacher, as well as being the concertmaster of the Vienna Philharmonic, is its leader. Phoebe's father was his protegé. He worked very closely alongside Rosé who, I believe, used to have him sit in occasionally as second violinist in the quartet. Isn't that right, Phoebe?'

Phoebe nodded.

'Well,' concluded our teacher, 'nothing quite like working with outstanding players to best learn the tricks of the trade; and nothing quite like learning to lead by learning to follow.'

As for the days Phoebe had spent in her father's company, they had been as much devoted to violin study as they had been to each other. Together they had worked on improving the range and subtlety of her tone and, in doing so, had increased her versatility. As a result, Phoebe was able to weave in and out as she pleased.

She relished her varied role. Sometimes her mellow tones blended with Pim's and mine, othertimes she sang out with her characteristic brilliance. Always, she was sensitive to Della's lead. After all, she had learnt the first violin part as well as her own. Now it stood her in very good stead, for Della needed every bit of support.

We flirted briefly with minor harmonies before returning again to the waltz. The hours of practice we had devoted to those difficult progressions paid off a hundredfold. Della was tiring and there was no respite. Sheer mastery was keeping her going and still she managed to play with grace and charm, flitting blithely from phrase to phrase. But I hated to think what she was feeling inside. And who was to know? It seemed to have little bearing on her playing for she tossed off her final plucked notes as gay as could be.

Enough was enough. There is only so much a 'cello can take of frivolity, however high the demands may be to achieve it, and the opportunity to voice my concerns came in the third movement. The whirligig of the Scherzo gave way to the solace of the Nocturne. Once again, it was my turn to lead and, briefly closing my eyes and caressing the old 'cello, I sang with all my soul.

While I played, Della had a chance to rest. She sat, worn and pale, and with my song I tried to comfort my poor, sick friend. At the same time, I could not help but sing my sorrow, ever accompanied by Phoebe and Pim's gentle harmonies. No doubt Della shared my troubles, for her reply, so high and sweet, was full of tender consolation. Underneath, Pim's viola quietly voiced a more introspective melody and Phoebe's chords complemented my own low, pondering notes.

With a sudden key change from contemplative A major to friendly F major and an upwards rush of notes, Della initiated an attempt to lift our spirits. It was carried through by Phoebe and reminded us of happier times once more. Our memories, however, were short lived. Della's venture into the minor carried with it the protest that had crept into the first movement of the Haydn. Pim attempted consolation by playing my theme, but to no avail. I could not help my sorrows. None of us could and our running passages were expressed with more pathos than ever before. Given the utter exhaustion on Della's face, who knew how long it would be before we would play together again? One last time Della and I returned to our opening theme, echoing phrases mourning our plight. And when Della took up the melody on her own, I could not help my tears. Onto my 'cello they fell as I plucked my strings in resignation. I heard Phoebe gulp and glanced at her. Her lower lip was trembling. Pim, who was usually so stalwart, sniffed. Meanwhile, Della, her notes quietly soaring above our own, seemed to have entered another world.

Our beautiful melody faded into a sweet, soft chord, and then into utter stillness.

I quickly pulled the serviette from my pocket, took off my glasses and wiped my face. To my surprise, I saw a strange beige stain on the serviette. I had forgotten about the face powder and smiled a little at the thought.

'You all right?' Pim nudged me.

'Aye,' I nodded and peered at her. Her eyes, too, were moist.

'Yourself?' I asked.

Pim nodded and checked her tuning.

I returned my glasses to my nose. As I did, I saw Mr David in the audience.

'Pyjamas,' I recalled and I used that thought to push aside my cares while I checked my strings.

To think that sitting all in a row in that concert hall were five people who once had dressed in ancient robes for the sake of a wedding breakfast. Of those five, the three gentlemen had donned petticoats and corsets and kicked their way through a can can. A little further along sat a finely dressed woman who had downed a couple of brandies before performing a dance of veils for her husband. Next to her sat a tall, quiet man who, despite his own suffering, delighted in the good he saw about him and expressed it in his art.

Looking out at my father and my grown-up friends, I knew that, of the many things I had learnt over the last few months, nothing on this earth lasts forever. The years and seasons come and go as they please, but in this world neither the brightest joy nor the deepest sorrow will ever endure. However pleasant, however painful they may be, all things eventually pass. We only have the present; and the present is what we must embrace with all our heart. To love the present moment is the Art that is our life – not to say that there is nothing outside the here and now, far from it. It is precisely in the present that we face Eternity, for in the present we meet Him who is always present. We meet God Who Is; God Whom we must learn to trust.

And what faced us now was no longer the poignant Nocturne, but the Finale. It was a cheeky frolic through notes.

The time had come to indulge in a little nonsense.

Della and Phoebe began together. Their introduction was a demure yet haunting parody of the first movement's theme. Pim and I, playing in our lowest register, feigned indifference in a reply which was mockingly sinister. Again the violins teased, and again viola and 'cello shrugged them off.

I could not resist sending Della a brief Quasimodo look as I plucked out our theme at a lively pace. I was rewarded with a giggly smile. Pim, capable as ever, gabbled away on her strings. She was soon matched by Phoebe. Then Della added her tuppenceworth before leading into another happy melody.

It was astonishing how similar Borodin's Finale was to the last movement of the *Fifths*: the homage was present in the use of the fifth motif and of the first violin's descant. Particularly true to the Haydn spirit were the musical jokes that were bandied throughout. The Finale abounded in chatty counterpoint; there were unexpected returns of the opening phrase intimating an end which did not come; there was even a viola solo. There was fun for us all. We revelled in the constant horseplay, tossing off accents and pitting three notes against two (always a joy). Cantering rhythms rollicked from second violin to viola to 'cello while melodies cavorted from part to part.

The end was near. In unison now we played our opening theme, leaving our audience in suspense. I took the lead, my pizzicato imitating that of a double bassist in a jazz band. Pim made her entry, then Phoebe, then Della. I farewelled the melody that had so delighted us, while Della plucked her strings as if her violin were a ukulele. Quietly we played, and while I gambolled with triplets in the bass, Della, Phoebe and Pim took their leave and wallowed in subtle harmonies.

The crescendo followed, and we made sure it would be one we would never forget. After a final plunge into the first motif, Phoebe repeated it softly, then Pim, then Della, while I signalled the end with a sustained low A. Up the octave and ever louder I played my A. Della soared to the heavens and Phoebe and Pim worked the first motifs with ever increasing force. Della's scintillating high D sang out in sheer ecstasy and Phoebe, Pim and I brought the themes into a jubilation of chords and concluded with a single celebratory note.

Truly, there was nothing quite like a good old bicker over a quartet!

Our final note died away and still Della held her bow in mid-air. None of us could lower our bows until she lowered hers and it seemed that she was not ready to put it down. Della knew, as we all did, that the moment her bow was lowered our world was going to change. She also knew, as we all did, that there was no going back.

Down came the bows.

Silence followed.

We exchanged looks.

What to do now?

We stood.

There was thunderous applause.

We curtsied and bowed. The audience clapped and clapped. A loud 'Brava!' was heard from none other than Phoebe's father and it was quickly echoed round the hall. People even stamped their feet. We bowed again and received more applause and cheers. Again we bowed and resolved that it was time to go. Still they clapped. We hesitated as to what to do. The audience laughed at our bewilderment and clapped some more. Somehow we all came to an agreement that it was time to leave, and, with a final bow, we walked into the wings.

51

By the time we entered the hall, the adjudicator was making his way to the stage. Mary and Beth waved us hello and we sat together to listen to what he had to say.

'It's Mr Pippin. He's the Director of the Conservatorium,' Phoebe whispered to me. 'He's very English.'

'Shhh!' whispered Pim.

'"If music be the food of love, play on; Give me excess of it,"' the adjudicator began in an exceedingly well elocuted voice.

'Many of you here today will probably know these famous lines, spoken by the lovelorn Duke Orsino, that open Shakespeare's *Twelfth Night*. Perhaps, being musicians, they are the *only* lines from Shakespeare you do know!'

Embarrassed laughter followed. Evidently, Mr Pippin had a good sense of his audience.

'Well,' he continued, 'whatever you may think of Mr Shakespeare, or the Duke Orsino, whose foolish infatuation and false melancholy is a parody of true love; as musicians you will most likely acknowledge that these famous lines carry an important assumption about music: the assumption that music is the food of love. Perhaps, for many of you, that assumption is the reason why you play music.

'You might also be asking yourselves what Shakespeare has to do with the adjudication of a chamber music competition. You might even be considering whether Mr Pippin has messed up his appointments and is today delivering the lecture he ought to be giving to the literary society next Tuesday. It would not be the first time,' he smiled.

More laughter.

'He's very absent minded,' whispered Phoebe.

'But I will hasten to inform you that I have not confused my appointments,' he added. 'Somehow those lines impressed themselves upon me as I listened to the music played today; for today we feasted upon some of the most beautiful works ever written. The performances we were privileged to hear demonstrate the extraordinary capacity music has for nourishment, not of course for our body, but for our heart and soul.

'And so, while I listened I asked myself, what is it about music that nourishes us? Why is it that some melodies please us "like the sweet sound, That breathes upon a bank of violets; Stealing and giving odour" while others do not? Why is it that the same music, like that played for Shakespeare's duke, can please us one moment and fail to satisfy the next? Why is it that we prefer the tune played by one musician over the same tune played by another? Surely the tune is the same, what was it that made the difference? What are the qualities of music that make this so? And I began to consider not whether music is the food of love – that is a given – but what is the food of music? And upon those considerations I made my decision regarding today's performances.

'Is it technique? I asked myself. Certainly fine music cannot be made without a considerable degree of technical competence. What we heard today was the fruit of hours of rehearsal, of years of private study. None of this can be achieved without dedication, without a constant striving for perfection. The string player especially must work long and hard to develop the quality of his tone and the accuracy of his pitch and intonation before he can even begin to shape his phrases. Technical flaws will ultimately undermine a musical performance. Yet technique alone is not enough. Today we heard several competent performances of very difficult works. That is, we heard a high standard of playing. Yet it left us cold. Why was that? Why did it not satisfy? Technique is part, it seems, but it is not all.

'Is it knowledge? I asked. Any musician needs to understand how a piece fits together in order to perform it as a cohesive whole. His knowledge of structure and harmony comes to bear upon the work that he might grasp its beauty and present it on a platter for the delight of the listener. To structure and harmony must be added an appreciation of musical style. This afternoon our competitors were required to perform two works: one by Haydn, the Father of the String Quartet, and another by a later composer. Classical restraint, for the most part, was contrasted with Romantic expression. Some groups succeeded with the Haydn but struggled with the later work. For others it was the opposite. There were a few performances which evinced a good grasp of both Classical and Romantic style but lacked emotional conviction. They satisfied our minds, but they did not move our hearts. Like technique, knowledge is critical, but on its own it is not enough.

'Is it a sense of ensemble? In the case of the string quartet, we are not looking at the technical skills and musical understanding of a solo player. Those demands are placed on four musicians who, in addition, must work in total concordance. Not only must they be able to play their own parts well, they must appreciate how their part fits with the others. In performance they need to make constant adjustments to their playing in order to maintain unity. In fact, I would go so far as to say that the sense of ensemble became the major deciding factor in terms of performance success, for not only did it demand the ability to play well, but the ability to entertain. This afternoon, there were two groups which seemed more bent on having a tug of war than on playing in a quartet. On the other side of the spectrum were two groups in which the rapport between the players made for very compelling performances, despite the occasional error or stylistic oversight. To one of these two ensembles I awarded the prize of Highly Commended and that goes to the Apollo Quartet. To the other, I awarded First Prize.'

Everyone applauded and at the same time ruminated as to the identity of the winning group.

'Which one was the Apollo Quartet?' I whispered to Phoebe.

'The one who played the Schubert this morning.'

'*Death and the Maiden* was it?'

'Yes.'

'But before I announce the winner,' Mr Pippin resumed, 'I will ask my final question since it has a direct bearing upon my choice: What is the basis for this rapport? Is it hours of rehearsal? Essential. Is it technique? Critical. Is it a common regard for music? Certainly. But there also needs to be a regard for each other. And that regard, is it not love?

'Now, when I talk of love I am not talking here of its caricature. Duke Orsino's lovesickness has no place in this context. Nor am I talking of romantic attachments. What I refer to is an individual's wholehearted gift of himself to another: a mutual or in the case of a quartet a fourfold sharing of personalities which somehow manages to infuse the music that is played. For, although music demands considerable knowledge and ability, considerable time and effort, if it is to be the food of love – if it is to move us, to uplift us, that is – must it not be fed by love?

'Listening today, I think there was one quartet which understood this more than all the others, and it was not the quartet I expected. When the four players appeared on stage they looked like lambs in search of their mothers. Ah, but when they performed, what a feast they set before us! They showed genuine pleasure in each other's company and, with their almost flawless playing, proved themselves remarkably capable musicians. Their Haydn was a captivating blend of restraint and rusticity performed with a sound understanding of instrumental roles. As for the Borodin, not only did they demonstrate considerable virtuosity, they took us through every chamber of our hearts, and I don't think there was a dry eye among us when they finished.

'What is particularly remarkable about this ensemble is that the average age of the members is only fifteen years old. I refer, of course, to the three young ladies and the young gentleman of the curiously and rather aptly named House of Cards Quartet who, I am proud to announce, are the winners of this our fourth annual quartet competition. To you I say, "Play on, give me excess of it!" You delighted us today and we look forward to hearing more from you. I am sure we will hear plenty in the years to come.'

52

'I don't believe it,' Della remarked as we watched the Apollo Quartet clapped onto the stage. 'Did we really win?'

'We certainly did,' smiled Pim.

'Come on!' Phoebe urged me in an excited whisper. 'We have to go!' Had I dallied any longer she would have pushed me out of my seat.

I stood and waited in the aisle while the others passed.

'How are you feeling, Delleen?' I asked.

Della looked up and smiled.

'We did it, old thing,' was all she said.

'Aye, we did it indeed we did,' I gently replied. 'Lead us on!'

Slowly we processed down the aisle. We could not walk quickly, not so much because of my limp, but because Della simply did not have the energy. Pim had to help her up the stairs to the stage. Once on the platform, however, she held herself as tall as she could, and, as leader of our quartet, walked out to receive the prize: a large and very impressive trophy. We followed her and were soon absorbed with curtsies, bows and all manner of handshakes and congratulations while we each were presented with smaller versions of the same trophy. I had an odd taste of what it was like to be a boy, for Mr Pippin's handshake to me was far more vigorous than the handshakes he gave to my friends. Determined not to be found out, I made a point of matching it.

We acknowledged the claps and cheers of our audience. Della and Phoebe together raised the trophy and the applause increased. But something was missing. In fact, it was not so much something as someone, and that someone sat several rows from the front in the form of a plain, bespectacled woman. I passed my trophy to Pim and, stepping forward, held my hands out towards Mrs Epstein and clapped for all I was worth. My friends quickly followed suit. Everyone craned their necks to find out who it was we were applauding. Mrs Epstein nodded at us, extended her hands in return and could not hide her pride.

And there were more congratulations to be had from fellow competitors, many of whom were known to Pim and Phoebe, on the way back to our room. We gathered our instruments and bags and made our way to the foyer.

'See the conquering heroes come! Sound the trumpets beat the drums!' sang Mr Raye, Mr Epstein and Mr David in harmony.

I came face to face with my father and felt myself blush. I was still wearing the suit.

'I couldn't perform in a frock, Da,' I apologised. 'Not in front of all them people. I couldn't do it, Da. Not with a calliper on my leg.'

'The way you played, lass, it wouldn't matter what was on your leg,' he smiled. 'Now, will I shake your hand or give you a hug?'

'Always a hug, Da.'

'Then a hug is what I'll give you. Well done, Luighseach. Do you think we could gather everyone for a photograph before we part?'

'Aye, we could. But Da—'

'What is it, Luighseach?'

'Delleen Sotheby's poorly.'

Daid looked over at Della, who was talking with her mother and Mrs Epstein, and nodded.

'All the more reason to take a photograph while we can, lass.'

Daid organised his box brownie and flash with his usual quiet efficiency, made his announcement and positioned the four of us for the photograph. Mrs Epstein joined us for a second photograph.

'And is there not another quartet would like its photograph taken?' he asked with typical insightfulness as he smiled at Mr and Mrs Epstein, Mr David and Mr Raye.

Mr David looked at Miss Bray who encouraged him. Mr and Mrs Epstein sent each other a surprised glance. Phoebe noticed her father suddenly looking at the floor and immediately took charge.

'Come on, Daddy,' she began, 'you stand here. Mrs Epstein, you stand in second violin position. Come on, Mr Epstein, stand next to Mrs Epstein, and you, Mr Birstall, on the other side for the 'cello. There!' she declared, beaming at Daid. 'The Klimt Quartet!'

'A battered and broken Klimt Quartet, I'm afraid, Possum,' Mr Raye remarked sadly but affectionately.

'But still together,' Phoebe replied.

'Yes, so to speak,' he nodded at his friends. 'After all these years: still together.'

'And now,' Daid was enjoying the occasion, 'shall we take a picture of yous all together?' He seemed to have a composition already in mind, so quickly did he guide us all to a suitable place.

Mr Pippin walked past while Daid was making some final alterations.

'Congratulations!' he called in a very affable tone. 'Jolly good! Well done! Would you allow me to take the photograph?' he asked Daid.

Daid agreed and they introduced themselves over handshakes.

'You must be very proud of your son,' Mr Pippin noted the obvious similarities between me and my father.

'Indeed I'm very proud of Luighseach,' Daid replied with a nod at me and immediately explained to Mr Pippin a few details concerning the camera before joining me in the back row. For once, in unfamiliar company, he did not anglicise my name. Daid, I could be sure, was not going to give my game away.

More introductions were made after Mr Pippin joined us for a final photograph which was taken, this time, by Pim's brother. Mr and Mrs Epstein, being well known to Mr Pippin, took charge. One person, however, needed hardly any introduction. Mr Pippin recognised Phoebe's father almost immediately:

'Roderick Raye, my dear fellow! After all these years! How *are* you?'

'This will be interesting,' I overheard Mrs Epstein mutter.

'It's the first time Roddy's had anything to do with the music establishment since the War,' she explained to me. 'I don't think he ever realised how highly regarded a musician he was, and thanks to you lot he's only now realising how much he still is able to give. Reuben, do you think he'll cope?'

'Knowing Roderick, he will. But he wouldn't have had to cope, Annie, if they'd given him a job when he needed it,' Mr Epstein replied.

'True,' acknowledged Mrs Epstein. 'Well, all I can say now is, thank heavens for Phoebe.'

If Mr Raye had been like a child going to the zoo at the beginning of the day, he was like a child coming home from the zoo at the day's end. One look into his dark, penetrating eyes and it was clear he was exhausted. Phoebe, however, had become highly attuned to her father's idiosyncratic manners and intense moods. She stood staunchly by him and, despite her years, participated actively in the conversation. As for the conversation, it seemed to end on very amiable terms, for Mr Pippin passed her father his calling card.

Mrs Sotheby requested everyone's attention.

'I have a couple of tables reserved at the Wentworth Hotel,' she announced in a very cordial manner. 'You are all most welcome to join us for a celebration supper.'

'Oh Mummy, must we?' Della quietly objected while everyone reconsidered their plans.

'Don't be ridiculous, darling,' Mrs Sotheby dismissed her daughter with a wave of a gloved hand. 'Of course we must! Winning a competition and not celebrating? What a ludicrous idea.'

Mrs Epstein who, like me, had been keeping a careful eye on Della, made her own assessment of the situation.

'Della, are you quite well?' she asked.

'No, Mrs Epstein, I'm afraid I'm not very well at all,' Della murmured as her legs gave way.

Daid caught her just in time.

53

'Sick again!' replied the class when Della's name was called at roll call on Monday morning.

And there followed the usual prattle about the illnesses and afflictions of various relatives once, twice and thrice removed. Of course, everyone had a story about the Influenza and everyone had a story about the War; and, of course, the main perpetrator was Frances Mahony.

'Arrah! Frances Mahony, will you never put a stop to all your silly talk?' I could stand it no longer.

'I have a right to talk about my grandmother if I want,' retorted Fanny.

'I'm not saying you don't,' I replied. 'What I am saying is that if she'd been truly ill as you say, you wouldn't make light of it the way you do.'

'I'm not making light of it,' Fanny answered. 'How could you make light of the Influenza? Hundreds of people died from the Influenza, not to mention the War. Didn't they, Sister Magdalene?'

'Then why is it that whenever the subject arises you don't be mentioning your father?' I didn't wait for Sister Magdalene.

'Because my father has nothing to do with it, that's why.' This time Fanny's response was not quite so flippant.

'Did he not lose a leg in the War?' I questioned. 'For you never talk about that. Not ever in all your idle chatter did I ever hear you mention your da.'

Fanny turned silent and glared at me.

'Well, you're not making light of it now, are you?' I asked her.

'That will be all, thank you, Lucy,' concluded Sister Magdalene. 'And while poor Della might be absent, I think I can mark that *you* are present,' she added as she turned back to her roll.

'Except, Sister Magdalene,' inserted big Kathleen. 'Are you sure it's Lucy Straughan and not Louis Straughan who's here this morning?'

'Well, she's not wearing trousers, Kate, so it must be Lucy,' tittered Fanny. 'Louis Straughan?' she imitated Sister Magdalene. 'Present, Sister Magdalene,' she answered in a low voice and burst into laughter.

How did they know that? Who told them? Amidst all the giggling, I glanced round and spotted Mary Byrne. Mary blushed. Clearly she had been the one responsible for the news but she had never intended the information be used for ill-purpose.

My morning only grew worse. When we were half-way through our History lesson, a message was delivered. I was required to report immediately to Sister

Bellarmine.

When I entered the Head Mistress' office, I was very relieved to find Pim standing at the head mistress' desk. She grinned a hello.

Sister Bellarmine stood opposite.

'I would like to offer the two of you my congratulations,' she began. 'I believe you gave a very successful performance at the Conservatorium on Saturday.'

'Yes, Sister Bellarmine. Thank you, Sister Bellarmine.' Pim, who was very used to speaking with the Head Mistress, knew that the best reply was a prompt one.

'Ordinarily, I would ask you to perform for the school,' resumed Sister Bellarmine. 'On this occasion, however, Della Sotheby is too ill and Phoebe Raye is no longer with us, so a performance will not be possible. You also have examinations in a week's time. Philomena, I trust you are prepared for your matriculation?'

'Yes, Sister Bellarmine.'

'Very good. May you continue to make good use of your study time. That will be all, thank you, Philomena. Lucy,' she indicated I was not to leave. 'I need to speak of a matter which concerns you.'

Pim, who had not yet left the room, immediately guessed what the matter was.

'Excuse me, Sister Bellarmine,' she interrupted, clearing her throat, 'if it's about the trousers, Sister Bellarmine, I think you ought to know that I was the one who put her up to it. She wouldn't have done it if I hadn't suggested it.'

'Thank you, Philomena, I will bear that in mind,' Sister Bellarmine replied. Apparently it was about the trousers. 'God be with you.'

Sister Bellarmine waited for Pim to leave.

'Sit, Lucy,' she indicated a chair. 'I have heard from a reliable authority that on Saturday you dressed as a boy and performed in a public venue disguised as a boy. Is this true?'

'It is, Sister Bellarmine.'

'It seems that news of this has already spread around the school. Living with the scandal you have caused I think will be sufficient punishment. Now, Lucy, regardless of the hand Philomena Connolly played in the matter, what I want is for you to explain to me in your own words why you did it. I beg your pardon?' Sister Bellarmine caught me muttering.

'I said, I thought examinations began next week,' I replied.

'Lucy,' Sister Bellarmine cautioned. Her voice, however, did not sound quite as severe as I expected.

'I'm not wanting to explain.'

'Lucy,' Sister Bellarmine persisted. 'Was it because of the callipers?'

'Well, I'm not a nun and I've no intention of becoming one. I wasn't going to perform in a habit!'

'And I'm very relieved that you didn't. Child, I do not wish to discuss whether or not you have a vocation. That is for God to reveal and you to discern. Either way, a religious habit is not a disguise. I wear my habit because I have nothing to hide. I am happy to be the person God has made me and I am happy to accept His Holy Will. I don't think the same could be said of you. Did you disguise yourself as a boy to hide the fact that you are crippled?'

I blinked hard and hoped that Sister Bellarmine did not see the tears that had smarted into my eyes.

'I have it on good authority that you are an exceptionally talented cellist,' Sister Bellarmine abandoned the argument.

I said nothing. Instead, I took off my glasses and began to clean them.

'I had heard similar remarks in the past but did not put anything by them because the sources were not entirely trustworthy. Too often excessive praise arises from excessive sentiment. In your case, however, it seems that the commendations are justified.'

I maintained my silence.

'I am not asking you to admit your talent, Lucy,' Sister Bellarmine persevered, her voice strong, her wimpled face stern. 'What I wish to say to you is that you have no need to be ashamed of the person you are. Shame only for sin, Lucy, and even then may it be turned to sorrow and firm purpose of amendment. Aside from possessing a wonderful gift – and, yes, Lucy, music is a wonderful gift – you are also burdened with a handicap. Believe it or not, it too is a gift. Both are from God, dear child. There is no need to be ashamed of the person you are – every aspect of that person – even the so-called crippled parts. We are all crippled, Lucy, each of us in our own way, just as we all have our talents. God loves us regardless and it is up to us to love Him with all He has given us. From your demeanour, I think you understand that very well.'

I sniffed and looked away.

'If you understand what I have said, can you live by it?'

Sister Bellarmine was going to make sure that I did.

'Now, instead of your quartet giving a performance,' she continued, 'I would like you to perform a 'cello solo at the school assembly on Friday. You will wear your uniform and you will wear the callipers.'

'I've not a 'cello,' I avoided consent.

'You may borrow a 'cello from the school if you need one. I will ask Sister Alberta to arrange one for you.' Immediately she made a note of the matter, rang the bell and passed the note to her secretary.

'I'll not play without Phoebe Raye to accompany me,' I presented a second obstacle.

'You may ask Phoebe. What will you play?'

Short of truancy there was to be no escape. Besides, Sister Bellarmine was wise to truancy.

'Schumann,' I conceded.

'Very good. I played the piano when I was your age. I enjoyed playing Schumann. Do you know *Scenes from Childhood?*' I had heard Phoebe play the piece and nodded. 'What did he write for the 'cello?' asked Sister Bellarmine.

'There are five pieces I know that he wrote.'

'One piece will do for Friday. Which will you play?'

'*Vanitas Vanitatem mit humor.*'

'I see,' Sister Bellarmine replied. 'Well, Lucy, I am glad it will be "mit humor",' she added, restraining what seemed to be a wry smile. 'You may go now, Lucy. God be with you.'

I picked up my crutches and rose from the chair.

'Lucy,' Sister Bellarmine looked up from her papers. 'I am praying for Della Sotheby. Let us hope she makes a good recovery.'

'Do you know what the trouble is, Sister Bellarmine?' I asked.

'I have not been told, Lucy. If she rests I understand she has every prospect of getting well, and I expect they will do all they can to help her. Pray for her, child. Place it all in God's hands. At this stage, it is the best and only thing you can do.'

And I did pray. I prayed with all my heart and I began to frequent the place I was least likely to be seen when at school: the school chapel. Since Della was accustomed to visit the chapel when troubled it became the place where I felt closest to her. Its quiet and seclusion, its beauty and order suited my desire for peace and solitude.

Most particularly, I began to visit in the early morning. My arrival usually coincided with the end of Mass. I would sit in a spare pew and take solace in the soothing Gregorian chanted by the nuns in their stalls. And while the 'Ubi Caritas' floated through the chapel vault, I would close my eyes in prayer.

What to pray about? While I was sick Daid certainly had not spared any prayers for my recovery. I did not die. Instead, I ended up crippled and had to accept that my fate was somehow part of God's divine plan. Over the past months I had become more accepting of the idea, but when it came to praying for Della it didn't seem right to dictate to God how I wanted things to turn out. I could pray that she be cured, certainly; but I knew full well that God had a way of doing things all His own and who was I to question it? So I stared at the tabernacle in the sun-filled sanctuary and the crucifix which hung above it, and mulled over the circumstances of my friend's illness.

''Twas so slow and sinister, Da, yet 'twas quick too,' I remarked to my father when he brought home the photograph he had taken at the Conservatorium. Della had always seemed a little frail, but what a difference there was between the dainty, Ariel figure of Mr Birstall's earlier photo which took pride of place on my desk and the pale and haggard face that struggled to smile in my father's picture. 'She was thin and tired the week before but not nearly as sick as she was at the competition. And she said nothing, Da! Nothing! All for the sake of a silly quartet!'

'A silly quartet is it now? Well, Luighseach, I never thought I'd hear you say such a thing as that.'

'Well, Da, and what was more important I'm asking you, the music or the friendship?'

'Lass, I'm thinking the one was so bound in the other 'twas almost impossible to separate them, although I think you can answer that question for yourself. The music will come and go only as much as there's an instrument to play and a lad or a lassie to play it. There will always be friendship.'

'And what sort of friendship is it that doesn't share its suffering?'

'Will you be doubting your friendship with the lass? Well, if she's not shared her sufferings with you in the past – and I don't think that's entirely true – you can be sure she'll be sharing them with you now. Will you be helping her through them, come what may, or will you be like two travellers taken separate paths on a forked road?'

'I'd never leave her, Da.'

'I know, Luighseach. And you can be sure that the last thing Delleen Sotheby would want to do is to hurt yourself.'

But I was hurt. I could not help being hurt. I was hurt and angry, worried and afraid. I did not want to be so, but I could not help myself.

And that was the problem: I could no longer help myself.

Oh, to get inside that tabernacle! From my place in the dark body of the chapel I wanted to stretch forward like the branches of a tree in a dark forest struggled towards the light. I wanted to be inside the mind and heart of God Himself. I wanted to know what He wanted. Also like a tree, however, I was fixed to the ground by a tangle of roots: a confused mess of desires and feelings that rendered me helpless and immobile.

'Hey Lucy, what's up?' It was Pim who was on her way out after the conclusion of Mass.

'Is it Della?' she asked.

I nodded.

She sat next to me and gave me a hug.

'She'll be right, you'll see.'

'You don't know that, Pimmy,' I sniffed.

'You don't know that she won't either, Lucy. What about a Rosary? Mum swears by the Rosary.'

'Aye,' I agreed. 'So does my Da.'

That morning Rosary became a custom for Pim and me, and it was not long before we were joined by others. It seemed I was not the only girl who visited the chapel before school. All manner of students, younger and older, popped in to say a prayer, particularly since exams were drawing close. Some merely genuflected in the aisle; others tarried a little longer in a pew. All of them knew Della. As news of Della's illness circulated, many of them brought their beads and sat with us. Even Frances Mahony cast her flippancy aside and prayed a decade or two.

It was a prayerful spirit that infused our days. The Hail Marys before and after class were no longer acts of subjugation on the part of mistresses. Although accompanied by distracted glances at Della's vacant desk, they were now the fervent prayers of classmates. Soon, news began to spread that Della's illness was more serious than anyone expected. Doctors' appointments were arranged. X rays were taken. Devout though he might have been, Daid was visibly relieved when my results were returned in the negative. Of Della herself, though, we received little information other than she had been sent to a sanatorium in the mountains where she was certain to receive special care.

There was little need to explain why. Everyone knew.

Della had tuberculosis.

As for Phoebe, she had news of a very different kind when I saw her on Friday and we had time to chat after our performance at the school assembly.

'Guess where I'm off to next week,' she announced.

'Please to God 'tis not a sanatorium,' I replied.

'No, silly. I'm right as rain,' Phoebe did not seem at all concerned about Della. How much had she been told? I wondered. Probably not much, I concluded. 'And no doubt Mrs Epstein has her reasons,' I thought to myself and kept silent.

'I'm going to Ballarat to visit my grandparents,' she excitedly informed me. 'And guess who's coming?'

'Not your da?'

She nodded with glee.

'And will you manage?'

'Of course I will. I know what to do.' And indeed for the past month Phoebe had devoted herself to learning how to do for her father all the things her mother used to do for him. She was determined to look after him.

'Some weeks ago I found out my grandparents' address and I wrote them,' she explained. 'My grandmother wrote back and told me I was welcome to come and visit, so I made arrangements. Dad was very worried when I told him what I had planned. He didn't like the idea of me travelling all that way by myself on a train.'

'Indeed, indeed. The like of you scheming such a thing as that. And how long will it take you?'

'Overnight from Sydney with a change at Albury and then on to Melbourne. Change at Spencer Street, then tally ho to "The Bally Rat",' she concluded in a manner that was very much like her father. 'Nearly two whole days,' Phoebe had her journey all worked out.

'Two days in a train all by yourself is it? Little wonder your da was worried.'

'He didn't like the idea of my visiting my grandparents alone, either. I can look after him as much as I please, he says, but he won't have me batting for him. So he decided to come. We're leaving on Monday.'

'They're both mad as hatters so they should get along quite well together, and doubtless they'll return with enough stories to fill a book,' remarked Mrs Epstein to me during my lesson the following Monday night. 'Heaven only knows how they'll fare with the Raye clan at large. From what I understand, as far as his father is concerned, Roddy's one redeeming feature is that he fought for his King and Country. You can imagine what Roddy feels about that. As for his mother, she visited him in hospital soon after he returned from France. He told me he didn't cope very well with it and he hasn't seen her since. If it wasn't for Phoebe, I doubt he would ever see either of them again. They say time heals, Luighseach. Let's hope it's true.'

'And what of Delleen, Mrs Epstein? Do you think she'll get better?'

'I hope so, Luighseach.'

'I feel as if I made her sick. She wouldn't have pushed herself so hard if it hadn't been for myself wanting the quartet so much.'

'Luighseach, Della wanted that quartet as much as you, as much as Phoebe and as much as Pim. Even if there had been no quartet she would have pushed herself,' Mrs Epstein advised me. 'When I first met Della Sotheby, which was only two years ago, she was a little girl who desperately wanted to succeed at something.'

''Twas that important, Mrs Epstein?'

'That's an unusual question coming from you,' observed my teacher. 'Consider it from Della's point of view: her father was a decorated war hero, her step-father is a successful businessman, her mother is a society doyenne, her brother is a champion cricketer. All of them, in their own way, have been successful. Once she glimpsed that she could succeed on the violin there was no holding her back. True, she will never be a soloist – she has neither Phoebe's proficiency nor her stamina and she knows it – but she is a wonderful chamber musician. She was going to be the best she could possibly be and she succeeded on many levels. And she has you to thank for it— Yes, Luighseach,' Mrs Epstein stopped me, 'To thank. Do you think it's right to deny a person the chance to be the best they could possibly be, Luighseach?'

''Twould be very wrong to do that, Mrs Epstein.'

'Even if it means they might die in the process?'

'There's always a risk you might die is there not, Mrs Epstein? Besides, you'd die inside if you didn't strive for something.'

'Very true. So why do you give them the chance?'

'Because you love them.'

Mrs Epstein nodded. 'And sometimes, Luighseach, love means letting go. Now listen to me,' she cautioned. 'You'll make yourself sick if you keep worrying like this. Who can say how an illness as unpredictable as Della's has been affected by the year's happenings? Who can say how else it might have come about? You cannot blame yourself. Instead, look at what you've given each other and treasure it. My dear girl, in watching and listening to the two of you play on that stage, no one could deny the beauty of that friendship and the music it made. That, Luighseach, will transcend time and space.'

And so, for the last few weeks of term, there was no Della and there was no Phoebe. Once examinations began, there was hardly any Pim and no Pim at all when they finished, for Pim was at liberty to go home where she was needed to help run the guesthouse. There was hardly any 'cello either. My 'cello, it turned out, was beyond repair, so any 'cello practice was restricted to short afternoon sessions with the old 'cello in Miss Bray's workroom. Certainly, I had the companionship of my classmates, particularly Mary Byrne who proved good company, but the world I had been very happy to be part of had fallen to pieces and I began to feel lonely all over again.

Then something happened which changed all that and it happened on Strathfield station early one Wednesday afternoon.

'Hello Lu,' sounded a familiar and very English voice.
I looked up and standing before me was Wally Sotheby.
'Practising?' he asked.
I blushed. He was right. I had been fingering a passage on a crutch.
'Dell does that,' he remarked. 'Spoons, rulers, armchairs. Nothing's safe. I was hoping to see you. I've been meaning to pass you this.'
He pulled from his pocket a folded piece of paper.
'It's the address of the sanatorium she's staying at,' he explained. 'I thought you might like to write to her.'
I took the paper gratefully. 'Thank you, Wally,' I smiled. 'Thank you very much. And you'll tell me true now, won't you? How is she?'
'I can't say she's well, Lu,' Wally seemed to appreciate being asked and welcomed the opportunity to be perfectly frank. 'She's not. All she can do is have complete rest and fresh air. It should bring her round. It did before.'
'Before, you're saying?'
He nodded. 'She had influenza badly when she was little, then a few years ago she had a pretty nasty bout of Pneumonia. She recovered well, though. Doctors thought a warmer climate would continue to help her. That's why we moved to Australia. And it has. It's helped her a lot. May I sit?'
I made room for him.
'Are— are you well?' he asked.
'Aye, I am, thanks be to God. And what brings you here so early?' I inquired. School was not due to finish for another couple of hours.
'I had an exam this morning. Since I've nothing scheduled this afternoon I've

permission to go home. What about you? You're not truanting are you?'

'I'm going swimming,' I replied.

'Really?' he was very impressed.

'Well, to tell you the truth 'tis therapy,' I admitted. 'The doctor—'

'The doctor?' he echoed, a broad smile slowly spreading across his face. 'Did you see the doctor?'

'Aye, I did,' I replied as I looked at him appreciatively. If it had not been for Wally's encouragement I would never have made the decision. 'And the doctor recommended I learn to swim to help my legs grow stronger. Every Wednesday now I go swimming. I daresay it's not really swimming for I use my arms mostly and what I can of my legs and I do exercises besides, but—'

'Enjoying it?'

'Aye, I am. And if I can get my right knee stronger I'll only need to wear a half brace on that leg.'

'I say, that's terrific! So you won't have to have an operation?'

'Doctor Little would prefer not to operate if possible and I'm pleased about that. Even the thought of hospital—' I broke off, thinking about Della.

'Well that's about the best bit of news I've heard in weeks. Tell you what, when you can swim I'll take you rowing.'

'You'll do what?'

'Would you like to come? We could hire a boat and row a section of the river. I—I could row you if you want but I have a feeling you'd enjoy it more if we rowed together. You'd be terrific with a pair of oars. In fact, I reckon you're as strong as any chap. It would be awful fun. What do you say?'

His enthusiasm was infectious.

'I'd like that very much indeed.'

'Shake on it?' he held out his hand and I shook it. 'Good. By the way, congratulations,' he added. 'For the competition, I mean.'

'Thank you,' I replied and grew quiet.

'Heard you were tops. Heard about the trousers, too,' he remarked drily and nudged me.

'Now don't you start up about it, for 'tis nothing but trouble's come of them trousers ever since,' and I told him what happened with Fanny and with Sister Bellarmine.

'Well then, I won't tell you what my mother said,' he replied.

'I don't care what your mother said!' I could well imagine what Mrs Sotheby had to say.

He laughed.

''Tis not funny!' I protested. 'You're lucky you're a boy. If you wore callipers they'd be covered up and no one would notice. Not so myself. It's not fair! Look at them! They're ugly! They're the ugliest things in all the world! I wish I was a boy!'

'I don't. I'm jolly glad you're a girl. And the callipers might be ugly, but you're not. Lu, you could never be ugly.'

Astonished, I stared at him.

He was not teasing.

'But— I wear glasses,' I objected.

'You have beautiful eyes.'

'I still wear glasses.'

'So do I,' he shrugged. 'And it doesn't change the fact that you have beautiful eyes.'

'I limp.'

'I don't.'

'Aye, you're lucky.'

'You're plucky.'

'My nose is too long.'

'What's that got to do with being plucky, Pinocchio?'

'Pinocchio, you're saying? So you do think it's too long?'

'No. I think you exaggerate.'

'My chin juts out.'

'Only when you're being stubborn— like you are now.'

'My mouth's too big.'

'It's expressive. You've a huge smile that blows everyone's cares away.'

'Well, whatever you say, you cannot say I'm pretty.'

'No, you're not. You're more than that. What do you want to look like anyway? Mary Pickford?'

I felt the colour rush to my cheeks.

'You're not serious?' he laughed. 'You want to look like Mary Pickford? Crikey! Lucy, you'd look awful!' and he struck a series of melodramatic pouts and poses. They looked so silly that I could not keep from smiling.

'I say. Is that your train?' he asked in response to a distant toot.

'Aye, it is.'

'Would you mind if I came with you?'

'What do you want to come for?'

'I'd like to.'

'I'd be very glad of your company,' I replied. 'Tell you the truth I'm a little nervous for 'tis the first time I'll be catching the tram by myself. I can ask for help if I need, but 'tis hard sometimes to do that. Would you help me with the tram?'

'Nothing would give me more pleasure,' he replied. 'Where are we going?'

'To Darling Point it is.'

And so, every Wednesday afternoon, for the next few weeks, that is what he did.

Our train trips passed all too quickly. We seemed to have so much to talk about and the differences in our respective backgrounds made for such interesting conversation that we were always caught by surprise when the train arrived at

Central. Unlike Della, who groaned every time I pulled out Dudeney's *Amusements*, Wally enjoyed the puzzles therein. He readily provided the answer to how many runs the Captain scored in 'Slow Cricket' and it was puzzles of all descriptions that occupied us during quieter times.

As for the tram, I could have been royalty the way he escorted me. It was never any trouble to him to help me with the steps and he would always make sure I had a seat. If he noticed anyone staring at me, he would stare back at them until they began to feel uncomfortable, or else he would politely point out something wrong with their attire – be it a button undone, a loose thread or a shirt stain – and wink mischievously at me. Best of all were the nonsense tales he fabricated about my callipers. He would make eye contact, size up his victim and, toward the end of our journey, would spin his story. His proper English accent, his glasses, his height and build gave him an air and an authority that not many people would dare dispute.

'Have you heard of a scold's bridle?' he would ask.

Of course the victim had not heard of a scold's bridle, and he would explain the iron contraption used by husbands of olden times to prevent their wives from nagging.

'Well, they're a bit like that. They've been locked on,' he would continue in a very serious tone, indicating my callipers. 'Her father did it so she wouldn't be able to walk out with me. We're going to get them sawn off. Come on, Lu. Here's our stop.'

Our destination was a private establishment that up until recently had been used as an ex-servicemen's home. It was now a convalescent hospital for children with polio. Wally would wait for me to have my session, at the end of which I usually had to go in search of him. I would find him in all sorts of places: on the verandah discussing the cricket with a boy on crutches, reading a story to a smaller child, in a ward helping distribute meals; or else pushing a wheelchair across the grounds, having taken the patient on an excursion to look at the bridge construction. He seemed to derive genuine pleasure from spending his afternoon this way. Perhaps it provided an outlet for doing what he wished to do for his sister and could not. Whatever the reason, he quickly became a welcome visitor.

Although I enjoyed the challenge, I found water therapy exhausting. For that reason, Wally insisted on taking a taxi home and on paying for the trouble. Daid, in response, once he had overcome the initial shock of seeing me climb out of the cab in the company of a boy, invited him in for tea.

His presence at our table would have brought a smile to my mother's face. Wally had a healthy appetite. Ordinarily six sausages, a bowl of mashed potato and a few vegetables fresh from the garden provided us with an ample meal and something leftover for the morning's breakfast. On his first visit, however, Wally helped himself to four of the six sausages, ate more than half the potato and helped himself to seconds of all the vegetables. Daid was better prepared the next time, and from then on Wally was always assured of a hearty meal.

The conversation was curious, too. No dinner table taboos here. All manner of topics were discussed both during our meal and during the washing up, a task which seemed to intrigue Wally as much as it did Della. Daid wanted to know what Wally had planned now that he'd finished school. Was he off to the Varsity or was it a job he was after? And what did he think of Trade Unions? And what of Mr Lang? Was it just to have a White Australia policy did he think? And what did he have to say about the forthcoming Ashes test? Wally had plenty to say about the forthcoming Ashes test, as he did about politics and future hopes. So, surprisingly, did Daid.

But the mood changed with the Rosary. Wally politely refused Daid's invitation to join us and took his leave.

'Well, you can be sure we'll be praying for your sister, lad, and yourself besides,' Daid replied.

'What good's it going to do?' was Wally's surly response. 'It's not going to make her better.'

'Perhaps not,' replied my father, 'but our Good Lord has His ways, and however things come about, lad, we can be sure of His grace.'

Wally bid a curt good-bye. The ensuing weeks, however, saw him sitting in our parlour, brooding while we prayed. He never joined us, nor did he make any remark. He watched us conclude our prayers with the Sign of the Cross after which he would depart quietly, having given my father a respectful handshake, and return for more the following Wednesday.

In the meantime, there was a letter from Della:

Thursday, 22nd November, 1928
Feast of St Cecilia

Dear Luighseach,

Thank you ever so for your letter. As I read it I could hear your lively brogue and I felt as if I had spent lunchtime with you all over again, sitting on the lawn at school. I am glad exams went well and am quite thankful I did not have to sit them. Certainly you will take the lion's share of the prizes and you have my hearty congratulations in advance.

Have you heard any more from Phoebe? Mummy forwarded me a postcard from Ballarat but it has nothing on it save 'Love from Phoebe' in enormous handwriting. Why could she not write small and write more? It's frightfully lax of her. Please enlighten me. I might as well be Robinson Crusoe given the rate at which news travels here.

But a postcard with 'Love from Phoebe' was all the news I too had received. Since Pim and Mrs Epstein had been recipients of an identical card with an identical inscription, I could only report that no one was any the wiser.

The letter continued:

Speaking of news, old thing, you have a serious duty to continue to provide me with every skerrick of piffle, however trivial or frivolous you might think it. The same can be said for the more important things. I must know what is going on! I don't wish to miss out on <u>anything</u>, do you understand?

It is beautiful here. Not quite the Hydro Majestic but it has a very pleasant aspect and tranquil atmosphere. I spend much time on the verandah taking the air. In fact, I've taken so much air I am sure I will soon float away like a hot air balloon! Honestly, Luighseach, I have never had to work so hard at resting in my entire life! But, rest I must. I am commanded to rest. Doctor's orders! I manage some respite by reading and yesterday finished 'A Tale of Two Cities'. Now I'm reading 'Nicholas Nickleby'. Let's see if I can read all Dickens' novels before I leave. I have to be quite surreptitious about it because I am not to over-exert myself in anything. Really! When has reading ever been a burden? With little over a month till Christmas, however, I will be hard pressed to achieve my goal, and, believe you me I intend to be home for Christmas. I feel myself growing stronger daily and the doctor assures me I should be well enough to travel home soon.

How I long to see you again! I have missed you so much, old thing. Do write often; and if you don't hear from me as much as you might, know that you are always in my heart and in my prayers.

I remain ever your dear friend,

Mary Arondelle 'Delleen' Sotheby

''Tis what she doesn't say that worries me more,' I remarked to Wally when we next met.

'You know what she's like, Lu, she hardly ever thinks of herself. Besides, you've spent months in hospital, when it comes to writing, what would you have to say when one day's the same as the next? Hardly the thing to talk about, let alone write, I reckon.'

'She says she'll be home soon. Is it true, do you think?'

'Can't say. I hope so. She wants to be home more than anything else. I miss her too.'

I gave his hand a squeeze. He nodded and squeezed it back and did not say much after that.

The following Wednesday, however, Wally did not come. I let the train pass and waited in case he might appear. There was no sign of him and I resigned myself to catching the train and tram alone.

I finished my session and found Daid waiting for me instead.

''Twas Wally telephoned this afternoon, Luighseach,' he explained. 'He sent his apologies for not coming today but 'twas to the mountains he had to go.'

'He's gone to see Delleen, Da?'

'He's bringing her home, lass.'

'So soon, Da? And she's better already? Will I be able to see her?'

'In time to be sure you will, Luighseach. All in God's good time.'

54

'Lucy?'

I looked away from the window and stared blankly at Sister Magdalene.

'There is a lot of truth in the statement, don't you think?'

Which statement?

I scanned the blackboard for clues. All that was written was another list of names and dates:

Rousseau, 1712-1778
Diderot, 1713-1784
Voltaire, 1694-1778

No Fibonacci numbers there. No prime numbers either. The class began to giggle. I was notorious for my inattentiveness in History.

Why pay attention? It was Friday afternoon, exams had finished, and why bother with the French Revolution when it was nearly one hundred degrees outside and my little friend was home again?

'That if God did not exist, it would be necessary to invent Him,' prompted Sister Magdalene.

'Well,' I sighed. 'Thanks be to God, Sister Magdalene, we've been spared of the trouble.'

What laughter ensued was quickly suppressed by the arrival of Sister Bellarmine. Instantly, we rose to our feet. Greetings were made and Sister Bellarmine exchanged a few quiet words with Sister Magdalene while we sat.

Sister Bellarmine prepared to address us.

'Girls, what I have come here to say concerns Della Sotheby. It is my sad duty to inform you that Della will not be returning to school. While we will continue to pray for a cure or miracle, it seems that God is calling Della to Himself. I trust you will understand that this is a very difficult time for her family and that Della needs rest. Della wishes very much to see her friends but the nature of her illness demands that any contact must be strictly limited. Her mother has requested that you please refrain from spontaneous visits. You will be invited to come when it is suitable; kindly respect these wishes. In the meantime, it will be far more effective to remain prayerful and to trust in God's Holy Will. Thank you, Sister Magdalene. Let us now stand and we will pray a Hail Mary together.'

The bell sounded the end of school. The 'Sub Tuum Praesidium' was prayed and a very subdued class filed out of the room.

'Lucy,' Sister Magdalene gently called me back.

'What is it, Sister Magdalene?'

'I need to pick the flowers for Holy Mass tomorrow. It's the Feast of the Immaculate Conception and we need to have the chapel beautifully adorned. Would you help me?'

'I don't know I'll be much help, Sister,' I replied.

'I think you will give me all the help I need. I'll do the picking. I want you to choose the flowers. Come with me, child.'

I was compelled to follow Sister Magdalene to the Nun's Garden. The garden was situated between the chapel and the convent and ordinarily was out of bounds to students. It was in full bloom.

'I've never seen so many roses,' I remarked.

'Do you like flowers, Lucy?' she asked.

'Aye, I do,' I nodded, 'very much.'

'Which roses do you like most? These yellow ones here?'

''Tis the pink ones over there that I like best, Sister.'

'Then they are the ones we shall pick. Choose a range of blooms, child. We want a pleasing arrangement for tomorrow, but one that will last more than a day.'

Sister Magdalene let me choose all the roses I wanted. I soon exhausted the pinks and decided next upon the white roses nearby. Bloom after bloom was carefully placed in her basket and all the while Sister Magdalene chatted. What a hot day it had been, she remarked, and would the weather continue till Christmas? Did I have any plans for the coming holidays? And how were my 'cello studies progressing?

It came to a point, however, at which I could take no more.

'Lucy,' Sister soothed.

'Why is it that everyone I love is taken away from me?' I sobbed.

'Everyone, Lucy?'

'It feels like everyone, Sister,' I grimaced and shrugged through my tears.

'Much to your annoyance,' replied Sister Magdalene, 'I'm going to answer that with another question. What reason did you have for choosing each of these flowers?'

'They're the most beautiful, Sister.'

Sister Magdalene agreed. 'And they will look beautiful on the altar tomorrow, Lucy. They will give Our Lord and Our Lady and everyone who sees them a great deal of pleasure. And now I will ask you a further question. Should the garden complain that we have taken the roses?'

I sniffed and shook my head. How could a garden complain?

'Since we have made the garden,' Sister gently proceeded, 'we are free to take the roses as we please and it does the garden a lot of good to have its flowers picked. Provided we cut the stems correctly, the garden will produce all the more. Besides, we did not pick the flowers to use them wantonly. We took them to treasure, because we delighted in them. They will be put to the highest purpose: to adorn the altar for Holy Mass.

'Lucy, just as these roses are our flowers, so are we God's flowers and, good gardener that He is, He will pick us as He sees fit. You can be sure God loves Della as much as you, dear child. He loves us all and He will pick us when we are most beautiful. Some of us will be in full bloom, others hardly open, many He will allow to bud, bloom and fade. Della is being picked as a young rose. Your mother died young, didn't she?'

'Only twenty-six years old she was, Sister. 'Tis now passed eight years nearly to the day since she died.'

'Well, Lucy, you can be sure that on your altar in Heaven there is a vase with at least two beautiful flowers that will bloom forever more. You can gaze on those flowers and delight in their perfection – perfection as God sees it. I suppose it doesn't help much, but take heart, dear girl. You can be sure that my prayers will be with you as much as they are with Della.

'There, there, child. Sometimes it is very hard to accept God's Holy Will; and it's quite all right to be upset. It shows you've a big heart. Well, Lucy, that big heart's about to become even bigger.'

'She's my friend, Sister Magdalene,' I cried. 'She's my best friend.'

'She always will be, child. And so is God. He's not punishing you, Lucy. He's not leaving you alone to suffer all by yourself. He's asking you to draw close to Him. Have faith, dear child. All is not lost. Now, will someone be home for you this afternoon?'

'I'm not going home.'

'Where are you going?' Sister looked concerned.

'To Miss Bray's shop I'm going for to play the 'cello.'

'To sing what's in your soul?'

'Aye.'

'Well, Lucy, he who sings prays twice; and with an instrument as soulful as a 'cello, I think the same could be said. Just remember, child, you are never alone. Not for a minute. In fact,' she glanced aside, 'there's someone here for you right now.'

I turned around and there near the chapel was Mary Byrne.

'I was waiting for you at the front gate,' Mary explained. 'You didn't come so I went looking for you. Are you catching the train? We can catch the train together if you want.'

Mary and I travelled together as far as Lewisham. Although we said very little, I greatly appreciated her company. She bid me good bye, leaving me to travel to Newtown by myself.

Miss Bray greeted me when I entered her shop.

'Lucy, you're not here to play the 'cello, are you?' she inquired.

Of course I was. Miss Bray knew that.

'I'm afraid it's been sold, dear,' she said. 'Only this afternoon. There's another—'

But I did not want to hear about any other 'cellos.

How could she sell it? How could she? I knew the 'cello wasn't mine. I had no right to it. Yet of all the times to sell it, why did it have to be the time I needed it most?

And, as I wandered homewards, I began to cry all over again and was forced to stop in front of shop after shop to push my tears away.

'He's only an instrument,' I tried to remind myself. 'He's not a person. Only wood and gut he is. 'Tis silly to be upset about him. I never owned him and I've no right to behave as if I did.'

'But he's my Voice!' I cried. 'I've lost my Voice! Dear God in Heaven, whatever will I do now?'

As usual when he arrived home before me, Daid was waiting out on the front steps with Danny. In their company was Wally. Down the steps he came and opened the front gate for me.

'I'm so very sorry you found out like that,' he apologised. 'I couldn't believe my ears when I learned that my mother asked the school to break the news. Are you all right?'

I sadly shook my head.

'How's Delleen, Wally?' I sniffed. The 'cello was nothing compared with Della. 'Please tell me how she is.'

'It's in her spine as well as her lungs, Lu,' he began. 'The doctors say there's nothing more they can do. Mother's employed a nurse and we're doing everything we can to make her comfortable. Dell says not to worry. You know what she's like, but—'

Strong and manly though he was, Wally could no longer hide his feelings. 'I don't know how I'm going to get through this, Lu,' he choked. 'First my father and now my only sister. Why, Lucy? Why?'

Poor laddie. The sunshine did not beam in his blue eyes the way it usually did when I looked at him. I freed myself of a crutch, reached up and gently brushed aside a lock of hair that had fallen over his forehead.

'She can't move her legs, Lu,' he whispered.

My hand slowly drifted from his forehead to his shoulder and from his shoulder to his back. The only thing to do was to give him comfort.

'I'm not steady like you,' he quietly continued as he held me close. 'I've seen you angry and I've seen you sad, I've seen you suffer and I've seen you frustrated, and you've every reason to be, but I've never known you to resent anyone or anything because of your own loss whereas I want to smash the world to pieces and yet I can't because I know it will be futile to even try. But you, you—' he loosened his hold and gazed at me intently.

'Wally, lad, if only you knew how I felt inside.'

'You could hate me and yet you don't.'

'Hate you?' I repeated, looking at him straight in the face. Whatever made him say that? 'I could never hate you.'

'Come on, lad,' Daid took him by the arm. 'Come and have a cup of tea.'

'Look at you! Look at the two of you!' he cried. 'Do you ever think who I am?'

'You're yourself, lad,' remarked Daid as he guided him to our parlour.

'Sir, I'm the illegitimate son of an Anglo-Irish officer of the British Army and every time I look at that beautiful woman,' he gesticulated at Mam in the wedding portrait, 'I cannot help but think that she was killed by a man like my father.'

'Don't say that, Wally.'

'It's true, Lucy, and what do you do to me? You welcome me into your home with open arms. You feed me when your cupboards are nearly bare. You'd give me the coat off your back if I needed it.'

'We'd do that for anyone, lad,' said Daid. 'I'll go and put that kettle on. Sit yourself down by the hearth there.'

Wally did not sit, however. He stood close to me and touched me gently on the elbow. 'Despite everything that's happened to you, there's not an ounce of bitterness, not an ounce of hatred in you, Lucy. Why?'

It seemed to be a matter that had weighed on his mind for some time, and, given what he had confided in me about his father, it was only right that I should tell him what I had carried in my heart for so long.

''Twill be eight years ago tomorrow that Mam died you know, Wally,' I sighed and smiled a little at the photograph that hung directly opposite where we stood. 'And you're right: a man like your father shot and killed her. But there's something you don't know. That shot was not the first one fired. 'Twas my own people fired first and they shot a soldier. He fell down wounded and crying with pain. Only then was Mam shot and she too fell and could not speak. After that a cry went up that a child was there and the shooting stopped. 'Twas fearfully quiet. The groans of the wounded soldier were no more to be heard and Mam lay there with a half smile on her face. Then an officer came towards me. Perhaps he, too, was like your father. I suppose he spoke gently but I was so afraid. I couldn't talk. I couldn't move. He had to prise me off my mother. He carried me to a nearby house and it was there that I waited while Daid was fetched. Later, you know, that officer visited my da and offered to help us. Long they talked by the fire and it was through him that we were able to leave the country. But back in the street there, two people were dead: an English soldier and my darling Irish mother. They might have been different in this world, Wally, but from that moment they were both the same. They'd both gone to God and who was I to judge? 'Tis a scene and a thought that will never leave me. I can't hate, Wally. I can't. I can't hate anyone. And I could never hate yourself.'

And indeed, who was I to judge? I felt like nothing that day; and now, eight years later, that same nothingness, that powerlessness, that utter hopelessness haunted me all over again. I was no one. I was nothing. But, over the years, simple affection and tender-heartedness, patience and understanding had helped me accept Mam's death. And I knew that affection and tender-heartedness, patience and understanding would help Wally accept what was happening to Della. I also knew that it was up to me to give it.

Once again I took his hand. Once again I felt the strength of his arm around my waist and I let go my hold on my crutches and leant on him. I looked across at Mam and I could have sworn at that moment that she looked at me and smiled. All of a sudden my nothingness was transformed into something that seemed far beyond myself and yet at the same time seemed so much a part of me. It seemed so innate, so natural to me. It was not quite a feeling; it was a deeper motion and it welled up from the depths of my spirit:

It was a willing.

Somehow I knew what I had to do and I vowed I would do it with all my soul. I would accept and I would do everything I could to help Wally do the same.

'You'll get through, Wally Sotheby.'

'You'll stand by me, won't you?'

'Aye, I will. We'll stand by each other.'

'She wants to see a priest, Lu.'

'Then you fetch her a priest.'

'How do I do that? I've never had anything to do with priests.'

'Then let you come to Mass with me tomorrow.'

'On a Saturday?'

'Aye. Ordinarily I don't go to Mass on a Saturday but it happens to be the anniversary of Mam's death and it would mean a lot to me if you were there.'

'Of course I'll come.'

'We can talk to Father Callaghan after that. He'll be pleased to help.'

There was a rattle of cups. Wally steadied me and stood erect while Daid entered with the tea tray.

'And how is your mam, Wally?' Daid asked and passed Wally his tea.

'You know what she's like,' Wally sighed as he sat and stirred his sugar. 'On with the show....'

''Twill be hard for her the next few weeks and more, I'm thinking,' my father quietly observed.

'Mrs Mahony was with her most of this morning,' Wally replied. 'She's agreed to look after Leila and Henry while Dell's at home so mother can prepare for the funeral. I left her this afternoon looking at samples of black crepe with her dressmaker.'

'She's going to need you, lad,' Daid remarked.

'Me?' Wally scoffed. 'She can't bear the sight of me.'

'Aye, she won't if you're hostile to her. 'Tis comfort she needs, Wally. Are you man enough to give her comfort?' I'd never known my father to be quite so firm with anyone other than myself. 'And when will your step-father be home?'

'He cabled from Ceylon, sir. He's expected home a few days before Christmas.'

'Well, you'll be the man in the house till your step-father returns and let you take good care of your mother at least till then.'

Early the following morning, Wally met us outside St Joseph's for Mass. Since he had a cricket match to play, he was dressed in his whites over which he wore an orange and black striped blazer and matching cap.

'Folk will be thinking you're a hornet on a seaside holiday. What is it you put in there?' I smiled at him and indicated his duffle bag.

'All my gear: bat and pads among other things. I say, I feel frightfully underdressed for church,' he remarked, noticing the sidelong glances of parishioners. 'Are you quite certain this is all right?'

'If it's clean and ironed and mended, then there's nothing wrong with it,' I replied. ''Tis a little bright is all.'

'You think this is bright?' he challenged me. 'Well, the last time I attended church I wore a red military jacket with brass buttons and gold braid, navy trousers with a red stripe down the side, and shoes that were polished till they shone like mirrors.'

'Faith! 'Tis little wonder they call you Toffee. And how long is it since you been to church?'

'Apart from school chapel, it would be a couple of years, I reckon. Dell usually takes herself to Mass on Sundays and sometimes succeeds in dragging Mother and Leila along with her. Other than that the family tends to make a show at Christmas and Easter: usually Anglican for one and Catholic for the other. Last year I managed to get out of both. I say, is it really all in Latin?'

'Aye, it is. Even the homily, you know.'

'Homily? What? Do you mean the sermon's in Latin?'

'Aye, indeed, indeed it is,' but I could not keep a straight face. 'Well, to tell you the truth the homily will be in English if Father has time for one. Father Callaghan's Irish, though, so I don't know how you'll go understanding him.'

'I don't seem to have too much trouble understanding you,' he replied with a smile I was glad to see. 'By the way, how will I know what to do?'

'Follow himself there,' I nodded at Daid, 'for I do mostly sit. And don't worry about going to Holy Communion. Not everyone will go if they've not fasted so you won't feel left out.'

All in all, Wally managed quite well. He was very relieved to find some similarities between my Missal and the Book of Common Prayer, between the liturgy and what he recalled of his own attendance at Sunday services, and so had some idea of what was going on. We introduced him to Father Callaghan who remembered Della from my concert and who promised to oblige by visiting on Sunday afternoon and offering the day's Mass for her.

'Do you really believe all that? You know, all that Body and Blood of Christ stuff?' he asked me afterwards. 'Dell's tried to tell me a few bits and bobs in the past, but I've never been all that religious. I mean, I believe in God, but I've never really bothered about it beyond going to church. How can you believe in that anyway?'

'Well,' I confessed, ''tisn't like a mathematics equation, although sometimes I wish it were that straightforward. And if you asked the like of Sister Augustine, she'd give you a talking to about transubstantiation and a goodly dose of St Thomas Aquinas, and that's all fine. But I don't need proofs for 'tis deep down in my heart that I believe and I cling to it. In the past few weeks I've held on to it very hard indeed and I'm not going to let go any time soon. I don't need to invent God, Wally Sotheby. I know He exists and I know that He loves me more than I could ever dream. I put my trust in Him and He doesn't leave me alone in my sorrow. In fact,' I looked up at him and smiled, 'He seems to know what I need better than I know myself.'

55

If there was any reason for celebrating my birthday, the fact that it coincided with the last day of school was reason enough. I took one final look at the tall, lanky figure in the worn shirt and box-pleated tunic that was reflected in the cracked glass of my wardrobe, crossed my eyes, waggled my fingers in front of my nose and blew a raspberry.

Daid was waiting in the hallway.

'Lá breithe sona dhuit, a Luighseach,' he greeted me with the sign of the cross on my forehead, a kiss and a hug and brought me to the kitchen.

'Boxty today is it for breakfast, Daidí?'

'It is,' he replied.

Together we modelled small white worlds of mashed potato, squashed them flat, tossed them in oats and fried them golden brown.

Half-way through breakfast and Daid had a special request to make.

'It being the last day of school, lass, and your birthday, do you not think I could take your photograph?'

I knew I could not refuse him. Not a single photograph did he have of me in my uniform and it was well and truly time that he did.

'Aye, Da. You can take my photograph,' I sighed.

'Then let you finish your tea and clean your teeth and come to the parlour, for 'tis there that I set up my camera.'

I did as bidden and met Daid outside the parlour door. He opened the door for me.

'In you go, Luighseach,' he said.

In I went.

The camera was perched on its tripod. It was pointed towards the bay window, the place where I most liked to practise. There Daid had placed a chair for me. Leaning against the chair was something I never expected to see again.

'Daid!' I whispered.

'Go on, lassie,' he coaxed.

'Is it mine?'

'Aye, it is,' he replied.

'And you mean to say you been holding on to it for a whole week without breathing a word and leaving myself without any 'cello to play?'

'Luighseach, you're not going to be upset over it all, are you?'

'I'm trying not to be,' I sniffed. 'I cannot believe it, is all. And it's really my very own?'

'Aye, 'tis yours to keep. Your very own 'cello. A little money I been putting aside over the years, hoping that one day I might buy it for you. Well, the day finally came and what better occasion than my darling lass's sixteenth birthday to give it?'

'Oh, Da!'

'And is that giving you pleasure?' my father beamed at me, his own eyes glistening.

'Aye, it is!'

'And will you let me take your photograph?'

'With the 'cello?'

'Aye, with the 'cello and hopefully not too many tears. And let you not worry about the train this morning for I'll drive you to school. I don't think Sister Bellarmine will mind a little lateness on such a special day as today.'

I picked up the old 'cello and the bow I so liked to use with him. He was very out of tune, so I immediately set to work adjusting his strings. Within minutes I was warming him up, and with every stroke of my bow I cherished the deep delight that at last that mulled and hearty sound was truly mine.

We were driving up the hill towards King Street when we heard a shout.

'Yoohoo! Lucy!'

Mrs Murphy came waddling out carrying a large tin in one arm and waving vigorously with the other.

'I thought I'd missed you,' she panted as she reached my sidecar. 'I didn't think you'd be driven to school and it's just as well I caught you for you've saved me a trip. I was about to take the train there myself.'

She passed me the tin and told me to open it. Inside was a chocolate cake with cherries on top.

'I iced it this morning,' she said. 'I couldn't let you go to school on your birthday without a cake to share with your class. There should be enough for everyone and I included a knife. Stay there, Lucy. You can give me a hug when you return the tin. God bless and have a happy day, dear,' she added before she waved us off.

And the cake was not the only surprise. Daid picked me up from school that afternoon. He set me down at our front gate before taking the motorcycle round the back to the shed. Our front door opened and out came Phoebe and Pim.

'How grand it is to see you both again!' I couldn't think who to hug first. 'Pimmy! And little Phoebe!'

'Lil gave me the day off specially,' said Pim. 'Family sends their regards: Many happy returns from the Connollys.'

'And when did you come home, Phoebe Raye?'

'Two days ago.'

'And you been away how long?'

'Nearly a whole month, I think,' chatted Phoebe. 'We intended to spend a week but there was so much to do and so many people to see we had to stay longer. My grandmother insisted we stay. But she didn't have to insist. We would have stayed anyway.'

'Well, come inside and tell me all about it, only let me change first and sort my legs out. 'Twill be the last of this uniform till February, you know.'

'Except for prize giving on Saturday,' reminded Pim.

'We put some presents in the parlour,' Phoebe informed me. 'So be quick and come and open them!'

I was about to open my gifts when Danny barked and trotted out to the front door.

Danny was never wrong about visitors and this visitor was someone he particularly liked. It was Wally and he was holding an enormous bunch of roses.

'I hope I'm not too late,' he smiled. 'Happy birthday, Lu. May I come in?'

'To be sure you can.'

He passed me the roses. 'For you. Do you like them?'

'I do indeed, very much!' They were the creamiest of whites with a soft pink blush.

'I would have picked camellias but they're not in bloom. So I'm afraid you had to settle for roses,' he explained a little awkwardly. 'Once Hammond was certain he knew what I was doing, he gave me free rein, although I don't think he expected me to pick quite so many. Apparently they're called Madame Ernest Calvat or something like that. I'm afraid my French isn't all that good.'

'And neither is mine,' I replied.

'And this is from Dell,' he handed me another gift. 'She apologises for not wrapping it but she didn't think you'd mind.'

It was a book of poems by Gerard Manley Hopkins – one of her own. On the flyleaf was a bookplate with the St Dominic's crest. It read:

Presented

to

Mary Arondelle Sotheby

Summa Cum Laude

English Literature III

1927

Above it she had written in her feathery scrawl:

To my dear Irish friend, Luighseach Ní Sruitheáin, who is certain to love these poems as much and even more than me.

'Tell her thank you, will you?' I gulped. 'And will you join us for some tea?'

'That's what I'm here for,' he replied as he entered the parlour and greeted Pim and Phoebe.

'Here, this one's from me,' Pim passed me her present which I unwrapped. '*The Innocence of Father Brown*,' I read the title.

'It seemed like your sort of book,' she remarked. 'Read any Father Brown?'

I had not read any Father Brown. 'Mystery stories is it?' I asked as I examined the contents.

'This big present here is from me,' Phoebe passed me a large and heavy item. 'Well, it's from Dad and me.'

I undid the string and brown paper and uncovered the painting of the harbour I had seen in Mr Raye's room. 'For myself is it?'

'Dad thought that seeing you liked it so much that day you might like to put it somewhere, although where you'll put it I don't know. It's getting a bit full in here.'

'Aye, we're filling the hallway now, but I'll be putting this one in my room above the fireplace. Thank you! Thank you everyone, and tell your da thank you too, Phoebe.'

'You can tell him yourself. You'll see him soon enough.'

Daid came in, having put away the motorcycle and attended to the garden. He admired my gifts and made his greetings. Pim suggested we go to the dining room for our celebration. Apparently they had planned a special birthday dinner.

'And you'll be looking forward to the second Test tomorrow, Wally?' Daid asked Wally while they walked together.

'Don't you start, Mr Straughan,' Wally replied with a slight groan.

'To be sure you were glad of the victory the other week?'

'I can't say I am, sir.'

'So 'tis the Australians you're barracking for after all?'

'Des does,' he replied, referring to his step-father. 'He has a soft spot for the colonies. He says Australian cricket's a credit to the Empire.'

'Is that so?' Daid gave the idea a brief moment's consideration. 'Well, I'm thinking it's nothing like a contest to sort things out, is there?'

'I don't know about that, sir. I'm playing cricket tomorrow and I'm going to be toast regardless of which side I'm playing for.'

'Well, lad,' Daid gave him an encouraging pat on the back. 'You ought to hold your head high and be proud of the victory. Was it not a decisive win by the English in Brisbane? And how many runs was it they scored?'

'They won by six hundred and seventy five runs,' came the guilt-ridden correction. 'I say, sir,' Wally approached the matter cautiously. 'You don't barrack for the English do you?'

'Mother of God, lad!' Daid feigned shock. 'What a question is that to ask an Irishman!'

It turned out that Pim had devoted part of the afternoon to preparing a feast in our kitchen. Out she came, with Phoebe in tow, carrying a platter of prawns and oysters fresh from the markets, a just-baked loaf of bread and new churned butter. It was a summer feast indeed!

Phoebe could no longer wait to tell about her trip.

'And you had a safe journey?' I asked her.

'Dad was a bit upset,' she replied. 'The last time he visited Ballarat was when he took my mother down for Christmas. He wanted to show her more of where he grew up, hoping that a change of scenery might help her. It only made things worse, for the trip ended up in a horrible argument over Christmas dinner in which the entire family put pressure on him to enlist. I told him he didn't have to go but he was determined. He was very keen to show me all the things he wanted to show my mother and never did.

'So we arrived at Ballarat and we were met by my Aunt Rachel. She's my father's other sister and she's much kinder than my Aunt Sara. My father didn't expect to see her with her hair all grey. She looks after my grandparents. She made me this dress, too. Do you like it?'

We all said we did. Indeed it had been quite a pleasant surprise to see Phoebe in a more modern style of dress.

'Aunt Rachel took us to one of the grandest homes you have ever seen,' she resumed. 'It was the house where Dad grew up. My grandmother was overjoyed to see him again. I didn't know what to expect of my grandmother but I never expected her to look the way she did.'

'And how was that?' I was curious.

'Well, I've always wondered why my father looks like a gypsy and now I know. My grandmother is part Chinese! I have a Chinese great-grandfather. His name was Li Yeung Peng, although everyone called him Billy Penn, Billy being short for William and William sounding a bit like Li Yeung, you see.'

'Didn't your father ever tell you that?' queried Pim.

'He never thought to,' Phoebe laughed. 'You see, he never thought of his grandfather as Chinese. He showed me a photograph of Great-Grandfather with a top hat and frock coat and his eyes are exactly like Dad's. Not too many Australians can boast they have Chinese blood, Dad says, so I ought to consider it a privilege. Anyway, my grandparents still have the servants who knew my father before he went away – although not as many as they used to and the house is a little run down because of it – and the servants couldn't believe their eyes when they saw Dad. Hatty the cook made him all his favourites.

'And Dad was a bit surprised to find his room exactly as he left it. His first full-size violin was there and all the medals he'd won in the eisteddfods. My grandmother had even framed the notices for the concerts he gave before he left for Vienna as well as some he'd sent her from Vienna itself. She told me he used to ride all over the countryside with his violin on his back performing wherever he could. In fact, the reason why he eventually chose the violin over the piano was because he couldn't take a piano on horseback. His gramophone recordings are there, too, as well as a beautiful picture of him in concert dress. And on the mantelpiece in the drawing room there's a photograph of him in his light horse uniform and he has a very defiant glint in his eye. Near it is another photograph of him which has been framed with the medal he was awarded and the notice describing what he did to earn it. Dad took one look at it, stamped his stick on the floor, muttered something that sounded like "You cocky bastard" (pardon me) and walked away.

'Anyway, Dad became quite a celebrity. Every morning he'd make an excursion to the barber for a shave. It usually took a couple of hours because news started going round that he was in town and fellows he knew began to wander down. The barber did a roaring trade while Dad was there. We paid so many calls and received so many calls and ate so many cakes and scones that Dad said he'd end up as paunchy as Felix the Cat if we kept it up any longer. Most people hadn't seen him since he left for Vienna, which was more than twenty years ago, and they were very glad to see him again. Lots of fellows his age never came back from the War, you see. We even met his first violin teacher who's very old now and I played for him. Dad showed me all over the town, took me to the theatres where he used to play, to all the shops, to all the tea rooms, to the gardens – everywhere! And everywhere we went there was someone to talk to. It was exhausting!

'Then my Uncle Alec came to visit. He's my father's oldest brother. Dad's the baby of the family. Uncle Alec married late – just after the War ended – so I have a family of young cousins neither of us ever knew about. They were very eager to meet Uncle Roderick who up till now has been a mysterious bohemian hero who haunts the family.'

I smiled at that description. 'Did you know Mr David calls him Puccini's Bushman? He told me if Puccini had lived to write an opera set in Australia he'd find all the inspiration he'd need in your da,' I explained.

'I can believe it,' acknowledged Phoebe. 'Of course, all the silly Gregory Allegri stories came out and more,' she continued. 'And the day after that Dad took me horseriding. Dad was mortified when I told him I'd never been on horseback before, so he had my aunt's mare saddled and he showed me what to do. Then he decided to ride himself and he demanded they have another horse saddled for him. He spent a long time patting it and talking to it. In the end he buried his head in the horse's neck and cried.'

'Had he been on a horse since the War?' Pim asked and explained to Wally what happened.

'No,' Phoebe replied. 'And he did ride, eventually, although he needed help to mount. He spent the entire afternoon in the saddle. You should have seen him on that horse.'

'Good?' asked Pim.

'It was beautiful. He didn't gallop or do any jumping although Aunt Rachel said once upon a time he would have even if he did have wooden legs and the use of only one arm. It was the way he controlled the horse. He could make it go forwards and backwards, sideways, step high, turn round and round – anything he wanted once he found his seat. Unfortunately, though, he was so stiff afterwards he could hardly walk and for the next few days all he could do was sit on the verandah with my grandfather. But it didn't stop him. He was at it again nearly every other day for the rest of the holiday even if it meant hobbling around between times.'

'You've not yet said anything about your grandfather,' I noted. 'What's he like?'

'Let's see,' considered Phoebe. 'He's ninety years old, which is quite a bit older than Grandmother, but he's well for his age and very stern. I was quite afraid of him. He didn't stop complaining the entire time we were there. Dad was very late rising after two days of travelling and Grandfather complained he was lazy. He kept on saying that apart from the army my father never did a decent day's work in his life. Apparently when Dad was growing up Grandfather viewed music practice as leisure, not work, and never considered working nights and giving concerts a proper job. Dad went to the barber's and Grandfather complained his moustache made him look like a dandy and that his ties were too bright. He complained when Dad went to Mass and kept on passing comments about the Mark of the Beast and the Whore of Babylon all through Sunday dinner. Dad went to the pub and Grandfather, who's never touched a drop of alcohol, started ranting about temperance. Dad lit a cigarette and Grandfather complained he smoked too much. He complained whenever Dad used the telephone. He complained that there were too many visitors, he complained that there were too few visitors. He complained that there were no visitors.'

'And what did your da say to all that?'

'Nothing. Dad said absolutely nothing. Years ago, Aunt Rachel said, it would have been the source of endless quarrels, but Dad said he's seen enough pointless fighting to last him the rest of his life. I told Dad I thought him very like Grandfather. He was a bit shocked to hear it but when I heard that Grandfather came out all the way from Scotland when he was sixteen years old to seek his fortune on the goldfields, it seemed to me that he has the exact same dogged, daredevil determination as my father. After all, Dad did the same thing in going to Vienna at the very same age. And the funny thing was, that all the time my father was home, Grandfather was always nearby, listening to all his quips and stories. Then, you wouldn't believe what happened.'

'What?'

'Well, a couple of days before we decided to return home, Grandfather took us out. We rode in the carriage out of the town, through an enormous arch and down a very wide avenue. There were trees growing on either side. It turned out that each of the trees – and there are thousands of them – represent a boy from the town who served in the War. Grandfather showed Dad the tree he planted for him. It's an elm and it has a plaque with "Roderick John Raye Trooper 13th Lighthorse" on it. Grandfather's been helping to look after that tree ever since it was planted ten years ago. Dad wanted to see all the other trees and he and Grandfather visited as many as they could and Dad and Grandfather talked of what they remembered of all the boys they knew who went to fight. Then Dad started to cry again and Grandfather put his arm on his shoulder and let him cry and didn't complain that he cried. I suppose it was Grandfather's way of saying he was grateful Dad came back and how sorry he was about the War. Deep down, I think, he's really very proud of my father. They laid a wreath at the Arch of Remembrance the following day and Grandfather stopped complaining after that.

'Then we had to leave. Grandmother was very sad. She said we'd brought the old house to life again and she didn't know what she was going to do with it quiet. It seems that wherever my father goes everything suddenly becomes very busy and very lively. And amidst all the comings and goings, Dad was making trunk calls to Sydney and sending telegrams, mainly to Mr Birstall of all people. He was up to something and I didn't find out what it was until we got back.'

'And what was it?'

'He showed me yesterday after we went to see Della.'

'You saw Della?' I echoed slowly.

'Haven't you seen her yet?' Phoebe was genuinely surprised that I hadn't.

'How is she?'

'She's much better, she says, although I thought she looked very pale and weak. Dad says she's very sick. She said to give you her love.'

'And yourself?' I warily asked Pim. 'Is it you seen Delleen?'

'This morning,' Pim confessed. 'I'm going to Moss Vale on Monday to give Rose a hand with the baby,' she elaborated. 'She's due any day now. I had to see Dell. It'd probably be my only chance before—well, you know...'

'And what was it your father was up to?' I quietly returned to the former topic.

'He took me to our house!' Phoebe excitedly replied. 'And he's had it all cleaned up, Lucy. He's made it beautiful again and guess who's going to live there?'

'Who is it?'

'We are! We're moving this weekend. And there's more. Mr and Mrs Epstein are coming to live there too. They're going to live on the top floor. Dad says the house is way too big for the two of us and Mr and Mrs Epstein need a place to live without worrying about being evicted. Mrs Epstein's eyesight isn't getting any better and moving every year or two doesn't help. It's the least we can do for them given all they've done for us. He's even engaged his favourite nurse to help keep house. We're going to use most of the bottom floor for music studios. Dad's taking on a couple of students and Mr Pippin's asked him to do some examining. It's about time we filled that old house to the brim with music, like it used to be, said Dad. Oh dear! Lucy, please don't cry.'

But I could not help crying.

'Really, Lu, it's not that Dell doesn't want to see you,' Wally knew the reason for my tears. 'Nothing could be further than the truth. She's afraid.'

'Afraid of myself is it? Are we not best friends? A week she's been home now and most of the class has seen her and Phoebe here and Pim and not myself!'

'Crikey, she's not afraid of you. I've tried to tell her how much you want to see her I don't know how many times. Every day Mother asks her if she wants to see

you. Mother always mentions you first and Dell always says not yet. It's not "no",
Lu. It's "not yet".'

'She asked after you at least three times while I was there,' said Pim.

'And it was her idea to have a birthday for you,' added Phoebe. 'You can
be such a dark horse about some things. We wouldn't have known it was your
birthday if it wasn't for Della.'

'I don't suppose this is any consolation, Lu,' said Wally, 'but Dell can't cope.
She can be bright and cheery with everyone else and pretend nothing's really the
matter, but she knows that the moment she sees you she's going to have to face
what she doesn't want to face. She doesn't want to go. I promise, though, cross
my heart, I'll make sure you see her before it's too late.'

'Guess it's a bit like dessert, Lucy,' observed Pim with a dry smile. 'I reckon
she's saving the best till last.'

Phoebe looked at each of us with a confused, concerned expression. 'Is— is
Della really going to die?'

It seemed to be the first time it had really occurred to her.

'Can't they make her better?' she queried.

'There's absolutely nothing they can do,' said Wally.

'I suppose that's what everyone's been trying to tell me,' she murmured. 'Do
you mean we're never going to play together any more?' Phoebe's eyes were filling
with tears. 'But— but she can't go. What are we going to do? I didn't say good
bye.'

'She doesn't want to say good bye,' Wally replied. 'Listen, the best thing you
could have done was what you did the other day: come with a bucketful of news.
And tell your father thanks heaps for reading to her. He read her a chapter from
Nicholas Nickleby and did a topping Mr Squeers impersonation. I'm afraid I'll be
hard pressed to do better.'

'You don't understand. I must say good bye,' insisted Phoebe.

'They'll make sure you say good bye, Phoebe,' Daid reassured her and nodded
at Wally. 'Will you come and help me serve the ice cream?'

'Ice cream, Da?' that was a treat. 'You know, I cannot get used to the idea of
ice cream on my birthday. Back home 'twould be Mass in honour of St Lucy,
snow outside and treacle pudding.'

'Too hot for treacle pudding, Lucy.'

'Aye, but I'm fond of it all the same.'

Wally and I stood on the front porch, having waved Pim off on the tram and
Phoebe with Mr Epstein.

'I suppose I ought to go myself,' he began after we had talked for some time.

'Thank you again for the roses. I put them in my room. 'Twill be lovely to wake
up tomorrow and see them on my bedside table. They're beautiful, Wally.'

'Like you. You're beautiful.'

'But—'

'No buts,' he put a finger to my lips and smiled. 'I know, you gimpy girl. And I'd even go so far as to say that those funny, spindly, stringy legs in those rotten callipers have made you beautiful. Well, you're beautiful to me if that counts for anything.'

I had seen that look of his before. Wally meant every word and I knew that any retort of mine would have cut him to the core. Besides, I did not want to hurt him.

'And that's what you think, is it?'

He took my hands. 'I like you an awful lot. In fact, I like you so much that— Well, I wondered if you'd be my girl. That is, if you felt the same way about me. You don't have to say straight away and you can say no if you prefer. I want you to know how I feel, that's all. Did you have a happy day?'

'Aye, I did. I cannot but be very thankful for all that's been given to me.'

'Luighseach!' Daid called from inside.

'I'm thinking I better go in now.'

'Will you be swimming on Wednesday?'

'I will.'

'May I see you then?'

'You may.'

'Till Wednesday then. And for now, Happy Birthday, Lu.'

And before I knew what had happened, he raised my hand to his lips and kissed it. Then he dashed down the steps and ran towards the station.

56

And so it was that my last 'cello lesson for the year was held, not at Petersham, but at Phoebe's house. The wrought iron gate that opened onto the property was still in a shabby state, but what a transformation had taken place within! All the undergrowth had been cleared and a new lawn had been laid, showing off the giant poplar tree in all its summer splendour. Gone was the broken swing and, to right and left, garden beds had been tilled and prettily planted. It seemed Roderick Raye's humour knew no bounds for a statue of Venus at her toilette had been positioned in such a way that the goddess seemed to have taken refuge behind a shrub. One look in the opposite direction made it perfectly clear why: Venus had been caught in the act by a confident Mars.

The master of the house himself came out to greet us.

'And how's Miss Lucy Long?' he welcomed me. Evidently his penchant for pet names had been extended my way. No doubt he was referring to my height, but I had a notion he was implying a good many other things besides. I thanked him for the painting.

'You still like it?' he asked.

'Aye, I do, and I hung it up in my room.'

'You make sure you get yourself a curach someday, eh?' he winked. 'And it's as much a thank you present as it is a birthday present. You've been a good friend to my daughter. Thank you,' he added quietly and introduced himself again to Daid.

'Do you think the garden beautiful?' asked Phoebe.

'It is indeed. And another pretty frock you're wearing there, Phoebe Raye?' I admired her summer dress.

'Dad arranged with Mrs Sotheby's dressmaker to have some new clothes made especially for me. It was a welcome home surprise!'

'Had to do something for my little girl,' remarked her father, 'else people round here will start thinking she's spent the last few years of her life in an orphanage! Tut, tut, tut! Can't have that, can we, Possum?'

'Come and see inside,' Phoebe led me in. The vestibule had been cleaned and decorated with potted palms, and a vase of lilies stood on the hallstand. The wallpaper had been repaired and the timber glowed.

'I have to show you the portrait,' she said.

I was shown into the room that had once been her aunt's studio. It now served as her father's studio and on its walls were displayed his own paintings. There was an entire regiment of portraits. All of them were soldiers and they were all painted in Mr Raye's curiously childlike style, with staring medieval eyes and sometimes disturbing faces set against very plain backgrounds.

'They're like icons,' I remarked, fascinated and not a little overwhelmed by the array. 'But none of them are saints, I'm thinking.'

'They all have their personalities, don't they?' Phoebe replied. 'Dad can't stand the euphemisms people use when they talk about the War. You know, phrases like "war heroes" and "the fallen" and "supreme sacrifice". He hates that sort of thing.'

'Mother of God, the head of that one's upside down and it isn't joined to its body! What on earth put it into his head to paint like that?'

'That's what he remembers,' Phoebe explained. 'It was my mother's idea originally. "If you can't talk about your dreams," she told him, "paint them. Tell me in paint and for once I don't care that you can't use your right hand. Use your left, but please, Roddy, tell me." That's what she said. Most of those men are dead. The ones still alive are mostly the ones that look strange, like that one with the lob-sided face. That's Tom. He lives in the home in North Sydney. There's a German one here: Kurt. He plays the oboe. Dad knew him from the Academy in Vienna and they happened to meet in France because Kurt was taken prisoner of war and Dad had to escort him to camp. Dad has a story about each of those men. Oh, and this is me!'

On the easel was an unfinished portrait of Phoebe. It had been executed in a similar style. In the top left corner was simply written 'Possum' and, in fact, Mr Raye had made Phoebe look like a possum. He had exaggerated her large, round eyes and long lashes, elongated her nose, and made much of her hair which fell over her shoulders in ringlets. She was wearing the same pretty dress she now wore and was holding her violin, standing it on her lap with her fingers over its shoulder.

'The brooch I'm wearing is Dad's regimental badge: the Dancing Devil. He gave it to me. Do you like the painting? I've been sitting for it most of today.'

'I like it very much. A fine portrait it is.' And, in its intriguingly whimsical way, it was a very fine portrait for it had captured Phoebe beautifully.

'Excuse me, Luighseach, have you come to see an exhibition or are you here for a 'cello lesson?' called Mrs Epstein from the door.

'I'm thinking 'tis going to be a late night,' I left Dad engrossed in conversation with Phoebe's father and followed Mrs Epstein to her new studio. The contents of her former music room, including the piano, had found their way into the front room. A process of sorting out had commenced and I wondered to myself if it would ever be finished.

'I imagine they have a lot in common,' enjoined Mrs Epstein. 'Here, I have something for you.'

It was not like Mrs Epstein to give presents.

'"To the one student I never thought would play as well as she does",' I read on the front cover of the music she had given me. '"Best wishes and warm regards for your sixteenth birthday, Luighseach, Mary Anne Epstein". The Brahms *Double*

Concerto. A concerto, Mrs Epstein?'

'Phoebe's been pestering me for months about it. It would be good for you to get your teeth stuck into something like this.'

'A concerto?' I repeated.

'There's no rush to learn it. You can take your time. We'll worry about an orchestra later.'

'A concerto, Mrs Epstein?'

'Yes, Luighseach. A concerto. Don't you want to play a concerto?'

'I—'

'I think you'll enjoy it. I'm not going to put you on the spot and make you sight-read it now so have a look at it over Christmas. What I would like to focus on is Handel's *Messiah,*' Mrs Epstein handed me some more music. 'Rehearsals start on Wednesday and there'll be three performances next week in the Town Hall. We're sorely in need of an extra cellist. I've spoken to your father about it and he's quite happy for you to do it. Will you?'

As usual, the question was a rhetorical one.

'Incidentally, I'm not the one asking the favour,' she continued, 'although I heartily endorse the idea. It's high time you did some orchestral work. The invitation comes from Mr Pippin who will be conducting. He suggested I ask that splendid young lad of mine,' here she gave me one of her looks. 'It took me a while to work out who he meant. You can share my desk. Phoebe's playing second violin, Reuben's playing viola and Roddy's managed to get himself into the tenors. It should be fun. The *Messiah* always is. For a musician, Christmas isn't Christmas without Handel's *Messiah.* And there's an added bonus: you'll earn some pocket money and a ticket for your father.'

It was pointless telling Mrs Epstein no.

'Good,' Mrs Epstein concluded. 'Now, you'll need a black dress that will comfortably accommodate your 'cello. Tea length I believe it's called. I have a spare one that will probably fit you. I will leave you to explain yourself to Mr Pippin on Wednesday, you scallywag,' she finished with a smile.

Out came the music and we spent a good portion of the lesson sitting side by side, just as we would in an orchestra, playing together, and pausing to discuss bowings and fingerings whenever necessary.

'That really is a superb instrument, Luighseach,' Mrs Epstein decided it was time for a break.

''Tis the one I used at the competition. I've always loved this 'cello.'

'And so you should. It has a name, you know.'

'A name, Mrs Epstein?'

'Oh yes. We know it very well. Its name is Cyrano.'

'What is it?'

'It's Cyrano. Cyrano de Bergerac – a hero who was famous for his ugliness as much as he was for his beautiful poetry – at least that's what Roddy called it and

I believe the name stuck. You know who used to own it, don't you?' Mrs Epstein realised I was a little baffled.

'And is there a reason why I should?'

'I suppose there isn't, but it used to belong to Ailine Devereaux. Roddy constantly teased her about it. The two of them used to enact silly courtships with their instruments, Roddy pretending his violin was the lady and Ailine turning her cello into the gentleman. Ailine sold Cyrano to Dulcie Bray to pay for her passage to France.

'Don't worry, Luighseach, it does us all a lot of good to see that cello in your hands. After all, it is only an instrument and is totally dependent on the person who plays it. In this case, I couldn't think of anyone better to play it than you. Speaking of Miss Bray, have you heard the news?'

'About the wedding, you mean, Mrs Epstein?' Mrs Epstein shared my smile. 'Aye, Mr David and Miss Bray told us yesterday afternoon when they came for a cup of tea. Daid's going to be the photographer for the occasion.'

'They've asked Reuben and me if we'd provide some music,' my teacher informed me. 'We thought we'd put a string quartet together. We need a cellist and we'd like it very much if you'd play with us. It would mean a lot to Davy if you did.'

'It would mean a lot to myself, too, Mrs Epstein.'

'I thought so. We'll work on the programme a little later. The wedding's not till February. There will be some Haydn of course. Phoebe's agreed to play first violin.'

'And how does Phoebe feel about that?'

'For once I think she's a bit daunted by the prospect – and so she should be. One thing is to want to be first violinist, but it is quite another to find oneself in the leader's position. She'll have her father helping her along, though. You realise we're going to be up against a conspiracy, don't you?'

'Aye,' I smiled. 'But we'll outnumber them three to two.'

'Good,' Mrs Epstein agreed. 'So you'll do it?'

'Aye, I will. I miss playing quartets,' I sighed. 'They'd become a part of me, Mrs Epstein.'

'Phoebe feels the same way. Now, I have a very big favour to ask you,' she sighed. 'It concerns Della.'

'Is it you seen her, Mrs Epstein?'

'No, I haven't yet. But I did speak to Mrs Sotheby the other day. She telephoned me to ask if you could play at the wake.'

'She did what?'

'She wants a quartet, Luighseach.'

'She can't be serious, Mrs Epstein.'

'Luighseach, this is not going to be an easy thing for any of us to do, and, I assure you, it was not an easy thing for Mrs Sotheby to ask. But think what that poor woman is going through, what the family is going through. They dearly want to bring some music back into their home, and as far as I'm concerned I will support them in whatever way I can. If it's a string quartet they want, then a string quartet they will have. Pim's agreed and will be coming up from Moss Vale for the funeral. In the meantime, Mr Epstein will play viola in her place, I will take second violin, and, since she already knows Della's part, Phoebe will take first. Phoebe desperately needs to play. She is still clinging to the possibility that Della will get better. Listen, I know it's hard, Luighseach—'

'But it's not fair, Mrs Epstein!' I cried. 'Why should Delleen die? Why should she die? Polio nearly killed me when I was eight years old. Why did it not? It's not fair!'

'Whoever said anything about it being fair?' answered my teacher. 'Not much in life is fair, I'm afraid, as you well know. It's just the way things are. I remember feeling like that when I lost Joseph. Being told I could never have any more children was like receiving a death sentence. And then to see other mothers blessed with five, six, seven children, and all of them healthy, was a sight I couldn't bear for many years. Why should that happen?

'To make matters worse, some people said it was my punishment for marrying a Jewish man while others would tell Reuben it was his punishment for marrying a Christian. What a simple-minded idea! To think we can mould divine wisdom like putty in our puny hands, according to our own petty notions. If we can't even read the minds of our best friends how can we pretend to read the mind of God? Maybe we won't see the purpose of it till the end of time itself.

'Meanwhile, Life goes on and, no Luighseach, sometimes it doesn't seem fair. Be thankful for Della, be thankful for yourself. But you must lead your own life. Della is a part of your life, as you are part of Della's. It's time to take your leave for the moment. I had to do the same thing to a tiny baby years ago. Since then, I have had many children. There, there, Luighseach. Everything has a way of working out. It might not seem so at the moment, but you'll see.'

'Aye, Mrs Epstein. Deep down I know it will and I trust that it will, but 'tis hard all the same.'

'I know it's hard. But try not to make it any harder than it is. You will play, won't you? I mean, we can't ask Kathleen Doherty, can we?' she joked.

'Indeed we cannot, Mrs Epstein.'

'Indeed we cannot. We'll do the *Lark*, which I believe is Della's personal favourite. The first movement will probably be enough.'

'And is that why you don't go to Holy Mass, Mrs Epstein?' I ventured to ask my teacher something I had wanted to know for a very long time.

'What? Now don't you start!' I knew I would receive a scolding. 'Yesterday I had Roderick chide me about my Sunday obligations like a mother superior would a postulant. What on earth made you bring that up?'

'Phoebe Raye once said you didn't go to Mass any more because you did something good and it's worried me ever since. Was marrying Mr Epstein the good thing that you did?'

'Yes it was. It still is, even though it has been very hard – more because of the War than anything else. As for the facile judgements people make— well, I wish they would mind their own business,' replied my teacher as she gave further thought to her explanation. 'You see, Luighseach, I have always tried to do what is right and I have never understood how anyone could tell me that to love a man who is not of the same faith is not right. As for demanding that he give up something as intrinsic as his beliefs merely to satisfy a religious or legal formality, well, I couldn't think of anything more abhorrently false.

'If it wasn't for Roddy and the efforts he made to find us a priest, I doubt we would ever have married at all. To live in sin, however, even if you love each other, is not right either, is it?'

I gravely shook my head.

'And then, when Roddy and Juliette married, I had to swallow every ounce of pride. To see those two at the altar and the grandness of the wedding – Roddy, to all effects having converted out of expedience and Juliette beginning to show she was with child – well, frankly, it seemed to fly in the face of every principle to which I had tried to hold fast, particularly when the entire affair was sanctioned by the institution that had made the celebration of my own marriage so difficult. If it wasn't for the fact that Roddy is such a loyal friend and that he and Juliette seemed so genuinely happy together – at least at first – I would have turned my back on them. Just as well I didn't for it seems I've been proven very wrong in many ways,' she sighed. 'Talk about a topsy turvy world. Roddy's become quite devout in his own inimitable way— and that's something I wouldn't have expected from the very man who, twenty years ago, used to tease me incessantly about wanting to be a nun.'

'And why didn't you become a nun? Was it because you fell in love with Mr Epstein?'

'Insatiable curiosity!' my teacher fondly reprimanded me. 'Mind you be careful or you'll get your nose tweaked. Yes, Luighseach, in part it was; but more to the point, being a nun was not my vocation as it turned out. Roddy, savvy as ever, was very right to tease. I think if I had ended up a nun I would have been like one of those sisters in the convent of Porte Royale: as pure as an angel and as proud as the devil himself. You're not thinking of becoming a nun, are you?' she asked in a very wary tone.

I shook my head.

'Well, I'm very relieved about that. You're too good a cellist to be in a convent.'

'But how did you know that you loved Mr Epstein? How do you know when you love someone, Mrs Epstein?'

'A man, do you mean?'

I nodded.

'Well,' Mrs Epstein looked at me and smiled one of those special smiles of hers, 'I think that's best answered by considering it the other way round. How do you know when a man loves you? Does he honour you? Is he kind to you? Does he listen to you? Is he patient with you? Is he there for you when you're weak or sick or sad? Does he really care about the person you are? Does he value all that you have to give? Does he want the best for you, more even than you might want for yourself? And if you can answer yes to all of those questions, then that man probably loves you. Conversely, if you try to do the same for that man, want the same for that man, then I think it would be pretty safe to say that you love him. There are feelings attached, too – very beautiful feelings – and it brings a very deep joy. That sort of friendship is the love that marriage is built on and it's very precious. Does that help?'

It helped very much indeed.

'And that's why you married Mr Epstein?'

'Yes, it is.'

'And 'tis why you didn't marry Mr Raye?'

'You're very bold. Yes, it is, along with the fact that he never asked my hand. It was never that sort of a friendship. Besides, being married to Roderick Raye, for all his brilliance and warmth of heart, would be like having custody of a child who, the moment you turned your back, would be in the duck pond, up the highest tree or down in the cellar uncorking the ginger beer and at the end of the day would have to tell you every detail of his exploits and more. Roddy's a very, very dear friend, but not my idea of a husband by any means. I think Juliette ended up bringing out the best in him if his relationship with Phoebe is any gauge. I wish I had known her better,' she sighed. 'But she was four years younger than me, which is a lot when you are only in your twenties. By the way, have you seen Roddy's portrait?'

Mrs Epstein indicated the pictures she had hung and we walked over to study them. They were the paintings I had seen in Ailine's studio.

'They're Ailine's are they not?'

'She left them behind.'

'There was a landscape, too, you know.'

'With the ruined church? Yes, there was. We haven't worked out what to do with that one. It upset Roddy terribly. During the War he rode through village after village like that, with homes, buildings, churches – many of which had stood for centuries – razed to the ground, leaving families homeless and starving, mothers without their babies and little children without their parents. What's more, the retreating German army had planted mines in their wake. Roddy saw five of his mates blown apart. He had to bury what remained of them. Horrible.'

'And you're not telling me that's a portrait of Mr Raye?' I pointed at the painting of the strange, fragmented face with the violin and music.

'Yes it is. It's Roddy in his uniform. See the feather? It's from the Lighthorseman's slouch hat. You can make out the hat from that patchwork of green and brown. And there's the moustache and cigarette, the oriental eyes, and the scars on the temple and cheek are patterned in that section there. She's even painted the neck of his violin with the cigarette burn as his own neck. It's Roddy all right, with his head full of music – a walking, talking violin if ever there was one. Of course he's much, much more than that. In fact, it's a good reminder of the mistake we made about him – well, it is for me at any rate.'

'And do you truly like that painting?' I never realised Mrs Epstein had such an interest in art.

'Yes, I do. Very much.'

'And that one too?' I indicated the mother and child picture.

'Yes, I do, in a different way. It's a self portrait, but I tell you I see as much of myself in that picture as I do Ailine. Three hours of life – three short, precious hours. To be able to portray such desolation, how did she know?'

'She had a child herself,' drawled a voice from behind.

We both turned round to find Mr Raye at the door. How long had he been standing there?

'It was the reason why they left Vienna so quickly all those years ago,' he explained as he joined us. 'Turned out Jules and me were the least of Fleur's worries. Poor old Ailine got herself in a spot of trouble.'

'I had no idea,' Mrs Epstein continued to look at the painting. 'What happened?'

'She had to give the little one up,' he said. 'The only reason I know is because Jules was very upset about it.'

'I can imagine. Poor Lina. Why didn't she say anything?'

'What could you say, Annie, when your sister and your friends were all courting and marrying and having children themselves? Anyway, that was why she went back to France: to look for her child.'

'And did she find the little one?'

'She found her. In the same institution as she left her. She took me to see her when I was on leave. After all, an uncle is entitled to see his niece, isn't he? Her name was Sabine and the poor little girl couldn't do anything for herself,' he sadly shook his head at the memory. 'She knew her mother, though. She died a few weeks later. Got the news before Bellicourt. Reckon it sent Lina round the twist. That little girl was probably the only person she ever really cared for. Doesn't excuse what happened afterwards, mind you, but it partly explains it.'

'So you think—' I ventured a question about Phoebe's mother.

'Think?' he interrupted me. 'I know Lina did it. She deliberately left that violin in the attic. She wanted me to find it, to drive me mad with it. Tell you what, she didn't need a violin to do that. You seen a hawk before?'

'Aye, I seen hawks.'

'You've seen how they hover over their prey before they swoop?'

'Aye.'

'Well, that's how old Lina was when she visited me last year, save for one peculiar thing. For a split second she lost her composure when I asked her about the violin. She was surprised I didn't know. She quickly covered it up and I didn't put two and two together until Possum came along with that fiddle tucked under her chin.'

'And you know for sure she was in the country those years ago?'

'Police have found some evidence. And there's a witness. A little girl who was seven when it happened.'

'Phoebe is it?'

Mr Raye nodded. 'It was the Sunday afternoon before Jules died. We were picnicking in the garden. Possum was off on an adventure and ended up having a natter with someone at the front gate. Jules called her away. She didn't like it when passers-by stopped to catch the sideshow of the legless cobber at number thirty-four. Well, Possum kept on chatting so Jules came down to the gate to fetch her. By that time, the visitor had moved on. Possum said it was a very nice lady who was just like Bobeshi, which was her name for Fleur. Jules only had a glimpse, but she said later she could have sworn it was Lina. Anyway,' he sighed, 'Possum can't remember it ever happening, and, well, who's going to believe me?'

'And will it come to justice, do you think?'

'Justice?' he repeated. 'What do you mean by that?'

'Will it ever come to trial?'

'I hope it doesn't. For one, Lina's skipped the country and there's insufficient evidence to tie her to the crime. Even if she is caught and charged, consider this, Lucy Long. If she's tried in a court of law and found not guilty, she walks. If she's found guilty, she swings. I don't call that justice, do you?'

'But if she murdered—'

'She has it on her conscience and, as far as I'm concerned, justice is already being brought to bear. But if she swings? Then I've committed the same vile act as she, with an executioner as my henchman. It might be legitimised in a court of law, but I can't live with that. The punishment cries to Heaven as much as the crime itself. Don't know whether you've experienced it, but it's like this: When you've been forgiven – as I have – by someone you have grievously offended – as I have – how can you condemn someone who has harmed you?'

'One can still forgive and see the cause of justice served, Roddy,' remarked Mrs Epstein.

'It's not justice, Anne.'

'Don't you think you're being a bit utopian?' questioned Mrs Epstein.

'Yes, well, perhaps there isn't any place on this earth for such thinking, but I'd prefer it that way than the other and I'll be damned if I don't. As for poor Jules, there'll be a proper requiem for her, and that's justice truly done on one front at least. You'll come, won't you?' he asked me.

'Aye, of course I will.'

'Good. Now listen,' he nudged me. 'Your "Da" was wondering whether it would be all right to stay a little longer.'

I smiled. I fully expected a request of that sort.

'Then I'll fix some supper,' he concluded, his eyes brightening with pleasure.

'You all right to do that?' asked Mrs Epstein.

'Reckon I can rustle up a bottle of wine, a loaf of bread and a round of cheese. Fed every king and peasant since Adam was a boy,' he remarked as he left.

'I'll make some cocoa for the girls when I've finished,' Mrs Epstein called after him.

He raised his stick in reply.

We did not get home till midnight. Following a late supper, Phoebe, Mr Epstein, Mrs Epstein and I played quartet after quartet.

Daid and Mr Raye, meanwhile, talked and talked.

57

It was not until after Christmas that I saw Della. Daid and I arrived at the Sotheby house and were welcomed inside and escorted up the stairs by Wally. Daid was shown into Della's room; and while he was inside getting my cello set up, Wally and I waited on the landing.

'How are your legs?' he asked.

'They're fine, thanks be to God,' I replied. For the past week I had been wearing a half brace on my right leg. I was permitted to wear it for only part of the day and I still had to use crutches, but I was able to walk without having to lift my leg quite so high to clear my foot. The strain and effort involved had markedly lessened and my limp was not so pronounced. I also had the advantage of using crutches over longer distances and walking without them if I so wished once I had reached my destination. I appreciated the freedom.

'You've no idea what it's like to be able to use your knee again, Wally.'

'No, I don't,' he smiled. 'It's good to see you walking better. To this day, I don't know how you managed to climb these stairs with both legs braced. I tried it once.'

'You what?'

'Once after you visited Dell— crikey it must have been round about Easter. I tried to climb the stairs straight-legged and then I tried to go down the way you do. You had me stumped and you've had me stumped ever since.'

Daid emerged.

'Time for you, Luighseach,' he said. 'She needs you now. Wally, would your parents be downstairs?'

Della lay on a snowdrift of pillows. She seemed as if made of glass wrapped in tissue paper, so thinly did her skin enclose her delicate bones. Her hands, which rested on the coverlet, were like the claws of a fledgling that could barely grip a branch. Every care had been taken to make sure that she was not merely comfortable but also pretty. Her nightdress, which was pure white, was embroidered and lacy. Her hair, which had been brushed and neatly styled, was clipped at the side as always with a jewelled slide; but it had lost its soft wave and golden sheen. She was not wearing her glasses as she usually did, and her eyes appeared small and weak as a result. They seemed lit from a strange internal source, however, like a torch set deep within a cavern bearing a single testimony to the fact that her spirit had not yet left her.

'Hello, old thing,' she whispered.

'Delleen,' I replied as I sat in the chair next to her bed.

'You look well,' she began after a pause.

'I wish I could say the same of yourself. Do you be comfortable there? Is it a wee glass of water that I can pour for you?'

'No, no,' she sighed. 'I must look an awful fright. If I pull through this I will be quite hunchbacked. I don't know what Mummy will do with a real Quasimodo for a daughter. I'm such a disappointment, but then I never was very pretty.'

''Tis not like yourself to talk like that, Delleen,' I was surprised and saddened to hear her speak of herself in this way. 'You've always made the very best of yourself.'

'Mummy insists on it. It only takes a little extra effort to look your best, she says.'

'And you look your best right now sitting against all them pillows. You're like a snow queen on a snowy throne.'

'More like a poor captive, bound to my bed by sheets and coverlets, bound by my own wretched body,' she lamented and coughed, a hollow, hacking cough which left her worn and weakened.

'Thank you for the book you gave me for my birthday,' I tried to divert the conversation to something I knew really mattered to her. 'I like it very much.'

'Which one was it?' she asked.

''Twas a collection of poems by Hopkins, Delleen.' Did she not remember?

She smiled slightly. 'I'm glad you like it. No point in hanging on to it.'

'You won it, Delleen.'

'That was a first,' she tried to smile but coughed instead. 'Never won a prize for literature before,' she gasped. 'I hear quite a lot of congratulations are in store for you. You duxed the form.'

'Aye, I did, and I received a pile of books into the bargain. 'Twill keep me busy all summer, reading all them books. I don't deserve it, mind you.'

'Nonsense. You're by far the best in the class at maths.'

'But English and History, Delleen. I only did well on account of the fact I can memorise dates and details and argue a point. Them prizes should have been yours.'

'I was never very good at exams,' she sighed. 'You've been made Head Prefect, too, I hear?'

'Aye. Now, that was a surprise, I'm telling you.'

'Everyone's awfully pleased about it. They all tell me that. Mary said it couldn't happen to anyone better and I quite agree.'

'Well, 'twas Sister Bellarmine said to me that if Mr Roosevelt can be elected governor of the state of New York, then Lucy Straughan can be head girl of St Dominic's. Apparently Mr Roosevelt himself had polio, you know.'

'And what else has been happening? I have loved reading your letters. Do tell me what else you've been up to.'

She was too weak to talk and lay back to wait what I had to say.

'First of all, 'tis the *Messiah* I ought to tell you about. Do you remember Mr

Pippin from the Conservatorium?' Della nodded. 'Well, he was conducting. Mrs Epstein introduced me at my first rehearsal and he took one look at me, Delleen, and clapped his hand to his forehead so and said, "Heavens above!" you know how he speaks, Delleen, "I don't believe it!" he said, "You're a girl!" Everything said and done, though, he was quite happy for me to play. And, Delleen, you'll not believe what a wonderful piece of music it was. There we were – a full orchestra in the Sydney Town Hall with a choir and four soloists.'

'Mrs Epstein said you could hardly play for crying at one point.'

'Aye, well, when the soprano sang the "Come unto Him" aria, it went straight to my heart, you know, Delleen, such comfort did it give. Sister Magdalene told me that he who sings prays twice, well, that night no truer words could be said. And when everyone stood for the Hallelujah chorus I felt like standing myself save I was playing the 'cello. To be sure I'll be doing the *Messiah* every year.'

'Phoebe says she's Messiahed out.'

'Aye, and that's because her da's been singing the *Messiah* at the top of his voice the entire week before Christmas as well as all the performances and not a conversation can be had without him quoting bits of it and punning or making up nonsense words and all. Things like singing "And we like sheep" over the Sunday roast, you know. 'Tis well and good it's only once a year, she said to me when we finished. Even when she was helping him with his legs he had the hide to sing "How beautiful are the feet of them who bring the Gospel of peace" in a high voice like a woman.'

Della was in too much pain to laugh.

'And the Saturday before Christmas, Daid and myself spent the day watching Wally play cricket.'

'He hit a six.'

'Aye, he did. Pow! Into the stands! And then he hit another one. Then they bowled him a Yorker, plumb onto the middle stump. Off flew the bails and off walked your brother, out for a mere eighteen runs.'

'Wally said you were getting very good at following the cricket.'

'Well,' I continued, 'he didn't like seeing such a low score for that innings, so he made a point of taking a few wickets. Three for forty-three, I think he managed in the end.'

'He was pleased with that. And did you have a good Christmas?' she asked.

'Indeed we did. We spent Christmas Eve singing carols at the Birstall's house. You heard about Mr David did you not?'

Della had not, so I passed her the news of the coming wedding.

'Everyone was there: Mr and Mrs Epstein, Phoebe and Mr Raye, Daid, myself, Mr and Mrs Birstall, Mr David and Miss Bray and more besides. And after that we heard Midnight Mass.'

'I love going to Midnight Mass,' she murmured. 'I usually go with Mummy. I couldn't this time.'

'Never mind, Delleen.'

'Wally went with her instead.'

'He did that, did he?'

She nodded slightly.

'And to be sure he did so for your sake.'

'Perhaps. Tell me more, old thing.'

'Well now, on Christmas Day we enjoyed a fine roast chicken dinner with Mrs Murphy. Following that, on Boxing Day, we took a picnic to Centennial Park and yesterday we visited Pim and her family.'

'Is Pim back from Moss Vale?'

'She came up for Christmas but travelled back today. Her Aunt Rose, you know, gave birth to a baby girl. They called her Charlotte Marie and she'll be baptised come the feast of the Holy Family so we'll be catching the train down to Moss Vale for that. Anyway, apart from Aunt Rose, all her family were there: her sister Annie with her children, and her brother with his, and Peggy with little Caroline there for the first time in years, and Father Johnny and Sister Scholastica. And her sister Gracie will be marrying Billy Bailey and her brother Benny's marrying his Daphne. So that makes three weddings and a baptism so far, next year. Of course there was enough food to feed an army, children galore and a cricket game on the front lawn that lasted most of the afternoon. Daid even played and managed to score a few runs. 'Twas funny seeing my da play cricket, you know, for he's not all that inclined to the like of such games, but he's been needing to keep pace of late with Wally, I'm telling you.

'And the day after tomorrow I'm off to the pictures to see *The Jazz Singer* with Hilda Geraghty. A talking picture it is would you believe, and we're needing to travel into town for to—

But Della had begun to cry. I pulled out my handkerchief, sat on the bed and dabbed her tears.

'I'm sorry, Delleen. 'Twas silly of me to chatter so.'

'It's my fault, old thing. It's silly of me to cry. Oh it hurts!'

'Shhh. There, there now, 'tis not a thing in the world the matter with a few tears. I brought my 'cello there to play especially for you. Can you credit it, Delleen, not ever did I play *The Swan* for you. Do you remember when you asked me all those months ago and I couldn't play for fear? Well, 'tis about time I played it for you. Would you like that?'

'Very much, old thing. Thank you,' she gasped.

'Then lay back quietly now and close your eyes and I'll play it. If Phoebe was here she'd play the piano and you'd be able to hear the ripple of the water and see the light shimmer on the lake. But 'tis only myself the one playing, so you'll be putting up with a lone swan instead.'

And so I played for her. I did my best to touch my tones with sunshine, and to conjure the whitest of swans gliding through the water. I dearly wanted to soothe and cheer her with my music, but it seemed to have the opposite effect.

'I feel as if I've been penetrated by some vile act of fate, as poor Leda was by the duplicitous Zeus,' she struggled to speak.

'Delleen, Delleen,' I had to scold her. 'Of all the ways to think about swans, why would you think of such a thing as that?'

'Luighseach, I was so very, very certain I would get better this time, but I seem to be sicker than ever. Why should it happen to me?'

'I'm afraid I don't know,' I returned to her bedside and took her hand again. ''Tis the sickness making you sad and you'd not be the first one, I can tell you that. I've thought similar thoughts many a time. It might be hard, Delleen, but try to think a little differently.

'What you're talking of is a silly myth. That Zeus, why he's a perversion, a pagan god bent on deception and trickery. What's happening to yourself is not a vile act of fate, nor is it a cruel deception. 'Tis simply nature taking its course. That pain you're feeling will only last a short time more. You're sick and you've not much longer to live and you know that's the truth, but let you have faith. God acts in harmony with nature, not against it. He's there. And if you pray and trust you'll find He's like a beautiful swan, silent and graceful, that will glide towards you, open His wings and let you nestle there as a mother swan does her cygnet. Did you ever see such a sight? Did you ever watch the swans on the lake?'

'Sometimes, old thing, in London, when I was little. We'd feed the swans and ducks in Hyde Park.'

'Aye, you did, to be sure. And there are swans aplenty in Galway. I used to love watching the swans. And did you ever see the little cygnets riding on their mothers' backs?'

She nodded.

'So let you think that when you think of swans, for swans are gentle and faithful. They'll do anything to protect their little brood. Why, you've a room full of swans with them swans on your pretty wallpaper! You know, in Galway, when I'd walk with Mam, we often saw an old man with the swans. Not a single tooth was there in his mouth nor was there a single dark hair on his head and he was near bent over with age. He loved the swans, that old man did, and he'd raise his stick at any lad who dared throw stones at them. 'Twas a sin to harm a swan, he said, for the swans carried our souls to Heaven. And to harm any of the swans would be to harm Paddy and Maire and Biddy and Mícheál and all his other brothers and sisters whose souls they'd borne away.'

'But what has been the point of it all, old thing?' she mourned. 'What have I given? What will I leave? I've a silver trophy sitting on my bookcase over there and the more I look at it the more futile it seems to be. We'll never play together again. Phoebe's terribly upset about it. We should never have done it.'

'Delleen—'

'My poor mother! How will she manage? And my brother! Oh, Luighseach what is to become of everything? What is to become of me?'

'Sh, sh, sh. Listen now, to be sure your life's merely a drop in time, but despite what you say, 'tis much you've achieved. And even more important than how you've lived is how you've loved, Delleen. I cannot tell you how much your love has meant to myself. I'll never forget that, Delleen, not ever. And while you'll stop living here and now, you'll never stop loving and we'll never stop loving you. Let you think where you're heading. Let you think of Heaven now. To be sure, you'll be let in on a few secrets when you get there. My Mam will be there. She'll know you, for I've told her all about you, and mind you give her a big hug and a kiss from myself. And Phoebe's mam will be there and your da. To think you'll see your daid again.'

'Do you think he'll be there?'

'Imagine it,' I continued. 'Perhaps he'll come for you in his aeroplane. He'll fly down, whoosh! Just like that! And he'll land right there in your back garden and make a fine mess of your mother's lawn and flowerbeds. Then he'll hop out of his 'plane and say, "And how's my Mary Arondelle?" And he'll sweep you up in his arms and take you on board. Perhaps you'll be his navigator, Delleen.'

'Perhaps,' she smiled. 'Perhaps I will.'

There was a knock at the door.

'Time to go, I'm afraid, Lu,' said Wally as he entered. 'You all right, Dell?' he tenderly asked his sister.

Della nodded.

Wally and I packed my 'cello.

I was about to bid Della good-bye when she looked up at the two of us and smiled a smile of such radiance it was as if she had been suddenly restored to health.

'You know, Luighseach, old thing,' she began, 'With your dark hair and fair skin, you are very like a swan yourself.'

'A rather lame and short-sighted old swan, I'm afraid, Delleen.'

'They're always a little awkward on land, aren't they?' she replied. 'But no one can deny their stately beauty. Stately and serene and so very faithful: yes, you're very like a swan. Dia dhuit, a Luighseach,' she murmured. And for the first time that morning, she seemed genuinely at peace.

'Dia is Muire dhuit agus Pádraig, a Dhelleen,' I replied.

Wally accompanied me down the stairs.

'She hasn't much longer,' he sighed. 'The doctor's surprised she's lasted this far. But, she had to see Des and she had to have Christmas. She could well hold on for New Year. Wouldn't be like Dell to miss a fireworks display.'

'I feel so helpless, Wally. Is there not anything I can do?'

'We all feel like that, Lu. And you've done a lot.'

''Tis nothing I've done.'

'Nothing? Do you think caring is nothing? Your caring has meant everything to me, as it has to Della: all the letters you've sent her, the prayers you've prayed, the affection you have. You cry and I cry through you. I wipe your tears and I know I'm giving the comfort I can't give my sister. It has been such a consolation to me knowing that you care about her so very much. As for Dell— well, you saw her face back then.'

'She's like a sister to me, Wally.'

'I know. You're like a sister to her.'

Della died a few days later, in the early hours of New Year's Day. When we next visited her, she was laid out in her prettiest of frocks, her room filled with white roses. There, at her bedside, Daid and I prayed our Rosary. Wally sat with us and occasionally joined our prayers.

'Tell me she died peacefully, Wally?' I asked him.

'She did, Lu. Typical Dell, she insisted Mother and Des go to the Mahony's for cocktails. She's always loved seeing them dressed to the nines. They came home early and Des let off some fireworks for her at midnight. We watched them from her window. I stayed with her after that. She wanted to pray the Rosary but she could barely speak, so I prayed it with her. Just as well I had some idea of how it went,' he gave me a wink. 'She fell asleep while we were praying. I must have fallen asleep as well because the next thing I knew it was dawn. Mother woke me and told me she'd gone.'

'And how's your mam?'

'Not too good, I'm afraid. She's exhausted. We all are.'

I nodded. Wally looked as if he'd barely slept for a week.

'You know, Lu,' he continued, 'you're probably the only person I can say this to— and I hope you don't think I'm being too morbid, but, it was beautiful. It was a beautiful death. She slipped away so gently and graciously. And the peace! Mum and I sat with her. The sun was coming up. Then the birds began to sing. We sat there, holding Dell, listening to the birds and watching the sunlight gradually stream into her room. She died as she lived, Lu.'

'Indeed she did. 'Twas a sweet and tender song her life.'

'Apparently the last thing she said was, "He loved you, Mummy". Mum didn't know what she was talking about, but I knew Dell meant The Captain so I told Mum about our father, showed her the ring, everything. Oh, Lu!'

'You told your mam?' It was the first time Wally had ever spoken anything of any worth to his mother. 'There, there,' I held him close. 'Cry all you like, laddie.'

'I want that peace!' he sobbed. 'Not the peace that was her death, but the peace that was her life! She was so very, very good!'

'Well, as my Da's said to me many a time, Wally lad, you can only learn to walk by walking.'

58

Red-eyed and weary, Pim, Phoebe and I waited with our instruments in Mrs Sotheby's parlour. Mrs Epstein waited in the hall where she kept an eye on the drawing room proceedings. In the drawing room itself, Mr Sotheby was giving a final address. I tried to think through *The Lark*, but Schubert's 'The Lord is my Shepherd', which the school choir had sung at the requiem, was still very much in my mind. I conceded to Schubert, hugged my 'cello and sighed.

'When will you be going back to Moss Vale, Pim?' I asked her.

'Thursday,' she replied. 'You coming down for the Baptism?'

'Aye. 'Twill be grand to see Aunt Rose again and meet the new baby.'

'I'll be staying down there for the rest of the year. Rose's got her hands pretty full with four little ones, so I'm giving her a hand. Be seeing a bit more of Hughie, too.'

'And do you be keen on him?'

'You could say that,' she smiled.

'And does he be keen on yourself?'

'You could say that.'

''Twill be the last time we play together for a while?'

'I'm afraid so. It's been good, though, hasn't it?'

'Aye, Pimmy. It's been very good indeed.'

'I hear you two are playing with Mr and Mrs Ep,' she remarked.

'Oh yes,' enjoined Phoebe in a tone which suggested she was still a little overwhelmed by the challenge. Playing in a quartet with our teacher and her husband had introduced the two of us to another very vibrant, but demanding musical world. 'We've quite a few jobs ahead, haven't we, Lucy?'

'Good for you,' encouraged Pim. 'Reckon you'll both do well. All the best with it.'

'We called ourselves the Hirondelle Quartet, for Della's sake, Pim,' Phoebe added. 'Mrs Sotheby told me Arondelle comes from French for swallow, like the bird, not the verb. That's what hirondelle means in French. Do you think it's a good name?'

'It's a beaut name.'

Mrs Epstein knocked softly on the open door. 'We're on, girls,' she announced. 'One last call.'

We picked up our instruments and set off across the hall.

'Just a minute!' Phoebe called, and before we knew it she was dashing up the stairs.

'Phoebe! Come back here!' ordered Mrs Epstein, to no avail.

'Go in without me!' Phoebe replied from the landing.

And so we entered without her. The drawing room was filled with people we knew. All our families were there and all my school friends with their families, many of whom had cut their summer holidays short. Of our mistresses, only Sister Bellarmine and Sister Magdalene had come to the wake. In their white habits, they stood out like great beacons in a sea of black suits and frocks. They both smiled warmly in my direction and Sister Magdalene wiped her eyes with an enormous handkerchief.

Phoebe hurriedly pushed her way inside and we looked in astonishment at what she had brought with her. Instead of her own violin, she carried Della's violin case. She opened it, tenderly took the violin out from its paisley scarf and rapidly began to tune.

'I had to,' she whispered as we made a few final adjustments. Pim rolled her eyes and Mrs Epstein shook her head and sighed, but neither reaction was a protest. For my part, I had to fight the tears. When at last I looked up ready to play our opening note, I was very grateful to see Wally standing opposite, a little behind Phoebe.

'Break a leg,' he mouthed.

And so we began *The Lark*. And so, also, Della's canary began to trill as he always did whenever he heard the violin. It had been a long time since I had heard a skylark sing merrily from the heavens, and as I played I took consolation that from high above, Della, too, was singing with us.

We finished the first movement. Then, amidst applause and sniffs, Mrs Sotheby appeared. Alongside Mr Sotheby, she had been busy the entire morning, groomed to perfection, receiving the condolences of hundreds of people. When Daid and I had paid her our respects, she responded graciously and without a tear. She did not cry at the funeral; she did not cry at the cemetery; nor did she cry as she welcomed friend after friend into her home. Now, with faultless composure, she held out her hand to Phoebe and gave her a kiss of thanks on each cheek. Her thanks she also extended to Mrs Epstein. But it only took one look from our teacher before she began to shake.

'There, there,' I heard Mrs Epstein say as they hugged. 'Sixteen beautiful years. You've a lot to be thankful for. She is a credit to you.'

'Come on, Mum,' Wally whispered. 'Come on. It's all right.'

And he gently escorted her out of the room.

In the back garden, a game of blindman's buff was in full force. Henry Sotheby was in the unfortunate position of having to chase after a crowd of children, among which could be seen his sister and the younger Mahony girls. They dodged his groping arms and indulged in all manner of taunts.

Meanwhile Kismet, Della's canary, continued blithely to trill his pretty song. His cage, however, appeared as if it had not been cleaned for some days.

'Poor little fellow,' I said to him as I unlatched the door and removed his water container. There was a jug of iced water on the table on the verandah which had been placed there for the benefit of the children. From it I filled the container and returned it to the cage.

''Tis up to us to take good care of you,' I continued, 'for 'twould be a sorry end indeed if you were left to fend for yourself.'

The floor of the cage was filthy, so I decided to pull it out and give it a clean. It was not quite the easy task I expected. The end of the tray jammed in the cage and it took a bit of a shake before I freed it. In the process, husks and feathers and droppings began to scatter all over the verandah. When I finally managed to release the tray it came out so quickly that the remaining mess slid directly to the floor and I lost my balance and fell backwards.

Someone chuckled, and there at the back door was Wally.

'You certainly know how to put your foot in it,' he smiled and helped me to my feet. 'There should be a dustpan and broom under the tablecloth here.'

Sure enough, there was, and Wally began to sweep up the mess, which he then deposited under one of the azalea bushes near the verandah.

'Mother never liked Dell tipping the bird droppings on the plants,' he continued, squatting beside the shrub. 'So Della used to dig it in a bit so she wouldn't notice,' and Wally, too, set to work with a garden trowel that had been left in the soil for precisely that purpose. 'The bush never seemed to mind. It's probably one of the healthiest plants in the garden, and that's saying something. There,' he dusted his hands and returned to the verandah.

'How's your mam?' I asked him.

'She's had a bit of a rest. She's gone back to the guests now, so I'm off duty for a little while,' he grinned. Since Mrs Sotheby's collapse, Wally had been fully engaged in playing the host. 'By the way, I suppose I ought to give this back to you.'

He passed me Dudeney's *Canterbury Puzzles*.

'I'm afraid Dell never read it,' he remarked.

'Aye, not a one for numbers and puzzles was Delleen.'

'I read it, though. And all your annotations. I enjoyed it. I—I tried to keep all your notes in the right places.'

'Thank you,' I replied. 'You can keep it if you want. To be sure 'tis been with you so long 'tis as much your own as it is mine.'

'Thanks,' he smiled appreciatively. 'And you know you're most welcome to borrow it any time you like.'

'I'll remember that,' I laughed.

'I say, would you like some water?' he asked.

'Aye, I would.'

'Are you feeling all right?' he asked as he pulled up a chair for me and passed me the glass he had poured. 'I don't know how you managed to play that piece. And thanks. It meant an awful lot.'

'To tell you the truth, I don't know how I managed it either, Wally Sotheby.'

'But you are feeling all right, aren't you?' he asked again, a little more anxiously.

'Aye,' I reassured him. 'You know, Wally, I don't want this to sound callous or selfish, but would you believe I'm happy?' I began to confide. ''Tis the oddest feeling, only I expected to be engulfed with sadness like I was when Mam died and I'm not. I don't feel as if Delleen's really gone. Somehow she's still here and I feel so blessed to have known her. 'Tis as if she's blessed me in return and I haven't lost her at all. In fact, I've found another friend, a deeper, truer friend than I could ever imagine, and he always seems to be there for me, as he is right now.' I looked at him, and despite my tears I could not help a smile.

Wally nodded. 'You know,' he replied, 'I feel the same way. Perhaps it hasn't really hit and I'm fooling myself, but somehow it's as if I've been made the richer for it. My sister has given me a friend, and she seems to share my every thought; she revels in my happiness and understands my sorrow. She's strong and faithful, clever and true and ever so wise, and I love her,' he took my hand and I smiled at the ardour in his sky blue eyes.

'I love you, Lucy Straughan,' he said.

'Well, if love is the joy and warmth that bathes my heart and seems to make my very being blossom, aye, then I love you, too, Wally Sotheby.'

'Do you really?'

'Aye, I do,' I laughed and cried at the same time. 'I love you.'

'Does that mean you'll be my girl?' he asked.

'Aye, it does. And I will. I'll be your girl.'

'There you are!' Phoebe stormed out onto the verandah. 'Lucy! Everyone's been looking everywhere for you! You have to come inside! We're going!'

'Better go, then,' Wally stood up and offered me his arm. Willingly I took it. In turn, he took my crutches with his free hand and we walked into the house together.

Daid was waiting in the hall with Mr and Mrs Sotheby and my dearest friends. It was a curious group that met us, for the moment they saw us they all began to smile, everyone in exactly the same way. I could not help smiling in return and nor could Wally.

'Well, folks,' began Mr Raye in the style of Al Jolson. 'Ah see Miss Lucy ain't tarryin'.'

'Wait a minute! Wait a minute, sir!' replied Wally with an enormous grin. 'You ain't seen nothin' yet! I tell you, you ain't seen nothin'!' Despite his proper accent, he was a very good mimic.

489

We made our good-byes.

'It seems I have acquired another daughter,' said Mrs Sotheby as she took my hand.

'Well, if that's the case, ma'am,' I replied, 'then I seem to have acquired another mother.'

'A daughter not of my own choosing, mind you,' she warned me.

'Well, we don't really have a say in such matters, do we, ma'am?'

'Which is why we must make the most of what we have,' she added with a smile. 'Now, Lucy, we will be spending the remainder of the summer at the seaside. When we return, we would very happy for you to come and visit. As you know, we receive on Wednesdays, but you are welcome any time. In fact, as I was telling your father, you both must come for luncheon. That would be very nice. Good-bye dear,' she kissed me on each cheek, 'and God bless you.'

Wally saw us to the motorcycle, helped me in and waved us off.

We had not driven far when Daid suddenly pulled over to the side of the road and stopped the motor.

What had happened?

Daid took off his goggles.

'The lad asked my permission to walk out with you and indeed I gave it,' he informed me in a very serious manner. 'But he knows that if any courting's to begin he'll be needing to think about his obligations. Young Wally Sotheby's not a Catholic, Luighseach.'

'But he's good, Daid!' I urged. 'He's good and kind and thoughtful and he makes me laugh so. I'm happy when I'm with him, so happy that I'm dancing inside.'

'And outside, too, Luighseach,' Daid replied. 'Never did I see your eyes dance the way they been dancing lately. Let's pray that God will give him the gift of faith, for I'm telling you now, lass, as I told the lad himself, I'll not let you go if He doesn't.'

'I think God's done that already, Da.'

Off we drove to South Head, and together we walked to the cliff. We gazed out over the ocean, which was brilliantly blue and glittering with the summer sun, and held our hats against the sea breeze. Behind us, the bridge was awaiting another piece of arch.

'Do you remember that hot summer's day when first we sailed through them

490

heads there?' said Daid.

'I do, Da.'

'Aye,' my father paused as he so often did on that single word. 'I remember looking down at my small, sad, thin little lass; my poor little girl who wouldn't say a word, and wondering what would ever become of you. And now beside me there's a fine young woman who can look out across that exact same sea and smile.'

'So much has passed, Da.'

'Aye, Luighseach, so much has passed. And we've even more to look forward to.'

'Aye, we do, Da, we do indeed.'

Daid gave me a hug and we turned and headed back for home.

CPSIA information can be obtained
at www.ICGtesting.com
Printed in the USA
FSOW03n1940140415
6364FS